Marketing Research

State-of-the-Art Perspectives

Marketing Research

State-of-the-Art Perspectives

Handbook of the
American Marketing Association &
Professional Marketing Research Society

Chuck Chakrapani, PhD
Editor

Library of Congress Cataloging-in-Publication Data

Marketing research: state-of-the-art perspectives: handbook of the
American Marketing Association and the Professional Marketing Research Society/
edited by Chuck Chakrapani.
     p. cm.
  Includes bibliographical references and index.
  ISBN 0-87757-283-6
    1. Marketing research. I. Chakrapani, Chuck.
    II. American Marketing Association.
    III. Professional Marketing Research Society.

  HF5415.2 .M3582 2000
  658.8'3 — dc21   00-035565

  ISBN: 0-87757-283-6 American Marketing Association
  ISBN: 0-920741-15-0 Professional Marketing Research Society

Published by the American Marketing Association in conjunction with the
Professional Marketing Research Society

American Marketing Association
311 S. Wacker Drive, Suite 5800, Chicago, Illinois 60606 USA
  Francesca Van Gorp Cooley, Editor
  Elisabeth Nevins, Copy Editor
  Mary Loye, Interior Design and Compositor

Cover design by Liz Novak

Manufactured in the United States of America

Contents

For the visionaries

F. CHRIS COMMINS
whose vision made this book possible

&

PAUL E. GREEN
whose vision defined marketing research in its adolescent years

With deep respect and admiration
CHUCK CHAKRAPANI

Introduction

Chuck Chakrapani

THE OBJECTIVE

The objective of this book is to provide a solid and authoritative introduction by a team of experts to marketing research as it is practiced at the beginning of the third millennium. For the beginning researcher, this book is an expert introduction to marketing research, best used in conjunction with a basic textbook; for the experienced researcher, this is a reference book and a supplementary exposition.

THE RATIONALE

This book started with our[1] desire to bring out a book on marketing research that would be up-to-date and what could be described as the state-of-the-art book. No one, of course, aims to write a book that is dated. So in a sense, all good books are "state-of-the-art" books. However, in practice, most books tend to be strong in the author's area of specialization but weaker in other areas. An author who specializes in market modeling may not be fully familiar with the current developments in computerized qualitative data analysis; similarly, an author who specializes in interpreting and communicating research results may have no specialized knowledge of sampling techniques. Because marketing research is becoming more and more specialized, we thought it might be a good idea to bring out a book in which each chapter is written by an expert or an ongoing practitioner in that area.

---

[1]"Our" refers to a small group of people from the PMRS and AMA. Please refer to the Acknowledgments for details.

In choosing the experts, we did not want to confine ourselves to North America. After all, basic marketing research principles are the same around the world. So we decided to approach experts wherever we could find them. Our final list includes contributors from the United States, Canada, England, Scotland, and Australia. Because the authors were drawn from different countries, we decided not to meddle with the national spelling and other linguistic styles of the authors. Thus, you will find American, British, and Canadian linguistic styles, depending on the contributor.

A word of warning: Experts can and do disagree among themselves. Because this book reflects the state-of-the-art thinking, you will find that more than one point of view is being expressed here.

So here we have a book that covers the whole spectrum of marketing research as seen by experts in each area. However, it is by no means encyclopedic in its coverage. To the extent possible, the authors have tried to eschew jargon and pedantry. We kept the length of the book to a manageable level, which resulted in some compromises. We reluctantly had to give up coverage of a few topics, even though some researchers may consider them important, and rightly so. We hope the compromises were reasonable and the final content reflects the bulk of marketing research as it is practiced today.

THE STRUCTURE

This book has six parts.

The first part "Discovering Lawlike Relationships" is a macro view of marketing research. We are all taught how to convert data into information. But how is information converted into identifiable relationships (or lawlike relationships) that we can use with confidence? How do we go from data to information to knowledge? What is our core body of knowledge? In this section, Andrew Ehrenberg and John Bound and Eric Marder present two different—but not necessarily contradictory—ways to elicit lawlike relationships. These original thinkers from both sides of the Atlantic explain how marketing research can move from solving an immediate problem at hand to identifying the enduring lawlike relationships that are the hallmark of any science.

The next three parts—"Gathering Data," "Analyzing Data," and "Searching for Structure"—are central to marketing research. The exposition is somewhat less detailed than what would be found in a marketing research textbook and is meant to serve as an overview of the field.

"Gathering Data," the second part, contains contributions from Ken Deal, Vinay Kanetkar, Brian Fine, Peter Chan, and Naomi Henderson that expertly explain the nuances of data collection, both qualitative and quantitative.

"Analyzing the Data," the third part, deals with the basic skills that all modern marketing researchers are required to have. Here we learn from Naresh Malhotra how to go from data to information. Ian Dey introduces relatively new ways of analyzing qualitative data using computer programs. Brian Everitt explores the production and use of graphical techniques.

"Searching for Structure," the fourth part, attempts to extend data analysis to identify usable patterns and quantify them. David Gascoigne, Bill Neal, and Peter Peacock explore different aspects of market modeling.

The fifth part, "Exploring Special Areas," is a sampler of many specialized areas of marketing research. Although research principles are common across different subject areas, each specialized area has its own specialized needs. I simply chose expert practitioners for each field and asked them to define and write about their special subject. Contributors to this section had considerable freedom in defining, summarizing, and presenting their field of expertise. Some tended to summarize their field (e.g., David Lyon), whereas others offered a viewpoint (e.g., Roger Wimmer). Various special issues are explored by Humphrey Taylor (opinion research), Roger Wimmer (advertising research), Jim Barnes (customer relations research), Howard Moskowitz (product and packaging research), David Lyon (pricing research), Doss Struse (international marketing research), and Ruth Corbin and Neil Vidmar (legal research). Because marketing research covers so many specialized areas, the topics chosen should be considered a sampling rather than an exhaustive list.

The sixth part, "Envisioning the Future," contains a quick look at the future. Jack Honomichl, who has been one of the keenest observers of the research scene for many decades, offers some excellent insights into where we are headed.

Because this book was conceived to be the voice of marketing research experts at the turn of the millennium, only a minimal review was carried out. This was a deliberate decision; I consider this book more as a record of how the experts view their field of specialization at the dawn of the third millennium and less as a standard exposition of the subject matter. So, although this book includes most of the standard materials covered in marketing research textbooks, it goes much further—it also accommodates the disparate views of different experts.

I hope you find our efforts worthwhile. I will always be interested in hearing your reactions. You can reach me at chakrapani@cheerful.com or through the publisher.

— Chuck Chakrapani

Acknowledgments

"The preface world is an idyll peopled by super-intelligent conscientious colleagues.... They all have a sense of humor ... which is 'unfailing'...." So observed a rather cynical Neil M. Kay in his book, *The Emergent Firm*. But as far as this book is concerned, my world has been such an idyll.

It all started with Chris.

Chris Commins was organizing a grand marketing research conference to commemorate the year 2000 as well as the 40th anniversary of the Professional Marketing Research Society (PMRS) of Canada. He suggested that it would be a good idea to put together a collection of reprints of the best papers that appeared in the *Canadian Journal of Marketing Research*, of which I am the editor. I wondered if it would be better instead to create a book that would summarize the state of the art of marketing research instead of a "look-back" publication. Chris agreed with me. I was quite pleased that we were in agreement on principle.

For reasons that still baffle me, Chris did not seem to realize that this was just a theoretical discussion. Instead, he called me back the following day to find out when I could start on the project. The resources needed to complete the project were not insignificant, but Chris wasn't about to back down. He would support the project until it became a reality. Maybe he would apply for a special grant, maybe he'd get a few corporate sponsors.

I started working on the project, and it started growing in scope. At some point, it became clear to me that making the project successful would require a lot more resources and access to markets than what we had in mind. It wasn't a small project any more. Joanne McNeish of the PMRS suggested that I find a publisher. The most logical choice for this, to my mind, was the American Marketing Association. AMA, the largest association of marketers in the world, has access to the specialized market and has goals that are similar to those of the PMRS. I discussed the proposal with AMA's Francesca Van Gorp Cooley, who was enthusiastic about the project and confirmed AMA's interest in participating in a matter of days.

Clearly, the three people I needed to deal with from the time the project was just an idea to the time it became a viable proposition — *Chris Commins, Joanne McNeish*, and *Francesca Van Gorp Cooley* — deserve special thanks for making the book possible.

My idyllic world did not end there.

When I approached various experts, some of them not known to me personally, they were surprisingly willing to support the project. I was struck by the generosity of the contributors—some eminent academics, some heads of large organizations, and others noted consultants—in terms of the time and effort needed to write an authoritative chapter in the area of their specialization on fairly short notice. In fact, it is their book. As the editor of the book, I am delighted that they cared to work with me on this project. My heartfelt thanks go to the great team of contributors: *Prof. Jim Barnes, Prof. John Bound, Peter Chan, Dr. Ruth Corbin, Prof. Ken Deal, Prof. Ian Dey, Prof. Andrew Ehrenberg, Prof. Brian Everitt, Brian Fine, David Gascoigne, Naomi Henderson, Jack Honomichl, Prof. Vinay Kanetkar, Dave Lyon, Prof. Naresh Malhotra, Eric Marder, Dr. Howard Moskowitz, Bill Neal, Prof. Peter Peacock, Doss Struse, Humphrey Taylor, Prof. Neil Vidmar,* and *Dr. Roger Wimmer.*

In addition, Elisabeth Nevins deserves thanks for reconciling divergent writing styles and expertly copyediting the book.

There are others who supported the project, even if they perhaps didn't even know it. There are too many of them, but I'll name only three (this book—and life—is too short to name them all): *Lynd Bacon,* who has been always helpful in locating any source, any e-mail address, any Web site, be it a topic area or a person; *Rosemary Cliffe,* who is always willing to act as the touchstone when I am not sure of my concepts; and *Christine Mole,* my exceptional assistant, whose contributions to my projects are so pervasive that it has become hard to isolate her specific contributions to my work. Thanks Lynd. Thanks Rosemary. Thanks Chris.

Part I
Discovering Lawlike Relationships

Research is the quest for knowledge. It is about discovering what we do not know or know only partially. It is also about reconfirming what we already know to make sure that what we have known all along continues to hold true.

Although knowledge is based on information, information is not knowledge. Information accumulates quickly, knowledge does not. Just as information is digested data, true knowledge is digested information. Although it is relatively easy to go from data to information, it is not easy to go from information to knowledge. As we move from data to knowledge, we are extending the applicability of what we find, we are generalizing what we know. The higher the level of generalization, the greater the evidence we need.

We can also view it in another way. Marketing research's main function is traditionally seen as providing information to the marketer. For example, research might show that, for the product under consideration, a price increase of 10% will result in a sales decrease of 8%. This is information, and applied marketing research is concerned mainly with this type of relationship. Although this finding helps the marketing decision maker, it does not add anything significant to our marketing knowledge. If we come across a similar product, will this relationship hold? If the relationship is found to work in the United States, can we assume it will also work in Europe? If not, what are the limits of the applicability?

Obviously, the breadth of applicability defines the usefulness of any relationship. Compared with data or information, knowledge has much wider applicability. To have relevance as a significant discipline, we need to accumulate knowledge. This makes knowledge our discipline. We need to outgrow the definition of marketing research as a discipline that simply collects, analyzes, and interprets data. The first chapter expounds on this theme.

1

But how do we go from information to knowledge? How do we know that what worked for products A, B, and C will also work for products F, G, and H? What do we know about the relationship between attitude and usage? What do we know about how advertising works?

In most cases, we don't have precise answers to questions like these. However, we can get interim answers to such questions. Such interim answers are the result of accumulated information. Gradually, some consistent patterns emerge. Such patterns are what we call "lawlike relationships." They are not "laws," because the predictions we make are not precise like laws of physics[1] but are "precise enough" for marketing purposes. Discovery of lawlike relationships eventually leads to knowledge.

But what is the process by which we move from information to lawlike relationships to knowledge? Different experts have different views on this. In this section, we present two major approaches.

Ehrenberg and Bound's (Chapter 2) approach is based on understanding the structure of the data and looking for patterns. The researcher looks for patterns in the data, mostly at an informal level. Such patterns form the rudiments of a model. Informal pattern recognition is necessary to avoid ending up with facts without models or the converse, models without facts—creation of theories the validity of which is unknown. New studies are used to validate and extend the theory and identify the exceptions. New information is constantly being interpreted with the help of prior knowledge. The chapter by Ehrenberg and Bound explores lawlike relationships that lead to knowledge developed mainly using this approach.

Marder's (Chapter 3) approach is related, but different. Like Ehrenberg and Bound, Marder starts with data and information. However, instead of continuing the process of accumulation and generalization until the very end, Marder uses an axiomatic approach to knowledge. Marder contends that, at some point, when enough information is accumulated, certain relationships become so obvious and self-evident that they become "axioms." The researcher then explicitly states these axioms, develops further hypotheses, and thereby extends the applicability of the axioms. The chapter by Marder is based on this approach.

In summary, this part deals with marketing research as a discipline and a source of knowledge. It is about the ends rather than the means. It's about solving different classes of problems rather than a single problem. It is as much about exploration as about discovery—discovery of lawlike relationships that lead to knowledge.

From a logical point of view, these chapters should perhaps be placed toward the end, because it is the end product. I have chosen to place them at the beginning to remind us of our final goal, which is knowledge, and to emphasize that, in the final analysis, knowledge is our discipline.

---

[1]It can be argued, as Andrew Ehrenberg effectively does, that even laws of physics are only lawlike relationships. But we do not explore this any further here.

1
Knowledge as Our Discipline[1]

Chuck Chakrapani

Marketing research is at a crossroads. What is at stake is the survival of marketing research as a profession. The way marketing research has been positioned and practiced over the years appears to be at odds with the new information age and management decision requirements. There seems to be an immediate need to redefine our discipline and our role in management decision making.

Many solutions have been offered to get marketing research back on track (Adams 1999; Mahajan and Wind 1999). They include highly concrete suggestions like repositioning ourselves, developing core competencies, achieving integrated skills that encompass qualitative and quantitative research techniques, modeling, experimentation, and database analyses. Undoubtedly, they are worthwhile suggestions. But the roots of the problem might go deeper. In my opinion, the current crisis in marketing research is the result of marketing research having no core body of knowledge. If we do not address this issue, I believe we will face recurring problems, even if we overcome the current crisis. It is this issue of creating a core body of knowledge and developing our identity as practitioners of a worthwhile and practical discipline that is the subject of this chapter. It revolves around four major themes:

1. Traditionally, marketing research has been considered a discipline that primarily uses scientific methods to collect, ana-

---

[1]This chapter has benefited immensely from the insightful comments I received from Rosemary Cliffe, Larry Gibson, and Bill Neal.

I borrowed the phrase "knowledge as our discipline" from Andrew Ehrenberg, who used the phrase as a title to one of his early papers. He is also a strong proponent of the concept of "lawlike relationships." Phrases like "facts without models" and "models without facts" were coined by him. Although Andrew was kind enough to let me use his concepts and phrases, my views are not necessarily a faithful representation (or even a pale reflection) of his views on these topics.

lyze, and interpret data relevant to marketing of goods and services. The acceptance of this definition has prevented marketing researchers from being meaningful partners in the decision-making process.

2. The practice and goal of marketing research should not be just to provide "input" to decision makers but to gather data and interpret them in light of what is already known and to be a part of the decision-making process.

3. To have continued relevance to management and marketing, we should develop a core body of knowledge. Such knowledge should be supported by extensive empirical evidence.

4. There is no substitute for empirical evidence. Statistical analysis on limited data cannot take the place of empirical evidence.

Because these four themes are interrelated, the exposition is not necessarily sequential. Rather, the themes are interwoven throughout the chapter.

A LIMITING DEFINITION

In his paper, "Quo Vadis, Marketing Research?" Larry Gibson (2000) makes an interesting observation. In 1961, the American Marketing Association defined marketing research as

> The systematic gathering, recording, and analyzing of data about problems relating to the marketing of goods and services.

Implied in this definition is the idea that marketing researchers have no direct involvement in the process of marketing decision making. Their role is to provide support to the real decision makers by providing the information asked for by them. Sadly, some variation of such descriptions of marketing research were accepted by academics, as evidenced by the following quotes from textbooks:

> Marketing research is the systematic process of *purchasing relevant information* for marketing decision making (Cox and Evans 1972, p. 22; emphasis added).

> The primary purpose of marketing research is to *provide information for decision making* (Kinnear and Taylor 1979, p. 17; emphasis added).

> *Only the manager has a clear perspective as to the character and specificity of the information needed* to reduce the uncertainty surrounding the decision situation (Kinnear and Taylor 1979, p. 25; emphasis added).

By inference, marketing researchers have nothing to contribute to the character and specificity of the information needed to reduce the uncertainty surrounding the decision situation; *only the manager* has a clear perspective on these matters. This idealized version of the decision maker as someone who has a clear perspective on what he or she needs to make sound decisions is as much a myth as the concept of the "rational man" of the economic disciplines of yesteryears. Both these romanticized portraits—decision maker with a clear perspective and rational man who optimizes his well-being/returns—sound enticing and plausible in theory but are seldom obtained in practice.

Marketing researchers have a lot to contribute to the character and specificity of the information needed to reduce the uncertainty surrounding the decision. Many an inexperienced researcher has been unpleasantly surprised by the disappointment expressed by the decision maker when exactly what has been asked for is delivered. Experienced researchers generally know that probing the decision maker is an important part of clarifying the perspective and identifying the information required. In some cases, it can even be argued that only the market researcher has a clear perspective as to whether the information asked for by the decision maker will provide meaningful and effective input to the decisions about to be made. To borrow a turn of phrase from Clemenceau, decision making is too important to be left solely to the designated decision maker.

That market researchers systematically gather, record, and analyze data about problems relating to the marketing of goods and services is incontrovertible. Yet by defining marketing research in terms of its narrow functional roles rather than by its broad overall goals, we have acutely limited the growth of marketing research as a serious discipline striving to create a core body of knowledge. We cannot confuse what we do (gather and interpret data) with our purpose (to derive lawlike relationships that contribute to our understanding of the marketing process). To define ourselves by our functional roles rather than by our overall goals is similar to a university defining itself as a collection of buildings with employees whose job it is to publish papers and lecture students who pay. In a rapidly changing world, like the one we find ourselves in today, defining anything by its functional role rather than by its overall goals seriously undermines its relevance as things change.

The results of a narrow functional definition have led to a tunnel vision in our profession. Its consequences have been far-reaching and not in positive ways either. At the dawn of the twenty-first century, marketing research stands at the threshold of irrelevance, as the following facts indicate:

❑ In 1997, *Financial Times* of London published a 678-page book, *The Complete MBA Companion*, with the assistance of three major international business schools: IMD, Wharton, and the London Business School. The book had 20 modules that covered a wide range of subjects relevant to management. Marketing research is not one of them. The term "marketing research" is not even mentioned in the index.

❑ In 1999, *Financial Times* published another book, *Mastering Marketing Management*, this time with the assistance of four major international business schools: Kellogg, INSEAD, Wharton, and the London Business School. The book had 10 modules and covered the entire field of marketing. Again, marketing research is not one of them. No module discussed the topic of marketing research directly. Rather, there were some indirect and sporadic references to the uses of marketing research in marketing. Apparently, the field of marketing can be mastered without having even a passing familiarity with marketing research.

❑ The following books, many of them business bestsellers, completely ignore marketing research: Peters and Waterman's *In Search of Excellence* and *A Passion for Excellence,* Porter's *Competitive Advantage,* Rapp and Collins's *Maximarketing,* and Bergleman and Collins's *Inside Corporate Innovation* (Gibson 2000).

❑ Mahajan and Wind (1999) list many specific instances in which decision makers completely discount the role of marketing research in marketing decision making altogether.

❑ AMA's (2000) Attitude and Behavior Conference was preoccupied with concerns about marketing research becoming completely irrelevant. Many speakers pointed out that marketing researchers have been changing their department names to "Consumer Insights" or "Marketing Measurement and Information Systems" to redefine their role and function, as well as to ensure that they are not ignored because of their moniker: market researchers.

A FLICKER AT THE END OF THE TUNNEL

Yet things have been changing for a while. The changes have been too slow to be perceptible to the naked eye. As a precursor for changes to come, in 1987, AMA revised its definition of marketing research and stated that

> Marketing research is the use of scientific methods to identify and define marketing opportunities and problems; generate, refine, and evaluate marketing actions; monitor marketing performance; and improve our understanding of marketing as a process (*Marketing News* 1987, p. 1).

This extended definition acknowledged that information is used to identify and define marketing opportunities and problems; generate, refine, and evaluate marketing actions; monitor marketing performance; and improve understanding of marketing as a process. Marketing research is the function that links the consumer, customer, and public to the marketer through information. Finally, the extended definition also acknowledged that marketing research:

1. Specifies the information required to address these issues,
2. Designs the method for collecting information,
3. Manages and implements the data collection process,
4. Analyzes the results, and
5. Communicates the findings and their implications.

Thirteen years before the dawn of the third millennium, AMA acknowledged that marketing research is much more than collecting and analyzing data at the behest of the "decision makers"; it is a discipline in its own right and is involved in improving our *understanding of marketing as a process.* With this new definition, marketing research is not a content-free discipline that concerns itself (using methods heavily borrowed from other disciplines) with eliciting information with no thought given to accumulating, codifying, or generalizing the information so elicited.

Things did not improve overnight when the AMA revised its definition of marketing research. The discipline did not recover quickly from its self-inflicted wounds. The advent of new technologies—the Internet, data mining, and the like—brought with it a host of other specialists who started encroaching upon the territory traditionally held by marketing researchers and minimizing their importance even further. A road map was needed for the discipline that seemed to have lost its way. The ailing profession needed prescriptions. Recognizing the need, AMA's *Marketing Research* published a cover story by Mahajan and Wind, *Rx for Marketing Research*, in 1999.

As one of the prescriptions to reviving the role of research, Mahajan and Wind (1999) completely reversed the earlier view that "only the manager has a clear perspective as to the character and specificity of the information" (Kinnear and Taylor 1979, p. 22) and stated that the "biggest potential in the use of marketing research is … in helping management ask the right strategic questions." They went on to suggest that "marketing researchers need to give it a more central role by connecting it more closely to strategy processes and information technology initiatives" (Mahajan and Wind 1999, pp. 11–12).

Mahajan and Wind (1999) were not alone in recognizing that market researchers are not simply order takers whose function it is to provide information asked for by decision makers. The president and CEO of Hasbro, Herb Baum, in an interview with Michelle Wirth Fellman (1999, p. 5) spelled it out even more explicitly: "[Market research] could improve productivity, if the department were to run with the permission, so to speak, to initiate projects rather than be order takers.… I think they [market researchers] would be more productive if they were more a part of the total process, as opposed to being called in cafeteria style to do a project."

Why is it even necessary for someone else to remind us of our proper role in decision making? Over the years, we have been trying to position ourselves as professionals providing reality checks that are critically needed to make multimillion dollar decisions; refining techniques that increase the sophistication, reliability, and validity of information; and eagerly exploring anything that will increase the precision of our input — be it neural nets or a single source database — and yet, as we discussed, the discipline of marketing research itself is facing irrelevance and even possible extinction. Part of the problem is the way we defined ourselves. Our functional rather that goal-oriented definition of ourselves had devastating effects on the way marketing research was taught and in the way marketing researchers were perceived by themselves and by others. As we will see, there are other reasons as well.

But we have more immediate concerns: How do we reclaim our relevance to the marketing decision processes? Where do we begin? Following Lewis Carroll's advice, we "begin at the beginning."

CONSEQUENCES OF USING INFORMATION AS KNOWLEDGE

What makes us marketing researchers? There must be an underlying premise to our discipline. There must be a point of view that defines our interests. There must be an underlying theme that motivates us and makes us define ourselves as practitioners of the profession.

That underlying theme cannot simply be the collection, analysis, and interpretation of data. This theme has not served us well in the past and has led us to a place where we are already discussing how we can effectively continue to exist as a profession and reestablish our relevance without facing imminent professional extinction.

The underlying theme that propels a marketing researcher, it seems to me, should be much more than the collection, analysis, and interpretation of data. I would like to propose that it is the search for marketing knowledge.

The quest for knowledge is not unique to marketing researchers. It is common to all researchers. Many scientific paradigms are based on inductive reasoning, followed by a deductive verification of the hypotheses generated by induction. Accumulating specific data enables us to generalize (see Figure 1). It is no different in marketing research. In marketing research, we also have the opportunity to follow the scientific process of accumulating data in order to derive lawlike relationships. Marketing researchers seek knowledge at various levels of abstraction. Consider the following marketing questions that move from very specific to very generalized information:

❏ How many consumers say that they intend to buy brand X next month?

❏ How many consumers say that they intend to buy the product category?

❏ How many of the consumers who say that they intend to buy the brand are likely to do so?

❏ Can the intention–behavior relationship be generalized for the product category?

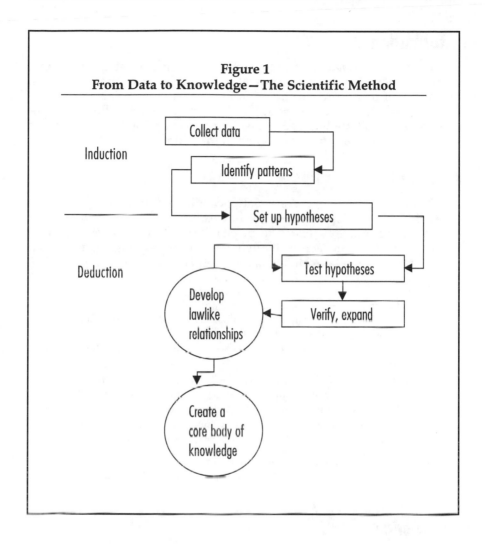

Figure 1
From Data to Knowledge—The Scientific Method

Induction

Collect data

Identify patterns

Set up hypotheses

Deduction

Test hypotheses

Develop lawlike relationships

Verify, expand

Create a core body of knowledge

❑ Can it be generalized across all product categories?
❑ Can we derive any lawlike relationships that will enable us to make predictions about consumer behavior in different contexts?

Clearly, these questions require different degrees of generalization. We need to accumulate data first so we can derive lawlike relationships. In Ehrenberg and Bound's (2000) model, we go from data to information to lawlike relationships to arrive at knowledge. Because our discussion is focused on deriving lawlike relationships that lead to knowledge, we review these concepts briefly here.

Information

The term *information* refers to an understanding of relationships in a limited context. For example, correlational analysis may show that loyal customers of firm x are also more profitable customers. This is information because, though it is more useful than raw data, it has limited applicability. We don't know whether this finding is applicable to other firms or even to the same firm at a different point in time.

Lawlike Relationships

By increasing the conditions of applicability of information, we arrive at lawlike relationships. In the preceding example, if it can be shown that loyalty of customers is related to profitability of a firm across different product categories and across different geographic regions, we have what is known as a lawlike relationship. The other characteristics of lawlike relationships (Ehrenberg 1982) are that they are

1. *General, but not universal.* We can establish under what conditions a lawlike relationship holds. Exceptions do not minimize the value of lawlike relationships;

2. *Approximate.* Absolute precision is not a requirement of lawlike relationships;

3. *Broadly descriptive and not necessarily causal.* In our example, our lawlike relationship does not say that customer satisfaction leads to profits; and

4. *Of limited applicability* and may not lend themselves to extrapolation and prediction. (The lawlike relationships cannot be assumed to hold in all contexts; they have to be verified separately under each context.) It is good to remember in this context Box's (1965) famous statement: "All models are wrong, but some are useful."

Knowledge

Accumulation of lawlike relationships leads to knowledge. In the words of Ehrenberg and Bound (2000, pp. 24–25), "Knowledge implies having a wider context and some growing understanding. For example, under what different circumstances has the attitude–behavior relationship been found to hold; that is, how does it vary according to the circumstances? With knowledge of this kind, we can begin successfully to predict what will happen when circumstances change or when we experimentally and deliberately change the circumstances. This tends to be called 'science,' at least when it involves empirically grounded predictions that are routinely successful." These four aspects are summarized in Figure 2.

Unlike in many other disciplines, the gathering of lawlike relationships has been less vigorously pursued in market research. Whenever we

---

Figure 2
From Data to Knowledge

Data	Undigested information
Information	Digested data in a limited context
Lawlike Relationships	Information generalized to a variety of contexts
Knowledge	Growing understanding of lawlike relationships

---

are asked by nonresearch professionals how some marketing variables work (for example, the relationship between advertising expenditure and sales, the relationship between attitude and behavior), we are painfully reminded how little accumulated knowledge we really have on the subject despite our professional credentials.

A Note on the Phrase "Core Body of Knowledge"

In general usage, the phrase "core body of knowledge" also refers to the skill set a person is expected to have to qualify for the title market researcher. However, in this chapter, the term refers to marketing knowledge derived through the use of marketing research techniques.

PRACTICAL USES OF LAWLIKE RELATIONSHIPS

As practitioners of an applied discipline, we can argue that it is the method itself (which may include several aspects such as sampling, statistics, data collection and analysis methods, and mathematical model building in a limited context), not the knowledge generated by the method, that should be of concern to us. Such an argument has some intrinsic validity. However, this view is shortsighted, because it is wasteful and ignores the feedback that knowledge can potentially provide to strengthen the method.

Consider the lawlike relationship that attribute ratings of different brands roughly follow the market share. In general, larger brands are rated more highly on practically all brand attributes, and smaller brands are rated low on practically all brand attributes (Ehrenberg, Goodhardt, and Barwise 1990; McPhee 1963). A lawlike relationship such as this will enable the researcher to understand and interpret the data much better. For example, while comparing two brands with very different market shares, the researcher may realize that it may be unproductive to carry out significance tests between the two brands because practically all attributes favor the larger brand. Instead, the researcher may look at mean-corrected scores to assess whether there are meaningful differences, after accounting for the differences between the two brands that may be due to their market share.

When we use lawlike relationships, our analysis becomes more focused. In the preceding example, we would be more interested in those attributes that *do not* conform to the lawlike relationship (e.g., the large brand being rated low on a given attribute). Because lawlike relationships are a summary of prior knowledge, using them forces us to take into account what is already known.

As another example, if we can uncover a lawlike relationship between advertising and sales in different media, then we can use this to build further models and simplify and strengthen data analysis. Confirmed theories become prior knowledge when we analyze new data. As these examples show, knowledge can play an important role in marketing research, not just from a theoretical point of view, but from a practical point of view as well.

It is also true that the more we know about how marketing variables actually work, the more focused our data collection will be. From a practical point of view, firms do not have to pay for irrelevant data, information that does not in any way contribute to marketing decision making.

Braithwaite (1955, p. 1) explains the importance of formulating lawlike relationships this way: "The function of science … is to establish general laws covering the behaviors of the empirical events or objects with which the science in question is concerned, and thereby to enable us to connect together our knowledge of separately known events, and to make reliable predictions of events as yet unknown." We need to connect what we know through "separately known events" to derive knowledge that we can then use to predict what is not yet known. Deriving knowledge and using it to predict (e.g., success of new products, the relationship between advertising and sales, the relationship between price and quality) seem to be worthy goals for marketing researchers.

Knowledge, therefore, is not a luxury but a powerful tool that can contribute to the collection of relevant data, avoidance of irrelevant data, and more focused analysis of the data so collected. Because knowledge leads to more relevant data and more focused analysis, we can lower the cost of research while increasing its usefulness to decision making. Knowledge contributes to more relevant and cost-efficient research.

WHY DON'T WE HAVE A CORE BODY OF KNOWLEDGE?

Given all the benefits of having a core body of knowledge, we must ask ourselves why we failed to develop it, despite the fact that every other science has been steadfastly accumulating lawlike relationships. How is that even the presence of some of the brightest minds that any profession can boast of—from Alfred Politz to George Gallup, from Hans Zeisel to Andrew Ehrenberg, from Louis Harris to Paul Green—failed to propel us into rethinking our role in decision making until now? There are many reasons, including

- ❏ The way the marketing research has been taught,
- ❏ The way marketing research has been perceived over the years,
- ❏ The divergent preoccupations of academics (quantitative methods and model building) and practitioners (solving the problem at hand as quickly and cost effectively as possible),
- ❏ Lack of immediate rewards, and
- ❏ An overconcern about confidentiality.

All of these reasons, except for the last two, are expounded in different places in this chapter. Lack of immediate rewards and overconcern about confidentiality are discussed next.

Lack of Immediate Rewards

To be a market researcher, one does not necessarily have to generalize knowledge. In many other disciplines, this is not the case. Specific information is of use only to the extent that it contributes to a more generalized understanding of the observed phenomenon. In marketing research, information collected at a given level of specificity does not need to lead to any generalization for it to be useful. It can be useful at the level at which it is collected. For example, the question, "How many consumers say that they intend to buy brand X next month?" is a legitimate one, even if it does not lead to any generalization about consumers, brands, products, or timelines. It does not even have to be a building block to a higher level of understanding. For marketing researchers, information is not necessarily the gateway to knowledge. Information itself is often the knowledge sought by many marketing researchers.

Maybe because of the way we defined ourselves, no one seems to expect us to have a core body of knowledge. If no one expects this of us, if there is considerable work but not commensurate reward for it, why bother? Because there is no tangible reward, there is no immediacy about it either. When there is never an immediacy, it is only natural to expect that things will not get accomplished.

Overconcern About Confidentiality

The bulk of all market research data is paid for by commercial firms that rightfully believe that the data exclusively belong to them and do not want to share them with anyone, especially with their competition. This belief has such intrinsic validity that it clouds the fact that, in most cases, confidentiality is not particularly relevant.

Let us consider data that are few years old and do not reflect current market conditions. In such cases, data are of little use to competitors — the data are dated, and the market structure has changed. It is because of such concerns that many firms repeat similar studies year after year. Although old data are of little use to current marketing decision making, they could be of considerable use to researchers trying to identify the underlying marketing relationships. Yet, as experience shows, it is extremely difficult to get an organization to release past research data, even when concerns of confidentiality have no basis in fact. The concept of confidentiality is so axiomatic and so completely taken for granted in many businesses that it is not even open for discussion. It is as though the research data come with a permanent, indelible label "confidential" attached to them. A case can be made that nonconfidential data held confident do not promote the well-being of an organization but simply deprive it of the generalized knowledge that can be built on such data.

WHAT TAKES THE PLACE OF KNOWLEDGE?

In the previous section, I suggested that nonconfidential data held confident do not promote the well-being of an organization but simply deprive it of the generalized knowledge that can be built on such data. Let me elaborate. Our not having a core body of knowledge has led to at least two undesirable developments: development of models without facts and proprietary "black box" models with largely unverifiable claims. Neither of these developments has served decision makers well.

Models Without Facts

All empirically based models attempt to codify lawlike relationships in observed data. Although they are simplifications and do not precisely reflect reality, the reality represented by good models is adequate enough to be useful. Unfortunately, the same cannot be said of all purely statistical models with no empirical content ("models without facts").

Because we have defined ourselves as essentially collectors and interpreters of data, all we are left with are facts. So those who do realize the importance of models, especially in the academe, have attempted to build models with sparse data sets and substituted advanced statistical analysis for empirical observation. It is not uncommon to find research papers that attempt to develop elaborate marketing models based on just a single set of data supported by complex mathematics. Unfortunately, no amount of mathematics, no number of formulas, and no degree of theorizing can compensate for the underlying weakness: lack of data. When we use models without facts, we do not end up with a core body of knowledge but with, as Marder (2000, p. 47) points out, a "premature adoption of the trappings of science without essential substance."

Market researchers who are serious about developing a core body of knowledge do not, and should not, believe in premature theorizing and model building. Unfortunately, as Marder (2000) points out, academics who mainly develop theories and models do not have the vast resources needed to test them; practitioners who have access to data are not necessarily interested in theory building.

Much of the academic work in our discipline concentrates on quantitative aspects of sampling, analysis, methodology, and model building. And even here, we have borrowed extensively from the methods developed by other social sciences such as statistics (most multivariate techniques), psychology (factor analysis), sociology (path analysis), biologists (cluster analysis), and agriculture (experimental designs). Although these aspects of marketing research are very important, they are not substitutes for developing a core body of knowledge that transcends data collection and interpretation, no matter how sophisticated the underlying techniques are.

As it stands, we have the two solitudes: facts without models and models without facts.[2] However, the basis of all sciences is empirical data. To the extent our models and theories are not extensively supported by empirical data, we can presume we have a core body of knowledge.

What is of concern to us is those who are at the extremes, as in Figure 3: those who develop models with no significant empirical base (models without facts) and those who collect data without consolidating their knowledge (facts without models).

Both these extremes are undesirable. However, models without facts can be more damaging, because they elevate unconfirmed theorizing to the status of lawlike relationships. If we were to make a choice between the two, lack of knowledge is preferable to false knowledge. No amount of theory or quantitative analysis can supplant the need for empirical data. Application of experimental designs and mathematical modeling to data may enrich our analysis once we have the data, but we cannot replace empirical data with mathematical models.

Models we build need confirmation. There are two meanings of the word "confirm" (Poundstone 1988). In common usage, "confirm" is used in the absolute sense, to mean that something is established beyond a reasonable doubt. Whatever doubts we had about the issue before, we don't have them now. However, in science, hardly any experiment, data, or statistical technique can be proved with such absolute confirmation. So "confirmation" in social sciences does not mean that we know with certainty how something works but rather that we have not found any evidence

---

[2]What I describe as facts without models may have *some* underlying models, and models without facts may have *some* underlying facts. The terms are used as shorthand descriptions of the gross imbalance between facts and models in these two approaches.

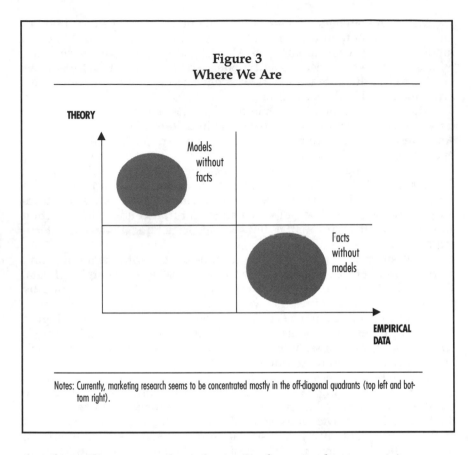

Figure 3
Where We Are

THEORY

Models without facts

Facts without models

EMPIRICAL DATA

Notes: Currently, marketing research seems to be concentrated mostly in the off-diagonal quadrants (top left and bottom right).

thus far to disprove our hypothesis. Confirmation here means incremental, not absolute, confirmation. That is why it is highly unsatisfactory to derive lawlike relationships on the basis of a single set of data, no matter how extensive the data and analysis happen to be.

As Karl Popper (1992a) points out, a new theory must have greater empirical content. It should also make more testable predictions than the old theory. We cannot create a new theory or lawlike relationship that is based on a poor empirical foundation with no explicit means for testing the theory's soundness. Applying complicated statistical methods to a single set of data is riddled with a variety of problems and is not likely to lead to knowledge.

Black Box Models

The second outcome of the lack of a strong core body of knowledge is the proliferation of black box models. These are "proprietary" models developed by commercial vendors that are claimed to predict marketing successes of different marketing activities. For example, there are black box models that purport to predict future sales volumes of new products or forecast the success of a commercial yet to be aired. Because the mechanics of the models are not revealed to the buyer, the buyer necessarily has to rely on the persuasion skills and promises of the vendor. Black box models do not allow the buyers to evaluate for themselves the reasonableness and correctness of the assumptions and procedures involved.

Black box models implicitly assume to have uncovered some lawlike relationship. Yet they are of unknown validity and suspect because "the necessarily simple concepts behind a *good* method can hardly be kept a secret for long" (Ehrenberg and Bound 2000, p. 40). Claims of precise predictability by proponents of black box models can at times stretch one's credulity. If such precise knowledge were possible, it is only reasonable to assume that it would not have eluded the thousands of other researchers who work this rather narrow field of inquiry. We can of course never be sure, because there is no way to subject these models to scientific scrutiny. If proponents of the model cannot prove the validity of the model, neither can we disprove its lack of validity. This leads us to our next point.

We are uncomfortable with black box models not necessarily because there may be less to them than meets the eye, but because they lack the hallmark of scientific models: *refutability* (Popper 1992b). As Kuhn (1962) argues, even science is not protected from error. One main reason the scientific method is accepted in all disciplines is that science is self-correcting. Its models are open, and anyone can refute it with the use of logic or empirical evidence. Any knowledge worth having is worth scrutinizing. The opaqueness of black box models makes them impervious to objective scrutiny. Consequently, in spite of their scientific aura and claims to proprietary knowledge, black box models contribute little to our core body of knowledge. Unfortunately, the less we know about marketing processes, the more marketers will be dependent on black boxes of unknown validity.

WHERE WE HAVE TO BE

As we review the process by which we got here, some broad themes begin to emerge:

1. We have defined ourselves too narrowly to be of relevance in a changing environment;

2. Even though we swim in a sea of data, a false sense of absolute confidentiality has prevented many firms from sharing their data with others, even when such data were outdated;

3. Because we frequently use information as knowledge and because nobody seems to expect this of us, we have failed to develop a core body of knowledge;

4. As a result, models without facts and black models have replaced genuine knowledge; and

5. To regain our rightful position in the decision making process, we need to redefine ourselves and build a core body of knowledge.

As indicated at the beginning of this chapter, many concrete suggestions have been offered by many professionals in this field. Mahajan and Wind (1999) offer the following prescriptions: focus on diagnosing problems, use new information technology, take an integrated approach, and expand its strategic impact. Adams (1999) suggests that issues such as self-esteem, positioning, core competencies, and business analysis need to be addressed. These issues are of considerable importance. Yet for such functional nostrums to be effective in the long run, we need to define our identity in terms of our goals. We need to develop a core body of knowledge.

A SLOW MARCH TOWARD A CORE BODY OF KNOWLEDGE

In a way, perhaps we have known all along that we need a core body of knowledge. Marketing researchers such as Ehrenberg and Marder have independently tried to develop such a core body. We can assume that academics who attempted to build models, though they did not have access to large volumes of data, did so in an attempt to develop a core body of knowledge. But not enough has been done, and we continue to lack a core body of knowledge.

In marketing research, lawlike relationships are orphans. Applied researchers tend to concentrate on gathering and interpreting information, whereas academics tend to concentrate on methodology and techniques. Academics are mainly concerned with the *how well* (techniques and methods), whereas applied researchers are mainly concerned with the *how to* (implementation and interpretation). Academics act as enablers, whereas applied researchers use the techniques to solve day-to-day problems. But, as we have been discussing, a mature discipline should be more than a collection of techniques and agglomeration of facts. It should lead to generalizable observations. It should lead to knowledge.

We can think of knowledge as our discipline. Not just information, not just techniques. Information and skills imparted through techniques are not only ends in themselves (though they often can be), but also means to an end. That end is knowledge, and therefore, knowledge is our discipline. Marketing research can be thought of as a collection of techniques, an approach to solving problems as well as a means of uncovering lawlike relationships, which is our final goal.

From an overall perspective, we need to merge facts with models, theory with practice. Models that cannot be empirically verified have no place in an applied discipline like marketing research. Figure 4 is a conceptual illustration of merging facts with models. To arrive at knowledge, we convert data into information and information into lawlike relationships and merge empirical facts with verifiable theory.

I think the last point is worth emphasizing. Marketing research should be more than just an approach to solving problems—it should result in an uncovering of lawlike relationships in marketing. It should not be just a collection of tools—it should also be what these tools have produced over a period of time that is of enduring value. Market researchers should be able to say not only that they have the tools to solve a variety of problems, but also that they have developed a core body of knowledge using these tools. In short, marketing research is not just a "means" discipline, but an "ends" discipline as well.

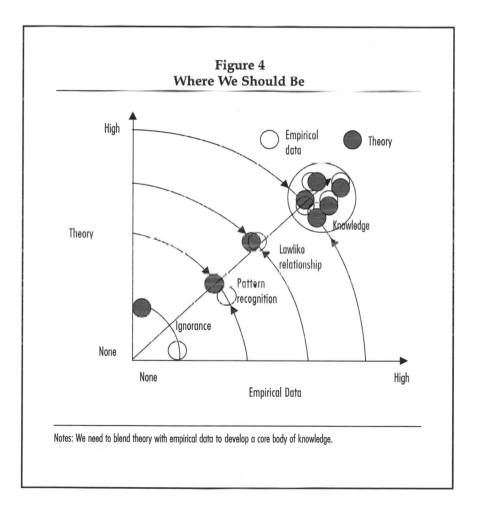

Figure 4
Where We Should Be

Notes: We need to blend theory with empirical data to develop a core body of knowledge.

Differences in Emphasis?

There is not much controversy surrounding the method of developing a core body of knowledge: collect data; observe patterns; set up hypotheses; test, refine, and expand hypotheses; and derive lawlike relationships. In practice, however, researchers differ in their emphasis. Even when we review the works of two researchers such as Ehrenberg and Marder, who each devoted several years in an attempt to create a core body of knowledge, we find differences in their approaches. Ehrenberg and Bound (2000) recommend setting forth informal hypotheses (pattern detection) on the basis of very little data. However, they rely on extensive empirical evidence to confirm their initial hypotheses. Marder (2000), in contrast, waits for the accumulation of so much empirical evidence that he starts with laws (or axioms) instead of hypotheses. If we consider Marder's axioms similar to the five axioms set forth by Euclid (from which he derived a whole subset of mathematics), then it is doubtful whether axioms can work in the same way in marketing research as they do in fields such as mathematics. Although mathematics can be a strictly deductive system that does not directly concern itself with the truth values of its propositions outside the system, the same cannot be said of applied disciplines. Even in mathematics, the axiomatic approach leads to paradoxical results (Whitehead and Russell 1910–1913), and one needs to go outside the system to resolve its truth value (Godel 1931). However, if we consider Marder's axioms as higher-order hypotheses that are based on extensive empirical data, then his axioms are similar to Ehrenberg's lawlike relationships. Whereas Ehrenberg and Bound generally express lawlike relationships in an algebraic form (e.g., "$b_{N/P} = Db_N$"), Marder expresses them in a more abstract fashion (e.g., "congruent choice situations have equal choice vectors").

In general, marketing researchers differ in the amount of evidence they need to accept a given pattern as strong enough to warrant testing and the amount and nature of confirmatory evidence they need to elevate preliminary hypotheses into lawlike relationships.

KNOWLEDGE AS OUR DISCIPLINE

Developing lawlike relationships and creating a core body of knowledge are marketing research's contribution to the understanding of marketing as processes. We cannot overemphasize that marketing research does not exist solely to provide information to decision makers, but also to develop a core body of marketing knowledge. Marketing research does not simply provide input to decision makers, but is also a part of the decision-making process. Marketing research is not peripheral to, but an integral part of, marketing decision making. To treat it otherwise impoverishes both marketing and marketing research.

To develop a core body of knowledge, we need to reexamine and perhaps discard many currently held beliefs, such as

- ❑ The sole purpose of marketing research is to collect and analyze data,
- ❑ Marketing researchers cannot directly participate in the decision-making processes,
- ❑ It is acceptable for decision makers to have an implicit faith in models that cannot be put through transparent validity checks (proprietary black boxes),
- ❑ Marketing researchers can be an effective part of the decision-making process without possessing a core body of knowledge,
- ❑ All data are forever confidential, and
- ❑ Lawlike relationships can be uncovered with the sheer strength of mathematical and statistical techniques without our first having to build a strong empirical base.

We need to work consciously toward creating a core body of knowledge. We deliberately need to share information and data. We need to discourage secret knowledge and unwarranted confidentiality. We need not to be content with just immediate solutions to marketing problems.

For those of us who have long believed that marketing research is more than a glorified clerical function, it has been obvious that a substantial part of marketing research should be concerned with developing knowledge that contributes to our understanding of marketing as a process.

For anyone who accepts this premise, it is self-evident that knowledge is our discipline. If it had not been so in the past, it should be so in the future.

BIBLIOGRAPHY

Adams, Tony (1999), "'A New Dimension' for Market Researcher," *Marketing Research: A Magazine of Management & Applications,* 11 (3), 32–33.

American Marketing Association (1961), *Report of Definitions Committee of the American Marketing Association.* Chicago: American Marketing Association.

——— (2000), "The Leadership Imperative," Attitude and Behavioral Research Conference, Phoenix, AZ (January 23–26).

Box, G.E.P. (1965), "Mathematical Models for Adaptive Control and Optimization," *AI. Ch. E. –1. Ch. Chem. E. Symp.,* Series 4, 61.

Braithwaite, R. (1955), *Scientific Explanation.* Cambridge: Cambridge University Press.

Cox, Keith K. and Ben M. Evans (1972), *The Marketing Research Process.* Santa Monica, CA: Goodyear Publishing Company.

Ehrenberg, A.S.C. (1982), *A Primer in Data Reduction.* Chichester, England: John Wiley & Sons.

——— and John Bound (2000), "Turning Data into Knowledge," in *Marketing Research: State-of-the-Art Perspectives,* Chuck Chakrapani, ed. Chicago: American Marketing Association, 23–46.

———, G.J. Goodhardt, and T.P. Barwise (1990), "Double Jeopardy Revisited," *Journal of Marketing,* 54 (3), 82–89.

Fellman, Michelle Wirth (1999), "Marketing Research is 'Critical'," *Marketing Research: A Magazine of Management & Applications*, 11 (3), 4–5.

Financial Times (1997), *The Complete MBA Companion*. London: Pitman Publishing.

—— (1999), *Mastering Marketing*. London: Pitman Publishing.

Gibson, Larry (2000), "Quo Vadis, Marketing Research?" working paper, Eric Marder Associates, New York.

Godel, Kurt (1931 [1992 translation]), *On Formally Undecidable Propositions of Principia Mathematica and Related Systems*, B. Meltzer, trans. New York: Dover Publications.

Kinnear, Thomas C. and James Taylor (1979), *Marketing Research: An Applied Approach*. New York: McGraw-Hill.

Kuhn, Thomas (1962), *The Structure of Scientific Revolutions*. Chicago: University of Chicago Press.

Mahajan, Vijay and Jerry Wind (1999), "Rx for Marketing Research," *Marketing Research: A Magazine of Management & Applications*, 11 (3), 7–14.

Marder, Eric (2000), "At the Threshold of Science," in *Marketing Research: State-of-the-Art Perspectives*, Chuck Chakrapani, ed. Chicago: American Marketing Association, 47–71.

Marketing News (1987), "New Marketing Definition Approved," (January 2), 1, 14.

McPhee, William N. (1963), *Formal Theories of Mass Behaviour*. Glencoe, NY: The Free Press.

Popper, Karl (1992a [reprint]), *The Logic of Scientific Discovery*. London: Routledge.

—— (1992b [reprint]), *Conjectures and Refutations: The Growth of Scientific Knowledge*, 5th ed. London: Routledge.

Poundstone, William (1988), *The Labyrinths of Reason*. New York: Doubleday.

Whitehead, A.N. and Bertrand Russell (1910–1913 [1962 reprint]), *Principia Mathematica*. Cambridge: Cambridge University Press.

2
Turning Data into Knowledge

Andrew Ehrenberg and John Bound

I n this chapter, we describe informally how we have, over the years, developed knowledge and understanding from observed data.

The process crucially involves the analysis of a sequence of many sets of data in turn (usually called MSoD). The same observed pattern may recur under different circumstances, thus building up piecemeal into a lawlike relationship. The process is slow — often a matter of fumbling. But in the end, it produces results, though so far, it has done so more often in the physical and biological sciences than in social science and marketing, for which this MSoD approach has not yet been widely practiced.

A contrasting approach is to seek the instant solutions supposedly provided by one of the popular statistical analytic techniques, such as multiple regression or factor analysis. These are usually applied to just a single set of data (SSoD) and therefore cannot and do not lead to generalisable findings.

To discuss these issues, we use a running example about customer retention and brand switching in the car market.

THE PROGRESSION:
DATA → INFORMATION → KNOWLEDGE

The basic progression is from some isolated data to relationships among data (i.e., information) and then to deeper understanding and knowledge.

Data

Research into marketing and day-to-day commercial or administrative operations (e.g., loyalty schemes) currently produces data in almost unimaginable profusion. But often, this is to no apparent purpose.

Statisticians unfortunately hinder the process of turning any such data into information. They have largely accustomed themselves during the past 150 years to just extending the results observed in a small and isolated sample to the larger population from which it was sampled (using their careful logic of probabilistic inference).

But statisticians' methods are seldom able to summarize and describe data in a way that communicates. Indeed, they have long been scornful of "mere" descriptive statistics and, hence, were helpless once the data deluge started.

Classical sampling inference itself became largely trivial when sample sizes started to run into thousands or millions. But "statistical inference" was, in any case, never more than an item of preventative hygiene to guard against the errors and biases than can occur with small data sets. Data about large populations, whether observed directly or inferred from a small sample, are seldom turned into usable information by textbook methods of statistical inference.

Information

When relationships *are* found in data (i.e., saying how this varies with that), it is the beginning of information, not just data. Finding relationships may be attempted by using one of the innumerable statistical techniques that are on the market (e.g., correlation and regression, factor, conjoint or other forms of multivariate analysis, explicit "data mining"; Hair et al. 1998). Innumerable associations can thus be found in any big database. But in our experience, these statistical procedures have seldom, if ever, led to lastingly useful results; no lasting results from ten years ago, say, seem to be quoted in the literature.

To be useful, a relationship needs, in our view, to be part of a generalisable pattern, as we will illustrate subsequently. It can then, for example, be used predictively. In contrast, an isolated result is of little practical or theoretical use because it is isolated; it only happened once. "Good" analysis therefore turns on linking up MSoDs and, in particular, linking a new result to *previous* findings. This means using prior knowledge.

Critics sometimes complain that they have no prior knowledge. But in any given area of study, that can happen once at most. As soon as someone has analyzed some data and established a relationship (e.g., how certain attitudes vary with behavior), it constitutes prior knowledge for use in analyzing any new data of broadly that kind (e.g., buyer behavior, attitudes, promotions). The first step with any new data then is not to seek a new relationship again (e.g., a best fit regression for that data) but to test whether the previous relationship still persists. For this, no "sophisticated" statistical techniques are needed.

Knowledge

Knowledge is more conceptual than mere information. Information is still only some linked bits of data. Knowledge implies having a wider context and some growing understanding. For example, under what different circumstances has the attitude–behavior relationship been found to hold; that is, how does it vary according to the circumstances? With knowledge of this kind, we can begin successfully to predict what will happen when circumstances change or when we experimentally and deliberately change the circumstances. This tends to be called "science," at least when it involves empirically grounded predictions that are routinely successful.

It may seem easy to agree with this view of science in broad general terms. But successfully applying it in marketing tends to be less obvious. Indeed, many have despaired of finding generalisable knowledge in marketing, or in the social sciences more generally, and have declared it to be all too complex. Yet experience has shown that it need not be so; there are already many examples of regular and predictable relationships in marketing (see, e.g., Bass 1994). The running example that is set out in the next section is a case in point (see also Ehrenberg 1968; Ehrenberg and Bound 1993).

We believe that the main stumbling block in developing lawlike relationships is that statistically minded researchers usually try to find an instant solution to a practical problem, without first investing in longer-term R&D to establish what, if any, generalisable relationships exist in the data. This is like astronomers trying to predict the date of an eclipse without having studied the movements of the planets.

A Running Example: Regularities in the Car Market

To illustrate the research process, we use a specific example from our recent work—a "hook to hang things on." This work established the nature of customer retention and brand switching in the car market (Ehrenberg and Bound 2000). As is outlined in the next section,

1. We in effect started with an isolated datum, namely, that repeat buying of Mercedes cars in France in 1989 was 65%.

2. We next noted two patterns ("information"): (a) that it also was roughly 65% in the preceding three years (the other French data available for Mercedes) and (b) that repeat rates for other makes were lower than for Mercedes.

3. We then saw more relationships, such as that repeat buying generally decreases with decreasing market share and an explanation for this (the "Double Jeopardy" [DJ] phenomenon). We also observed how DJ holds in different countries despite their different market share structures and that Mercedes was an exception. This was the beginning of knowledge: understanding, insights, and theory slowly building up.

This analysis process did not start from scratch. It followed previous work during many years in which similar regularities had been found for grocery and other products, though not for anything like motor cars (which can cost 10,000 times as much to buy as a jar of coffee, say, and are in solus-site distribution). In effect, therefore, we knew what to look for (we had hypotheses). But the results need not have worked out like those for other products; automobiles might have been different.

We believe that starting with prior results and building on them is a universal approach to establishing and extending new knowledge. It is slow but can get faster as experience in an area grows. Instant revelations are few, but they still have to be carefully checked.

REPEAT BUYING OF CAR MAKES: AN EXAMPLE

We now outline how the nature of repeat buying of different brands or makes of motor cars, such as Ford and Renault, was recently established (e.g., Ehrenberg and Bound 2000). As we have noted, this followed 40 years of work on the repeat buying of frequently bought grocery products from soap to soup (e.g., Ehrenberg 1959, 1972; Ehrenberg and Uncles 2000). The blow-by-blow history of this longer-term development is outlined in a later section.

Data

In 1989, Mercedes was reported to have a repeat buying rate of 65% in France. Thus, two-thirds of those previously owning a Mercedes bought a Mercedes again as their new car that year.

This was just an isolated datum. In the *HBR* editors' language, "What's the so what?" Is 65% high, low, or normal—as many as 65% buying Mercedes again or only 65%? And what are the implications? To tell required more data.

Information

Repeat buying of Mercedes in France in the three preceding years, 1986 to 1988 (the only available cases), was 58%, 62%, and 62%, respectively, and then 65% in 1989, as noted (average 62%). So we have the beginning of *information*: a pattern. Repeat buying of Mercedes in France was generally approximately 60% for these four years and slightly increasing.

But what was repeat buying like for other makes and in other countries? If it differed, why was that? And did the increase in repeat buying recur?

Repeat buying and switching data for all the other car brands in France in the four years were already available, as in Table 1. It was, however, not of much help in this undigested form (i.e., the traditional way the data were first provided to us by Renault France, to whom we are indebted).

Table 1
Repeat-Buying and Switching of 15 Leading Car Makes: The Original Counts, France 1989

NEWLY PURCHASED MAKE

PREVIOUS MAKE	Alfa	BMW	Cit	Fiat	Ford	GM	Lada	Merc	Peu	Ren	Rov	Saab	Seat	VW	Volv	Total Sample
Alfa Romeo	97	5	19	19	14	7	0	3	27	35	5	1	6	17	4	268
BMW	4	163	20	9	14	6	0	19	39	40	6	3	4	29	4	374
Citroen	6	13	1811	136	98	67	21	15	464	477	29	1	28	90	10	3311
Fiat	11	5	69	526	50	49	12	3	134	148	27	1	17	82	5	1165
Ford	4	10	45	53	696	76	8	8	121	146	20	1	23	60	7	1312
GM	2	7	20	23	50	362	7	4	68	80	7	0	12	39	4	710
Lada	0	0	12	13	11	12	63	0	25	76	4	0	3	7	0	180
Mercedes	2	17	3	3	5	2	0	136	4	10	3	1	1	5	3	210
Peugeot	13	23	273	164	125	168	34	23	2923	728	47	2	60	199	20	4962
Renault	22	37	353	334	308	254	40	33	895	4861	78	4	106	310	24	7775
Rover	2	4	18	25	30	3	6	1	30	45	115	0	6	40	2	337
Saab	1	2	0	1	0	0	0	2	0	0	0	10	0	2	1	20
Seat	2	0	13	10	10	11	0	0	10	29	3	0	36	13	0	137
VW/Audi	6	21	50	51	45	59	2	10	177	115	13	3	25	772	9	1417
Volvo	1	3	11	5	4	6	0	3	9	17	3	2	4	18	78	169
Total sample	209	367	3184	1647	1829	1297	233	313	5839	7937	440	36	394	1936	204	26774

Table 1 required much rearrangement before we, as analysts, could understand it, let alone present it meaningfully to anyone else. Otherwise, it was just providing us with a puzzle:

Here are some data. I can't understand it. Perhaps you can.

What we needed was attempts at "pattern recognition." But for this to be possible, the data had to be made more user-friendly, as in Table 2.

Now, we could use unashamed eyeballing to try to spot apparent patterns and subpatterns (or at least to recognize them once one has been told what they are, as we are doing here). Thus, in Table 2, one can now see fairly easily that

1. The repeat buying percentages in the leading diagonal in the table are very high compared with the switching figures, mostly about 50% or so.

2. The switching figures themselves are mostly similar in each column compared with their column average. (The figures in the Saab row jump around by 5 percentage points because they are based on a subsample of only 20).

3. The percentages in the Av. Switching row decrease 50-fold from the Large Local market leaders on the left to the small Luxury makes on the right (from 11% down to 0.2%).

4. This gradient largely recurs for each make in the rows of the table.

5. The average switching percentage (3.5%) shown on the right is about half the average penetration (6.5%). This leads to the initial normative "prediction" that the average switching levels in each column might be approximately $0.5 \times$ penetration for each make, as is also shown near the bottom of the table. (This turns out to be broadly so, at least to a fairly close degree of approximation. The correlation is approximately 0.95).

6. In more detail, however, the Av. Switching % are somewhat lower than these "predictions" for the first three makes (labeled by us the "Large Locals" here), slightly higher for the next eight makes, and then markedly higher for the four Luxury makes.

7. Further inspection of Table 2 shows that this Low → High → Higher pattern for the average switching does not occur in most of the individual rows.

8. Instead, one can see clusters; for example, switching between the three Large Local makes in the upper left-hand corner was higher than the column averages, and switching was very high (relative to column averages again) among the four Luxury makes in the lower right-hand corner. (It was these apparent patterns that led us to form the provisional clusters of "Large Local" makes and so on as this kind of analysis proceeded).

Table 2
More Reader-Friendly Switching and Repeat Buying Percentages

FRANCE 1989 / PREVIOUS	Large Local ‖			NEW PURCHASE / Other European								Luxury				Av.
	Ren	Peu	Cit	VW	Ford	Fiat	GM	Rov	Seat	Lada	Alfa	Merc	BMW	Volv	Saab	
Renault	(63)	12	4.5	4.0	4.0	4.3	3.3	1.0	1.4	.5	.3	.4	.5	.3	.1	
Peugeot	15	(59)	5.5	4.0	3.9	3.3	3.4	.9	1.2	.7	.3	.5	.5	.4	.0	
Citroen	14	14	(34.7)	2.7	3.0	4.1	2.0	.9	.8	.6	.2	.5	.4	.3	.0	
VW Audi	8	12	3.5	(54.5)	4.5	3.6	4.2	.9	1.8	.1	.4	.7	1.5	.6	.2	
Ford	11	9	3.4	4.6	(53.0)	4.0	5.8	1.5	1.8	.6	.3	.6	.8	.5	.1	
Fiat	13	12	5.9	7.0	4.3	(45.2)	3.2	2.3	1.5	1.0	.9	.3	.4	.4	.1	
GM	11	10	2.8	5.5	7.0	3.2	(51.0)	1.0	1.7	1.0	.3	.6	1.0	.6	.0	
Rover	13	9	5.3	11.9	8.9	7.4	.9	(34.1)	1.8	1.8	.6	.3	1.2	.6	.0	
Seat	21	7	9.5	9.5	7.3	7.3	8.0	2.2	(26.3)	.0	1.5	.0	.0	.0	.0	
Lada	9	14	6.7	3.9	6.1	7.2	6.7	2.2	1.7	(37.8)	.0	.0	.0	.0	.0	
Alfa Romeo	13	10	7.1	6.3	5.2	7.1	2.6	1.9	2.2	.0	(36.2)	1.1	1.9	1.5	.4	
Mercedes	5	2	1.4	2.4	2.4	1.4	1.0	1.4	.5	.0	1.1	(64.8)	8.1	1.4	.5	
BMW	11	10	5.3	7.8	3.7	2.4	1.6	1.6	1.1	.0	1.1	5.1	(43.6)	1.1	.8	
Volvo	10	5	5.5	13.7	2.4	3.0	3.6	1.8	2.4	.0	.6	1.8	1.8	(46.2)	1.2	
Saab	0	0	.0	10.0	.0	5.0	.0	.0	.0	.0	5.0	10.0	10.0	5.0	(50.0)	
Av. Switching	11	9	4.8	6.4	4.5	4.5	3.4	1.4	1.4	.5	.9	1.6	2.0	.9	.2	3.5
.5 × Penetration	15	11	4.9	3.7	3.4	3.1	2.4	.8	.7	.4	.4	.6	.7	.4	.1	3.2
Penetration	30	22	9.8	7.4	6.9	6.2	4.8	1.6	1.5	.9	.8	1.2	1.4	.8	.1	6.5

Notes: Data from Table 1 expressed as horizontal switching percentages and car makes ordered by size within provisional groupings with column averages, rounding, and "predictive" norms D × Penetration, with D = 0.5. See "Switching Between Car Makes" section. D = Av. Switching/Av. Penetration = 3.5/6.5 ≈ 0.5.

None of these patterns is apparent in the undigested format of Table 1, not even now that we know what the patterns are. Seeing them was, we stress again, a matter of actually looking at the data in a more user-friendly form, as in Table 2, and then eyeballing to see what could be seen. Making the results less personal and subjective was a second and conceptually separate step, as we note in the next section, though it is, in practice, overlapping. (When looking at Table 2, one "peeks" at other years' data to see whether the same things are showing up.)

The process involved in changing Table 1 into Table 2 used half a dozen so-called Data Reduction guidelines or rules, such as rounding, ordering by size, using averages, and so forth, which have been described previously (e.g., Ehrenberg 1975, 1977, 1981, 1982). Table 2 also reproduces the judgmental reordering of the car makes into subcategories or clusters ("Large Local," "Other European," and "Luxury") within which the results seemed more consistent. This had slowly been noted by a visual inspection and by checking against the other available data.

Knowledge

We have not hesitated to stress the eyeballing that occurred. This was, in our view, not only unavoidable if we were to get some feel for the previously unknown and opaque data, but also highly desirable. We had to actually *look at the data.*

Eyeballing is obviously subjective and judgmental, but so are the supposedly rigorous statistical techniques that are so often used instead (e.g., choosing any one of the many kinds of regression, factor, or correspondence analyses that are available).

Objectivity in the results could be increasingly achieved by simple replication—looking to establish whether the initial results are consistent and generalisable across other different sets of data. The more these data sets differ from one another in their circumstances and background conditions, the stronger are any ensuing empirical generalisations and conclusions (e.g., Lindsay and Ehrenberg 1993).

To see patterns and exceptions in the repeat rates themselves more easily than in Table 2 (and in the seven other such big tables that were available), we formed something like Table 3, which reproduces just the average penetrations and repeat rates in each country. The table also gives certain theoretical predictions that were developed and are briefly explained in a subsequent section.

Table 3 shows more clearly than before how the observed repeat rates are approximately 50% (e.g., on average and for the separate makes), as are the theoretical predictions. Crucially, the different makes therefore mostly had very similar repeat-loyalty. In addition, the agreement with the theory showed that the results for cars in Table 3 were *normal.* (The theory successfully reflects the observed findings of this kind in more than 50 other product categories.)

Table 3
Repeat Buying and Market Penetrations

France 1986-89	Pene-tration	Repeat Buying O	Repeat Buying P	Britain 1986-89	Pene-tration	Repeat Buying O	Repeat Buying P
Large Local	%			**Large Local**	%		
Renault	29	61	65	Ford	27	69	63
Peugeot	22	55	61	Rover	16	54	58
Citroen	12	55	56	GM	14	58	57
Other European				**Other European**			
Ford	7	51	54	VW/Audi	5	54	53
VW/Audi	7	52	53	Peugeot	5	43	52
Fiat	6	44	53	Renault	4	48	52
GM	5	51	52	Fiat	3	50	52
Rover	2	(36)	51	Volvo	3	57	51
Seat	1	(31)	51	Citroen	2	52	51
Lada	1	(39)	50				
Alfa	1	(37)	50	**Japanese**			
				Nissan	6	55	53
				Toyota	2	50	51
				Honda	1	47	50
				Mazda	1	52	50
Luxury				**Luxury**			
BMW	2	50	51	BMW	2	52	51
Mercedes	1	(62)	51	Mercedes	1	(62)	51
Volvo	1	45	50	Saab	1	49	50
Saab	0	48	50	Porsche	0	47	50
Average	6	48	53	Average	5	53	53

Notes: Observed = O; Predictions = P = 50% + 0.5 × penetration. ( ) = Deviations O to P of 10 points or more.

Exceptions

Three exceptions to this make-by-make similarity of the repeat rates in Table 3 stood out:

1. Much lower repeats, down in the 30% range, for four small makes in France, much lower also than predicted. (We have

no data to help explain these cases as yet but they were mostly consistent across the four years.)

2. A small consistent downward DJ trend in both countries: As discussed subsequently, car makes with lower market shares or penetrations[1] had lower repeat rates (e.g., the Other European makes at about 50% versus the Large Locals, with repeat rates closer to 60%).

3. The repeats for Mercedes were high at just more than 60%. This occurred in both countries for seven of the eight surveys. (It presumably is linked to this make's exceptional reputation and is discussed further subsequently. The surprise perhaps was that consistent make-related "exceptions" were not more common.)

The Double Jeopardy Phenomenon

The downward trend in repeat rates with market penetration that occurred in Table 3 was quickly recognized as an instance of DJ, an already known and very general phenomenon that says that small brands are "punished" twice for being small. They have fewer buyers than the big brands, and these few buyers do not buy them as often or like them as much attitudinally (Ehrenberg, Goodhardt, and Barwise 1990; McPhee 1963). The explanation of DJ was known to be as follows:

Double Jeopardy is a statistical selection effect that relates purely to market share or penetration. It is not a matter of a brand's "strength" or "equity." This is demonstrated by DJ being predicted by the Dirichlet model (see the "A Theoretical Model" section), which depends only on each make's market share, not on any attributes of the specific brands.

To find the statistical selection mechanism, consider for simplicity just two brands, a large "L "and a small "S." Buyers of each will also tend to buy other brands in the category, as is normal (consumers are generally polygamous). What is more, customers of each brand buy the whole category (i.e., any brand) at approximately the same average rates (e.g., Ehrenberg 1972; Ehrenberg and Uncles 2000).

Customers of L will also tend to buy S, but they do so fairly infrequently, in line with S being small. Buyers of L therefore have to buy L itself relatively often (to make up their total category rate of buying).

Conversely, customers of S tend also to buy L but do so relatively often because L is large. They therefore buy S relatively less often compared with how often customers of L buy L. That is the DJ trend being caused by "statistical selection," namely, that the repeat buying (or brand loyalty) varies with market share and is independent of the identity and

---

[1]With, at most, one purchase of a new car being made in a year, annual penetrations (percentage of car owners buying a new car) here are equal to the makes' market shares.

nature of the particular brand. Table 4 recounts a popular anecdote to illustrate statistical selection in a more general form.

The car data in Table 2 provide a direct test, or a "natural experiment," to show how DJ is a matter of market share or penetration, not of the idiosyncratic properties or "equity" of the individual brands as such. Table 5 (formalized here from our initial notes) summarizes the DJ effect

---

Table 4
Statistical Selection and National Intelligence

When a Scotsman emigrates to England, the average intelligence of both countries goes up. This is not because the Scots and the English both become more intelligent. Instead, it is due to statistical selection, in two steps:

1. Only a rather dumb Scotsman emigrates to England. Hence, the average intelligence in Scotland will go up.

2. But even a dumb Scotsman is more intelligent than the English. Therefore, on his arrival, the average intelligence in England also goes up.

Table 5
Average Market Penetrations and Repeat Buying

1986-89	*FRANCE* Av. Penetration	Av. Repeat % 0	P	*BRITAIN* Av. Penetration	Av. Repeat % 0	P
Average	%			%		
Large Local*	20	56	60	19	60	59
Other European	1	50	52	3	52	52
Japanese	—	—	—	2	52	51
Luxury	1	50	51	1	52	51
Exceptional						
Low repeats†	1	(36)	50	na	na	na

Notes: Observed = O, and Predicted = P.
*Renault, Peugeot, and Citroen in FRANCE; Ford, GM, and Rover in BRITAIN.
†Rover, Seat, Lada, and Alfa Romeo in FRANCE.

Table 6
Share and Repeat: High and Low Go Together

1986-89	Pene-tration	Repeat % 0	Repeat % P
High Shares/Penetrations	%		
Renault in France	29	61	65
Ford in Britain	27	69	63
All Large Locals in own country	20	59	60
Low Shares/Penetrations			
Renault in Britain	4	48	52
Ford in France	7	51	54
All Large Locals in other country	4	47	52

Notes: Observed = 0, and Predicted = P.

in two countries. Large Locals—crucially made up of different large makes in the two countries—have high shares and higher repeat rates in each country (near 60% rather than near 50%).

Table 6 shows a more explicit comparison for specific makes that we explored: It shows how a make with a high penetration in one country was small in the other (e.g., Renault in France versus in Britain). The repeat buying levels match this variation: high Renault repeat buying in France at 61% observed (and 65% predicted) versus lower Renault repeat buying in Britain at 48% (and 52% predicted).

The Mercedes Story

We noted previously that the repeat levels of Mercedes car buying in France varied from year to year between a low of 52% and a high of 65%. Table 7 shows how this was found to be a systematic upward trend from 1986 to 1989 consistently over the two countries.

Repeat buying of Mercedes therefore increased by a remarkable 10 points or so. This is despite the make's more or less steady penetration or market share (it varied irregularly from year to year by an average ±2 in either country). The trend therefore was not a case of repeat buying

Table 7
Mercedes: The Increase in Repeat Buying

	Britain	*France*
1989	65	65
1988	65	64
1987	63	62
1986	58	52
Av.	61	64

increasing because penetration had increased, together in the tandem DJ fashion. Nor did repeat buying for other car makes increase. Instead, an unusual "real" increase in repeat loyalty for Mercedes has occurred, which requires further study.

SWITCHING BETWEEN CAR MAKES

To complement the analysis of repeat buying for a make such as Mercedes, we also explored the extent to which previous Mercedes owners switched to other makes if they made a new car purchase in a given year. Table 2 shows the observed switching data for France in 1989, and we summarised the initial results of eyeballing these data just after Table 2. We now discuss a little more fully how our understanding of the data evolved.

Brand Switching: The Duplication of Purchase Law

The basic finding was that the number of new car buyers in the analysis year who switched to other makes varied with the percentage who bought each of these makes at all in that year (i.e., the makes' market penetrations in 1989). This came from noting how the average duplications and penetrations (at the bottom of Table 2) decreased together from left (for Renault) to right (for Saab).

This relationship of switching to penetration was recognized as a case of the "duplication of purchase law," which had already been widely established for packaged goods in nonpartitioned markets (e.g., Ehrenberg 1972; Ehrenberg and Uncles 2000). For cars, this reads:

The % of the previous owners of make P who switch
to the new make $N \simeq D \times$ the penetration of N,
where P is previous make, N is newly bought make,
and $\simeq$ is approximately equal.

Put at its simplest, more people switch to a big make than to a small one.

The proportionality factor D (the duplication coefficient) reflects the likelihood of switching from the previous make P to a different make N, relative to how many people bought N at all in that year. Thus,

$$D = \frac{\%\ of\ owners\ of\ P\ who\ switch\ from\ P\ to\ N}{\%\ who\ buy\ N\ at\ all}.$$

For Table 2, the D values for individual makes were roughly 0.5. Thus, 15% of Peugeot's previous owners switched to Renault, which is half of Renault's overall penetration of 30%. And 0.3% or 0.4% switched to a Volvo, which is approximately half its 0.8% penetration. This was the main switching pattern: The levels of switching were broadly half of each make's penetration. (As noted previously, the correlation for Table 2 is r = 0.95.)

We also noted deviations and subpatterns. The average switching to each of the first three makes in Table 2 was lower than the predicted 0.5 penetration norms (Renault–Citroen). For the rest, it was higher. Indeed, for some makes (e.g., BMW and Mercedes) average switching was more than twice as high (though still small in absolute terms).

Extended scrutiny of all the results suggested that these deviations reflected consistent clusters or submarkets in each of the four years in Britain as well as in France (as is confirmed in Table 8). Using provisional labels, the clusters were thought to be

- ❑ *Large Local*: Three larger makes, mostly locally produced (Renault, Peugeot, and Citroen in France; Ford, GM, and Rover in Britain).
- ❑ *Other European*: Smaller European-made makes in that country (e.g., Ford, GM, VW, Fiat in France; Renault, Peugeot, VW, Fiat in Britain).
- ❑ *Japanese*: In Britain only (a low import quota operated in France).
- ❑ *Luxury*: BMW, Mercedes, Volvo, Saab, Porsche (Volvo only in France, where it had a higher technical specification; Porsche was itemized only in Britain for 1988–89 in the given data).

This suggested that the clustering we had evolved from the intuitive inspection of the data was in fact relatively sophisticated. Thus, the individual Large Local makes differ between the two countries. Renault, for

Table 8
Duplication Coefficients D by Submarket, Year, and Country

France and Britain 1986–89		Large Local*				Other European				Japanese				Luxury			
PREVIOUS		86	87	88	89	86	87	88	89	86	87	88	89	86	87	88	89
Large Local*	Fr	.5	.5	.5	.5	.6	.6	.6	.6	—	—	—	—	.5	.5	.4	.4
	Br	.5	.5	.4	.6	.5	.5	.5	.5	.5	.4	.5	.5	.3	.3	.2	.3
Other European*	Fr	.4	.5	.5	.5	.8	.9	.9	.9	—	.6	.5	—	.8	.8	.7	.6
	Br	.5	.4	.4	.4	.9	.7	.7	.7	.6	.6	.5	.5	.6	.6	.5	.6
Japanese	Fr	—	—	—	—	—	—	—	—	—	—	—	—	—	—	—	—
	Br	.4	.3	.4	.3	.6	.6	.6	.6	1.2	1.8	1.3	1.4	.5	.5	.4	.6
Luxury	Fr	.2	.3	.2	.3	.6	.5	.5	.8	—	—	—	—	3.2	4.3	3.7	4.7
	Br	.3	.3	.5	.3	.6	.6	.6	.6	.4	1.1†	.5	.6	3.2	3.5	4.4	3.8

NEW PURCHASES

Notes: D = average switching/average penetration within and between makes in the four clusters.
*Specific makes differ in the two countries (see text).
†Outlier.

example, is large in France but not in Britain, and the converse it true for Ford. The Other European groupings correspondingly differ in part. Yet the results for these clusters appear consistent.

The clusters were derived from the differing likelihoods of switching between pairs of makes, as expressed by their D values. Table 8 shows how these followed simple and consistent regularities across the eight available data sets.

The two main patterns were:

1. D values are mainly of the order of 0.5 (i.e., between about 0.3 and 0.7), as already noted.
2. Higher switching within three clusters (shown in bold): Ds of about 0.8 for Other European, 1.4 for Japanese makes (in Britain), and about 4.0 for Luxury makes.

Three much smaller subpatterns were noted also to generalise across the eight data sets, as discussed in our initial paper (Ehrenberg and Bound 2000), as are the wider sales implications (or the *lack* of such implications) of these findings.

A Theoretical Model

The duplication of purchase law noted previously can be expressed algebraically as $b_{N/P} = Db_N$. (This relates the percentage, $b_{N/P}$, of owners of make P who switch to make N to N's penetration, b_N.)

It follows that the theoretical predictor of the repeat buying rates is $100(1 - D) + D \times$ the penetration of the brand (see Ehrenberg and Bound 2000 for details). This shows a make's predicted repeat level to be 50% + 0.5 × its penetration when the D are mostly approximately 0.5, as in Table 8. The theoretical formula applied to any nonpartitioned market (i.e., with the same D, such as 0.5, for all pairs of makes). For a small make with a penetration of 1% or 2%, say, the predicted repeat is 51%. For a leading make like Renault in France or Ford in Britain with a share of almost 30% at the time, the predicted repeat rate is approximately $50 + 0.5 \times 30 = 65\%$. This was much as was observed, as is shown in Table 3.

Wider Theory

These algebraic repeat buying and brand switching models had long ago become part of a still wider theory of buyer behavior, the Dirichlet (see Ehrenberg 1988, Chapter 13; Ehrenberg and Uncles 2000). For near stationary and nonpartitioned markets, the Dirichlet assumes steady split loyalty individual repeat buying and brand choice propensities that vary from consumer to consumer. The preceding formulae then follow as simplifying approximations. (This theory has also successfully predicted a wide range of other brand performance measures, which are not available for the limited two-purchase data for cars.)

THE TRADITIONAL SSoD TECHNIQUES

Many different statistical techniques for analyzing data are put forward in the literature and research seminars or training courses (i.e., multiple regression/econometrics, cluster analysis, correspondence or factor analysis, discriminant analysis, perceptual mapping, multidimensional scaling, CHAID, conjoint analysis, neural networks, fuzzy logic, and many more; e.g., Hair et al. 1998). Each technique also has many variants. There is no generally preferred approach, and no consensus on the use of such techniques has evolved. Yet the results generally differ; therefore, at most, one can possibly be correct (but this seems probabilistically unlikely).

This lack of consensus has recently been explicitly illustrated by the so-called Car Challenge, a rare comparison of the results put forward in different analyses. We asked some 21 experienced analysts in the United States and Europe to tackle our 1986–89 car switching data (as in Table 1). They could each work in their own chosen way instead of being constrained to using a single and perhaps unfamiliar method. The 21 analytic approaches that were used differed markedly and, more disturbingly, so did the reported results (see Colombo, Ehrenberg, and Sabavala 1999; the full entries are reproduced in Colombo [1999]).

What is common to virtually all the analysis techniques used in the Car Challenge—as also in the statistically orientated literature more generally—is that each technique would be applied to just a SSoD. Here, for example, each might use Table 1 for France in 1989. No attempt was usually made to compare and/or integrate the results from two or more sets of data (e.g., France and Britain or two or more years)—the so-called MSoD approach mentioned previously.[2]

Other features common to the SSoD techniques are the following:

1. They adopt some deliberate (or "arbitrary") maximizing/optimizing principle (e.g., least squares, some specific form of factor rotation), usually without any explicit justification (even though least squares was invented by Gauss as long as 200 years ago, and factor rotation by Thurstone and others in the 1920s).

2. None of the procedures has yet led to any lasting substantive results (such as here, that loyalty levels of competitive brands of motor cars are very similar).

3. Nor has the use of these statistical analysis techniques generally led to much subject matter theory or lasting explanations.

---

[2]A partial exception is statisticians' use of "hold-out samples." This is, however, essentially concerned with guarding against sampling errors. It uses hold-outs, which are as similar as possible to the main data (at times even randomly selected) rather than being as different as possible, as is needed in searching for generalisability.

4. The result of an SSoD analysis is seldom if ever used as the input to any subsequent analysis of other data (e.g., given that the repeat buying levels in France 1988 were generally about 50%, few analysts in the Car Challenge asked how other years and countries compared with that).

5. There is almost universally a narrow focus merely on statistical inference from the available sample. The concern is with goodness of fit and whether the sample result really happened ("is significant"), not with describing what the result actually is. It may, for example, be reported that brand switching correlates significantly with market share, but not that in an unpartitioned market switching is actually proportional to the brands' market penetrations.

6. Many users of these statistical techniques appear to be very poor at noting and then describing any such patterns in their data (mainly, perhaps, because they have not been trained to do so).

7. The analysis procedures themselves often seem to range from being opaque to being obscure, that is, "grey boxes" if not "black boxes." Deliberately seeking to keep one's analysis technique *Confidential* or *Proprietary* is surprisingly widely tolerated, as if that were both ethical and feasible, yet the necessarily simple concepts behind a *good* method can hardly be kept secret for long.

8. Little or no "looking at the data" is practiced or even well thought of. Might it not bias the analyst to know what his or her data are like?

9. The outcome is that analysts mostly apply analysis procedures they do not really understand to a single set of new data, which, by definition, they also do not yet understand, with predictable outcomes (i.e., nothing much).

SSoD are like mules, having neither pride of ancestry (prior knowledge) or hope of posterity (being reusable). There is therefore a strong need for a radically different approach.

A THIRD WAY

Rather than either practicing initial pattern recognition on new data (as illustrated previously in this chapter) or applying some arbitrary statistical techniques (as outlined previously), there is a third way of tackling new data. This is to use any prior knowledge that is already available.

This becomes feasible (and even, we believe, *de rigeur*) when previous analyses — or usually an *accumulation* of previous analyses — have provided some results on which to build. Once prior results exist, they should not, and strictly speaking *cannot*, be ignored. Having to start literally from scratch can therefore happen, at most, once.

In our running example here, we now know for car makes in France and Britain, 1986–89, that switching was usually proportional to overall market penetration, that repeat buying was similar for different makes, that there were also certain regular exceptions (e.g., the DJ trend and Mercedes' high repeat buying), and how all this has been quantified.

Such prior knowledge can now simplify and enrich the analysis of any further data, old or new, in the car market or any other market. Do these already known patterns recur or not? This is easier and more objective to establish than relying yet again on the arbitrary choice of one of the exploratory technique-oriented statistical procedures discussed in the preceding section. Nor is there then any need for further unaided pattern recognition. Indeed, using a prior result as the comparison norm becomes increasingly acceptable the more widely and consistently the same pattern has been reported.

A SPECIFIC CASE HISTORY: DOUBLE JEOPARDY

We now briefly sketch in the dozen or so main piecemeal stages of the historical development of the DJ result in the second section as an example. (The duplication of purchase law in the third section typically followed a similar progression of piecemeal stages.)

First, in the study of purchase frequencies, our own work started some 40 years ago with examining the frequency distribution of purchases of a brand over a year, namely, how many light, medium, and heavy buyers there were.

The immediate cause was that, in the late 1950s, the sales of Cadbury's Drinking Chocolate (CDC) were consistently overreported by the Attwood Consumer Panel in Great Britain. Attwood's then-technical director, Douglas Brown, suggested calibrating the distribution of 1, 2, 3, 4, and so on purchases theoretically and then possibly being able to identify some excess heavy buyers who could be censored out, thus reducing the average purchase rate of the brand. (Doug Brown later became the "B" in the so-called AGB or Audley-Gapper-Brown consumer panel operation in Britain—first the rival then the successor of Attwood when it came to be called "Audits of Great Britain".)

Second, after various theoretical tryouts (e.g., with the Poisson distribution), the negative binomial distribution (NBD) was found to give a good fit and also provide a sensible theoretical rationale (Ehrenberg 1959). Indeed, the fit of the NBD to various sets of CDC-type data was so good that there were no "excess heavy buyers," and the Attwood Consumer Panel's reporting problem for those particular products remained.

Third, the NBD was subsequently found to fit for some other product categories, as has been confirmed many thousand times since. It was also found that the NBD gave a good fit for data in different lengths of time periods (e.g., a month, a year) and that its theoretical underpinning (Poisson-Gamma) explained this.

The NBD pattern was therefore discovered by serendipity, that is, by looking to explain exceptions and instead stumbling across an unexpected regularity. (But as Pasteur said, "Fortune favours the prepared mind.")

Fourth, certain consistent deviations were also found at about this time and subsequently explained (e.g., the so-called variance discrepancy [Chatfield 1967; Ehrenberg 1959, 1972], which typically has not been of the slightest general interest since).

Fifth, during the following few years, it was slowly realized that the frequency of purchase as modelled by the NBD and, in particular, the average purchase frequency were possible measures of repeat buying loyalty.

One stumbling block in reaching this now-obvious (but also controversial) insight was that the analyses had initially been conceived in terms of the number of units bought (a sales-related approach) rather than as purchase occasions (as proposed by James Rothman), which was consumer-related.

Sixth, some ten years after the initial paper, Grahn (1969) noted that the means of the NBD for different brands were much the same. Different brands had much the same average purchase frequencies or repeat buying loyalties. (This was subsequently found to recur also with all other possible measures of loyalty.) It was widely verified (for more than 500 brands), and new examples continue to be found.

It is now a major feature of branding that brands generally differ greatly in penetration (with small brands having few customers) but minimally in their repeat buying loyalty, their customers' average frequencies of purchase.

Seventh, this, for the first time, related buying of each brand across the different brands. Before Grahn (1969), nobody (including us) had ever thought to compare different brands' average purchase frequencies because it was not expected by anyone that they would follow any kind of regular pattern. Hence, no one had looked.

This initial failure to see the pattern was in large part caused by the data usually being badly reported (as is still largely the case). In particular, the purchase rates of different brands would usually be set out as in Table 9: in alphabetical order (rather than ordered by market share), to more than two digits (which makes numbers difficult to take in), without averages (to provide a visual focus), and without any theoretical norms or benchmarks (e.g., Ehrenberg 1982). Table 9 shows a part of Table 3 set out in this totally unhelpful but customary form.

Eighth, it was then slowly realized that, for large brands and in long time periods, penetrations tend to be very high (near 100%). Unlike the finding in the previous point, such penetrations therefore do not vary much from brand to brand. In contrast, average purchase frequencies *do* then vary greatly. The basic concept in all this is the sales equation:

$$\text{Sales} = \text{Penetration} \times \text{Average Purchase Frequency.}$$

Therefore, if penetrations for brands with different market shares do not differ, their average purchase frequency must. (Theoretical formula-

Table 9
Repeat Buying and Market Penetrations: France 1986–89

	Pene-tration	Repeat Buying
Alpha	1.4	37.1
Citroen	12.6	54.8
Fiat	5.9	48.6
Ford	6.3	50.3
GM	5.0	40.8
Lada	0.9	39.1
Peugeot	29.3	61.0
Renault	22.4	54.7
Rover	1.9	36.2
Seat	1.2	30.8
VW/Audi	6.3	52.1

Notes: Part of Table 3 with brands in alphabetical order, too many digits, no averages, and no theoretical norm.

tions such as the w(1 – b) formula in our tenth point and the Dirichlet model in our eleventh point now take care of this feature automatically.)

Ninth, somewhat later again (still the early 1970s), we realized that this relationship between small brands having low penetrations and *slightly* lower average purchase frequencies was an instance of the DJ phenomenon, which had already been noted, named (as Double Jeopardy), and theoretically explained by William McPhee (1963) some years earlier in a nonmarketing context (along the lines noted previously but more mathematically).

This explanation of DJ—that it is due not to brands but to market share (as illustrated in Tables 5 and 6)—is still widely misunderstood. Marketers have an almost unconquerable compulsion to think of brands as differing from one another not just in their brand name and their size but also in their "Brand Equity" (e.g., Aaker 1991).

Tenth, also in the early 1970s, our colleagues Gerald Goodhardt and Chris Chatfield realized that if buying of different brands was independent and if a brand's customers' average rates of buying the whole category were much the same from brand to brand (as, in practice, is virtually the case in both respects), then the formula w(1 – b) φ w$_o$, a constant for different brands, would hold. Here, b stands for a brand's penetration, w represents the average purchase frequency per buyer of the brand, and w_o is the average purchase frequency of a very small brand (i.e., in the limit as b tends to zero; see Ehrenberg 1988, p. 225, for a fuller description of Goodhardt's proof). This reflects the Double Jeopardy phenomenon. In particular, it says that the DJ effect is numerically very small for low penetrations b (as occurs for small brands and/or short time periods).

Eleventh, in the early 1970s still, the much more general Dirichlet model of buyer behavior began to be developed (Chatfield 1975; Ehrenberg 1988, Chapter 13; Goodhardt and Chatfield 1973; Goodhardt, Ehrenberg, and Chatfield 1984). This automatically incorporated the DJ effect as one of its many predictions.

Twelfth, subsequently much work has been done on the practical applications and implications of the DJ phenomenon and the Dirichlet-type results more generally (including for very different products like cars and services, as summarized in Ehrenberg and Uncles [2000]).

Thirteenth, in particular, a parallel range of results about television viewing (e.g., repeat viewing and switching between programs and channels) was developed in 100 or so reports mainly for the Independent Television Authority (ITA, now the IBA) in the United Kingdom and for the BBC, CBS, and NBC (e.g., Barwise and Ehrenberg 1988; Goodhardt, Ehrenberg, and Collins 1987). A $1–$2 million updating and extension of this work is currently under active consideration.

Fourteenth, among many "new" aspects of buyer behavior generally, and DJ in particular, to be pursued much more systematically in the new century are (1) the nature of dynamic market situations and (2) the market behavior of stockkeeping units (SKUs, including pack sizes, flavors, specific car models, product formats, and so on).

The SKUs are what manufacturers and service providers make and distribute, what retailers stock and sell, and what consumers buy and use. *Brands* are only what are advertised and promoted. Yet little or nothing is, so far, known about SKUs (e.g., Fader and Hardie 1996; Singh and Ehrenberg 2000).

CONCLUSIONS

Research into marketing issues has traditionally centered on data collection. This usually concerns just a single set of data (SSoD), though it is often large and complex (e.g., a survey). Much attention is paid to sample design, measurement techniques, tests of significance (perhaps), and the recording and graphing of voluminous cross-tabulations, and sometimes one-off modelling. Few, if any, lasting and thus usable results have been reported from this approach, however. The results are merely the most up-to-date just-out-of-date data, typically presented in splendid isolation.

Little attempt is usually made to develop the generalisable knowledge and insights that can come, we believe, or indeed *know*, from combining a variety of such studies over time. The process has been illustrated in this chapter with a recent case history that establishes some general aspects of customer retention and brand switching in the car market. (To learn more about how something like "brand loyalty" develops probably also needs deliberate experimentation; e.g., Ehrenberg and Charlton 1972; Ehrenberg, Charlton, and Pymont 1972.)

This has led to apparently stable relationships for brand loyalty and market structures that closely resemble those already found in many other markets, such as that loyalty measures differ little between brands, brand switching is mostly in line with market share, and stable clusters of more closely substitutable brands can be consistently identified. Such increasingly "lawlike" findings can therefore be applied predictively in the future.

The basic analytic steps described here were

1. Initial subjective pattern recognition for an ad hoc SSoD;
2. Generalizing the results across many sets of data (MSoD) obtained under different circumstances;
3. Replication also increasing the objectivity of the findings (e.g., different investigators agreeing);
4. Pinpointing exceptions (which tend, however, to be unexciting once they have been explained); and
5. The results providing benchmarks for further empirical studies, for building explanatory theory, and for practical applications.

BIBLIOGRAPHY

Aaker, David A. (1991), *Managing Brand Equity*. New York: The Free Press.

Barwise, T. Patrick and Andrew S.C. Ehrenberg (1988), *Television and Its Audience*. London: Sage Publications.

Bass, Frank M. (1994), "Empirical Generalizations and Marketing," *Marketing Science*, 14 (3), 61–66.

Chatfield, Christopher (1967), "Some Statistical Models for Buyer Behaviour," doctoral dissertation, University of London.

——— (1975), "A Marketing Application of a Characterisation Theorem," in *Statistical Distributions in Scientific Work*, Vol. 2, G.P. Patil, S. Kotz, and J.K. Ord, eds. Dordrecht: D. Reidel.

Colombo, Richard (1999), "Approaches to Analyzing Brand Switching Matrices," New York: Fordham University [available at http://www.bnet.fordham.edu/public/mrktg/rcolombo/Cars.htm].

———, Andrew S.C. Ehrenberg, and Darius Sabavala (1999), "The Car Challenge," working paper, London: South Bank University.

Ehrenberg, Andrew S.C. (1959), "The Pattern of Consumer Purchases," *Applied Statistics*, 8, 26–41.

——— (1968), "The Elements of Lawlike Relationships," *Journal of the Royal Statistical Society A*, 131, 280–329.

——— (1972 [1988 2d ed.]), *Repeat-Buying: Facts, Theory and Applications*. London: Edward Arnold (Griffin) [New York: Oxford University Press]. Reprint available at www.marketing.unisa.edu.au/MSC/JEMSintro.html.

———— (1975), *Data Reduction*. Chichester and New York: John Wiley & Sons.

———— (1977), "Rudiments of Numeracy," *Journal of the Royal Statistical Society A*, 140, 277–323.

———— (1981 [1992]), "The Problem of Numeracy," *The American Statistician*, 35 (May) [*Admap*, (February), 37–40].

———— (1982 [1994]), *A Primer in Data Reduction*. Chichester and New York: John Wiley & Sons.

———— and John Bound (1993), "Predictability and Prediction," *Journal of the Royal Statistical Society A*, 156, 167–206.

———— and ———— (2000), "Customer Retention and Brand-Switching in the Car Market," working paper, South Bank University, London.

———— and Peter Charlton (1972), "An Analysis of Simulated Brand-Choice," *Journal of Advertising Research*, 12, 21–33.

————, ————, and Brian Pymont (1972), "Buyer Behaviour Under Mini-Test Conditions," *Journal of the Market Research Society*, 14, 171–83.

————, Gerald Goodhardt, and Patrick Barwise (1990), "Double Jeopardy, Revisited," *Journal of Marketing*, 54 (3), 82–91.

———— and Mark D. Uncles (2000), "Understanding Dirichlet-Type Markets," working paper, South Bank University, London.

Fader, Peter S. and Bruce G.S. Hardie (1996), "Modeling Consumer Choice Among SKUs," *Journal of Marketing Research*, 33 (November), 442–52.

Goodhardt, Gerald J. and Chris Chatfield (1973), "Gamma-Distribution in Consumer Purchasing," *Nature*, 244 (5414), 316.

————, Andrew S.C. Ehrenberg, and Chris Chatfield (1984), "The Dirichlet: A Comprehensive Model of Buying Behaviour," *Journal of the Royal Statistical Society A*, 147, 621–55.

————, ————, and Martin A. Collins (1987), *The Television Audience*. Aldershot: Gower.

Grahn, Gary L. (1969), "The Negative Binomial Distribution Model of Repeat-Purchase Loyalty: An Empirical Investigation," *Journal of Marketing Research*, 6 (1), 72–78.

Hair, Joseph F., Rolph E. Anderson, Ronald L. Tatham, and William C. Black (1998), *Multivariate Data Analysis*, 5th ed. Upper Saddle River, NJ: Prentice Hall.

Lindsay, Murray R. and Andrew S.C. Ehrenberg (1993), "The Design of Replicated Studies," *The American Statistician*, 47 (3), 217–28.

McPhee, William N. (1963), *Formal Theories of Mass Behaviour*. Glencoe, NY: The Free Press.

Singh, J. and Andrew Ehrenberg (2000), "Buying Patterns for SUVs," presented at Academy of Marketing Doctoral Colloquium, Derby.

3
At the Threshold of Science

Eric Marder

Marketing research is at the threshold of becoming a science. Such a development does not take place suddenly. It isn't possible to pinpoint a single event that accomplishes the transition. Theories and techniques evolve gradually, take a step forward in some places, a step backward in others. This is especially true for "marketing research," which brings together many unconnected, in some cases mutually exclusive, practices under a single umbrella—so that practitioners of one persuasion may hardly recognize, or wish to be associated with, what travels under the same label elsewhere.

Notwithstanding the inevitable setbacks, the confusion of terminology, and the premature adoption of the trappings of science without its essential substance, a "science" that deals with the problems and data that have been broadly referred to as marketing research is beginning to take shape. To qualify as such, marketing research must meet several requirements. Most important, it must provide an effective "reduction" of experience. The phenomenological world presents us with an unlimited number of ways an event can be examined and measured. Science simplifies this world. It reduces the unlimited number of variables to a relatively small number. And it replaces an unlimited number of unique *facts* with a few general *principles*, sometimes known as axioms or laws. These laws are usually a synthesis of logic and empirical evidence and often appear to be "obvious," if not downright tautological. (A body at rest will continue at rest....) They are intended to be as general as possible, so the largest number of facts or events can be summarized or explained by the smallest number of laws. And they are intended to be universal—not just true at one time, in one place, not just under some particular set of circumstances, but everywhere, always, over as broad a range of events as possible. To the extent they meet this requirement, they constitute knowledge that can be passed on. A schoolboy today can calculate the time it takes for a stone dropped from a high building to reach the ground, a computation that was beyond the power of Aristotle. This is not because the schoolboy is more intelligent than Aristotle, but because he is equipped with truths, formulated by Galileo, that are as relevant in twentieth century America as they were in sixteenth century Europe. If truths are not readily transmittable, if the methods employed in an inquiry require special talents, if different practitioners tackling the same problem cannot be expected to arrive at the same conclusion, we may be dealing with an art, but we are not yet dealing with a science.

Finally, laws don't just remain sterile. They "go somewhere." They lead to explanations and/or predictions, to solutions of problems that were impossible or more difficult to solve before the laws were available. And they lead to the discovery and/or formulation of further truths derived from these laws, not by replacing them, but by building on them.

Where does today's marketing research stand in relation to these requirements? There is the marketing research of the academic journals, the marketing research of the many corporations around the world, and the marketing research of the commercial vendors. Typically, these define problems differently, define variables differently, and employ different nomenclature. And yet some common denominators are beginning to emerge. This raises the question whether these common denominators can be identified. Are there any propositions that are truly universal? And what might these propositions look like?

An effort to address these questions led to the formulation of some basic propositions that can be regarded as axioms or laws. The detailed rationale for these laws, supported by a large body of empirical evidence, has been presented elsewhere (Marder 1997). This chapter deals with the inferences that can be drawn from the laws. It explores their implications for how we do marketing research and for the view that marketing research may indeed be at the threshold of becoming a science.

PREDICTING CHOICE

One way or another, marketing research deals with choice: measuring and analyzing the choices people make, predicting what choices they would make under various future conditions, and assessing different ways of influencing these choices. Accordingly, we may think of marketing research as the practical application of a general theory of choice.

In formulating such a theory, we start by defining its basic variables. First, there is some collection of items from which people choose. Each such item is called a "brand." The entire list is called a "competitive frame." By definition, the brands that make up a competitive frame face one another in head-on competition. Typically, each brand is identified by a name. When several offerings carry the same name, they may be collectively thought of as a single brand, or they may be treated as separate brands, in which case the fragmentation creates a new (more detailed) competitive frame. These terms are used in their most general sense. A "brand" could be a named coffee, a named personal computer, a named telephone service provider, a particular candidate for president, a particular health care plan, a particular religion, and so forth.

A "customer" is anyone called upon to make a choice (any kind of choice) among the brands of a competitive frame. And a "marketer" is anyone seeking to influence customers to choose some particular brand or brands. Each customer has beliefs about each brand. These may be detailed and extensive or minimal, and they may or may not be factually correct. Collectively, these beliefs are called the customer's "information" about the brand.

A "choice situation" is any unique occasion on which a customer is called upon to choose among the brands of a competitive frame. In each such situation, each brand has some "accessibility." This is a measure of the environmental factors that make some brands easier to choose than others. For example, a brand that is prominently displayed on the shelf is easier to choose (has higher accessibility) than a brand that is kept in the back room and can be obtained only by asking for it.

Collectively, the information a customer has about the brands in a choice situation is called the "information vector" or just the "information" of the choice situation. The accessibilities of all the brands are called the "accessibility vector" or just the "accessibility" of the choice situation. And the shares (percentages) with which the various brands are chosen are called the "choice vector." Two or more choice situations are said to be "congruent" if they have the same competitive frame, the same information, and the same accessibility. Given these definitions, we can formulate a law succinctly.

The First Law: The Law of Congruence

Congruent choice situations have equal choice vectors.
—Marder 1997, p. 36

What this law says is that choice depends only on the brands in the competitive frame, on the information the customer has about these brands, and on their accessibilities. It does *not* depend on the particular manner in which the choice is made. Consider two choice situations: (1) picking a brand off a supermarket shelf and (2) picking a brand from a list in a questionnaire. Provided the competitive frame is the same, the information about the brands is the same, and the accessibility of the brands is the same, the choices will be the same as well. This law is deceptively simple. On the one hand, it is self-evident. If everything else is the same, you may say, it should hardly surprise us that the choices will be the same as well. And so they will be, as demonstrated empirically (Marder 1997, Chapter 5). On the other hand, the law has far-reaching, and sometimes surprising, implications for marketing research, for how things can and should be done, and for how they should not be done. And it turns out, again and again, that failures in research design can be traced to a failure to keep in mind what the law teaches us.

Suppose we want to estimate the potential of a new brand. We could give the respondents a description of the new brand and ask them whether they will buy it. An unreasonably large number will say that they will do so. This may lead us to use finer gradations. A popular measurement tool is the so-called top box scale ("will definitely buy, probably buy, probably not buy, definitely not buy") in which, conservatively, only respondents who check the top box ("will definitely buy") are counted. Once again, we obtain patently absurd buying claims. If we continue to ask the question for a large enough number of brands, we accumulate, before long, buying reports that exceed all physical constraints. The respondents say that they will buy more than they could possibly consume even if they spent all their time doing nothing but buying and consuming (Marder 1997, pp. 164–66). Given such findings, researchers sometimes blame the respondents, charging them with fallibility and exaggeration. But if we are mindful of the First Law, we see that the respondents are in fact reasonable. Given the way the question is posed, their de facto options are to buy the brand or to buy nothing. Their answer, therefore, amounts to saying implicitly that if this brand were the only one available, they would buy it. In doing so, they are giving the right answer to the wrong question.

From the perspective of the First Law, we proceed as follows: We define the competitive frame in which the new brand will ultimately compete. We create a choice situation (in the interview) that is *congruent* with the choice the customer will face in the marketplace after the new brand has been introduced. We present to the respondent a list of all brands in the competitive frame, including the proposed new brand, and we request the respondent to choose among those brands. This measurement yields a realistic "deserved share" — deserved in the sense that it is the share the brand could be expected to achieve if all brands had equal accessibility and if customers came to have the same information about the brands as they had at the time of filling in the questionnaire. Subject to these conditions, the measurement is consistent with the First Law. The particular tool I have employed for this purpose since the early 1960s (STEP) shows each brand on a separate page, represented by a picture, a price, and a brief statement of its benefits, followed by three sensitizing questions. After exposure to all of the brands in the competitive frame, the respondents distribute 10 adhesive labels among the pages (brands) in the booklet to indicate how likely they would be to buy each, assuming all were available at the prices shown in the booklet.

Although the mechanics of STEP are intended to be an effective implementation of the First Law, it is important to distinguish between what is fundamental and what is incidental. The respondents could use 10 labels, or 20, or 5, or only 1, which is equivalent to asking them to simply choose a single brand from the list. (There is reason to believe that the 10 labels, representing as it were 10 separate choice opportunities, result in greater sensitivity than just a single choice [Marder 1997, Appendix B], but this is a matter of relative efficiency, not of fundamental validity.) The brands could be represented by information in different form, though it is important to keep in mind precisely what is to be measured. The brands could be shown on separate pages, on a single sheet, on a list, on a shelf. These options are implementational variants only. They may make the test more efficient or more attractive, but they have no bearing on its ultimate structure. The only real requirement is consistency with the First Law: using the correct competitive frame (the frame that can be expected to exist in the marketplace), using relevant information (an estimated representation of the information that will exist in the marketplace), and inducing the respondent to *choose* among the brands of the competitive frame.

Suppose we need to evaluate one or more variants of the new brand (different brand names, different package designs, different sizes, different selling claims, different prices, and so on.). We may be tempted to ask the respondents which variant they prefer, but such a design, which is used all too often, again violates the First Law. The question that needs to be answered is, holding everything else constant, what share would the brand achieve in world 1 in which it might have brand name A, compared with world 2 in which it might have brand name B? The First Law requires that we set up a controlled experiment, representing these alternative worlds—one group in which the test brand has name A, a second group in which it has name B. This design, and only this design, maintains the proper congruence between the measuring instrument and the potential marketplace.

Suppose we are given two formulations of a product, a sweet one and a sour one, and are asked to predict which will do better in the market. A common product testing technique is "paired comparisons," which has been used extensively by major packaged goods manufacturers, including, according to press reports, by Coca-Cola in its problematic introduction of "New Coke." The simplest type of paired comparisons test might give the respondents both the sweet and the sour product and ask them which one they like better or which one they would be more likely to buy. If the sweet one wins 80:20, this would be taken as overwhelming evidence for the "superiority" of the sweet one. But from the perspective of the First Law, we see instantly that the test can't be right. The sweet and sour products are not intended to be available in the market simultaneously.

The paired comparisons test is often implemented in a more sophisticated way. A principal competitor is selected. One group tests the sweet product versus the competitive product. The other group tests the sour product versus the competitive product. Suppose the results in the two groups are sweet product versus competitor 40:60 and sour product versus competitor 20:80. Once again, the sweet product has won overwhelmingly. But it may not work this way in the market. Why? It happens there are already nine sweet brands on the market. The tenth sweet brand can expect a share of approximately 10%. But there are no sour brands on the market. And though relatively few customers want a sour product, the single sour brand, competing against nine sweet ones, gets a share of 15%. The problem with the paired comparisons test is not that it gives the wrong answer, but that it gives the right answer to the wrong question.

Anyone thinking in terms of the First Law can see that this paired comparisons test is in effect asking, "What share would my sweet or sour brand get in a world in which all brands other than one competitor had gone out of business?" In such a world, the sweet brand might indeed achieve a higher share than the sour brand. But the First Law requires us to take the full competitive frame into account, and when we do so, the result reverses, as it does in the marketplace. It may, of course, happen under some circumstances that paired comparisons tests produce the right result. When this happens, however, it is due to a fortuitous convergence of the data rather than to the intrinsic ability of the test to generate the right answer. Conversely, an outright reversal is not merely a theoretical possibility but occurs in actual practice (Marder 1997, Chapter 9).

How then should the product test be conducted? If we expose respondents to the product, giving them an opportunity to use it under properly structured real-life conditions and then require them to make choices in the full competitive frame (including the test product), we can expect realistic predictions of what would happen if the test product actually came to market (Marder 1997, Chapters 8 and 10).

The important point is that the First Law provides the kind of reduction that is the hallmark of science. The persistent application of the law dramatically simplifies design considerations for a wide range of problems that have traditionally been thought of as different and have been approached differently: concept tests, name tests, packaging tests, strategy tests, price tests, copy tests, and product tests. Examined from the perspective of the First Law, all these problems are just special cases of a single, general problem: to estimate the incremental deserved share of some chunk of information. And the appropriate technique for tackling all of them is the same: to expose respondents to some information— either on the very pages of the questionnaire or some time before they receive the ostensibly unrelated questionnaire—to induce them to make choices among the brands of the full competitive frame and to note differences in brand shares obtained by the test brand as the information delivered to the respondents (in words, pictures, or actual product experience) is varied systematically.

In light of the First Law, this generality is totally obvious, yet methods that ignore the law, including top box and paired comparisons, continue to be used widely. Perhaps the First Law itself is then not as obvious as one might have supposed at first, and a real purpose is served in spelling it out explicitly, so it can become part of the routine equipment of every practitioner.

DESIRABILITY AND CHOICE

Measuring choice is one thing. Understanding how it comes about and how it can be influenced is another. To do this, we enlist two additional variables, desirability and beliefs. Desirability measures the extent to which people like a brand, a variable that is related to, but different from, choice. The distinction between these variables can be surprisingly deceptive. When we ask people how probable it is that they will buy (choose) a brand, are we dealing with desirability or with choice? When we ponder whether to use an "absolute" scale or a "constant sum" scale, are we distinguishing between measurement instruments or between variables?

As it happens, there is a simple test to determine whether we are dealing with desirability or choice. If, when rating brands, we can continue to append brands without affecting the prior measurements, we are dealing with desirability. But if any change in the set of brands requires a new measurement of all brands, we are dealing with choice. The question, "Use a 0–10 scale to indicate how likely you are to buy (choose) each of the following brands," may appear to measure choice, but adding brands does not invalidate the previously collected ratings. It therefore measures desirability. Conversely, the question, "Which of these eight brands do you like best?" may appear to measure desirability, but we cannot add brands to the list without needing to redo the entire measurement. The question therefore measures choice.

Notwithstanding the difference between desirability and choice, there is an intimate relationship between them. The nature of this relationship must be formulated explicitly. For this purpose, we define brand strength (S) as S = DA (where D is desirability and A is accessibility) and express the relationship as in the following law:

The Second Law: The Law of Primacy

An individual for whom, at the moment of choice, n brands are tied for first place in brand strength chooses each of these n brands with probability 1/n.

—Marder 1997, p. 177

Basically, this is saying that, holding accessibility constant, people choose the brand they like most, and if several brands qualify, they choose each of these brands with equal probability. But what makes people like one brand more than another? This is specified in a corollary:

The Second Law Corollary: Desires and Beliefs

An individual's desirability for a brand is an aggregation of the desirabilities of the characteristics the individual believes the brand to have.

This is saying that people like a brand to the extent they believe that it will give them what they want, which in turn means that people like *most* (and hence choose) the brand they believe will give them *more* of what they want than any other brand in the competitive frame.

Some clarifications may be in order. The corollary refers to characteristics of a brand but does not impose limitations on how many characteristics there are or how they are to be defined. Characteristics can be objective (like shape, dimensions, or particular features of a brand), or subjective (like reliability, quality of construction, or reputation), or global (like the synthesis of multidimensional aspects that cannot be broken into further subparts, for example, the originality of a painting). The corollary refers to an aggregation but does not specify the particular function to be used. The aggregation can be the sum of the desirabilities, the product, or any other function that aggregates the contributions of the various characteristics into a total desirability of the brand. The corollary refers to beliefs of the respondents but does not specify how these are measured. Given a set of mutually exclusive characteristics, the characteristic the respondent believes describes the brand best is scored 1; the others are 0.

At first glance, the law and its corollary may seem to be saying very little. People choose the brand they like most. What other brand should they choose, one they like less? People like a brand if they believe it has the characteristics they want. What other brand should they like, one they believe doesn't have the characteristics they want? Aren't both the law and the corollary tautologies? And even if they are not, aren't they just saying things that are obvious? I certainly hope that this is so and that we can therefore readily accept what the law and the corollary are saying and turn to the implications they have for how we do marketing research.

The most important implication of the Second Law is that it is indeed possible to use desirability to predict and/or understand choice, provided that this is done properly. If we ask respondents to rate the desirability of a number of brands and then average the scores obtained, we may find that, though brand A beats brand B on the average, brand B does better than brand A in the market. Applying the Second Law, however, we score the brand that received the highest rating from a respondent 1 and all other brands 0. If several brands, say three, are tied for first place, we score each of them 1/3 and all others 0. This will yield an indirect (implied) measure of choice. Thus, the Second Law not only states that choice *can* be computed from measurements of desirability, but also specifies how this is to be done.

Because the Law says that people choose the brand they like most, it should make no difference whether a respondent simply chooses a brand from a competitive frame (direct choice) or whether she rates the desirabilities of all the brands and the analyst subsequently designates the brand that received the highest score as her "chosen" brand (implied choice). The result should be the same. If the chosen brand is next removed from the competitive array, we should be able to repeat the process to identify the respondent's second choice and continue until the set is exhausted. This means that the choice-rank vector obtained directly from the respondents and the desirability-rank vector inferred analytically from their desirability scores should be the same. And so they are, as demonstrated in Figure 1, which shows the average desirability rank for different first-choice ranks and the average first-choice rank for different desirability ranks. Some people might regard this as a small or obvious finding, but it demonstrates empirically that choice can indeed be inferred from desirability. And it happens that choice modeling—doubtless one of the most important developments in marketing research during the past 30 years—requires just such inferences. The Second Law therefore has direct practical relevance. Just as the First Law can be thought of as the axiom that governs choice experiments, so the Second Law can be thought of as the axiom that governs choice modeling.

CHOICE MODELING

Suppose we want to evaluate the potential of two brand names (name A and name B). A two-group experiment, consistent with the First Law, will measure the "deserved share" of each name. Suppose we want to find out simultaneously whether the brand should be sweet or sour. We need only split each of the groups (A and B) and expose half to the sweet product and half to the sour product. Suppose we also want to find out the value of 150 calories per glass versus 10 calories per glass. We need only split the groups again. The experiment now consists of eight groups that represent every combination of the three dimensions. In principle, this process can be continued indefinitely. Provided the experiment remains consistent with the First Law (each respondent sees only *one* test stimulus and responds to the full competitive frame), the observed shares will be definitive.

Although this is true on the conceptual level and can be implemented as long as the number of dimensions studied remains small, it becomes impossible to implement in practice as the number of dimensions increases. Covering 20 dichotomous dimensions, for example, would require $2^{20} = 1,048,576$ experimental groups. Under these circumstances, choice modeling is used in lieu of a choice experiment. Choice modeling should be thought of as a "fallback" method, forced on us by practical

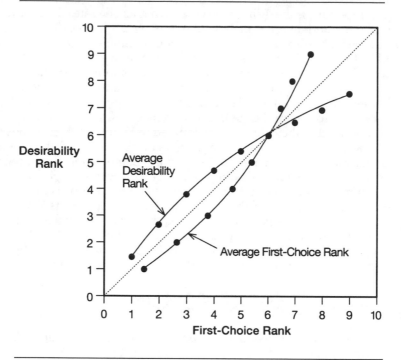

Figure 1
Relationship Between Desirability Rank and First-Choice Rank; Spectrum Study (N = 6633)

considerations, to be used when necessary in the hope that it will generate reasonable estimates of the deserved shares that would have been obtained if it had been possible to conduct an experiment.

Choice modeling collects input data from a sample of respondents, consolidates these data in a computer model, and invites the user to pose "what if" questions, sometimes called "simulations," of the form: "How much business would I get if I introduced a product (or modified an existing product) with characteristics A, B, C,...?" Each of these questions can be thought of as simulating a group in a controlled experiment, and each answer can be thought of as an estimate of the deserved share that would have been generated in such an experiment.

From its very outset in the early 1970s, choice modeling developed on two parallel tracks: conjoint analysis (Green and Rao 1971; Green and Wind 1973, 1975; Johnson 1974) and SUMM (single unit marketing model; Marder 1968, 1973, 1974). These have had very different histories. Conjoint analysis has grown dramatically, built on an extensive academic literature. It has developed many forms, off-shoots, and refinements and has become the most widely known and used form of choice modeling. SUMM has developed in private, in interactions between a commercial research organization and its clients, with no publications between 1974 and 1997 and has, until recently, been virtually unknown in the academic community.

Both conjoint analysis and SUMM start with a "map" of the product category. This identifies the characteristics to be included in the model. There are no firm rules for the selection of these characteristics, other than that it is desirable that they be mutually exclusive and comprehensive, including everything that could reasonably be expected to influence brand choice.

Conjoint analysis estimates the desirabilities of the characteristics (partworths) indirectly from overall ratings of different combinations of characteristics, uses these partworths together with objective brand descriptions to determine the overall desirabilities of the brands, and computes brand shares from these. SUMM measures the desirabilities of the characteristics directly (such measurements have been referred to as "self-explicated" in the literature), measures beliefs to determine which characteristics the respondents believe the various brands possess, and combines desirabilities and beliefs to compute brand choice.

Detailed expositions of conjoint analysis and SUMM are available elsewhere. In particular, there is an excellent review article of conjoint analysis (Green and Srinivasan 1990) and a full description of the rationale and methods of SUMM (Marder 1997, Chapters 16–20). In addition to SUMM, several other self-explicated models, including the self-explicated stages of so-called hybrid models, have appeared over the years (Edwards and Newman 1982; Green 1984; Green, Goldberg, and Montemayor 1981; Green, Krieger, and Agarwal 1991; Huber 1974; Johnson 1991; Srinivasan 1988; Srinivasan and Park 1997; Srinivasan and Wyner 1989). The methods used by these models have been generally similar to one another (Green and Srinivasan 1990) and also to the method used in the early generations of SUMM (Marder 1974, Appendix D). Setting aside specific differences among these methods and the many varieties of conjoint analysis and concentrating on the core assumptions of conjoint analysis and SUMM, we encounter three fundamental issues that apply generally to the design of all choice models: individual versus aggregate analysis, indirect versus direct (self-explicated) measurement of desirabilities, and inclusion of belief measurements. Let us explore what guidance, if any, the Second Law can give us with respect to these issues.

Individual Versus Aggregate Analysis

Suppose we measure 50 variables for 1000 respondents. We can report the data analyzed across the 1000 respondents by computing means, correlations, multiple correlations, and so on, all of which amounts to "aggregate analysis." Or, we can combine all 50 variables in some way for one respondent, use the information to determine which choice this respondent is most likely to make, and then go on to make a similar determination for each of the other respondents, which constitutes "individual analysis."

Individual analysis has been an integral aspect of SUMM from the beginning. It is, in fact, built right into SUMM's name (single unit marketing model). Conjoint analysis, which was originally implemented with aggregate analysis, now also employs individual analysis. There are, however, some variants of conjoint analysis and some self-explicated models that employ aggregate analysis, in whole or in part.

Although the Second Law is not explicit in this regard, it definitely requires individual analysis. The Law says that an individual chooses the brand she likes most. This asserts that there is a direct connection between what the individual likes and what she chooses, a connection that is inevitably lost the moment the desirability data are aggregated across a population. To be sure, we are usually interested in estimating the choices made by an entire population, but actual choices are made by individuals, not by groups. And no matter how many other people may choose a brand, the choice a particular respondent makes ultimately depends only on that particular respondent's desires and beliefs. And even if aggregate analysis should generate empirically acceptable results in some cases, such results are fortuitous. Aggregate analysis is demonstrably inappropriate for the study of choice. It is conceptually inconsistent with the Second Law and must be rejected on that ground.

Indirect Versus Direct Measurement of Desirabilities

Conjoint analysis and SUMM are based on different, in fact incompatible, assumptions. Conjoint analysis assumes that respondents cannot report directly the relative desirability of characteristics and that these must therefore be inferred analytically from differences in choices among so-called profiles or brands (the Decomposition assumption). Conversely, SUMM assumes that respondents *can* report the relative desirability of characteristics, provided these are measured properly (the Measurability assumption).

Because the Decomposition assumption implicitly asserts a negative, it cannot be proven as such. It remains vulnerable to evidence that what it asserts *cannot* be done *can* in fact be done. As it happens, a considerable amount of such evidence is available (Marder 1997, pp. 248–49, 411–12), some of it right in the conjoint analysis literature (Green, Carmone, and Wind 1972; Green, Krieger, and Agarwal 1991; Leigh, MacKay, and

Summers 1984; Srinivasan 1988, 1996; Srinivasan and Park 1997), culminating in the conclusion that "the-self explicated approach is likely to yield predictive validities roughly comparable to those of traditional conjoint analysis" (Green and Srinivasan 1990, p. 10). This evidence suggests that conjoint analysis may be a relatively complicated effort to deal with a problem that has a simpler and more straightforward solution. For the present purpose, however, it does not matter whether the Decomposition assumption or the Measurability assumption will ultimately prevail. We are only interested in determining the Second Law's implications for choice modeling. And because neither the Second Law nor its corollary specify how the desirabilities of characteristics are to be measured, both conjoint analysis and SUMM are compatible with the Second Law and its corollary in this respect.

The Measurement of Beliefs

Conjoint analysis, at least as usually practiced, treats the characteristics of products (brands) as objectively given. After devoting substantial effort to determining the desirability of characteristics (their partworths), it asks what share a product (brand) with some particular set of objectively specified characteristics would achieve. In doing so, conjoint analysis assumes that it is possible to describe brands, including competitive brands, entirely in terms of their objective characteristics (the Objective Reality assumption). Conversely, SUMM assumes that brands cannot be described properly by their objective characteristics and must be described by the characteristics the respondents *believe* the brands to have (the Beliefs assumption).

The corollary of the Second Law asserts explicitly that the desirability of a brand depends on the "characteristics the individual believes the brand to have." It thus requires the measurement of beliefs. By definition, SUMM is compatible with this requirement. Conjoint analysis, at least as usually practiced, is incompatible with it. This is not an intrinsic limitation of conjoint analysis. Belief measurements could be incorporated into conjoint models, and this should be done whenever possible. Given conjoint's struggle with capacity problems, however, it is not ordinarily practical.

Even the most cursory consideration of this issue leads to the conclusion that the corollary is right and that the omission of beliefs is conceptually indefensible. Imagine a medication that (1) costs $100 per pill, (2) produces a loss of one pound of body weight per pill, and (3) results in a ten-year increase in life expectancy for anyone who takes it once. The pill's impact on life expectancy is an objective fact, but if almost no one has heard of it and if those who have do not believe it to be true, it should not surprise us that demand for the pill is low. If people came to believe that the pill really did increase life expectancy, however, demand would rise dramatically. The pill itself would not have changed, but people's beliefs about it would have.

Obviously, there are cases in which beliefs don't have to be measured explicitly. We can assume that 100% of respondents would, if asked, express the belief that a four-door car model has four doors and that this belief can therefore be attributed to 100% of the respondents (and incorporated into the model) as though the respondents had actually expressed it overtly. Such "objective" characteristics, however, are a special case. If we were dealing with safety, different respondents would have different beliefs about different brands, and we would no longer be entitled to assume that 100% of the respondents would believe a car to be safe just because it happened to be safe by engineering standards. So what counts ultimately is not the objective reality but the beliefs about that reality.

CONTRIBUTIONS TO THEORY

Quite apart from the Second Law's implications for specific research techniques, the law also leads to the discovery of orderly relationships among the basic variables. These relationships may appear to be abstract, but they have practical consequences. Far from being digressions, they go to the very heart of the matter, for if we are asking whether marketing research has begun to qualify as a science, the discovery of fundamental relationships among its basic variables may ultimately be more important than any particular improvement in any of its tools. What then are some of the theoretical implications of the Second Law?

The Second Law states that people choose the brand they like most. This is an all-or-nothing translation of desirability into choice. But aren't there other ways of measuring choice, in particular, probabilistic ways? One such probabilistic measurement, the division of labels among brands (used in STEP), has already been discussed. In dividing ten labels, the respondents make ten separate choices in rapid succession, each label representing one choice. If it is really true, as the Second Law asserts, that respondents choose the brand they like most and if each label really represents a separate choice, then all respondents should allocate all ten of their labels to only one of the brands, which is not what happens empirically. The Law does, however, allow for an exception. If n brands are tied for first place, each of these brands should receive $1/$nth of the labels. This implies that all label allocations should be confined to ideal "tie types" and generate the following "tie score" patterns: 10, 0, 0, 0, 0, 0, ..., 5, 5, 0, 0, 0, 0, ..., 3.3, 3.3, 3.3, 0, 0, 0, ..., 2.5, 2.5, 2.5, 2.5, 0, 0, ..., 2, 2, 2, 2, 2, 0, ..., and so on. This too does not happen. The empirical responses include patterns such as 9, 1, 0, 0, 0, 0, ..., 8, 2, 0, 0, 0, 0, ..., 6, 4, 0, 0, 0, 0, ..., and so on. But when we examine the data more closely, we find that these apparently inconsistent patterns can be reconciled with the ideal tie types. If we take every empirical label allocation (STEP score) and replace it with the score corresponding to its closest ideal tie type, the resulting tie score shares are identical to the STEP score shares (Marder 1997, p. 183).

Plotting the "first choice" obtained directly from the respondents against the number of labels assigned to the chosen brand yields the S-curve shown in the upper portion of Figure 2. But when these numbers

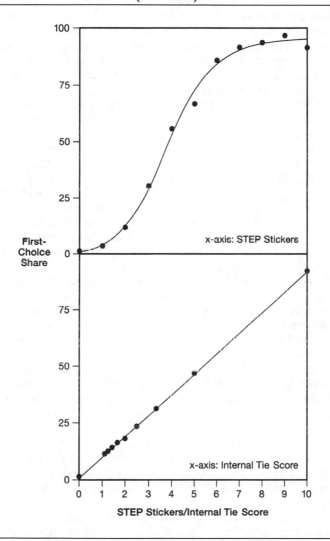

Figure 2
First-Choice Share vs. STEP Stickers/Internal Tie Score
Spectrum Study
(N = 6633)

Source: *The Laws of Choice: Predicting Customer Behavior* by Eric Marder (p. 185). Copyright © 1997 by Eric Marder. Reprinted with permission of The Free Press, a Division of Simon & Schuster.

(of labels) are transformed into their corresponding tie scores, the relationship becomes perfectly linear, as shown in the lower portion of Figure 2. Thus, the tie scores derived from the Second Law define the difference between multiple and single measures of choice and provide a simple device for translating the former into the latter when that may be required.

Equally striking is the relationship between the number of labels and the desirability rank respondents assign to a brand. The Second Law requires that this be a monotonically decreasing function. It is indeed a monotonically decreasing function, but not just any such function; it is a very particular one, a perfect negative exponential, as shown in Figure 3. This general finding holds with striking uniformity for many product categories (Marder 1997, pp. 184–91).

An extension of the tie concept leads to a method for translating desirability scores into probabilities of choice, the "Semimax" method, which is suitable for use in choice experiments and choice modeling. Although the Second Law provides for ties, it does not define what is meant by a "tie." In the set 45, 45, 45, 12, 2, 0, 0, 0, the three 45s are certainly tied. But what about the set 45, 45, 44, 12, 2, 0, 0, 0, 0? It doesn't seem reasonable to treat the two 45s as tied for first place and leave the 44 out of consideration altogether. We know that all measurements are subject to error and that it is not only possible but also probable that the difference between 45 and 44 is no more than a chance fluctuation. This suggests loosening the definition of a tie to include approximate or de facto ties, but how far should the definition be loosened?

The Second Law divides all brands of the competitive frame into two groups: those that are tied for first place (however that is defined) and all others. If we call the first group the "strong" brands and the second group the "weak" brands, the Law requires that each of n strong brands be scored $1/n$ and that the weak brands be scored 0. But if the term "tie" does not have to be taken literally, the Law only requires that we draw some line to distinguish between the strong and the weak brands. The loosest, internally consistent way to draw that line is to treat all brands that have desirability scores equal to or larger than half the maximum desirability ($d \geq d_{max}/2$) as strong brands, on the ground that they are closer to d_{max} than to 0, and all other brands as weak brands, on the ground that they are closer to 0 than to d_{max}. This defines a way of converting desirability scores into Semimax scores, probabilistic measures of choice. Figure 4 shows the relationship between such Semimax scores and explicit probabilistic scores (STEP) and demonstrates that the two are indeed equivalent.

Thus, the Second Law and its corollary not only serve to place conjoint analysis and SUMM into their proper context, but also lead to refinements in measurement techniques. Most important, they contribute to a deeper understanding of the relationships among the basic variables of marketing research: desirability, beliefs, and choice.

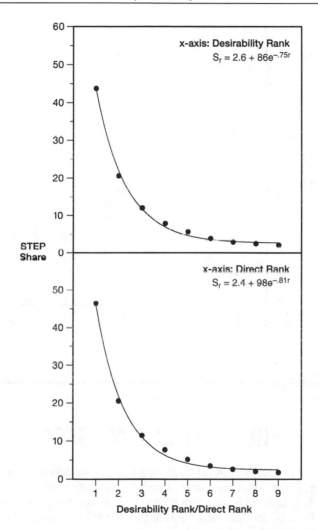

Figure 3
STEP Share vs. Rank
Spectrum Study
(N = 6633)

x-axis: Desirability Rank
$S_r = 2.6 + 86e^{-.75r}$

x-axis: Direct Rank
$S_r = 2.4 + 98e^{-.81r}$

STEP Share

Desirability Rank/Direct Rank

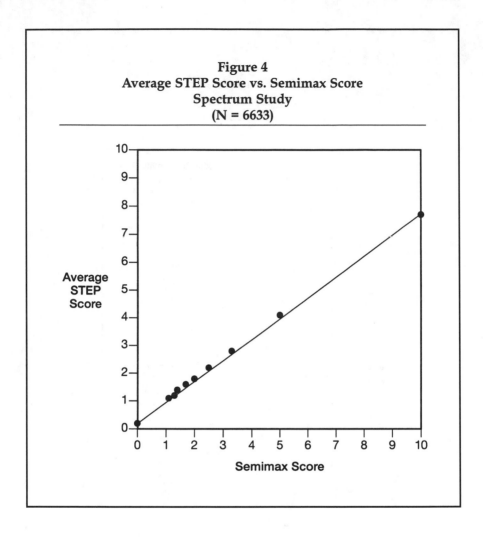

Figure 4
Average STEP Score vs. Semimax Score
Spectrum Study
(N = 6633)

THE EFFECT OF A MESSAGE

One way or another, everything we have considered so far has dealt with determining what messages need to be delivered to customers to influence their brand choice. The generic question has been, "What must I promise (and by implication be able to deliver) to induce the customer to choose my brand?"

When the appropriate message has been constructed and delivered (in the form of an advertisement, a coupon, or a product sample), this message will produce an effect. It will influence customers' beliefs about the brand, the desirability of the brand, and finally their choice of the brand. Specifically, the "effect" of a message is defined as the number of share points by which the probability of choosing the brand changes as a result of exposure to the message.

We know from learning experiments and everyday experience that people forget things. We should, therefore, expect that effects produced by messages will be "forgotten." We must, however, allow at least the theoretical possibility that a portion of these effects will persist. In considering this possibility, we must keep in mind that we are talking about *effect* — defined here as an increment in the probability of choosing a brand — and that it is possible for the effect of a message to persist even if the message itself is forgotten. Such persistence turns out to be the case, empirically, for advertising, coupons, and free product samples, as shown in Figures 5 and 6, and gives rise to a law:

The Third Law: The Law of Persistence

> The effect produced by a message is made up of two components: a transient effect and an intrinsic effect. The transient effect decays rapidly. The intrinsic effect lasts indefinitely.
>
> —Marder 1997, p. 363

Unlike the first two Laws, this Law is surprising. It says that some portion of the effect produced by a message lasts indefinitely. In that case, why doesn't the brand's share build to 100%? It doesn't because the persistence of effects does not apply only to our brand, but to competitive brands as well. These brands also send out messages that produce effects, and these effects too last indefinitely, countering our messages in a helter-skelter of effects that finally settles into a balanced steady state.

One might argue that the Third Law is spurious because the empirical data offered in its support come from commercial products and because messages for such products are self-reinforcing. The customer receives a message. The message induces her to buy the brand. She has experience with the brand and continues to buy it, which creates a steady flow of additional messages. And it is these additional messages and the effects produced by them that result in the apparent persistence of the original effect. This persistence, however, is not merely apparent. As the data demonstrate, it is real and, for purposes of marketing research, decisive.

The Third Law has special implications for product and advertising testing. It requires that a certain amount of time be provided between delivery of the message and the measurement. The Law does not specify how much time. It tells us only that the transient effects can be expected

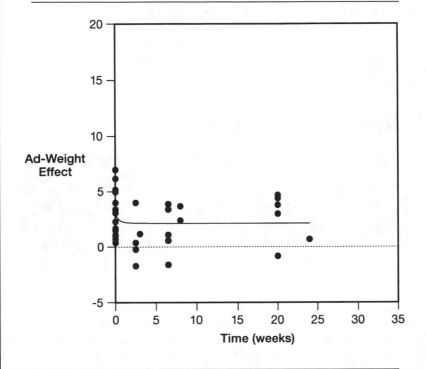

Figure 5
Effect of Advertising in Post-Advertising Period
14 Ad-Weight Studies
$(N' = 22{,}564, E_t = 2.1 + 7.8e^{-1.8t})$

to decay rapidly. On the basis of the available empirical results, we can say that "rapidly" probably means somewhere between two and eight weeks. The lower estimate (two weeks) is derived from an experiment in which the deserved share of a sampled brand remained approximately constant between week 2 and week 5 after delivery of the free sample (Marder 1997, pp. 107–108). The upper estimate (eight weeks) is derived from the analysis of the coupon and sample experiments in which the effects remained constant from week 8 on. In any case, it is necessary to provide intervals of several weeks between message delivery and measurement.

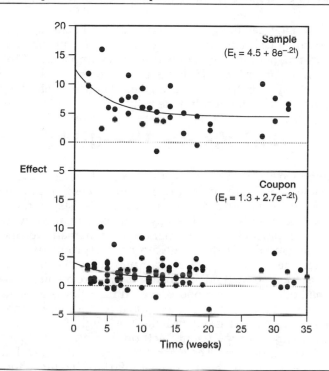

Figure 6
Effect of Sample and Coupon Over Time Consolidated
(N'_{Sample} = 10,063, N'_{Coupon} = 31,780, $N'_{Control}$ = 19,983)

Sample
($E_t = 4.5 + 8e^{-.2t}$)

Coupon
($E_t = 1.3 + 2.7e^{-.2t}$)

Effect

Time (weeks)

Source: *The Laws of Choice: Predicting Customer Behavior* by Eric Marder (p. 362). Copyright © 1997 by Eric Marder. Reprinted with permission of The Free Press, a Division of Simon & Schuster.

The Law also says that the intrinsic effect of a message can be expected to remain constant. It is, therefore, not necessary to measure that effect at many points in time. A single point, after the transient effect is gone, will do. If this were not so, it would be next to impossible to design a valid test of advertising effectiveness, because each such test would have to provide for measuring residual effects at many points in time after the advertising had stopped. As things stand, we can rely on the law and assume that effects, measured several weeks after message delivery, will remain approximately the same for a long time afterward, or indefinitely in the language of the Law.

Indefinitely is certainly not forever, but it is at least eight months, because that is how far our actual data points extend, and doubtless a year or two or more, based on the projection of the observed trends. The actual time may, however, be limited by conditions in the market. If, for example, we observed an effect and the brand was subsequently removed from the shelf, the shares among both the exposed and nonexposed respondents would suddenly go to zero and the effect would vanish. In the absence of such dislocations of the competitive frame, the Third Law holds.

Thus, the Law has both an inhibiting and a liberating effect on the design of product tests and advertising tests. On the one hand, it requires an initial waiting period to allow the transient component of the effect to dissipate. On the other hand, it allows measurements to be conducted at any reasonable point in time thereafter, free of concern that the particular time chosen will affect the result materially.

OUTLOOK FOR THE FUTURE

Although we must expect marketing research to evolve and accumulate increasing knowledge, there are powerful forces that pull in the other direction. By its very nature, marketing research exists in an institutional environment that is not always friendly, and occasionally downright hostile, to its development. Most detrimental is the demand for inexpensive research, a demand that is almost always counterproductive.

Consider the following stark example: A marketer must make a yes–no decision. Two methods for helping him are available: a standard method, method A, and a method B, which he believes to be marginally better. It doesn't matter what the methods are. Method A might be judgment, method B a focus group. Method A might be a choice model, method B a controlled experiment. Method A might be 500 respondents, method B 2000 respondents. The marketer happens to know that his standard method A gives him the right answer 90% of the time, and he properly believes that this is good—indeed, excellent. He understands that a better method B is available and that it would give him the right answer 95% of the time, but he considers this benefit negligible. It amounts to saying that either method would give him the right answer most of the time and that the better method B would give him the right answer only once more often in 20 times than method A. Assuming that method B is much more expensive, we don't expect the marketer to choose method B.

But examining the economics, we see that if the value of the correct decision happens to be $10,000,000, the marketer could afford to pay up to 5% of $10,000,000 = $500,000 more *per study* for the incremental value of method B. Why then is it so unlikely that he would do so? Isn't he used to cost/benefit analyses, and isn't he capable of making the simple calculation we have just made? He certainly is, and he is not irrational, but in his world, not all dollars are created equal. The dollars his company will lose because of a bad decision won't be visible for a long time, if ever—

most likely not until he has moved to another job—but the dollars he spends on research will show up on his current profit/loss statement. Under these circumstances, he will probably prefer a $10 million invisible loss caused by a poor decision to an immediate $1 million "expense." In effect, his environment encourages him to shop for the "insurance policy" that has the lowest premium, optimistically ignoring the fact that the premium is so low precisely because the insurer often will not pay when a claim is made.

The research community aids and abets this inclination by offering him "quick and dirty" research, which is not only damaging in its own right, but also has unfortunate second-order effects. When a really astute marketer looks at what sometimes passes as "marketing research" and finds it to be irrelevant to his problems, he concludes, with some justification, that he doesn't "believe" in marketing research, a judgment he then extends from the particular practices to which he happens to have been exposed to the field as a whole.

One manifestation of this tendency is the extent to which focus groups have become fashionable in recent years. Focus groups and other forms of qualitative research can make real contributions when used for the purpose for which they were designed: to identify alternatives and formulate hypotheses. But when they are turned into substitutes for quantitative studies and are used to justify business decisions, they are totally out of their depth. Yet precisely this is happening increasingly, not only because focus groups are quicker, cheaper, and easier to do than the necessary experiments, but also because they are sufficiently flexible to support particular desired conclusions.

What does all this imply for the future of marketing research? The future depends on the outcome of a tug-of-war between two forces that pull in opposite directions. On the one hand, there is the real desire for valid answers. On the other hand, there is the equally real desire to avoid any answers that might seem to be too expensive or unpleasant or embarrassing. In this tug, the desire for truth, and hence the willingness to support the kind of rigor that is essential for the development of a science, loses most of the time. It does, however, prevail occasionally—only in some companies, only with difficulty, and only with the support of unusually rational, disciplined, and committed executives. And it is on those rare people that the future depends.

Marketing research faces an equally serious internal problem: the need to combine conceptual thinking, call it "theory," with rigorous empirical evidence, call it "data." By and large, members of the academic community are more likely than commercial practitioners to be interested in theory but usually don't have the budgets to develop massive empirical evidence. Members of the commercial sector have greater access to the necessary resources but are less likely to be interested in theory. The important contributions will have to come from "straddle" practitioners, members of either community who combine a passion for theory with an ability to secure commercial support for the large-scale experiments that are necessary to generate definitive evidence. If any of those practitioners should find the Laws that have been presented useful or, alternatively, if they should undertake to design experiments to refute them, the Laws will have served their purpose. But this will not be enough. The Laws, their successors, or their replacements will need to be a springboard for growth—not of a flat structure in which method after method, theory after theory, and law after law are placed alongside one another, but of a hierarchical structure built on a base that supports successive tiers of knowledge. Only when this happens will marketing research have come into its own as a science.

BIBLIOGRAPHY

Edwards, W. and J. R. Newman (1982), *Multiattribute Evaluation*. Beverly Hills, CA: Sage Publications.

Green, Paul E. (1984), "Hybrid Models for Conjoint Analysis: An Expository Review," *Journal of Marketing Research*, 21 (May), 155–59.

——, F.J. Carmone, and Y. Wind (1972), "Subjective Evaluation Models and Conjoint Measurement," *Behavioral Science*, 17 (May), 288–99.

——, Stephen M. Goldberg, and Mila Montemayor (1981), "A Hybrid Utility Estimation Model for Conjoint Analysis," *Journal of Marketing*, 45 (Winter), 33–41.

——, Abba M. Krieger, and Manoj J. Agarwal (1991), "Adaptive Conjoint Analysis: Some Caveats and Suggestions," *Journal of Marketing Research*, 28 (May), 215–21.

—— and R. Rao (1971), "Conjoint Measurement for Quantifying Judgmental Data," *Journal of Marketing Research*, 8 (August), 355–63.

—— and V. Srinivasan (1990), "Conjoint Analysis in Marketing: New Developments with Implications for Research and Practice," *Journal of Marketing*, 54 (October), 3–19.

—— and Yoram Wind (1973), *Multiattribute Decisions in Marketing: A Measurement Approach*. Hinsdale, IL: The Dryden Press.

—— and —— (1975), "New Way to Measure Consumers' Judgments," *Harvard Business Review*, 53 (July/August), 107–17.

Huber, G.P. (1974), "Multiattribute Utility Models: A Review of Field and Field-Like Studies," *Management Science*, 20 (June), 1393–402.

Johnson, Richard M. (1974), "Trade-Off Analysis of Consumer Values," *Journal of Marketing Research*, 11 (May), 121–27.

—— (1991), "Comment on 'Adaptive Conjoint Analysis, Some Caveats and Suggestions'," *Journal of Marketing Research*, 28 (May), 223–25.

Leigh, T.W., David MacKay, and John O. Summers (1984), "Reliability and Validity of Conjoint Analysis and Self-Explicated Weights: A Comparison," *Journal of Marketing Research*, 21 (November), 456–62.

Marder, Eric (1968), "SUMM (Single Unit Marketing Model)," presentation at Advertising Research Foundation Conference (October).

—— (1973), "SUMM (Single Unit Marketing Model)," presentation at American Marketing Association Conference, Attitude Research Across the Sea (Winter).

—— (1974), *The Finances of the Performing Arts, Vol. II, A Survey of the Characteristics and Attitude of Audiences for Theater, Opera, Symphony and Ballet in 12 U.S. Cities*. New York: The Ford Foundation.

—— (1997), *The Laws of Choice: Predicting Customer Behavior*. New York: The Free Press.

Srinivasan, V. (1988), "A Conjunctive-Compensatory Approach to the Self-Explication of Multiattributed Preferences," *Decision Sciences*, 19 (Spring), 295–305.

—— (1996), "Conjoint Analysis and the Robust Performance of Simpler Models and Methods," presentation at American Marketing Association's Annual Marketing Research Conference (September).

—— and Chan Su Park (1997), "Surprising Robustness of the Self-Explicated Approach to Customer Preference Structure Measurement," *Journal of Marketing Research*, 34 (May), 286–91.

—— and G.A. Wyner (1989), "CASEMAP: Computer-Assisted Self-Explication of Multi-Attributed Preference," in *New Product Development and Testing*, W. Henry, M. Menasco, and H. Takanada, eds. Lexington, MA: Lexington Books, 91–111.

Part II
Gathering Data

Data are the foundation of marketing research. Gathering data is central to our discipline, and it is the foundation on which we build theories and models. We cannot build good models on bad data.

In Chapter 4, Ken Deal outlines the research process. He sets the stage by following a research project from the moment of conception to providing research results to the client and beyond. This chapter serves as an overall introduction to designing and carrying out a marketing research project.

There are many ways to collect data, not all of them interchangeable. Vinay Kanetkar (Chapter 5) outlines several of these methods, both qualitative and quantitative. This chapter is followed by extensive references to facilitate further exploration. A newly emerging method of data collection, the Internet, is of special interest. Brian Fine explores this medium and its potential in Chapter 6.

One of the first technical problems faced by any marketing researcher is how to choose a sample. The way we select a sample can affect our results. Sampling procedures also must take several factors into consideration: cost, accuracy, effort, and time. Peter Chan (Chapter 7) outlines different sampling procedures currently in use in marketing research.

Then there is qualitative research. It plays a special role in marketing research. From its early beginnings as focus groups held in moderators' rooms, qualitative research has changed a lot. Now it includes many innovative techniques, such as the open frame, getting over the wall, historical ally, ethnographics, mock juries, and ad labs, to name a few. Naomi Henderson explores these techniques and many more in Chapter 8.

4

The Process of Marketing Research

Ken Deal

The learning is in the process, not the destination.

—Anonymous

Well, of course, that's the old maxim. The reality is that learning occurs at different levels and for different reasons. Those involved in the marketing research process learn from it, and those who use the research findings to make better marketing decisions learn from that process. The fundamental value is that learning both takes place in processes and creates value for organizations and their customers.

For learning to be most effective, conventional processes need to be questioned regularly, critically, and creatively. We begin this chapter with a viewpoint of an extremely effective and highly renowned academic and consultant:

It is harder for a market researcher to get inside a consumer's mind than it is for a consumer to turn his mind inside out.

—Russell L. Ackoff, Ackoff's Best

Ackoff, Anheiser-Busch Professor Emeritus of Management Science at the Wharton School of Business, University of Pennsylvania, and founder and Chairman of INTERACT, a Philadelphia-based educational consulting firm, continues to be an active consultant in a variety of business sectors. He has been highly valued by his clients for designing studies that creatively and effectively answer marketing problems. He writes:

> Producers often try to find out what consumers want by asking them. This seldom yields useful information because consumers either don't know what they want or they try to provide (or avoid) answers they think are expected of them. In many cases a better way consists of using the consumer to *design* products or services; for example, a chain of men's stores, although successful, failed to attract the type of customer its owner wanted. He wanted to reach upwardly mobile professionals and businessmen by offering high-quality designer clothing at discount prices. But this method failed; rather it drew bargain hunters from lower income segments of the population. Repeated questionnaires addressed to potential buyers the firm wanted to attract yielded results that, when applied, failed to bring them into the stores.

> The owner and his executives sought help from a research group with a reputation for unconventional approaches to marketing problems. This group selected 15 representatives of the targeted customer population and invited them to attend a Saturday session designing their ideal men's store. The identity of the sponsoring firm was not revealed but several of its executives took part incognito.

> The representatives of the targeted population produced a very creative design of a men's store. When done, the identity of the sponsor was revealed and a comparison was made of the sponsor's stores with the one newly designed. The principal differences were wide and had not been revealed by any of the earlier research....

> Similar consumer design groups have been used for other types of product and service, and even to write advertising copy. They have always been creative and informative (Ackoff 1998, p. 145).

It is important for marketing researchers to be flexible to address the needs of marketing decision makers. Understanding and feeling comfortable with the conventional process can afford researchers the freedom of mind to adapt more innovative research paradigms to solve new problems.

Marketing research projects have beginnings, middles, and ends. This chapter is divided into the three main phases of marketing research: beginning with the marketing need, the project proposal, and the questionnaire; progressing through sampling, fieldwork, data cleaning, data analysis, and statistical analysis; and ending with interpretation of findings, reporting, presenting, and feedback.

The basic process of marketing research has remained essentially the same for decades. The components of that process have changed dramatically. In this chapter, the overall process is described and the key dynamics of change are presented. In several parts, other chapters are referenced for more detailed handling of the topics. Because of the nature of these topics, this chapter is written mainly from the practitioner's viewpoint.

AT THE BEGINNING: THE DESIGN STAGES

Marketing information includes information about the market environment and information that directly enhances the marketing decision-making process. Marketing research has been moving through a process in which organizations have dramatically expanded their definitions and needs for marketing information. Look at the range of information retrieval disciplines that now exist. And then ask whether those disciplines are components of marketing research. It might not be too outlandish to think that marketing research has dropped the ball on adapting to the needs of modern information technology.

Marketing information includes both *market* and marketing information. Marketing is an extremely complex and imprecise task. The challenges run from actions that can seem to be precise (e.g., pricing or media planning) but are not to decisions that are explicitly broad and creative, such as advertising. However, all of these areas require challenging cooperation between the need for understanding the terrain and investigating the complexities of marketing decisions.

Marketing research has evolved to include a much broader scope of activities than existed 30 years ago. But how should marketing research and the scope of marketing research be defined today?

Jocelyn (1977) differentiates between marketing research and the marketing information system (MIS). He defines marketing research as the "process for collecting MIS and special project data" and notes that

> An efficient marketing organization is likely to discover that its marketing information needs fall into two basic categories. The first is needed for repetitive decisions. The second accumulates information, opportunities, and/or problems of a nonrepetitive nature which require the modification of marketing strategies. It is the first category that applies to the design and implementation of a marketing information system.... Once the important variables are determined (which may require marketing research itself) and the quota decision is known, the organization should systematize the collection, interpretation, and reporting of such information so that it is available when needed. Marketing research activities, including primary and/or secondary data collection, are necessary to make a marketing information system operational.
>
> The second category of information needs deals with nonrepetitive situations. This category covers such problems as an unan-

ticipated decline in market share, a failure to penetrate new markets, and the rejection of a new product. Nonrepetitive situations may also represent opportunities such as selecting a new location for a retail outlet, the testing of a new product or service idea, or the expansion of channels. Here is where the "marketing research project" comes into play (Jocelyn 1977, p. 21).

So, the design, gathering, analysis, presentation, and use of information about markets, consumers, market offerings, and competitors, as well as opportunities for new and repetitive marketing decision making, constitute the challenges of marketing research.

Marketing research has many roots. It might be said that marketing research began with Arthur C. Nielsen Sr. designing a system for accounting for the sales of items in his uncle's drug store. Certainly, this process had a dramatic affect on marketing, but it is a routine task now. At the time, it was a response to a very practical unsolved problem. This evolution from attempting to solve an immediate problem to maintaining a system for providing market information has spawned many marketing research services. Nielsen's response to a marketing need evolved into the syndicated services of ACNielsen and other MISs that produce market information on a systematic schedule.

The essence of custom marketing research is a reaction to solving an immediate, nonrepetitive marketing problem. The research function is designed for this to benefit research buyers and users. The benefit is information that provides the basis for making better marketing decisions. In turn, better marketing decisions should provide increased value to customers, as well as to corporate stakeholders. The essential motivation of any decision-making focus of marketing research is management action.

In 2000, the range of methodology available to the researcher throughout the research process to help solve the immediate marketing problem is vast. There is still a choice whether to use an interviewer-administered or self-administered field methodology. However, the richness of implementation has expanded far beyond mail, telephone, mall, and in-home administration.

Consider Internet surveys. The ability to combine methodologies in an inexpensive medium for mass data collection has never been encountered before in marketing research. As a medium for the presentation of questions and the eliciting of answers, the Internet has many commendable features, though many question its sampling properties.

An Internet survey is self-administered. However, this medium has many features in common with interviewer-administered surveys. For example, in self-administered surveys, it is very difficult, if not impossible, to have respondents answer preliminary questions without looking ahead to later questions that might provide information that would bias or negate the usefulness of earlier questions. Because the Internet can shield later pages until earlier questions are answered, unaided brand awareness

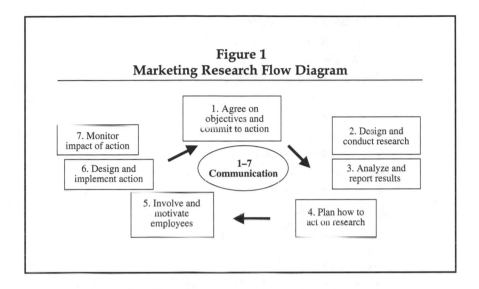

Figure 1
Marketing Research Flow Diagram

questions can be asked prior to asking aided awareness questions pertaining to some brands that were not mentioned in the unaided question.

Also, some sophisticated methodologies, such as conjoint analysis and discrete choice modeling, can be conveniently executed on the Internet. Product profiles can be shown to respondents in color with successive choice sets provided. Adaptive conjoint analysis, pioneered commercially by Sawtooth Software, can be executed on the Internet, whereas previously, this methodology could only be used in personal interviews using personal computers.

A fairly detailed path for marketing research is used in this chapter. Prior to this meticulous model, a concise flow diagram used by Schmalensee and Lesh (1999, p. 25) will be used (see Figure 1). One key point of their article, "How to Make Research More Actionable," was to make researchers understand that the agenda of management does not always recognize the importance of marketing research and the relevance of the marketing research process.

Researchers understand that the objective of conducting marketing research is not simply to have a report of findings. Action should be the natural result of research being interpreted for management and shown to be relevant to making better marketing decisions. Schmalensee and Lesh (1999, p. 25) contend that "wonderful research often sits on the shelf because most researchers and managers see only their part of the process and are unable to move their organizations through the entire process."

Recent developments in marketing information and research have dramatically expanded the scope of marketing research, but has the nature of the marketing research process changed? Traditionally, the marketing research process has been the following:

1. Define the marketing problem/opportunity;
2. Define the marketing research problem;
3. State the objectives;
4. State the research questions;
5. State the hypotheses;
6. Call for proposals;
7. Select a supplier;
8. Design the research study;
9. Design and execute the qualitative research;
10. Design the questionnaire;
11. Design the sampling;
12. Select the field methodology;
13. Pretest the questionnaire and refine;
14. Execute the fieldwork;
15. Capture the data and edit, clean, and prepare them for data analysis;
16. Analyze the data;
17. Provide the research findings for marketing decision making;
18. Continue to monitor the client's needs for information; and
19. Consider Research Ethics.

These procedures are as relevant for the researchers of today and tomorrow as they were for those of yesterday. So, are there no differences? Of course there are. And these define the remainder of this chapter.

Define the Marketing Problem

This stage, as shown in Figure 2, is the second-most dangerous of the process and is usually the responsibility of the marketing manager. Although some marketing problems develop, exist, and fester for a long period of time, others surface quickly, become targeted, and are addressed rapidly through a research study.

When the marketing researcher becomes involved with the marketing problem, the marketing problem should become more tightly defined and stated as part of a request for proposals (RFP) or the protocol for the project. It is interesting that sometimes an RFP is developed without a statement of the marketing problem. And sometimes when bidders ask for the marketing problem, the definition is not forthcoming. Often, the outside consultant does not have the presence within the firm to push for and receive this information. However, if the project sponsors want research findings that are relevant and able to provide direction for marketing decisions, this information should be provided.

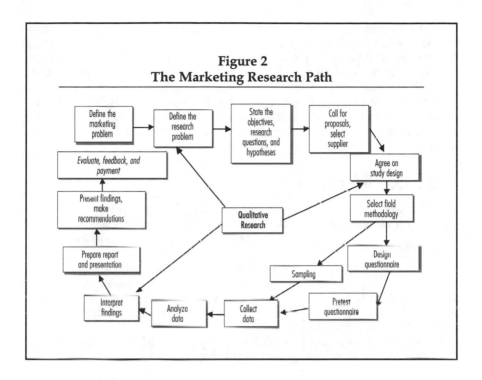

Figure 2
The Marketing Research Path

The marketing problem is the central focus for the marketing decision maker and should be stated in conjunction with the market research problem. The need for additional marketing insight through information is the typical key driver of the liaison between marketing and marketing research called the marketing research project. The marketing problem encompasses much more ground than can be addressed by the marketing research process.

Define the Marketing Research Problem

At the heart of the marketing research problem definition is the need to better understand the world. Understanding is based on having a theory of how the marketing that includes the problem area works, proposing a process for testing that theory, and then executing the process and considering the findings.

As mentioned by Wind (1997), theory provides the direction for conducting marketing research. In many cases, research questions are advanced in the RFP and used in the proposal. However, research questions are a very rudimentary means for directing the research enterprise, and often, no theory is developed to justify and guide the research process.

The marketing problem is larger than the marketing research problem. For example, how to price a new product that extends an existing line can be addressed with marketing research. The research study should provide recommendations that will help the marketing manager better price the product. However, the marketing manager must take into consideration many aspects of the product, the company, the market, customers, and competitors before finalizing the price decision. Marketing research can provide valuable insights, but it does not solve the problem. That is the job of the marketing manager.

State the Objectives

The study objectives need to be orderly, clearly stated, and achievable. One of the hazards mentioned by many researchers is having a client ask, "Now, why did we do this research?" after the findings have been presented. Embarrassment pervades the internal and external environments at that point, not to mention the threats to future business by being involved in "the research project with no purpose." Equally difficult are projects with multiple sponsors, each of whom intends the project to ideally meet his or her needs. The many-headed monster is sometimes conceived by many contributors.

As Schmalensee and Lesh (1999, p. 26) note, "Many researchers say they will not conduct the research until they:

1. Verify the research objectives with all key decision makers.
2. Verify the commitment to action before doing the research."

These requirements signify the importance of the research to those most concerned with the justification of the research and with the use of the findings.

State the Research Questions

The research questions are vague indicators of the minimum that needs to be achieved by the research. However, the development of research questions seems to be easier for many people than does the statement of hypotheses. Whereas research questions are important and convey the main thrust of the research venture, the research hypotheses provide more direct links to the questionnaire and future analysis.

State the Hypotheses

The hypotheses are critical to the success of the project and the ability of the project to connect to anything real. This relates to the previous statements regarding theory. It is to the benefit of the research buyers that the RFPs be informative, self-contained, and comprehensive. For this to be true, the marketing and research problems must have been thoroughly understood and translated into the relevant marketing concepts, hypotheses, and theories. A theory of the marketer's world could be the missing link.

The words "theory" and "hypotheses" relate in many managers' minds to "academic," "not useful in practice," and "waste of money." However, many marketing and marketing research managers have experienced several, if not many, projects conducted by very "practical" research suppliers that have not answered the core marketing needs of the research.

There seems to be a disconnection between the two worlds of "practice" and "theory." However, thoughtful marketing research managers often come to the conclusions that theory can take a marketing problem, translate it into research objectives that can be achieved by practical research, and produce action-oriented findings that provide the information and insights needed for solving the hard marketing problems.

How can this happen when it is often not expected? The basic reason relates to the ability to start with a problem and clearly prescribe a method for garnering the information needed for solving it.

Stating the null and alternative hypotheses will tend not to be understandable by all readers and might lead to a lack of confidence in the practicality of the final findings. The hypotheses should be stated as "alternative" hypotheses, which are usually what the marketer believes to be the true state of the market. For example, if the marketer believes that heavy users are upscale compared with light users, then the hypothesis should be stated as: "Heavy users of our product have demographic profiles that are more upscale than are those of light users." As soon as those demographic variables that will be used to identify economic conditions of sample respondents are defined, the hypothesis is understandable by the client because it probably was noted by him or her first and is part of the "conventional wisdom" of the marketing department. Figure 3 provides a structure that can be used to illustrate the network of constructs and hypotheses.

The development of the key hypotheses of the study provides building material for the questionnaire and sampling phases that follow. Also, the hypothesis testing provides much of the most interesting material for the report and presentation.

Call for Proposals

The proposal process produces a tremendous variety of experiences for consultants and clients. When an experienced and well-trained research professional prepares an RFP, equally experienced and well-trained consultants should understand the project needs clearly. Difficulties arise when

1. There is a lack of understanding of the real needs of the marketing decision makers by the marketing research manager,
2. The author of the RFP is not experienced or knowledgeable enough to translate the marketing needs into a document usable for developing a proposal, or

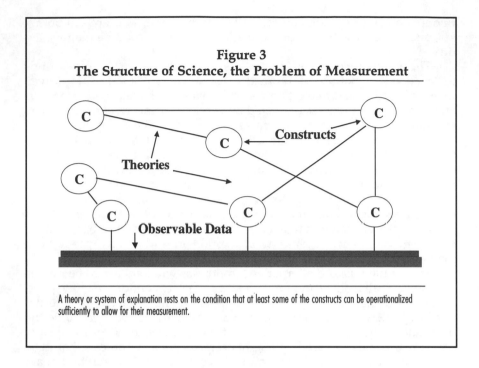

Figure 3
The Structure of Science, the Problem of Measurement

A theory or system of explanation rests on the condition that at least some of the constructs can be operationalized sufficiently to allow for their measurement.

3. The research consultant is not experienced enough to take a good RFP and produce a proposal that satisfies the research and marketing needs of the client.

Researchers from both the client and consulting sides of marketing research can recite cases in which there was inadequate input from the other party. Step 1 is the most dangerous of these three steps. If the RFP reflects the needs of management but is written poorly, an experienced consultant can elicit the needed information and, essentially, rewrite the RFP to higher standards. A marketing research client who is aware of his or her lack of knowledge will consult with one or more research suppliers before writing the RFP. The process will be greatly improved because of this collaboration.

Most researchers will notice distinct differences between the proposal or bidding process required by government agencies and that of private businesses. It is fairly common for government agencies to have very strict requirements for announcing an RFP, receiving proposals, and selecting a supplier. These characteristics include a fairly long, formal, and well-documented RFP, a very specific format for the proposal and appendices, a definite final time for submitting the proposal, a formal set of criteria by which the candidates will be evaluated, and a prescribed announcement protocol. These stages might seem overly extensive and rigid to marketing researchers in private corporations. However, the process was developed to serve particular needs that do not exist in private corporations.

Proposals developed for private corporations can vary from a simple price quote, literally on one sheet of paper, to extremely lengthy and detailed documents for critical, complicated, and pivotal research projects. The latter often are similar to the types of proposals required for government agencies.

Another difference between proposals for government and those for private business is the number of proposals sought by the manager responsible for the project. Very often, private companies will request that three to five consultants submit proposals. Sometimes, however, projects are sole sourced, and there is only one proposal.

Sole sourcing is sometimes available to government departments when the total price of the contract is less than a set dollar limit. However, many consultants have experienced situations in which the consulting community at large is asked to bid on a contract. This might produce 20 to 30 bids. When the project is of modest size, the total costs expended by the many consultants might be valued at more than the total project cost.

Those who must decide on the winning proposal look for the following qualities:

1. The consultant is known to be of high quality and has resources available for achieving the project objectives within the time horizon and within the budget;

2. All of the points of the RFP have been covered by the proposal;

3. The proposal shows how the project will be executed, provides written and visual explanations of the tasks and timing, and explains the flow of the project and how each step contributes to achieving the overall objectives, including

   ❑ Give specifics,

   ❑ Outline the steps of the project,

   ❑ Suggest procedures,

   ❑ How will it be done?

   ❑ What methodology will be used?

   ❑ Paint pictures of the methodology, and

   ❑ Show that you are eager to roll up your sleeves and get involved;

4. The proposal takes a practical and safe path to achieve the objectives;

5. (Sometimes) the proposal asks for the development of a basic theoretical approach to the topic and the explanation of innovative new approaches to measurement or field methodology;

6. The consultant produces findings that can lead to marketing action and are not just produced as an interesting set of tables and graphs; and

7. The consulting firm has executed the type of study previously or there is every reason to believe that the consultant can execute the project.

Consultants look forward to meeting the prospective client prior to the proposal being written. This important meeting can provide both sides with a wealth of information. The consultant should ask the following questions at or before that meeting:

❑ What is the agenda for this preproposal meeting?

❑ Will you provide a complete briefing on the project? What is the background? What marketing decisions will be based on the research findings? What are the specific objectives? What is wanted, and what is not wanted? How will the findings be used and by whom?

❑ How do you see me fitting into this project?

❑ How can I help you the most?

❑ How much has been designed up to this stage?

❑ What are your thoughts on the design and work strategy?

Sometimes the client wants to see innovative approaches to achieving the research objectives. When this occurs, it is important that the innovation is achievable and framed as potentially providing insight that is not attainable using standard methodology. It is very important that innovative approaches are imbedded in a framework of practical, generally accepted marketing research methodology.

Marketing research clients need to know that the end result will be useful and relevant to the marketing client. A certain level of safety is expected in every project. However, some research managers truly search for new procedures to assist their internal clients and extend their capabilities. This desire should never be assumed by the consultant. However, it should not be ignored either.

Select a Supplier

Selecting a supplier of marketing research services is similar to the procurement problem that affects many other aspects of business. Certainly, some research managers rely on the expertise of staff in procurement and/or human resources to assist with the selection of the best supplier. However, most marketing research contracts are managed on an ad hoc basis.

Strategic procurement planning is appropriate in some marketing research projects. Steele and Court (1996, p. 29) portray the strategic procurement process as in Figure 4.

Because marketing research projects range from the recovery of secondary data to focus groups to large purchases of syndicated data, the procurement process is handled in a wide variety of ways. Small ad hoc studies are usually handled informally and sometimes require little more

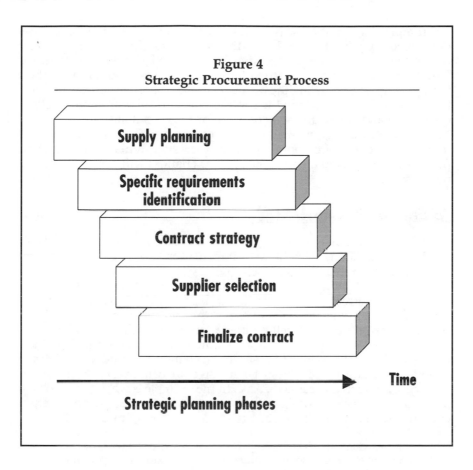

Figure 4
Strategic Procurement Process

Supply planning

Specific requirements identification

Contract strategy

Supplier selection

Finalize contract

Time

Strategic planning phases

than a price quote that accompanies a brief statement of objectives, methodology, deliverables, and timeline. Large studies, especially for government agencies and highly managed firms, require all bidders to follow very specific stages and formatting of the proposal, followed by a detailed contract with legal recitals.

It is certainly easy for two parties to any transaction to have differences of opinion. Intellectual property rights is an area of increasing concern for all parties. The client wants to ensure that it gets all that it pays for and that privileged information remains internal to the organization. Marketing research often is conducted to achieve or maintain competitive advantage. No company wants to give that dominant position away.

Consultants usually are hired to solve an organization's problem, either immediate or long-term. Some contracts are written that essentially lay claim to everything done by the consultant during the course of the project for the client organization. If this includes intellectual property rights, then it is the consultant's responsibility to inform the client where the contract ends.

If a problem solution was contracted for and new methodology was developed to solve that problem, the consultant should own the new methodology unless it is specifically provided for in the contract. However, if a contract is awarded to develop a new proprietary method for assessing and modeling the diffusion of new pharmaceutical products throughout the market, then the contract will probably provide for client ownership and adequate compensation for the consultant.

The larger issues of intellectual property rights, contract development, and the role of corporate procurement staff in marketing research projects are a developing area. Substantial changes will occur during the next several years.

Design the Research Study

Research design involves reconciling the marketing decision maker's needs for marketing insight and information and the initial design attempts of the research client with the suggestions of the research consultant. The marketing manager should have a good idea of the needed insight and information, the research manager usually has a firm vision of what the end product will look like, and the consultant has specified and priced the project using a well-defined plan of research and analysis.

Although Jocelyn (1977) refers to repetitive tasks and nonrepetitive marketing needs, there are also situations in which there is a fundamental desire to understand how people conduct themselves in their investigation of need-satisfying products and services. An extreme example is when the need is so basic that the researcher designs experiments to better understand the effect of each of several variables on the key marketing output measure. That is,

> Researchers in marketing experiment to learn about what products to make and how to influence the dynamics of supply and demand. Experiments are run in laboratories to develop a fundamental understanding of consumer behavior and in the field, to test and fine tune marketing action plans. One goal of planning and designing these experiments is to efficiently learn about the effects of marketing mix variables on consumer demand, i.e., to estimate effect sizes. Researchers often have some idea of the direction of these effects. For example, it is known a priori whether a particular manipulation will lead to an increase (or decrease) in the dependent variable. The experiment is then designed to maximally learn about, or quantify, consumer reaction to the experimental manipulations (Allenby, Arora, and Ginter 1999).

The form of the marketing research process must produce the information needed for more insightful marketing decisions. In some cases, this process might have been ideally designed several years in the past and should be applied as it has been many times. In others, the affiliated researchers and marketers face the challenge of creatively designing a process that innovatively and powerfully elicits the needed information from customers.

The most productive research studies are managed by project teams composed of client and consultant personnel. Whereas too many people can unnecessarily prolong project phases, too few can result in completed projects that might have benefited from additional input from informed and involved parties.

Design and Execute the Qualitative Research

Naomi Henderson is a highly respected qualitative researcher. In Chapter 8, she provides a broad presentation of qualitative research. Therefore, just a brief introduction to qualitative research is attempted here.

Although qualitative research can contribute to almost any quantitative study and produce valuable insights on its own, it is not always conducted. The reasons often given for this include

❏ The study is routine, and we don't think that qualitative research will add any additional insight at this stage.

❏ There is not time to conduct qualitative research and the survey within the timeline.

❏ The budget will not support both, and we feel that the survey will provide the greatest value.

❏ We have heard that qualitative research is of no value on projects such as this.

The first reason listed is legitimate. The last is not. The middle two might or might not be. Every research project is different, even if it is because of the differences in context and personnel from one study to the next, and should be assessed for the appropriateness of qualitative research on the basis of its own needs.

Certainly there are studies that have been conducted several times previously, have gained recognition for their validity and reliability, and have been noted for their contribution to marketing insight and improving marketing decisions. Perhaps qualitative research had been executed before the historically first round of a study several years earlier. In these situations, qualitative research might add nothing or very little to the overall study.

To be fair, there are some studies for which a very high percentage of the overall knowledge about a topic can be achieved using qualitative research. In fact, some problems can be executed only using qualitative research because of the subject material, the budget, or both.

To express the range of interpretation of qualitative research and ensure that readers understand the difference between qualitative research and surveys, statements similar to Figure 5 are commonly inserted at the beginning of focus group reports.

Figure 5
A Note Regarding Qualitative Research

Focus group findings can be extremely helpful for understanding the ways in which customers think and act. Significant value can be extracted from the in-depth comments that naturally flow during focus groups but are rare in surveys.

Along with the substantial benefits of focus groups come limitations. Focus groups reflect the attitudes of small groups of people. They are not surveys, and the findings should not be projected to the entire population. The findings from one group might be different from those of another group conducted with different participants.

Some statements made by focus group participants tend to be consistent with our everyday experiences and are totally believable. Other findings might seem to hold a lot of truth and may be strengthened with additional focus groups or surveys. A few findings from focus groups are surprising and should be treated with caution and definitely investigated further. These last two situations should be handled carefully to avoid unwise marketing decisions based on very small samples.

The findings herein should be regarded as tentative insights about the marketplace rather than as proven facts. This is inherent in the nature of this and any other qualitative research conducted with small numbers of individuals.

In the research process, qualitative research is usually conducted prior to any quantitative research. However, researchers increasingly appreciate the value of returning to customers for comments based on the survey research findings. Some survey findings are fairly obvious and need no further investigation, but others have meanings that can be discerned only with additional qualitative research. Some researchers prepare study findings in easily understood charts and present these to focus group participants to better understand their interpretation of the market.

Other times, the findings from the survey are rendered into the next marketing phase—perhaps a new product formulation or advertising copy—and presented to focus groups. Although these responses need to be treated in context, this careful additional step can reduce the risks of marketing errors at the next stage due to misinterpretation of survey findings.

Focus group research has its own process, methodology, and rules of practice. The main components of focus groups are presented in Figure 6. The focus group component of the marketing research industry is effectively organized around structure, content, and process. There are networks of moderators in many countries that depend on recruiting, focus room facilities, and other support personnel to provide these valuable services.

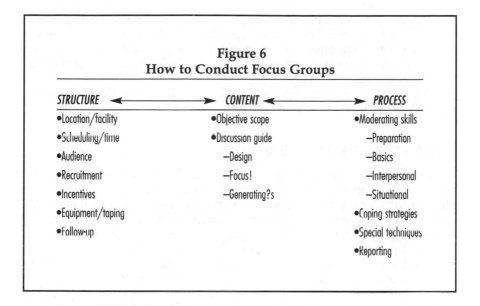

Figure 6
How to Conduct Focus Groups

STRUCTURE	CONTENT	PROCESS
•Location/facility	•Objective scope	•Moderating skills
•Scheduling/time	•Discussion guide	—Preparation
•Audience	—Design	—Basics
•Recruitment	—Focus!	—Interpersonal
•Incentives	—Generating?s	—Situational
•Equipment/taping		•Coping strategies
•Follow-up		•Special techniques
		•Reporting

Select the Field Methodology

The manner of eliciting information from respondents is intimately entwined with the design of the questionnaire and the sampling. Internet surveys have recently been added to the traditional methods of self-administered mailed questionnaires, telephone interviews, and face-to-face interviews. Newer methods added slightly before Internet surveys are interactive voice recognition telephone surveys, distribution of questionnaires on diskettes, and e-mail distribution of questionnaires. There are also hybrid methods, such as when telephone recruiting, faxed information, and telephone elicitation of responses are combined in one study.

In some projects, the field methodology is almost self-selecting. For example, if the product and other visual tools must be shown to respondents during the field process, telephone and self-administered methods without an interviewer present are not acceptable. If the budget can accommodate face-to-face interviews in the respondents' homes or offices, this is the most effective methodology. However, if the budget is not adequate, the questionnaire can be executed in shopping mall interviews with respondents selected from mall shoppers.

Naturally, each of the modes of fieldwork has a beneficial use and advantages over others. Although face-to-face interviews with respondents randomly selected from the relevant population offer the greatest flexibility and control, they are also the most expensive. Internet questionnaires have a level of flexibility formerly unknown, except in face-to-face interviews, along with very low costs. However, many question the sampling procedures of Internet surveys.

For many projects, telephone interviews provide the best compromise among conventional field practices. The telephone is fast, includes interviewer-to-respondent direct connection, is relatively less expensive than in-home/office interviews, and does not suffer from the sample bias of mall intercepts.

Because Chapter 5 of this book deals with data collection, the details of this topic will be left to that material.

Design the Questionnaire

Questionnaire design is the core of the marketing research project. All work prior to this stage is focused on producing a questionnaire that will elicit valid and reliable information on which to test the research hypotheses and achieve the study objectives. After the fieldwork begins, all hopes are pinned on the questionnaire for producing the raw material that leads to the insight needed for improved marketing decisions.

The theory developed around the marketing problem brings into being the key marketing concepts and hypotheses, and these in turn drive the survey questions. Certainly, many questionnaires are developed without formal theories being developed or hypotheses being stated explicitly. However, having hypotheses stated prior to questionnaire design can enhance clarity and promote faster questionnaire design and analysis of data.

The two most obvious parts of questionnaire design are the following:

1. Phrasing the questions and
2. Laying out the physical questionnaire page.

Question Phrasing

Two main modes exist for communication in questionnaires: oral and written. Because people most often write material to be read silently by others, self-administered questionnaires are typically easier to develop for most researchers. The writing seems more natural. And, if it is a self-administered questionnaire, it will be exactly what is needed.

However, interviewer-administered questionnaires are spoken communication, which means that someone speaks and the other person listens and then speaks back. This speech should be natural, pleasant, and understandable.

Note: The value of any communication is the response that you get.

This principle should be uppermost in the minds of all who create questionnaires. "In other words, it is not what you intend to communicate, or what you think that you communicate, but what the other person perceives you as communicating that matters. For practical purposes, the meaning of your communication is determined by the way in which the other person responds to you. If his response is what you intended, then you are successful. If his response is not what you intended, then your communication has not succeeded in getting your outcome. In this case, you need to do something else" (Woodsmall and Woodsmall 1998, p. 5).

Answers to survey questions allow analysts to test hypotheses. There is often less time spent wondering what to analyze during the testing phase, because there should be a clear trail between the hypotheses and the questions. The results of the hypothesis testing, combined with the overall findings from the survey, provide the foundation on which to base better marketing decisions.

Questionnaire design is similar to advertising in some ways. Both need to communicate simply and effectively. Whereas advertising communication is directed from the media to the audience, questionnaires must be developed to support ease of communication back from the audience to the interviewer or research staff. This two-way fluid communication is a demanding task.

The following quote was found many years ago in an advertising textbook. Although the source has since been lost, the wisdom of the advice of Arthur Kudner, a well-known advertising copywriter, will always be relevant and important. The story goes that Mr. Kudner walked into his teenage son's bedroom one night to find the boy writing an essay for his high school English course. To make a long story short, his son was using long words that he did not understand. Kudner wrote this note to his son:

> Never fear big, long words. Big, long words name little things. All big things have little names. Such as life and death, peace and war, dawn, day, night, hope, love and home. Learn to use little words in a big way. It's hard to do, but they say what you mean. When you don't know what you mean, use big words. They often fool little people.

The words, phrases, complete questions, and sections all must be scrutinized during questionnaire construction. Belson (1981, pp. 370–87), Payne (1951), Bradburn and Sudman (1980), and others have spent much time and effort investigating and categorizing the dos and don'ts of question wording. The insights provided by these researchers include the following:

1. Each question must relate to a hypothesis, research question, or objective of the study.
   a. Are the questions valid; that is, do they measure what they were intended to measure?
   b. Was each question tailored to the needs of this study, or were compromises made so that the answers to some questions can be compared with those of prior studies?
   c. Each question costs money; they should all be worthwhile.
   d. Each additional question increases the likelihood of tired respondents terminating their participation.
2. Ensure that each word, phrase, and question has one, and only one, meaning.

     a. No ambiguous words or phrases.

     b. Each question asks only one question. For example, "pleas-
ant" and "helpful" are two concepts with two different
meanings.

3. The questions and parts thereof must relate to phenomena
that are meaningful to respondents.

     a. Hypothetical situations often produce useless information.

     b. If the natural answer is some form of gray, don't ask for a
black or white answer.

4. Keep the words to the minimum. Can lengthy questions be
broken down into two or three components?

5. Don't force a scale that is not appropriate for the answer.
Although agree/disagree scales are often used, a scale that is
more closely connected to the question elicits better answers.

6. Be careful of long batteries of scaled questions. They can
cause respondents to disengage from the process.

7. Phrase all questions with the respondent in mind.

     a. Is the least capable respondent able to understand the
question, read the page, and understand the interviewer?

     b. If answering the question might embarrass the respondent,
is there another way to ask it?

     c. What is the most natural way to present the questions and
garner responses?

Spoken communication, especially when face-to-face, is the highest
level of human dialogue. The greatest amount of information can be
exchanged during the shortest period of time. In face-to-face communication, 7% of the information content is due to the words, 38% is based on
the voice tonality, and 55% is derived from body language cues.

This principle provides hope for increased effectiveness in communication as well as warnings. In the previous example, Ackoff (1999) found
great value in having an advisory team inform the clothing chain owner
about customer needs. Qualitative researchers are able to elicit a great
deal of information during focus groups and in-depth personal interviews. Much of this is due to the ability of one person to understand
another much better when communicating orally and in person.

Basic laws of administering survey questionnaires over the telephone
or face-to-face include the following:

1. The interviewer is to read exactly what is written on the questionnaire and

2. The interviewer is to record exactly the words spoken by the
respondent in answering the questions.

Consequently, because additional information can be sent and
received through changes in tonality of the voice and body expressions,

interviewers must be well trained in executing the survey script and recording information. Interpreting body language and tonality correctly for survey purposes requires a level of understanding that must be taught separately from normal interviewing skills.

Even simple words and phrases are open to (mis)interpretation. For example, the following five-word question, composed of single syllable words, can be read, heard, and interpreted in five different ways depending on the words accented most strongly and the intonation of the interviewer's voice (Payne 1951, p. 204):

❏ **WHY** do you say that?
❏ Why **DO** you say that?
❏ Why do **YOU** say that?
❏ Why do you **SAY** that?
❏ Why do you say **THAT**?

Sometimes interviews, whether telephone or face-to-face, are audio recorded, and skilled interpreters further analyze the tapes after the interviews have been fully recorded using conventional survey methodologies. Typically, focus groups are audio and video recorded to allow the researcher to review the tapes and extract important information beyond the spoken words.

Questionnaire Layout

The physical layout of questionnaires is very important. In self-administered questionnaires, great care should be taken with all aspects of the page layout of the questionnaire.

Respondents are precious to marketing researchers. Without respondents, marketing research firms would largely be out of business, and marketers would need to guess more often. These fine people should not have to work hard to provide their input to the survey process. The research team needs to prepare a self-administered questionnaire that

1. Presents the questions in their entirety;
2. Sequences the questions properly and shows respondents where to go next on the pages;
3. Is attractive in appearance and clean; that is, its physical design is easy to read and contains no "extra ink";
4. Provides for ease-of-answering; and
5. Can be returned to the survey firm with minimal effort.

Some self-administered questionnaires are electronically presented to the respondents, either on a computer using computer-assisted personal interviewing (CAPI) technologies or over the Internet, by e-mail, or by a mailed diskette. The same requirements hold.

Most telephone interviewing uses computer-assisted telephone interviewing (CATI) software. This places the questionnaire on the computer so that the interviewer reads the questions on the computer screen and types the answers into the computer. Sometimes paper-and-pencil aids are used, and interviewers might be required to write out answers to open-ended questions.

When telephone interviews are conducted using paper-and-pencil questionnaires, care must still be taken to ensure that the interviewer can maintain a flowing conversation with the respondent. Good page layout can lighten the interviewing burden. Also, the page designer must ensure that the answering format provides for easy recording of answers and is conducive to fast data entry, which minimizes the incidence of errors. Field firms that use paper-and-pencil surveys must have quality control systems aimed at maintaining the integrity of respondents' answers throughout the process.

Whether interviewing is done using CATI, CAPI, or paper-and-pencil questionnaires, field houses should maintain quality by either monitoring the interviews or calling respondents back to verify a certain percentage of each interviewer's output, usually 10% to 15%. Ideally, the interviewers and other staff used for verification are not used for primary interviewing.

Design the Sampling

The essential task of sampling is to ensure that the relevant population is identified and that the process of drawing the sample is conducted in an efficient and effective manner. Once again, there is an excellent chapter a little later in this book by Peter Chan (Chapter 7) that will treat this topic in greater depth.

Sampling has two main tasks: to design the sampling process and determine the size of the sample. Executing these tasks can be relatively easy or extremely complex.

Statistical inference relies on samples that are randomly selected from the relevant population(s) and representative of those populations on key characteristics. Obtaining a truly random sample is not simple. But there are ways, such as

❑ Using random digit dialing for telephone surveys;
❑ Randomly selecting sample listings from complete customer lists provided by the client firm; or
❑ Using street directories to select the sample for in-home interviews.

Most of the terminology of sampling is fairly descriptive:

❑ The **universe** is composed of all people who can qualify to be part of the study;

❑ The **sample frame** is the means by which the population is physically accessed, for example, client lists of customers or the telephone directory; and

❑ The **sampling unit** is the smallest entity of a sample that will constitute one unit of analysis, perhaps an individual, a household, or a company.

Sampling at the beginning of the twenty-first century has been streamlined from previous years. The process has been automated to the point of being able to buy samples in ways, such as on CDs, that might not have been imagined by many practitioners two decades ago. The key changes in sampling have been speed of sample access and breadth of sample frames.

It is still difficult for organizations to provide good samples from their customer databases that are fully usable by the consultant. However, it is now easier than ever to augment those lists with, for example, telephone numbers. These services are available from several suppliers that will take the incomplete list and fill in as much of the missing information as possible. Also, CDs of residents are available for purchase. These CD lists can be used to complete some of the missing information in the sample list, either by the client or the consultant.

Sampling procedures often fall under the following headings:

1. Simple random sampling, for which some mechanism is used to ensure that each sample unit in the population has an equal chance of being drawn into the sample as any other sample unit;

2. Systematic sampling, for which a random starting point is chosen in the sample frame, and thereafter, every nth sample unit is chosen to be part of the sample; or

3. Stratified sampling that involves "stratifying" the population into subgroups and sampling to ensure that each subgroup is represented in the sample:

   a. PPS (probability proportionate to size) or proportionate sampling is developed to ensure that the same proportion of the sample is captured within each subgroup as exists in the population within the same subgroup and

   b. Disproportionate sampling is when the population proportions in the subgroups are not maintained. This is typically conducted when the overall sample size is so small that the number of respondents within some strata would be too small to statistically analyze as needed. The final sample will probably oversample from small population subgroups and undersample from large population subgroups.

IN THE MIDDLE: FIELD, EDITING, CODING, TABBING

Pretest the Questionnaire and Refine

Pretesting the questionnaire is vital to the success of field research. In repetitive studies, this perhaps can be bypassed and is in most cases. However, when conducting research in new areas, danger lurks for the unsuspecting researcher with a fresh, nonpretested questionnaire.

As mentioned previously, the value of any communication is the response that you get. Pretesting enables the researcher to see and hear those responses and gauge whether the research communication process called fieldwork is likely to produce the anticipated value. Pretests should be conducted face to face. This is the only way in which vital information is not lost. Remember, paying attention and correctly interpreting the tonality of respondents' voices and their body language when reacting to a pretested questionnaire can provide a tremendous amount of valuable communication.

Pretesting a self-administered questionnaire in a face-to-face interview can be done in two ways. The first is to translate the questionnaire to the interviewer-administered format for question-and-answer wording and page layout. This is quite a bit of work. Also, one might wonder whether the questions and answers will translate between the two formats. They will, mostly. The greatest temptation is to use the greater flexibility of face-to-face interviews to garner more information than intended for the self-administered version. Resist this urge and translate as closely as possible.

The second way is to have the interviewer simply read the questions along with the respondent. This can work well and stays very close to the original field intentions. The interviewer needs to be a keen and sensitive interpreter of the answers, voice, and body language of the respondent. All of these might cause the interviewer to ask additional questions that are intended to tease the meaning out of a curt reply, raised eyebrows, grunt, giggle, or unusual body position.

A respondent who feels that a question is poorly worded in a self-administered questionnaire might simply not answer; in a telephone pretest, the intention of the question might be guessed and then answered. Both of these actions either provide no information or are misleading. In a face-to-face pretest, the respondent's exhale of frustration should cause the interviewer to ask if something is wrong or if greater clarification is needed.

After fieldwork begins, the tendency will be to carry on and complete the quota. So, pretesting might be the last good opportunity to challenge the questionnaire. Losing this opportunity can jeopardize the whole project. If, for some reason, a pretest is not conducted, at least ensure that the first day or two of fieldwork is closely monitored and reported to the project director.

Execute the Fieldwork

Beginning the survey fieldwork is like the opening night of a simple play between one actor and one audience member who is a key participant. All the work on both the client side and the consultant side has been devoted to producing a work, the questionnaire, that communicates well with the audience, the sample.

The beginning of field operations is the project's nexus to reality. Fieldwork provides the critical grounding of the theories, concepts, and hypotheses. Up to this stage, concepts would have been developed, theories advanced, and an instrument proposed. However, without the fieldwork, there would be no opportunity to judge whether the theories were relevant. There would be little, if any, value to the organization.

Data collection methods are the focus of Chapter 5 by Vinay Kanetkar. This topic will be handled very superficially here for that reason.

The field methodologies used in modern marketing research are tremendously varied: from observational procedures to focus groups to Internet surveys. Each method has its advantages and difficulties. Research considerations for selecting the fieldwork method include the following key features, among others:

1. Time horizon for completion of all field procedures;
2. Budget available for the field;
3. The nature of the sample frame and the size and type of sample and sampling;
4. Whether the questions can be abstracted from the normal, real-life environment of the customer's interaction with the product;
5. Whether the respondent needs to be shown something, taste food, smell something, or handle an article;
6. Whether the respondent may not have access to certain information until the "correct" time;
7. Whether the questions or sequence of questions need to be tailored to the specific responses of the respondent; and
8. Whether respondents with special and varied needs must be accommodated within the field process.

Depending on the needs of the process, the following survey field methodologies might be used:

1. Observation, with or without experimentation;
2. Telephone elicitation, by either personal interviews or interactive voice recognition;
3. Face-to-face interviews in respondents' homes or offices or in a central location such as a shopping mall; or

4. Electronic presentation of questions and visual stimuli and capturing responses, including keypad responses, diskette questionnaires, e-mail surveys, and Internet surveys.

There are other concerns for the field process, including the prospect of the main contractor subcontracting the fieldwork to another firm. Although some clients prefer that one contractor do all work, this is usually not a concern. Companies that conduct only fieldwork execute many excellent surveys. They are true professionals that prefer to focus their activities only on this one facet of the research process. They typically provide excellent service and value. The key point for the client to confirm is that the main contractor has experience in working with field houses and can effectively manage and assess the contribution made by the subcontractor.

Capture the Data and Edit, Clean, and Prepare Them for Data Analysis

This part of the process is observed by very few. As a middle stage, it is often considered a mechanical part of marketing research that is essential but typically hidden from view. Professional marketing researchers understand the importance of this phase of the process. Sampling and nonsampling errors were mentioned previously. Thorough attention to the integrity and importance of accurate representation of respondents' answers reduces or eliminates a potential source of error of the nonsampling kind.

The majority of survey fieldwork is now conducted using CATI systems. This automates the data capture process and reduces errors because respondents' answers are typed directly into the computer. Still, errors of entry can be made. In some cases, logical errors can be caught during the analysis phase. However, the inputting of a 6 instead of a 3 on a 10-point scale might never be found and becomes another instance of nonsampling error.

AT THE END: DATA ANALYSIS, REPORTING, AND FEEDBACK

Analyze the Data

Data analysis can range from basic production of stub-and-banner tables to sophisticated and elaborate statistical analysis. For many researchers, the transition from fieldwork to data analysis marks a major triumph of the research process. The external functions that can be tortured by the vagaries of the world are mostly left behind. When the data are in the computer and have been prepared for analysis, there is little that others can cause to go wrong.

The most basic data analysis exercise is when stub-and-banner tables are produced according to the specifications of the client. For a telephone study that was conducted using a CATI system, the process is one of providing tabular specs to the CATI programmer and receiving the tables. The analysis based on the tables would probably involve the investigation of relationships and the presentation of those key relationships in tables and graphs for the final report and presentation. Sometimes requests for additional tables result from this investigation.

The common format for many research studies involves the following stages:

1. Receive clean data,

2. Convert data to analysis format,

3. Perform statistical analysis to test hypotheses and investigate research questions, and

4. Simplify statistical findings to graphs and diagrams suitable for report and presentation.

Although each of these stages is important, the first, receiving clean data, is absolutely vital to any analysis. Data that are dirty or have been incorrectly entered or formatted can wreak havoc later in the process. Basic tests of data patterns should be conducted. These involve running basic frequency distributions, graphs, and crosstabs to understand the data. The hypotheses advanced at the beginning of the study can begin to be investigated through simple visualization of the data. This visualization can be the most important stage in discovering data problems. Higher-level statistical analysis often has a more difficult time unearthing bad data than do the techniques for exploratory data analysis that have been developed and championed by Tukey (1977) and Ehrenberg (1982).

Converting the data to the analysis format has been taken from a tortuous preprocessing stage ten years ago to a level that is almost automatic currently. The newest versions of the popular statistical application SPSS translate data from several different formats to SPSS format. Several other programs include this function. DBMS/COPY from Conceptual Software provides a fantastically wide range of conversions that cover most statistical programs, as well as spreadsheets and database applications. After converting the data into the analysis format, there will often be work needed to prepare the data for analysis and presentation, for example, entering variable and value labels.

Statistical testing should be conducted to test hypotheses that were specified at the project design phase of the study. Because the basics of hypothesis testing and quantitative analysis will be covered in Chapters 9 and 10 by Naresh Malhotra and then expanded by several others, no additional explanations will be provided here.

An extensive process is represented, as in Figure 7, by Peter Peacock (1998) as the "knowledge-discovery process" used in data mining. Peacock's article presents the essential details necessary for

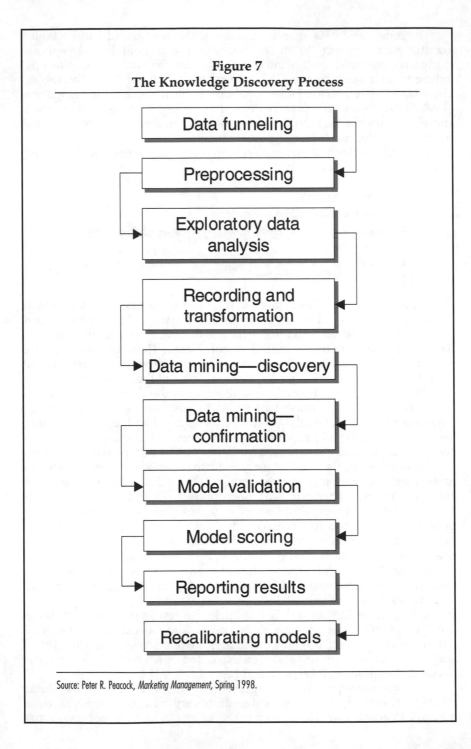

Figure 7
The Knowledge Discovery Process

Data funneling

Preprocessing

Exploratory data analysis

Recording and transformation

Data mining—discovery

Data mining—confirmation

Model validation

Model scoring

Reporting results

Recalibrating models

Source: Peter R. Peacock, *Marketing Management,* Spring 1998.

effectively establishing a higher level of customer knowledge on the basis of information contained in customer databases and enhanced with primary marketing research. His process involves the following elements:

- ❏ Data funneling is the gathering of relevant corporate data and pruning for effective integration;
- ❏ Preprocessing is cleaning the data, transforming variables, and formatting the data in preparation for analysis;
- ❏ Exploratory data analysis (EDA) involves a set of procedures and data analysis techniques to discover patterns in the data and relationships among variables;
- ❏ Recoding and transformation involves converting pre-processed variables into variables that are more amenable to statistical data mining methodologies;
- ❏ Data mining—discovery uses statistical methodologies and information technology processing to discover patterns, similarities, and dissimilarities among variables and customers by using, for example, decision trees such as CART, CHAID, and others;
- ❏ Data mining—confirmation tests hypotheses that were advanced before the data mining process or as a result of the EDA or the analysis of the previous step;
- ❏ Model validation to determine the quality of the model and its predictive validity;
- ❏ Model scoring uses the validated predictive model to generate predicted values for each customer and then further analyzes the similarities among groups of customers using clustering procedures;
- ❏ Reporting the findings to decision makers; and
- ❏ Recalibrating the model on a schedule of regular updates based on new customer information, testing the last phase of the model, cycling through the analysis, and recalibration procedures and rescoring.

The data mining process is obviously dynamic by its very nature. However, the general process of marketing research is itself one of hypothesizing, gathering, analyzing, testing, applying, challenging, and repeating. All aspects of marketing are truly dynamic and require data and findings that are tuned to today and the future but have learned from the past.

Provide the Research Findings for Marketing Decision Making

As with the data analysis, the provision of research findings can best be achieved after close consultation between the client and the consultant.

The consultant should strive to supply the research findings in formats that can be used easily and effectively by the client. This often involves a report tailored to the client's needs and usable by the client immediately.

Clients of marketing research should provide good feedback to their suppliers. Most consultants are eager to please their clients. Feedback provides the vehicle for change and improvements.

Consultants should strive to make their clients look like heroes by meeting all study objectives with a high-quality, clearly written, and illustrated report that is delivered on time. Clients often work under incredibly difficult workloads and time deadlines. Supplying the report and presentation slides provides the means for the client to save time and satisfy their managers.

Continue to Monitor the Client's Needs for Information

After the final report has been submitted and the presentation made, the use of the findings lies primarily in the hands of the client. The consultant should inquire to determine whether there is anything else needed and whether the initial expectations have been met. Every consultant looks forward to continued business from clients. Although this depends on the satisfaction of the client with the consultant's work, the need for additional work will be dictated by challenges to the client's business rather than the consultant's desire to continue or expand an existing project or begin a new project.

Consider Research Ethics

Should ethics be considered part of the research process? Yes. Ethics and conventions of good practice pervade every part of the marketing research process. Marketing research professional associations have statements of ethics and good practice and a director or a board of review that passes judgment on ethical issues in the profession.

The main ethical focus in marketing research is that the human rights of all parties are respected. Respondents are the primary concern of most marketing research clients and consultants. Respondents cooperate in surveys either because they understand that the process will eventually provide benefits to the public or because they feel compelled to cooperate because of interest, a desire to help the researchers, or financial incentives. As is mentioned in Chapter 5, incentives can convince people to participate in surveys. However, the amount of money or prizes offered is typically very small.

Respondents are commonly promised confidentiality and anonymity. To ensure that the researcher keeps this promise, the research firm maintains ownership of survey questionnaires. Other ethical issues include the following, as just a few examples:

1. Research clients are provided with value for the money spent,
2. Research suppliers are informed when a contract has more than one bidder, and
3. Selling and fund-raising under the guise of marketing research is unethical.

CONCLUSION

The ability to follow the research process to completion depends on being adaptable to the range of customer needs, as well as to the dictates of design, execution, and analysis methodologies. The simpler data requirements have shorter processes, whereas more complex methodologies, such as data mining, have fairly long methodologies.

However, let's not be fooled by looking at the immediate process and failing to see the total process. For if the motivational source for marketing research is a marketing problem, then the raison d'etre is to provide the information needed to better solve that problem through more insightful marketing decisions. Very little marketing research is contracted because someone sees marketing research as the end result. It is an excellent process for supplying insightful information, and that is all.

BIBLIOGRAPHY

Ackoff, Russell L. (1999), *Ackoff's Best*. New York: John Wiley & Sons.

Allenby, Greg M., Neeraj Arora, and James L. Ginter (1999), "Designing Informative Field Experiments," working paper, Marketing Department, Max M. Fisher College of Business, Ohio State University.

Belson, William A. (1981), *The Design and Understanding of Survey Questions*. Aldershot, Hants, England: Gower Publishing Co. Ltd.

Bradburn, Norman M. and Seymour Sudman (1980), *Improving Interview Method and Questionnaire Design*. San Francisco, CA: Jossey-Bass Publishers.

Ehrenberg, A.S.C. (1982), *A Primer in Data Reduction*. New York: John Wiley & Sons.

Jocelyn, Robert W. (1977), *Designing the Marketing Research Project*. New York: Petrocelli/Charter.

Payne, Stanley L. (1951), *The Art of Asking Questions*. Princeton, NJ: Princeton University Press.

Peacock, Peter R. (1988), "Data Mining in Marketing: Part 2," *Marketing Research: A Magazine of Management & Applications*, 7 (Winter/Spring), 23–36.

Schmalensee, Diane H. and A. Dawn Lesh (1999), "How to Make Research More Actionable," *Marketing Research: A Magazine of Management & Applications*, 11 (Winter), 15–25.

Steele, Paul and Brian Court (1996), *Profitable Purchasing Strategies*. London: McGraw-Hill.

Tukey, E. (1977), *Exploratory Data Analysis*. Reading, MA: Addison-Wesley.

Wind, Jerry (1997), "Start Your Engines," *Marketing Research: A Magazine of Management & Applications*, 9 (Winter), 4–11.

Woodsmall, Marilyne and Wyatt Woodsmall (1998), *People Pattern Power*. Washington, DC: The International Research Institute for Human Typological Studies.

5

Data Collection Methods and Marketing Research: A Comparison and Review of Alternatives

Vinay Kanetkar

There are many different methods to collect market research data. Some methods are qualitative, such as in-depth interviews or focus groups, whereas others are quantitative. In qualitative methods, researchers have used humanistic- and semiotic-based approaches to gather information about customers. Other methods rely on observations using either a human observer or some other recording devices, including computers or video cameras. Recent advances in computers and associated software products have enabled researchers to gather detailed information about the actors (manufacturers, retailers, suppliers, competitors, and consumers) in the marketplace. There are also traditional questionnaire-based methods. More recently, computers have been used to facilitate respondent and researcher interaction, including computer-assisted interviewing with audio and/or video support, as well as electronic mail–based surveys.

New technologies along with methodological advances bring about new insights about the marketplace and displace old "thumb rules" or heuristics with better and often knowledge-based rules. It is this dynamic that is explored in this chapter—specifically, the nature of data collection tools and rules that are often used and issues that the researcher must resolve and decide.

Moreover, our theoretical understanding about the tool itself is central. To some extent, each method has strengths and weaknesses, and many of these are explored in comparative studies. There are two types of comparative studies in the literature, those that explore within method and those that explore between methods. We explore both of these types of studies here.

Prior research and experiments with regard to data collection methods provide a valuable methodological foundation but limited understanding about the match between decision context and data collection methods. More specifically, we propose that there might be a relationship between validities (internal and external), which are benefits associated with data collection methods and costs. This benefit–cost (Value Map) concept then is used to explore challenges and opportunities to advancing the state of our understanding about data collection methods.

This chapter is organized as follows: In the next two sections, we summarize various data collection methods and describe each method with associated study design details. A short summary of research studies is presented to help design research study. In the following section, we provide a summary of various comparative methods studies. These studies are often between-methods studies. In the next section, we present a classification approach, as well as the nature of the relationship between benefits and costs. In the last section, we offer concluding comments about data collection.

QUALITATIVE DATA COLLECTION METHODS

In this section, various qualitative data collection methods are described briefly to provide an understanding about various design elements, that is, the nature of the tasks for researchers and respondents and the format for data collection. For each method, study steps are presented with the assumption that the research team has already made decisions about the product/service and decision context for which the data are to be collected. In addition, literature about particular data collection methods, especially about design elements and the type of precautions researchers may take to ensure better quality data at lower costs, is provided.

Depth Interviews

A depth or long interview involves open discussion between interviewer and respondent. On the basis of the initial response, the interviewer probes for elaboration and meaning. Answers to these questions lead to subsequent interviewer questions. The respondent is often asked to answer open-ended, semistructured questions with *depth* and *breadth* as topics. The researcher may verify responses by comparing other information sources, including documents. This method enables the researcher to develop detailed descriptions of individual situations.

Long interviews enable the researcher to generate data that provide a high degree of internal consistency, and respondents' answers are often verified against a variety of other sources. A typical long interview study may involve less than ten respondents. Consequently, it is difficult to project the results of a long interview to the population. Woodside and Wilson (1995) report a study in which a long interview lasted more than two hours. Moreover, interpreting and describing customer behaviour typically is more time consuming than other data collection approaches. To conduct depth interviews, the following steps are essential:

- ❑ Development of interview guide and potential individuals to be interviewed;
- ❑ Initial contact and interview scheduling (time, location, and desired format);
- ❑ Recording of interviews;
- ❑ Coding, analyzing, and interpreting collected information; and
- ❑ Report writing.

Focus Groups

A focus group is a research technique used to collect data through group interaction on a topic determined by the researcher (Morgan 1996). The goal in a focus group is to learn the opinions and values of those involved with products and/or services from diverse points of view (Lunt and Livingstone 1996). Many sources argue that a focus group should have 6 to 12 people as respondents, though there is limited published evidence to suggest that the quality or quantity of data would suffer if groups were smaller or larger. Focus groups are cheaper and faster to complete than individual depth interviews. Focus group data collection outcomes depend on a skilled moderator to maintain the free flow of ideas and keep structure to the discussion. Although focus group findings may be convergent with survey research results, it is difficult to generalize findings to the population (Hall and Rist 1999). Moreover, a typical focus group lasts for 90 minutes and can easily generate 30 pages of transcript. Consequently, determining key findings and their applicability to marketing decision may be a challenging task for the moderator. Additional material pertaining to focus groups is provided in Chapter 8 in this volume.

The Humanistic Perspective

The humanistic perspective assumes that each of us is capable of constructing multiple realities. Furthermore, the researcher and the study topic and knowledge are constructed jointly and interactively as a result of interaction with respondents. Finally, cause and effect cannot be separated, and research about the marketplace and consumers is value laden. Data collection through a humanistic perspective involves the researcher spending considerable time with respondents and often sharing living experiences. The researcher may make detailed recordings using audio or visual means, as well as maintain a diary of events, activities, and inter-actions. At the conclusion of data collection, researchers share their inter-pretation of the collected data with respondents and ask for their inter-pretation. In conclusion, this method provides not only a detailed understanding of customer behaviour, but also a holistic context of it. This is a relatively new method for data collection purposes in marketing. Belk, Wallendorf, and Sherry (1989) report on a study about buyer–seller interactions at flea and antique markets and find that trading of sacred objects (products that are owned for a long duration) by a seller requires that he or she be concerned about future use and upkeep of the objects (see also Wallendorf and Arnould 1991).

Semiotics

Semiotics is the study or science of signs. More specifically, signs are central to human communication and understanding. These signs include gestures, music, language, food, clothing, possessions, advertisements, and brand usage. Levy (1959) presented the first study in marketing that dealt with brand logos and meanings as perceived by consumers. There have been many subsequent efforts to use semiotics principles to collect marketing research information (see Hirschman, Scott, and Wells 1998; McCracken 1986; McQuarrie and Mick 1999; Mick 1986; Parker 1998). There are at least two distinct approaches that are used to understand meanings. First, there is archival tradition. Researchers gather a large sam-ple of stimuli (symbols, brand names, advertisements, or historical records of consumption process), which are content-analyzed to provide themes, conflicts, commonalities, and differences. Second, another approach relies on buyer or user response, with particular emphasis on understanding meanings associated with stimuli. Researchers may gather current stimuli that are sold or used in the marketplace. Selected stimuli are then pre-sented to current users or buyers. Researchers may conduct in-depth inter-views to understand user associations, meanings, and use contexts.

Projective Techniques

Projective techniques stimulate free-flowing associations that can uncover and identify deep, normally unconscious feelings (see Hollander 1988; Levy 1986; Shore and Cooper 1999). These techniques are designed so that respondents can express honest and often sensitive or embarrass-ing opinions about products and services. In general, projective tech-niques use ambiguous stimuli (words, sentences, pictures, or combina-tions), and the respondent is asked to describe, expand on, or build a story about the stimuli. There are several alternative projective techniques, including the Thematic Apperception Test (TAT), sentence completion, shopping list, word association (Reilly 1990), and storytelling. Because of the vagueness of the technique, there is a great deal of flexibility and challenge in designing and creating an appropriate stimulus set for a particular marketing decision. To collect data using a projective technique, in general, the following steps must be followed:

- ❏ Development of stimulus material, including pictures, words, or sentences to be completed;
- ❏ Respondent task(s) and response format;
- ❏ Recording of responses;
- ❏ Coding, analyzing, and interpreting collected information; and
- ❏ Report writing.

Fram and Cibotti (1991) summarize the shopping list studies that originated from Haire's (1950) classic work involving instant coffee versus ground coffee. To conduct a shopping list study, researchers must construct two or more shopping lists, each of which contains one or more items that are unique to it. The respondent then is asked to comment about a buyer who might have one of the shopping lists. Typically, each respondent is shown only one shopping list. Respondent comments are then content-analyzed for common themes, conflicts, and differences. Fram and Cibotti (1991) conclude that projective techniques provide reliable and stable (based on five replications over a 15-year period) understandings about consumer perception. Because the results were also replicated in two other countries, projective techniques provide reasonable external validity. Moreover, a more recent replication of Haire's study indicates that, as perception about instant coffee has changed, so has customer reactions.

Storytelling

Storytelling as a data collection tool enables researchers to gather personal anecdotes with emotions, as well as implicit and unspoken impulses respondents may have about products or services. In this method, respondents are asked to tell stories about stimuli (pictures or words) and provide a connection between them. The central idea behind storytelling is to allow respondents to express the emotions behind their choices (Lieber 1997). This works well when respondents may not want to admit a particular aspect of decision making because it is socially not appropriate or when respondents have not thought about the issues. One particular advantage of storytelling is that, with 15 to 20 respondents, researchers can obtain new and useful insights about customer behaviour. There are several variations of this technique. For example, researchers may ask respondents to make sketches, take photographs, or prepare video recordings and then write a story with the help of the visual aid. Researchers may ask for clarification about the meaning of symbols and signs to respondents. Finally, researchers are required to content-analyze stories and derive major and minor themes in relation to the marketing problem at hand.

Nominal Group Technique

The nominal group technique involves structured interviews with a group of respondents, which minimizes spontaneous interaction (Claxton, Ritchie, and Zaichkowsky 1980). Although there are many variations in the nominal group technique, a basic structure for data collection consists of the following steps: First, a group of six to ten respondents is gathered at one place, and each person is asked to come up with ideas about the product/service or topic under consideration. Second, each member is asked to present one idea without discussion. The process of idea presentation is continued until all ideas are presented. Third, all ideas are discussed for clarification, combination, and evaluation (Langford 1994). The researcher is allowed to express the importance of certain ideas or any other constructive comments about the ideas. At this stage, respondents are not allowed to criticize others in the group. Fourth, each respondent is asked to rate or rank the pooled ideas for degree of importance in helping meet topic objectives. Fifth, after a brief discussion about rating/ranking, the group is asked to form a consensus.

Unlike focus groups, the nominal group technique has not received a great deal of attention in the marketing field. At least, there is limited or no published literature. This may be due to the structure that is imposed by the method. There is, however, extensive literature dealing with the nominal group technique as a group decision-making tool (see Dennis and Valacich 1994 for some experimental research).

There are many qualitative methods that can be used to collect customer information. One unique aspect of all qualitative methods is that they require a small number of respondents and provide "deeper" and subconscious-level feelings about marketing stimuli. There are also differences across these methods. Techniques such as focus groups and nominal groups impose structure to gather information, and consequently, gathered information may be directly used by marketing managers. In contrast, many projective techniques, such as word association or storytelling, require the researcher to impose structure on the collected information.

QUANTITATIVE DATA COLLECTION METHODS

In this section, various quantitative data collection methods are described. These include face-to-face and telephone interviewing, questionnaire-based methods, direct observations, scanner-based data collection, and computer-based methods.

Face-to-Face and Telephone Interviewing

Face-to-face and telephone interviewing are modes of data collection in which an interviewer administers a structured set of questions to a respondent, and the respondent is requested to provide response information within a specified time period. In the case of face-to-face, or in-person, interviewing, both individuals (interviewer and respondent) are at the same physical location, whereas for telephone interviewing, the interviewer may be using a central or distributed telephone facility.

Telephone interviewing is relatively inexpensive to gather survey data compared with face-to-face interviews. With multiple telephone operators, it is possible to conduct many more interviews in a shorter time period. Moreover, respondents can be contacted according to their preferred time, and repeated follow-ups can be made at a reasonable cost. Before we present issues pertaining to telephone interviewing, we provide some steps needed to complete telephone, or for that matter questionnaire-based, methods:

- ❑ Decide on mode of administration (telephone, face-to-face, mail, or mall intercept);
- ❑ Decide on sampling, including frame (element, respondent selection, timing);
- ❑ Design measurement instrument, which involves
    - ❑ Determine response format, open-ended or structured,
    - ❑ Determine content of individual questions,
    - ❑ Determine form of response to each question,
    - ❑ Determine wording for each question,
    - ❑ Decide on question sequencing, for example, general to specific, important questions first, or question skipping, and
    - ❑ Decide on physical characteristics of questionnaire;
- ❑ Pretest instrument;
- ❑ Train interviewer to minimize variation across interviewers;
- ❑ Conduct interviews or, in the case of mail surveys, send survey instrument to respondents;
- ❑ Code, analyze, and interpret collected information; and
- ❑ Write report.

We first examine telephone interviewing, then proceed to face-to-face interviewing.

There are four different challenges with respect to using telephone interviewing as the only data collection technique for the general population (Groves et al. 1988). The first concern is the *sampling frame*, or the list from which a telephone number is obtained. (We do not review this here because it is reviewed in Chapter 7.[1]) The second concern is *coverage*, that

---

[1]For completeness, note that there are four alternative approaches to obtain a random sample of telephone numbers: two-stage random dialing, list-assisted sampling based on directory samples and telephone number samples, and dual-frame sampling.

is, the proportion of households included in the sampling frame to the total population. The third challenge is *nonresponse*, that is, those individuals who were contacted but could not be reached for various reasons, including "person not at home." Finally, there is a challenge to minimize *interviewer-related effects* on responses. We briefly review the last three challenges subsequently.

Massey (1988) reports a summary of studies comparing telephone coverage across 22 countries. As might be expected, countries with low telephone ownership in the household sector are likely to have lower coverage. Massey (1988) reports that telephone ownership is related to the sociodemographic status of the household, as well as the relative cost of delivering telephone service to the household. For example, in the United States, blacks, lower-income households, and those unemployed may not own a telephone and may contribute to noncoverage bias. In Canada, the number of households without a telephone is small, but telephone surveys may not have adequate coverage for young men or those with less than a postsecondary level of education. Massey (1988) also suggests that, in addition to sociodemographic variables, spatial distances among relatives and friends and government policies toward telephone installation may contribute to telephone ownership.

In the United States, Thornberry and Massey (1988) compare health-related practices for those with telephones and those without them. Based on a National Health interview survey in 1985, these authors report that the incidence of smoking and not wearing a seat belt was significantly higher among nontelephone households compared with telephone households. Moreover, nontelephone households are less likely to install a smoke detector in their homes and exercise regularly compared with telephone-owning households. The authors also report that telephone coverage may work in the same direction as response rate, whereas, as respondents become older, their telephone coverage increases and the response rate decreases. Thornberry and Massey (1988, p. 48) conclude that "the potential of having substantial bias due to under coverage and/or nonresponse is very real in surveys based only on telephone households."

Quantitative Surveys and Nonresponse

Groves and Couper (1998) present a conceptual framework of factors that contribute to survey participation (see Figure 1). The framework is useful because it brings together various modes of data collection as well as myriads of factors that may influence response rate. The conceptual framework, broadly speaking, argues that controllable (survey design and interviewer characteristics) and uncontrollable (social and respondent environment) factors result in an interaction between respondent and interviewer, which in turn results in an outcome about participation. We briefly review this framework and provide empirical support for four factors: social and respondent factors, survey design, and interviewer characteristics and their influence on survey participation.

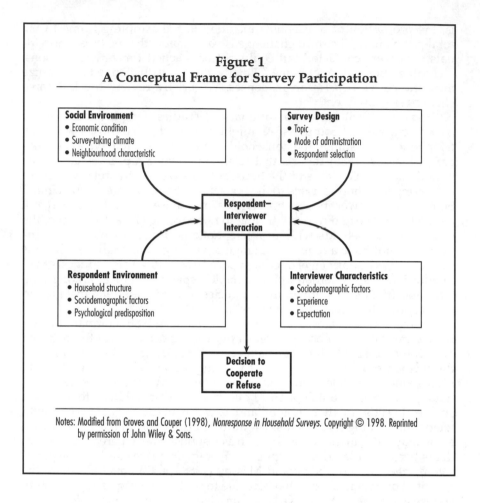

Figure 1
A Conceptual Frame for Survey Participation

Notes: Modified from Groves and Couper (1998), *Nonresponse in Household Surveys*. Copyright © 1998. Reprinted by permission of John Wiley & Sons.

Survey is a social event, and one would expect that social- and group-level factors have bearing on response rates. At the societal level, survey participation is governed by societal norms about societal responsibility and legitimacy of social institutions in both the private and the public sector. No one questions whether such effects exist. However, obtaining empirical evidence is often confounded by survey design and different contact protocols to reduce nonresponse.

Within a given society, there are response rate variations that are systematic across groups of respondents. For example, those living in urban areas tend to have lower response rates than rural respondents. The evidence about the urban–rural variation in response rates is well documented across many countries (see Groves and Couper 1998). Factors influencing this effect may be mediated or moderated by crime rate, social disorganization, and population density. Groves and Couper (1998) test more specific hypotheses that suggest that crowding, fear of crime, and high levels of stimulus input in urban areas lead to avoidance of contact with strangers (interviewers) and result in lower response rates.

There is extensive literature about nonresponse rate as influenced by household characteristics such as number and ages of household members and type of dwelling, as well as respondent's age, sex, marital status, education, and income. If we argue that the decision to participate in a survey by the respondent is based on quick and shallow decision making or heuristics,[2] then we could argue that various demographic variables enhance the decision-making heuristics of reciprocation, authority, consistency, commitment, scarcity, social validation, and liking (Cialdini 1984). Because these heuristics are also applicable in mail surveys, we review the important ones subsequently.

Reciprocation heuristics suggest that a respondent would be more willing to participate in a survey if there was a repayment of a perceived gift, favour, or concession or a perceived sense of obligation. This concept is closely related to the concept of social exchange (see Childers and Skinner 1996; Evangelista, Albaum, and Poon 1999). Another heuristic that respondents may use is authority. That is, if the request to participate comes from an appropriate authority or legitimate sponsoring organization, then greater participation may result. Conversely, those individuals who perceive themselves as not part of the larger society may perceive authority negatively and refuse to participate.

The consistency or self-perception heuristic asserts that, after making a commitment, respondents are more willing to comply with requests to participate. Allen and Colfax (1968) have argued that the consistency heuristic depends on salience, favourability (affective feeling toward participation in a survey), and availability of information in memory and that these lead to a better participation rate. A concept related to consistency is the commitment and involvement heuristic (see Evangelista, Albaum, and Poon 1999).

Groves and Couper (1998) report that the effect of various demographic factors, such as socioeconomic status and age, may be mediated by social environment as well as the heuristic of reciprocation and authority. Evangelista, Albaum, and Poon (1999) report that the consistency–committment heuristic is more applicable than reciprocation. Helgeson (1994) reports on a phenomenological study of responding to mail surveys and finds that attention and exchange or reciprocation are important in influencing survey participation.

A third factor that influences participation in surveys is survey design. Design elements include the mode of administration, the topic, and respondent selection. Although most of these elements are fixed for a study and across all respondents, the choice of various tactical elements

---

[2]This is known as decision making based on peripheral cues. In contrast, decision making that involves attribute comparisons is considered rational decision making.

(nature and form of incentive, advance letter, persuasive tactics) may have a substantial impact on participation. There are, however, many design factors that are determined during the survey design stage, and we review those for which empirical evidence is available. First, if a survey allows more callbacks and callbacks are scheduled at different times of the day, it is likely to result in contact, and the probability that a respondent would participate increases (Weeks, Kulka, and Pierson 1987). Second, many studies have found that if the survey-sponsoring organization is perceived positively by respondents, it is likely to have a positive impact on response rate (see Presser, Blair, and Triplett 1992). Third, sending an advance notification in the form of either a telephone call or a written letter, influences the likelihood of participation in surveys (see Dillman, Gallegos, and Frey 1976). Fourth, providing *some incentive*, especially at the time of contact, has a positive influence on survey participation (see Berlin et al. 1992; Church 1993). Fifth, topic saliency has a positive influence on survey participation (see Couper 1997; Groves and Couper 1998). In these studies, the authors note that people are more likely to participate in health surveys than political ones and that those with an interest in the political arena versus those without it are more likely to participate in surveys.

The fourth factor in Groves and Couper's (1998) framework that influences survey participation is interviewer characteristics. Particularly, sociodemographic factors such as age, race, sex, and socioeconomic status, as well as experience and interviewer expectation, may facilitate interaction between the respondent and the interviewer and thus contribute to a higher response rate. The studies measuring the effect associated with the interviewer are limited. We review three main findings. First, the interviewer's skills at persuading and the degree to which the interviewer is not distracted by other activities have a positive influence on response rate (Singer, Frankel, and Glassman 1983). Second, more experience (generally more than six months) in conducting surveys has a positive influence on the interviewer's ability to convince respondents to participate (Groves and Fultz 1985). Third, if the interviewer creates a positive attitude toward a survey, then he or she is likely to convince the respondent to participate (Singer, Frankel, and Glassman 1983).

Mail Surveys

Self-completed mail surveys involve sending a questionnaire to a sample of respondents. The survey organization requests the respondents to complete the questionnaire and mail it back to the survey organization. Mail surveys must also address challenges with respect to the *sampling frame, coverage*, and *nonresponses*, as we discussed in the context of telephone and face-to-face interviews. One particularly different challenge for mail surveys is the issues surrounding question wording and interpretation by respondents, questionnaire format, response mode effects, and the consequences on responses that result from these. Because the sampling and coverage issues are not different from those discussed previously, we concentrate on nonresponse and questionnaire design, or the cognitive aspect of survey design (see Schwarz 1999; Sirken et al. 1999).

Mail survey studies typically get approximately a 10% to 20% response rate and are relatively inexpensive to conduct. Consequently, researchers have been investigating a variety of survey design features that may influence respondents' willingness to participate in a survey. Note that the survey nonresponse framework suggested by Groves and Couper (1998) can be used to interpret various mail survey experiments. The literature, however, has followed a simple three-stage (prenotification, concurrent, and follow-up) framework to interpret findings.

During the past 15 years, there have been five reported meta-analytic studies that we were able to find (see Armstrong and Lusk 1987; Church 1993; Jobber 1986; Jobber and O'Reilly 1998; Yu and Cooper 1983). We provide a short summary of some of the findings that have appeared consistently across various studies. First, sending prenotification helps increase response rate on average by approximately 5%. If prenotification is done by telephone, response rates can go up by 15% to 20%.

Second, there are many studies published that deal with monetary and nonmonetary incentives and their consequences on response rates. Consistent with the notion of reciprocation (see Childers and Skinner 1996; Groves and Couper 1998), incentives create a sense of obligation, which leads to survey participation. Experimental evidence suggests that monetary incentives are more effective in creating reciprocation than nonmonetary incentives are. Moreover, to create obligation, the incentive amount could be as small as 25¢. Most experimental research finds that a token incentive amount ($1 or $2) is sufficient to create obligatory feelings and thus improves response rate by 15% to 20%. A promise of a monetary incentive or a lottery to be awarded randomly may not be as effective as providing the cash amount along with the questionnaire.

Third, nonmonetary incentives (e.g., a special coin, writing pen) have a small but statistically significant effect on response rate (no more than 2% to 3%). Fourth, inclusion of return stamped envelope, maintaining the anonymity of respondent, and sponsorship by a university or not-for-profit organization all contribute to increase response rate. Fifth, paper colour of the questionnaire and assigning a deadline do not appear to have any effect on response rate. However, a short questionnaire (fewer pages) or one with closed-ended questions tends to get a better response rate. Sixth, a follow-up reminder or mailing a new copy of the questionnaire improves response rate.

Mall Intercept

Mall intercept as a method of data collection requires that the interviewer approach a shopper and ask that individual to participate in a research study. This method is popular among applied researchers because it allows researchers to conduct face-to-face interviews at a lower cost and faster than is possible using door-to-door or in-home interviews (see Gregory 1996). In addition, respondents may have the opportunity to inspect the product, packaging, logos, and other stimuli that may be central to the research project.

Sudman (1980) has suggested that sampling in the mall be done so that shoppers are chosen randomly. This includes sampling from different locations in the mall and using different entrances, times of day, and days of the week. All these procedures may lead to a higher occurrence of those respondents who visit malls frequently and shop for a longer duration. In addition, it is possible that the average mall shopper may be different from the average population. Consequently, a complex weighting as well as quota sampling should be undertaken (see Nowell and Stanley 1991) to minimize sampling frame biases.

There are three articles (Bush, Bush, and Chen 1991; Bush and Parasuraman 1984; Hornik and Ellis 1989) that deal with methodological comparisons of mall intercepts and other modes. We provide a summary of their key findings. Mall intercept data are comparable to telephone interviewing in terms of response rate and quality of data (defined as degree of nonmissing responses and the averages on key dependent variables). Survey administration by the respondent or the interviewer had no effect on data quality or attitude toward the survey itself. A refusal rate of 44%, or response rate of 56%, is common for this method. Moreover, several tactical approaches can be used to recruit respondents. The following approaches have been suggested in the literature to improve recruitment efforts: matching gender of interviewer and respondent, gazing and looking at respondents, and offering incentives or donations to charities.

Diary Survey

A diary survey is a self-completed questionnaire form on which a respondent is asked to write information at a regular interval or soon after an event has occurred. Diary surveys are not different from other forms of structured interviews, and respondents are asked to keep records of events as they occur. Moreover, in general respondents are asked to keep records of factual information, such as the radio station to which they listen or the shopping centre they visit. Note, however, that recording of events on a regular basis is a challenging task for respondents, who often follow heuristics to answer questions. Sudman, Bradburn, and Schwarz (1996) suggest that responding to survey questions requires a respondent to remember proceeds along the following steps:

1. Interpreting the question;
2. Generating an opinion;
3. Judgment stored previous?
   a. If yes, recall prior judgment,
   b. Form response, and
   c. Edit response;

4. If no, access relevant information;
5. Decide on use of that information;
6. "Compute" the judgment;
7. Form response; and
8. Edit response.

Note that Sudman, Bradburn, and Schwarz's (1996) steps enable us to understand the question context, telescoping, averaging, and self-generated validity (creating responses that are consistent with previous responses).

Observational Methods

Direct observation as a systematic method for data collection involves recording events or a time sequence and measurements by an observer. The observer may be a person not involved with the event or recording devices such as time-lapse photography or video recording. There are two broad classes of observational research: overt and covert. In overt observational studies, the researcher openly requests permission to observe a situation and plans to make his or her identity, objectives, and intentions known (Stafford and Stafford 1993). This form of observational data collection is ethical, but participants may react to the researcher's intrusion. This clearly is a situation in which there is a threat to internal validity. In a covert observational technique, the researcher's identity remains concealed. One particular technique is called mystery shopping studies, in which the researcher assumes the disguised role of a customer to gauge service providers' responses. Such covert observational methods might provide greater validity but raise questions about ethics. Note that scanner data collection is also a covert form of direct observation. However, the scanner data collection method often maintains respondent anonymity, and household identity is not revealed to anyone other than personnel within the data collection organization. Direct observational techniques are particularly useful for understanding children (see McGee 1997; Rust 1993), as well as situations involving specialized events (Seaton 1997).

Scanner data are collected by stores or households and typically contain detailed product descriptions of price, package size, flavour, and brand name. Store-level scanner observations are usually aggregated for a week for a particular universal product code (UPC). Additional information about store decisions also can be gathered to account for store promotions such as in-store displays, deals, and size and location of feature advertising in store advertising. Stores typically follow a fixed pattern of promotion, such that promotions start on Sunday or Wednesday and shelf space allocated for a particular UPC is fixed. It is common to find as many as 100 brand/size/flavour combinations for a simple product category such as automatic dishwashing detergent. A particular store may carry a small subset of these UPCs. More complex product categories, such as crackers and cookies or cereals, can have as many as 1200 different UPCs, and a store may stock approximately one-third of these varieties.

Scanner panel data is an overt observational data collection approach. The unit of observation is usually the household. Each household or panel member is provided with an electronic means (e.g., a handheld device to scan groceries at home, store cards with magnetic coding to identify a household) to maintain the household's purchase history. Scanner data detail the purchase histories for a large number of panelists over two to three years. The data collection organization also may collect additional information that could be mapped together with purchase history. For example, IRI and ACNielsen in the United States provide information about the store environment in which the panelist may have shopped, demographic information about the household, and, in some cases, the household's television viewing patterns. Given detailed information about the choices that households make and extensive prior information, researchers can creatively understand the effect of various marketing mix variables on choices.

Although much of the research based on scanner data has remained in the marketing journals (e.g., *Journal of Marketing Research, Marketing Science*, and *Journal of Marketing*), several methodological manuscripts have recently appeared in other disciplines as well. For example, Jones's (1997) article dealing with demand for food products (milk and cereal) used scanner data, and the results appear in an agricultural economics journal. More recently, the *Journal of Econometrics* published a special issue dealing with marketing models, and nearly half the papers were based on scanner data (e.g., Allenby and Rossi 1999; Chiang, Chib, and Narasimhan 1999; Erdem, Keane, and Sun 1999). Although scanner data have provided marketing researchers with better understandings of household choices, various antecedents of choice are rarely investigated. Moreover, most of the applications and modelling of scanner data have been confined to frequently purchased packaged goods, though there is some recent evidence that researchers are using point-of-sale data to understand purchase behaviour in appliance markets (Ioannidis and Silver 1997).

New data collection technologies often result in better understanding about customers. Scanner data collection is no exception. We highlight several insightful findings (Schmittlein 1993). Most marketing researchers argue that the customer decision process moves from problem definition to alternative generation, evaluation of alternatives, and then choice. Scanner data–based research suggests that the sequence of decision making might be shopping trip decision, store choice, and product category choice, followed by brand and quantity choice. This paradigm argues that in many product categories, customers engage in decision making while they are in the store. Also, price and store promotions have major effects on brand sales,[3] and the effect of television advertising is small and often statistically not significant. Price competition between high-quality

---

[3]An average price elasticity of –1.7 is a reasonable guess, if one knows nothing about customers.

brands and lower-quality brands is asymmetric. That is, when high-quality brands lower their price, they steal unit share away from other brands in their own tier and from brands in the tier below, but the reverse, with respect to lower-tier brands, is likely to happen. Finally, most marketers believe that 80% of purchases are made by 20% of customers, called the "80/20 law." Based on scanner data, it looks like 50% of volume is purchased by 20% of the customers for packaged goods product categories, which suggests a "50/20 law."

Computer-Assisted Data Collection Methods

In this subsection, we present developments in computer-based data collection methods. We first present a brief history, followed by online research methods. We conclude with comments about electronic focus groups.

Computer-assisted survey information collection (CASIC) attempts to replace paper-and-pencil questionnaires to gather information from respondents. Computer-assisted telephone interviewing (CATI) was the first technology used to control and speed up centralized telephone interviewing and at the same time reduce postinterview processing time. The CATI system reduces costs, increases timeliness, and improves data quality relative to paper-and-pencil telephone surveys. The first CATI system was introduced in 1966 (e.g., see Couper and Nicholls 1998). Computer-assisted personal interviews (CAPI) are a more recent development. They enable researchers to keep track of quotas and complex questionnaire routing, which often results in improvements in data quality. The evolution of computerized technology to gather information about customers now includes computerized self-administered questionnaires (CSAQ), disk by mail, electronic mail surveys, and many variations in computer-assisted self interviewing (CASI), including audio CASI (ACASI) and video CASI (VCASI). There are three dominant reasons for using the CASIC technology for data collection. First, CASIC methods reduce the time for data collection, especially postinterview data processing. Second, cost reductions may result if data collection occurs repeatedly or for a large number of respondents. Third, CASIC methods allow improvement in data quality in terms of improved gathering of sensitive information, a decrease in respondent memory errors, and the ability to randomize items that may be subject to order bias. To conduct computer-based surveys, the researcher needs to follow the steps that were listed in the section dealing with face-to-face interviewing. In addition to those steps, the researcher needs to write code to display question(s) and response formats and a mechanism to gather responses.

Recent comments in *Marketing News* (James 2000) suggest that, within five years, 50% of marketing research spending will be directed toward computerized online research. To provide analysis of such a realization, we review the nature of electronic-based survey measurement. There are at least three distinct approaches to gather survey information from respondents. For the first approach, one can devise an e-mail–based survey in which each individual would receive a questionnaire. Respondents then would have a choice of responding by either e-mail or paper (fax or postal mail system). This approach is practical, technically feasible, fast, and inexpensive. There are, however, issues pertaining to coverage (currently, less than half the population has access to computers, and fewer are knowledgeable about e-mail usage), creation of the sampling frame, and the nature of the questionnaire that each respondent receives.

The second approach that is practical and feasible is to use hypertext mark-up language (html) or its variation to write code that mimics a survey environment for a respondent. This method requires that the respondent have access to an electronic browser, as well as access to e-mail technology. With an electronic browser, the respondent uses screens to respond to prepared questions. This method is likely to be quick and inexpensive and allows one to include graphics and audio and visual inputs for data collection. To be respondent-friendly, the program needs a programmer with knowledge of html and the limitations of that language.

The third approach uses the World Wide Web to create an interface between the respondent and the researcher. The Web enables the researcher to include audio and visual inputs and gather information (numerical, verbal, audio) electronically. Web-based survey respondents would need to have access to e-mail, as well as a browser capable of data entry. The researcher's task would include writing complex software that would simulate a paper-and-pencil type of survey instrument (King 2000).

Electronic focus groups (E-focus) attempt to simulate traditional focus groups in an electronic environment. These can be faster, involve more geographically diverse respondents, and be more flexible and convenient to the respondent than conventional focus groups can. The current technology, however, limits visual and sensory inputs from the moderator. Moreover, E-focus do not provide a direct means to communicate with other respondents. Although we have no independent assessment about outcomes at E-focus, we would expect that the responses one gathers in E-focus should be similar to those from traditional focus groups. Moreover, whether there are cost differences between these two methods depends on the number of focus groups conducted using the e-format. In conclusion, E-focus groups are likely to evolve as an alternative method of data collection and may attract a different group of respondents currently not served by existing methods.

DATA COLLECTION METHODS COMPARED

When making a decision about a particular data collection method, marketing researchers want to know the nature of the collected information and its consequences on costs. To assist in such a pursuit, we reviewed the literature for comparative studies, especially those that compared one method with another for data collection purposes. This resulted in a large set of published articles. We review the set of comparisons that were possible.

Focus Groups Compared with Other Data Collection Methods

Fern (1982) reports on the relative effectiveness and efficiency in generating ideas using moderated group discussion (focus group), open-ended group discussion, and individual interviews. He concludes that focus group participants generated 60% fewer ideas per person than did people in individual interviews. Moreover, individual interviews generated better-quality ideas than did group discussion. Not surprisingly, moderated group discussions had more and better ideas than unmoderated group discussions. One may be tempted to think that focus groups are not as productive as individual interviews. Note, however, that one focus group takes no more than three hours of the moderator's time, and the moderator may interact with eight to ten individuals. In contrast, eight individual interviews would require almost three times as much time to complete. Thus, considering the costs of individual interviews, a focus group as a method of data collection is the more economical approach.

More recently, Wight (1994) and Kitzinger (1994) report studies related to health, sexual preferences, and AIDS using individual interviews as well as focus groups. In these studies, the same individuals participated in both methods, and the order in which each participated in each form of interview was randomly assigned. Both studies find that female participants produced identical responses and that order of interview (whether focus group first or individual interview first) had no effect on the data collected. However, male participants tended to conform to their views if they participated in the focus group first, whereas there were large discrepancies when the male participants first faced an individual interview and then the focus group. Therefore, focus groups may encourage response behaviour that conforms to group thinking, at least among some population groups.

Bristol and Fern (1996) conducted a study to compare feelings during focus groups, nominal group techniques, and open-ended individual interviews. There were three major findings in this research. First, the focus group participants felt more excited, more informal, and less relaxed than participants in nominal group technique interviews. Second, focus group participants felt less anonymous, less confident, more personal, less relaxed, and less laid-back than individual interview respondents. Third, nominal group technique participants felt less anonymous, less free, and less confident than individual interview respondents.

Three studies (Folch-Lyon, de la Macorra, and Schearer 1981; Saint-Germain, Bassford, and Montano 1993; Ward, Bertrand, and Brown 1991) compare surveys with focus groups and find that results or summary measures from both methods are convergent. We highlight differences between the methods. First, on sensitive topics, respondents were more constrained by the nature of comments that are socially acceptable and appropriate. Second, surveys were able to indicate better responses to yes-or-no types of answers and specific behaviours and experiences, whereas focus groups tended to provide open-ended and nonspecific comments. Third, surveys typically could cover a large set of topics, but designing surveys with deeper meanings is harder and it is more difficult to elicit responses. Thus, we might be tempted to conclude that, in using focus groups rather than other methods, a deeper understanding of a topic is gained, whereas surveys and other methods provide breadth of information. Lunt and Livingstone (1996) suggest that survey methodology relies on reliability and external validity but that less attention is paid to content and the internal validity of responses.

Projective Technique (TAT) Compared with Questionnaire Methods

It was difficult to find research that compared response to TAT as a qualitative method with questionnaire-based data collection. One recent meta-analysis examined the correlation between questionnaire-based measures of *need for achievement* and TAT scores on the same topic. Spangler (1992) examines 105 studies and concludes that TATs and questionnaire-based measures of achievement have low correlations (0.088), though they are statistically significant. Thus, we may conclude that projective techniques may be measuring different aspect of values than questionnaire-based measures. Moreover, TAT–based measures of achievement better predicted behaviour such as job placement and examination grades than questionnaire-based measures. This supports the argument that projective methods provide better understanding of inner motives that are consistent among respondents, whereas questionnaire-based measures may provide surface-level or top-of-mind responses.

Face-to-Face, Telephone, and Mail Survey Methods Compared

Designing a survey is a complex task. Designing a fair survey experiment is even more challenging. De Leeuw and van der Zouwen (1988) report the first meta-analytic comparison of experiments involving face-to-face interviews and those involving telephone interviews. They found 31 published studies from 1952 to 1986 and compared the response rate and data quality reported in these studies. Although response rate, on average, was better by 6% for face-to-face interviews, the studies did not find major differences in terms of data quality (proportion of missing values, social desirability bias, similarity of response distribution). This is a remarkable and useful finding, because the cost of collecting face-to-face interview data can be eight times that of mail surveys (Groves and Kahn 1979). In addition, face-to-face interviewing takes considerably more time to complete because of travel.

We found 15 studies published in the past ten years in which the data collection mode was compared for data quality. In many of these studies, responses pertained to health and the health-related industry, which is similar to the meta-analysis summary provided by de Leeuw and van der Zouwen (1988). According to a comparison of response rates obtained from 6 studies for telephone and face-to-face interviews, the latter mode is better only by 5%. In two other comparisons, mail versus telephone and mail versus face-to-face, no major differences were indicated in response rates, and the differences tended to be bimodal. That is, in some studies the mail mode outperformed telephone, and vice versa. There was one consistent finding across the various studies that was striking. All three modes generally tended to have similar responses. In studies in which the researcher is seeking answers to sensitive questions or questions for which there are socially desirable answers, mode differences are statistically significant. In particular, respondents answering telephones generally were more positive (more satisfied, less critical of service provider) compared with other modes of data collection. Van Wijck, Bosch, and Hunink (1998) report the only study that employed within-group design (same person interviewed twice, first on the telephone and then in a face-to-face interview, and vice versa). The study found no difference in the mode of data collection for time trade-off versus the standard gamble. We review several of these studies in more detail subsequently.

McHorney, Kosinski, and Ware (1994) report on a comparison of responses obtained using telephone and mail as modes of data collection for health-related information. Respondents were selected from a prior sample in which they had participated in a similar study. The data collection mode for an individual was assigned randomly. The authors report higher response rates for mail (79.2%) compared with telephone (68.9%) interviews. There were several findings that reveal the strengths and weaknesses of mode of data collection, as well as confounding in sampling and relevant comparisons. First, those respondents who answered mail surveys were younger (on average by five years), less likely to be minorities or married parents, more educated with higher income, and more likely to be employed compared with mail survey nonrespondents. These differences were less pronounced in the telephone survey sample. Second, mail surveys contained more missing variables than telephone interviews. Third, a comparison of reliability (consistency of responses to similar questions) for the concept of social functioning was less reliable in mail surveys. Similarly, reliability estimates for general health perception were lower for telephone surveys. Fourth, mail respondents reported significantly higher responses to allergies, back pain, and dermatitis compared with telephone interview respondents. Therefore, if only mail survey measures were used in health policy decision making, it would indicate that the population is sicker than would be suggested by alternative modes.

De Leeuw, Mellenbergh, and Hox (1996) compare telephone, face-to-face, and mail survey modes of data collection using the estimated structural equation models about the concept of well-being. They report response rates of 68% for mail, 51% for face-to-face, and 61% for telephone interviews. The authors ensured that each group had at least 250 respondents. The study concluded that, though the three modes of data collection generally indicated similar models, the relative importance of various attributes that contributed to well-being differed. For example, in the mail survey, respondents indicated that "social network" and "income" were the most important attributes, whereas "social network" was only important in face-to-face interviews and "income" was the most important predictor of well-being in the telephone interviewer sample.

Mail Compared with Electronic Mail

It is not surprising that marketing researchers are debating whether the postal mail system can be substituted by e-mail as a mode of data collection, especially for those populations in which respondents have access to e-mail. Most e-mail surveys are tested in professional groups, such as employees of a single organization or members of a professional association. In such cases, sampling frame and coverage is less of a concern. Note that studies that have collected demographic data have found that male respondents with a nonminority background and managerial status tend to be more likely to respond to e-mail surveys compared with postal mail surveys. We located 14 research papers that had some element of e-mail as part of their survey research. On the basis of these studies, we would conclude that mail surveys had higher response rates by approximately 16%. There were only 4 studies that randomly assigned respondents to survey modes (e-mail or postal mail). Schaefer and Dillman (1998) find that postal mail surveys had more missing values and shorter answers to open-ended questions than e-mail surveys did. Others (Couper, Blair, and Triplett 1999; Tse 1998; Tse et al. 1995) have found no statistically significant differences between e-mail and postal mail modes of data collection.

E-mail surveys offer new ways to collect customer information, and there is growing recognition of this within the market research community. E-mail surveys arrive back approximately one week faster to the survey organization than mail surveys. There are, however, various technological and instrumentation difficulties associated with e-mail as a data collection tool. First, it is impossible to know about those who refuse to participate in the survey and those who do not use e-mail for the purpose of communication. Second, it is difficult to ensure that all respondents receive the identical survey instrument when conducting e-mail surveys. This is partly due to the variety of software tools that respondents may use in their work environment. Third, inclusion of graphics and other methods of improving response rate are difficult to implement, given that the graphic standards used by respondents may vary. Fourth, there does not appear to be much cost savings when using e-mail compared with postal mail when all costs are counted. For example, Couper, Blair, and Triplett (1999) report that the cost was almost the same for both methods (approximately $1.70 per respondent).

DATA COLLECTION METHODS: A SYNTHESIS

The preceding literature review provides a comprehensive understanding about data collection methods. Although a great deal is known, there are concerns regarding the match between the managerial decision context and the data collection context. In other words, there is extensive knowledge about data collection methods but little known about the bundle of *benefits* that a method can provide the researcher and, ultimately, the client or marketing manager. In addition, we know about methods that are currently in use, but we need to look ahead and think of alternatives that may be insightful in the future. To accomplish such a task, we first propose a classification scheme that could be used to classify a variety of data collection methods. We then follow with an approach to understanding the benefits and costs of data collection methods.

Classification of Data Collection Methods

There are many different approaches to classify data collection methods (see Table 1). Each marketing research textbook follows its own approach. For example, the method used in this article is based on the distinction that one needs to separate measurement context (what behaviour to be measured?) and data gathering method.[4] This is different from the scheme that Churchill (1999) proposes with two broader types of methods: communication-based versus observational. We believe that there are two broad measurement contexts within which data collection may occur. First, there is marketplace behaviour, whether historical or current. Second, there is respondent behaviour under conditions that simulate the marketplace. In such a situation, respondents are asked about their actions, knowledge, and feelings toward presented stimulus material. For each context, there are several subcategories of measurement context. For example, marketplace behaviour can be viewed from physical traces, public and/or private records, use of quasi experiments, or observational studies. Similarly, simulated marketplace behaviour may be conducted

---

[4]We thank John Liefeld for suggesting this distinction about data collection.

Table 1
Measurement Context and Data Collection Methods

Measurement Context		Data Collection Methods
Marketplace Behaviour	Physical traces	Natural or controlled methods
	Public records	Actuarial, political, judicial, government, mass media, Internet tracking, competitive intelligence
	Organizational records	Sales invoices, industrial and institutional data, scanner data.
	Quasi experiments	AD-Tel experiments, store scanner experiments, field experiments
	Passive observations	Physical signs, expressive movement, video recording
	Contrived observations	Eye tracking, pulse, pupil dialation
Simulated Marketplace Behaviour	Group discussion	Focus groups, nominal group techniques, Delphi groups
	Probing individual	Projective techniques, storytelling, word association, sentence completion
		Face-to-face: Door-to-door surveys, mall intercept
		Telephone interviews: CATI, telephone, paper
		Self-completed surveys: Mail, e-mail, Internet, Web-based surveys
	Experiments	Laboratory experiments, conjoint studies

by probing individuals or groups of individuals at the same time. Moreover, probing can provide verbal or pictorial reports or numerical information. Finally, one may also simulate marketplace behaviour by conducting experiments, as is common in laboratory experiments and conjoint studies.

Our classification scheme has several insights. First, we can evaluate the effect of new data collection methodologies within the context of measurement. That is, Internet-based surveys may replace mail-based surveys if they happen to reach the same set of customers. Second, there are many approaches to gather marketplace information, but these methods can only provide information about the past. Third, by probing individuals, though we may sacrifice something about real events, we can consider causal relationships and obtain insights about customer behaviour. Fourth, it is not surprising that each method within a particular cell follows its unique research tradition, analytical methods, and approaches to derive knowledge about customers. It is also not surprising that researchers have compared their preferred method within a particular cell rather than comparing across the cells.

Data Collection Methods: Benefits and Costs

Many textbooks indicate strengths and weaknesses of some data collection methods but do not provide structure to relate these methods to marketing decision contexts for which they might be applicable. With this as a background, we propose a framework that provides a mechanism to understand the bundle of benefits (value) that marketing managers receive as a result of gathering data for decision-making purposes. It is understood that to receive benefits, marketing managers must incur costs. To accomplish this task of determining benefit and cost, we suggest that there is an implicit assumption about the nature of decisions that marketing managers face and the desired level of reliability and internal and external validity that market researchers can deliver. This assumption then is used to describe measures that can be used to qualitatively assess these validities. Note that by reliability, we are referring to the degree to which measures may be reproduced, or the degree of consistency. We also note that for any measurement, satisfactory levels of reliability must be achieved. By internal validity, we refer to our ability to attribute the effect that is observed to the variables under consideration and not to other factors. Finally, by external validity, we refer to our ability to extrapolate the observed effects to the target population.

There are many purposes for which marketing managers collect data. If we assume that the purpose of data collection is to facilitate managerial decision making, then we must have a set of decisions for which information is sought. One approach to characterize various decisions that marketing managers face is to think of the *desired level* of reliability and internal and external validity. In an ideal situation, marketing managers want a high level of internal and external validity, but such a situation would cost much and take a considerable amount of time to design the study. In contrast, in the concept- and idea-generation stage of product development or advertising research, many marketing managers are seeking a variety of inputs and are less concerned with validities. Between these two extremes, there are many decision situations with varying degrees of desired internal and external validity. Let us first examine a method to assess external validity.

To assess external validity, we need to know whether findings could be projected to the target population (Cook and Campbell 1979). Moreover, this assessment requires that researchers prespecify a target population, products, and time. The sample is then drawn to represent the population. The second aspect of external validity is whether results could be replicated to other products, organizations, respondent groups, and times. Most researchers, in practice, would be satisfied if they could demonstrate that the sample drawn and those who participate reflect the population. Note two components that we include to assess external validity: sampling and participants in the study. Consequently, we propose that two indicators capture this validity:

❑ *Sampling control* is about the researcher's ability to obtain respondents from the desired population. This includes the ability to create sampling frames and sampling units, as well as determine the sampling error and coverage-related errors.

❑ *Response rate* refers to the ratio of individuals who participated in the study to the number of individuals that were part of the sample for the study. Using measures of response rate, we are assuming that a higher response rate creates a better correspondence between the population and the sample.

It must be noted that most research reports do not indicate anything about sampling control, whereas there is a great deal of numerical information available about response rates.

To assess internal validity, we need to ensure that at least the following effects did not occur:

❑ *History effect*, which occurs when the observed effect may be due to an event that is not part of the research;

❑ *Maturity effect*, which occurs when the respondent becomes older, wiser, stronger, and more experienced during the study phase;

❑ *Testing effect*, which occurs when the respondent becomes familiar with a test and produces responses that are inconsistent with his or her own views;

❑ *Instrumentation effect*, which occurs when the observed effect may be due to a change in the measurement instrument;

❑ *Selection effect*, which occurs when the process of selecting respondents for the study leads to the observed effect; and

❑ *Mortality effect*, which occurs when individuals participate in some part of study but not in other parts.

It is clear that external and internal validities are delivered by market researchers, and marketing managers are expected to pay for those values in terms of money and time required to complete delivery of a particular service. We use the following criteria:

❑ *Cost* refers to the total money needed to complete data gathering activities, including design of measuring instruments, collection of a sample observations, and provision of simple summary measures of collected variables.

❑ *Speed* refers to total time needed to complete data-gathering activities.

Marketing researchers want to know the values associated with these described methods, along with their benefits and costs. Table 2 provides a summary of the nature and type of information that will facilitate decision making about alternative methods.

CONCLUDING COMMENTS

In this chapter, several useful and insightful methods that are used in the market research area have been presented. For each method, we have suggested appropriate operational details so that a novice researcher can organize research activity. Another and equally important aspect of this review has focused on experimental studies to understand the limitations of each method.

We have noted that new methods of gathering data often provide new insights about marketplace actors. We have also noted that advances in scanning technology, along with efficient software to process scanner based databases, have led to different ways of thinking about consumers. In frequently purchased packaged goods, consumers make decisions about the shopping trip and then about products when they are in the store. Note, however, that scanner-related data collection has marginally affected the traditional methods of data collection, such as focus groups or telephone surveys.

We could use scanner data collection as an exemplar to understand the consequences of Internet and Web-based data collection on traditional market research activity. First, we would expect that as the Internet is adopted for data collection, we will get new insights about customer decision making and problem solving—namely, problem definition, search for alternatives, evaluation of alternatives, choice, and postchoice behaviours. Second, these new insights will affect how we collect data in traditional data collection methods. For example, we might ask about the role of price or distribution in the problem-definition stage as opposed to currently, when we exclusively focus on the choice stage of customer decision making. Third, new technology always makes it possible to include new groups of customers who were not served before by the market research businesses. Fourth, there might be a small reallocation of budgets away from computer- or mail-based data collection methods.

Table 2
Desired Information about Alternative Data Collection Methods

| Data Collection Method | External Validity | | Internal Validity | | | | | Costs | |
	Sampling Control	Response Rate	History	Maturity	Testing	Instrumen-tation	Mortality	Cost	Speed
Natural or controlled methods									
Actuarial, political, judicial, government, mass media, Internet tracking, competitive intelligence									
Sales invoices, industrial and institutional data, scanner data									
AD-Tel experiments, store scanner experiments, field experiments									
Physical signs, expressive movement, video recording									
Eye tracking, pulse, pupil dialation									
Focus groups, nominal group techniques, Delphi groups									
Projective techniques, storytelling, word association, sentence completion									
Face-to-face: Door-to-door surveys, mall intercept									
Telephone interviews: CATI, telephone, paper									
Self-completed surveys: Mail, e-mail, Internet, Web-based surveys									
Laboratory experiments, conjoint studies									

Acknowledgments

The author thanks Lisa Avery, Chuck Chakrapani, Ken Deal, and John Liefeld for their insightful comments on a previous draft.

BIBLIOGRAPHY

Allen, I.L. and J.D. Colfax (1968), "Respondents' Attitudes Toward Legitimate Surveys in Four Cities," *Journal of Marketing Research*, 5 (4), 431–33.

Allenby, Greg M. and Peter E. Rossi (1999), "Marketing Models of Consumer Heterogeneity," *Journal of Econometrics*, 89 (1/2), 57–78.

Armstrong, Scott J. and E.J. Lusk (1987), "Return Postage in Mail Surveys: A Meta-Analysis," *Public Opinion Quarterly*, 51 (2), 233–48.

Belk, Russell W., Melanie Wallendorf, and John Sherry (1989), "The Sacred and the Profane in Consumer Behaviour: Theodicy on the Odyssey," *Journal of Consumer Research*, 16 (1), 1–39.

Berlin, M., L. Mohadjer, J. Waksberg, A. Kolstad, I. Kirsch, D. Rock, and K. Yamamoto (1992), "An Experiment in Monetary Incentives," in *Proceedings of the Section on Survey Research Methods*. Alexandria, VA: American Statistical Association, 393–98.

Bristol, Terry and Edward F. Fern (1996), "Exploring the Atmosphere Created by Focus Group Interviews: Comparing Consumers' Feelings Across Qualitative Techniques," *Journal of the Market Research Society*, 38 (2), 185–95.

Bush, Alan J., Ronald F. Bush, and Henry C.K. Chen (1991), "Method of Administration Effects in Mall Intercept Interviews," *Journal of the Market Research Society*, 33 (4), 309–19.

———— and A. Parasuraman (1984), "A Self Disclosure Approach to Assessing Response Quality in Mall Intercept and Telephone Interviews," *Psychology and Marketing*, 1 (1), 23–39.

Chiang, Jeongwen, Siddhartha Chib, and Chakravarthi Narasimhan (1999), "Markov Chain Monte Carlo and Models of Consideration Set and Parameter Heterogeneity," *Journal of Econometrics*, 89 (1/2), 223–48.

Childers, Terry L. and Steven J. Skinner (1996), "Toward a Conceptualization of Mail Survey Response Behavior," *Psychology and Marketing*, 13 (2), 185–209.

Church, Alan H. (1993), "Estimating the Effect of Incentives on Mail Survey Response Rates: A Meta-Analysis," *Public Opinion Quarterly*, 57 (1), 62–79.

Churchill, Gilbert A. (1999), *Marketing Research: Methodological Foundations*, 7th ed. Orlando, FL: The Dryden Press, Harcourt Brace College Publishers.

Cialdini, Robert B. (1984), *Influence: The Psychology of Persuasion*. New York: William Morrow.

Claxton, John D., Brent Ritchie, and Judy Zaichkowsky (1980), "The Nominal Group Technique: Its Potential for Consumer Research," *Journal of Consumer Research*, 7 (3), 308–13.

Cook, Thomas D. and Donald T. Campbell (1979), *Quasi-Experimentation: Design and Analysis of Issues for Field Settings*. Boston: Houghton Mifflin Company.

Couper, Mick P. (1997), "Survey Introductions and Data Quality," *Public Opinion Quarterly*, 61 (2), 317–38.

————, Johny Blair, and Timothy Triplett (1999), "A Comparison of Mail and E-Mail for a Survey of Employees in U.S. Statistical Agency," *Journal of Official Statistics*, 15 (1), 39–56.

———— and William L. Nicholls II (1998), "The History and Development of Computer-Assisted Survey Information Collection Methods," in *Computer-*

Assisted Survey Information Collection, M.P. Couper, Reginald P. Baker, Jelke Bethlehem, Cynthia Z.F. Clark, Jean Martin, William L. Nicholls II, and James M. O'Reilly, eds. New York: John Wiley & Sons, 1–17.

de Leeuw, Edith D., Gideaon J. Mellenbergh, and Joop J. Hox (1996), "The Influence of Data Collection on Structural Models: A Comparison of a Mail, a Telephone and a Face-to-Face Survey," *Sociological Methods and Research*, 24 (4), 443–72.

———— and Johannes van der Zouwen (1988), "Data Quality in Telephone and Face-to-Face Surveys: A Comparative Meta-Analysis," in *Telephone Survey Methodology*, R.M. Groves, Paul P. Biemer, Lars E. Lyberg, James T. Massey, William L. Nicholls II, and Joseph Waksberg, eds. New York: John Wiley & Sons, 283–300.

Dennis, Alan R. and Joseph S. Valacich (1994), "Group, Sub-Group, and Nominal Group Idea Generation: New Rules for a New Media," *Journal of Management*, 20 (4), 723–36.

Dillman, Don A., J.G. Gallegos, and J.H. Frey (1976), "Reducing Refusal Rates for Telephone Interviews," *Public Opinion Quarterly*, 40 (1), 66–78.

Erdem, Tulin, Michael P. Keane, and Baohong Sun (1999), "Missing Price and Coupon Availability Data in Scanner Panels: Correcting for the Self-Selection Bias in Choice Model Parameters," *Journal of Econometrics*, 89 (1/2), 177–96.

Evangelista, Felicitas, Gerald Albaum, and Patrick Poon (1999), "An Empirical Test of Alternative Theories of Survey Response Behaviour," *Journal of the Market Research Society*, 41 (2), 227–44.

Fern, Edward F. (1982), "The Use of Focus for Idea Generation: The Effects of Group Size, Acqaintanceship, and Moderator on Response Quantity and Quality," *Journal of Marketing Research*, 19 (1), 1–13.

Folch-Lyon, E., L. de la Macorra, and S.B. Schearer (1981), "Focus Group and Survey Research on Family Planning in Mexico," *Studies in Family Planning*, 12 (12), 409–32.

Fram, Eugene H. and Elaine Cibotti (1991), "The Shopping List Studies and Projective Techniques: A 40-Year View," *Marketing Research*, 3 (4), 14–22.

Gregory, Ellen (1996), "Cost/Quality Issues Plague Mall Intercepts," *Marketing Research*, 8 (2), 46–47.

Groves, Robert M., Paul P. Biemer, Lars E. Lyberg, James T. Massey, William L. Nicholls II, and Joseph Waksberg (1988), *Telephone Survey Methodology*. New York: John Wiley & Sons.

———— and Mick P. Couper (1998), *Nonresponse in Household Surveys*. New York: John Wiley & Sons.

———— and N.H. Fultz (1985), "Gender Effects Among Telephone Interviewers in Survey of Economic Attitudes," *Sociological Methods and Research*, 14 (1), 31–52.

———— and Robert L. Kahn (1979), *Surveys by Telephone: A National Comparison with Personal Interviews*. New York: Academic Press.

Haire, Mason (1950), "Projective Techniques in Marketing Research," *Journal of Marketing*, 14 (April), 649–56.

Hall, Amy L. and Ray C. Rist (1999), "Integrating Multiple Qualitative Research Methods (or Avoiding the Precariousness of a One-Legged Stool)," *Psychology and Marketing*, 16 (4), 291–304.

Helgeson, James G. (1994), "Receiving and Responding to a Mail Survey: A Phenomenological Examination," *Journal of the Market Research Society*, 38 (4), 339–47.

Hirschman, Elizabeth C., Linda Scott, and William B. Wells (1998), "A Model of Product Discourse: Linking Consumer Practice to Cultural Texts," *Journal of Advertising*, 27 (1), 33–50.

Hollander, Sharon L. (1988), "Projective Techniques Uncover Real Consumer Attitudes," *Marketing News*, 22 (1), 34.

Hornik, Jacob and Shmuel Ellis (1989), "Strategies to Secure Compliance for a Mall Intercept Interview," *Public Opinion Quarterly*, 52 (4), 539–51.

Ioannidis, Christos and Mick Silver (1997), "Estimating the Worth of Product Characteristics," *Journal of the Market Research Society*, 39 (4), 559–70.

James, Dana (2000), "The Future of Online Research," *Marketing News*, (January 3), 1, 11.

Jobber, David (1986), "Improving Response Rates in Industrial Mail Surveys," *Industrial Marketing Management*, 15 (3), 95–107.

——— and Daragh O'Reilly (1998), "Industrial Mail Surveys: A Methodological Update," *Industrial Marketing Management*, 27 (2), 95–107.

Jones, Eugene (1997), "An Analysis of Consumer Food Shopping Behavior Using Supermarket Scanner Data: Differences by Income and Location," *American Journal of Agricultural Economics*, 79 (5), 1437–43.

King, Nelson (2000), "What Are They Thinking? A Review of Survey Software," *PC Magazine*, (February 8), 162–78.

Kitzinger, Jenny (1994), "The Methodology of Focus Groups: The Importance of Interaction Between Research Participants," *Sociology of Health and Illness*, 16 (1), 103–21.

Langford, Barry E. (1994), "Nominal Grouping Sessions," *Marketing Research*, 6 (3), 15–21.

Levy, Sidney J. (1959), "Symbols for Sale," *Harvard Business Review*, 37 (July/August), 117–24.

——— (1986), "Dreams, Animals, Fairy Tales and Cars," *Psychology and Marketing*, 2 (2), 163–71.

Lieber, Ronald B (1997), "Storytelling: A New Way to Get Close to Your Customer," *Fortune*, 135 (2), 102–108.

Lunt, Peter and Sonia Livingstone (1996), "Rethinking the Focus Group in Media and Communication Research," *Journal of Communication*, 46 (2), 79–98.

Massey, James T. (1988), "An Overview of Telephone Coverage," in *Telephone Survey Methodology*, R.M. Groves, Paul P. Diemer, Lars E. Lyberg, James T. Massey, William L. Nicholls II, and Joseph Waksberg, eds. New York: John Wiley & Sons, 3–24.

McCracken, Grant (1986), "Culture and Consumption: A Theoretical Account of the Structure and Movement of the Cultural Meaning of Consumer Goods," *Journal of Consumer Research*, 13 (June), 71–84.

McGee, Tom (1997), "Getting Inside Kids' Heads," *American Demographics*, 19 (1), 52–59.

McHorney, Colleen A., Mark Kosinski, and John E. Ware Jr. (1994), "Comparison of Costs and Quality of Norms for the SF-36 Health Survey Collected by Mail Versus Telephone Interview: Results from a National Survey," *Medical Care*, 32 (6), 551–67.

McQuarrie, Edward F. and David Glen Mick (1999), "Visual Rhetoric in Advertising: Text-Interpretive, Experimental, and Reader-Response Analysis," *Journal of Consumer Research*, 26 (June), 37–54.

Mick, David Glen (1986), "Consumer Research and Semiotics: Exploring Morphology of Signs, Symbols and Significance," *Journal of Consumer Research*, 13 (September), 196–213.

Morgan, David L. (1996), "Focus Groups," *Annual Review of Sociology*, 22, 129–52.

Nowell, Clifford and Linda R. Stanley (1991), "Length-Biased Sampling in Mall Intercept Surveys," *Journal of Marketing Research*, 28 (4), 475–79.

Parker, Betty J. (1998), "Exploring Life Themes and Myths in Alcohol Advertisements Through a Meaning Based Model of Advertising Experiences," *Journal of Advertising*, 27 (1), 98–112.

Presser, Stanley, Johny Blair, and T. Triplett (1992), "Survey Sponsorship, Response Rates and Response Effects," *Social Science Quarterly*, 73 (3), 699–702.

Reilly, Michael D. (1990), "Free Elicitation of Descriptive Adjectives for Tourism Image Assessment," *Journal of Travel Research*, 28 (4), 21–26.

Rust, Langbourne (1993), "Observations: How to Reach Children in Stores," *Journal of Advertising Research*, 33 (6), 67–72.

Saint-Germain, Michelle A., Tasmen L. Bassford, and Gail Montano (1993), "Surveys and Focus Groups in Health Research with Older Hispanic Women," *Qualitative Health Research*, 3 (3), 341–67.

Schaefer, David R. and Don A. Dillman (1998), "Development of a Standard E-Mail Methodology: Result of an Experiment," *Public Opinion Quarterly*, 62, 378–97.

Schmittlein, David (1993), "A Decade of Scanner Data Research, 1983–1993: What Have We Learned?" paper presented at "New Direction and Current Issues in the Analysis and Use of Scanner Data," Toronto, Ontario.

Schwarz, Norbert (1999), "Self-Reports," *American Psychologist*, 54 (2), 93–105.

Seaton, A.V. (1997), "Unobtrusive Observational Measures as a Qualitative Extension of Visitor Surveys at Festivals and Events: Mass Observation Revisited," *Journal of Travel Research*, 35 (4), 25–30.

Shore, Gene and Peter Cooper (1999), "Projecting the Future," *Journal of the Market Research Society*, 41 (1), 33–45.

Singer, Elenor, M.R. Frankel, and M.B. Glassman (1983), "The Effect of Interviewer Characteristics and Expectation on Response," *Public Opinion Quarterly*, 47 (1), 68–83.

Sirken, Monroe G., Douglas J. Herrmann, Susan Schechter, Norbert Schwarz, Judith M. Tanur, and Roger Tourangeau (1999), *Cognition and Survey Research*. New York: John Wiley & Sons.

Spangler, William D. (1992), "Validity of Questionnaire and TAT Measures of Need for Achievement: Two Meta-Analyses," *Psychological Bulletin*, 112 (1), 140–54.

Stafford, Marla Royne and Thomas F. Stafford (1993), "Participant Observation and the Pursuit of Truth: Methodological and Ethical Considerations," *Journal of the Market Research Society*, 35 (1), 63–76.

Sudman, Seymour (1980), "Improving the Quality of Shopping Center Sampling," *Journal of Marketing Research*, 17 (4), 423–31.

———, Norman M. Bradburn, and Norbert Schwarz (1996), *Thinking about Answers: The Application of Cognitive Process to Survey Methodology*. San Francisco: Jossey-Bass Publishers.

Thornberry, Owen T. and James T. Massey (1988), "Trends in United States Telephone Coverage Across Time and Subgroups," in *Telephone Survey Methodology*, R.M. Groves, Paul P. Biemer, Lars E. Lyberg, James T. Massey, William L. Nicholls II, and Joseph Waksberg, eds. New York: John Wiley & Sons, 25–49.

Tse, Alan C.B. (1998), "Comparing the Response Rate, Response Speed and Response Quality of Two Methods of Sending Questionnaires: E-mail vs. Mail," *Journal of the Market Research Society*, 40 (4), 353–61.

————, Ka Chun Tse, Chow Hoi Yin, Choy Boon Ting, Ko Wai Yi, Kwan Pui Yee, and Wing Chi Hong (1995), "Comparing Two Methods of Sending out Questionnaires: E-mail Versus Mail," *Journal of the Market Research Society*, 37 (4), 441–46.

van Wijck, Esther E.E., Johanna L. Bosch, and Maria G.M. Hunink (1998), "Time-Tradeoff Values and Standard-Gamble Utilities Assessed During Telephone Interviews Versus Face-to-Face Interviews," *Medical Decision Making*, 18 (4), 400–405.

Wallendorf, Melanie and Eric J. Arnould (1991), "'We Gather Together': Consumption Rituals of Thanksgiving Day," *Journal of Consumer Research*, 18 (1), 13–31.

Ward, Victoria M., Jane T. Bertrand, and Lisanne F. Brown (1991), "The Comparability of Focus Group and Survey Results: Three Case Studies," *Evaluation Review*, 15 (2), 266–83.

Weeks, M.F., R.A. Kulka, and S.A. Pierson (1987), "Optimal Call Scheduling for Telephone Surveys," *Public Opinion Quarterly*, 51 (4), 540–49.

Wight, Daniel (1994), "Boys' Thoughts and Talk About Sex in a Working Class Locality of Glasgow," *The Sociological Review*, 42 (4), 702–37.

Woodside, Arch G. and Elizabeth J. Wilson (1995), "Applying the Long Interview in Direct Marketing Research," *Journal of Direct Marketing*, 9 (1), 37–56.

Yu, J. and H. Cooper (1983), "A Quantitative Review of Research Design Effects on Response Rates to Questionnaires," *Journal of Marketing Research*, 20 (1), 36–44.

SUGGESTED READINGS

Aquilino, William S. (1998), "Effects of Interview Mode on Measuring Depression in Younger Adults," *Journal of Official Statistics*, 14 (1), 15–29.

Armacost, Robert L., Jamshid C. Hosseini, Sara A. Morris, and Kathleen A. Rehbein (1991), "An Empirical Comparison of Direct Questioning, Scenario, and Randomized Response Methods for Obtaining Sensitive Business Information," *Decision Sciences*, 22 (5), 1073–90.

Armstrong, Scott J. and Thomas J. Yokum (1994), "Effectiveness of Monetary Incentives: Mail Surveys to Members of Multinational Professional Groups," *Industrial Marketing Management*, 23 (2), 133–36.

Arnett, Robert (1990), "Mail Panel Research in the 1990s," *Applied Marketing Research*, 30 (2), 8–10.

Beebe, Timothy J., Patricia A. Harrison, James A. McRae Jr., Ronald E. Anderson, and Jayne A. Fulkerson (1998), "An Evaluation of Computer-Assisted Self-Interviews in a School Setting," *Public Opinion Quarterly*, 62 (4), 623–32.

Biner, Paul M. and Heath J. Kidd (1994), "The Interactive Effects of Monetary Incentive Justification and Questionnaire Length on Mail Survey Response Rates," *Psychology and Marketing*, 11 (5), 483–92.

Bonnel, Patrick and Michel Le Nir (1998), "The Quality of Survey Data: Telephone Versus Face-to-Face Interviews," *Transportation*, 25 (2), 147–67.

Bowles, Tim (1989), "Data Collection in the United Kingdom," *Journal of the Market Research Society*, 31 (4), 467–76.

Brennan, Mike (1992), "The Effects of a Monetary Incentives on Mail Survey Response Rates: New Data," *Journal of the Market Research Society*, 34 (2), 173–77.

————, Don Esslemont, and Dean Hini (1995), "Obtaining Purchase Predictions via Telephone Interviews," *Journal of the Market Research Society,* 37 (3), 241–50.

———— and Janet Hoek (1992), "The Behavior of Respondents, Nonrespondents, and Refusers Across Mail Surveys," *Public Opinion Quarterly,* 56 (4), 530–35.

Brown, Stephen (1995), "Postmodern Marketing Research: No Representation without Taxation," *Journal of the Market Research Society,* 37 (3), 287–310.

Burton, Scot and Edward Blair (1991), "Task Conditions, Response Formulation Processes, and Response Accuracy for Behavioral Frequency Questions in Surveys," *Public Opinion Quarterly,* 55 (1), 50–79.

Buttle, Francis and Gavin Thomas (1997), "Questionnaire Colour and Mail Survey," *Journal of the Market Research Society,* 39 (4), 625–26.

Campen, Cretien Van, Herman Sixma, Jan J. Kerssens, and Loe Peters (1998), "Comparison of Costs and Quality of Patient Data Collection by Mail Versus Telephone Versus In-Person Interviews," *European Journal of Public Health,* 8 (1), 66–70.

Chawla, Sudhir K., P.V. (Sunder) Balakrishnan, and Mary F. Smith (1992), "Mail Response Rates from Distributors," *Industrial Marketing Management,* 21 (4), 307–10.

———— and Rajan Nataraajan (1994), "Does the Name of the Sender Affect Industrial Mail Response?" *Industrial Marketing Management,* 23 (2), 115–15.

Chen, Henry C.K. (1996), "Direction, Magnitude and Implications of Non-Response Bias in Mail Surveys," *Journal of the Market Research Society,* 38 (3), 267–76.

Chowdhury, Jhinuk, James Reardon, and Rajesh Srivastava (1998), "Alternative Modes of Measuring Store Image: An Empirical Assessment of Structured Versus Unstructured Measures," *Journal of Marketing: Theory and Practice,* 6 (2), 72–86.

Cohen, Ronald Jay (1999), "What Qualitative Research Can Be," *Psychology and Marketing,* 16 (4), 351–68.

Cook, Richard L. and Thomas R. Stewart (1975), "A Comparison of Seven Methods for Obtaining Subjective Descriptions of Judgment Policy," *Organization Behavior and Human Performance,* 13 (1), 31–45.

Couper, Mick P. and Benjamin Rowe (1996), "Evaluation of a Computer-Assisted Self-Interview Component in a Computer-Assisted Personal Survey," *Public Opinion Quarterly,* 60 (1), 89–105.

de Leeuw, Edith D., Joop J. Hox, and Ger Snijkers (1995), "The Effect of Computer-Assisted Interviewing on Data Quality: A Review," *Journal of the Market Research Society,* 37 (4), 325–44.

Diamantopoulos, Adamantios, Bodo B. Schlegelmilch, and Lori Webb (1991), "Factors Affecting Industrial Mail Response Rates," *Industrial Marketing Management,* 20 (4), 327–39.

Dickinson, John R. and A.J. Faria (1995), "Refinements of Charitable Contribution Incentives for Mail Surveys," *Journal of the Market Research Society,* 37 (4), 447–53.

———— and Douglas L. MacLachlan (1996), "Fax Surveys: Return Patterns and Comparison with Mail Surveys," *Journal of Marketing Research,* 33 (1), 108–13.

Dillman, Don (1978), *Mail and Telephone Surveys: The Total Design Method.* New York: John Wiley & Sons.

————, Michael D. Sinclair, and Jon R. Clark (1993), "Effects of Questionnaire Length, Respondent-Friendly Design, and a Difficult Question on Response Rates for Occupant-Addressed Census Mail Surveys," *Public Opinion Quarterly,* 57 (3), 289–304.

———, Eleanor Singer, Jon R. Clark, and James B. Treat (1996), "Effects of Benefits Appeals, Mandatory Appeals, and Variations in Statements of Confidentiality on Completion Rates for Census Questionnaires," *Public Opinion Quarterly,* 60 (3), 376–89.

———, Kirsten K. West, and Jon R. Clark (1994), "Influence of an Invitation to Answer by Telephone on Response to Census Questionnaires," *Public Opinion Quarterly,* 58 (4), 557–68.

Erdman, Harold P., Marjorie H. Klein, and John H. Greist (1985), "Direct Patient Computer Interviewing," *Journal of Consulting and Clinical Psychology,* 53 (6), 760–73.

Faria, A.J. and John R. Dickinson (1992), "Mail Survey Response, Speed and Cost," *Industrial Marketing Management,* 21 (1), 51–60.

Feldman, Jack M. and John G. Lynch Jr. (1988), "Self-Generated Validity and Other Effects of Measurement on Belief, Attitude and Intention," *Journal of Applied Psychology,* 73 (4), 421–35.

Fiset, Louis, Peter Milgrom, and John Tarnai (1994), "Dentists' Response to Financial Incentives in a Mail Survey of Malpractice Liability Experience," *Journal of Public Health Dentistry,* 54 (2), 68–72.

Fowler, Floyd Jackson, Jr., Anthony M. Roman, and Zhu Xiao Di (1998), "Mode Effects in a Survey of Medicare Prostate Surgery Patients," *Public Opinion Quarterly,* 62 (1), 29–46.

Fox, Christine M., K. Lynne Robinson, and Debra Boardley (1998), "Cost-Effectiveness of Follow-Up Strategies in Improving the Response Rate of Mail Surveys," *Industrial Marketing Management,* 27 (2), 127–33.

Gajraj, Ananda M., A.J. Faria, and John R. Dickinson (1990), "A Comparison of the Effect of Promised and Provided Lotteries, Monetary and Gift Incentives on Mail Survey Response Rate, Speed and Cost," *Journal of the Market Research Society,* 32 (1), 141–62.

Gendall, Philip, Janet Hoek, and Mike Brennan (1998), "The Tea Bag Experiment: More Evidence on Incentives in Mail Survey," *Journal of the Market Research Society,* 40 (4), 347–51.

———, ———, and Don Esslemont (1995), "The Effect of Appeal, Complexity and Tone in a Mail Survey Covering Letter," *Journal of the Market Research Society,* 37 (3), 251–68.

Gfroerer, Joseph, Doug Wright, and Andrea Kopstein (1997), "Prevalence of Youth Substance Use: The Impact of Methodological Differences Between Two National Surveys," *Drug and Alcohol Dependence,* 47 (1), 19–30.

Gilpatrick, Thomas R., Robert R. Harmon, and L.P. Douglas Tseng (1994), "The Effect of a Nominal Monetary Gift and Different Contacting Approaches on Mail Survey Response Among Engineers," *IEEE Transactions of Engineering Management,* 41 (3), 285–902.

Green, Kathy E. (1996), "Sociodemographic Factors and Mail Survey Response," *Psychology and Marketing,* 13 (2), 171–84.

Greenwald, Anthony G., Catherine G. Carnot, and Rebecca Beach (1987), "Increasing Voting Behavior by Asking People if They Expect to Vote," *Journal of Applied Psychology,* 72 (3), 315–18.

Greer, Thomas V. and Ritu Lohtia (1994), "Effects of Source and Paper Color on Response Rates in Mail Survey," *Industrial Marketing Management,* 23 (1), 47–54.

Haggett, Sarah and Vincent-Wayne Mitchell (1994), "Effect of Industrial Prenotification on Response Rate, Speed, Quality, Bias and Cost," *Industrial Marketing Management,* 23 (2), 101–10.

Hahlo, Gerry (1999), "Examining the Validity of Re-Interviewing Respondents for Quantitative Surveys," *Psychology and Marketing,* 16 (4), 291–304.

Hall, Melvin F. (1995), "Patient Satisfaction or Acquiescence? Comparing Mail and Telephone Survey Results," *Journal of Health Care Marketing,* 15 (1), 54–61.

Hoch, Stephen J. (1987), "Perceived Consensus and Predictive Accuracy: The Pros and Cons of Projection," *Journal of Personality and Social Psychology,* 53 (8), 221–34.

Hoffman, Douglas K., Vince Howe, and Donald W. Hardigree (1991), "Ethical Dilemmas Faced in the Selling of Complex Services: Significant Others and Competitive Pressures," *Journal of Personal Selling and Sales Management,* 11 (4), 13–25.

James, Jeannine M. and Richard Bolstein (1990), "The Effect of Monetary Incentives and Follow-Up Mailings on Response Rate and Response Quality in Mail Surveys," *Public Opinion Quarterly,* 54 (3), 346–61.

—— and —— (1992), "Large Monetary Incentives and Their Effect on Mail Survey Response Rates," *Public Opinion Quarterly,* 56 (4), 442–53.

Jobber, David, Hafiz Mirza, and Kee H. Wee (1991), "Incentives and Response Rates to Cross-National Business Surveys: A Logit Model Analysis," *Journal of International Business Studies,* 22 (4), 711–21.

—— and John Saunders (1988), "An Experimental Investigation into Cross-National Mail Survey Response Rates," *Journal of International Business Studies,* 19 (3), 483–89.

John, Esther M. and David A. Savitz (1994), "Effect of a Monetary Incentive on Response to a Mail Survey," *Annals of Epidemiology,* 4 (3), 231–35.

Johnston, Jerome and Christopher Walton (1995), "Reducing Response Effects for Sensitive Questions: A Computer-Assisted Self Interview with Audio," *Social Science Computer Review,* 13 (3), 304–19.

Jones, Peter and John Polak (1993), "Computer-Based Personal Interviewing: State-of-the-Art and Future Prospects," *Journal of the Market Research Society,* 35 (3), 221–33.

Kalafatis, S.P. and F.J. Madden (1995), "The Effect of Discount Coupons and Gifts on Mail Survey Response Rates Among High Involvement Respondents," *Journal of the Market Research Society,* 37 (2), 171–84.

—— and M.H. Tsogas (1994), "Impact of the Inclusion of an Article as an Incentive in Industrial Mail Surveys," *Industrial Marketing Management,* 23 (2), 137–43.

Kaldenberg, Dennis O., Harold F. Koenig, and Boris W. Becker (1994), "Mail Survey Response Rate Patterns in a Population of the Elderly," *Public Opinion Quarterly,* 58 (1), 58–68.

Karimabady, H. and P.J. Brunn (1991), "Postal Surveys to Small Manufacturers," *Industrial Marketing Management,* 20 (4), 319–26.

Klose, Allen (1991), "A Commercial and Industrial Mail Survey in the Caribbean: A Multi-Country Comparison," *Journal of the Market Research Society,* 33 (4), 343–46.

—— and A. Dwayne Ball (1995), "Using Optical Mark Read Surveys: An Analysis of Response Rate and Quality," *Journal of the Market Research Society,* 37 (3), 269–86.

Koff, Bernard (1992), "How to Assess Primary Data Collection Techniques," *Medical Marketing and Media,* 27 (1), 56–59.

Krysan, Maria, Howard Schuman, Lesli Jo Scott, and Paul Beatty (1994), "Response Rates and Response Content in Mail Versus Face-to-Face Surveys," *Public Opinion Quarterly,* 58 (3), 381–99.

LaGarce, Raymond and Linda D. Kuhn (1995), "The Effect of Visual Stimuli on Mail Survey Response Rates," *Industrial Marketing Management*, 24 (1), 11–18.

Lankford, Samuel V., Barton P. Buxton, Ronald Hetzler, and James R. Little (1995), "Response Bias and Wave Analysis of Mailed Questionnaires in Tourism Impact Assessments," *Journal of Travel Research*, 33 (4), 8–13.

Lester, Richard K., Michael J. Piore, and Kamal M. Malek (1998), "Interpretive Management: What General Management Can Learn from Design," *Harvard Business Review*, 76 (2), 86–96.

Lynn, Peter (1998), "Data Collection Mode Effects on Responses to Attitudinal Questions," *Journal of Official Statistics*, 14 (1), 1–14.

———, Rachel Turner, and Patten Smith (1998), "Assessing the Effect of an Advance Letter for a Personal Interview Survey," *Journal of the Market Research Society*, 40 (3), 265–72.

MacGregor, Donald, Sarah Lichtenstein, and Paul Slovic (1988), "Structuring Knowledge Retrieval: An Analysis of Decomposed Quantitative Judgment," *Organizational Behavior and Human Decision Processes*, 42 (3), 303–23.

Martin, Charles (1994), "The Impact of Topic Interest on Mail Survey Response Behaviour," *Journal of the Market Research Society*, 36 (4), 327–38.

McKee, Daryle O. (1992), "The Effect of Using a Questionnaire Identification Code and Message About Non-Response Follow-Up Plans on Mail Survey Response Characteristics," *Journal of the Market Research Society*, 34 (2), 179–91.

McKenna, Christopher K. (1992), "Nominal and Focus Group Work Well Together," *Marketing News*, 26 (1), FG2, FG15.

McNaughton, Rod B. (1999), "Disk by Mail for Industrial Survey Research," *Industrial Marketing Management*, 28 (3), 293–304.

Mehta, Raj and Eugene Sivadas (1995), "Comparing Response Rates and Response Content in Mail Versus Electronic Mail Surveys," *Journal of the Market Research Society*, 37 (4), 429–39.

Menon, Geeta, Barbara Bickart, Seymour Sudman, and Johnny Blair (1995), "How Well Do You Know Your Partner? Strategies for Formulating Proxy-Reports and Their Effect on Convergence to Self-Reports," *Journal of Marketing Research*, 32 (1), 75–84.

Murphy, Paul R. (1991), "Exploring the Effects of Postcard Prenotification on Industrial Firms' Response to Mail Surveys," *Journal of the Market Research Society*, 33 (4), 335–41.

Nebenzahl, Israel D. and Eugene D. Jaffe (1995), "Facsimile Transmission Versus Mail Delivery of Self-Administered Questionnaires in Industrial Surveys," *Industrial Marketing Management*, 24, 167–75.

Noble, Iain, Nick Moon, and Dominic McVey (1998), "'Bringing It All Back Home...' – Using RDD Telephone Methods for Large Scale Social Policy and Opinion Research in the UK," *Journal of the Market Research Society*, 40 (2), 93–120.

Oppermann, Martin (1995), "E-Mail Surveys – Potentials and Pitfalls," *Marketing Research*, 7 (3), 29–33.

Paxson, M. Chris (1992), "Follow-Up Mail Surveys," *Industrial Marketing Management*, 21, 195–201.

Pol, Louis G. (1992), "A Method to Increase Response when External Interference and Time Constraints Reduce Interview Quality," *Public Opinion Quarterly*, 56 (3), 356–59.

────── and Thomas G. Ponzurick (1989), "Gender of Interviewer/Gender of Respondent Bias in Telephone Surveys," *Applied Marketing Research*, 29 (2), 9–13.

Richardson, Lynne D., John E. Swan, and Cecilia McInnis-Bowers (1994), "Sampling and Data Collection Methods in Sales Force Research: Issues and Recommendations for Improvement," *Journal of Personal Selling and Sales Management*, 16 (4), 31–39.

Schlegelmilch, Bodo B. and Adamantios Diamantopoulos (1991), "Prenotification and Mail Survey Response Rates: A Quantitative Integration of the Literature," *Journal of the Market Research Society*, 33 (3), 243–55.

Schuldt, Barbara A. and Jeff W. Totten (1994), "Electronic Mail vs. Mail Survey Response Rates," *Marketing Research*, 6 (1), 36–39.

Schwarz, Norbert, Barbel Knauper, Hans J. Hippler, Elisabeth Noelle-Neumann, and Leslie Clark (1991), "Rating Scales: Numeric Values May Change the Meaning of Scale Labels," *Public Opinion Quarterly*, 55 (4), 618–30.

Steele, Thomas J., W. Lee Schwendig, and John A. Kilpatrick (1992), "Duplicate Responses to Multiple Survey Mailings: A Problem?" *Journal of Advertising Research*, 32 (2), 26–33.

──────, ──────, and Nina M. Ray (1989), "Do Multi-Wave Mailings Lead to Multi-Response in Mail Surveys?" *Applied Marketing Research*, 29 (2), 15–20.

──────, ──────, and Michael D. Reily (1989), "Modes of Address and Response Rates in Mail Surveys," *Applied Marketing Research*, 29 (1), 19–21.

Sturgis, Patrick and Pamela Campanelli (1998), "The Scope for Reducing Refusals in Household Surveys: An Investigation Based on Transcripts of Tape-Recorded Doorstep Interactions," *Journal of the Market Research Society*, 40 (2), 121–39.

Synodinos, Nicolaos E. and Jerry M. Brennan (1988), "Computer Interactive Interviewing in Survey Research," *Psychology and Marketing*, 5 (2), 117–37.

Taylor, Anne W., David H. Wilson, and Melanie Wakefield (1998), "Differences in Health Estimates Using Telephone and Door-to-Door Survey Method—Hypothetical Exercise," *Australian and New Zealand Journal of Public Health*, 22 (2), 223–26.

Taylor, Stephen and Peter Lynn (1998), "The Effect of a Preliminary Notification Letter on Response to a Postal Survey of Young People," *Journal of the Market Research Society*, 40 (2), 165–73.

Unzicker, Deborah K. (1999), "The Psychology of Being Put on Hold: An Exploratory Study of Service Quality," *Psychology and Marketing*, 16 (4), 327–50.

Warriner, Keith, John Goyder, Heidi Gjertsen, Paula Hohner, and Kathleen Mcspurren (1996), "Charities, No; Lotteries, No; Cash, Yes: Main Effects and Interactions in Canadian Incentives Experiment," *Public Opinion Quarterly*, 60 (4), 542–62.

Wilson, K., B. Roe, and L. Wright (1998), "Telephone or Face-to-Face Interviews? A Decision Made on the Basis of a Pilot Study," *International Journal of Nursing Studies*, 35 (6), 314–21.

Wright, Debra L., William S. Aquilino, and Andrew J. Supple (1998), "A Comparison of Computer-Assisted and Paper-and-Pencil Self-Administered Questionnaires in a Survey on Smoking, Alcohol, and Drug Use," *Public Opinion Quarterly*, 62 (3), 331–53.

Zanes, Anne and Euthemia Matsoukas (1979), "Different Setting, Different Results? A Comparison of School and Home Responses," *Public Opinion Quarterly*, 43 (4), 550–57.

6
Internet Research: The Brave New World

Brian Fine

BACKGROUND AND HISTORY

The growth of the Internet has resulted in what may be regarded as a major paradigm shift in the fields of marketing and market research. We can consider the influence of the Internet at two levels: as a breakthrough medium that is capable of accomplishing tasks that could not have been accomplished hitherto and as the replacement technology capable of doing what we have been doing, perhaps better, faster, and cheaper.

The Internet as a Specific Field of Interest

As a channel of communication and interaction, the Internet is worthy of investigation in its own right. Any marketer entering this new arena would need to know the following:

1. How does this channel work, what are the dynamics of access and interaction?
2. Who are the users of this channel; what are their profiles in demographic, attitudinal, behavioural, and psychographic terms?
3. How does this channel fit into the lifestyle of users, when is it accessed, for how long and for what reasons?
4. How does one access users of the Internet, customers and potential customers; how will they find you, your site and your messages?
5. How does usage of the Internet fit into the total context of media usage, entertainment, and shopping behaviour? What are the cross-usage characteristics in terms of media consumption and on- and offline purchasing?

The Internet as a Replacement Technology

With the increasing penetration of Internet usage, we are seeing the profile of Internet users move from the skewed demographics and values of the "early adopters" to a user profile that comes closer to the population profile. As this trend gains momentum, we can safely predict the increased use of the Internet as an alternative methodology for collecting data. It will be added to the researcher's options of mail, face-to-face, and telephone surveys. At one stage, telephone survey methodology was frowned on by the purists as an inadequate replacement for random face-to-face surveys. Changes in culture and increasing refusal rates, along with more sophisticated weighting procedures, have resulted in telephone surveys using computer-assisted telephone interviewing (CATI) becoming a major method of survey data collection.

Protagonists of this new methodology, such as Gordon Black and David Clemm of Harris Interactive, claim that Internet research will become the new benchmark in survey methodology (Black 1998). With weighting procedures such as propensity weighting, the Internet will enable researchers to replicate telephone surveys at a fraction of the cost and with infinitely greater speed (Taylor 1999/2000).

The Internet medium enables the researcher to access larger samples in a very tight time frame. At the time of writing, very large Internet panels are already in operation, and the bulk of respondents on an Internet panel respond within 48 hours of a survey invitation.

A CONCEPTUAL MARKETING FRAMEWORK

Before proceeding to develop a research framework and appropriate research tools for the Internet, one must first generate hypotheses that relate to how marketing works on the Internet. Recent experience indicates that there are five core areas of marketing activity on the Internet:

1. Branding,
2. Image (brand equity) building,
3. Information provision,
4. Relationship management, and
5. Transactions.

Each of these areas requires differing marketing and advertising strategies to be successful. The layout and format of sites and pages needed to achieve one set of objectives will be less appropriate for other objectives.

The delivery systems to achieve each set of objectives are rapidly changing, and we have seen the progression from banner ads to "rich media" and digital audio photographs to streaming media. The success of these systems depends on both the technology used by the publisher and the sophistication, speed, and capacity of the equipment used by the receiver.

Segmentation of users and prospective users of an Internet site should also be considered in developing strategies. The "needs" of users is one segmentation that is relevant in planning an Internet strategy. For example, in the financial sector, users' needs may range from price value to speed, access, and convenience to level and quality of service provided to unique and different product or service features. Each of these needs groups would have differing priorities, which are likely to affect the delivery mechanism and the resultant research design to assess performance of the site.

A CONCEPTUAL MARKET RESEARCH FRAMEWORK

In the same way as we have developed a conceptual marketing framework, we must also consider a conceptual framework for market research. Before embarking on research design and analysis, we must identify the issues that may influence validity and reliability of market research on the Internet. The issues of importance here are the sample, questionnaire, and analysis.

The Sample

How representative is an Internet sample in enabling projection to

- ❏ The Internet universe,
- ❏ The general population (either residential or business),
- ❏ Specific client databases, or
- ❏ Visitors to a specific site?

Each of these target groups will differ in its sampling needs. Sending an e-mail to a database enables us to better control who is invited. This can be carried out by an e-mail questionnaire or by sending an invitation that directs the respondent to a specific site or server to complete an online questionnaire.

Sampling of respondents who visit a site can occur by inviting all visitors to click on a banner ad or to participate in a "pop-up" survey on the site. One can also use the "1 in n" approach, in which a random selection of visitors is given the opportunity to participate.

All of these target groups and sampling methods are less than desirable, in that participants "self-select" whether they will participate. It is difficult to control and monitor the nonresponse and the profile of the nonresponse. Protagonists of online surveys, however, argue that telephone, face-to-face, and mail surveys all suffer from self-selection bias, and it is equally difficult to profile those not participating. Although this argument has some validity, we should remember that self-selection in this context is not an "either–or" proposition. Rather, it is a matter of degree. All methods involve selection in the sense that a respondent is free to refuse to respond to a survey. However, it is also known that the more impersonal the medium, the greater the self-selection is. For example, the response rate for mail surveys is far lower than that for either telephone or door-to-door surveys.

The ultimate solution to ensure representativeness for all methodologies lies in the ability of the researcher to weight the data to the population they are purported to represent, in addition to ensuring that the data so weighted will reasonably represent the universe under consideration.

The Questionnaire

The medium is unique in that it is a hybrid of both personal interviews (with the ability to control order of exposure and use visual materials) and mail interviews (which require self completion). Researchers need to understand the strengths and weaknesses of the medium in designing questionnaires.

Internet questionnaires offer several advantages, such as the ability to use colour and graphics and to control rotations, filters, and exposure to visual prompts (including audio and visual material such as television commercials). They also offer the respondents the ability to access the survey at their convenience. But there are some weaknesses too. For example, there is no person-to-person interaction and control (for guidance and clarification), an increased potential for dropping out, a high degree of self-selection, slow downloading of visual materials especially if a respondent has a low-level computer, and the need to work with shorter questionnaires to maintain interest.

The Analysis

Analysis of Internet data is far more time-consuming than other methods because of the need for extensive weighting procedures to enable us to represent the Internet universe of the population at large and the need to clean and edit data received and assess the nonresponse bias in the sample. Other than these issues, the Internet enables us to sample larger populations and discrete niche target groups at a lower cost in a fraction of the time taken by traditional research.

APPLICATIONS AND NEEDS

At a practical level, the Internet opens a parallel universe of users to that existing in the field of classical research. What does this mean to research? Here are some likely scenarios.

Expanding Field of Measurement

Marketing models that relate to new product development and measurement of mature categories and brands all apply. In addition, there is a whole new field of measurement that relates to understanding and measuring the integration of the Internet with more traditional fields of communication (television, radio, newspapers, magazines, outdoor, direct mail) and product sales channels (wholesale, retail). In this latter area, consulting skills and knowledge of the classical paradigm and research techniques are extremely relevant. A new hybrid set of skills will be needed to service the research needs of e-marketers.

Greater Technical Expertise

Research skills and knowledge of sampling, research design, and analysis will become even more critical. This will need to be supported by a understanding of the dynamics of this new medium, and research companies will need strong "back-end' technical support and "Internet-savvy" consultants.

More Sound Knowledge Base

As in the traditional research model, the passing fads of just trying new techniques will be replaced by sound understanding of how information from the research will add value to marketing and communication decisions and ultimately result in more profitable brands and organisations. The range of information needs include the following:

❑ Understanding how the new channel works (methods of access, reasons for access, strengths and limitations);

❑ Measurement of user profiles and where to reach them for communication and marketing, as well as for research;

❑ Measurement of user needs from this medium, both generically and within specific category and product segments;

❑ Testing new product concepts, branding (e-brands can be different), packaging, pricing communication, and customer satisfaction;

❑ Tracking effectiveness of e-commerce strategies and relative performance of the brand, product/service, and strategy in a competitive context; and

❑ Tracking the overlap and discreet benefits of differing channels of communication, sales, and delivery.

These needs are likely to spawn a host of branded and packaged research techniques, including usage and attitude surveys; product concept tests; advertising concept tests; advertising pretesting; advertising tracking; brand equity measurement and tracking; customer satisfaction, loyalty, and advocacy measurement; choice modelling; pricing surveys; qualitative research; omnibus surveys; research across differing target markets such as business, residential, and hard-to-find specialist target groups such as doctors and health-impaired groups; audience measurement; and multivariate techniques.

In addition to these well-worn areas, new areas will grow quickly. These include research to develop and assess Web sites, e-business auditing and measurement, customer service and fulfillment measurement, measurement of usage and measurement using WAP (Wireless Area Protocol) devices, measurement of actual "click throughs" of banner ads and pathway analysis of those who ended up clicking on an ad and those who did not, specialist single-source databases that combine offline exposure to advertising (e.g., cable, television meters) with online exposure (e.g., in-PC measurement) with off- and online shopping (e.g., shopper cards such as Catalina), and fusion of databases, both off- and online.

A CLIENT/RESEARCH USER BASELINE

A helpful rule in developing new products and (research) techniques is to go to the market first and establish whether there is a need for them and, primarily, what there is a need for.

In Australia, AMR Interactive conducted a benchmark survey (n = 109) in August 1999 with a group of clients that included

- ❏ Managers (in major marketing organisations) responsible for Web commerce development;
- ❏ Marketers involved in e-commerce development for major financial institutions;
- ❏ Marketing managers of major computer/information technology companies;
- ❏ E-media specialists in ad and media placement agencies; and
- ❏ Business development managers in Internet service providers (ISPs), portal providers, and Web developers.

The survey covered the following areas: awareness of Internet measurement techniques, knowledge of Internet measurement techniques, usage of Internet measurement techniques, satisfaction with Internet measurement techniques, and areas of need. In addition to providing some important guidelines on where researchers should focus, the survey was designed to provide a benchmark against which to measure changes in all of these areas as the medium matures. Although the results presented in the next section may not hold for every country, they provide some insights that may be of value in general.

THE RANGE OF RESEARCH NEEDS

According to the benchmark survey, users of Internet research were using, to various degrees, 14 key measures:

1. Own site user profiling,
2. User profiles (market),
3. Penetration measures,
4. Penetration (Australia versus other markets),
5. "Click-through" analysis,
6. Use of Net for information,
7. Purchasing/transaction measurement,
8. Use for e-mail or information,
9. Measurement of relative site usage,
10. Use of Internet versus other media,
11. Categories accessed on Net,
12. Usership and audit surveys,
13. Processes/dynamics of use, and
14. Web site needs.

Figure 1 shows the varying penetration of usage of these various techniques and measurements. More interesting, it also identifies unfulfilled needs in terms of interest in using measurements not previously used. Users were also asked their satisfaction with the techniques (Figure 2).

METHODOLOGIES IN USE—THEIR METRICS, STRENGTHS, AND WEAKNESSES

A review of existing techniques being used in Internet research identified five key areas: server log file analysis, site-centric measures, online user surveys, offline user (and potential user) surveys, and PC panels. Table 1 describes each of these techniques, along with their strengths and weaknesses. From the table, it can be seen that

❏ Log file analysis provides measures of multiple sites but has serious limits and gaps;

❏ Site-based measures can give great detail about activity but are narrow, incomplete, and often biased;

❏ Online surveys can be a rich source of additional data but can suffer sample bias and need validation;

❏ Offline surveys can add greater depth to understanding of users but add questions about memory decay to those raised for online surveys; and

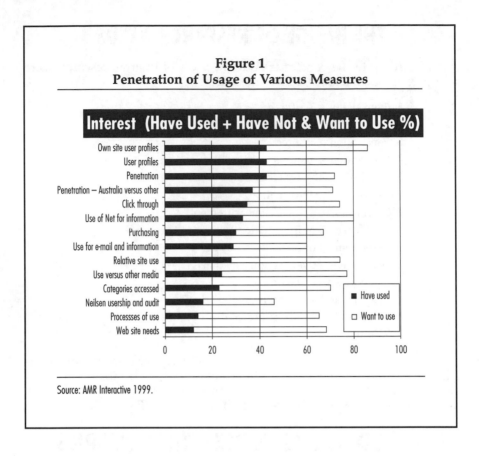

Figure 1
Penetration of Usage of Various Measures

Source: AMR Interactive 1999.

❏ In-PC panel overcomes many problems of ISP and site-centric measures but raises issues of cost, sample bias, and what cannot be captured in this way.

THE NEED FOR INTEGRATION AND TRIANGULATION OF METHODOLOGIES

We need to understand the market at several levels — as consumers and businesses, as an Internet audience, and as Internet users or (soon to be) users.

We also need to understand online and offline activities and different methodologies for each of the sources. When we review the strengths and weaknesses of different approaches (Table 2), we note that we can counterbalance the weakness of any single method by using a combination of approaches. Consequently, we may need to develop a holistic approach to

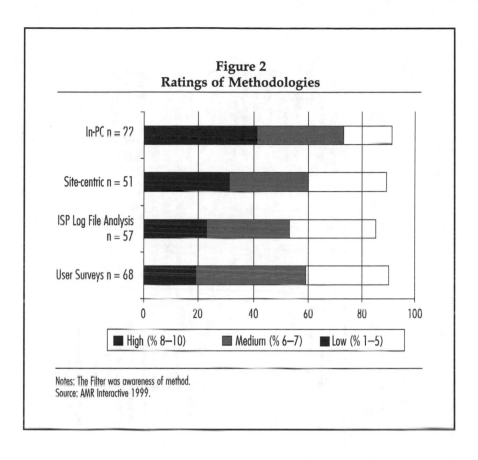

Figure 2
Ratings of Methodologies

Notes: The Filter was awareness of method.
Source: AMR Interactive 1999.

research and measurement. It should cover the three areas of "e-activity": demand side, online interaction, and supply side. Some components of each of these areas are shown in Table 2.

THE WAY FORWARD: FUTURE APPLICATIONS, METHODS, AND ISSUES

The Internet field is rapidly changing. Based on current trends, some projected scenarios for the near future are as follows:

❏ The Internet will extend its reach beyond computers to other devices in the home, such as playstations, microwaves, refrigerators, and televisions, as well as become more accessible through mobile telephones and WAP devices.

Table 1
Five Key Areas of Internet Research

	Server Log File Analysis (SLF)	Site-Centric Measures	Online User Survey	Offline User Survey	PC Panel
DESCRIPTION	Analysis of ISP server log files to determine number of pages served, by domain name, by date/time.	Software to record and analyze number of pages served, by domain name, by date/time for a site. Can be provided by ISP or Web master or use downloaded shareware.	Analysis of user responses to Web-based questionnaire by pop-up survey or e-mailed invitation.	Analysis of user responses to paper questionnaire.	Analysis of usage data collected by application on the user's PC, across a large sample of users (similar to "People Meters" used for television ratings). Can be supplemented by questionnaire data obtained at recruitment and in subsequent special surveys.
POSSIBLE METRICS	Number of pages, by domain name, site section, date and time, user's server suffix (e.g., .com, .UK, .au).	Number of pages, by domain name, site section, date and time, user's server suffix (e.g., .com, .au). Time spent by site area. Click through on ads. Potential to capture user details with "pop-up" questionnaires.	Preferences and stated usage by segment, including type of sites, specific Internet activities, reasons for preferences and usage, location of access (home, work), amount of time spent online, relationship to other media (switching, boosting). Exposure and response to specific site features. Demographics.	Preferences and stated usage by segment, including type of sites, specific Internet activities (e.g., e-mail), reasons for preferences, location of access (home, work), amount of time spent online, use versus other media.	Same as server log file analysis, but also captures cached pages usage. Same as surveys but with actual data plus duration of page view and inter- and intrasite traffic flow.

Table 1
Continued

Server Log File Analysis (SLF)	Site-Centric Measures	Online User Survey	Offline User Survey	PC Panel
STRENGTHS				
"Real-time" analysis. Identifies top sites visited (based on hits or impressions). Tracks change in visits. Identifies overseas sites visited relative to Australian sites.	Measure time spent on site. Detail on areas of site visited. Detail on where use came from (e.g., portal, ISP, equipment used). Potential user profiles through pop-up questionnaire. Measure other sites visited through "cookies."	Detailed diagnostics. Cross-PC usage (home, work, education). Unique individual. Detailed demographics and values. Details of multimedia usage. Check motivation for use. If pop-up, short delay after use.	Amount of detail. Can include nonusers to measure reasons for nonuse and future intentions. Complete control over data collection process (e.g., sample, question order).	Detailed activity measures at individual level sites visited (reach, frequency) and time spent at site. Detailed demographics of users (recruitment survey). Can filter user on the basis of data (e.g., filter or tab by site). Detailed data on use of browsers or ISPs.
WEAKNESSES				
Can't determine number of users. Limited to ISPs that take part (thus biased). Caching (source of bias). Hits potentially more misleading than impressions. No "duration of page view" data. No demographics, diagnostics, other effect measures.	Hard to determine number of users. Limited to one site, no measurement of popularity relative to other sites. Sample bias, one site, self-selection, multiple replies, "pseudo users." No demographics, diagnostics, effect measures (unless pop-up used).	Sample bias due to sites used, heavy, experienced users, incentive self-selection. Not "real time." Difficult to validate responses, except for preferred sites (validate with server log files). Pop-up potential for repeated response by one user.	Can only validate for preferred sites (validate with server log files). Memory decay. Overclaiming of major sites/brands. Not "real-time" measurement. Sampling issues (e.g., finding users of low volume sites). Cost.	Quality depends on sample quality (size, selection to avoid bias by) recruitment channel, incentives used, self-selection. Reasons not captured (unless by pop-up or follow-up surveys, but can be done). Cost. Multiple users/one PC, can miss use through other PCs.

❑ Collection of research data will become more immediate and closer to the events being measured. Intermediaries such as interviewers will become less prevalent, and technology will become more pervasive.

❑ Methods of data collection will change radically with increased penetration of Internet access, and the business models being used by research organizations will need to be transformed.

❑ Lower data collection costs will allow growth in use of market research and enable larger samples and more discreet target groups to be accessed in the same budgets.

❑ The qualitative research paradigm will shift from that we know today, though current methods will still be advantageous in many cases.

❑ The range of techniques available to researchers will expand, and studies will be about the new media, convergence, and new marketing and communication opportunities.

❑ Methodologies will expand to include access panels, pop-up surveys, observation analysis of behaviour, and use of CATI, computer-assisted personal interviewing (CAPI), and WAP devices. Methodologies will also need to consider hybrid approaches and fused data from on- and offline population groups. These technology changes and this chapter will require refreshing in the not-too-distant future.

Table 2
Three Basic Areas of Measurement

Demand Side	Online Interaction	Supply Side
•Number of subscribers	•Hours online	•ISP industry structure and trends
•Number of users	•Pages viewed	•ISP network issues
•Sociodemographics of users	•Top ten domains	
•Loyalty	•User volume and share	
•Value by segment	•Time at site/page	
•Reasons for use	•Transactions	
•Intended future use		
•Offline purchase behaviour		

With all of these changes comes a need to review our standards, our ethics, and the principles by which we have worked. Hopefully, these will keep pace with the urgency driving the technology changes.

BIBLIOGRAPHY

Black, Gordon S. (1998), "On the Internet as a Replacement Technology," paper presented at the American Association of Public Opinion Research Annual Meeting, St. Louis, MO (May 8).

Taylor, Humphrey (1999/2000), "Does Internet Research Work?" *International Journal of Market Research*, 42 (1), 51–63.

SUGGESTED READINGS

Fine, Brian, Gary Wilkinson, and Andrew Sergeant (1999), "The e-Activity Research Initiative," presented at Workshop for Internet Marketers, Sydney, Australia (November).

Porritt, Don and Brian Fine (1999), "On Measuring the Web," presented at Workshop for Internet Marketers, Sydney, Australia (September).

Wit, Karlan and Ray Poynter (1998), "Research on the Internet," *ESOMAR Handbook of Market and Opinion Research*, 4th ed. (Chapter 33). Amsterdam: ESOMAR Secretariat.

7
Sampling Techniques

Peter Chan

Quantitative survey research involves the collection and analysis of data using appropriate and valid methods. In most cases, a census of any population is both prohibitively expensive and statistically unnecessary. Therefore, samples are normally used to represent the population that is of interest to the researcher.

Although there are many factors that make up a well-executed and valid survey, one of the major components of any sample survey is the sample design. It dictates the precision of the survey estimates and is the foundation on which projections to the total population are built.

Sampling theory is a complex statistical field. Broadly speaking, sampling can be viewed as having two components. The first is defining the population to be sampled and determining the manner in which this will be done. The second is determining how the collected data will be treated. In one sense, they are opposite sides of the same coin, because a sample design should not be finalized without an appreciation of how the resulting data will be treated to provide valid estimates for the population surveyed.

All surveys should start with a sampling plan that explicitly recognizes that the estimation procedures to be used are integral parts of the sampling procedures. The estimating procedures must be explicit to ensure that the consequences of all stages of a sample design are appreciated.

Every sample design requires that there is a corresponding mathematical formula to estimate the parameters and the sampling variance. The more complex the sample design, the more complex will be the estimating formula. Most computer software used by survey researchers to analyze the data do not have the flexibility to allow advanced estimation formulae to be incorporated into the analyses, which thereby limits the analysis of data collected by advanced sampling techniques.

There are many new techniques currently being developed to handle real-life problems, particularly in the agricultural and wildlife areas, but the aim of this chapter is to describe and comment on the more common techniques used in market and social research surveys. This is done in four main sections:

1. The components of survey sampling,
2. A review of the types of sampling techniques commonly used,
3. The application of those techniques within different data collection modes, and
4. Weighting and statistical estimating.

Finally, some observations are made about possible future developments and challenges.

THE COMPONENTS OF SURVEY SAMPLING

From the survey researcher's perspective, sampling is not the most exciting part of the research process. However, it is the foundation upon which all research conclusions will be based. Therefore, the important dependency of the estimation process (weighting) on the sample design cannot be ignored. With a better understanding of the pros and cons of the different designs, researchers can make more intelligent decisions when choosing the sample design that can best achieve their cost or precision objectives. This requires an appreciation of the important components of sampling.

Universe and Sample

Before any survey can take place, we must define carefully the target survey universe. The survey design must be consistent in providing statistical inferences about the survey universe. Who provides the information or from where the information is obtained is an operational and design issue and should not be confused with universe definition.

If a researcher is interested in studying the attitudes of adults, then the universe should be defined as the adult population, 18 years of age and older. If the research is to estimate the penetration rate of computer ownership in households, then the universe should be defined as all households, even though that information will likely be provided by any adult member living in the household. In a study of the advertising expenditures of business corporations, an appropriate universe definition might be all headquarters of businesses and the informant could be the advertising manager. However, if a survey is interested in finding out business customer satisfaction with courier services, then branch offices of all business corporations would be the suitable survey universe and the mailroom operator could be the informant.

Often, a market researcher's mandate is to provide, within the same survey, information about different universes, as in the case of a multipurpose study. Data about individuals and their households are often required from the same research survey. Therefore, a multipurpose design is often used in survey research. We can look at how this can be achieved by designing a proper sampling plan after we introduce some basic sampling concepts.

The Sample Frame

When the survey universe is defined, a search for the appropriate sample frame begins. Examples of frequently used sample frames in North America include telephone directories (both white pages and yellow pages), census files, taxation files, postal code listing and conversion files, and many other commercial lists maintained by list brokers. Sometimes more than one list or source is required to represent the universe properly, and sometimes a frame will need to be built from scratch. The real world is not always nicely organized, and it is quite common that a suitable sample frame simply does not exist. In such cases, a more complex sample design will need to be developed to make the best use of alternative frames.

Errors and Biases

Because we only include and measure a random subset of the units from a universe, the survey estimate will likely vary from the true value in the universe, and therefore, some amount of error can be expected. Two types of error are incurred during the process and are referred to as sampling and nonsampling errors.

A sample will always be subject to errors because not every unit in the universe is included in the sample and measured. When we repeat sampling of the same universe, we do not expect all the independent samples to produce identical estimates. Each sample could have a slightly different mix of the units from the universe, and if the universe is not homogeneous, then it is obvious that the sample estimates, such as the mean or proportion of some variables, will vary from sample to sample.

Using the random sampling process, the independent sample estimates will form a distribution and center around the true value of the universe. When a particular sample is picked, its estimate has an expected probability of being within a certain range from the true value. For sufficiently large samples, 95% of all possible samples will have a sample estimate within two standard errors of the true value. Five percent of all samples will produce estimates farther away. If this error range is narrowed to one standard error of the true value, then only 90% of the samples qualify.

The survey error, which is the expected difference from the true value, is conditioned by the level of uncertainty we are willing to accept. This level of uncertainty is called the *confidence level*, and 95% or 90% is commonly chosen. In general, if the sampling process follows a random procedure, such that the theoretical probability of a unit being selected in the sample can be determined, then sampling error can be quantified statistically.

The sampling error is usually reported as a margin of error or confidence limit. It is normally reported plainly as "The survey result is precise to within plus or minus X%, 19 times out of 20 (for 95% confidence)."

When the error can be quantified, we should also be able to control or pre-specify the probable error and confidence level when designing a survey.

The magnitude of the sampling error mainly depends on the variability of the data in the universe, known as *variance*, and on the sample size. Increasing the sample size has the direct effect of reducing the sampling error. Although it is desirable to have as small a sampling error as possible by increasing the sample size, it is also crucial to control the cost of the survey. It would be imprudent to spend unnecessary dollars to achieve insignificant improvements in survey precision. However, the necessary precision should never be compromised if the research objective requires it.

Unfortunately, the nonsampling error cannot be as easily quantified. It encompasses a wide range of measurement errors due to misinterpretation by respondents, wording bias in the questionnaire, interviewer bias due to all kinds of execution inaccuracies, and many other systematic errors not controllable by the survey design, including the inability to interview all members of the selected sample (nonresponse). Readers can refer to Biemer (1991) for further reading on nonsampling error.

In principle, a well-thought-out survey, with well-trained interviewers and careful execution, should minimize much of these types of errors. However, because there are too many unknowns and uncontrollable circumstances in the real world that may introduce bias, there is no guarantee that they will be totally removed.

Sample Size

Although sampling error is inversely related to sample size, its relationship is nonlinear and will reach diminishing returns after attaining a certain sample size. A typical relationship is shown in Figure 1.

As can be seen from this graph, for the percentage estimate, the reduction of sampling error slows down significantly when the size reaches 380. Because the variance function for a percentage will reach a maximum at the 50% level, we can use this worst-case assumption to estimate sample size requirements, and as a result, a size of 400 is often recommended when percentages are the data format required. However, the calculation of sample sizes will differ for other estimates, such as the mean of a rating scale. This is because we cannot assume a maximum value for the variance of a numerical variable, such as the rating scale, without first collecting the data. In such cases, we normally need to rely on estimates from other sources.

The following is the general formula for estimating minimum sample size for any desired level of precision:

$$n = \frac{V}{\dfrac{A^2}{Z^2} + \dfrac{V}{N}},$$

where

n = minimum sample size;
N = population size;
V = variance of target variable in the population;
A = accuracy desired expressed in decimal (e.g., 0.01, 0.05); and
Z = number of standard deviation units of the sampling distribution corresponding to the desired confidence level. This can be looked up from the Normal probability distribution table. For a 95% confidence level, the Z value is 1.96.

As an illustration, suppose we need to determine the minimum sample size for estimating a proportion and would like the accuracy to be no more than 0.05 with a 95% level of confidence. The worst-case assumption of a half–half split will generate the maximum variance of V = 0.25. Substituting A = 0.05 and Z = 1.96 and further supposing that N = 100,000, the computed value of n is 384.

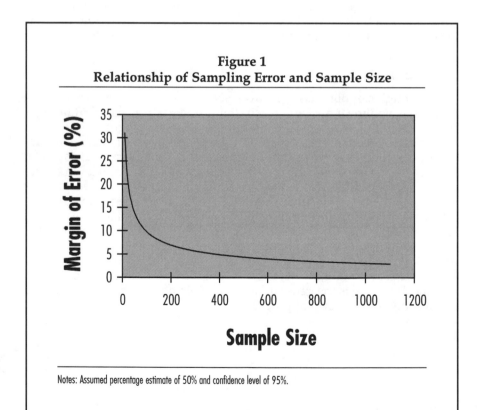

Figure 1
Relationship of Sampling Error and Sample Size

Notes: Assumed percentage estimate of 50% and confidence level of 95%.

SAMPLING TECHNIQUES

There are many types of sampling, because researchers are continually being challenged by new problem areas and seek to find the most cost-effective way of meeting those challenges. However, most methods used are one of the following types or slight variants.

Simple Random Sampling

The simplest sampling technique, as suggested by its name, is simple random sampling. This is the most straightforward technique, like drawing numbered balls from an urn. In practice, all units, called primary sampling units (psu), in the universe are assigned a sequential number, and random numbers are generated to determine which units are to be selected. In this method, every psu has an equal probability of being selected in the sample.

In some situations, the psus, by design, might not be selected with equal probability. In these circumstances, the selection probabilities must be known, and the proper estimating formula, known as the estimator, must be applied to provide an unbiased statistical estimate.

Systematic Random Sampling

Sometimes the characteristics of the sample frame may prohibit the application of simple random sampling. For example, a telephone directory has so many entries that sequential numbering of the psus would be unnecessarily cumbersome.

A simpler alternative is to use systematic sampling, for which one chooses 1 in every k entries. In the telephone directory application, one starts by estimating the total number of listings by, for example, counting the number of listings on a typical page and multiplying the result by the total number of pages.

The estimated total number of listings is divided by the required gross sample size to determine the skip interval. The skip interval is further divided by the average number of listings per page so that the number of pages to be skipped between each selection can be determined. On each selected page, a sample unit is chosen by selecting the predetermined entry, such as the 51st number in column 2. The procedure is continued until the required gross sample size is reached.

Stratified Random Sampling

For practical or design reasons, we might need to divide the universe into different parts, called strata, and treat each stratum as an independent sample. For example, in Canada, there are five geographical regions: Atlantic, Ontario, Quebec, Prairies, and the West. To use the data in conjunction with national estimates, we must organize the total sample into five separate subsamples. This is stratified sampling; in this case, the strata are the five regions.

Apart from giving better control of the execution of the sample drawing, stratified sampling also has practical and statistical advantages. In the five Canadian regions example, if each region is to receive its proper proportion of the sample, then the Atlantic region (which is relatively small) could end up with a sample size too small to be accurate if analyzed in isolation. With stratified random sampling, one can disproportionately give each stratum a target sample size to fulfill the analytical requirements.

Another reason for using stratified sampling is to reduce sampling cost. When a stratum is known to be more homogeneous relative to other strata, then that stratum can be undersampled to save on sampling costs and still maintain the overall statistical precision. For example, a particular industry is required by government to follow certain safety standards. All operating companies in that industry will have more or less the same company policy with respect to safety. Therefore, there is very little new information to gain about safety in the work environment whether 100 or 1000 companies are surveyed. In this case, stratifying companies with regard to whether they are subject to similar regulatory requirements allows the use of a stratified random sampling design to reduce sampling costs (by having a smaller sample) or sampling error (if sample size remains unchanged).

Cluster Sampling

Cluster sampling is often used to reduce the cost of data collection. It can take various forms. The most common type occurs with face-to-face interviewing, when a simple random sample would be prohibitively expensive because of the cost of having interviewers travel great distances between respondents. A more effective alternative is to have interviews conducted at a limited number of locations. A sample of locations is selected as the first-stage sample, and households are selected as a second stage. The third stage is the selection of a respondent from within the household.

Another type of clustering is when more than one person is interviewed within the same psu. An example might be a study of the beverage consumption habits of consumers for which a seven-day diary is to be used. If the survey plan is to have all household members record their beverage consumption in a diary, then effectively, we build the data by clusters of people within households.

Both examples of the cluster sampling technique provide an efficient way of collecting data. The characteristic of cluster sampling is that the primary sampling unit is a cluster of sampling elements (e.g., household members), and when the psu is selected, all members of the cluster are included. However, cluster sampling is a trade-off between the cost of a sample of size X and the effective sample size for variance estimates, which will be less than X. All clustering will reduce the effective sample size. There are mathematical functions for calculating the impact of any clustering used. Therefore, using assumptions of the within-psu correlation of sample members for the items being measured, it is necessary to consider when a cluster of a particular size might cancel out the supposed cost efficiencies.

Multistage Random Sampling

The most frequently used sampling technique is probably multistage random sampling. If telephone interviewing is the data collection method, we rarely wish to interview all members in the household when we make a call, unlike what can occur in some forms of cluster sampling. We want only to interview one household member using a simple random sampling technique. Therefore, we have a two-stage random selection to get to the respondent. The first stage is to select the telephone household, and the second stage is to select a person from that household.

In area probability sampling for door-to-door interviews, three- or even four-stage random sampling might be used. This is illustrated in a subsequent section.

Adaptive Sampling

Relative to sampling techniques discussed previously, adaptive sampling is a more recently developed sampling technique. When the members of the study universe are inherently rare and difficult to sample or estimate, adaptive sampling offers an alternative method that goes beyond the conventional set of techniques to achieve efficiency while using the conventional methods to the greatest advantage possible.

It builds on the notion that there is some natural clustering of the psus when the units share similar characteristics. For example, in studying commercial species of shrimp using trawl sampling, in which a net is towed behind the research vessel at selected locations, it was found to be very time consuming if a vast area was to be covered. However, biologists also found that shrimps typically concentrate in just a few areas but that the areas keep changing because of the shrimps' schooling movements. Adaptive sampling was used to trawl predetermined sections of the ocean, and if the catch was greater than a set quantity, an adjacent section not in the original sample was also trawled. By using adaptive sampling, the sampling effort was greatly reduced, but the yield of shrimp improved significantly.

Consider as another example a survey of homeowners who have replaced their furnaces with a newer high-efficiency type furnace. Houses in the same neighborhood usually have more or less the same age of household furnace. Furnace replacement usually happens when the old one breaks down or because of a desire to improve energy conservation. When a furnace replacement takes place in one home, the neighbors may also be stimulated to follow. A clustering of "replacement" homeowners could be developed. To efficiently sample this population, we could use the adaptive sampling technique. A random sample of households is drawn. If the sampled household is a "replacement" household, then automatically, the next-door neighbor is included in the sample. The inclusion will continue as long as the neighbor of the neighbor is also a qualified "replacement" household. Thompson and Seber (1996) provide comprehensive coverage of this technique.

Quota Sampling

Another type of sampling method widely used in market research is quota sampling. As the name suggests, in quota sampling, any person is eligible to be interviewed providing he or she has the prespecified characteristics and people with those characteristics are still required (the quota is not full). The most common control variables are age, sex, income, geography, and users of a particular product category. The demographic variables are normally interlaced.

If the quotas' relationships to the control variable are reasonable and close to what random sampling of the population would produce, then quota sampling is similar to stratified sampling. Instead of prestratifying the sample frame, the quota verification and assignment process by the interviewer becomes a poststratification of the sample.

Normally, quota sampling is needed because random sampling of the universe does not produce the required sample size for the control variable or because the sample requires more control to ensure that the structure of the universe is better reflected by the sample. Hence, the quota on the control variable is usually higher than what might be achieved by a random sample. Because of this, a considerable amount of field work effort is needed to fill all quotas, especially at the later stages of field work when the entire effort is dedicated to filling the hard-to-get quota cells.

The desperate need to fill the quotas requires giving the interviewers some latitude to decide who should be included in the sample. This takes away the randomness required by probability sampling. Incrementing a quota cell could also affect another quota cell; therefore, it is a sequential process with continuous refinement and, thus, nonrandomness. In general, the normal sampling error formulae cannot be applied with any confidence to the results of quota samples.

Sudman (1966) proposed the probability sampling with quotas technique to impose more stringent control on the interviewer, allowing (in theory) no interviewer discretion in choosing the household to which to administer the questionnaire. Stephenson (1979) conducted analyses to compare the probability quota sample with the full probability sample. He concluded that data from a survey carefully conducted with the "probability sampling with quotas" design are acceptable.

An alternative to using quota sampling to obtain a larger sample size of the control variables is to oversample. This is done by first obtaining a random sample of the universe, called the cross-section sample. When the required cross-section size is reached, the interviewers screen every new sample unit for the qualification on the control variables and interview only those qualified. The screening data must be retained, and the screen-in rate is calculated to provide a weighting factor to blend the oversample to the cross-section sample.

Other Nonprobability Sampling Techniques

Probability sampling is usually required for opinion and policy research because of accuracy and generalization requirements. For commercial applications, a more relaxed condition often prevails. As a result, several convenient or purposeful sampling techniques have been used to obtain samples of hard-to-find people. Snowball sampling is one of those techniques. When a person of the required type is found, he or she is interviewed. Then the person is asked for the names and contact information of any other people he or she knows who have the hard-to-find characteristic. When the referred people are contacted, the process is repeated, and the chain continues. This sampling technique is very effective when the incidence of qualifiers in the general population is very low and there is a network among the qualifiers to which snowballing can apply. However, unlike adaptive sampling, this is a nonprobability method.

Surveys based on custom-built panels of consumers are also common in market research. One of the advantages of this data collection method is the higher response rate than that of other conventional methods. To sample from such a database or panel, it is assumed that the target universe is predominantly characterized by demographic control variables such as age, sex, income, household composition, and geographical regions. If these control variables have been taken into account, then the heterogeneity among the consumers is simply a result of random distribution. Therefore, to construct a sample from a panel to represent any universe, it is necessary to randomly draw members from the panel by controlling for the key demographic variables.

A panel sample is not a probability sample in the traditional sense, and the sampling error cannot be computed. A pragmatic way to give panel samples some measure of precision is to judgmentally increase it by a factor. A 50% inflation factor to the variance is not uncommon for this kind of sample.

APPLICATION OF SAMPLING TECHNIQUES

To handle many of the real-life applications of survey sampling, the basic techniques discussed are often combined to suit the situation, the needs, and the available resources. A few applications are described in this section to illustrate how theory is applied in practice.

Sampling Technique for Door-to-Door Survey

Suppose that we would like to conduct a national door-to-door survey of adults. Unlike some other countries, the United States and Canada do not provide voter list for public access, and there is no sample frame of adults. However, aggregate census data are accessible.

To draw a sample of adults, we start with the smallest geographical unit of the census, which is known as census block in the United States and enumeration area (EA) in Canada. Although I use Canada to illustrate the sampling procedures, the technique is the same whether used in the United States or in any other country with similar availability of information. Only the terminology differs.

An EA is the smallest geographical unit of census data published by government statistical department and is first stratified by province or state. Then the EAs within each province (or state) are sorted with respect to some appropriate geographical ordering.

The EA is the psu, and the sorted list is the sample frame for the corresponding stratum (i.e., province). For simplicity, the systematic sampling technique is applied in order to draw a sample of EAs with equal probability.

The number of EAs to be sampled depends on the number of adults required in total for the stratum. Because a door-to-door survey involves travel by interviewers, more than one interview per EA is usual. The next stage involves the sampling of households within the selected EAs. To do this, an EA map showing the streets is obtained. A random start point and a random direction are marked on the map, and the interviewer is instructed to attempt to make contact with every kth house until the required sample size for the EA is reached.

When a successful contact is made with a member of the household, a third stage of random sampling is required to select a respondent. The interviewer compiles a list of all adult members in the household, and a random selection of one adult from this list is made. This sampling process is executed similarly for each stratum. In practice, there are more advanced methods for selecting a respondent, and these are covered subsequently. The procedure described encompasses several sampling techniques introduced previously and may be called a stratified three-stage random sampling.

This sampling procedure is not statistically efficient because the EAs (psus) are selected with equal probability. It implies that the EAs with more houses have the same chance to be chosen as the smaller EAs. Consequently, the respondents are not chosen with equal probability. Therefore, the sample estimate will be statistically biased if the estimating procedure does not take this into account. A better sampling method is to select the EAs with probability proportionate to their size, which is the total number of households in the example.

One way to select psus with probability proportionate to size is first to compute, on the sample frame, the running cumulative sum of the size variable (i.e., number of households) and then divide the grand total by the sample size required to obtain the skip interval. To select the psus, a starting point is obtained by selecting a random number between 1 and the skip interval. Then we look for the psu that has the cumulative sum just exceeding the start-up value and retain that psu as the first selected unit. To select the next unit, the start-up value is incremented by the skip interval value. Again, the cumulative sum of the psu list is compared with this incremented value, and the psu with the cumulative sum just exceeding the search value is selected. The process is continued until the required number of psus is obtained.

Sampling Techniques for Telephone Survey

The telephone survey is a much more economical means of data collection than the door-to-door survey. Telephone service is widely available and relatively inexpensive. The widespread ownership of telephones implies that good coverage of the population is ensured. In addition, the telephone survey eliminates expensive traveling costs. It generally requires a shorter field time and provides a broader dispersion of the sampling units than the door-to-door survey, due to no clustering. Several telephone sampling methodologies are commonly used in market and survey research.

Directory Telephone Sample

Telephone directories are easily accessible in most developed countries, especially in North America. Using the directories as the sample frame is a common method for generating a telephone sample. Sequential sampling is commonly applied because of the huge size of the directories. However, there are a few disadvantages to using the directories. Telephone directories are published only once a year. From the date that a new telephone or change of number is initiated, it could take up to a year for the directories to reflect the change. Different regions' or cities' telephone directories do not necessarily publish at the same time. Therefore, a sample frame built by combining more than one directory does not reflect the most current inventory of the telephone households. As well, it is difficult to pin down the exact date the sample frame represents.

In practice, these issues are usually ignored. Their impact has not been studied but is assumed to be small. However, care must also be taken with the use of overlapping directories to avoid certain telephone households with a higher chance of being selected than others.

The major problem with directory sampling is the incompleteness of the frame. As the general public has become more concerned about its privacy being invaded or personal data being disclosed, more and more telephone households are opting to have unlisted numbers. The level of unlisted telephone households has been as high as 50% to 60% in the United States, especially in high crime areas. The level of unlisted numbers in Canada is believed to be lower than in the United States and may be (in some neighborhoods) approximately 15% to 20%. For this reason, researchers should be concerned about the undercoverage associated with the use of telephone directories as a sampling frame. Nevertheless, in the United States and Canada, telephone directory sampling is a popular method for market research surveys that do not require stringent representation of the universe because of its ease of use and reasonable hit rate of reaching telephone households.

Plus-Digit Random Telephone Sample

To avoid the pitfalls of unlisted telephone households in a directory sample, a plus-digit method can be used. The plus-digit method takes a directory sample as the seed sample and alters each selected telephone number by adding a random digit to it. It is an attempt to give the unlisted telephone households a chance to be included in the sample.

It works on the assumption that unlisted numbers are randomly spread among all working telephone numbers. The hit rate of finding a telephone household ranges from 65% to 70% in North America, with a better hit rate in larger cities. The plus-digit sample has been the most popular telephone sampling method when universe coverage is an important concern. The disadvantages of the plus-digit sample are the wasted dialing to 30% to 35% of nonusable numbers and the loss of geographical identity when the listed seed number has been altered. The loss of geographical identity may or may not be crucial to a particular survey, so it must be evaluated on a case-by-case basis. For a survey covering a large geographical area, such as a province, the plus-digit telephone number will still be within the province because area codes follow provincial boundaries. Experience suggests that plus-digit samples have a very high probability of staying within the same area as the seed sample, and therefore, geographical identity is not a real problem. Other surveys that specifically target small geographical areas will be more likely to have some selected numbers fall outside the target area, and some effort to confirm the location of the respondents is recommended.

Random Digit Dialing (RDD) Sample

Because the plus-digit sample usually builds upon the seed sample drawn from a published telephone directory, the outdated nature of the directory could omit some new residential areas that may be assigned to new telephone exchanges (first six digits, including area code, of the ten-digit telephone number) by the telephone company. In such cases, the new area will never have a chance to be included in the plus-digit sample. A telephone sampling methodology that can overcome this is the full random digit dialing (RDD) method.

The selection process starts with a compiled list of working telephone exchanges, and for each exchange, a series of four-digit random suffixes are added to create the telephone sample. Full RDD sampling is the most statistically reliable form of telephone sampling, but it does have some practical drawbacks.

First, because four-digit suffixes range from 0000 to 9999, for a total of 10,000 possibilities, the chance of hitting nonoperating telephone numbers is quite high. Experience suggests that as many as 70% of the numbers selected by RDD sampling are nonissued or nonresidential numbers. Therefore, the screening of the sample to obtain the subset of working telephone numbers becomes a costly part of the interviewing budget.

Second, the compilation of current working telephone exchanges is not simple. Some regional telephone companies are willing to provide information as to which exchanges have live numbers; others are not as cooperative. When the geographic coverage of the sample becomes very broad, compiling a list of current telephone exchanges becomes a costly task and sometimes can run into difficulties.

Third, given the large number of possible four-digit suffixes that can be generated, the chances of an RDD telephone number falling outside the target area is proportionately higher. However, this sampling technique remains the purest and easiest to understand method.

Waksberg-Mitofsky Random Digit Dialing Sample

To make full RDD more efficient in reaching the population of telephone households without incurring a large amount of time in screening for working telephone numbers, Waksberg (1978) developed a clustering approach to the full RDD method. The method consists of two stages and can be briefly described as follows:

1. Determine all telephone exchanges for the survey universe. Telephone subexchanges (i.e., first seven digits of the telephone number) could also be used if feasible.

2. From the telephone exchanges, construct a series of eight-digit telephone blocks, each with a potential of 100 numbers—for example, 416-924-00, 416-924-01 ... to 416-924-99. These blocks of 100 numbers form the sample frame for selecting primary sampling units.

3. Randomly select *m* psus of telephone blocks and generate one RDD telephone number from each psu. The sample size *m* is predetermined.

4. Call each psu's RDD number to establish whether the number dialed is a residential household. Retain those psus that are residential and discard those that are not. This completes Stage 1 sampling.

5. In Stage 2, additional telephone numbers are drawn and dialed from each retained psu until *k* residential numbers per psu have been reached. The value of *k* is a predetermined number to reach the required sample size.

The method has the advantage of not requiring any knowledge of the first- and second-stage selection probabilities of the sampling units, but it does produce an equal probability sample of a residential telephone sample. The efficiency of the Waksberg-Mitofsky method increases when the nonresidential and nonoperating numbers cluster sequentially.

The choice of the number of clusters m in Stage 1 and the cluster size k for Stage 2 is a balancing act. On the one hand, we do not want to have too small a cluster (i.e., small k) that defeats the efficiency of the two-stage dialing. On the other hand, too big a cluster, which implies fewer psus, might reduce the universe coverage. Experience is needed to guide the selection of the choice of m and k values.

Although the Waksberg-Mitofsky method is statistically attractive and more efficient than full RDD, it does have a few operational challenges. Because it is a two-stage approach, all Stage 1 call outcomes must be resolved before Stage 2 can proceed. Also, the method requires that the retained psus in Stage 1 are completely determined before the second-stage cluster RDD sample can be generated. Then it requires a fixed number of residential numbers per cluster in order to maintain the equal sampling probability property (a self-weighting design). Sometimes many callbacks are required to determine whether an RDD number is a residential number, particularly if the number repeatedly rings with no answer. Operating this sequential process, which affects both data collection administration and sample management, creates logistical difficulties.

It is impossible to determine ahead of time how many RDD telephone numbers are needed per cluster without completely finishing the callbacks and ascertaining the sample status. Current research on how to handle repeated "no answer" calls suggests replacing the psu in Stage 1 with a new one and retrying. For Stage 2, unanswered numbers also get replaced. Another suggestion is to retain the unanswered psu and include the unanswered RDD number in the cluster size of k.

Recognizing the awkward sequential nature of the Waksberg-Mitofsky method, Brick and Waksberg (1991) developed a modified approach to the method. The modification retains the process in selecting psus of telephone blocks in Stage 1, as in the original method. For Stage 2, instead of requiring a constant number of sampled residential numbers per cluster, it uses a constant number of telephone numbers per cluster. Unlike residential telephone numbers that need to be confirmed by calling the number, random telephone numbers require no confirmation. With a constant number of telephone numbers per cluster, the sampled numbers can be designated in advance, eliminating the sequential process. It should be noted that follow-up effort is still necessary to determine which sampled telephone numbers are residential in both the first and second stages of sampling.

This modification has good features for administration of the survey operation. It is simpler than the original method. The sample can be virtually preselected, and no costly control operations are needed. However, the modification removes the self-weighting property, and the sample design weight needs to be developed from the data. It also introduces some statistical bias to the survey estimates. Brick and Waksberg (1991) claim that the bias is fairly small, but it does exist. Finally, the modified method loses the original feature of predetermining the sample size. This is because it is not known how many residential telephone numbers can be achieved from dialing a constant number of telephone numbers per cluster.

Techniques in Respondent Selection

In a multistage population survey, the last stage of sampling usually involves a random selection of a qualified person. Having a random selection simplifies the statistical estimation of population parameters because the selection probability is uniform and easily obtained. The application of such probabilities is discussed in the weighting and estimation section. For the moment, we focus on how the selection can be done.

Kish (1949) proposed the full enumeration of the household members and, using a random number table, randomly selecting one person for interview. This procedure takes up a significant amount of interviewing time, and the request for such private information can be viewed as somewhat invasive. This can lead to a higher refusal rate, especially with telephone surveys. Troldahl and Carter (1964), in an attempt to improve on Kish's method, proposed an alternative method that requires only that two questions be asked before a respondent is selected:

1. How many persons 18 years of age or older live in your household, counting yourself?
2. How many of them are men?

Four selection matrices (see the Appendix) are used. Using the answer to the two questions as a basis, the youngest or oldest man or woman will be picked. The four matrices are sequentially rotated throughout the sample to give each matrix an equal chance of being used.

It is obvious that the Troldahl-Carter (T-C) method is biased because it gives a middle-aged person no chance of selection in a household with more than two adults. Bryant (1975) proposed a modification in the T-C method to account for the changing patterns in household composition and to compensate for the traditionally higher refusal rate among men. Bryant proposed a disproportionate assignment of the T-C matrices to compensate for the shortage of men among the respondents. Instead of repeating the matrix assignments of (1,2,3,4), Bryant's (T-C-B) disproportionate assignments are (1,2,3,4), (1,2,3), (1,2,3,4), (1,2,3), and so forth. Because the T-C Matrix 4 in the Appendix selects women more often, Bryant's assignment reduces the female selection probabilities and boosts those of men.

Czaja, Blair, and Sebestik (1982) conducted an experiment that created two versions of the T-C-B method by addressing the second question to men in one version and to women in the other. The two versions of the T-C-B method, as well as the Kish method, were applied to actual telephone surveys, and the effects of the methods were analyzed. The T-C-B (women) version and Kish methods perform similarly in the achieved cooperation rate, with T-C-B (men) trailing slightly behind. In practice, all three methods are used by market researchers.

The T-C selection method can be extended to cover more selection variations of a designated respondent among the household members. A larger number of selection matrices must be made and randomized across the sample. With a more elaborate set of selection matrices, the selection probabilities can be better balanced, giving all members of the household their fair chance to be included in the survey.

One of the easiest respondent selection methods, after a household is selected, is the recent birthday method. In a telephone survey, the respondent selection method should be simple, reliable, quick, and not invasive, because the person answering the telephone can easily refuse the interview at the outset. The recent birthday method is a recommended technique for telephone surveys. The interviewer simply asks the question:

> To determine whom to interview, could you tell me, of the people who currently live in your household who are 18 years of age or older, who had the most recent birthday?

The selection method is random and fulfills the equal probability characteristic. O'Rourke and Blair (1983) conducted a telephone survey experiment that compared the recent birthday method with the Kish selection procedure. The results showed a much lower refusal rate for the recent birthday method than for the Kish selection procedure. The respondents' characteristics for the two samples were virtually identical. The birthday method is easy to administer and easy for the informant to answer. Their findings concluded that "the birthday method of respondent selection is an adequate, noninvasive probability procedure" (O'Rourke and Blair 1983, p. 432).

Design Effect and Effective Sample Size

We have discussed some examples of the use of cluster sampling to improve data collection efficiency. We have also alluded to a trade-off between ease of data collection and statistical loss. This is now discussed more fully.

If all the elements within a cluster are identical, there is little to be gained in terms of information by interviewing 100 people instead of 1 person. Unfortunately, it is often the case within a small geographical cluster that the degree of variation is low. This degree of variation in the data affects the statistical efficiency of using cluster sampling.

The similarity, or homogeneity, of the elements within a cluster is generally measured by the intraclass correlation r. The correlation can theoretically range from –1 to +1. But negative correlations are rare, and values between 0 to 0.2 are common in survey research. It varies from one survey question to another, but the value is usually small.

Because a survey is done by a group of interviewers and each is responsible for conducting a portion of the target sample, clustering effect by interviewers is indirectly created. Such clustering may not be part of a sample design but is sufficient to cause the intraclass correlation to be nonzero.

Collins and Butcher (1983) have provided theoretical and empirical discussions regarding the interviewer effect on sample precision. Mathematically, the variance of an estimate based on a cluster sample is $[1 + (m - 1)r]$ times the variance of a simple random sample of the same total size, where m is the number of elements within the cluster. If cluster size varies, then m is the average of such sizes. The square root of this multiplying factor is called the *design factor*.

Each question in a survey can have a different intraclass correlation r. It is not that easy to compute, and the quantity is usually small. Therefore, the design effect is often ignored by survey researchers. However, it is expected that any complex sample design will cause the sampling variance to be larger than that of a simple random sample design.

The idea of multiplying the design factor by the variance of the simple random sample to estimate the likely error is attractive. It avoids the need to perform tedious and difficult variance computation for the complex sample design. Empirical work is needed to establish a typical intraclass correlation and, therefore, the design factor to be used.

Whenever we design a survey, we are confronted with the choice of the sampling methodology and the size of the sample. Each sampling design possesses advantages and disadvantages with respect to the survey requirement. From a theoretical standpoint, choosing a sample design with the smallest variance appears to be trivial. However, the rationalization of the decision in practice often requires consideration of the cost.

A larger sample usually leads to smaller variance but generates a higher field cost. Evaluating this trade-off becomes more difficult when different sampling designs and methodologies are being considered. It adds one more component to the cost and sample size decision model. Market researchers can choose an easier trade-off criterion by asking the question: "For the sample design and sample size under consideration, what is the equivalent sample size using simple random sampling, such that the theoretical variance would be identical?"

By knowing the design effect, we can determine what sample size is needed to produce the same sampling variance using a more complex design, such as cluster sampling, as would be obtained by using a simple random sampling. This is called the *effective sample size*. It is calculated by dividing the actual sample size by the design factor. For the nontechnical market researcher, effective sample size offers an easy-to-understand measure for trading off cost (sample size) and precision when different methodologies are compared.

The use of the effective sample size calculation is not restricted to cluster sampling. With a little bit of algebraic work on the analytical sampling variance function, the effective sample size can be computed for any given design. For example, a disproportionate stratified sample's effective sample size may be calculated as follows:

$$n = \frac{1}{\sum \left(\frac{N_i}{N}\right)^2 \frac{1}{m_i}}$$

where

n = effective sample size,
N_i = population size of the ith stratum,
N = total population, and
m_i = sample size of the ith stratum.

STATISTICAL ESTIMATION AND WEIGHTING

The majority of survey results are presented in terms of averages (means) and percentages. Such calculations are simple arithmetic exercises, in principle. However, when applying such simple arithmetic calculations to survey data, there is a tendency to assume that the data are collected by a survey that has used simple random sampling. This is usually an incorrect assumption.

For every sampling technique, it is necessary to assess how the parameters, such as means and percentages, are computed from the collected data. The mathematical formula used is called the *statistical estimator*. Because different sampling designs and techniques use different selection probabilities from the sample frame, the ultimate selection probability of the elements in the sample will be affected.

To produce a statistically unbiased estimate of the survey parameters, the selection probability must be taken into consideration in a correct manner. Statistically unbiased estimates are important because they enable researchers to make a probability statement about the precision of the survey estimates.

In the case of the simple random sampling technique, every element is selected with equal probability. When this equal probability property is factored into the derivation of the estimator for the mean, no change to the arithmetic average is required. Because a percentage or proportion is just a special case of calculating averages (assigning 1 to present and 0 to absent), no new estimator is needed for percentages. A sampling design that requires no special manipulation of the data to estimate the mean is called a *self-weighting design*. Simple random sampling is one such design. It is always advantageous to develop a self-weighting design, if at all possible, because the potentially complex derivation of the estimator is eliminated and no special estimating computer program is needed to compute the means and percentages.

Some market researchers tend not to concern themselves with statistical estimators. However, there is another type of data adjustment that is more visible, namely, data weighting. On the surface, weighting of survey data appears to be a simple adjustment of data by multiplying different groups of people by a factor. However, the actual development of the weight factor is not trivial. When considering weighting, we should regard the final weights as having two parts. There is a design weight and an adjustment weight. In a lot of cases, the statistical estimator we discussed previously has been incorporated into the design weight part and, therefore, is not noticed by the nonstatistician.

Design Weight

Design weights can be used to correctly estimate the population parameter by taking the sample design into account. Here we use examples of a few sample designs to illustrate this.

The most common situation in which weighting is required is when stratified sampling is used. In a national survey, estimates at the regional (stratum) levels are often required. To ensure reliable estimates at the regional level, adequate sample sizes per region are required. Such sample size requirements at the stratum level can lead to the achieved regional samples being disproportionate to the true distribution. Consider the following numerical example:

	Universe		Sample	
Stratum A	30,000	75%	200	50%
Stratum B	10,000	25%	200	50%

If the data are not statistically weighted, the aggregate sample estimate will be inaccurate and biased. To properly represent the target universe, the sample should have the same proportionality as in the universe for Strata A and B. However the example shows that the sample has underrepresented A but overrepresented B. Although individual stratum estimates are still possible and are correct without weighting, the aggregate sample estimate will be inaccurate.

To correct the aggregate estimate, the Stratum A contribution to the estimate must be increased, and the Stratum B contribution reduced. Numerical factors need to be computed for each stratum such that they will inflate the Stratum A portion of the sample and deflate the Stratum B portion. For Stratum A, the factor is 0.75/0.5 = 1.5, and for Stratum B, the factor is 0.25/0.5 = 0.5. These are design weights.

In general, the statistical weight for the ith stratum in a stratified sample is calculated by dividing the proportionality of the stratum in the universe by the proportionality in the sample:

$$\text{Weight for Stratum } i \ = \ \frac{N_i \, / \, N}{n_i \, / \, n}.$$

N and n denote the universe and sample size, respectively, and N_i and n_i are the corresponding sizes for the ith stratum.

Some survey analysis software do not require the weights to be explicitly calculated. By specifying the universe distribution as part of the computer input, the program will carry out the computation internally and apply them to the data being analyzed.

Another type of design weight is the correction for the respondent selection processes used, as described previously. For example, a face-to-face survey is often started by randomly selecting a household and then selecting a qualified individual at random. This kind of sample involves two random selections from two separate sample frames. The first sample frame is the universe of all households. The second frame is the list of qualified individuals within a selected household. When the survey is intended to represent the population of qualified individuals, the survey analysis must take steps to weight the data.

Suppose the universe consists of households with no more than four adults, distributed as in Table 1. There are 15,000 adults in the one-adult household, 50,000 adults in households with two adults, and so on. When a simple random sample of 1000 households is drawn, the distribution by household type is exactly the same as that in the universe. Because we only interview one randomly selected adult, we will have 1000 individuals in the sample, distributed as in Table 1.

It is clear that people living in one- or two-adult households are over-represented, but those living in larger households are underrepresented.

Table 1
Hypothetical Universe and Sample

Number of People 18 Years of Age or Older in Household	Universe		Sample	
	Households	People	Households	People
1	15,000	15,000	150	150
2	25,000	50,000	250	250
3	30,000	90,000	300	300
4	30,000	120,000	300	300
Total	100,000	275,000	1000	1000

Table 2
Illustration of Selection Probability and Weighting

Number of People 18 Years of Age or Older in Household	Households	People	Probability	Weight	Weighted People
1	150	150	1.0	1.0	150
2	250	250	0.5	2.0	500
3	300	300	0.33	3.0	900
4	300	300	0.25	4.0	1200
Total	1000	1000			2750

For example, the universe has 43.6% of individuals living in four-adult households, but the sample has 30% of these individuals. If the analysis is based on the actual data without applying the design weight, then the results will be incorrect.

To properly weight the data in this example, the selection probability of the individual must be considered. The respondent in the one-adult household has 100% chance of being selected, whereas the one living in the two-adult household has only 50% chance. Table 2 shows the selection probability.

The weight for this second-stage sample is the inverse (reciprocal) of the selection probability. When the weight is applied to the 1000 individuals in the sample, a weighted count of 2750 respondents is obtained. The distribution of the weighted sample of individuals is exactly the same as that of the universe and is the correct way of weighting this kind of sample. This kind of weight factor is referred to as *conversion weight*. The conversion weight is an application of the Horvitz and Thompson's (1952) estimator in sampling theory.

There is a situation in which the conversion weight should not be applied. If the survey estimate is about the universe of households, then the conversion weight should not be used. For example, if we want to estimate the incidence of home security systems, then this piece of information is common across all members of the household and the base for the computation is at the household level, not the individual level. Because the selection of household is based on simple random sampling, which is a self-weighting design, the application of conversion weight would be inappropriate.

It is not unusual for a survey to be designed that will produce both household and individual data. Clearly, it is important that the correct weighting scheme is applied to the populations as is appropriate to the particular data being analyzed.

Adjustment Weights

There are many different reasons the actual sample might not reflect the universe, even after careful execution of the sample plan and proper application of the design weight. Therefore, another type of weighting is used to achieve a sample profile (usually in demographic or regional terms) that is closer to the profile of the target universe. These are called *adjustment weights*.

Adjustment weights should normally be calculated and applied to the sample data to which the design weights have been applied. A multiplying factor is applied to some or all of the respondents in the sample for the purpose of bringing the final weighted sample distribution to mirror that of the universe. The adjustment weight has very little to do with the sample design.

An example of the application of adjustment weights is the alignment of the sample to the age by sex profile of the true population. This is done using a cell-by-cell prorating that is frequently referred to as *cell weighting*. This part of weighting allows manual correction of over- or underrepresentation of certain population segments due to uncontrollable factors such as nonresponse.

Younger people and men are, in general, harder to interview in a survey. As a result, most samples will underrepresent their contribution if the data are left untreated. Adjustment weights provide corrections to the sample on the basis of known universe characteristics. The choice of variables used in adjustment weighting is judgmental and has no probability base. Of all the variables collected by a survey, only a few variables can be considered, because the sample cannot afford to be split into too many cells. Therefore, the choice of the variables is important. They should be appropriate to the purpose of the study, and in this sense, the understanding of the study is as important as any statistical routine.

The judgmental aspect of choosing variables for adjustment weights provides the researcher with the opportunity to increase the "comfort" factor of the data. However, excessive adjustment weighting, in terms of the size of the weight factor and the number of cells, will compromise the random sampling properties. Therefore, adjustment weighting should be applied with prudence. Otherwise, the accuracy of the survey estimates becomes questionable.

Rim Weighting

There are occasions when the researcher regards two or more variables as key, but due to sample size, it is inappropriate to use full matrix weighting, as indicated previously. In such circumstances, a compromise weighting system can be used. This is called *rim weighting*.

An example of applying rim weighting might be in a financial survey in which the critical variables are believed to be ownership of a credit card and personal income. So we wish to align the survey data to known population parameters for those two variables.

The work involved in applying rim weighting has been described by Deming and Stephan (1940), and at that time, it was a complex operation. However, the increase in computing power available today permits rim weighting to be more accessible to survey researchers.

Rim weighting is an iterative process that searches for the adjustment factors that will produce the target marginal distributions simultaneously when the factors are applied to the sample. The process starts by comparing one control variable with the target marginal distribution; on the basis of the comparison, cell weights are determined. This set of weights is retained and applied to the data, the second control variable (weighted) is compared with the second target marginal distribution, and cell weights are again computed and multiplied by the first set of weights. With these fresh combined weights in place, the first control variable is checked again and another set of cell weights for the first variable is determined to be multiplied by those established previously. Retaining the combined weights, the second control variable is considered in a similar way. This process is repeated over and over again until the changes in the weights are negligible.

Deming and Stephan (1940) demonstrated that this method normally converges to the least squares optimization solution. A major advantage of using rim weighting is that target weighting on key variables may proceed even when the targets are not available on an interlaced basis, as required by cell weighting. A larger number of variables can be balanced simultaneously using rim weighting, which cannot be achieved by cell weighting.

Different Countries with Different Methods

The commonly used sampling techniques described in the preceding sections may not necessarily be as prevalent in other countries. It is possible that these techniques may not work as well in other countries. Some of the reasons for this could be related to cultural, economical, or technological factors, as well as to the infrastructure of the society.

Taylor (1995) surveyed 35 leading survey research firms in 13 countries including those in North America and Europe, Australia, Japan, and South Africa. He found that a vast difference exists in standard research practices among the countries.

FUTURE DEVELOPMENTS AND PROBLEMS

The past 20 years have seen a considerable change in the types of surveys used and techniques applied. There is little doubt that the changes over the next 20 years will be greater, though the nature of the change is difficult to predict. However, some of the pressures, problems, and opportunities are already with us, and the resulting changes should be seen within less than 5 years. Therefore, to conclude this chapter, comments are made on several current developments.

Sampling the Internet

Everybody knows the Internet is developing very rapidly. Advertisers and marketers are watching this medium with eagle eyes. Market researchers are no different. From a data collection point of view, putting aside the cost of investment in the technology, the Internet is potentially much cheaper than telephone surveys or even mail surveys.

How to sample Netizens (Internet users)? We have two problems to deal with in order to answer the question. First, if we apply the first principle of sampling, we must have a frame. For the Internet, there is no frame. The Internet user population is constantly growing, and the user profile is changing at the same rapid pace. Three years ago, Netizens were predominantly men. Now, women are becoming a significant part of this population. With the current growth rate, any frame that may exist today will become outdated tomorrow.

Second, by putting up some banner announcements and inviting cooperation with a survey on certain Web pages, the Internet survey is like making a public announcement on the television network. How many people see it and have enough interest to participate is totally out of the researchers' control. The self-selection aspect of those Netizens who respond creates a bias of unknown proportions. Employing the 1-in-kth sample selection will not eliminate self-selection bias. As well, Netizens are notorious for not revealing their identify for privacy reasons. The identity of the person actually responding to the survey can therefore be suspect. Is it really a "he," or is it in fact a "she"? Doing a random survey of Netizens through banner ads or some other similar approach to solicit responses is certainly problematic in terms of data quality.

A possibly efficient and reliable way to survey Netizens may be to approach the issue in the same way as one would in conducting a panel survey. This requires that a special panel of Internet users is established and, in addition, that frequent surveys are made of the general population to update the current profile of the Netizen population. The panel is then adjusted with the introduction of new members.

Sampling Techniques for the Future

The growth of telephone numbers in North America has increased tremendously as more business and residential users are installing additional telephone lines to connect facsimiles and be online with the Internet. The large pool of machine-connected telephone numbers inadvertently translates into a decrease in dialing efficiency of any randomly generated telephone sample. Piekarski, Kaplan, and Prestegaard (1999) have reported their observations of the growth in telephone numbers and the potential impact on RDD sampling in the United States.

A household with multiple telephone lines for both voice and data purposes has a greater chance of being included in any telephone sample compared with a household with a single-line service. This increase in telephone line usage implies that the traditional probability of selection assumption must be reconsidered. Depending on the sampling technique, some extra weighting to compensate for this selection bias is warranted.

Another phenomenon in the telecommunications industry that is having a considerable impact on telephone sampling is the rapid increase in the use of mobile telephones. The decline in ownership cost has transformed and will continue to transform the ownership relationship from "telephone and household" to "telephone and individual."

More and more single-person households will opt for a mobile telephone instead of a standard residential telephone. Also, mobile telephone numbers are not listed anywhere, and they operate with a different set of exchanges. Therefore, a telephone sample with total coverage and without duplication will be more difficult to construct. Considering the growth rate and all these changes in the telecommunications world, we can predict that telephone sampling will face increasingly difficult challenges in the future.

Survey results that are aimed at providing a high level of precision will continue to demand random probability sampling methods. Market research sometimes can compromise precision if the marketer is using the research to provide marketing direction and not to estimate market share. Given the continuous upward trend in refusal rates for random surveys, marketers will become more and more sensitive to the high cost of conducting random population surveys. The push for cost savings will put pressure on the market researcher to search for alternate sampling sources that will have lower refusal rates.

At the same time, computer technology continues to advance rapidly, making it more and more powerful, affordable, and user-friendly. This will create an increasing demand for more information to be on a digital platform. More and more customer databases, consumer databases, and government databases will be available for marketers to access. It is quite likely that we will see mega-databases created by merge–purging many databases within and across industries. Also, consumer panels have characteristics that could make them a natural for the application of such mega-databases. If so, panel sampling may become a very effective and acceptable way of conducting market research.

Appendix
Troldahl-Carter Selection Matrices: Descriptions of Selected Respondent by Household Size

Number of Men 18 Years of Age or Older in Household	Number of Persons 18 Years of Age or Older in Household			
	1	2	3	4 or more
Matrix 1				
0	Woman	Oldest woman	Youngest woman	Youngest woman
1	Man	Man	Man	Oldest woman
2	—	Oldest man	Youngest man	Youngest man
3	—	—	Youngest man	Oldest man
4+	—	—	—	Oldest man
Matrix 2				
0	Woman	Youngest woman	Youngest woman	Oldest woman
1	Man	Man	Oldest woman	Man
2	—	Oldest man	Woman	Oldest woman
3	—	—	Youngest man	Woman or oldest woman
4+	—	—	—	Oldest Man
Matrix 3				
0	Woman	Youngest woman	Oldest woman	Oldest woman
1	Man	Woman	Man	Youngest woman
2	—	Youngest man	Oldest man	Oldest man
3	—	—	Oldest man	Youngest man
4+	—	—	—	Youngest man
Matrix 4				
0	Woman	Oldest woman	Oldest woman	Youngest woman
1	Man	Woman	Youngest woman	Man
2	—	Youngest man	Woman	Youngest woman
3	—	—	Oldest man	Woman or youngest woman
4+	—	—	—	Youngest man

BIBLIOGRAPHY

Biemer, Paul P. (1991), "Measurement Errors in Surveys," in *International Conference on Measurement Errors in Surveys*. New York: John Wiley & Sons.

Brick, J. Michael and Joseph Waksberg (1991), "Avoiding Sequential Sampling with Random Digit Dialing," *Survey Methodology*, 17 (1), 27–41.

Bryant, Barbara E. (1975), "Respondent Selection in a Time of Changing Household Composition," *Journal of Marketing Research*, 12 (May), 129–35.

Collins, M and B. Butcher (1983), "Interviewer and Clustering Effects in an Attitude Survey," *Journal of the Market Research Society*, 25 (1).

Czaja, Ronald, Johnny Blair, and Jutta P. Sebestik (1982), "Respondent Selection in a Telephone Survey: A Comparison of Three Techniques," *Journal of Marketing Research*, 19 (August), 381–85.

Deming, W.E. and F.F. Stephan (1940), "On a Least Squares Adjustment of a Sampled Frequency Table when the Expected Marginal Totals Are Known," *Annuals of Mathematical Statistics*, 2.

Horvitz, D.G. and D.J. Thompson (1952), "A Generalization of Sampling Without Replacement from a Finite Universe," *Journal of the American Statistical Association*, 47, 663–85.

Kish, Leslie (1949), "A Procedure for Objective Respondent Selection Within the Household," *American Statistical Association Journal*, (September), 380–87.

O'Rourke, Diane and Johnny Blair (1983), "Improving Random Respondent Selection in Telephone Surveys," *Journal of Marketing Research*, 20 (November), 428–32.

Piekarski, Linda, Gwen Kaplan, and Jesica Prestegaard (1999), "Telephony and Telephone Sampling: The Dynamics of Change," paper presented at AAPOR Annual Conference, St. Petersburg, FL (May 15).

Stephenson, C. Bruce (1979), "Probability Sampling with Quotas: An Experiment," *Public Opinion Quarterly*.

Sudman, Seymour (1966), "Probability Sampling with Quotas," *Journal of the American Statistical Association*, 61, 749–71.

Taylor, Humphrey (1995), "Horses for Courses: How Survey Firms in Different Countries Measure Public Opinion with Very Different Methods," *Journal of the Market Research Society*, 4 (3).

Thompson, Steven K. and George A.F. Seber (1996), "Adaptive Sampling," *Wiley Series in Probability and Statistics*.

Troldahl, Verling C. and Roy E. Carter Jr. (1964), "Random Selection of Respondents Within Households in Phone Surveys," *Journal of Marketing Research*, 1 (May), 71–76.

Waksberg, Joseph (1978), "Sampling Methods for Random Digit Dialing," *Journal of the American Statistical Association*, 73 (361), 40–46.

SUGGESTED READINGS

INTERNET

Banks, Randy (1998), "The Internet and Market Research: Where Can We Go Today?" paper presented at The Internet, Marketing & Research 5 seminar, Computing Marketing & Research Consultancy Ltd., London (June 8–9).

Coates, Dan and Matthew Froggatt (1997), "On-Line Recruitment & Web Sampling," paper presented at The Internet, Marketing & Research 4 seminar,

Computing Marketing & Research Consultancy Ltd., London (December 15–16).

Coomber, R. (1997), "Using the Internet for Survey Research," *Sociological Research Online*, 2 (2).

Dahlen, Michael (1998), "Controlling the Uncontrollable. Towards the Perfect Web Sample," in *The Book of Papers from the Worldwide Internet Seminar 1998*. Paris: ESOMAR.

Dietrich, Don (1999), "Consumer Segmentation Results Using RDD vs. Mail Panel vs. Internet Sample… There Is A Difference!" paper presented at the 20th Annual Marketing Research Conference, American Marketing Association, San Diego, CA (September 26–29).

Gonier, Dennis E. (1999), "The Emperor Gets New Clothes," in *The Future of Research: Online*. Los Angeles: ARF, 8–13.

Johnson, Tod and Steve Coffey (1998), "New Media Audience Measurement. Sample Design and Recruitment Strategy Considerations," in *The Book of Papers from the Worldwide Internet Seminar 1998*. Paris: ESOMAR.

Schillewaert, N., F. Langerak, and T. Duhamel (1998), "Non Probability Sampling for WWW Surveys: A Comparison of Methods," *Journal of the Market Research Society*, 4 (40), 307–13.

Yoffie, Amy J. (1998), "The 'Sampling Dilemma' Is no Different On-line," *Marketing News*, 32 (8), 16.

OTHER

Kish, Leslie (1910 [1965]), *Survey Sampling*. New York: John Wiley & Sons.

Satin, A. (1993), *Survey Sampling: A Non-Mathematical Guide*, 2d ed. Ottawa: Statistics Canada.

Robert, M.G. (1989), *Survey Errors and Survey Costs*. New York: John Wiley & Sons.

8

Qualitative Research Techniques: Taking the Best of the Past into the Future

Naomi R. Henderson

CURRENT PRACTICES

Born in the 1930s, qualitative market research (QLMR) had a modest childhood. Soap and car manufacturers made the first requests for "group discussions." Respondents sometimes received product samples or coupons in lieu of stipends. The settings were casual and informal. Moderators were more likely to be men than women. "Depth interviewing" was the descriptive term for the process.

As a mature industry, now more than 60 years old, focus groups are still the most common form of QLMR, and the term has become commonplace in the language of Americans (Henderson 1994). Journalists and television reporters now refer to insights from focus groups when reporting on political campaigns. Focus groups are the stimulus for laugh tracks on sitcoms like *Frasier* and *Murphy Brown*. References to focus groups can be found in movies like *Network*, and mock focus groups are part of the "authentic" look to some current ad campaigns for telecommunications and coffee. A billboard in England for a high-priced luxury car has the headline "Rejected by Focus Groups."

Every day, average Americans are calling research companies in their area and asking: "Can you put me in your databank?" Qualitative market research has come a long way from focus groups in the homes of recruiters. Fancy facilities, with state-of-the-art equipment for sending focus group pictures by satellite, make it possible for clients to stay in their home city and see the focus group "live." Telephone focus groups bring the Delphi technique up-to-date with communications technology, and a skilled moderator can listen to tone, pacing, pitch, and volume, as well as the silences between words, to glean nuances to support participants in responding without the use of visual cues. Group sessions with handheld devices blur the line between quantitative and qualitative research. Online focus groups make it possible for everyone to stay right in their offices or at home in pajamas and give new meaning to the concept of "serial interviewing." The only factor missing, to date, is holographic focus groups, and somebody is probably working on that!

Focus groups started in the homes of recruiters and then moved to research settings with small, one-way mirrors and microphones. Facilities have expanded to host backrooms of 18 to 20 people in tiered seating with lighted workstations to plug in laptops to capture data using a variety of software programs. Mirrors are now wall-sized and double thick with expensive video cameras that can be manipulated by operators in another room using joysticks to move in for close-ups and out for long pan shots of the group experience. Stipends have grown from product samples and coupons to cash payments that allow respondents to buy themselves and their families a wonderful meal in a gourmet restaurant or make a hefty payment on one of their credit cards.

Clients are more savvy than in the past, asking moderators to conduct exercises and lines of questioning that get at "how," "in what way," and more than simply "why?" Clients paste easel sheets in the viewing room with headers and pass out colored Post-It notepads to capture "ahas," "new insights," and adjectives that describe products, services, and experiences.

Respondents are asked to do more than just talk about their experiences. They may be asked to draw pictures, create collages, or work in pairs or teams to create new ideas. Business executives are asked to role play products in exercises such as "If this product could talk, what would it say?" Housewives are told to imagine that they are on the Board of Directors for a major corporation and they are charged with selling 1000 more cases of product monthly and must do so without lowering the price! It is amazing to watch moms, who don't work in corporate America, model the behavior of the pompous CEO and the penny-pinching CFO. And it is interesting to see them arguing with the "Director of Research" and the "Marketing VP" about how to move 1000 cases of dog food so that they can be sure to get the quarterly bonus.

The age range of respondents has expanded beyond those in the workplace with salaries to include teens with buying power and children who can provide insights on toys and games and childhood experiences to help companies understand the "youth viewpoint." Seniors are asked to talk about health and insurance and planning for retirement. Individuals way out on the bell curve, such as prostitutes, mothers of triplets, PLAs (People Living With AIDS), and women under 40 who suffer from incontinence, are asked to share their beliefs and experiences in QLMR settings.

In this last decade of the twentieth century, there are some factors related to current practices that can be noted in qualitative research:

- ❏ Group sizes for focus groups are dropping from 12 to 10 respondents down to 8 to 6 respondents as clients discover that "more is not better."
- ❏ Minigroup (4 to 6 people) respondents are on the increase for some types of studies to allow deeper conversations about products, services, issues, and ideas.
- ❏ Shorter sessions are being used (e.g., one hour) focused on one specific aspect, such as an ad campaign and two minor variations.
- ❏ Triads are replacing one-on-ones and dyads to maximize research schedules for observers.
- ❏ Research models of "known pairs" or "friendship pairs" are increasing to mine the rich shared experiences of respondents, both as a dyad model and as several sets within a group.
- ❏ In-house moderators (who work for the client company) are increasing as companies seek ways to maximize research budgets.
- ❏ Requests for PowerPoint presentations of findings are seen more often.
- ❏ Video reports that let respondents "tell the story" are being asked for by clients.
- ❏ "Cheaters and repeaters" (professional respondents) are being weeded out through more diligent methods including database management and more vigilant qualitative researchers.
- ❏ More trained moderators are in the workplace than ever before.
- ❏ Universities are providing degrees in "market research" as a distinct science and working toward building the "body of knowledge" needed in this field.

❏ Clients are asking moderators to elicit more than top-of-mind responses from respondents and to mine second and third levels of perception and belief.

❏ Clients are more "savvy" about QLMR techniques and procedures and ask for more activities in group discussions to better understand respondent viewpoints.

❏ The range of QLMR methodologies is increasing; for example, ethnographic research, once the sole province of anthropologists, is now a common QLMR practice through the use of video cameras, tape recorders, and disposable cameras.

❏ Qualitative consultants are taking training in allied disciplines such as NeuroLinguistic Programming (NLP) or Synectics or courses at the Creative Problem Solving Institute to expand the range of options to offer clients.

❏ The dialogue about certifying qualitative researchers is escalating as the industry ages and standards need to be more concrete in what services clients are buying.

❏ More and more nonprofit organizations are adding QLMR studies to their research requirements to fully meet the needs of the target groups they serve.

❏ Schools and churches are finding QLMR insights useful for short- and long-range planning.

❏ Start-up companies are using QLMR projects to help fine-tune business plans.

❏ Timing for QLMR projects is no longer limited to evenings. Breakfast groups are common at 7:30 A.M., and groups on Saturdays with either kids or adults are on the rise. QLMR sessions at conferences are also on the increase.

❏ Payments to respondents are increasing, and costs for all services in QLMR are increasing.

❏ Clients expect reports to be more than a reporting of what happened, with emphasis on pointing to directions for strategic planning.

❏ Demands for "master moderators" are on the increase — moderators with long histories of moderating and familiarity with multiple product or service categories.

❏ Qualitative research is growing among minority populations, and bilingual moderators are in demand.

❏ QLMR is growing internationally with companies conducting concurrent studies in five or more countries as a traditional research model.

❏ The number of male moderators is increasing as men find the tools to bring active listening models into play.

❏ There is evidence that the traditional consumer is now an "informed consumer" and can talk with knowledge about "product erosion," "maximizing shelf space," and "cannibalizing product lines."

❑ There is acceptance of QLMR as a research tool with the same values for decision making as the more concrete survey data collection models.

(Note: Some of these trends come from informal interviews with members of QRCA, the Qualitative Research Consultants Association, a U.S.-based organization with nearly 800 members in 22 countries at the close of 1999.)

For every 100 qualitative researchers, there are 100 qualitative research techniques, all aimed at providing insights related to POBAs (perceptions, opinions, beliefs, and attitudes) under a broad umbrella of studying social phenomena. Rossman and Rallis (1998) have identified eight characteristics that fit both qualitative research and the individuals who conduct it:

Qualitative Research

1. Takes place in the natural world,
2. Uses multiple methods that respect the humanity of study respondents,
3. Honors what emerges and does not seek to match preconceived plan, and
4. Is fundamentally interpretive.

The Qualitative Researcher

5. Views social phenomena holistically,
6. Reflects on his or her own systematic role in the research,
7. Is sensitive to his or her own biography and how it shapes the research, and
8. Uses complex reasoning that is multifaceted and iterative.

If these eight items are the frame into which all qualitative research models fit (i.e., focus groups, ethnographic research, mock juries, taste tests, and the like), it is clear that many research tools are needed to access respondent POBAs. Using the right tools will provide clients with insights that support long- and short-range planning efforts. Poor use of qualitative tools and techniques makes the qualitative experience a long and onerous affair.

As a trainer of qualitative researchers for the past two decades, it has become necessary to teach the "classic" tools of this industry, as well as keep an eye out for new techniques that provide opportunities to obtain richer answers from consumers and members of target groups.

This chapter focuses not only on "classic" qualitative research techniques, but also on some innovative solutions to getting more than top-of-mind answers from a variety of respondents.

Stages of a Qualitative Interviewing Event

Qualitative market research typically follows the following four stages, regardless of whether the session is a traditional two-hour focus group, a 30-minute in-depth interview, or a six-hour extended session. The four stages simply take more or less time according to the time set aside for the event:

Stage 1: Introduction,

Stage 2: Rapport and reconnaissance,

Stage 3: In-depth investigation, and

Stage 4: Closure.

In Stage 1, the researcher's main activity is to create sufficient and appropriate rapport so that respondents feel safe in sharing POBAs with one another and the researcher. Stage 1 also sets the direction for the discussion, and the moderator demonstrates willingness to listen to diverse points of view without judging.

Stage 2 requires the researcher to provide respondents with a narrowing field of questions that create a floor of understanding about the basic issues being discussed. For example, if the study was about premium dog food and the reasons to buy it rather than store-brand dog food, the Stage 2 discussion would determine such issues as what brands are purchased and for what reasons, as well as the image of specific brands.

Stage 3 starts approximately one-third of the way into the interview and generally takes up the majority of time set aside for the particular research mode. In traditional two-hour focus groups, this section would start at about the 40-minute mark and last until about the 95-minute mark.

Stage 4 is the last portion of the time set aside for the research mode. When done well, it ties up the key insights gleaned thus far in the group. It allows respondents one last forum to come to closure on any ideas previously discussed.

Experienced moderators have a fairly large repertoire of interviewing tactics, which contribute to successful interviewing events. Chief among them are the following qualities:

1. Convey an open, accepting attitude and genuine interest in and respect for each respondent;
2. Allow more open-ended than closed-ended questions;
3. Allow respondents to do most of the talking;
4. Encourage all respondents to participate fully;
5. Encourage respondents to hold and state their own opinions, regardless of what others may believe;

6. Use exercises appropriately to garner deeper information; and

7. Vary behavior to meet demands of each new interviewing event.

Standard Focus Group Elements

As QLMR has evolved from related disciplines of cognitive anthropology, sociology, human ethology, ecological psychology, holistic ethnography, and sociolinguistics (Atkinson, Delamont, and Hammersley 1988; Jacob 1987), it has followed a "standard" framework for interviewing selected target populations. Those elements include the following:

❑ Set timelines (e.g., 120 minutes, 30 minutes, or six hours);

❑ Trained interviewer, moderator, or researcher;

❑ Open-frame format, loose structure that allows for respondent "gold mines" to emerge;

❑ Fixed number of respondents across a series of interview events;

❑ Respondents share common traits;

❑ In group settings, respondents typically do not know one another;

❑ Respondents have "generic" study context, not "specific" context;

❑ Respondents generally receive stipends for participation;

❑ Research setting created in facilities or in the field to accurately document activities and, where possible, provide for observers;

❑ Discussion has a clear purpose and stated desired outcomes;

❑ Four stages for each research interview event;

❑ Allowance for bias of group influence;

❑ Allowance for bias of researcher; and

❑ Knowledge that reported behavior may differ from actual behavior.

Krueger (1988) provides a detailed description of these elements, and Rossman (1999) indicates that though the questions in a focus group setting that embrace these elements may appear "deceptively simple," the goal is to promote participants' expression of their views through the creation of a supportive environment.

In addition, QLMR pulls from disciplines, such as NLP, which is the study of subjective experience. First developed by Bandler and Grinder in the late 1970s, NLP is defined as how human beings generalize, distort, or delete their sensory experience and how they act to produce a given result in themselves or others. It seeks to define or outline the things we do subconsciously or unconsciously and demystifies the outcomes that are created when we think or act (Grinder and Bandler 1976).

The NLP techniques are a good partner to qualitative research techniques. They provide tools to access below top-of-mind responses with the support and approval of respondents because "NLP, like psychology, encompasses the whole spectrum of human behavior" (Chakrapani 1991).

Classic Techniques

Several QLMR practitioners have written about the industry, and Goldman and McDonald (1987) still have one of the clearest definitions:

> qualitative research addresses the nature of structure, attitudes, and motivations, rather than their frequency and distribution ... the underlying goal is to explore, in depth, the feelings and beliefs people hold, and to learn how those feelings shape overt behavior.

To adequately explore feelings and beliefs, an "environment" has to exist in which POBAs can emerge. Five items need to be in place to create that environment:

1. Trust between moderator and respondents,
2. Respect for what respondents have to say,
3. Steady pace to keep discussion moving along,
4. Variety of simple activities that keep interest level up, and
5. Methods of asking questions that do not "lead" respondents.

Because the goal of QLMR is then to explore the feelings and beliefs (or POBAs), classic techniques, like those outlined next, are designed to provide platforms so that respondents can share behavioral and rational information concurrently.

Creating Trust

Levels of trust begin the moment the interviewer sees a participant. That first eye contact on the part of the interviewer should be accompanied by a smile and a sense of welcoming by word and deed. Rapport is deepened in the first stages of the interview event when the following activities take place:

1. State clear purpose;
2. Provide adequate disclosures about mike, mirrors, and observers;
3. Provide key ground rules for participation; and
4. Ask easy opening questions.

Respecting Respondents

Although many observers and some qualitative researchers make fun of respondents, an attitude of respect is a coin that doubles and triples the investment made. It takes a respondent some measure of courage to come out, alone, to a research session in which questions are asked that reveal motivations and beliefs! A good qualitative researcher knows that when true respect is in the interviewing event, the amount of data increases and the depth of that information is often deep and rich. When these classic techniques are in place, the information pool is as large as a lake:

1. Honor the world where the respondent stands,
2. Listen actively, and
3. Suspend judgment.

Maintain a Steady Pace

The "I ask–you answer" model of qualitative interviewing is interesting for about five minutes, and after that, it is more interesting to watch paint dry! When the pace of a qualitative interviewing event is crisp and moves right along, respondents tend to stay interested, and they respect the rigor of planning that means no wasted moments. They learn to answer in headlines rather than novellas, and they tend to be willing to give answers without first overthinking them. Some ways to establish and maintain a steady pace include

1. Changing activities approximately every 20 minutes,
2. Writing and asking good questions and then following up with appropriate probes, and
3. Managing the timeline for the session so respondents work quickly but without rushing.

Provide a Variety of Simple Activities that Keep Interest High

Like the pacing activities, the inclusion of simple activities can keep interest high and forward client learning. The following are just a few:

1. Ask short questions to get long answers,
2. Stand and ask questions from different areas in the room from time to time so "authority" is not rooted in the researcher's chair,
3. Ask questions that access different models of listening,
4. Provide written and spoken instructions for all activities,
5. Find alternatives to charting responses on easel,
6. Use manipulatives to forward discussion (e.g., file cards, product sorts, worksheets),

7. Make abstract content more specific through the use of easel drawings, and

8. Use projective techniques that allow quick access to deeper thinking.

Ask Questions that Don't Lead Respondents

If part of the answer is in the question itself, it is a poor question and "tips off" the respondent as to what is being asked. Directly leading the respondent to conform to a particular viewpoint is risky, as the following two samples illustrate:

Poor Q: You like sport-utility vehicles, right?

Better Q: What do you like about sport-utility vehicles?

Poor Q: Why do you grocery shop on the way home? Is that because it is convenient?

Better Q: When do you usually grocery shop, and what are some reasons for that time frame?

Taylor and Bogdan (1984) list these factors as critical to the interviewing process:

❑ Being nonjudgmental,
❑ Letting people talk,
❑ Paying attention,
❑ Being sensitive,
❑ Probing for clarity,
❑ Using cross-checks to get same data in different ways, and
❑ Staying in rapport throughout the whole session with respondents.

Specific Techniques to Gain More than Top-of-Mind Responses

Every qualitative researcher has a "toolbox" of techniques that fit his or her personality and research style. An interview with any set of ten such researchers would probably find some subset of these common tools:

❑ Product obituaries or eulogies,
❑ Board of Directors,
❑ Sentence completions,
❑ Role-play exercises,
❑ Picture sorts,

❏ Product sorts,

❏ Collages,

❏ Custom worksheets,

❏ Debate teams,

❏ Writing stories,

❏ Drawing exercises,

❏ "What-if" scenarios,

❏ Product transformations,

❏ Comparisons,

❏ Associations,

❏ Secret pooling,

❏ Personifications,

❏ Balloon drawings,

❏ Easel drawings, and

❏ Show/tell items (e.g., concepts).

These activities can be sorted into two categories: visual interventions and process interventions. An "intervention" is any activity that interrupts the "I ask–you answer" model of interviewing. Simple interventions include listing items on an easel and circling one for deeper discussion. A complicated intervention may be making a collage that describes the "personality of a brand."

Visual interventions are those that require respondents to look at existing items and make comments. This could include looking at two different laglines for a product or reviewing a brochure that tells the user how to program the new VCRs on the television screen.

Process interventions are those that require respondents to do something and then talk about what they did. It is in the arena of process interventions that most qualitative researchers either create their own or use traditional models, such as those outlined in the preceding list.

Regardless of what type of intervention is used with respondents, their effectiveness tends to stem from adherence to these procedures:

1. Plan the intervention,

2. Organize the materials,

3. Write instructions for the researcher and participants,

4. Test the intervention if it is new to the researcher,

5. Set aside sufficient time for respondents to complete the exercise quickly but without rushing,

6. Praise the first person to respond,

7. Decide when to use private writing before public disclosure of information by respondents,

8. Remain cognizant of order bias, and

9. Realize that the data come from the discussion following the intervention, not from the intervention itself.

Innovative Techniques

Sometimes researchers need to create new techniques to meet client needs that range from discussions about preparing for death from AIDS to finding new uses for paper towels. Over the years, the following techniques have provided useful respondent insights for a variety of service-, product-, or issue-based QLMR projects.

Open Frame

The simplest form of this technique is to draw a rectangle in the middle of the easel paper, approximately 14 inches by 10 inches. Inside that rectangle, a word or short phrase is placed with ten or so lines radiating out from the edges of the rectangle like spokes from a square wheel. Respondents are asked to either provide a definition of the term or phrase or give an example. This works well when the term or phrase is abstract and has many meanings or definitions. Clients want to see what "pops up" in the aided conversation or hear the "language" of respondents as they provide answers. Some examples of words or phrase tested this way include

❑ Diabetic,

❑ Underinsured, and

❑ Family values.

Once, when a group of teenage girls were asked to indicate ways to prevent teen pregnancy, the conversation "bogged down" and then stopped. The moderator drew a face on the easel in place of the rectangle and gave these instructions:

> This is a 15-year-old teen who lives in the next county. She likes hoop earrings (draw hoops on diagram) and she likes headbands (draw headband on the figure). It is your job as an advisory committee to tell her how to avoid getting pregnant. What would you tell her?

The moderator drew lines radiating out from the face and as fast as the teens talked, key phrases were added to the chart. When the comments (about 20) trickled to a stop, the moderator circled two of the items (implants and birth control pills) and asked the group to talk more about those two items.

This technique illustrates the need to create simple methods to get respondents to access internal information in a new way. Often, the more simple the technique, the less the emphasis is on the process and the more the emphasis is on what respondents have to say.

Getting Over the Wall

Many QLMR projects ask respondents to focus on barriers, obstacles, or impediments to something. Early questions in this arena, such as "what prevents you from...," or "what gets in the way when you...," or "what are some reasons people have problems with...," will promote some conversation, but it can also generate "long stories." To quickly access a variety of obstacles across the experience base of participants, the following technique may be useful:

1. Draw a line down the middle of an easel paper like a side view of a brick wall;
2. On the left side, draw a stick figure facing the line;
3. On the left side of line, draw six to ten arrows that touch the line or "wall",
4. Ask the question: "How many different barriers or obstacles are there to...." As the first set of comments come forth, probe with "what else?"
5. Write the comments on the arrows, working quickly to build a long list fast; and
6. On the right side, mark three items that the group agrees are key obstacles or barriers and discuss those in more detail.

Historical Ally

After introductions, ask respondents to write down the name of someone famous from history who is no longer living but whom they admire. Let them know that later on in the group discussion, they will be calling on that person as support to help solve a problem.

At the appropriate time in the discussion, present the problem (e.g., "How can the state save money on trash pickup services?" or "What can be done to lower health care costs?" or "What would be a good name for this new product?"). Ask respondents to see the problem from the point of view of their historical ally and provide some comments to the room from that viewpoint.

Sample responses include

> Madam Curie would find a way to treat the trash with a chemical wash that will shrink the trash so there is less to take away.

> Abraham Lincoln would tell us that if each one of us paid more attention to the health of our neighbors, we would all be more healthy.

Salvador Dali would tell us to name the product something provocative so that the product would stand out from the competition.

Although the comments may be silly or fanciful, the delivery of such insights opens the door to other comments that are past the range of practical and closer to the arena of "creative problem solving." Sometimes a "detour" can be the shortest route to new information.

CURRENT TRENDS

Widening the Scope of QLMR

As qualitative research enters into another century, traditional focus groups, minigroups, and in-depth interviews are expanding to include other QLMR models.

Ethnographic Research

There is a flurry of interest in ethnographic research with video cameras, digital cameras, and throwaway cameras used by respondents to record bits of their lives prior to the discussion of products, services, and ideas. A car company asks researchers to visit homes of owners and nonowners and determine if there are any differences and to film the environment in which the car plays a role. A cereal company creates a research project that includes visits to families to see how breakfast is fixed and served and to photograph the pantry and the refrigerator contents to enhance the discussion with respondents. A day in the life of a terminally ill patient is filmed and discussed with family members to see what alternatives might be created to lessen stress.

This QLMR research tool is not used by every qualitative researcher, but the technique is definitely on the increase as more and more companies want to know how consumers and target audiences live and hope to gain insights that can be turned into better advertising elements or better products.

Guidelines for ethnographic research include

1. A clear study purpose so that fieldwork variables don't overshadow the research plan.
2. A team approach with one interviewer to talk with respondents and a different researcher to record (audio, video, or notes) insights and comments.
3. Sufficient time at the research setting (e.g., someone's kitchen, test drive in car, coffee shop) to conduct the full interview and sufficient time between interviewing events to allow for travel time, as well as set-up and take-down time.

4. Top-of-the-line recording equipment (audio and/or video), because observers will not be present and transcripts or audio and/or video reports will become the data to be analyzed.

5. A systematic way to keep materials for one interview together. Many researchers find that the large see-through plastic envelopes with string ties allow them to see elements such as recording tapes, disposable cameras, checklists, manipulatives, and stipend checks for respondents. Some researchers use blue envelopes for "users" and yellow envelopes for "nonusers" so that more cues are available for the researcher.

6. A questionnaire or research guide that avoids leading the respondent through a set of preformed ideas. Rather, the guide or research questionnaire should be sufficiently open-ended to promote storytelling, so that the respondents can explain and illuminate their lives and their decisions. A poor ethnographic question is, "What do you like about your car?" A better ethnographic question is, "If you sold your car, what features or qualities would you miss most and for what reasons?"

Known Pairs Research

Friendship pairs, married couples, and mothers with their children are being interviewed to expand on an understanding of how information and knowledge is shared when participants know one another and the barriers of "will I look good in this group setting?" are erased. The interchange between known pairs increases the depth of information about products, services, and ideas.

A manufacturer of nail polish products invited girlfriend pairs and girlfriend trios to a set of interviews in a research facility and asked them to bring their nail polish supplies to "do their nails" while they talked with the moderator. By observing their behavior (e.g., four pads soaked with nail polish remover), the moderator was able to ask the reasons for multiple pads rather than one pad used front and back. The client was able to create product extensions to meet this increased use of solvents.

Watching a family play a new board game and talking aloud about how easy or hard the directions were provided game developers with insights missed in the design stage.

A researcher needs to stay alert to "gold mines" of information in the interstitial conversations between respondents, as well as to the respondents' replies to the interviewer, while resisting the temptation to "join the conversation."

Extended Groups

Clients sometimes complain about having insufficient time to delve deeply into respondent POBAs, and if the sessions were longer, then more discussion about and among issues would be possible. To meet those needs, respondents are invited to attend sessions that last two to three hours in some cases and four to six hours in other situations.

In the extended sessions, respondents often complete behavioral tasks, such as collages and storyboards, or engage in creative activities, such as modeling in clay or drawing stories, that access more than top-of-mind experiences. On occasion, they may work in pairs or teams to complete a task.

Sometimes they participate in "field trips" during the research period, such as meeting at a facility and discussing shoe buying patterns of the past. After that initial 30-minute discussion, they enter a van and are driven to a nearby mall and given money to shop for shoes at a specific store while observers "eavesdrop" on the process. On the ride back to the facility, the participants compare shoes purchased and talk about how much money they saved. When the formal discussion resumes, specific questions are asked about elements of the shopping experience and factors about the store layout, helpfulness of staff, and pricing.

Another study might invite participants to a large parking lot with instructions to get into nine different cars and rate the ease/difficulty of buckling the seat belt, while an interviewer records notes and comments on a checklist form. When all respondents have tested all cars, they convene for a focus group discussion on specific cars with memory aids of photos and seat belt systems.

A toothpaste company asks respondents to meet for a four-hour session and build two collages. One collage presents images of how they see a specific brand, and the second collage is based on reading a concept statement that positions the brand on a whole new platform.

These longer sessions allow a wide range of topics and activities to be covered in detail without having to rush through a guide to keep to the 90- or 120-minute deadlines of standard focus group sessions. These longer sessions also allow for a fuller creative expression of insights to be gleaned from respondents.

Piggyback Groups

When one group of respondents watches a group and then is interviewed in turn, the "piggyback" research mode relies on current behavioral experiences rather than reported experiences. For example, a group of dentists in the same practice view a focus group of a set of patients that visited the practice during the past year. The patients are told that their dentist, along with others, is behind the mirror. Questions about the practice, as a whole, start off the session until respondents feel comfortable making positive and negative statements without judgment by the moderator. Specific comments on "how my dentist does X" are saved until later in the discussion. When the patients leave the research facility, the dentists are then interviewed about what they heard, using "live data" as a background for their comments.

A much deeper discussion about patient POBAs is possible when the dentists are talking about the patient group comments rather than remembering incidents or feelings from the past. To keep patients from being uncomfortable when talking about "my doctor" when they know he or she is behind the mirror, the moderator needs to put in place a clear set of guidelines for participation that encourages a range of comments without devolving into a "bash session."

Mock Juries

In this QLMR process, two sets of "jurors" are convened, and each hears a different strategy on the same case points. Then each deliberates, allowing lawyers to be "flies on the wall" in the jury deliberation process to see how case points and strategies affect the final votes.

Typically, this process is done on a Saturday and a Sunday because it can take as long as six hours for "jurors" to hear plaintiff and defendant case points, deliberate on those case points, and reconvene to discuss reasons for voting as they did. A fair amount of role playing is required for this research tool. For example, one lawyer has to play "judge" and instruct the jury. Another lawyer has to play a role different from his or her regular legal function (e.g., a defense firm doesn't have plaintiff lawyers on staff as a rule, so someone must pretend to be a plaintiff lawyer to make the case points for the mock jurors).

Mock juries typically have a long planning period (e.g., jurors must be found that are similar in most ways to the actual jury that could be seated for the actual trial), and time must be allotted for the legal team to create two distinct strategies for trying the case. In addition, a larger research facility is required because the room is often set up like an actual courtroom to give lawyers the practice they need in making case points and simulate the jury process for the participants. Additional time is also needed to recruit respondents for longer-than-average sessions.

Mock juries are worth every dollar they cost in cases in which a great deal of money rides on the outcome. A wrongful death suit is a good example of the value of using a mock jury process: A widow is asking for $9 million in damages from a bus company. A city bus ran up on the curb, striking and killing her husband. The law firm defending that widow needed to know which legal strategy would move it closer to the outcome it desired.

Mock juries are also useful in those cases in which it is unclear where sympathy might rest for the defendant. A good example is a case in which a teenage boy ran into a roof support stanchion in his high school gym during a basketball game and suffered a concussion that later caused his death. The parents sued the school. The legal firm for the school needed to know where the sympathy rested in the case: with the parents for losing their child or with the school that had been in the community for 55 years with no other accidents of this type on record.

When the outcome of a case depends on factors that verge on the emotional response of jurors rather than clear-cut case points, mock juries are an emerging way to "test the waters." Law firms use them to decide before committing to taking on a client or to choose an approach to mount at the actual trial.

Harnessing the Internet for QLMR Projects

Online focus groups, which use the power of the Internet to pull respondents from different states and countries into one linked session to report POBAs through cyberspace, provide a modern version of the Delphi technique.

Questions are emerging about the best uses for this type of research. Early adopters of this research tool are companies that are already using the Internet as a sales opportunity, such as car manufacturers, travel service companies, and companies that market communication products. A rising market for this type of research also includes users of catalog services and education programs. Also, children's research is growing in this field because computers are so commonplace in homes and schools and an easy medium to reach children. Corporations are exploring ways to reach busy executives and harried decision makers right at their desks.

Problems that have emerged include creating firewalls so that findings and raw data cannot be extracted by nonvested parties and ways to ensure that the respondent recruited is the respondent on the other end of the modem.

Some *Fortune* 500 companies are using this methodology to enhance findings discovered in face-to-face groups. Some recent uses include concept testing, customer service insights, feature testing of new products, Web page testing, and package testing.

Another barrier that must be overcome is the initial poor quality of "virtual qualitative facilities" and the resultant bad press of those early offerings. Although second- and third-generation technological advances have much improved the services of online focus groups, the initial problems still remain in the minds of some research buyers. As this technique increases in usage, the role of the moderator will change from listener to active participant, and a new hybrid researcher will be born.

Ad Labs

This is a streamlined focus group in which the entire focus is on one aspect of an advertising campaign. It could be the testing of a range of advertising approaches, or one campaign with five different taglines, or one approach with four different talent shots. Because the entire focus is on the impact of a campaign and its variations, there is little need for product background questions on product usage or image.

Groups are typically one hour or 75 minutes in length, and typically, three or four are conducted in one day. All the same tools and techniques of traditional focus groups are in place for this mode of QLMR, and advertising agencies are typically thrilled to have the whole focus on the communications component and not the attitude and usage elements of traditional research.

Although this list does not contain every new methodology, it does outline some of the more common ones and provides some insights into applications.

What Is the Future of QLMR Techniques?

In the last 10 to 15 years, the area of techniques and methods in QLMR has exploded. Some techniques were developed in response to client needs and some to handle the shifts in technology and communication. Techniques should not be confused with "tricks" or games to play on respondents (Henderson 1994). Appropriate QLMR techniques are ones that meet these criteria:

❑ Have a clear purpose,

❑ Provide a specific outcome related to study objectives,

❑ Allow respondents to participate in a way that does not demean or belittle them or their experiences,

❑ Are conducted by an experienced and trained moderator, and

❑ Move understanding about consumer behavior to a new and deeper level.

Some techniques have been borrowed from psychology or NLP. Some have been creatively developed to fit the information needs of specific companies or industries. In the hands of inexperienced moderators, these techniques can "bomb" when they are used without testing. Sometimes moderators feel pressured to show off a technique to entertain clients or create a sense of something proprietary to impress clients. Creative techniques used to "showcase" a moderator are also risky, and doubly so when that technique can be potentially damaging to respondents who are then held up to ridicule by the backroom when they fail to understand what is wanted or needed.

The Washington Post carried an article (Carlson 1993) entitled "Hocus Focus" in which consumers were demeaned in print. Part of the problem stemmed from the fact that neither the client observers nor the reporter they allowed to view the session understood the research underpinnings, and the moderator "played to the backroom" rather than held the flag for research rigor. That moderator did not serve as a good gatekeeper for the protection of respondents, and "moderating techniques" were done for "showtime quality" rather than as a legitimate research tool.

Barry Feig (1989), in an article for *American Demographics*, cautions researchers to avoid entertaining the client. He states that many researchers are afraid they might bore the client. He further cautions that "bored groups" or groups that don't go well are all part of the process of learning the respondents' viewpoints. One "aha" in a series may be worth the trip. Such was the case in the Arm & Hammer famous baking-soda-in-the-refrigerator campaign. A chance comment in a fairly dull focus group was the inspiration. The backroom was listening and built on the insight.

In the quest for "new, different, and better," qualitative researchers may erroneously place emphasis on the technique rather than the outcome produced.

SUMMARY

As the twentieth century blends into the twenty-first, qualitative researchers can look to the past and take forward classic techniques such as building rapport and respecting respondents, along with standard interventions, such as Board of Directors. Although new techniques will be added to the classic basics outlined in this chapter, qualitative researchers should always measure the benefits of doing "something new" against the gains it could provide and remember that new does not necessarily mean better. Good baseline QLMR techniques will go a long way to understanding the target groups that buy the products and services offered in the marketplace.

BIBLIOGRAPHY

Atkinson, P., S. Delamont, and M. Hammersley (1988), "Qualitative Research Traditions: A British Response to Jacob," *Review of Educational Research*, 58.

Carlson, Peter (1993), "Hocus Focus," *Washington Post Sunday Magazine*, (February 14), 21.

Chakrapani, C. (1991), "NLP & Its Applications to Marketing Research," *Canadian Journal of Marketing Research*, 10, 81.

Feig, B. (1989), "How to Run A Focus Group," *American Demographics*, (December), 31.

Goldman, A.E. and S.S. McDonald (1987), *The Group Depth Interview: Principles and Practice*. Englewood Cliffs, NJ: Prentice Hall.

Grinder, J. and R. Bandler (1976), *The Structure of Magic*. Palo Alto, CA: Science & Behaviour Books.

Henderson, N.R. (1994), "Asking Effective Focus Group Questions," *Quirk's Marketing Research Review*, 8 (December), 34.

Jacob, E. (1987), "Qualitative Research Traditions: A Review," *Review of Educational Research*, 51.

Krueger, R.A. (1988), *Focus Groups: A Practical Guide For Applied Research*. Newbury Park, CA: Sage Publications.

Rossman, G.B. and S.F. Rallis (1998), *Learning in the Field: An Introduction to Qualitative Research*. Thousand Oaks, CA: Sage Publications.

Taylor, S.J and R. Bogdan (1984), *Introduction to Qualitative Research Methods: The Search for Meanings*. New York: John Wiley & Sons.

SUGGESTED READINGS

Bandler, R. and J. Grinder (1979), *Frogs Into Princes*. Moab, UT: Real People Press.
——, ——, R. Dilts, and J. DeLozier (1980), *NeuroLinguistic Programming: Vol. 1, The Study of the Structure of Subjective Experience*. Cupertino, CA: Meta Publications.
Bronson, G. (1987), "Focus Groups for Lawyers," *Forbes*, (September 21), 70.
Collis, C. (1996), "Confessions of A Telephone Focus Group Skeptic," *Quirk's Marketing Research Review*, 10 (May), 12.
Dilts, R. (1983) *Applications of NeuroLinguistic Programming*. Cupertino, CA: Meta Publications.
Fern, E.F. (1982), "The Use of Focus Groups for Idea Generation: The Effects of Group Size, Acquaintanceship and Moderator on Response Quality and Quantity," *Journal of Marketing Research*, 19 (February), 67.
Fuller, G. (1996), "Qualitative Introductions: An Annotated Script For Meeting and Welcoming Focus Group Respondents," *Quirk's Marketing Research Review*, 10 (December), 17.
Gordon, R.L. (1980) *Interviewing Strategies, Techniques & Tactics*. Homewood, IL: The Dorsey Press.
Gordon, W. and R. Langmaid (1988), *Qualitative Market Research: A Practitioner's & Buyer's Guide*. Aldershot, UK: Gower.
Grinder, J. and R. Bandler (1981), *Trance-Formations. Neuro-Linguistic Programming and the Structure of Hypnosis*. Moab, UT: Real People Press.
Greenbaum, T.L. (1988), *The Practical Handbook & Guide to Focus Group Research*. Lexington, MA: Lexington Books.
Henderson, N.R. (1988), "Client Ground Rules for Observing Focus Groups," *Quirk's Marketing Research Review*, 2 (December), 14–17.
—— (1990), "Qualities of a Master Moderator," *Quirk's Marketing Research Review*, 4 (December), 19–20.
—— (1991), "Focus Groups for the Last Decade of the Twentieth Century," *Marketing Research: A Magazine of Management & Applications*, 3 (June), 11–17.
—— (1992), "Trained Moderators Boost the Value of Qualitative Market Research," *Marketing Research: A Magazine of Management & Applications*, 4 (June), 26–30.
—— (1995), "A Practical Approach to Analyzing and Reporting Focus Group Studies: Lessons from Qualitative Market Research," *Qualitative Health Research Journal*, 5 (4), 463–77.
—— (1998), "The Magic of Eight," *Quirk's Marketing Research Review*, 12 (December), 18–19.
—— (1999), "The Art & Science of Qualitative Research," working paper, Bethesda, MD.
Langer, J. (1991), "Focus Groups," *American Demographics*, (February), 23.
Merton, R.K. (1990), *The Focused Interview: A Manual of Problems & Procedures*. New York: The Free Press.
Patton, M.Q. (1990), *Qualitative Evaluation and Research Methods*, 2d ed. Newbury Park, CA: Sage Publications.
Rausch, M.J. (1997) "Qualities of a Beginning Moderator," *Quirk's Marketing Research Review*, 11 (December), 11.
Schnee, R.K. (1982), "Follow These Six Rules When Doing Qualitative Research for Evaluating New Product Ideas," *Marketing News*, (January 22), 6.
Templeton, J.F. (1994), *Focus Groups: A Guide for Marketing & Advertising Professionals*. Chicago: Probus Publishing.

Part III
Analyzing Data

Data analysis is the first major step in converting data into knowledge. Analyzing data, more than any other aspect of marketing research, has been the main concern of marketing researchers in recent years. Although techniques of marketing research—sampling, data collection, and the like—have not changed very much in recent years, techniques of data analysis have. The application of sophisticated techniques of data analysis, which began accelerating during the late 1960s, continues to be of central importance in marketing research. Not coincidentally, the growth of complex analysis in marketing research parallels the growing availability of inexpensive computing power.

Basic to data analysis in marketing research is the use of univariate and bivariate analysis. Most data analysis had been and still is based on cross-tabulations that describe the relationship between a dependent and an independent variable (e.g., the relationship between product usage and gender, the relationship between product usage and income). The accelerating access to computing power over the past 30 years or so has made it possible for us to go beyond univariate and bivariate analysis into multivariate analysis. Now we can answer many questions that cannot be answered using univariate and bivariate procedures, in addition to being able to analyze scores of variables simultaneously. Naresh Malhotra describes the basic and advanced techniques of quantitative data analysis in Chapters 9 and 10.

Another recent development in data analysis is the application of computer-aided techniques to qualitative data. Ian Dey of University of Edinburgh guides the reader through this fascinating new field. Dey (Chapter 11) discusses grounded theory, first proposed by Glaser and Strauss, in the current context to qualitative data analysis.

It is often said that "a picture is worth a thousand words." Unfortunately, not all pictures qualify for this distinction. So what is the role of graphics? In Chapter 12, Brian Everitt describes various graphical methods: pie charts, dot plots, histograms, stem-and-leaf, boxplots, scatterplots, and coplots. He discusses the application of scatterplots on derived variables as obtained in principal components analysis and correspondence analysis. Everitt effectively demonstrates the power of graphical methods in data analysis and presentation.

9
Quantitative Data Analysis: Univariate Techniques

Naresh K. Malhotra

We present a classification of statistical techniques. Then we discuss the major univariate techniques. We begin with frequency distribution, a basic but very useful procedure. Then we focus on tests of differences, discussing the parametric as well as the nonparametric tests in the case of one sample, two independent samples, and paired samples.[1]

A CLASSIFICATION OF STATISTICAL TECHNIQUES

Statistical techniques can be classified as univariate or multivariate. Univariate techniques are appropriate when there is a single measurement of each element in the sample or there are several measurements of each element, but each variable is analyzed in isolation. Multivariate techniques, in contrast, are suitable for analyzing data when there are two or more measurements of each element and the variables are analyzed simultaneously. Multivariate techniques are concerned with the simultaneous relationships among two or more phenomena. Multivariate techniques differ from univariate techniques in that they shift the focus away from the levels (averages) and distributions (variances) of the phenomena

---

[1]This material is based on Malhotra, Naresh K. (1999), *Marketing Research: An Applied Orientation*, 3d ed. Upper Saddle River, NJ: Prentice Hall. The reader should consult this text for more details, including numerical illustrations.

and concentrate instead on the degree of relationships (correlations or covariances) among these phenomena. We show how the various techniques relate to one another in an overall scheme of classification.

Univariate techniques can be classified on the basis of whether the data are metric or nonmetric. Metric data are measured on an interval or ratio scale. Nonmetric data are measured on a nominal or ordinal scale. These techniques can be further classified on the basis of whether one or two or more samples are involved. It should be noted here that the number of samples is determined on the basis of how the data are treated for the purpose of analysis, not how the data were collected. For example, the data for men and women may well have been collected as a single sample, but if the analysis involves an examination of sex differences, two sample techniques will be used. The samples are independent if they are drawn randomly from different populations. For the purpose of analysis, data pertaining to different groups of respondents (e.g., men and women) are generally treated as independent samples. However, the samples are paired when the data for the two samples relate to the same group of respondents.

For metric data, when there is only one sample, the z-test and the t-test can be used. When there are two or more independent samples, the z-test and t-test can be used for two samples and one-way analysis of variance (one-way ANOVA) for more than two samples. In the case of two or more related samples, the paired t-test can be used. For nonmetric data involving a single sample, frequency distribution, chi-square, Kolmogorov-Smirnov (K-S), runs, and binomial tests can be used. For two independent samples with nonmetric data, the chi-square, Mann-Whitney, Median, K-S, and Kruskal-Wallis one-way ANOVA (K-W ANOVA) can be used. In contrast, when there are two or more samples, the sign, McNemar, and Wilcoxon tests should be used (see Figure 1).

FREQUENCY DISTRIBUTION

Marketing researchers often need to answer questions about a single variable. For example,

❑ How many users of the brand can be characterized as brand loyal?

❑ What percentage of the market consists of heavy users, medium users, light users, and nonusers?

❑ How many customers are very familiar with a new product offering? How many are familiar, somewhat familiar, and unfamiliar with the brand? What is the mean familiarity rating? Is there much variance in the extent to which customers are familiar with the new product?

❑ What is the income distribution of brand users? Is this distribution skewed toward low-income brackets?

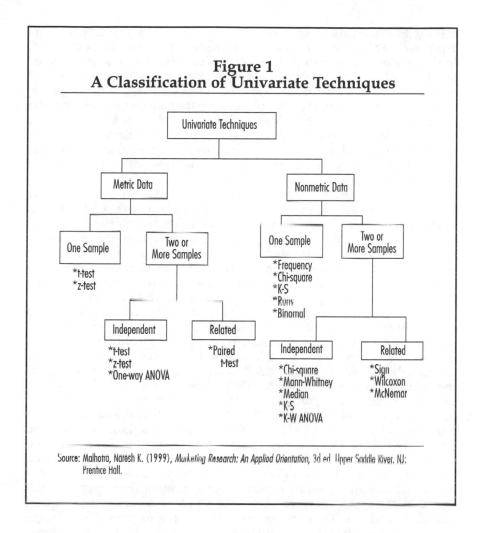

Figure 1
A Classification of Univariate Techniques

Source: Malhotra, Naresh K. (1999), *Marketing Research: An Applied Orientation*, 3d ed. Upper Saddle River, NJ: Prentice Hall.

The answers to these kinds of questions can be determined by examining frequency distributions. In a frequency distribution, one variable is considered at a time. The objective is to obtain a count of the number of responses associated with different values of the variable. The relative occurrence, or frequency, of different values of the variable is expressed in percentages. A frequency distribution for a variable produces a table of frequency counts, percentages, and cumulative percentages for all the values associated with that variable.

A frequency distribution helps determine the extent of item nonresponse. It also indicates the extent of illegitimate responses. If a variable has been measured on a 1-to-7 scale and 9 has been assigned to missing values, values of 0 and 8 would be illegitimate responses, or errors. The cases with these values could be identified and corrective action taken. The presence of outliers or cases with extreme values can also be detected. In the case of a frequency distribution of household size, a few isolated families with household sizes of ten or more people might be considered outliers. A frequency distribution also indicates the shape of the empirical distribution of the variable. The frequency data may be used to construct a histogram or a vertical bar chart in which the values of the variable are portrayed along the x-axis and the absolute or relative frequencies of the values are placed along the y-axis. From the histogram, one could examine whether the observed distribution is consistent with an expected or assumed distribution.

The most commonly used statistics associated with frequencies are measures of location (mean, mode, and median), variability (range, interquartile range, standard deviation, and coefficient of variation), and shape (skewness and kurtosis). The measures of location that marketing researchers are most interested in are measures of central tendency, because they tend to describe the center of the distribution. If the entire sample is changed by adding a fixed constant to each observation, then the mean, mode, and median change by the same fixed amount.

The measures of variability, which are calculated on interval or ratio data, include the range, interquartile range, variance or standard deviation, and coefficient of variation. The range measures the spread of the data. It is simply the difference between the largest and smallest values in the sample. As such, the range is directly affected by outliers. The interquartile range is the difference between the 75th and 25th percentile. For a set of data points arranged in order of magnitude, the pth percentile is the value that has p% of the data points below it and (100 − p)% above it. If all the data points are multiplied by a constant, the interquartile range is multiplied by the same constant. The variance is the mean squared deviation from the mean, and it can never be negative. When the data points are clustered around the mean, the variance is small. When the data points are scattered, the variance is large. If all the data values are multiplied by a constant, the variance is multiplied by the square of the constant. The standard deviation is the square root of the variance. Thus, the standard deviation is expressed in the same units as the data rather than in squared units. The coefficient of variation is the ratio of the standard deviation to the mean expressed as a percentage, and it is a unitless measure of relative variability. The coefficient of variation is meaningful only if the variable is measured on a ratio scale.[2]

In addition, measures of shape are also useful in understanding the nature of the distribution. The shape of a distribution is assessed by examining skewness and kurtosis. Skewness is the tendency of the deviations from the mean to be larger in one direction than in the other. It can be

---

[2]See any introductory statistics book for a more detailed description of these statistics, for example, Berenson and Levine (1999).

thought of as the tendency of one tail of the distribution to be heavier than the other. Kurtosis is a measure of the relative peakedness or flatness of the curve defined by the frequency distribution. The kurtosis of a normal distribution is zero. If the kurtosis is positive, then the distribution is more peaked than a normal distribution. A negative value means that the distribution is flatter than a normal distribution. Most computer programs for running frequencies will calculate and print all these statistics.

Hypotheses Testing Related to Differences

We focus on hypotheses testing related to differences. Hypotheses related to associations are covered in Chapter 10, on multivariate analysis.[3] A classification of hypothesis testing procedures for examining differences is presented in Figure 2. Note that Figure 2 is consistent with the classification of univariate techniques presented in Figure 1. The major difference is that Figure 1 also accommodates more than two samples and thus deals with techniques such as one-way ANOVA and K-W ANOVA, whereas Figure 2 is limited to no more than two samples. Also, one-sample techniques, such as frequencies, that do not involve statistical testing are not covered in Figure 2. (Note that one-way ANOVA is discussed in Chapter 10, because it provides a foundation for discussing ANOVA and MANOVA.)

Hypothesis testing procedures can be broadly classified as parametric or nonparametric on the basis of the measurement scale of the variables involved. Parametric tests assume that the variables of interest are measured on at least an interval scale. Nonparametric tests assume that the variables are measured on a nominal or ordinal scale. These tests can be further classified on the basis of whether one or two or more samples are involved, as explained previously.

The most popular parametric test is the t-test, conducted to examine hypotheses about means. The t-test could be conducted on the mean of one or two samples of observations. In the case of two samples, the samples could be independent or paired. Nonparametric tests based on observations drawn from one sample include the K-S test, the chi-square test, the runs test, and the binomial test. In the case of two independent samples, the Mann-Whitney U-test, the median test, and the K-S two-sample test are used for examining hypotheses about location. These tests are nonparametric counterparts of the two-group t-test. For paired samples, nonparametric tests include the Wilcoxon matched-pairs signed-ranks test and the sign test. These tests are the counterparts of the paired t-test. Parametric as well as nonparametric tests are also available for evaluating hypotheses relating to more than two samples (Sirkin 1994).

---

[3]Excellent discussions of ways to analyze cross-tabulation associations can be found in Hellevik (1984).

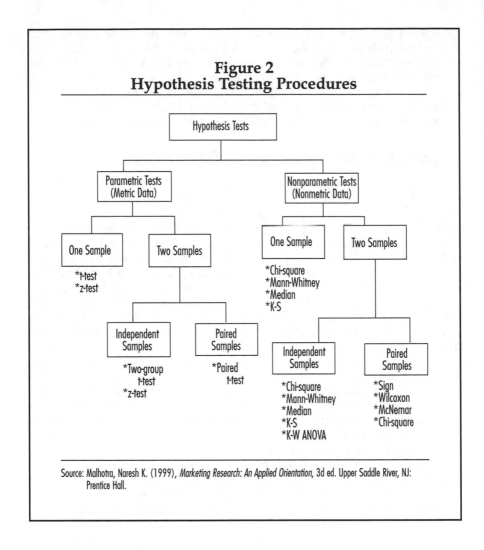

Figure 2
Hypothesis Testing Procedures

Source: Malhotra, Naresh K. (1999), *Marketing Research: An Applied Orientation*, 3d ed. Upper Saddle River, NJ: Prentice Hall.

Parametric Tests

Parametric tests provide inferences for making statements about the means of parent populations. A t-test is commonly used for this purpose. This test is based on Student's t-statistic. The t-statistic assumes that the variable is normally distributed, the mean is known (or assumed to be known), and the population variance is estimated from the sample. Assume that the random variable X is normally distributed, with mean μ and unknown population variance σ^2, which is estimated by the sample variance s^2. Recall that the standard deviation of the sample mean, $\overline{X}$, is estimated as $s_{\overline{X}} = s/\sqrt{n}$. Then, $t = (\overline{X} - \mu)/s_{\overline{X}}$ is t distributed with $n - 1$ degrees of freedom.

The t distribution is similar to the normal distribution in appearance. Both distributions are bell-shaped and symmetric. However, as compared with the normal distribution, the t distribution has more area in the tails and less in the center. This is because population variance σ^2 is unknown and is estimated by the sample variance s^2. Given the uncertainty in the value of s^2, the observed values of t are more variable than those of z, the standard normal variate. Thus, we must proceed a larger number of standard deviations away from 0 to encompass a certain percentage of values from the t distribution than is the case with the normal distribution. Yet, as the number of degrees of freedom increases, the t distribution approaches the normal distribution. In fact, for large samples of 120 subjects or more, the t distribution and the normal distribution are virtually indistinguishable. Although normality is assumed, the t-test is quite robust to departures from normality.

The procedure for hypothesis testing for the special case when the t-statistic is used is as follows:

1. Formulate the null (H_0) and the alternative (H_1) hypotheses.
2. Select the appropriate formula for the t-statistic.
3. Select a significance level, α, for testing H_0. Typically, the 0.05 level is selected.
4. Take one or two samples, and compute the mean and standard deviation for each sample.
5. Calculate the t-statistic assuming H_0 is true.
6. Calculate the degrees of freedom and estimate the probability of getting a more extreme value of the statistic. (Alternatively, calculate the critical value of the t-statistic.)
7. If the probability computed in Step 5 is smaller than the significance level selected in Step 2, reject H_0. If the probability is larger, do not reject H_0. (Alternatively, if the value of the calculated t-statistic in Step 4 is larger than the critical value determined in Step 5, reject H_0. If the calculated value is smaller than the critical value, do not reject H_0.) Failure to reject H_0 does not necessarily imply that H_0 is true. It only means that the true state is not significantly different from that assumed by H_0.
8. Express the conclusion reached by the t-test in terms of the marketing research problem.

We illustrate the general procedure for conducting t-tests in the following sections, beginning with the one-sample case (Cowles and Davis 1982; Verma and Goodale 1995).

One Sample

In marketing research, the researcher is often interested in making statements about a single variable compared with a known or given standard. Examples of such statements include the following: the market share for a new product will exceed 15%, at least 65% of customers will like a new package design, or 80% of dealers will prefer the new pricing policy. These statements can be translated to null hypotheses that can be tested using a one-sample test, such as the t-test or the z-test. In the case of a t-test for a single mean, the researcher is interested in testing whether the population mean conforms to a given hypothesis (H_0). The appropriate test statistic may be calculated as

$$t = (\overline{X} - \mu)/s_{\overline{X}}.$$

Note that if the population standard deviation was assumed to be known, rather than estimated from the sample, a z-test would be appropriate. In this case, the value of the z-statistic would be

$$z = (X - \mu)/\sigma_{\overline{X}}.$$

In the case of testing a hypothesis related to a population proportion, π, the t-statistic is estimated using the sample proportion, p, as follows:

$$t = (p - \pi)/s_p,$$

where

$$s_p = \sqrt{\frac{p(1 - p)}{n}}.$$

Two Independent Samples

Several hypotheses in marketing relate to parameters from two different populations. For example, the users and nonusers of a brand differ in their perceptions of the brand, high-income consumers spend more on entertainment than low-income consumers, or the proportion of brand loyal users in segment 1 is greater than the proportion in segment 2. Samples drawn randomly from different populations are termed "independent samples." As in the case for one sample, the hypotheses could relate to means or proportions.

Means. In the case of means for two independent samples, the hypotheses take the following form:

$$H_0: \mu_1 = \mu_2.$$

$$H_1: \mu_1 \neq \mu_2.$$

The two populations are sampled and the means and variances computed on the basis of samples of sizes n_1 and n_2. If both populations are found to have the same variance, a pooled variance estimate is computed from the two sample variances, as follows:

$$s^2 = \frac{\sum_{i=1}^{n_1} (X_{n1} - \overline{X}_1)^2 + \sum_{i=1}^{n_2} (X_{n2} - \overline{X}_2)^2}{n_1 + n_2 - 2}.$$

The standard deviation of the test statistic can be estimated as

$$s_{\overline{X}_1 - \overline{X}_2} = \sqrt{s^2 \left(\frac{1}{n_1} + \frac{1}{n_2} \right)}.$$

The appropriate value of t can be calculated as

$$t = \frac{(\overline{X}_1 - \overline{X}_2) - (\mu_1 - \mu_2)}{s_{\overline{X} - X_2}}.$$

The degrees of freedom in this case are $(n_1 + n_2 - 2)$.

If the two populations have unequal variances, an exact t cannot be computed for the difference in sample means. Instead, an approximation of t is computed. The number of degrees of freedom in this case is usually not an integer, but a reasonably accurate probability can be obtained by rounding to the nearest integer.

An F-test of sample variance may be performed if it is not known whether the two populations have equal variance. In this case, the hypotheses are

$$H_0: \sigma_1^2 = \sigma_2^2.$$

$$H_1: \sigma_1^2 \neq \sigma_2^2.$$

The F-statistic is computed from the sample variances as follows:

$$F_{(n_1 - 1), (n_2 - 1)} = \frac{s_1^2}{s_2^2},$$

where

n_1 = size of sample 1,

n_2 = size of sample 2,

$n_1 - 1$ = degrees of freedom for sample 1,

$n_2 - 1$ = degrees of freedom for sample 2,

s_1^2 = sample variance for sample 1, and

s_2^2 = sample variance for sample 2.

As can be seen, the critical value of the F distribution depends on two sets of degrees of freedom: those in the numerator and those in the denominator. If the probability of F is greater than the significance level α, H_0 is not rejected, and t based on the pooled variance estimate can be used. However, if the probability of F is less than or equal to α, H_0 is rejected and t based on a separate variance estimate is used.

A similar test is available for testing the difference between proportions for two independent samples.

Proportions. In the case involving proportions for two independent samples, the null and alternative hypotheses are

$$H_0: \pi_1 = \pi_2.$$

$$H_1: \pi_1 \neq \pi_2.$$

A z-test is used, as in testing the proportion for one sample. However, in this case, the test statistic is given by

$$Z = \frac{P_1/P_2}{S_{\overline{P}_1/\overline{P}_2}}.$$

In the test statistic, the numerator is the difference between the proportions in the two samples, P_1 and P_2. The denominator is the standard error of the difference in the two proportions and is given by

$$S_{\overline{P}_1/\overline{P}_2} = \sqrt{P(1/P)\left(\frac{1}{n_1} + \frac{1}{n_2}\right)},$$

where

$$P = \frac{n_1 P_1 + n_2 P_2}{n_1 + n_2}.$$

Paired Samples

In many marketing research applications, the observations for the two groups are not selected from independent samples. Rather, the observations relate to paired samples, in that the two sets of observations relate to the same respondents. A sample of respondents may rate two competing brands, indicate the relative importance of two attributes of a product, or evaluate a brand at two different times. The difference in these cases is examined by a paired samples t-test. To compute t for paired samples, the paired difference variable, denoted by D, is formed and its mean and variance calculated. Then the t-statistic is computed. The degrees of freedom are $n - 1$, where n is the number of pairs. The relevant formulas are

$$H_0: \mu_D = 0.$$

$$H_1: \mu_D \neq 0.$$

$$t_{n-1} = \frac{\overline{D} - \mu_D}{\dfrac{s_D}{\sqrt{n}}},$$

where

$$\overline{D} = \frac{\displaystyle\sum_{i-1}^{n} D_i}{n}, \text{ and}$$

$$s_D = \sqrt{\frac{\displaystyle\sum_{i=1}^{n} (D_i - \overline{D})^2}{n - 1}}.$$

The difference in proportions for paired samples can be tested by using the McNemar test or the chi-square test, as explained in the following section on nonparametric tests (Harnett 1982; Kanji 1993).

Nonparametric Tests

Nonparametric tests are used when the independent variables are nonmetric. Like parametric tests, nonparametric tests are available for testing variables from one sample, two independent samples, or two related samples (Lancaster 1969; Pett 1997).

One Sample

Sometimes the researcher wants to test whether the observations for a particular variable could reasonably have come from a particular distribution, such as the normal, uniform, or Poisson distributions. Knowledge of the distribution is necessary for finding probabilities corresponding to known values of the variable or variable values corresponding to known probabilities. The K-S one-sample test is one such goodness-of-fit test. The K-S compares the cumulative distribution function for a variable with a specified distribution. A_i denotes the cumulative relative frequency for each category of the theoretical (assumed) distribution, and O_i is the comparable value of the sample frequency. The K-S test is based on the maximum value of the absolute difference between A_i and O_i. The test statistic is

$$K = \text{Max} \, | A_i - O_i |$$

The decision to reject the null hypothesis is based on the value of K. The larger K is, the more confidence we have that H_0 is false. For $\alpha = 0.05$, the critical value of K for large samples (more than 35) is given by $1.36/\sqrt{n}$. Alternatively, K can be transformed into a normally distributed z-statistic and its associated probability determined.

The chi-square test can also be performed on a single variable from one sample. In this context, the chi-square serves as a goodness-of-fit test. It tests whether a significant difference exists between the observed number of cases in each category and the expected number. Other one-sample nonparametric tests include the runs test and the binomial test. The runs test is a test of randomness for the dichotomous variables. This test is conducted by determining whether the order or sequence in which observations are obtained is random. The binomial test is also a goodness-of-fit test for dichotomous variables. It tests the goodness of fit of the observed number of observations in each category with the number expected under a specified binomial distribution. For more information on these tests, refer to standard statistical literature.

Two Independent Samples

When the difference in the location of two populations is to be compared on the basis of observations from two independent samples and the variable is measured on an ordinal scale, the Mann-Whitney U-test can be used. This test corresponds to the two independent sample t-test for interval scale variables when the variances of the two populations are assumed to be equal.

In the Mann-Whitney U-test, the two samples are combined, and the cases are ranked in order of increasing size. The test statistic, U, is computed as the number of times a score from a sample or group precedes a score from another group. If the samples are from the same population, the distribution of scores from the two groups in the rank list should be random. An extreme value of U would indicate a nonrandom pattern, thereby pointing to the inequality of the two groups. For samples of less than 30, the exact significance level for U is computed. For larger samples, U is transformed into a normally distributed z-statistic. This z can be corrected for ties within ranks.

Researchers often wish to test for a significant difference in proportions obtained from two independent samples. As an alternative to the parametric z-test considered previously, one could also use the cross-tabulation procedure to conduct a chi-square test. In this case, we will have a 2 × 2 table. One variable will be used to denote the sample and will assume the value of 1 for sample 1 and the value of 2 for sample 2. The other variable will be the binary variable of interest.

Two other independent-sample nonparametric tests are the median test and K-S test. The two-sample median test determines whether the two groups are drawn from populations with the same median. It is not as powerful as the Mann-Whitney U test because it merely uses the location of each observation relative to the median, not the rank, of each observation. The K-S two-sample test examines whether the two distributions are the same. It takes into account any differences between the two distributions, including the median, dispersion, and skewness (Cheung and Klotz 1997).[4]

Paired Samples

An important nonparametric test for examining differences in the location of two populations based on paired observations is the Wilcoxon matched pairs signed-ranks test. This test analyzes the differences between the paired observations, taking into account the magnitude of the differences. It computes the differences between the pairs of variables and ranks the absolute differences. The next step is to sum the positive and negative ranks. The test statistic, z, is computed from the positive and negative rank sums. Under the null hypothesis of no difference, z is a standard normal variate with a mean of 0 and a variance of 1 for large samples. This test corresponds to the paired t-test considered previously.

Another paired sample nonparametric test is the sign test. This test is not as powerful as the Wilcoxon matched-pairs signed-ranks test because it only compares the signs of the differences between pairs of variables without taking into account the magnitude of the differences. In the spe-

---

[4]There is some controversy over whether nonparametric statistical techniques should be used to make inferences about population parameters.

cial case of a binary variable, where the researcher wishes to test differences in proportions, the McNemar test can be used. Alternatively, the chi-square test can also be used for binary variables.[5]

SUMMARY AND CONCLUSIONS

Univariate data analysis provides valuable insights and guides multivariate data analysis, as well as the interpretation of the results. A frequency distribution should be obtained for each variable in the data. This analysis produces a table of frequency counts, percentages, and cumulative percentages for all the values associated with that variable. It indicates the extent of out-of-range, missing, or extreme values. The mean, mode, and median of a frequency distribution are measures of central tendency. The variability of the distribution is described by the range, variance or standard deviation, coefficient of variation, and interquartile range. Skewness and kurtosis provide an idea of the shape of the distribution.

Parametric and nonparametric tests are available for testing hypotheses related to differences. In the parametric case, the t-test is used to examine hypotheses related to the population mean. Different forms of the t-test are suitable for testing hypotheses based on one sample, two independent samples, or paired samples. In the nonparametric case, popular one-sample tests include the K-S, chi-square, runs, and binomial tests. For two independent nonparametric samples, the Mann-Whitney U-test, median test, and the K-S test can be used. For paired samples, the Wilcoxon matched-pairs signed-ranks test and the sign test are useful for examining hypotheses related to measures of location.

As we move into the new century, data analysis will become more sophisticated. Yet there will always be a place for univariate techniques — not as a substitute for multivariate analysis but rather as a precursor to multivariate techniques. Nonparametric procedures have not been popular in the past. However, their popularity is likely to grow in the future. This will result from better trained marketing researchers and greater availability of relevant statistical software. In several instances, marketing research data are not well behaved. In such situations, the researcher can avoid making stringent assumptions by using nonparametric methods.

---

[5]The t-test in this case is equivalent to a chi-square test for independence in a 2 × 2 contingency table. The relationship is

$$\chi^2_{.95(1)} = t^2_{.05(n_1 + n_2 - 2)}.$$

For large samples, the t distribution approaches the normal distribution, and so, the t-test and the z-test are equivalent.

BIBLIOGRAPHY

Berenson, Mark L. and David M. Levine (1999), *Basic Business Statistics: Concepts and Applications*, 7th ed. Englewook Cliffs, NJ: Prentice Hall.

Cheung, Y.K. and J.H. Klotz (1997), "The Mann-Whitney-Wilcoxon Distribution Using Linked Lists," *Statistica Sinica*, 7 (July), 805–13.

Cowles, Michael and Caroline Davis (1982), "On the Origins of the .05 Level of Statistical Significance," *American Psychologist*, (May), 553–58.

Harnett, Donald L. (1982), *Statistical Methods*, 3d ed. Reading, MA: Addison-Wesley.

Hellevik, O. (1984), *Introduction to Causal Analysis: Exploring Survey Data by Crosstabulation*. Beverly Hills, CA: Sage Publications.

Kanji, Gopal K. (1993), *100 Statistical Tests*. Thousand Oaks, CA: Sage Publications.

Lancaster, H.O. (1969), *The Chi Squared Distribution*. New York: John Wiley & Sons.

Pett, Marjorie A. (1997), *Nonparametric Statistics for Health Care Research*. Thousand Oaks, CA: Sage Publications.

Sirkin, R. Mark (1994), *Statistics for the Social Sciences*. Thousand Oaks, CA: Sage Publications.

Verma, Rohit and John C. Goodale (1995), "Statistical Power in Operations Management Research," *Journal of Operations Management*, 13 (August), 139–52.

10
Quantitative Data Analysis: Multivariate Techniques

Naresh K. Malhotra

We present a classification of multivariate techniques. Then we discuss the major techniques of cross-tabulations, analysis of variance, regression, discriminant analysis, factor analysis, cluster analysis, multidimensional scaling, and conjoint analysis. Our emphasis is on the managerial applications, as well as on procedures for conducting these techniques.[1]

A CLASSIFICATION OF MULTIVARIATE TECHNIQUES

Multivariate statistical techniques can be classified as dependence techniques or interdependence techniques (see Figure 1). Dependence techniques are appropriate when one or more variables can be identified as dependent variables and the remaining as independent variables. When there is only one dependent variable, cross-tabulation, analysis of variance and covariance, regression, two-group discriminant analysis, and conjoint analysis can be used (Lenell and Robinson 1996). However,

---

[1]This material is based on Malhotra, Naresh K. (1999), *Marketing Research: An Applied Orientation*, 3d ed. Upper Saddle River, NJ: Prentice Hall. The reader should consult this text for more details, including numerical illustrations.

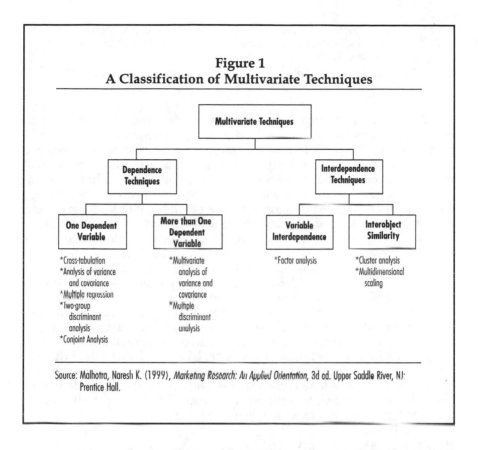

Figure 1
A Classification of Multivariate Techniques

Multivariate Techniques

Dependence Techniques

Interdependence Techniques

One Dependent Variable

More than One Dependent Variable

Variable Interdependence

Interobject Similarity

*Cross-tabulation
*Analysis of variance and covariance
*Multiple regression
*Two-group discriminant analysis
*Conjoint Analysis

*Multivariate analysis of variance and covariance
*Multiple discriminant analysis

*Factor analysis

*Cluster analysis
*Multidimensional scaling

Source: Malhotra, Naresh K. (1999), *Marketing Research: An Applied Orientation*, 3d ed. Upper Saddle River, NJ: Prentice Hall.

if there is more than one dependent variable, the appropriate techniques are multivariate analysis of variance and covariance, canonical correlation, and multiple discriminant analysis. In interdependence techniques, the variables are not classified as dependent or independent; rather, the whole set of interdependent relationships is examined. These techniques focus on either variable interdependence or interobject similarity. The major technique for examining variable interdependence is factor analysis. Analysis of interobject similarity can be conducted by cluster analysis and multidimensional scaling (Sirkin 1994).

CROSS-TABULATIONS

Cross-tabulations help answer questions about how variables link or associate with other variables. For example,

❑ How many brand-loyal users are men?

❑ Is product use (measured in terms of heavy users, medium users, light users, and nonusers) related to interest in outdoor activities (high, medium, and low)?

❑ Is product ownership related to income (high, medium, and low)?

The answers to such questions can be determined by examining cross-tabulations (Berenson and Levine 1999). Whereas a frequency distribution describes one variable at a time, a cross-tabulation describes two or more variables simultaneously. Cross-tabulation results in tables that reflect the joint distribution of two or more variables with a limited number of categories or distinct values. The categories of one variable are cross-classified with the categories of one or more other variables. Thus, the frequency distribution of one variable is subdivided according to the values or categories of the other variables. In general, the margins of a cross-tabulation show the same information as the frequency tables for each of the variables. Cross-tabulation tables are also called contingency tables. The data are considered qualitative or categorical, because each variable is assumed to have only a nominal scale.

Computation of percentages can provide more insights into the pattern of the relationship between the two variables. Because two variables have been cross-classified, percentages could be computed either columnwise, based on column totals, or rowwise, based on row totals. Which of these tables is more useful? The answer depends on which variable will be considered the independent variable and which the dependent variable. The general rule is to compute the percentages in the direction of the independent variable, across the dependent variable.

Statistics Associated with Cross-Tabulation

We discuss the statistics commonly used for assessing the statistical significance and strength of association of cross-tabulated variables. The statistical significance of the observed association is commonly measured by the chi-square statistic. The chi-square statistic (χ^2) assists us in determining whether a systematic association exists between the two variables. The null hypothesis, H_0, is that there is no association between the variables.

The strength, or degree, of association is important from a practical or substantive perspective. In general, the strength of association is of interest only if the association is statistically significant. The strength of the association can be measured by the phi correlation coefficient, the contingency coefficient, Cramer's V, and the lambda coefficient (Pett 1997).

General Comments on Cross-Tabulation

Although more than two variables can be cross-tabulated, the interpretation is quite complex. Also, because the number of cells increases multiplicatively, maintaining an adequate number of respondents or cases in each cell can be problematic. As a general rule, there should be at least five expected observations in each cell for the statistics computed to be reliable. Thus, cross-tabulation is an inefficient way of examining relationships when there are several variables. Note that cross-tabulation examines association between variables, not causation. To examine causation, the causal research design framework should be adopted.

Cross-tabulation is widely used in commercial marketing research, because (1) cross-tabulation analysis and results can be easily interpreted and understood by managers who are not statistically oriented; (2) the clarity of interpretation provides a stronger link between research results and managerial action; (3) a series of cross-tabulations may provide greater insights into a complex phenomenon than a single multivariate analysis would; (4) cross-tabulation may alleviate the problem of sparse cells, which could be serious in discrete multivariate analysis; and (5) cross-tabulation analysis is simple to conduct and appealing to less sophisticated researchers.

ANALYSIS OF VARIANCE

Analysis of variance and analysis of covariance are used for examining the differences in the mean values of the dependent variable associated with the effect of the controlled independent variables, after taking into account the influence of the uncontrolled independent variables. Essentially, analysis of variance (ANOVA) is used as a test of means for two or more populations. The null hypothesis, typically, is that all means are equal. For example, suppose the researcher was interested in examining whether heavy, medium, light, and nonusers of cereals differed in their preference for Total brand cereal, measured on a nine-point Likert scale. The null hypothesis that the four groups were not different in their preference for Total could be tested using ANOVA.

In its simplest form, ANOVA must have a dependent variable (preference for Total cereal) that is metric (measured using an interval or ratio scale). There must also be one or more independent variables (product use: heavy, medium, light, and nonusers). The independent variables all must be categorical (nonmetric). Categorical independent variables are also called factors. A particular combination of factor levels, or categories, is called a treatment. Analysis of variance involves only one categorical variable, or a single factor. The differences in the preferences of heavy, medium, light, and nonusers would be examined by one-way ANOVA. In one-way ANOVA, a treatment is the same as a factor level (medium users constitute a treatment). If two or more factors are involved, the analysis is termed n-way ANOVA (Jaccard 1997). If the set of independent variables consists of both categorical and metric variables, the technique is called analysis of covariance (ANCOVA).

One-Way Analysis of Variance

Marketing researchers are often interested in examining the differences in the mean values of the dependent variable for several categories of a single independent variable or factor. For example,

- ❑ Do the various segments differ in terms of their volume of product consumption?
- ❑ Do the brand evaluations of groups exposed to different commercials vary?
- ❑ Do retailers, wholesalers, and agents differ in their attitudes toward the firm's distribution policies?
- ❑ How do consumers' intentions to buy the brand vary with different price levels?

The answer to these and similar questions can be determined by conducting one-way ANOVA. Before describing the procedure, we define the important statistics associated with one-way ANOVA.

Conducting One-Way Analysis of Variance

The procedure for conducting one-way ANOVA involves identifying the dependent and independent variables, decomposing the total variation, measuring effects, testing significance, and interpreting results.

Identification of the Dependent and Independent Variables. The dependent variable is denoted by Y and the independent variable by X. X is a categorical variable with c categories. There are n observations on Y for each category of X. The sample size in each category of X is n, and the total sample size is $N = n \times c$. Although the sample sizes in the categories of X (the group sizes) are assumed to be equal for the sake of simplicity, this is not a requirement.

Decomposition of the Total Variation. In examining the differences among means, one-way ANOVA involves the decomposition of the total variation observed in the dependent variable. This variation is measured by the sums of squares corrected for the mean (SS). Analysis of variance is so named because it examines the variability or variation in the sample (dependent variable) and, based on the variability, determines whether there is reason to believe that the population means differ (Neter 1996).

The total variation in Y, denoted by SS_y, can be decomposed into two components:

$$SS_y = SS_{between} + SS_{within,}$$

where the subscripts "between" and "within" refer to the categories of X. $SS_{between}$ is the variation in Y related to the variation in the means of the categories of X. It represents variation between the categories of X. In other words, $SS_{between}$ is the portion of the sum of squares in Y related to the independent variable or factor X. For this reason, $SS_{between}$ is also denoted as SS_x. SS_{within} is the variation in Y related to the variation within each category of X. SS_{within} is not accounted for by X. Therefore, it is referred to as SS_{error}. The total variation in Y may be decomposed as

$$SS_y = SS_x + SS_{error},$$

where

$$SS_y = \sum_{i=1}^{N} (Y_i - \overline{Y})^2;$$

$$SS_x = \sum_{j=1}^{c} n(\overline{Y}_j - \overline{Y})^2;$$

$$SS_{error} = \sum_{j}^{c} \sum_{i}^{n} (Y_{ij} - \overline{Y}_j)^2;$$

Y_i = individual observation;
$\overline{Y}_j$ = mean for category j;
$\overline{Y}$ = mean over the whole sample, or grand mean; and
Y_{ij} = ith observation in the jth category.

Measurement of Effects. The effects of X on Y are measured by SS_x. Because SS_x is related to the variation in the means of the categories of X, the relative magnitude of SS_x increases as the differences among the means of Y in the categories of X increase. The relative magnitude of SS_x also increases as the variations in Y within the categories of X decrease. The strength of the effects of X on Y are measured as follows:

$$\eta^2 = SS_x/SS_y = (SS_y - SS_{error})/SS_y.$$

The value of η^2 varies between 0 and 1. It assumes a value of 0 when all the category means are equal, indicating that X has no effect on Y. The value of η^2 will be 1 when there is no variability within each category of X but there is some variability between categories. Thus, η^2 is a measure of the variation in Y that is explained by the independent variable X. Not only can we measure the effects of X on Y, but we can also test for their significance (Winer, Brown, and Michels 1991).

Significance Testing. In one-way ANOVA, the interest lies in testing the null hypothesis that the category means are equal in the population. In other words,

$$H_0: \mu_1 = \mu_2 = \mu_3 = ... = \mu_c.$$

Under the null hypothesis, SS_x and SS_{error} come from the same source of variation. In such a case, the estimate of the population variance of Y can be based on either between-category variation or within-category variation. In other words, the estimate of the population variance of Y

$$= SS_x/(c-1) = \text{Mean square due to } X = MS_x;$$

or

$$= SS_{error}/(N-c) = \text{Mean square due to error} = Ms_{error}.$$

The null hypothesis can be tested by the F-statistic on the basis of the ratio between these two estimates:

$$F = \frac{SS_x/(c-1)}{SS_{error}/(N-c)} = \frac{MS_x}{MS_{error}}.$$

Interpretation of Results. If the null hypothesis of equal category means is not rejected, then the independent variable does not have a significant effect on the dependent variable. However, if the null hypothesis is rejected, then the effect of the independent variable is significant. In other words, the mean value of the dependent variable will be different for different categories of the independent variable. A comparison of the category mean values will indicate the nature of the effect of the independent variable.

N-Way and Multivariate Analysis of Variance

N-way ANOVA is often interested in the effect of more than one factor simultaneously. A major advantage of this technique is that it enables the researcher to examine interactions among the factors. Interactions occur when the effects of one factor on the dependent variable depend on the level (category) of the other factors. The procedure for conducting *n*-way ANOVA is similar to that for one-way ANOVA. The statistics associated with *n*-way ANOVA are also defined similarly.

Multivariate analysis of variance (MANOVA) is similar to analysis of variance (ANOVA), except that instead of one metric dependent variable, we have two or more. The objective is the same, because MANOVA is also concerned with examining differences among groups. Whereas ANOVA examines group differences on a single dependent variable, MANOVA examines group differences across multiple dependent variables simultaneously. In ANOVA, the null hypothesis is that the means of the dependent variable are equal across the groups. In MANOVA, the null hypothesis is that the vector of means on multiple dependent variables are equal across groups. Multivariate analysis of variance is appropriate when there are two or more dependent variables that are correlated. If there are multiple dependent variables that are uncorrelated or orthogonal, ANOVA on each of the dependent variables is more appropriate than MANOVA (Novak 1995).

REGRESSION ANALYSIS

Regression analysis is a powerful and flexible procedure for analyzing associative relationships between a metric dependent variable and one or more independent variables (Draper and Smith 1998). It can be used to

1. Determine whether the independent variables explain a significant variation in the dependent variable (whether a relationship exists);
2. Determine how much of the variation in the dependent variable can be explained by the independent variables (strength of the relationship);
3. Determine the structure or form of the relationship (the mathematical equation relating the independent and dependent variables); and
4. Predict the values of the dependent variable.

Regression analysis deals with the nature and degree of association between variables and does not imply or assume any causality. Bivariate regression is discussed first, followed by multiple regression.

Bivariate Regression

Bivariate regression is a procedure for deriving a mathematical relationship, in the form of an equation, between a single metric dependent or criterion variable and a single metric independent or predictor variable. The analysis is similar in many ways to determining the simple correlation between two variables. However, because an equation needs to be derived, one variable must be identified as the dependent and the other as the independent variable. Bivariate regression can be used to address the following types of questions:

❑ Can variation in sales be explained in terms of variation in advertising expenditures? What is the structure and form of this relationship, and can it be modeled mathematically by an equation that describes a straight line?

❑ Can the variation in market shares be accounted for by the size of the salesforce?

❑ Are consumers' perceptions of quality determined by their perceptions of prices?

Conducting Bivariate Regression Analysis

The steps in conducting bivariate regression analysis involve plotting the scatter diagram, formulating the general model, estimating the parameters and testing for significance, determining the strength and significance of association, checking prediction accuracy, examining the residuals, and validating the model (Neter, Wasserman, and Kutner 1990). These steps are discussed briefly.

Scatter Diagram. A scatter diagram, or scattergram, is a plot of the values of two variables for all the cases or observations. It is customary to plot the dependent variable on the vertical axis and the independent variable on the horizontal axis. A scatter diagram is useful for determining the form of the relationship between variables. A plot can alert the researcher to patterns in the data or possible problems. Any unusual combinations of the two variables can be easily identified. If it appears from the scattergram that the relationship between X and Y is linear, how should the straight line be fitted to best describe the data?

The most commonly used technique for fitting a straight line to a scattergram is the least squares procedure. This technique determines the best fitting line by minimizing the vertical distances of all the points from the line. The best fitting line is called the *regression line*. The scatter diagram indicates whether the relationship between Y and X can be modeled as a straight line and, consequently, whether the bivariate regression model is appropriate.

Bivariate Regression Model. In the bivariate regression model, the general form of a straight line is as follows:

$$Y = \beta_0 + \beta_1 X,$$

where

Y = dependent or criterion variable,

X = independent or predictor variable,

β_0 = intercept of the line, and

β_1 = slope of the line.

This model implies a deterministic relationship, in that Y is completely determined by X. The value of Y can be perfectly predicted if β_0 and β_1 are known. In marketing research, however, very few relationships are deterministic. So the regression procedure adds an error term to account for the probabilistic or stochastic nature of the relationship. The basic regression equation becomes:

$$Y_i - \beta_0 + \beta_1 X_i + e_i,$$

where e_i is the error term associated with the ith observation. Estimation of the regression parameters, β_0 and β_1, is relatively simple.

Estimation of Parameters. In most cases, β_0 and β_1 are unknown and estimated from the sample observations using the equation

$$\hat{Y}_i = a + bx_i,$$

where $\hat{Y}_i$ is the estimated or predicted value of Y_i, and a and b are estimators of β_0 and β_1, respectively. The constant b is usually referred to as the nonstandardized regression coefficient. It is the slope of the regression line, and it indicates the expected change in Y when X is changed by one unit. The formulas for calculating a and b are simple. The slope, b, may be computed in terms of the covariance between X and Y (i.e., COV_{xy}) and the variance of X, as follows:

$$b = \frac{COV_{xy}}{S_x^2}$$

$$= \frac{\sum_{i=1}^{n} (X_i - \overline{X})(Y_i - \overline{Y})}{\sum_{i=1}^{n} (X_i - \overline{X})^2}$$

$$= \frac{\sum_{i=1}^{n} X_i Y_i - n\overline{X}\overline{Y}}{\sum_{i=1}^{n} X_i^2 - n\overline{X}^2}.$$

The intercept, a, may then be calculated using

$$a = \overline{Y} - b\overline{X}.$$

Normally, the regression coefficients have been estimated on the raw (untransformed) data. Should standardization of the data be considered desirable, the calculation of the standardized coefficients is also straightforward (Greenberg and Parks 1997).

Standardized Regression Coefficient. Standardization is the process by which the raw data are transformed into new variables that have a mean of 0 and a variance of 1. When the data are standardized, the intercept assumes a value of 0. The term *beta coefficient* or *beta weight* is used to denote the standardized regression coefficient. In this case, the slope obtained by the regression of Y on X, B_{yx}, is the same as the slope obtained by the regression of X on Y, B_{xy}. Moreover, each of these regression coefficients is equal to the simple correlation between X and Y:

$$B_{yx} = B_{xy} = r_{xy}.$$

There is a simple relationship between the standardized and nonstandardized regression coefficients:

$$B_{yx} = b_{yx} (S_x/S_y).$$

After the parameters have been estimated, they can be tested for significance.

Significance Testing. The statistical significance of the linear relationship between X and Y may be tested by examining the following hypotheses:

$$H_0: \beta_1 = 0.$$

$$H_1: \beta_1 \neq 0.$$

The null hypothesis implies that there is no linear relationship between X and Y. The alternative hypothesis is that there is a relationship, positive or negative, between X and Y. Typically, a two-tailed test is done. A t-statistic with $n - 2$ degrees of freedom can be used, where

$$t = \frac{b}{SE_b} \quad \text{and}$$

SE_b denotes the standard deviation of b and is called the *standard error* (Wang 1996).

Strength and Significance of Association. A related inference involves determining the strength and significance of the association between Y and X. The strength of association is measured by the coefficient of determination, r^2. In bivariate regression, r^2 is the square of the simple correlation coefficient obtained by correlating the two variables. The coefficient r^2 varies between 0 and 1. It signifies the proportion of the total variation in Y that is accounted for by the variation in X. The decomposition of the total variation in Y is similar to that for ANOVA. The total variation, SS_y, may be decomposed into the variation accounted for by the regression line, SS_{reg}, and the error or residual variation, SS_{error} or SS_{res}, as follows:

$$SS_y = SS_{reg} + SS_{res},$$

where

$$SS_y = \sum_{i=1}^{n} (Y_i - \overline{Y})^2,$$

$$SS_{reg} = \sum_{i=1}^{n} (\hat{Y}_i - \overline{Y})^2, \text{ and}$$

$$SS_{res} = \sum_{i=1}^{n} (Y_i - \hat{Y}_i)^2.$$

The strength of association may then be calculated as follows:

$$r^2 = \frac{SS_{reg}}{SS_y}$$

$$= \frac{SS_y - SS_{res}}{SS_y}.$$

It may be recalled from earlier calculations of the simple correlation coefficient that

$$SS_y = \sum_{i=1}^{n} (Y_i - \overline{Y})^2.$$

The predicted values ($\hat{Y}$) can be calculated using a regression equation. It can be seen that $SS_y = SS_{reg} + SS_{res}$. Furthermore,

$$r^2 = SS_{reg}/SS_y.$$

Another equivalent test for examining the significance of the linear relationship between X and Y (significance of b) is the test for the significance of the coefficient of determination. The hypotheses in this case are

$$H_0: R^2_{pop} = 0.$$

$$H_1: R^2_{pop} > 0.$$

The appropriate test statistic is the F-statistic:

$$F = \frac{SS_{reg}}{SS_{res}/(n-2)},$$

which has an F distribution with 1 and $n - 2$ degrees of freedom. The F-test is a generalized form of the t-test. If a random variable is t distributed with n degrees of freedom, then t^2 is F distributed with 1 and n degrees of freedom. Therefore, the F-test for testing the significance of the coefficient of determination is equivalent to testing the following hypotheses:

$$H_0: \beta_1 = 0 \text{ and}$$

$$H_1: \beta_1 \neq 0,$$

or

$$H_0: \rho = 0, \text{ and}$$

$$H_1: \rho \neq 0.$$

If the relationship between X and Y is significant, it is meaningful to predict the values of Y based on the values of X and estimate prediction accuracy.

Examination of Residuals and Cross-Validation. The final two steps in conducting bivariate regression are the examination of residuals and model cross-validation. A residual is the difference between the observed value of Y_i and the value predicted by the regression equation $\hat{Y}_i$.

Residuals are used in the calculation of several statistics associated with regression. In addition, scattergrams of the residuals, in which the residuals are plotted against the predicted values, $\hat{Y}_i$, time, or predictor variables, provide useful insights in examining the appropriateness of the underlying assumptions and regression model fitted (Mason and Perreault 1991).

Regression and other multivariate procedures tend to capitalize on chance variations in the data. This could result in a regression model or equation that is unduly sensitive to the specific data used to estimate the model. One approach for evaluating the model for this and other problems associated with regression is cross-validation. Cross-validation examines whether the regression model continues to hold for comparable data not used in the estimation. A special form of validation is called double cross-validation. In double cross-validation, the sample is split into halves. One half serves as the estimation sample, and the other is used as a validation sample in conducting cross-validation. The roles of the estimation and validation halves are then reversed, and the cross-validation is repeated (Cooil, Winer, and Rados 1987).

Multiple Regression

Multiple regression involves a single dependent variable and two or more independent variables. The questions raised in the context of bivariate regression can also be answered by multiple regression by considering additional independent variables:

- ❏ Can variation in sales be explained in terms of variation in advertising expenditures, prices, and level of distribution?
- ❏ Can variation in market shares be accounted for by the size of the sales force, advertising expenditures, and sales promotion budgets?
- ❏ Are consumers' perceptions of quality determined by their perceptions of prices, brand image, and brand attributes?

Additional questions can also be answered by multiple regression, such as

- ❏ How much of the variation in sales can be explained by advertising expenditures, prices, and level of distribution?
- ❏ What is the contribution of advertising expenditures in explaining the variation in sales when the levels of prices and distribution are controlled?
- ❏ What levels of sales may be expected given the levels of advertising expenditures, prices, and level of distribution?

The general form of the multiple regression model is as follows:

$$Y = \beta_0 + \beta_1 X_1 + \beta_2 X_2 + \beta_3 X_3 + \ldots + \beta_k X_k + e,$$

which is estimated by the following equation:

$$\hat{Y} = a + b_1 X_1 + b_2 X_2 + b_3 X_3 + \ldots + b_k X_k.$$

As previously, the coefficient a represents the intercept, but the bs are now the partial regression coefficients. The least squares criterion estimates the parameters in such a way as to minimize the total error, SS_{res}. This process also maximizes the correlation between the actual values of Y and the predicted values of $\hat{Y}$ (Cohen and Cohen 1983).

DISCRIMINANT ANALYSIS

Discriminant analysis is a technique for analyzing data when the criterion or dependent variable is categorical and the predictor or independent variables are interval in nature (Fox 1997). For example, the dependent variable may be the choice of a brand of personal computer (brand A, B, or C), and the independent variables may be ratings of attributes of computers on a seven-point Likert scale. The objectives of discriminant analysis are as follows:

1. Development of discriminant functions or linear combinations of the predictor or independent variables that will best discriminate between the categories of the criterion or dependent variable (groups);
2. Examination of whether significant differences exist among the groups, in terms of the predictor variables;
3. Determination of which predictor variables contribute to most of the intergroup differences;
4. Classification of cases to one of the groups on the basis of the values of the predictor variables; and
5. Evaluation of the accuracy of classification.

Discriminant analysis techniques are described by the number of categories possessed by the criterion variable. When the criterion variable has two categories, the technique is known as two-group discriminant analysis. When three or more categories are involved, the technique is referred to as multiple discriminant analysis. The main distinction is that in the two-group case, it is possible to derive only one discriminant function. In multiple discriminant analysis, more than one function may be computed (Johnson and Wichern 1998).

Examples of discriminant analysis abound in marketing research. This technique can be used to answer questions such as

❏ In terms of demographic characteristics, how do customers who exhibit store loyalty differ from those who do not?

❏ Do heavy, medium, and light users of soft drinks differ in terms of their consumption of frozen foods?

❏ What psychographic characteristics help differentiate between price-sensitive and non–price-sensitive buyers of groceries?

❏ Do the various market segments differ in their media consumption habits?

Discriminant Analysis Model

The discriminant analysis model involves linear combinations of the following form:

$$D = b_0 + b_1X_1 + b_2X_2 + b_3X_3 + ... + b_kX_k,$$

where

D = discriminant score,

bs = discriminant coefficient or weight, and

Xs = predictor or independent variable.

The coefficients or weights (b) are estimated so that the groups differ as much as possible on the values of the discriminant function. This occurs when the ratio of between-group sums of squares to within-group sums of squares for the discriminant scores is at a maximum. Any other linear combination of the predictors will result in a smaller ratio.

The assumptions in discriminant analysis are that each of the groups is a sample from a multivariate normal population and all of the populations have the same covariance matrix. The role of these assumptions and the statistics just described can be better understood by examining the procedure for conducting discriminant analysis (Klecka 1980).

Conducting Discriminant Analysis

The steps involved in conducting discriminant analysis consist of formulation, estimation, determination of significance, interpretation, and validation. These steps are discussed and illustrated within the context of a two-group discriminant analysis.

Formulation

The first step in discriminant analysis is to formulate the problem by identifying the objectives, the criterion variable, and the independent variables. The criterion variable must consist of two or more mutually exclusive and collectively exhaustive categories. When the dependent variable is interval or ratio-scaled, it must first be converted into categories. The predictor variables should be selected on the basis of a theoretical model or previous research, or in the case of exploratory research, the experience of the researcher should guide their selection.

The next step is to divide the sample into two parts. One part of the sample, called the estimation or analysis sample, is used for estimation of the discriminant function. The other part, called the holdout or validation sample, is reserved for validating the discriminant function. When the sample is large enough, it can be split in half. One half serves as the analysis sample, and the other is used for validation. The role of the halves is then interchanged and the analysis is repeated. This is called double cross-validation and is similar to the procedure discussed in regression analysis. Often, the distribution of the number of cases in the analysis and validation samples follows the distribution in the total sample (Fok et al. 1995).

Estimation

When the analysis sample has been identified, we can estimate the discriminant function coefficients. Two broad approaches are available. The direct method involves estimating the discriminant function so that all the predictors are included simultaneously. In this case, each independent variable is included, regardless of its discriminating power. This method is appropriate when, based on previous research or a theoretical model, the researcher wants the discrimination to be based on all the predictors. An alternative approach is the stepwise method. In stepwise discriminant analysis, the predictor variables are entered sequentially on the basis of their ability to discriminate among groups. This method is appropriate when the researcher wants to select a subset of the predictors for inclusion in the discriminant function. The next step is determination of significance.

Determination of Significance

It would not be meaningful to interpret the analysis if the discriminant functions estimated were not statistically significant. The null hypothesis that, in the population, the means of all discriminant functions in all groups are equal can be statistically tested. In SPSS, this test is based on Wilks' λ. If several functions are tested simultaneously (as in the case of multiple discriminant analysis), the Wilks' λ statistic is the product of the univariate λ for each function. The significance level is estimated on the basis of a chi-square transformation of the statistic. If the null hypothesis is rejected, which indicates significant discrimination, one can proceed to interpret the results.

Interpretation

The interpretation of the discriminant weights, or coefficients, is similar to that in multiple regression analysis. The value of the coefficient for a particular predictor depends on the other predictors included in the discriminant function. The signs of the coefficients are arbitrary, but they indicate which variable values result in large and small function values and associate them with particular groups (Morrison 1969).

Given the multicollinearity in the predictor variables, there is no unambiguous measure of the relative importance of the predictors in discriminating among the groups. With this caveat in mind, we can obtain some idea of the relative importance of the variables by examining the absolute magnitude of the standardized discriminant function coefficients. In general, predictors with relatively large standardized coefficients contribute more to the discriminating power of the function compared with predictors with smaller coefficients.

Some idea of the relative importance of the predictors can also be obtained by examining the structure correlations, also called *canonical loadings* or *discriminant loadings*. These simple correlations between each predictor and the discriminant function represent the variance that the predictor shares with the function. Similar to the standardized coefficients, these correlations must also be interpreted with caution.

Another aid in interpreting discriminant analysis results is to develop a characteristic profile for each group by describing each group in terms of the group means for the predictor variables. If the important predictors have been identified, then a comparison of the group means on these variables can assist in understanding the intergroup differences. However, before any findings can be interpreted with confidence, it is necessary to validate the results.

Validation

As explained previously, the data are randomly divided into two subsamples. The analysis sample is used for estimating the discriminant function; the validation sample is used for developing the classification matrix. The discriminant weights, estimated by using the analysis sample, are multiplied by the values of the predictor variables in the holdout sample to generate discriminant scores for the cases in the holdout sample. The cases are then assigned to groups on the basis of their discriminant scores and an appropriate decision rule. For example, in two-group discriminant analysis, a case will be assigned to the group whose centroid is the closest. The hit ratio, or the percentage of cases correctly classified, can then be determined by summing the diagonal elements and dividing by the total number of cases.

The extension from two-group discriminant analysis to multiple discriminant analysis involves similar steps (Hair et al. 1999).

FACTOR ANALYSIS

Factor analysis is a general name denoting a class of procedures primarily used for data reduction and summarization. In marketing research, there may be a large number of variables, most of which are correlated and must be reduced to a manageable level. Relationships among sets of many interrelated variables are examined and represented in terms of a few underlying factors. For example, store image may be measured by asking respondents to evaluate stores on a series of items on a semantic differential scale. These item evaluations can then be analyzed to determine the factors underlying store image.

In ANOVA, multiple regression, and discriminant analysis, one variable is considered as the dependent or criterion variable and the others as independent or predictor variables. However, no such distinction is made in factor analysis. Rather, factor analysis is an interdependence technique, in that an entire set of interdependent relationships is examined (Johnson and Wichern 1998).

Factor analysis is used in the following circumstances:

1. To identify underlying dimensions, or factors, that explain the correlations among a set of variables;
2. To identify a new, smaller set of uncorrelated variables to replace the original set of correlated variables in subsequent multivariate analysis (regression or discriminant analysis); or
3. To identify a smaller set of salient variables from a larger set for use in subsequent multivariate analysis.

Factor analysis has many applications in marketing research. For example,

❑ Factor analysis can be used in market segmentation for identifying the underlying variables by which to group customers. New car buyers might be grouped on the basis of the relative emphasis they place on economy, convenience, performance, comfort, or luxury. This might result in five segments: economy seekers, convenience seekers, performance seekers, comfort seekers, and luxury seekers.

❑ In product research, factor analysis can be employed to determine the brand attributes that influence consumer choice. Toothpaste brands might be evaluated in terms of protection against cavities, whiteness of teeth, taste, fresh breath, and price.

❑ In advertising studies, factor analysis can be used to understand the media consumption habits of the target market. The users of frozen foods may be heavy viewers of cable television, see a lot of movies, and listen to country music.

❑ In pricing studies, factor analysis can be used to identify the characteristics of price-sensitive consumers. For example, these consumers might be methodical, economy-minded, and home-centered.

Factor Analysis Model

Mathematically, factor analysis is somewhat similar to multiple regression analysis, in that each variable is expressed as a linear combination of underlying factors. The amount of variance a variable shares with all other variables included in the analysis is referred to as *communality*. The covariation among the variables is described in terms of a small number of common factors plus a unique factor for each variable. These factors are not overtly observed (Dunteman 1989). If the variables are standardized, the factor model may be represented as

$$X_i = A_{i1}F_1 + A_{i2}F_2 + A_{i3}F_3 + ... + A_{im}F_m + V_iU_i,$$

where

X_i = *i*th standardized variable,

A_{ij} = standardized multiple regression coefficient of variable *i* on common factor j,

F = common factor,

V_i = standardized regression coefficient of variable *i* on unique factor *i*,

U_i = the unique factor for variable *i*, and

m = number of common factors.

The unique factors are uncorrelated with each other and with the common factors. The common factors themselves can be expressed as linear combinations of the observed variables:

$$F_i = W_{i1}X_1 + W_{i2}X_2 + W_{i3}X_3 + ... + W_{ik}X_k,$$

where

F_i = estimate of *i*th factor,

W_i = weight or factor score coefficient, and

k = number of variables.

It is possible to select weights or factor score coefficients so that the first factor explains the largest portion of the total variance. Then a second set of weights can be selected so that the second factor accounts for most of the residual variance, subject to being uncorrelated with the first factor. This same principle could be applied to selecting additional weights for the additional factors. Thus, the factors can be estimated so that their factor scores, unlike the values of the original variables, are not correlated.

Furthermore, the first factor accounts for the highest variance in the data, the second factor for the second highest, and so on. Several statistics are associated with factor analysis.

Conducting Factor Analysis

The first step is to define the factor analysis problem and identify the variables to be factor analyzed. Then, a correlation matrix of these variables is constructed and a method of factor analysis selected. The researcher decides on the number of factors to be extracted and the method of rotation. Next, the rotated factors should be interpreted. Depending on the objectives, the factor scores may be calculated or surrogate variables selected to represent the factors in subsequent multivariate analysis. Finally, the fit of the factor analysis model is determined. We discuss these steps in more detail.

Problem Formulation

Problem formulation includes several tasks. The objectives of factor analysis should be identified. The variables to be included in the factor analysis should be specified on the basis of prior research, theory, and judgment of the researcher. It is important that the variables be appropriately measured on an interval or ratio scale. An appropriate sample size should be used. As a rough guideline, there should be at least four or five times as many observations (sample size) as there are variables.

Construction of the Correlation Matrix

The analytical process is based on a matrix of correlations among the variables. Valuable insights can be gained from an examination of this matrix. For the factor analysis to be appropriate, the variables must be correlated. Formal statistics are available for testing the appropriateness of the factor model. Bartlett's test of sphericity can be used to test the null hypothesis that the variables are uncorrelated in the population; in other words, the population correlation matrix is an identity matrix. In an identity matrix, all the diagonal terms are 1, and all off-diagonal terms are 0. The test statistic for sphericity is based on a chi-square transformation of the determinant of the correlation matrix. A large value of the test statistic will favor the rejection of the null hypothesis. If this hypothesis cannot be rejected, then the appropriateness of factor analysis should be questioned. Another useful statistic is the Kaiser-Meyer-Olkin (KMO) measure of sampling adequacy. This index compares the magnitudes of the observed correlation coefficients with the magnitudes of the partial correlation coefficients. Small values of the KMO statistic indicate that the correlations between pairs of variables cannot be explained by other variables and that factor analysis may not be appropriate.

Method of Factor Analysis

When it has been determined that factor analysis is an appropriate technique for analyzing the data, an appropriate method must be selected. The approach used to derive the weights or factor score coefficients differentiates the various methods of factor analysis. The two basic approaches are principal components analysis and common factor analysis.

In principal components analysis, the total variance in the data is considered. The diagonal of the correlation matrix consists of unities, and full variance is brought into the factor matrix. Principal components analysis is recommended when the primary concern is to determine the minimum number of factors that will account for maximum variance in the data for use in subsequent multivariate analysis. The factors are called principal components (Dunteman 1989).

In common factor analysis, the factors are estimated only on the basis of the common variance. Commonalties are inserted in the diagonal of the correlation matrix. This method is appropriate when the primary concern is to identify the underlying dimensions and the common variance is of interest. This method is also known as *principal axis factoring*.

Number of Factors

It is possible to compute as many principal components as there are variables, but in doing so, no parsimony is gained. To summarize the information contained in the original variables, a smaller number of factors should be extracted. The question is how many. Several procedures have been suggested for determining the number of factors. These include a priori determination and approaches based on eigenvalues, scree plot, and percentage of variance accounted.

A Priori Determination. Sometimes, because of prior knowledge, the researcher knows how many factors to expect and thus can specify the number of factors to be extracted beforehand. The extraction of factors ceases when the desired number of factors have been extracted. Most computer programs enable the user to specify the number of factors, allowing for an easy implementation of this approach.

Determination Based on Eigenvalues. In this approach, only factors with eigenvalues greater than 1.0 are retained; the other factors are not included in the model. An eigenvalue represents the amount of variance associated with the factor. Therefore, only factors with a variance greater than 1.0 are included. Factors with variance less than 1.0 are no better than a single variable, because, due to standardization, each variable has a variance of 1.0. If the number of variables is less than 20, this approach will result in a conservative number of factors.

Determination Based on Scree Plot. A scree plot is a plot of the eigenvalues against the number of factors in order of extraction. The shape of the plot is used to determine the number of factors. Typically, the plot has a distinct break between the steep slope of factors with large eigenvalues and a gradual trailing off associated with the rest of the factors. This gradual trailing off is referred to as the *scree*. Experimental evidence indicates that the point at which the scree begins denotes the true number of factors. In general, the number of factors determined by a scree plot will be one or a few more than that determined by the eigenvalue criterion.

Determination Based on Percentage of Variance. In this approach, the number of factors extracted is determined so that the cumulative percentage of variance extracted by the factors reaches a satisfactory level. What level of variance is satisfactory depends on the problem. However, it is recommended that the factors extracted should account for at least 60% of the variance. Interpretation of the solution is often enhanced by a rotation of the factors.

Rotation of Factors

An important output from factor analysis is the factor matrix, also called the *factor pattern matrix*. The factor matrix contains the coefficients used to express the standardized variables in terms of the factors. These coefficients, the *factor loadings*, represent the correlations between the factors and the variables. A coefficient with a large absolute value indicates that the factor and the variable are closely related. The coefficients of the factor matrix can be used to interpret the factors.

Although the initial or unrotated factor matrix indicates the relationship between the factors and individual variables, it seldom results in factors that can be interpreted, because the factors are correlated with many variables. Therefore, through rotation, the factor matrix is transformed into a simpler matrix that is easier to interpret.

In rotating the factors, we would like each factor to have nonzero, or significant, loadings or coefficients for only some of the variables. Likewise, we would like each variable to have nonzero, or significant, loadings with only a few factors or, if possible, with only one. If several factors have high loadings with the same variable, it is difficult to interpret them. Rotation does not affect the commonalties and the percentage of total variance explained. However, the percentage of variance accounted for by each factor changes. The variance explained by the individual factors is redistributed by rotation. Therefore, different methods of rotation may result in the identification of different factors.

The rotation is called orthogonal rotation if the axes are maintained at right angles. The most commonly used method for rotation is the varimax procedure. This is an orthogonal method of rotation that minimizes the number of variables with high loadings on a factor, thereby enhancing the interpretability of the factors. Orthogonal rotation results in factors that are uncorrelated. The rotation is called oblique rotation when the axes are not maintained at right angles and the factors are correlated. Sometimes, allowing for correlations among factors can simplify the factor pattern matrix. Oblique rotation should be used when factors in the population are likely to be strongly correlated.

Interpretation of Factors

Interpretation is facilitated by identifying the variables that have large loadings on the same factor. That factor can then be interpreted in terms of the variables that load highly on it. Another useful aid in interpretation is to plot the variables, using the factor loadings as coordinates. Variables at the end of an axis are those that have high loadings on only that factor and thus describe the factor. Variables near the origin have small loadings on both factors. Variables that are not near any of the axes are related to both the factors. If a factor cannot be clearly defined in terms of the original variables, it should be labeled as an undefined or a general factor.

Factor Scores

Following interpretation, factor scores can be calculated, if necessary. Factor analysis has its own stand-alone value. However, if the goal of factor analysis is to reduce the original set of variables to a smaller set of composite variables (factors) for use in subsequent multivariate analysis, it is useful to compute factor scores for each respondent. A factor is simply a linear combination of the original variables (Lastovicka and Thamodaran 1991). The factor scores for the ith factor may be estimated as follows:

$$F_1 = W_{11}X_1 + W_{12}X_2 + W_{13}X_3 + \ldots + W_{1k}X_k.$$

These symbols were defined previously.

Selection of Surrogate Variables

Sometimes, instead of computing factor scores, the researcher wishes to select surrogate variables. Selection of substitute or surrogate variables involves singling out some of the original variables for use in subsequent analysis. This allows the researcher to conduct subsequent analysis and interpret the results in terms of original variables rather than factor scores. By examining the factor matrix, one could select, for each factor, the variable with the highest loading on that factor. That variable could then be used as a surrogate variable for the associated factor.

Model Fit

The final step in factor analysis involves the determination of model fit (Basilevsky 1994). A basic assumption underlying factor analysis is that the observed correlation between variables can be attributed to common factors. Thus, the correlations between the variables can be deduced or reproduced from the estimated correlations between the variables and the factors. The differences between the observed correlations (as given in the input correlation matrix) and the reproduced correlations (as estimated from the factor matrix) can be examined to determine model fit. These differences are called *residuals*. If there are many large residuals, the factor model does not provide a good fit to the data, and the model should be reconsidered (Acito and Anderson 1980).

CLUSTER ANALYSIS

Cluster analysis is a class of techniques used to classify objects or cases into relatively homogeneous groups called *clusters*. Objects in each cluster tend to be similar to one another and dissimilar to objects in the other clusters. Cluster analysis is also called *classification analysis* or *numerical taxonomy*. We address clustering procedures that assign each object to one and only one cluster (Chaturvedi et al. 1997).

Both cluster analysis and discriminant analysis deal with classification. However, discriminant analysis requires prior knowledge of the cluster or group membership of each object or case included to develop the classification rule. In contrast, in cluster analysis, there is no a priori information about the group or cluster membership for any of the objects. Groups or clusters are suggested by the data, not defined a priori.

Cluster analysis has been used in marketing for a variety of purposes, including the following:

❑ *Segmenting the market*: Consumers may be clustered on the basis of benefits sought from the purchase of a product. Each cluster would consist of consumers who are relatively homogeneous in terms of the benefits they seek. This approach is called *benefit segmentation*.

❑ *Understanding buyer behaviors*: Cluster analysis can be used to identify homogeneous groups of buyers. Then, the buying behavior of each group may be examined separately. For example, respondents may be clustered on the basis of the self-reported importance attached to each factor of the choice criteria used in selecting a brand.

❑ *Identifying new product opportunities*: By clustering brands and products, competitive sets within the market can be determined. Brands in the same cluster compete more fiercely with one another than with brands in other clusters. A firm can examine its current offerings compared with those of its competitors to identify potential new product opportunities.

❑ *Selecting test markets*: By grouping cities into homogeneous clusters, it is possible to select comparable cities to test various marketing strategies.

❏ *Reducing data*: Cluster analysis can be used as a general data reduction tool to develop clusters or subgroups of data that are more manageable than individual observations. Subsequent multivariate analysis is conducted on the clusters rather than on the individual observations. For example, to describe differences in consumers' product usage behaviors, the consumers may first be clustered into groups. The differences among the groups may then be examined using multiple discriminant analysis.

Conducting Cluster Analysis

The first step in cluster analysis is to formulate the clustering problem by defining the variables on which the clustering will be based. Then an appropriate distance measure must be selected. The distance measure determines how similar or dissimilar the objects being clustered are. Several clustering procedures have been developed, and the researcher should select one that is appropriate for the problem at hand. Deciding on the number of clusters requires judgment on the part of the researcher. The derived clusters should be interpreted in terms of the variables used to cluster them and profiled in terms of additional salient variables. Finally, the researcher must assess the validity of the clustering process.

Formulating the Problem

Perhaps the most important part of formulating the clustering problem is selecting the variables on which the clustering is based. Inclusion of even one or two irrelevant variables may distort an otherwise useful clustering solution. Basically, the set of variables selected should describe the similarity between objects in terms that are relevant to the marketing research problem. The variables should be selected on the basis of prior research, theory, or a consideration of the hypotheses being tested. In exploratory research, the researcher should exercise judgment and intuition.

Selecting a Distance or Similarity Measure

Because the objective of clustering is to group similar objects together, some measure is needed to assess how similar or different the objects are. The most common approach is to measure similarity in terms of distance between pairs of objects. Objects with smaller distances between them are more similar to each other than are those with larger distances. There are several ways to compute the distance between two objects.

The most commonly used measure of similarity is the euclidean distance or its square. The euclidean distance is the square root of the sum of the squared differences in values for each variable. Other distance measures are also available. The city block or Manhattan distance between two objects is the sum of the absolute differences in values for each variable.

The Chebychev distance between two objects is the maximum absolute difference in values for any variable.

Use of different distance measures may lead to different clustering results. Therefore, it is advisable to use different measures and compare the results. Having selected a distance or similarity measure, we can next select a clustering procedure.

Selecting a Clustering Procedure

Clustering procedures can be hierarchical or nonhierarchical. Hierarchical clustering is characterized by the development of a hierarchy or treelike structure. Hierarchical methods can be agglomerative or divisive. Agglomerative clustering starts with each object in a separate cluster. Clusters are formed by grouping objects into bigger and bigger clusters. This process is continued until all objects are members of a single cluster. Divisive clustering starts with all the objects grouped in a single cluster. Clusters are divided or split until each object is in a separate cluster.

Agglomerative methods are commonly used in marketing research. They consist of linkage, error sums of squares or variance, and centroid methods. Linkage methods include single linkage, complete linkage, and average linkage. The single-linkage method is based on minimum distance or the nearest neighbor rule. The single-linkage method does not work well when the clusters are poorly defined. The complete-linkage method is similar to single linkage, except that it is based on the maximum distance or the furthest neighbor approach. The average-linkage method works similarly. However, in this method, the distance between two clusters is defined as the average of the distances between all pairs of objects, where one member of the pair is from each of the clusters. Thus, the average-linkage method uses information on all pairs of distances, not merely the minimum or maximum distances. For this reason, it is usually preferred to the single- and complete-linkage methods (Milligan 1980).

The variance methods attempt to generate clusters to minimize the within-cluster variance. A commonly used variance method is Ward's procedure. At each stage, the two clusters with the smallest increase in the overall sum of squares within cluster distances are combined. In the centroid methods, the distance between two clusters is the distance between their centroids (means for all the variables). Of the hierarchical methods, the average-linkage and Ward's methods have been shown to perform better than the other procedures.

The second type of clustering procedures, the nonhierarchical clustering methods, is frequently referred to as k-means clustering. Two major disadvantages of the nonhierarchical procedures are that the number of clusters must be prespecified and the selection of cluster centers is arbitrary. Yet nonhierarchical clustering is faster than hierarchical methods and has merit when the number of objects or observations is large. It has been suggested that the hierarchical and nonhierarchical methods should be used in tandem. First, an initial clustering solution is obtained using a hierarchical procedure, such as average linkage or Ward's. Second, the number of clusters and cluster centroids so obtained are used as input to nonhierarchical clustering.

Deciding on the Number of Clusters

A major issue in cluster analysis is deciding on the number of clusters (Everitt 1993). Although there are no hard and fast rules, some guidelines are available:

1. Theoretical, conceptual, or practical considerations may suggest a certain number of clusters. For example, if the purpose of clustering is to identify market segments, management may want a particular number of clusters.

2. In hierarchical clustering, the distances at which clusters are combined can be used as criteria. This information can be obtained from the agglomeration schedule or the dendrogram.

3. In nonhierarchical clustering, the ratio of total within group variance to between-group variance can be plotted against the number of clusters. The point at which an elbow or a sharp bend occurs indicates an appropriate number of clusters.

4. The relative sizes of the clusters should be meaningful.

Interpreting and Profiling the Clusters

Interpreting and profiling clusters involves examining the cluster centroids. The centroids represent the mean values of the objects contained in the cluster on each of the variables. The centroids enable us to describe each cluster by assigning it a name or label. If the clustering program does not print this information, it may be obtained through discriminant analysis (Dibbs and Stern 1995).

Often, it is helpful to profile the clusters in terms of variables that were not used for clustering. These may include demographic, psychographic, product usage, media usage, or other variables. For example, the clusters may have been derived on the basis of benefits sought. Further profiling may be done in terms of demographic and psychographic variables to target marketing efforts for each cluster. The variables that significantly differentiate between clusters can be identified by discriminant analysis and one-way ANOVA.

Assessing Reliability and Validity

Given the several judgments entailed in cluster analysis, no clustering solution should be accepted without some assessment of its reliability and validity. Formal procedures for assessing the reliability and validity of clustering solutions are complex and not fully defensible. Therefore, we omit them here (Funkhouser 1983; Klastorin 1983). However, the following procedures provide adequate checks on the quality of clustering results:

1. Perform cluster analysis on the same data using different distance measures. Compare the results across measures to determine the stability of the solutions.
2. Use different methods of clustering and compare the results.
3. Split the data randomly into halves. Perform clustering separately on each half. Compare cluster centroids across the two subsamples.
4. Delete variables randomly. Perform clustering on the basis of the reduced set of variables. Compare the results with those obtained by clustering based on the entire set of variables.

BASIC CONCEPTS IN MULTIDIMENSIONAL SCALING

Multidimensional scaling (MDS) is a class of procedures for representing perceptions and preferences of respondents spatially by means of a visual display. Perceived or psychological relationships among stimuli are represented as geometric relationships among points in a multidimensional space. These geometric representations are often called *spatial maps*. The axes of the spatial map are assumed to denote the psychological bases or underlying dimensions respondents use to form perceptions and preferences for stimuli (Cox 1994). It has been used in marketing to identify

1. The number and nature of dimensions consumers use to perceive different brands in the marketplace,
2. The positioning of current brands on these dimensions, and
3. The positioning of consumers' ideal brand on these dimensions.

Information provided by MDS has been used for a variety of marketing applications, including

❏ *Image measurement*: Comparing the customers' and noncustomers' perceptions of the firm with the firm's perceptions of itself.

❏ *New product development*: To look for gaps in the spatial map, which indicate potential opportunities for positioning new products. Also, to evaluate new product concepts and existing brands on a test basis to determine how consumers perceive the new concepts.

❏ *Assessing advertising effectiveness*: Spatial maps can be used to determine whether advertising has been successful in achieving the desired brand positioning.

❏ *Pricing analysis*: Spatial maps developed with and without pricing information can be compared to determine the impact of pricing.

❏ *Channel decisions*: Judgments on compatibility of brands with different retail outlets could lead to spatial maps useful for making channel decisions.

Conducting MDS

The researcher must formulate the MDS problem carefully because a variety of data may be used as input into MDS. The researcher must also determine an appropriate form in which data should be obtained and select an MDS procedure for analyzing the data. An important aspect of the solution involves determining the number of dimensions for the spatial map. Also, the axes of the map should be labeled and the derived configuration interpreted. Finally, the researcher must assess the quality of the results obtained. We describe each of these steps, beginning with problem formulation (Carroll and Green 1997).

Formulating the Problem

Formulating the problem requires that the researcher specify the purpose for which the MDS results would be used and select the brands or other stimuli to be included in the analysis. The number of brands or stimuli selected and the specific brands included determine the nature of the resulting dimensions and configurations. At a minimum, 8 brands or stimuli should be included to obtain a well-defined spatial map. Including more than 25 brands is likely to be cumbersome and may result in respondent fatigue.

The decision regarding which specific brands or stimuli to include should be made carefully. Suppose a researcher is interested in obtaining consumer perceptions of automobiles. If luxury automobiles are not included in the stimulus set, this dimension may not emerge in the results. The choice of the number of and specific brands or stimuli to be included should be based on the statement of the marketing research problem, theory, and the judgment of the researcher.

Obtaining Input Data

Input data obtained from the respondents may be related to perceptions or preferences. Perception data, which may be direct or derived, are discussed first.

In direct approaches to gathering perception data, respondents are asked to judge how similar or dissimilar the various brands or stimuli are, using their own criteria. Respondents are often required to rate all possible pairs of brands or stimuli in terms of similarity on a Likert scale. These data are referred to as similarity judgments.

The number of pairs to be evaluated is $n(n-1)/2$, where n is the number of stimuli. Other procedures are also available. Respondents could be asked to rank-order all the possible pairs from the most similar to the least similar. In another method, the respondent rank-orders the brands in terms of their similarity to an anchor brand. Each brand, in turn, serves as the anchor.

Derived approaches to collecting perception data are attribute-based approaches that require respondents to rate the brands or stimuli on the identified attributes using semantic differential or Likert scales. If attribute ratings are obtained, a similarity measure (such as euclidean distance) is derived for each pair of brands (Steenkamp, Van Trijp, and Ten Berge 1994).

Preference data order the brands or stimuli in terms of respondents' preference for some property. A common way in which such data are obtained is preference rankings. Respondents are required to rank the brands from the most preferred to the least preferred. When spatial maps are based on preference data, distance implies differences in preference. The configuration derived from preference data may differ greatly from that obtained from similarity data. Two brands may be perceived as different in a similarity map yet similar in a preference map, and vice versa. We continue to use the perception data to illustrate the MDS procedure.

Selecting an MDS Procedure

Selection of a specific MDS procedure depends on whether perception or preference data are being scaled or whether the analysis requires both kinds of data. The nature of the input data is also a determining factor. Nonmetric MDS procedures assume that the input data are ordinal, but the procedures result in metric output. The distances in the resulting spatial map may be assumed to be interval-scaled. In contrast, metric MDS methods assume that input data are metric. The metric and nonmetric methods produce similar results.

Another factor influencing the selection of a procedure is whether the MDS analysis will be conducted at the individual respondent level or at an aggregate level. In individual-level analysis, the data are analyzed separately for each respondent, which results in a spatial map for each respondent. Although individual-level analysis is useful from a research perspective, it is not appealing from a managerial standpoint. Marketing strategies are typically formulated at the segment or aggregate level, rather than at the individual level. If aggregate-level analysis is conducted, some assumptions must be made in aggregating individual data. Typically, it is assumed that all respondents use the same dimensions to evaluate the brands or stimuli but that different respondents weight these common dimensions differentially (Borg and Groenen 1996).

Deciding on the Number of Dimensions

The objective in MDS is to obtain a spatial map that best fits the input data in the smallest number of dimensions. However, spatial maps are computed in such a way that the fit improves as the number of dimensions increases. Therefore, a compromise must be made. The fit of an MDS solution is commonly assessed by the stress measure. Stress is a lack-of-fit measure; higher values of stress indicate poorer fits. The following guidelines are suggested for determining the number of dimensions:

1. *A priori knowledge*: Theory or prior research may suggest a particular number of dimensions.

2. *Interpretability of the spatial map*: In general, it is difficult to interpret configurations or maps derived in more than three dimensions.

3. *Elbow criterion*: A plot of stress versus dimensionality should be examined. The points in this plot usually form a convex pattern. The point at which an elbow or a sharp bend occurs indicates an appropriate number of dimensions.

4. *Ease of use*: It is generally easier to work with two-dimensional maps or configurations than with those involving more dimensions.

Labeling the Dimensions and Interpreting the Configuration

After a spatial map is developed, the dimensions must be labeled and the configuration interpreted. Labeling the dimensions requires subjective judgment on the part of the researcher. The following guidelines can assist in this task:

1. Even if direct similarity judgments are obtained, ratings of the brands on researcher-supplied attributes may still be collected. Using statistical methods such as regression, these attribute vectors may be fitted in the spatial map. The axes may then be labeled for the attributes with which they are most closely aligned.

2. After providing direct similarity or preference data, the respondents may be asked to indicate the criteria they used in making their evaluations. These criteria may then be subjectively related to the spatial map to label the dimensions.

3. If possible, the respondents can be shown their spatial maps and asked to label the dimensions by inspecting the configurations.

4. If objective characteristics of the brands are available (e.g., horsepower or miles per gallon for automobiles), these could be used as an aid in interpreting the subjective dimensions of the spatial maps.

Often, the dimensions represent more than one attribute. The configuration or the spatial map may be interpreted by examining the coordinates and relative positions of the brands. For example, brands located near one another compete more fiercely. An isolated brand has a unique image. Brands that are farther along in the direction of a descriptor are stronger on that characteristic. Thus, the strengths and weaknesses of each product can be understood. Gaps in the spatial map may indicate potential opportunities for introducing new products (Borg and Groenen 1996).

Assessing Reliability and Validity

The input data, and consequently the MDS solutions, are invariably subject to substantial random variability. Therefore, it is necessary that some assessment be made of the reliability and validity of MDS solutions (Malhotra 1987). The following guidelines are suggested:

1. The index of fit, or R-square, should be examined. This is a squared correlation index that indicates the proportion of variance of the optimally scaled data that can be accounted for by the MDS procedure. Thus, it indicates how well the MDS model fits the input data. Higher values of R-square are desirable, but values of 0.60 or better are considered acceptable.

2. Stress values are also indicative of the quality of MDS solutions. Whereas R-square is a measure of goodness of fit, stress measures badness of fit, or the proportion of variance of the optimally scaled data that is not accounted for by the MDS model. Stress values vary with the type of MDS procedure and the data being analyzed.

3. If an aggregate-level analysis has been done, the original data should be split into two or more parts. The MDS analysis should be conducted separately on each part and the results compared.

4. Stimuli can be selectively eliminated from the input data and the solutions determined for the remaining stimuli.

Correspondence Analysis

Correspondence analysis is an MDS technique for scaling qualitative data in marketing research. The input data are in the form of a contingency table, indicating a qualitative association between the rows and columns. Correspondence analysis scales the rows and columns in corresponding units, so that each can be displayed graphically in the same low-dimensional space. These spatial maps provide insights into (1) similarities and differences within the rows with respect to a given column category, (2) similarities and differences within the column categories with respect to a given row category, and (3) the relationship among the rows and columns.

The interpretation of results in correspondence analysis is similar to that in principal components analysis, given the similarity of the algorithms. Correspondence analysis results in the grouping of categories (activities, brands, or other stimuli) found within the contingency table, just as principal components analysis involves the grouping of the independent variables. The results are interpreted in terms of proximities among the rows and columns of the contingency table. Categories, which are closer together, are more similar in underlying structure.

BASIC CONCEPTS IN CONJOINT ANALYSIS

Conjoint analysis attempts to determine the relative importance consumers attach to salient attributes and the utilities they attach to the levels of attributes. This information is derived from consumers' evaluations of brands or brand profiles composed of these attributes and their levels. The respondents are presented with stimuli that consist of combinations of attribute levels. They are asked to evaluate these stimuli in terms of their desirability. Conjoint procedures attempt to assign values to the levels of each attribute, so that the resulting values or utilities attached to the stimuli match, as closely as possible, the input evaluations provided by the respondents. The underlying assumption is that any set of stimuli, such as products, brands, or stores, is evaluated as a bundle of attributes.

Similar to MDS, conjoint analysis relies on respondents' subjective evaluations. However, in MDS, the stimuli are products or brands. In conjoint analysis, the stimuli are combinations of attribute levels determined by the researcher. The goal in MDS is to develop a spatial map depicting the stimuli in a multidimensional perceptual or preference space. Conjoint analysis, in contrast, seeks to develop the partworth or utility functions that describe the utility that consumers attach to the levels of each attribute. The two techniques are complementary. Conjoint analysis has been used in marketing for a variety of purposes, including

❑ Determining the relative importance of attributes in the consumer choice process. A standard output from conjoint analysis consists of derived relative importance weights for all the attributes used to construct the stimuli used in the evaluation task. The relative importance weights indicate which attributes are important in influencing consumer choice.

❑ Estimating market share of brands that differ in attribute levels. The utilities derived from conjoint analysis can be used as input into a choice simulator to determine the share of choices, and thus the market share, of different brands.

❑ Determining the composition of the most preferred brand. The brand features can be varied in terms of attribute levels and the corresponding utilities determined. The brand features that yield the highest utility indicate the composition of the most preferred brand.

❑ Segmenting the market on the basis of similarity of preferences for attribute levels. The partworth functions derived
for the attributes may be used as a basis for clustering respondents to arrive at homogeneous preference segments.

Conducting Conjoint Analysis

Formulating the problem involves identifying the salient attributes
and their levels. These attributes and levels are used for constructing the
stimuli to be used in a conjoint evaluation task. The respondents rate or
rank the stimuli using a suitable scale, and the data obtained are analyzed. The results are interpreted and their reliability and validity
assessed (Wittink, Vriens, and Burhenne 1994). We now describe each of
the steps of conjoint analysis in detail.

Formulating the Problem

In formulating the conjoint analysis problem, the researcher must
identify the attributes and attribute levels to be used in constructing the
stimuli. Attribute levels denote the values assumed by the attributes. A
typical conjoint analysis study involves six or seven attributes. After the
salient attributes have been identified, their appropriate levels should be
selected. The utility or partworth function for the levels of an attribute
may be nonlinear. For example, a consumer may prefer a medium-sized
car to either a small or large one. In these cases, at least three levels should
be used. Some attributes, though, may naturally occur in binary form
(two levels); a car does or does not have a sunroof.

Constructing the Stimuli

Two broad approaches are available for constructing conjoint analysis
stimuli: the pairwise approach and the full-profile procedure. In the pairwise
approach, also called *two-factor evaluations*, the respondents evaluate two
attributes at a time until all the possible pairs of attributes have been evaluated. In the full-profile approach, also called *multiple-factor evaluations*, full or
complete profiles of brands are constructed for all the attributes. Typically,
each profile is described on a separate index card (Loosschilder et al. 1995).

It is not necessary to evaluate all the possible combinations, nor is it feasible in all cases. In the pairwise approach, it is possible to reduce the number of paired comparisons by using cyclical designs. Likewise, in the full-
profile approach, the number of stimulus profiles can be greatly reduced by
means of fractional factorial designs. Generally, two sets of data are
obtained. The *estimation set* is used to calculate the partworth functions for
the attribute levels. The *holdout set* is used to assess reliability and validity.

Deciding on the Form of Input Data

As in the case of MDS, conjoint analysis input data can be either nonmetric or metric. For nonmetric data, the respondents are typically

required to provide rank-order evaluations so that such data accurately reflect the behavior of consumers in the marketplace. In the metric form, the respondents provide ratings rather than rankings. In this case, the judgments are typically made independently. In recent years, the use of ratings has become increasingly common.

In conjoint analysis, the dependent variable is usually preference or intention to buy. In other words, respondents provide ratings or rankings in terms of their preference or intentions to buy. However, the conjoint methodology is flexible and can accommodate a range of other dependent variables, including actual purchase or choice.

Selecting a Conjoint Analysis Procedure

The basic conjoint analysis model may be represented by the following formula:

$$U(X) = \sum_{i=1}^{m} \sum_{j=1}^{k} \alpha_{ij} x_{i_1},$$

where

$U(X)$ = overall utility of an alternative,

α_{ij} = the partworth contribution or utility associated with the jth level $(j, j = 1, 2, ..., k_i)$ of the ith attribute $(i, i = 1, 2, ..., m)$,

k_i = number of levels of attribute i, and

m = number of attributes.

The importance of an attribute, I_i, is defined in terms of the range of the partworths, α_{ij}, across the levels of that attribute:

$$I_i = \{\max(\alpha_{ij}) - \min(\alpha_{ij})\} \text{ for each } i.$$

The attribute's importance is normalized to ascertain its importance relative to other attributes, W_i:

$$W_i = \frac{I_i}{\sum_{i=1}^{m} I_i},$$

so that $\sum_{i=1}^{m} w_i = 1$.

Several different procedures are available for estimating the basic model. The simplest, and one gaining in popularity, is dummy variable regression. In this case, the predictor variables consist of dummy variables for the attribute levels. If an attribute has k_i levels, it is coded in terms of $k_i - 1$ dummy variables. If metric data are obtained, the ratings, assumed to be interval-scaled, form the dependent variable. If the data are nonmetric, the rankings may be converted to 0 or 1 by making paired comparisons between brands. In this case, the predictor variables represent the differences in the attribute levels of the brands being compared.

The researcher must also decide whether the data will be analyzed at the individual respondent or the aggregate level. At the individual level, the data of each respondent are analyzed separately. If an aggregate-level analysis is to be conducted, some procedure for grouping the respondents must be devised. One common approach is first to estimate individual-level partworth or utility functions. The respondents are then clustered on the basis of the similarity of their partworths. Aggregate analysis is then conducted for each cluster. An appropriate model for estimating the parameters should be specified.

The estimation of the partworths and the relative importance weights provides the basis for interpreting the results (Carroll and Green 1995).

Interpreting the Results

For interpreting the results, it is helpful to plot the partworth functions. The utility values reported have only interval scale properties, and their origin is arbitrary.

Assessing Reliability and Validity

Several procedures are available for assessing the reliability and validity of conjoint analysis results (Malhotra 1982):

1. The goodness of fit of the estimated model should be evaluated. For example, if dummy variable regression is used, the value of R^2 will indicate the extent to which the model fits the data. Models with poor fit are suspect.
2. Test–retest reliability can be assessed by obtaining a few replicated judgments later in data collection.
3. The evaluations for the holdout or validation stimuli can be predicted by the estimated partworth functions. The predicted evaluations can then be correlated with those obtained from the respondents to determine internal validity.
4. If an aggregate-level analysis has been conducted, the estimation sample can be split in several ways, and conjoint analysis can be conducted on each subsample. The results can be compared across subsamples to assess the stability of conjoint analysis solutions.

OTHER MULTIVARIATE TECHNIQUES

In multiple regression, there is a single dependent variable, which is metric. In the special case in which there is a single, binary, dependent variable, logistic regression, also called the *logit model*, can be used. The logit model assumes that the random component or the error term follows standard Weibull or extreme value distribution. The dependent variable assumes one of two values; that is, the individual chooses or does not choose a particular alternative. When more than one alternative is involved, as in a discrete choice situation, the logit model generalizes to the multinomial logit model, which models the probability that an individual will select a particular alternative from a specified choice set.

The probit model is similar to the logit model in that the dependent variable is binary. However, the error term is assumed to have a normal distribution. Yet another limited dependent variable model is the tobit model. In this case, the dependent variable has a limiting value for a large number of cases. Suppose the dependent variable is the amount spent by a household in selected department stores during a specified time period. If a random survey of households is conducted, there would be a large number of households in the sample that would not have spent anything in specific department stores and would, therefore, have a value of 0. Thus, the dependent variable would have a limiting value of 0 for a large number of cases. If multiple regression is used in this situation, the parameters will be biased. The correct procedure to use is the tobit model.

The techniques that we have discussed so far examine only a single relationship at a time. In contrast, structural equation modeling (SEM) enables the researcher to examine a series of dependence relationships simultaneously. This technique allows for the possibility that one dependent variable becomes an independent variable in subsequent dependence relationships. For example, what variables determine customer value? How does customer value combine with store characteristics to influence preference to shop? How does preference to shop affect store patronage? Thus, SEM may be thought of as an extension of multiple regression. It estimates a series of interdependent multiple regression equations simultaneously, as specified by the structural model. The structural model is specified by the researcher on the basis of theory and past experience.

CONCLUSION

We have discussed the commonly used multivariate techniques. How should a researcher select a technique or set of techniques for a particular project? The selection of a data analysis strategy should be based on the earlier steps of the marketing research process, known characteristics of the data, properties of statistical techniques, and the background and philosophy of the researcher.

Data analysis is not an end in itself. Its purpose is to produce information that will help address the problem at hand. The selection of a data analysis strategy must begin with a consideration of the earlier steps in the process. One should consider the known characteristics of the data. The measurement scales used exert a strong influence on the choice of statistical techniques. In addition, the research design may favor certain techniques. For example, ANOVA is suited for analyzing experimental data from causal designs. The insights into the data obtained during data preparation can be valuable for selecting a strategy for analysis.

It is also important to take into account the properties of the statistical techniques, particularly their purpose and underlying assumptions. Some statistical techniques are appropriate for examining differences in variables, others for assessing the magnitudes of the relationships between variables, and others for making predictions. The techniques also involve different assumptions, and some techniques can withstand violations of the underlying assumptions better than others.

Finally, the researcher's background and philosophy affect the choice of a data analysis strategy. Researchers differ in their willingness to make assumptions about the variables and their underlying populations. In general, several techniques may be appropriate for analyzing the data from a given project. The experienced, statistically trained researcher will employ a range of techniques.

As we move into the next century, we will see an innovative application of existing techniques in areas in which they have not been used hithertofore. We will also see the development of new techniques designed to meet the challenges facing data analysts. In particular, there is a need to develop techniques that will reduce the data collection demands imposed on respondents and yet allow the estimation of parameters at the individual or disaggregate level. There is also a need to develop techniques that can analyze data as they are being collected by the respondents in an interactive manner. Thus, data collection and analysis can take place interactively and simultaneously.

BIBLIOGRAPHY

Acito, Frank and Ronald D. Anderson (1980), "A Monté Carlo Comparison of Factor Analytic Methods," *Journal of Marketing Research*, 17 (May), 228–36.

Basilevsky, Alexander (1994), *Statistical Factor Analysis & Related Methods: Theory & Applications.* New York: John Wiley & Sons.

Berenson, Mark L. and David M. Levine (1996), *Basic Business Statistics: Concepts and Applications*, 6th ed. Englewood Cliffs, NJ: Prentice Hall.

Borg, Ingwer and Patrick J. Groenen (1996), *Modern Multidimensional Scaling Theory and Applications.* New York: Springer-Verlag.

Carroll, J. Douglass and Paul E. Green (1995), "Psychometric Methods in Marketing Research: Part I, Conjoint Analysis," *Journal of Marketing Research*, 32 (November), 385–91.

———— and ———— (1997), "Psychometric Methods in Marketing Research: Part II, Multidimensional Scaling," *Journal of Marketing Research*, 34 (February), 193–204.

Chaturvedi, Anil, J. Douglass Carroll, Paul E. Green, and John A. Rotondo (1997), "A Feature-Based Approach to Market Segmentation Via Overlapping K-Centroids Clustering," *Journal of Marketing Research*, 34 (August), 370–77.

Cohen, Jacob and Patricia Cohen (1983), *Applied Multiple Regression Correlation Analysis for the Behavioral Sciences*, 2d ed. Hillsdale, NJ: Lawrence Erlbaum Associates, 181–222.

Cooil, Bruce, Russell S. Winer, and David L. Rados (1987), "Cross-Validation for Prediction," *Journal of Marketing Research*, 24 (August), 271–79.

Cox, T. (1994), *Multidimensional Scaling*. New York: Routledge, Chapman & Hall.

Dibbs, S. and P. Stern (1995), "Questioning the Reliability of Market Segmentation Techniques," *Omega*, 23 (December), 625–36.

Draper, N.R. and H. Smith (1998), *Applied Regression Analysis*, 3d ed. New York: John Wiley & Sons.

Dunteman, George H. (1989), *Principal Components Analysis*. Newbury Park, CA: Sage Publications.

Everitt, B. (1993), *Cluster Analysis*, 3d ed. New York: Halsted Press.

Fok, Lillian, John P. Angelidis, Nabil A. Ibrahim, and Wing M. Fok (1995), "The Utilization and Interpretation of Multivariate Statistical Techniques in Strategic Management," *International Journal of Management*, 12 (December), 468–81.

Fox, John (1997), *Applied Regression Analysis, Linear Models, and Related Methods*. Thousand Oaks, CA: Sage Publications.

Funkhouser, G. Ray (1983), "A Note on the Reliability of Certain Clustering Algorithms," *Journal of Marketing Research*, 30 (February), 99–102.

Greenberg, Edward and Robert P. Parks (1997), "A Predictive Approach to Model Selection and Multicollinearity," *Journal of Applied Econometrics*, 12 (January/February), 67–75.

Hair, Joseph F., Jr., Ralph E. Anderson, Ronald L. Tatham, and William C. Black (1999), *Multivariate Data Analysis with Readings*, 5th ed. Englewood Cliffs, NJ: Prentice Hall.

Jaccard, James (1997), *Interaction Effects in Factorial Analysis of Variance*. Thousand Oaks, CA: Sage Publications.

Johnson, Richard A. and Dean W. Wichern (1998), *Applied Multivariate Statistical Analysis*, 4th ed. Paramus, NJ: Prentice Hall.

Klastorin, T.D. (1983), "Assessing Cluster Analysis Results," *Journal of Marketing Research*, 20 (February), 92–98.

Klecka, W.R. (1980), *Discriminant Analysis*. Beverly Hills, CA: Sage Publications.

Lastovicka, John L. and Kanchana Thamodaran (1991), "Common Factor Score Estimates in Multiple Regression Problems," *Journal of Marketing Research*, 28 (February), 105–12.

Lenell, Wayne and Robert Boissoneau (1996), "Using Causal-Comparative and Correlational Designs in Conducting Market Research," *Journal of Professional Services Marketing*, 13 (2), 59–69.

Loosschilder, Gerard H., Edward Rosbergen, Marco Vriens, and Dick R. Wittink (1995), "Pictorial Stimuli in Conjoint Analysis-to Support Product Styling Decisions," *Journal of the Market Research Society*, 37 (January), 17–34.

Malhotra, Naresh K. (1982), "Structural Reliability and Stability of Nonmetric Conjoint Analysis," *Journal of Marketing Research*, 19 (May), 199–207.

——— (1987), "Validity and Structural Reliability of Multidimensional Scaling," *Journal of Marketing Research*, 24 (May), 164–73.

Mason, Charlotte H. and William D. Perreault Jr. (1991), "Collinearity, Power, and Interpretation of Multiple Regression Analysis," *Journal of Marketing Research*, 28 (August), 268–80.

Milligan, G. (1980), "An Examination of the Effect of Six Types of Error Perturbation on Fifteen Clustering Algorithms," *Psychometrika*, 45 (September), 325–42.

Morrison, D.G. (1969), "On the Interpretation of Discriminant Analysis," *Journal of Marketing Research*, 6 (May), 156–63.

Neter, John W. (1996), *Applied Linear Statistical Models*, 4th ed. Burr Ridge, IL: Richard D. Irwin.

————, William Wasserman, and Michael H. Kutner (1990), *Applied Linear Regression Models*, 3d ed. Burr Ridge, IL: Richard D. Irwin.

Novak, Thomas P. (1995), "MANOVAMAP: Geographical Representation of MANOVA in Marketing Research," *Journal of Marketing Research*, 32 (August), 357–74.

Pett, Marjorie A. (1997), *Nonparametric Statistics for Health Care Research*. Thousand Oaks, CA: Sage Publications.

Sirkin, R. Mark (1994), *Statistics for the Social Sciences*. Thousand Oaks, CA: Sage Publications.

Steenkamp, Jan-Benedict E.M., Hans C.M. Van Trijp, and Jos M.F. Ten Berge (1994), "Perceptual Mapping Based on Idiosyncratic Sets of Attributes," *Journal of Marketing Research*, 31 (February), 15–27.

Wang, George C.S. (1996), "How to Handle Multicollinearity in Regression Modeling," *Journal of Business Forecasting Methods & Systems*, 15 (Spring), 23–27.

Winer, B.J., Donald R. Brown, and Kenneth M. Michels (1991), *Statistical Principles in Experimental Design*, 3d ed. New York: McGraw-Hill.

Wittink, Dick R., Marco Vriens, and Wim Burhenne (1994), "Commercial Uses of Conjoint Analysis in Europe: Results and Critical Reflections," *International Journal of Research in Marketing*, 11 (January), 41–52.

11
Computer-Based Qualitative Data Analysis

Ian Dey

The notebooks are full, the cabinets packed, and the shelves overflowing with annotations, observations, and transcriptions. Finally, the fieldwork phase of the project is over. We have observed, absorbed, recorded, and accumulated every snippet of information that might be remotely relevant to our concerns. But what to do now with all these data? We are baffled by their complexity. Daunted by their sheer volume. Bewildered by their diversity. Yet from these myriad materials, we must somehow produce a single and succinct account—and be quick about it!

The mysteries of qualitative analysis, of how we produce that account, for the most part remain just that—impenetrable and unfathomable mysteries, more befitting a dark art than an exact science. But the advent of information technology promises to move us at least a little way along the path from inspired faith to a more reasoned and reasonable—and more rigorous—perception of how to proceed. This promise is most evident in attempts to articulate an analytic rationale within which software for qualitative data analysis (QDA) can be developed and applied. It is equally evident in discussions about how software may shape analysis through the explicit or tacit assumptions upon which it is based and used. It is even evident in skeptical responses to what the software offers, which are based on alternative but previously unarticulated views of what qualitative analysis is all about. Albeit in different ways, these responses to the computer have helped make the implicit more explicit and suggested procedures—or if not procedures, then at least clearer clues—as to how to proceed.

In comparison with the dearth of explicit and pragmatic procedures for qualitative analysis, the literature is replete with epistemological prescriptions and ontological canons that presume to permit this or prohibit that approach. Qualitative data analysis has more often been considered a weapon in an epistemological struggle—for example, to overcome positivism—than a set of tools for struggling with data. The proliferation of different methodologies (Renata Tesch [1990] identified more than 40 at the start of the decade) does little in itself to clarify the options that we can consider. Such clarification requires of the researcher a critical and reflective engagement with methodological accounts rather than a simple selection of what feels most comfortable from a range of rival perspectives.

Stimulated by changing technology, such an engagement can illuminate the issues we confront when analyzing qualitative data. It is not a matter of prescribing a methodology as much as trying to identify some tools of the trade and recognizing their limitations. And the tools of the trade are changing rapidly. When I undertook my first qualitative study, in the early 1970s, I used a card index system to record and duplicate data, laboriously writing out materials by hand. By the early 1980s, though desktop computers had arrived, so little software was available for qualitative analysis that I had to take a leaf from Disraeli's book ("When I want to read a novel I write it myself") and produce my own application. A decade later, one could at least pick and choose among various software packages, though most of these (like mine) were developed, released, and supported by qualitative researchers themselves. Now, a mere decade later, a wide range of software can be bought off the shelf, marketed, and sold on a commercial basis (see www.scolari.co.uk for free demonstrations of some of the main packages, including Atlast/ti, Code-A-Text, The Ethnograph, HyperResearch, Nud*ist, Nvivo, and WinMAX). The pace of change is so rapid that reviews of specific software are very quickly out-of-date.

With the development of software, the toolkit for analyzing qualitative data has expanded. The first packages were designed mainly to allow analysts to categorize data by attaching categories to segments of text. They set up simple systems (at least they were intended to be simple) to allow data to be categorized in an expeditious and straightforward way. These could increasingly exploit the computer's search functions, even to the extent of "automatic" assignation of categories to located text. The data could then be "retrieved" under category headings, and comparisons could be made of both exemplars within categories and data across categories. More sophisticated procedures allowed categories to be split or spliced, which permitted the development of multiple levels of categorization. This in turn prompted the development of graphic modes of representation, which allowed category relationships to be presented (and manipulated) through mapping onto a visual display. Visual representation has been extended to include links among various elements in the analysis, including, for example, analytic memos, as well as categories, in a network that allows immediate access to relevant data. Retrievals have also been extended, notably through the adoption of Boolean or related procedures. These allow categorized data to be retrieved under various combinations (e.g., AND, OR, NOT). These in turn can be combined with case conditions (e.g., including or excluding all the documents where X is true) to provide some powerful analytic tools for examining the data. Further (or alternative) conditions may be imposed on retrievals depending on other relationships within the data, such as order or proximity. If we prefer, instead of making inferences based on retrievals, we may interrogate the data through specifying hypotheses (if X, then Y) and "testing" to see how far these hold good across cases. Meantime, the advent of multimedia has allowed the extension of "data" from text to incorporate graphic forms (such as video), and with more sophisticated methods of inputting materials, the analyst can circumvent the need to transcribe large volumes of data.

In one of the most comprehensive efforts to report on software development, Weitzman and Miles (1995) considered programs in terms of a range of procedures, including their facilities for inputting, annotating, coding, linking, searching, retrieving, and graphic representation. They also considered the variety of ways in which programs could assist conceptual development or theory generation. Programs varied considerably in the range of facilities they offered, both across and within these groupings. For example, some programs offered no support for data linking, whereas others provided support for linking memos to text, codes to memos, or memos to codes. Clearly, the appropriateness of software support must be considered in relation to the specific tasks required of any particular analysis. Overall comparisons (e.g., Barry 1998) between programs should be considered with this in mind. However, even a selective checklist of functions against which to compare applications, such as in Table 1, demonstrates the range of procedures that software can already support.

Thus, the computer offers a novel and rapidly developing toolkit for the management and manipulation of data in qualitative analysis. These tools affect the way we conceptualize and analyze our data, as well as manage and manipulate them. In this respect, perhaps the most remarkable aspect of software development has been the associated resurrection of Grounded Theory as a common analytic framework through which these tools can be applied. This paradoxical alliance of new technology and old theory (Glaser and Strauss introduced Grounded Theory in 1967) provides an appropriate puzzle through which to review the role of computer-based qualitative analysis as the new century opens.

Given its ambiguities and internal contradictions, Grounded Theory is difficult to summarize for the uninitiated (Dey 1999). In the present context, it is enough to note that Grounded Theory aims to generate substantive theory through the systematic collection and analysis of qualitative data by identifying categories and connecting them through a process of

Table 1
Checklist of Software Functions

Functions	Program 1	Program 2
Direct input of data		
Importing of data		
Formatted data accepted		
Offline data accepted		
Data files revisable		
Nonstandard text units specifiable		
Coding by keyword		
Coding by phrase		
Coding on-screen		
Automated coding		
Multilevel coding		
Graphic display of codes		
Text editing		
Text annotation		
Memos attachable to text		
Memos attachable to codes		
Links within memos/codes/text		
Links between memos/codes/text		
Search by Boolean operators		
Search by wildcard operators		
Search by proximity in text		
Search of text/memos/codes/cases		
Hits can be shown in context		
Hits can be edited		
Hypothesis testing possible		
Multicase comparisons		
Hierarchical structure modelling		
Network structure modelling		
Matrix tabulation display		

"constant comparison." The centrality of "coding" to Grounded Theory is reflected in the key stages of analysis proposed: open coding of data to generate categories, axial coding to relate categories (in terms of a "coding paradigm" that focuses on conditions, strategies, and consequences), and selective coding around a core category.

One of the attractions of Grounded Theory to software developers and users undoubtedly lies in its early pioneering attempts (in the 1960s) to engage with the pragmatic question of just what to do with all that data. Grounded Theory (Glaser and Strauss 1967; Strauss and Corbin 1990) sets out more explicitly than ever before just how a qualitative analysis can be done. Whether by accident or design, the procedures supported by software packages closely parallel the Grounded Theory approach to data analysis, with its emphasis on coding data, constant comparison of the coded data, analytic annotation using memos, and graphic representation. Thus, Grounded Theory seems to offer a methodological framework that explains and justifies the procedures that software can support.

This has provoked a concern that qualitative analysis may be diverted by computer-based software along a particular channel:

> The widespread influence of computer-assisted qualitative data analysis is promoting convergence on a uniform mode of data analysis and representation (often justified with reference to grounded theory) (Coffey, Holbrook, and Atkinson 1996, abstract).

The extent of this symbiotic convergence may be exaggerated (Kelle 1997; Lee and Fielding 1996) — particularly given the ambiguities in Grounded Theory itself, in that there are varying and conflicting versions of the theory (cf. Glaser 1992; Strauss and Corbin 1990). But there is no doubt that in some shape or form, Grounded Theory has become a standard framework through which to account for and justify computer-supported methods of analysis. Because of this convergence, Grounded Theory offers a convenient frame of reference for critical reflection on the methodological tools that are supported by computer software. It prompts us to reflect not only on the use we can make of the search and filing functions of the computer, but also about the nature of categorization, the analysis of causality and process, and the role of theory and validation in qualitative analysis.

Thinking of software as a toolkit reminds us that tools are instruments that we use for our own purposes. However, we must also recognize our inclination to adapt these purposes to whatever tools lie at hand. If software enables us to classify with ease but analyze narrative links only with difficulty, then it may encourage us to favor classification over narrative analysis. There may be nothing intrinsically wrong with this — technology can transform the methodological possibilities before us and the benefits and costs associated with pursuing them—but we should at least be aware of what we are doing and what we leave undone.

In this respect, it is worth considering what the software for qualitative analysis can (and cannot) do. The particular range of functions supported depends of course on the software selected, but the general run of software tends to include some common procedures. After a brief mention of its role in managing data, I shall examine the use of software for searching, filing, and linking data and explore the methodological issues these raise in reference to Grounded Theory. My aim is to explore some of the analytic issues raised by the main trends in the use of software for qualitative analysis.

MANAGING DATA

Most obviously, software provides tools for managing data—for storing, filing, copying, accessing, and retrieving in ways that facilitate analysis and reduce the laborious processes previously required for this purpose. The data management functions of software may represent in themselves a major advance over traditional methods in terms of efficiency and reliability. They also open the way to more effective methods of archiving and sharing qualitative data and, even in this simple way, can transform the analytic process. What was previously a purely and intensely private dialogue conducted with the data is creeping slowly but surely into a more public domain. This is not without problems, of course (notably with regard to anonymity and confidentiality and the problem of informed consent if wider access becomes possible for data recorded for a particular purpose). But it also promotes a greater openness in qualitative analysis and a greater sensitivity to whether conclusions can stand up to the scrutiny of others. At the same time, improvements in the speed and security of retrieval can encourage more comprehensive and systematic use of data and help sustain a closer dialogue between data and ideas throughout the analytic process.

SEARCH FUNCTIONS

Important as it is, no one really gets excited about the management of data. The main contribution of the computer to qualitative analysis lies in its ability to search, display, copy, link, and file data during analysis. Because the computer is preeminently a tool for searching data, this facility has been much exploited by qualitative software, with some applications offering a wide range of more or less sophisticated options and procedures by which to hunt down data that match the specified search criteria. These may be simple, such as finding all the words that match a specified target, or complex, such as finding all the instances in which multiple targets appear in a specified order and distance. The speed and flexibility of data searches may vary, but even the simplest search by software through large volumes of data transforms the analytic process, because it allows us to distinguish patterns, identify contexts, compare exemplars, and cross-check citations in ways that were previously impractical. A linear reading of the text can now be overlaid by exploration of many different paths through the data.

Searches can become fast, systematic, reliable, and comprehensive, but never mechanical. Concern that search routines may displace analytic inquiry (even the language is suggestive) is misplaced, so long as we recognize that any search at all involves an interrogation of our data, and therefore, we need to understand both what we are asking of the data and why we are asking it. Even a simple search for occurrences of a single word in a text involves analytical judgments, for example, on how to take account of context or how to identify and what to do about errors of inclusion or omission. However, if we do not recognize this, our approach will certainly be mechanical (in the sense of being uninformed by critical inquiry), regardless of whether or not we are using the computer.

The computer's search facilities allow us not only to read but also to interrogate our data in a different way—to ask not only "what?" but "what if?" questions of the data. In full-blooded guise, we may view this as a form of hypothesis testing in which we can test whether the data confirm or refute the hunches that emerge during the analysis. This may be especially appropriate when we use the computer to find evidence confirming or refuting propositions that express relations between concepts (such as A correlates with B). But even if one hesitates to adopt the language (and the analytic baggage) associated with hypothesis testing, one can see the value of search procedures that allow the analyst continually to check claims against evidence. The Boolean algebra—connecting concepts through AND, NOT, and OR—provides a powerful toolkit for examining prima facie evidence of whether or how far putative relationships hold in the data.

These search tools can be used to explore data in their pristine state (such as fieldwork notes, observations, and interview responses), but they can also be used to interrogate the ideas produced through the analytic process itself. The annotations, memos, and categorizations employed in the course of the analysis can themselves be subject to further searches, though for some, this displacement in analytic focus may risk too great a departure from the disciplines of the data. However, by linking our abstractions directly to the data to which they refer, computer-based analysis may minimize the tension between retaining a sense of context and abstracting for the purposes of comparison.

The range and complexity of search functions, including the formal testing of hypotheses, perhaps provide one explanation for the symbiotic relationship between software for qualitative analysis and Grounded Theory. The latter places great emphasis on generating ideas from data, even to the extent of casting doubt on the value of "preconceived" ideas. Although the virtues of the tabula rasa approach are open to question, the use of data to develop and discipline theory is certainly consistent with the use of the computer to search data in a systematic and comprehensive way. This correspondence is most evident in the centrality in Grounded Theory of its methodology of constant comparison.

However, there is also some ambivalence in Grounded Theory about the need for such a systematic and comprehensive approach to analyzing qualitative data. This is reflected in two other methodological points that are much emphasized in Grounded Theory, expressed in the ideas of Theoretical Sensitivity and Theoretical Saturation.

Theoretical Sensitivity refers to the creative aspects of the analytic process and the importance of using data as a springboard for the generation of ideas. In Grounded Theory, these do not emerge of themselves through the routine application of analytic procedures but are generated through the way we as analysts interact with the data. Although preconceptions may be discounted, a rich and varied analytic experience must be brought to bear on the data. The analyst must not be blinkered and dogmatic but must foster an imaginative and fertile mind open to unexpected associations.

Data are important, from this perspective, mainly as catalysts that stimulate the theoretical imagination. This is expressed most emphatically (but also rather misleadingly) in the idea of Theoretical Saturation, which refers not to the exhaustion of all data sources through a systematic and comprehensive analysis, but to precisely the opposite. Saturation is reached at a point when no ideas are stimulated by the data, at which point the analyst is enjoined not to "exhaust" the data (and him- or herself!) but to turn to (or indeed generate) new data sources that may offer further stimulation.

Neither Theoretical Sensitivity nor Theoretical Saturation require or encourage a systematic search through data for the purposes of comparison. This ambivalence about whether and how to use data systematically reflects an underlying tension in Grounded Theory about the question of validation. Grounded Theory is conceived primarily as a means of generating theory, and the place of validation (or verification) in this enterprise has never been satisfactorily settled. On the one hand, validation is seen as incidental to theory generation, a task that can thankfully be relegated to some less theoretically inclined researcher and consigned to some later stage in the research process. Indeed, if we accept that social theories have a short shelf life and that their utility may depend on factors other than their veracity, validation may not be required at all. On the other hand, validation is seen as integral to the process of "grounding" the generation of theory by replacing the comfort of the armchair with the discipline of analyzing data. From this standpoint, subsequent validation can also be deemed irrelevant, because the generated theory has already been grounded in the process by which it has been generated.

Because theory is "discovered" through research, validation reduces to the question of consistency of ideas with the data from which they have been generated and can be taken as more or less given. This temptation is even more beguiling given the disposition to discount alternative interpretations of data. It is recognized that these alternatives may occur, but they are relegated to exploration in a further study in preference to focus on a "core category" or "main story" through which to apprehend the data. There is little place for entertaining diverse interpretations, though for Patton (1980), this ought to be the hallmark of qualitative analysis.

Given its rather cautious approach to testing ideas against data, it may seem ironical that Grounded Theory has been embraced so enthusiastically by developers and users of QDA software. If we subscribe to the canons of Theoretical Sensitivity and Theoretical Saturation, then the systematic and comprehensive search facilities of the computer are hardly required. We need no more than some fairly flexible ways of generating variation and comparisons in the data, with a view to stimulating ideas. This perhaps explains the obvious unease expressed by qualitative researchers regarding the "mechanical" use of the computer to manipulate data sets without much regard to their theoretical import.

To this end, it is common to counterpose the generation of theory with its validation, the latter being associated with a rather vulgar trade in numbers. However, this opposition may itself be of doubtful validity if we accept that a comprehensive analysis of all the data may in some cases offer a better basis for generating theory. It is not clear how we can identify patterns in our data without looking for consistency and variation across the data or, more crudely, without counting repetitions. Moreover, if we want to claim that the theory we generate is grounded in our data, then we are surely obliged to validate this for the data as a whole and not simply use part of the data as a heuristic tool. Otherwise, the opposition of a logic of discovery to that of validation in Grounded Theory may encourage either discovery without discipline (unsupported ideas) or discipline without discovery (no ideas at all)!

It is hard to underestimate the importance in qualitative analysis of confronting evidence that may not conform to our predilections. As we have seen, Grounded Theory has a rather ambivalent view of validation. Sometimes it is presented as an integral step in generating theory (by testing it against data), but sometimes it is relegated as a responsibility of other researchers and studies. This ambivalent attitude to validation in Grounded Theory—as in qualitative analysis more generally—probably stems in part from a suspicion of the role of numbers in qualitative analysis, because counting is often seen as an integral part of validation. This suspicion is the more surprising given the very central role that numbers play in everyday experience and discourse—and indeed, in qualitative analysis (Van Maanen 1982).

Numbers and meanings need not be seen as antithetical if we recall that we are trying to figure out the meaning of things and regard them as more or less significant. Then, numbers and meanings may be seen as mutually informative. Numbers can contribute to qualitative analysis in at least two ways. One is by allowing us to consider the weight of evidence that supports (or refutes) the ideas (and especially the generalizations) we generate from our data. Whether these hold good must in part be judged by how far they are empirically represented in the data. Of course, we must always be alert for that astounding moment of revelation when a short aside in some obscure corner of the data shifts the whole course of the study in a new and unexpected direction.

FILING FUNCTIONS

In addition to providing powerful search facilities, the computer is an excellent tool for filing materials. Its filing functions have been exploited mainly through the development of software applications that allow analysts to categorize data (commonly referred to as "coding" or "indexing"). The data can then be organized or accessed through the categories employed (by the coding scheme or the index system). This "recontextualisation" (Tesch 1990) of the data is widely (but not invariably) regarded as a critical step in the analytic process, but there is also a degree of analytic obscurity about what this step actually involves. Efforts to clarify the nature of coding have tended to counterpose different functions—factual and referential (Richards and Richards 1994), heuristic and representational (Seidel and Kelle 1995), reductive and complicative (Coffey and Atkinson 1996)—and emphasize the theoretical role of coding in generating ideas over its empirical functions in organizing data. The latter can then be presented as somehow "pre-theoretical," as in the invitation to "code first and think later" (Fisher 1997, p. 72). Analysis then focuses less on the conceptualization involved in creating and assigning categories (codes) than on their use for the purposes of data retrieval and comparison.

This inclination to consider categories (codes) as (at least initially) atheoretical is evident in the very language of coding (with its mechanical overtones), but it is also consistent with the ways in which categories and categorization are presented in Grounded Theory. Although Glaser and Strauss (1967, p. 36) define categories as "conceptual elements of a theory," the way categories are seen as generated and elaborated is not consistent with this conceptual emphasis. Categorization in Grounded Theory tends to be presented as a function of observation, such that categories derive naturally and automatically from the data on which they are based. Our categories are generated by analysis of data, only awaiting "discovery" (and not "invention") by the analyst. The relationship between categories and the data they represent is seen as unproblematic, because the categories are "indicated" by the data without ambiguity. A concept-indicator model of categorization is adopted, in which the meaning of categories as concepts is specified by the indicators through which they are derived. Although categories are seen as acquiring a (conceptual) life of their own, they are expressed entirely in terms of their indicators, which moreover may vary according to context.

This account of categorization conforms to the classical model of classification, whereby instances can be assigned unambiguously to specific classes according to a clearly established set of criteria. This also corresponds to a commonsense view of classification, which treats the identification of category members as a natural product of observation. These perspectives have both been influential in shaping Grounded Theory, through its roots in quantitative sociology and naturalist inquiry, and through this medium continue to influence the way categorization is conceived in QDA. The convergence of computer-based analysis and Grounded Theory over the centrality of coding data may stem from the pervasive influence of these models of classification.

However, the classical and commonsense models do not provide an accurate account of how categorization is achieved in practice. For this, we must turn to the evidence provided by studies in linguistics and psychology.

The basic flaw in the classical model is that it assumes that category membership is invariably based on a clear set of criteria by which we can discriminate unambiguously between members and nonmembers. But this is not how categorization operates in practice. Instead, psychological studies suggest that we tend to rely on prototypical examples in terms of which we assign membership on the basis of family resemblance (Rosch 1978). The closer the affinity with our prototypical example, the more disposed we are to include an instance as a category member. The use of prototypes implies that category membership is a matter of degree and that some members of categories are more typical of that category than others (McNeill and Freiberger 1994). It also implies that category boundaries are vague and ill-defined, because discrimination occurs not at the boundary but in terms of comparison with core instances.

Even rule-based approaches to classification cannot be taken as defining conditions that specify the necessary and sufficient conditions for membership. Thus, Harnad (1987) argues that we identify categories by discriminating between positive and negative instances among a range of "confusable alternatives." The categories we use acquire stability as they converge upon an adequate approximation of experience to date, but they are always provisional and subject to revision in the light of further experience. There is no invariant correspondence (established by and expressed in a set of rules defining membership) between the world "out there" and the categories through which we apprehend it but instead an evolving process of approximate and provisional convergence. Moreover, this is a process in which we focus selectively and contingently on those features that help us discriminate among putative members.

The classical model of classification implies a degree of certainty and rigidity in the use of categories that does not conform to psychological experience. Nor does the classical model accord well with linguistic usage. In his examination of the linguistic dimensions of categorization, Lakoff (1987) argues that categories can be understood only in terms of what he calls underlying "idealized cognitive models" that invest them with meaning. Categories acquire meaning, not through a set of indicators establishing correspondence with the world as experienced, but through the cognitive contexts supplied by these idealized models.

To contrast these views, consider the category "bachelor." In terms of the concept-indicator model, we might try to define a set of criteria for this concept that defines who can or cannot be included in this category that specifies gender (male), age range (adult), marital status (never married), and so on. However, this conceptualization is not as straightforward as it might seem at first. Consider the issue of cohabitation and whether a bachelor who cohabits but does not marry is still a bachelor. Or consider the issue of age and the point at which we might deem someone no longer a bachelor because they are "beyond it"! The boundaries are not exact, and our attempts to define them more precisely draw on some underlying assumptions (or models) of what bachelorhood is about. Thus, we might hesitate to describe celibate monks or sixth-form pupils as bachelors, for these do not conform to an underlying assumption that a bachelor is (1) capable of being sexually active and (2) could marry but chooses not to. In Lakoff's terms, such assumptions form idealized models that invest the category with meaning. Stereotypes may play an important part in these idealized models—in this case, stereotypical notions of how bachelors behave. Categories may also call on different and perhaps conflicting cognitive models. Thus, "motherhood" is a category whose meaning may vary according to the different models (e.g., working mother, biological mother) that invest it with meaning.

Lakoff (1987) suggests that many categories are derived from basic-level experience through various extensions. These include metaphorical extensions (transferring meaning across domains), metonymical extensions (extending meaning from part to whole), and image-schematic extensions (extending meaning from basic perceptual or bodily experience). Thus, the use of categories is bound by convention rather than logic. And logic itself is no more than a conventional extension of bodily experience based on a "container" model through which we differentiate between the states of being in or out of the container.

The Aristotelian logic that underpins the classical model (McNeill and Freiberger 1994, pp. 52–53) depends on categories that are exhaustive and mutually exclusive. Thus, the law of contradiction states that "A cannot be both B and not-B," whereas the law of the excluded middle states that "A must be either B or not-B." But if the meanings of categories are informed by idealized cognitive models and discrimination among members relies on comparison with stereotypical or prototypical exemplars, category boundaries become diffuse and permeable and lose their exhaustive and mutually exclusive character. For example, I may be deemed a bachelor in some respects but not in others depending on the cognitive models invoked; I can be "B" and "not-B" at the same time. Or, it may not make sense to classify me in either way if, for example, I am still in school even though of marriageable age.

The emphasis in Grounded Theory on the use of sensitizing concepts that are valued for their rich connotations, relevance, and utility rather than as an expression of a set of indicators accords well with the view that categories are created and informed by convention rather than defined by logic. However, in Grounded Theory, there is a tension between these rich concepts, animated by complex meanings implicit in practical experience, and the more systematic but "flat" specification of concepts required for formal theory. This tension stems in large measure from the assumption of a classical model of categorization, with its requirement for exhaustive and mutually exclusive categories. Becker and Geer (1982), in contrast, describe categorization in qualitative analysis as inclusive rather than exclusive, in that the aim is generally to include relevant data rather than classify them per se. The development of a classification scheme that organizes concepts into mutually exclusive and exhaustive categories can be seen as a subsequent stage in analysis, or even as a special case. Having adopted the classical model, Glaser and Strauss (1967) tried (though with questionable success) to reconcile the sensitizing and analytic aspects of categories by distinguishing between different levels of abstraction in theory—formal and substantive—and emphasizing the importance of application as well as accumulation of theoretical knowledge.

The use of computer software for qualitative analysis may reinforce the classical approach of Grounded Theory and underplay its more conventional, sensitizing, and practical use of categories. Because of its powerful filing functions, the computer makes it relatively easy (through the appropriate software) to assign categories to data, so that instances can be accumulated and variation analyzed along the lines suggested by Grounded Theory. The computer enables us to file all the relevant instances of a particular category and specify the set of criteria in terms of which categorical discriminations are made. However, this analytic thrust may also obscure and distort interpretation if we try to reduce the meaning of categories to the sets of examples (indicators) that are identified and accumulated through coding data.

To avoid fragmentation of meaning, it may be helpful to recognize and emphasize the ways in which categories interrelate. It may be useful to think in terms of category "strings" rather than sets, if this suggests that the relationships among categories are as important as the categories themselves. In a category string, the category is no more than one focus in a web of meaning represented by the string as a whole. Compare this with the image of a set of categories, in which each category belongs to the set by virtue of some characteristic held in common, perhaps no more than being used in the study in question.

Although analysis, strictly speaking, involves the breaking up of a whole into constituent parts, the better to perceive the relationships between the parts, it is important to consider complementary or alternative modes of investigation and interpretation. With the advent of computer-supported analysis and attendant claims to greater rigor, there is a risk (to which I have already succumbed in a previous text) that methods of interpretation less amenable to software emulation will be side-tracked. Thus, the role of intuition or holistic interpretation may be downplayed simply because these cannot be specified in the same terms as analytic procedures.

When we acknowledge that categorization proceeds largely along conventional rather than logical lines, it becomes more important to identify, examine, and elucidate the underlying cognitive contexts through which categories acquire their meaning. In this respect, the whole is more than the sum of the parts, just as the forest is more than a set of individual trees. There would be less danger of not seeing the forest for the trees if we were less inclined to discount the forest in the first place. As Lakoff (1987) argues, complex concepts are not simply a juxtaposition of simple concepts combined in an additive way, but depend on their own cognitive underpinnings. Thus, the idea of a forest is bound up with particular cognitive models (which may differ if I am thinking of it as a hiker, as a forester, or as a carpenter) that cannot ever be realized by thinking only in terms of individual trees.

Conversely, concepts cannot be understood except in terms of a whole of which they are part. In Grounded Theory, categories are described as concepts that can stand alone, which implies that their meaning can be grasped independently of the cognitive context of which they are a part. But if we use wood to make a chair, the back and the seat of the chair are parts whose meaning is inseparable from the idea of a chair, as something to sit on. Recognizing the significance of this part/whole interrelationship requires a more holistic interpretation than is allowed by the insistence that complex wholes are combinations of parts whose meanings are individual and separate. As Kosko (1994, p. 108) observes, "you can study arms and legs and organs and other parts and still not know how a human behaves." When we observe teachers or teaching, for example, the social contexts of the classroom or the school are vital to our interpretation of what is happening.

LINKING DATA AND CONCEPTS

The advent of the computer offers new opportunities that may not only support existing analytic strategies, but also transform them, rather as the telescope transformed study of the sky, though perhaps less dramatically! The filing functions of the computer merely enhance what was done before through the laborious use of card index systems and such. But it is not possible to use physical means to make connections among different parts of the data, at least in any systematic way. This requires electronic means, notably the arrival of Hypertext and the ability to make electronic connections that thread together disparate parts of a text or document. All this has suddenly become so familiar through the rapid development of the Internet that it is easily overlooked how recently this powerful tool has become available. Systematic linking enables us to make connections to explicate causal chains, explanatory frameworks, patterns of discourse, and so on, directly on the basis of the data.

Making connections and creating categories may be seen as complementary rather than antithetical analytic activities, because in the process of connecting different parts of the data (say two events), we may also connect the categories assigned to those events. This enables us to combine analyses on the basis of comparison and connection and examine how categories are related, not through concurrence, but through the observation of connections in the data themselves.

In making such connections, we ought to make as clear and explicit as possible the ground rules that govern our judgments. For example, we may want to make connections only if these are already in vivo, identified and recognized as such by our respondents. Or we may opt to exploit our privileged position as analyst and make connections on the basis of inference rather than direct observation. In either case, we ought to set out the criteria on the basis of which connections are identified. It is not essential to do so, but by making our criteria explicit, we go some way toward grounding our analysis more thoroughly.

If we extend Lakoff's (1987) discussion of categorization to include making connections, then we can assume that the judgments we make about connections will not always reflect clear and exhaustive definitions, rules, and propositions. We may be inclined to make connections on the basis of our sense of narrative, judging the significance of an event not by its inherent significance (for example, for participants) so much as by the dramatic role it can play in the evolution of a story that has captured our attention. If we are looking for a dramatic denouement to a sequence of events, then the chances are we will find it in the data. The daily sensationalist diet of media revelations suggests that we can rarely resist this temptation, no matter how it distorts or obscures the significance of an event in other respects. There is no reason to suppose that qualitative analysts are exceptional in this regard. The connections we make, as with the categories we create, are invested with meaning by underlying cognitive models.

It seems important that we make such models as clear and explicit as possible. It is common in qualitative analysis to distinguish between three types of notes: observational, methodological, and analytic. The first of these refers to observations recorded in the course of the research and constitutes our initial data. The methodological notes refer to the context through which the data are generated, such as the settings, recording devices, periods of observation undertaken, sources of information, and so on. These are important in allowing (and prompting) us to reflect on the quality of our data. The analytic notes refer to the thinking or theorizing we do about our data and the insights and inferences it generates. To these we should perhaps add a fourth form of notes that refers to the methodological issues raised and paths pursued during analysis. Do we opt to make connections only on the basis of in vivo evidence, and if so, why? Do we allow connections based on inference, and if so, what kind of evidence is required to support such inferences? By making these explicit, we can keep track of the process of conceptualization and show more effectively how we arrive at our conclusions.

The computer offers us the means to do this through its ability to link not only different parts of the data, but also these different elements in the analysis. Thus, we can link the categories or connections we are using with the criteria that we develop in employing them, with instant access to the latter as required or even simultaneous access with both data and conceptualizations displayed on the screen. This linking can help us be more thorough and systematic in applying concepts and provide an environment conducive to analytic integration.

Software is increasingly designed to enable analysts to make connections between different parts of the data. These connections can take a variety of forms. For example, we can make connections among all the parts of the data that represent episodes in a sequence of events, which may or may not be chronological. These connections, when made, allow a chain of events to be followed through the data without disturbing the original text. We could identify radial connections, in which a variety of events follow from a key incident recorded in the data. Or we could identify a focal point in the data that results from a wide range of factors, all of which can be connected to it. These examples involve simple connections, but clearly, we can use the computer to make all sorts of more complex connections, such as a combination of radial and focal connections.

These examples refer to causal connections, but there are other types of connections that may be of interest in qualitative analysis. Most obviously, we may be interested in identifying the connection between different parts of a discourse to identify and follow the threads of meaning, explication, or argument. For example, we may have obtained data on our respondents' views of a particular product and want to identify all the connections between their knowledge of the product and the judgments they make about it. Or we may want to connect all the contradictory statements about a product. Or we may identify a connection between use of the product and opinions formed about it, depending on context. We could connect these — use, context, and opinion — to form a triad that can then be compared with similar triads in this or other interviews.

Linking procedures offer us alternative modes of analysis of causal relations to classification based on relations of similarity and difference. Sayer (1992) has argued that classification along these lines has loomed large in social science, whereas "substantive" relations (such as those of causal connection) tend to be ignored. The problem lies in attempts to reduce substantive relations to those of similarity and difference on the basis of atomistic assumptions that we can observe only individuals and not the relationships between them. For Sayer, the individual is already involved in such relationships, notably those involving the exercise of power. To identify the individual in isolation from his or her involvement in interactions and relationships is already to abstract from the world as observed.

The atomistic model in which concepts are reduced to collections of individuals that share common characteristics can never recapture or restore this knowledge of contexts and relationships. This is also true of the filing functions embodied in software systems that support coding and retrieval of data. If parts of the data (such as text segments) have been filed under different headings, the relationships between those parts are fractured and lost to view. Much of the subsequent analytic effort is then devoted to identifying possible ways in which these fractured data parts can be reintegrated into some meaningful relationship.

In relation to causality, this process of fragmentation and integration involves the use of methods of constant conjunction that date back at least to David Hume (whose radical empiricism was responsible for much of our subsequent confusion about how to identify causal relations), though later systematized by John Stuart Mill. His "method of agreement" involves identifying as causes those circumstances that invariably precede the occurrence of an event, whereas the "method of difference" adds weight to this analysis by identifying as causes only those circumstances that are invariably absent if the event does not occur. The method of analytic induction typically involves identifying causes among possible alternatives by searching for cases in which a condition is present but the event is absent—a negative instance that allows one to discount the condition as a possible cause on the basis of the lack of agreement.

As Ragin (1987) observes, the main problems with analytic induction arise with respect to multiple and conjunctural causation. In the case of multiple causation, the methods of agreement and difference break down because an event may occur because of several different causes, each sufficient to preclude the event but none necessary to do so. Thus, any single cause may only be intermittently present when an event occurs, and it will be overlooked by a procedure that relies on constant conjunction. In the case of conjunctural causation, many causes are each necessary to produce an event, but none is sufficient to do so. Here again, causes will be discounted by an analysis based on constant conjunction simply because they do not invariably co-occur with the event if other conditions are absent.

Glaser and Strauss (1967) explicitly reject the method of analytic induction, as they reject the use of Grounded Theory to establish single and universal causal explanations of phenomena. Instead, they emphasize both the complexity of social processes and the need to analyze them in terms of their individual character. Thus, the focus of Grounded Theory seems to be on multiple and conjunctural forms of causation. However, Glaser and Strauss still rely on a modified form of analysis based on constant conjunction. The method of constant comparison is presented as the core of a Grounded Theory approach, and methods of data generation and analysis emphasize the vital role of comparing across data to identify patterns of similarity and difference. Whereas negative instances in analytic induction are used to reject putative causes, in Grounded Theory, they are regarded as evidence of further complexity in causal patterns. They are incorporated into the emerging theory as additional factors that modify the character of already identified relationships. Analysis proceeds through constant comparison of conditions and effects but without any rigorous attempt to control for the effect of intervening variables to isolate particular causal relationships. The "constant" in constant comparison seems to refer to the process of continual modification and adjustment of the emerging theory as new factors come to light.

Although this approach has the merit of addressing conjunctural and multiple forms of causation, it is not at all clear how causal relationships are to be identified or confirmed. Although the explicit logical analysis of the methods of agreement and difference is rejected, Grounded Theory continues to rely on the general logic of identifying causal patterns through constant comparison, that is, identifying causality in terms of where factors do or do not co-occur. This inference of causal relations from concurrence lacks any means of confirming causality through requirements, because any variation can always be explained away through further modifications of the theory. It is difficult to see how such an ad hoc approach can justify claims that relationships have been grounded in data or, for that matter, that this approach can produce theory that is simple and parsimonious. The resulting theory may be sufficient to account for the data in hand, but it is likely to be too dense and diverse to offer much theoretical purchase beyond the particular case. In Grounded Theory, this problem is addressed through the distinction between "substantive" and "formal" theory, to which we return in due course.

Meantime, let us consider how causality can be established without reliance on the rather limited logic of constant conjunction. An alternative approach assumes that causal relations can be identified directly through observation and experience rather than inferred indirectly through induction from regularities. From this perspective, our own experience provides grounds for causal inference, for example, through the ways in which we act upon the world and are acted upon in turn. Causality is inherent in the exercise of powers inherent in our capacity to act, as when I switch on the computer, type on the keyboard, and produce a text on the screen. This causal process is one that I can render intelligible through my understanding of how a computer operates. This understanding need not be very profound; I need not know how the electronic or logical processes operate to understand the connection between what my fingers are doing and what is happening on the screen. I only need, in Lakoff's (1987) terms, an idealized cognitive model of the processes involved in order to render the causal relationship intelligible. The evidence for causality does not depend on constant conjunction—for example, that every time I press the letter "G" on the keyboard, a "G" appears on the screen—but on understanding why this is so. Nor am I unsettled by negative instances, such as the appearance of a "©" instead of a "G" if I hold down the option key while hitting "G" on the keyboard. I do not elaborate my causal explanation—for example, to state that hitting "G" on the keyboard and holding down the option key produces "G" on the screen—to take account of further conditions (as suggested in Grounded Theory approach to variation in the data). Negative instances are only problematic if I have no intelligible account of why they occur. Although regularity may provide evidence for causal inference, it cannot establish causality and, indeed, may often mislead us.

How are causal explanations made intelligible? The answer lies partly in our bodily experience, which for toddler and scientist alike makes the world manipulable and intelligible. We develop theories that are consistent with our experience and help us explain it. These theories are not based only on observation, as though we were condemned to an entirely passive role, for we are entities engaged in the world and capable of interacting with it. It is through action and interaction that our theories are put to the test and prove more or less adequate or in need of refutation or refinement.

Glaser and Strauss (1967) hint at this approach when they suggest that confidence in our interpretations of our fieldwork stems from the practical know-how and experience acquired through spending time and learning how to get by in the field. But this remains only a hint, one that, given its requirement for in-depth study, is hard to reconcile with the more general emphasis on analysis through constant comparison, which, among other things, requires a continual search for new and varied settings to study through theoretical sampling. The practical test of theoretical knowledge is also implied by the emphasis on developing theory that is intelligible to those who are studied and applicable in the situations to which it refers. But this emphasis on the immediate and practical application of theory is overlaid by more ambitious claims to produce theory with a wider import. What is missing here is any means of generalizing from the particular to the general, because the basis for making theoretical claims about the particular are not made explicit.

This can be summarized by suggesting that, in identifying causality, we tend to rely more on identifying powers (how things work) than on identifying patterns (whether things concur). If we understand how something works (how an action produces an effect), then we make a causal relationship intelligible in a way that cannot be achieved through establishing concurrence. Yet the software that has become available for qualitative analysis encourages the identification of patterns of concurrence in the data. It does this in increasingly complex and sophisticated ways by exploiting the computer's capacity to conduct searches that can identify all the instances in which things concur under specified conditions. The complexity and sophistication of these procedures should not blind us, however, to the limited view of causality on which they are based. Overwhelmed by our newfound capacity to explore every kind of variation in the data, we may overlook the direct approach that tries to render processes intelligible by developing explanations of how things work. In practice, of course, we may tacitly rely on this approach in any case, because otherwise, we would quickly be lost in the complex maze of variation among myriad variables without some sense of where to look or what to look for. However, the preoccupation with identifying patterns in the data may obscure the value of identifying and explaining the processes that produce them.

In this respect, it is worth contrasting the view of pattern as surface regularity and the conception of pattern an underlying rule or set of rules that produces effects, regular or otherwise. The former can be illustrated by regular distribution of colors in a striped garment, but the latter can be illustrated by the pattern of instructions by which the garment is produced. Such patterns may or may not result in regularities; it is possible for a simple set of rules to produce a complex and infinitely variable product. The challenge of identifying patterns can be conceived in terms of identifying underlying rules that produce regularity or variation rather than in terms of identifying superficial regularities in the data. The former is more challenging but also more analytic and explanatory in its intent. It reduces rather than reproduces the complexity of the data by identifying a simpler set of "rules" in which the data can be understood.

This suggests analytic tasks for qualitative analysis rather different from the "rich description" that is often taken as its hallmark. Whereas rich description aims at rendering a description, identifying underlying rules must go beyond description to offer an account not only of the data, but also of why the data take the form they do. The dilemma of rich description is that a full and detailed description of the data is incompatible with the requirements for a parsimonious and limited account. The problem of reduction is recognized as inherent in qualitative data analysis, though mainly in terms of growing selectivity in focus (what is the main story?) and condensation of description through coding. The identification of underlying "rules" (or perhaps "processes" would be more apt) offers an altogether sterner analytic challenge, but one that ultimately may provide a more rewarding approach to the problem of data reduction.

CONCLUSION

Although Grounded Theory can claim to have encouraged theoretical ambitions in qualitative analysis, in some ways it may also have limited them. This is most likely if the caution to eschew preconceived ideas is taken as an injunction to begin analysis without any prior theorizing, which confuses, as I have remarked elsewhere, an open mind with an empty head. Despite the emphasis on theoretical sensitivity and the sensitizing role of categories in Grounded Theory, its heavy emphasis on inductive theorizing based on the data predominates. As a result, theory is conceived largely in terms of its applicability within a particular study, with little requirement to consider its relevance or consistency with other theories and evidence. Although a role is envisaged for formal theory as a way of generalizing beyond the particular (or substantive) study, existing formal theory seems rarely taken into account when it comes to generating further theory.

Theoretical ambitions are also at once enhanced and limited by the presentation of Grounded Theory as a hybrid mode of theorizing—a mixed method that seems a rather mixed blessing. Unlike intensive modes of theorizing that focus on holistic explanations of particular phenomena, Grounded Theory emphasizes the importance of systematic comparison across a range of settings. In place of the single case study, it proposes theoretical sampling of a range of settings (not cases) upon which analysis can be based. However, unlike extensive modes of theorizing that seek broad generalizations of universal import and typically rely on the quantitative analysis of variables abstracted from any particular time and place, Grounded Theory favors more intensive, qualitative forms of data collection and analysis.

It is not clear whether this merging of methods offers the best or worst of both. The combination of intensive methods and extensive logic may provide a more powerful methodological tool than either approach in isolation. However, intensive methods are costly and time consuming, and they therefore tend to be confined to the initial stages of research, though they are arguably of relevance throughout. And extensive methods may be difficult to employ effectively within the framework of an intensive approach, which precludes effective application of the logic of inquiry on which they are predicated.

Concerns about the risks of computer-based approaches to qualitative analysis tend to focus on the use of the computer's filing functions to code and retrieve data and the use of its search functions to emulate a form of variable analysis (including hypothesis testing) more familiar (and some would argue, more appropriate) in quantitative research (cf. Barry 1998; Kelle 1997). The worry is that counting will substitute for rather than inform conceptualization or that the humdrum tasks of managing data (which the computer can support) will be mistaken for the more challenging task of theorizing about it (which it cannot). Given the affinity between computer-based approaches and Grounded Theory, it is not surprising that the same concerns arise regarding the latter. Both the classical model of categorization and the central role assigned to constant comparison encourage a methodology of variable analysis, which in turn may be encouraged by the software emphasis on coding and comparison. Other aspects of Grounded Theory, such as intensive methods of theorizing, the sensitizing role of concepts, and the substantive analysis of causal relationships and process, may be eclipsed in the process.

To close on a suitably dramatic note, we can envisage two diverging paths, with software reinforcing a rather limiting preoccupation with classification and comparison on the one hand or opening up new possibilities for connecting data and linking ideas and data on the other. Experience elsewhere suggests a note of caution. The contribution of information technology to productivity growth over the past two decades has been marginal. Compared with the revolutions at the close of the nineteenth century — of electricity, telecommunications, transport, chemicals — the transformations wrought by information technology may be altogether more subtle. This may also be true of its application in qualitative data analysis, in which its contribution may be less transformative than either its advocates or its critics expect.

Although Grounded Theory has given a welcome impetus to the development and use of software in qualitative analysis, it remains to be seen whether it will continue to act as a catalyst. If it is to be a springboard for rather than a fetter on further development, we need to reflect critically on the methods it proposes and the theorizing it avows. We need to view Grounded Theory less as a means of legitimating computer-based methods and more as a means of considering their logic and limitations. In the process, we need to acknowledge and explore the ambiguities and contradictions in Grounded Theory itself.

The perplexing problem of finding a path through the data has plagued qualitative analysis from its inception. But the latest challenge of QDA is not only to produce an account of the data, but also to account for its production. It is no longer enough to tell it how it is. Now we need to give as much heed to the telling as to the tale. We need to consider the medium as well as the message.

BIBLIOGRAPHY

Barry, C.A. (1998), "Choosing Qualitative Data Analysis Software: atlas/ti and Nud*ist Compared," *Sociological Research Online*, 3 (3).

Becker, H. and B. Geer (1982), "Participant Observation: The Analysis of Qualitative Field Data," in *Field Research: A Sourcebook and Field Manual*, R. Burgess, ed. London: Allen & Unwin, 239–50.

Coffey, A. and P. Atkinson (1996), *Making Sense of Qualitative Data: Complementary Research Strategies*. Thousand Oaks, CA: Sage Publications.

———, B. Holbrook, and P. Atkinson (1996), "Qualitative Data Analysis: Technologies and Representations," *Sociological Research Online*, 1 (1).

Dey, I. (1999), *Grounding Grounded Theory: Guidelines for Qualitative Inquiry*. San Diego, CA: Academic Press.

Fisher, M. (1997), *Qualitative Computing: Using Software for Qualitative Data Analysis*. Aldershot: Ashgate.

Glaser, B. and A. Strauss (1967), *The Discovery of Grounded Theory: Strategies for Qualitative Research*. Chicago: Aldine.

Harnad, S. (1987), "Category Induction and Representation," in *Categorical Perception: The Groundwork of Cognition*, S. Harnad, ed. Cambridge: Cambridge University Press, 535–65.

Kelle, U. (1997), "Theory Building in Qualitative Research and Computer Programs for the Management of Textual Data," *Sociological Research Online*, 2 (2).

Kosko, B. (1994), *Fuzzy Thinking*. London: Flamingo.

Lakoff, G. (1987), *Women, Fire and Dangerous Things: What Categories Teach About the Human Mind*. Chicago: Chicago University Press.

Lee, R.M. and N. Fielding (1996), "Qualitative Data Analysis: Representations of a Technology: A Comment on Coffey, Holbrook and Atkinson," *Sociological Research Online*, 1 (4).

McNeill, D. and P. Freiberger (1994), *Fuzzy Logic: The Revolutionary Computer Technology that Is Changing Our World.* New York: Touchstone.

Patton, M.Q. (1980), *Qualitative Evaluation Methods.* London: Sage Publications.

Ragin, C.C. (1987), *The Comparative Method: Moving Beyond Qualitative and Quantitative Strategies.* Berkeley, CA: University of California Press.

Richards, T.J. and L. Richards (1994), "Using Computers in Qualitative Research," in *Handbook of Qualitative Research*, N.K. Denzin and Y.S. Lincoln, eds. London: Sage Publications, 445–62.

Rosch, E. (1978), "Principles of Categorization," in *Cognition and Categorization*, E. Rosch and B.B. Lloyd, eds. Hillsdale, NJ: Lawrence Erlbaum Associates.

Sayer, A. (1992), *Method in Social Science: A Realist Approach*, 2d ed. London: Routledge.

Seidel, J. and U. Kelle (1995), "Different Functions of Coding in the Analysis of Textual Data," in *Computer-Aided Qualitative Data Analysis*, U. Kelle, ed. London: Sage Publications, 52–61.

Strauss, A. and J. Corbin (1990), *Basics of Qualitative Research: Grounded Theory Procedures and Techniques.* London: Sage Publications.

Tesch, Renata (1990), *Qualitative Research: Analysis Types and Software Tools.* London and Philadelphia: Falmer Press.

Van Maanen, J. (1982), *Varieties of Qualitative Research.* London: Sage Publications.

Weitzman, E.A. and M.B. Miles (1995), *Computer Programs for Qualitative Data Analysis: A Software Sourcebook.* London: Sage Publications.

SUGGESTED READINGS

Archer, M.S. (1995), *Realist Social Theory: The Morphogenetic Approach.* Cambridge: Cambridge University Press.

Bryman, A. and R.G. Burgess, eds. (1994), *Analyzing Qualitative Data.* London: Routledge.

Creswell, J.W. (1998), *Qualitative Inquiry and Research Design: Choosing Among Five Traditions.* London: Sage Publications.

Denzin, N.K. and Y.S. Lincoln (1994), "Introduction: Entering the Field of Qualitative Research," in *Handbook of Qualitative Research*, N.K. Denzin and Y.S. Lincoln, eds. London: Sage Publications, 1–17.

Dey, I. (1993), *Qualitative Data Analysis: A User-Friendly Guide for Social Scientists.* London: Routledge.

Fielding, N.G. and R.M. Lee, eds. (1991), *Using Computers in Qualitative Research.* London: Sage Publications.

Forster, N. (1994), "The Analysis of Company Documentation," in *Qualitative Methods in Organizational Research: A Practical Guide*, C. Cassell and G. Symon, eds. London: Sage Publications, 147–66.

Glaser, B. (1978), *Theoretical Sensitivity.* Mill Valley, CA: Sociological Press.

——— (1992), *Emergence v. Forcing: Basics of Grounded Theory Analysis.* Mill Valley, CA: Sociology Press.

Hammersley, M. (1989), *The Dilemma of Qualitative Method: Herbert Blumer and the Chicago Tradition.* London: Routledge.

Lincoln, Y.S. and N.K. Denzin (1994), "The Fifth Moment," in *Handbook of Qualitative Research*, N.K. Denzin and Y.S. Lincoln, eds. London: Sage Publications, 575–86.

Lonkila, M. (1995), "Grounded Theory as an Emerging Paradigm for Computer-Assisted Qualitative Data Analysis," in *Computer-Aided Qualitative Data Analysis*, U. Kelle, ed. London: Sage Publications, 41–51.

Mar, C. and G. Rossman (1989), *Designing Qualitative Research.* London: Sage Publications.

Mason, J. (1996), *Qualitative Researching*. London: Sage Publications.

Melia, K.M. (1996), "Rediscovering Glaser," *Qualitative Health Research*, 6 (3), 368–78.

Ragin, C.C. (1995), "Using Qualitative Comparative Analysis to Study Configurations," in *Computer-Aided Qualitative Data Analysis*, U. Kelle, ed. London: Sage Publications, 177–89.

Robrecht, L.C. (1995), "Grounded Theory—Evolving Methods," *Qualitative Health Research*, 5 (2), 169–77.

Silverman, D. (1993), *Interpreting Qualitative Data: Methods for Analyzing Talk, Text and Interaction*. London: Sage Publications.

Strauss, A. (1987), *Qualitative Analysis for Social Scientists*. Cambridge: Cambridge University Press.

——— and J. Corbin (1994), "Grounded Theory Methodology: An Overview," in *Handbook of Qualitative Research*, N.K. Denzin and Y.S. Lincoln, eds. London: Sage Publications, 273–85.

——— and ——— (1997), *Grounded Theory in Practice*. London: Sage Publications.

12
Graphical Methods of Data Analysis and Presentation

B.S. Everitt

A good graph is quiet and lets the data tell their story clearly and completely.

—Wainer, 1997

A ccording to Chambers and colleagues (1983), "there is no statistical tool that is as powerful as a well chosen graph." And indeed, there is considerable evidence that there are patterns in data and relationships among variables that are easier to identify and understand from graphical displays than from, say, the alternative of simply tabulating the data. For this reason, researchers who collect data are constantly encouraged by their statistical colleagues both to make a preliminary graphical examination of their data and to use a variety of plots and diagrams to aid in the interpretation of the results from more formal analyses. But just what is a graphical display? A concise description is given by Tufte (1983).

Data graphics visually display measured quantities by means of the combined use of points, lines, a coordinate system, numbers, symbols, words, shading, and colour.

289

Figure 1
Percentage of Degrees in Science and Engineering Earned by Women in the periods 1959–1960, 1969–1970, and 1976–1977

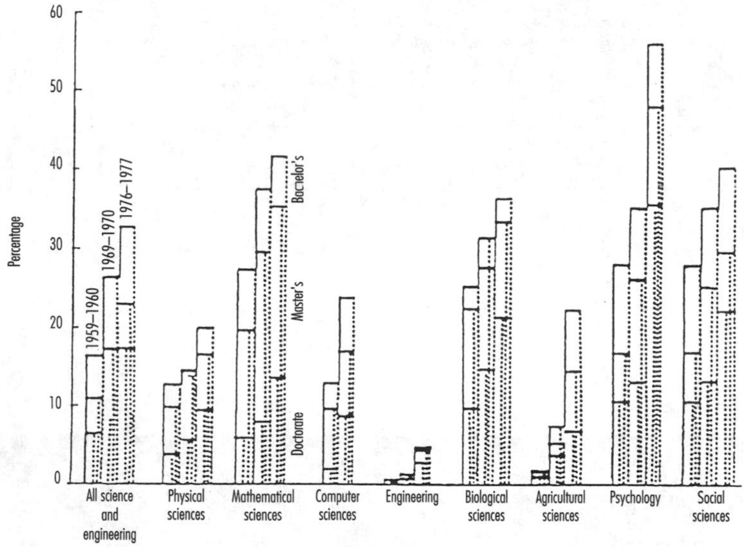

Reproduced with permission from Vetter (1980), American Association for the Advancement of Science.

Tufte (1983) estimates that between 900 billion (9×10^{11}) and 2 trillion (2×10^{12}) images of statistical graphics are printed each year. Some of the advantages of graphical methods have been listed by Schmid (1954):

- In comparison with other types of presentation, well-designed charts are more effective in creating interest and appealing to the attention of the reader;
- Visual relationships as portrayed by charts and graphs are more easily grouped and remembered;
- The use of charts and graphs saves time because the essential meaning of large measures of statistical data can be visualized at a glance;
- Charts and graphs provide a comprehensive picture of a problem that makes for more complete and better balanced

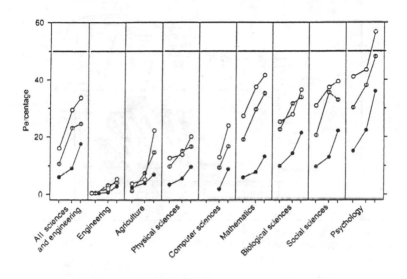

Figure 2
Percentage of Degrees Earned by Women for Three
Degrees, Three Time Periods, and Nine Disciplines

Notes: o – bachelor's degree, ø = master's degree, • = doctorate. The three points for each discipline and each degree indicate the periods 1959–1960, 1969–1970, and 1976–1977.
Reproduced with permission from Cleveland (1994).

understanding than could be derived from a tabular or textual form of presentation; and

❏ Charts and graphs can bring out hidden facts and relationships and can stimulate, as well as aid, analytic thinking and investigation.

Schmid's (1954) last point is reiterated by the legendary John Tukey (1977, p. vi) in his observation that "the greatest value of a picture is when it forces us to notice what we never expected to see."

Not all graphical displays are, of course, of the "well-designed" variety mentioned in the first item on Schmid's list. And unfortunately, it is often simpler to deceive with graphs, if this is the intention, than with other forms of data presentation. Because many poorly chosen and dishonest graphics are described by Tufte (1983) and Wainer (1997), we limit ourselves here to a single example of each.

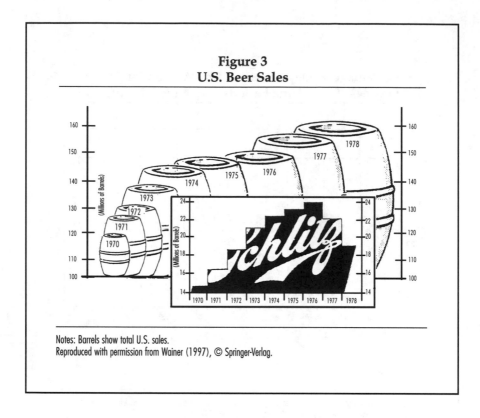

**Figure 3
U.S. Beer Sales**

Notes: Barrels show total U.S. sales.
Reproduced with permission from Wainer (1997), © Springer-Verlag.

The diagram in Figure 1 originally appeared in Vetter (1980); its aim is to display the percentages of academic degrees awarded to women in several disciplines of science and technology during three time periods. At first glance, the labels suggest that the graph is a standard divided bar chart with the length of the bottom division of each bar showing the percentage of doctorates, the length of the second division showing the percentage of master's degrees, and the top division showing the percentage of bachelor's degrees. In fact, a little reflection shows that this is not correct, because it would imply that in most cases the percentage of bachelor's degrees given to women is generally lower than the percentage of doctorates awarded. Closer examination of the diagram reveals that the three values of the data for each discipline during each time period are determined by the three adjacent vertical dotted lines. The top end of the left-hand line indicates the value for doctorates, the top end of the middle line indicates the value for master's degrees, and the top end of the right-hand line indicates the position for bachelor's degrees.

Cleveland (1994) discusses various problems with Figure 1, pointing out that its manner of construction makes it hard to connect visually the three values of a particular type of degree for a particular discipline and thus see change over time. Figure 2 shows the data replotted by Cleveland

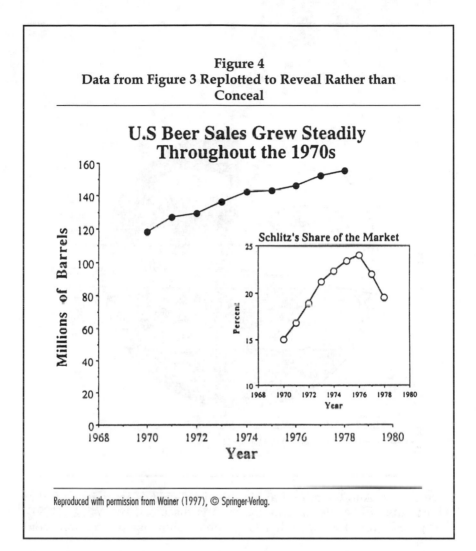

Figure 4
Data from Figure 3 Replotted to Reveal Rather than Conceal

in a bid to achieve greater clarity. It is now clear how the data are represented, and the design allows viewers to see easily the values corresponding to each degree in each discipline through time. Finally, the figure caption explains the diagram in a comprehensive and clear fashion. All in all, Cleveland appears to have produced a plot that would satisfy even that doyen of graphical presentation, Edward R. Tufte, in his demand that "excellence in statistical graphics consists of complex ideas communicated with clarity, precision and efficiency" (Tufte 1983, p. 13).

What, however, Tufte would think of Figure 3 must remain speculation. Here, volume of barrel is used to distort the perception of increases

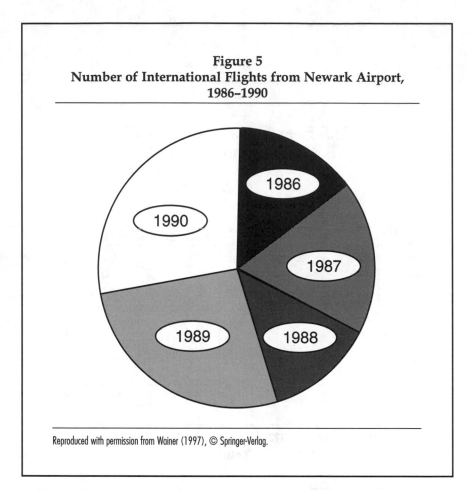

Figure 5
Number of International Flights from Newark Airport,
1986–1990

Reproduced with permission from Wainer (1997), © Springer-Verlag.

in beer sales. And the inset graphic showing Schlitz's share is too full of "chart junk" to be useful. This example is discussed by Wainer (1997), who gives Figure 4 as a more honest graph for showing information about beer sales.

Some suggestions for avoiding graphical distortion taken from Tufte (1983) are as follows:

❑ The representation of numbers, as physically measured on the surface of the graphic itself, should be directly proportional to the numerical quantities represented;

❑ Clear, detailed, and thorough labelling should be used to defeat graphical distortion and ambiguity. Write out explanations of the data on the graphic itself. Label important events in the data;

❑ To be truthful and revealing, data graphics must bear on the question at the heart of quantitative thinking: "Compared

Table 1
Expenditure on Food by Region

Region	Average Expenditure Per Household Per Week (£)	Average Percentage Spent on Food
ENGLAND		
North	150.2	20.8
Yorkshire and Humberside	157.3	20.3
East Midlands	169.8	20.3
East Anglia	188.2	18.1
South East	219.2	17.8
South West	189.5	19.0
West Midlands	166.4	20.4
North West	172.0	19.9
WALES	163.6	21.7
SCOTLAND	161.8	20.5
NORTHERN IRELAND	178.5	21.4

with what?" Graphics must not quote data out of context; and

❏ Above all else, show the data.

There is a vast range of graphical techniques now available for identifying patterns, diagnosing models, and generally searching for novel and perhaps unexpected phenomena. But in this chapter, we concentrate on the most common methods, many of which are relatively simple (though not simplistic). Nonetheless, the methods to be described are of the utmost importance for presenting and explaining data.

Large numbers of graphs are often needed to fully explore some data sets, and computers are needed to draw them for the same reasons that they are needed for numerical analysis, namely, that they are fast and accurate.

PIE CHARTS AND DOT PLOTS

Pie charts are one of the most familiar graphical forms. Invented by William Playfair in the late eighteenth century, they are widely used in the mass media, particularly in newspapers. An example, taken from Wainer (1997), is shown in Figure 5. Despite their popularity, they are held in low regard by almost all writers on graphics; Tufte (1983, p. 178), for example, in his book *The Visual Display of Quantitative Information*, remarks, "A table is nearly always better than a dumb pie chart; the only worse design than a pie chart is several of them...." And Wainer (1997) declares that pie charts are the least useful of all graphical forms. Perhaps the main problem with pie charts is their failure to order numbers along a visual dimension.

An alternative display that is always more useful than the pie chart is the *dot plot*. The two methods of presenting data can be compared using the data shown in Table 1, which gives the average expenditure per household per week in the 11 main regions of the United Kingdom, along with the average percentage of the total that is spent on food. Dot plots and pie charts of both variables are shown in Figure 6. It is very clear that the two dot plots are far more informative that the corresponding pie charts.

HISTOGRAMS, STEM-AND-LEAF DISPLAYS, AND BOX PLOTS

The data in Table 2 are the salaries offered in 72 randomly selected advertisements in *The Guardian* newspaper on days specialising in different occupations. The units are pounds sterling. When ranges are given in the advertisements, the midpoint of the range is used in Table 2.

Of interest here is whether there is a difference between advertised starting salaries in the two occupations. Various significance tests might be considered, such as the independent samples t-test, but prior to applying any such test, the data would need to be examined graphically to assess both their distributional properties and whether there was any evidence of outliers. Several graphical displays might be considered. Most commonly, histograms of the salaries in each occupational category would be constructed. These are shown in Figure 7. The histograms indicate that each set of salaries had a somewhat skewed distribution, which may have implications for significance testing. There is also evidence of a possible outlier among the education salaries.

The histogram is generally used for two purposes: counting and displaying the distribution of a variable. According to Wilkinson (1992, p. 7), however, "it is effective for neither." And Cleveland (1993, p. 8) comments,

> The histogram is a widely used graphical method that is at least a century old. But maturity and ubiquity do not guarantee the efficiency of a tool. The histogram is a poor method.

And in the 360 pages of Cleveland's book, the histogram makes only a single appearance!

Figure 6
A: Dot Plot of Average Expenditure Per Week

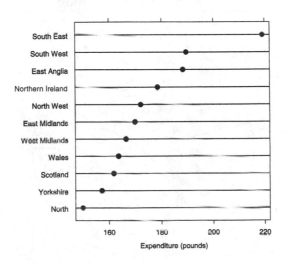

Expenditure (pounds)

B: Dot Plot of Average Percentage of Expenditure Spent on Food

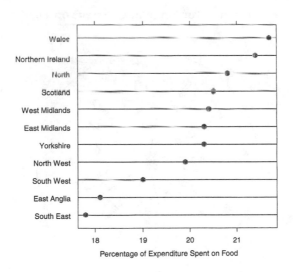

Percentage of Expenditure Spent on Food

Figure 6
Continued
C: Pie Chart for Expenditure

D: Pie Chart for Percentage Spent on Food

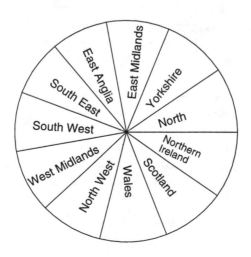

Table 2
Salaries in Different Occupations
(Units in Pounds Sterling)

(1) Creative, Media, and Marketing			(2) Education		
17703	13796	12000	25899	17378	19236
42000	22958	22900	21676	15594	18780
18780	10750	13440	15053	17375	12459
15723	13552	17574	19461	20111	22700
13179	21000	22149	22485	16799	35750
37500	18245	17549	17378	12587	20539
22955	19358	9500	15053	24102	13115
13000	22000	25000	10998	12755	13605
13500	12000	15723	18360	35000	20539
13000	16820	12300	22533	20500	16629
11000	17709	10750	23008	13000	27500
12500	23065	11000	24260	18066	17378
13000	18693	19000	25899	35403	15053
10500	14472	13500	18021	17378	20594
12285	12000	32000	17970	14855	9866
13000	20000	17783	211074	21074	21074
16000	18900	16600	15053	19401	25598
15000	14481	18000	20739	15053	15053
13944	35000	11406	15053	15083	31530
23960	18000	23000	30800	10294	16799
11389	30000	153798	37000	11389	15053
12587	12548	21458	48000	11389	14359
17000	17048	21262	16000	26544	15344
9000	13349	20000	21047	14274	31000

Histograms can often be misleading for displaying distributions because of their dependence on the number of classes chosen. Simple tallies of the observations are usually preferable for counting, particularly when shown in the form of a *stem-and-leaf plot*. Such a plot has the advantage of being able to show the "shape" of a frequency distribution while

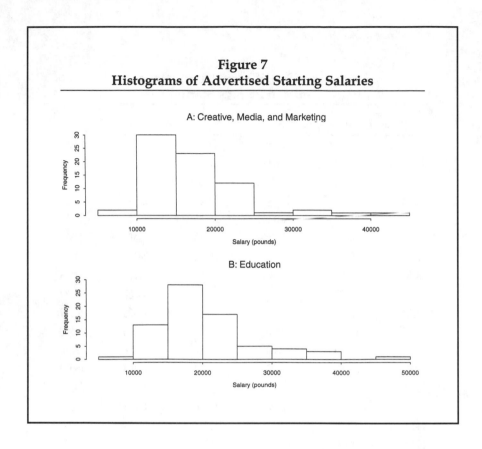

Figure 7
Histograms of Advertised Starting Salaries

retaining the values of the individual observations. The stem-and-leaf plots for the salaries data are shown in Figure 8.

Another valuable graphical display that could be used for the salaries data is the *box-and-whisker plot*, or *box plot* for short. This graphic is based on what is known as the *five-number summary* of a data set, the five numbers in question being the minimum, the lower quartile, the median, the upper quartile, and the maximum. The construction of the box plot from these numbers is described in Figure 9.

The box plots of the salaries data are shown in Figure 10. This diagram suggests the presence of several outlier observations in each occupation category and, somewhat surprisingly, at least to the author, that the level of education salaries is perhaps higher than that in creative, media, and marketing! Placing the box plots side by side, as in Figure 10, makes comparison of the salaries of each occupational category much simpler, and this advantage is magnified if there are several box plots to compare.

Figure 8
Stem-and-Leaf Plots of Advertised Starting Salaries

```
N = 72   Median = 16300
Quartiles = 13000, 20000

Decimal point is 3 places to the right of the colon

    9 : 05
   10 : 577
   11 : 0044
   12 : 00033556
   13 : 000023455689
   14 : 55
   15 : 0477
   16 : 068
   17 : 0056770
   18 : 002789
   19 : 04
   20 : 00
   21 : 035
   22 : 019
   23 : 0001
   24 : 0
   25 : 0
   26 :
   27 :
   28 :
   29 :
   30 : 0
   31 :
   32 : 0

High:   35000   37500   42000



N = 72   Median = 18043.5
Quartiles = 15053, 22500

Decimal point is 3 places to the right of the colon

    9 : 9
   10 : 3
   11 : 044
   12 : 880
   13 : 016
   14 : 349
   15 : 11111111136
   16 : 0688
   17 : 44444
   18 : 00148
   19 : 245
   20 : 1155567
   21 : 1117
   22 : 557
   23 : 0
   24 : 13
   25 : 699
   26 : 5
   27 : 5
   28 :
   29 :
   30 : 8
   31 : 05
   32 :
   33 :
   34 :
   35 : 047
   36 :
   37 : 0

High:   48000
```

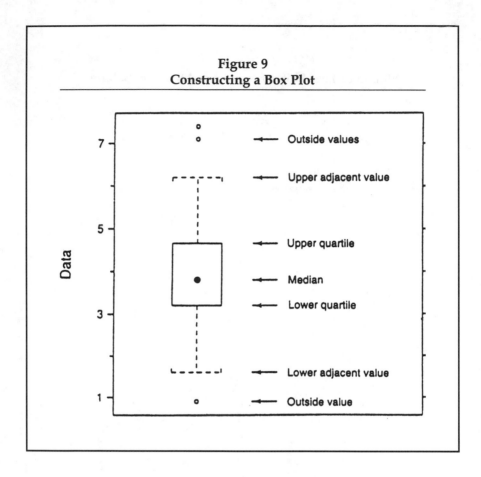

Figure 9
Constructing a Box Plot

THE SCATTERPLOT

The simple xy scatterplot has been in use since at least the nineteenth century. But despite its age, it remains, according to Tufte (1983, p. 47),

> the greatest of all graphical designs. It links at least two variables, encouraging and even imploring the viewer to assess the possible causal relationship between the plotted variables. It confronts casual theories that x causes y with empirical evidence as to the actual relationship between x and y.

A simple example of a scatterplot of the expenditure data from Table 1 is shown in Figure 11. Here, the points are labelled by a unique identifying label for each region. The diagram highlights the clear division of the regions into roughly North and South, with the members of the latter

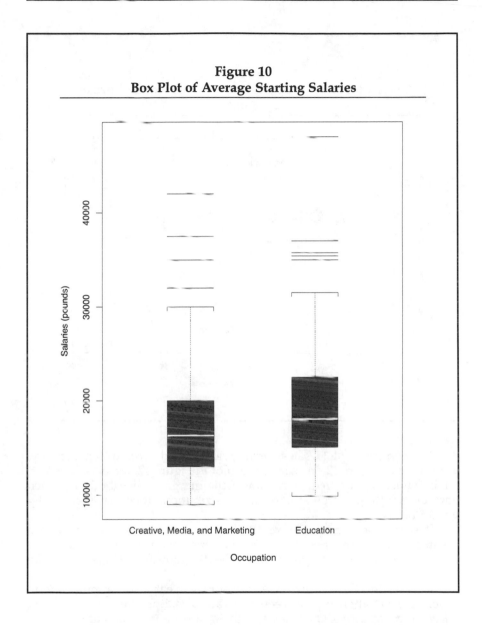

Figure 10
Box Plot of Average Starting Salaries

class having far higher expenditures, a smaller percentage of which is spent on food.

Now consider the data given in Table 3, which show ice cream consumption over 30 four-week periods, the price of ice cream in each period, and the mean temperature in each period. Of interest here is which element, price or temperature, has the most influence on ice cream sales.

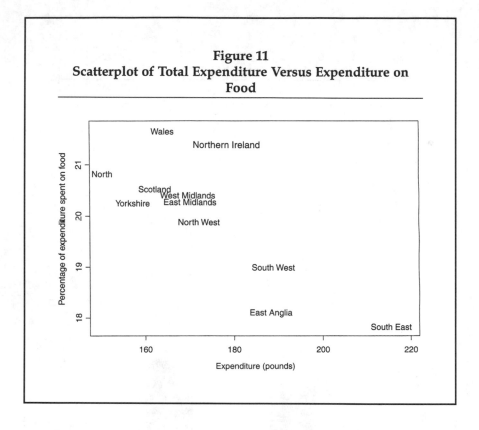

Figure 11
Scatterplot of Total Expenditure Versus Expenditure on Food

The two scatterplots, sales versus price and sales versus temperature, are shown in Figure 12. In each scatterplot in Figure 12, the bivariate scatter is framed with a frequency plot of the marginal distribution of each variable. Plotting marginal and joint distributions together is generally good practice.

It seems clear from Figure 12 that temperature affects sales to a greater degree than price does. This becomes even more obvious if we include the fitted linear regressions on the diagrams, as is shown in Figure 13.

In cases in which a linear relationship is clearly not appropriate to describe the relationship between two variables, it is often worth adding *a locally weighted smoothing curve* to the scatterplot. Details are given in Cleveland (1979), but essentially, such a curve is designed to accommodate data for which $y_1 = g(x_i) + \epsilon_i$, where g is a smooth function, and ϵ_i are random variables with mean zero and constant scale. Fitted values, $\hat{y}_i$, are used to estimate $g(x_i)$ at each x_i by fitting polynomials using weighted least squares, with weights larger for points near x_i and smaller otherwise.

As an illustration of this approach, we apply it to the data shown in Table 4, which gives age-specific life insurance premium rates for a sum

Table 3
Ice Cream Consumption

Period	Y (Pints Per Capita)	X_1 (Price Per Pint)	X_2 (Weekly Family Income)	X_3 (Mean Temperature °F)
1	.386	.270	78	41
2	.374	.282	79	56
3	.393	.277	81	63
4	.425	.280	80	68
5	.406	.272	76	69
6	.344	.262	78	65
7	.327	.275	82	61
8	.200	.267	79	47
9	.269	.265	76	32
10	.256	.271	79	24
11	.286	.282	82	28
12	.298	.270	85	26
13	.329	.272	86	32
14	.318	.287	83	40
15	.381	.277	84	55
16	.381	.287	82	63
17	.470	.280	80	72
18	.443	.277	78	72
19	.386	.277	84	67
20	.342	.277	86	60
21	.319	.292	85	44
22	.307	.287	87	40
23	.284	.277	94	32
24	.326	.285	92	27
25	.309	.282	95	28
26	.359	.265	96	33
27	.376	.265	94	41
28	.416	.265	96	52
29	.437	.268	91	64
30	.548	.260	90	71

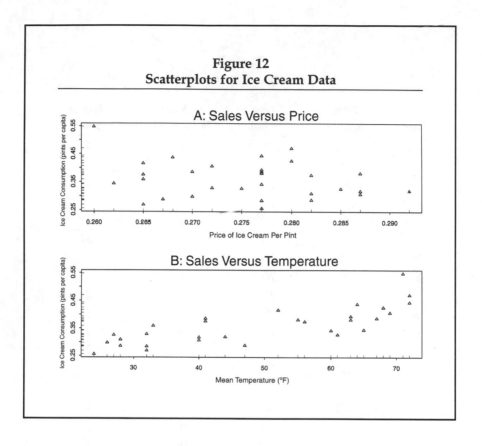

Figure 12
Scatterplots for Ice Cream Data

insured of $50,000. A scatterplot of the premium rates against age for each of the four groups is shown in Figure 14. The same scatterplot in Figure 15 shows the estimated locally weighted regression lines for each group.

Other examples of using locally weighted regression are given subsequently.

The Aspect Ratio of a Scatterplot

Two scatterplots with the same statistical information can appear different because our ability to process and recognize patterns depends on how the data are displayed. At times, the default display produced by a computer package may not be the most useful. For example, one important parameter of a scatterplot that can greatly influence our ability to recognise patterns in the plot is the *aspect ratio*, the physical length of the vertical axis divided by that of the horizontal axis. Most computer packages produce plots with an aspect ratio near 1, but this is not always the best value to use. To illustrate how changing this characteristic of a scatterplot can help clarify the structure in a set of data, we use the figures on

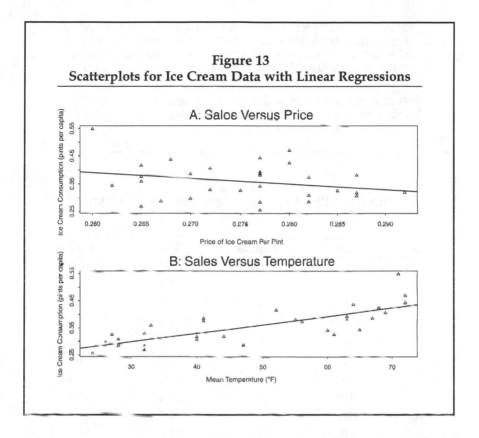

Figure 13
Scatterplots for Ice Cream Data with Linear Regressions

monthly sales of pairs of jeans, in 1000s, in the United Kingdom over six years, as is shown in Table 5. A scatterplot of sales versus month with an aspect ratio of 1 is shown in Figure 16. It is difficult to extract anything other than very "global" features from this diagram, such as the clear outlier and a possible yearly cycle in sales.

Now let us see what happens when the data are replotted with an aspect ratio of 0.3. The resulting scatterplot is shown in Figure 17. Now things are far clearer; there is a definite, if not particularly strong, cycle in jeans sales with sales peaking during spring and summer in most years. In 1981, sales were poor compared with the other five years. The outlier corresponds to June 1984, during which sales of jeans in the United Kingdom were particularly high.

Tufte (1983) makes the point that, in general, graphics should tend toward the horizontal, greater in length than in height. The jeans sales example certainly appears to suggest that horizontally stretched time-series data are more accessible to the eye. Tukey (1977, p. 492) makes a similar point in a little more detail:

Most diagnostic plots involve either a more or less definite dependence that bobbles around a lot, or a point spatter. Such plots are rather more often better made wider than tall. Wider-than-tall shapes usually make it easier for the eye to follow from left to right.

Perhaps the most general advice we can offer is that smoothly changing curves can stand being taller than wide, but a wiggly curve needs to be wider than tall.

Table 4
Insurance Premiums for a Sum Insured of $50,000

Age	Male		Female	
	Smoker	*Nonsmoker*	*Smoker*	*Nonsmoker*
33	130	100	110	95
34	135	105	110	95
35	140	105	115	100
36	145	110	120	100
37	155	110	125	105
38	160	115	130	105
39	170	120	140	110
40	180	125	145	115
41	195	130	155	120
42	210	140	165	130
43	230	145	175	135
44	250	155	190	145
45	270	170	205	155
46	295	180	225	165
47	325	200	245	180
48	360	215	265	195
49	395	235	290	210
50	435	260	320	230
51	485	285	350	250
52	535	315	380	275
53	590	350	420	305
54	650	390	460	335
55	715	435	505	370

Simply changing the aspect ratio will, of course, not be the solution in all cases. For some data sets, some transformation of the data may be necessary before altering the aspect ratio becomes helpful (for more details, see Cook and Weisberg 1994).

The Bubble Plot

The basic scatterplot can accommodate only two variables, but there are ways in which it can be enhanced to display further variable values. One particularly simple technique is the *bubble plot*. Here, two variables are used to form a scatterplot in the usual way, and then the values of a third variable are represented by circles with radii proportional to the values and centered on the appropriate point in the scatterplot.

The bubble plot can be illustrated using the ice cream data in Table 3. Using temperature and price to form the basic scatterplot and ice cream sales for the circles leads to Figure 18. This diagram illustrates that price and temperature are largely unrelated and, of more interest perhaps, demonstrates that consumption remains largely constant as price varies and temperature varies below 50°F. Above this temperature, sales of ice cream increase with temperature but remain independent of price. The

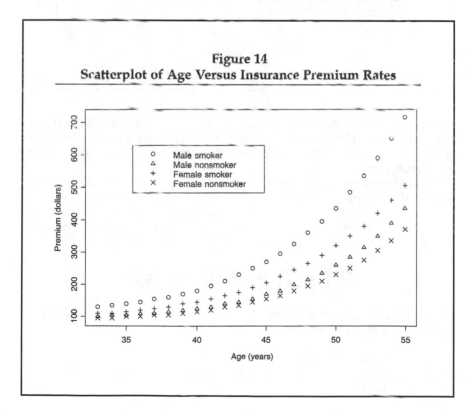

Figure 14
Scatterplot of Age Versus Insurance Premium Rates

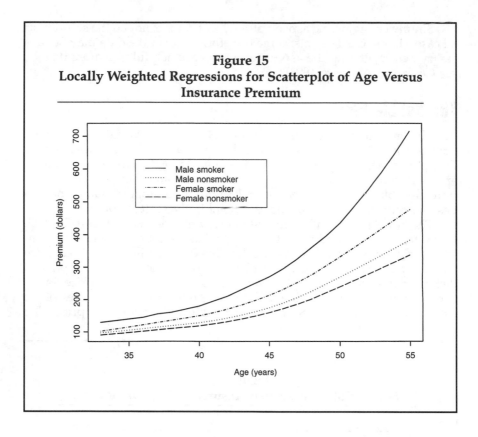

Figure 15
Locally Weighted Regressions for Scatterplot of Age Versus Insurance Premium

maximum consumption corresponds to the lowest price and highest temperature. One slightly odd observation is indicated in the plot; this corresponds to a month with low consumption despite low price and moderate temperature.

An alternative to the bubble plot for displaying the relationships among three variables is a three-dimensional plot, as is shown in Figure 19. This becomes more helpful if a "smoothed" surface is fitted to the observations, as is shown in Figure 20. This diagram reflects the comments made previously with respect to the bubble plot of these data.

THE SCATTERPLOT MATRIX

The data in Table 6 show the values of four demographic variables for the 50 states of the United States. The variables are as follows:

❏ Urban: Percentage urban areas,
❏ Income: Percentage of population earning more that $25,000 per year,

Table 5
Jeans Sales in the United Kingdom in 1000s

Month	1980	1981	1982	1983	1984	1985
January	1998	1927	1969	2149	2319	2137
February	1968	1959	2044	2200	2352	2130
March	1937	1889	2100	2294	2476	2154
April	1827	1819	2103	2146	2296	1831
May	2027	1824	2110	2241	2400	1899
June	2286	1979	2375	2369	3126	2117
July	2484	1919	2030	2251	2304	2266
August	2266	1845	1744	2126	2190	2176
September	2107	1801	1699	2000	2121	2089
October	1690	1799	1591	1759	2032	1817
November	1808	1952	1770	1947	2161	2162
December	1927	1956	1950	2135	2289	2267

❏ Taxes: Taxes in millions of dollars, and

❏ Density: Population density.

To look at the relationship among the four variables, we might begin by examining the scatterplots for each pair of variables, perhaps labelling the points to identify each state. This becomes considerably more informative if the scatterplots are arranged in the form of a *scatterplot matrix*.

A scatterplot matrix is defined as a square, symmetric grid of bivariate scatterplots (Cleveland 1994). This grid has p rows and p columns, each one corresponding to a different one of the p variables. Each of the grid's cells shows a scatterplot of two variables. Because the scatterplot matrix is symmetric about its diagonal, variable j is plotted against variable i in the ijth cell, and the same variables appear in cell ji with the x and y axes of the scatterplots interchanged. The reason for including both the upper and lower triangles of the grid, despite its seeming redundancy, is that it enables a row and a column to be visually scanned to see one variable against all others, with the scales for the one variable lined up along the horizontal or the vertical.

The scatterplot matrix for the demographic variables of the states of the United States is shown in Figure 21. The diagram suggests that several pairs of variables are nonlinearly related and that on some variables,

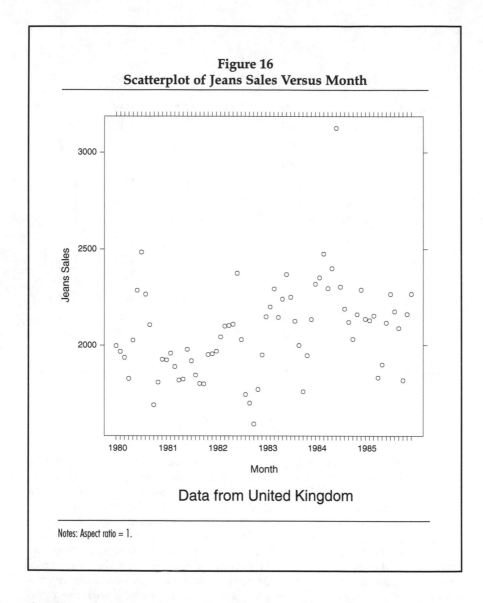

Figure 16
Scatterplot of Jeans Sales Versus Month

Data from United Kingdom

Notes: Aspect ratio = 1.

there are some very clear outliers. For these data, perhaps a much more sensible scatterplot matrix would be that based on the variable values after a log transformation. This is shown in Figure 22.

The relationships among the transformed variables appear rather more straightforward than those among the raw data. On the whole, the relationships are now linear, though only in the case of log (density) and log (taxes) are they particularly strong, as can be seen in Figure 23, in which simple linear regression lines have been added to each panel. The

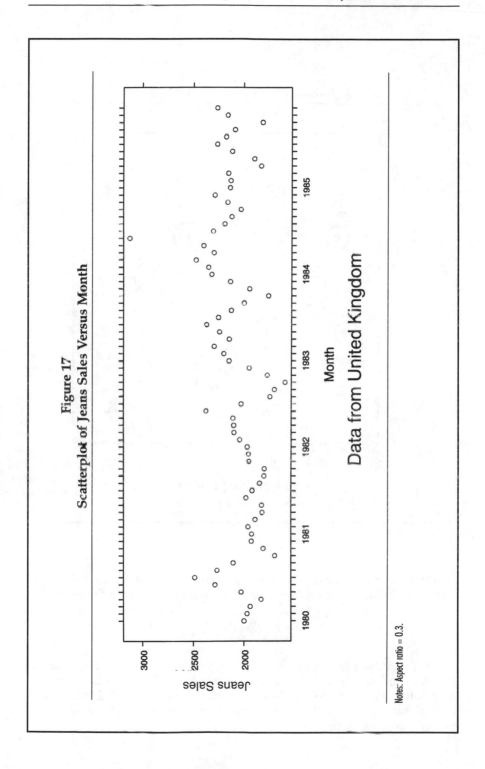

Figure 17

Scatterplot of Jeans Sales Versus Month

Data from United Kingdom

Notes: Aspect ratio = 0.3.

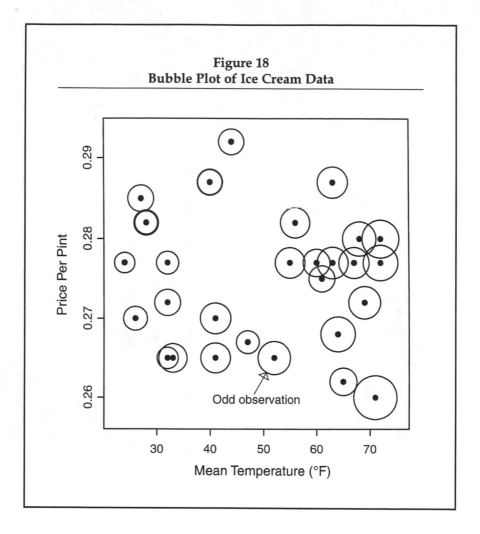

Figure 18
Bubble Plot of Ice Cream Data

locally weighted regression curves for each scatterplot are also shown in Figure 23. In most cases, these depart only moderately from the linear fits.

COPLOTS

The *conditioning plot,* or *coplot,* is a particularly powerful visualisation tool for studying how two variables are related, conditional on one or more other variables being held constant. There are several varieties of conditioning plot, the differences among which are largely a matter of presentation rather than real substance.

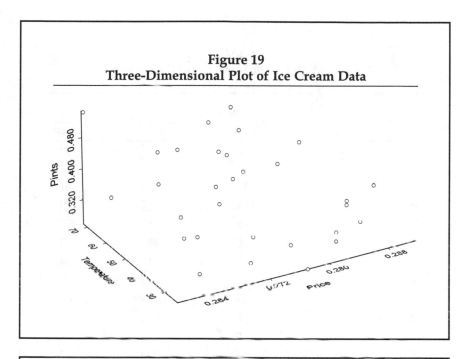

Figure 19
Three-Dimensional Plot of Ice Cream Data

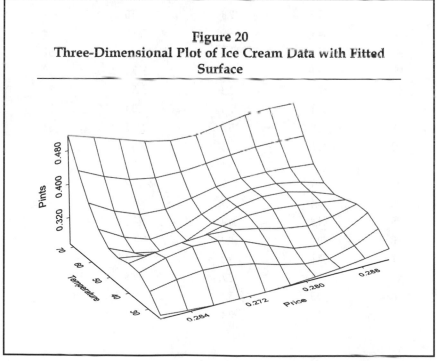

Figure 20
Three-Dimensional Plot of Ice Cream Data with Fitted Surface

Table 6
Data on 50 States for Health and Demographic Characteristics

State	Demographic Variables			
	Urban	*Income*	*Taxes*	*Density*
AL	58.4	26.2	297.7	68
AK	48.8	2.9	53.8	1
AZ	79.5	3.0	406.9	16
AR	50.0	18.3	162.2	37
CA	90.9	7.0	7365.3	128
CO	78.7	3.0	589.7	21
CT	77.3	6.0	981.5	624
DE	72.1	14.3	67.1	277
FL	80.5	15.3	1203.9	126
GA	60.3	25.8	629.0	79
HI	83.0	1.0	125.9	120
ID	54.3	0.3	112.2	9
IL	83.0	12.8	3130.0	199
IN	64.9	6.9	1247.2	144
IA	57.2	1.2	676.6	51
KS	66.1	4.7	522.1	28
KY	52.4	7.2	305.2	81
LA	66.1	29.8	500.1	81
ME	50.9	0.3	224.7	32
MD	76.6	17.8	996.8	397
MA	84.6	3.1	1929.5	727
MI	73.9	11.2	2184.7	156
MN	66.4	0.9	924.3	48
MS	44.5	36.8	189.8	47
MO	70.1	10.3	958.5	68
MT	53.6	9.3	191.1	5
NE	61.6	2.7	384.9	19
NV	80.9	5.7	136.3	4
NH	56.5	0.4	210.4	82

Table 6
Continued

State	Demographic Variables			
	Urban	Income	Taxes	Density
NJ	88.9	10.7	2475.6	953
NM	70.0	1.9	85.3	8
NY	85.6	11.9	7453.4	381
NC	45.0	22.2	526.3	104
ND	44.3	0.4	110.5	9
OH	75.3	9.1	2372.9	260
OK	68.0	6.7	334.7	37
OR	67.1	1.3	540.5	22
PA	71.5	8.6	2362.9	262
RI	87.0	2.7	200.3	905
SC	47.6	30.4	230.4	86
SD	44.6	0.3	174.1	9
TN	58.8	15.8	546.9	95
TX	79.8	12.5	1971.8	43
UT	80.6	0.6	167.6	13
VT	32.2	0.2	122.5	48
VA	63.1	18.5	819.5	117
WA	72.6	2.1	653.4	51
WV	39.0	3.8	167.7	72
WI	65.9	2.9	1181.7	81
WY	60.4	0.7	70.4	3

A simple coplot can be illustrated on the demographic data in Table 6. In Figure 24, taxes are related to incomes, *conditional on* population density. In this diagram, the panel at the top of the figure is known as the *given panel*; the panels below are *dependence panels*. Each rectangle in the given panel specifies a range of values of population density. On a corresponding dependence panel, tax is plotted against income for those states whose population densities lie in the particular interval. To match density intervals to dependence panels, the latter are examined in order from left

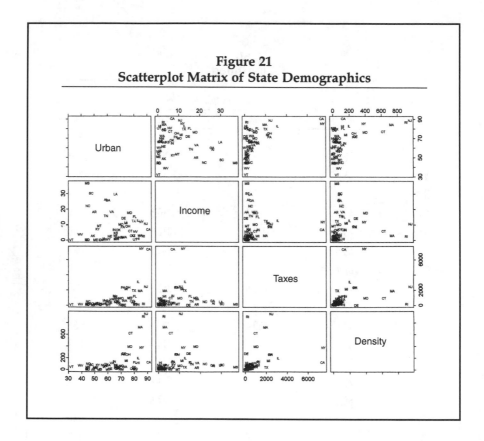

Figure 21
Scatterplot Matrix of State Demographics

to right in the bottom row and then again from left to right in subsequent rows.

Here, linear regressions and locally weighted regressions are added to each dependence panel. There is perhaps some evidence that the linear relationship between tax and income (both log transformed) appears to become stronger as population density increases.

SCATTERPLOTS ON DERIVED VARIABLES

In the previous sections, we have concentrated on graphing the raw data. But scatterplots and the like are equally important when used on variables derived from some analysis that are thought to summarize the data in some meaningful manner. Three examples will serve to illustrate the possibilities.

Figure 22
Log Transformation Scatterplot Matrix of State Demographics

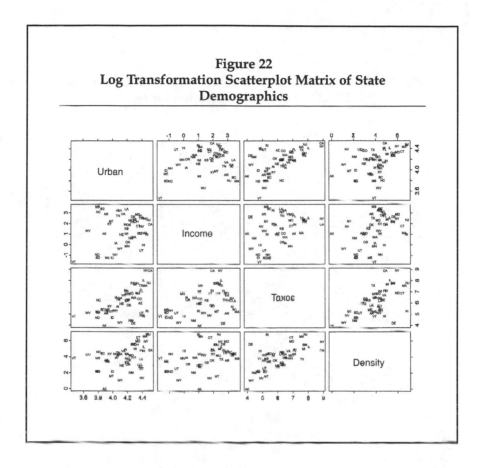

Principal Components Analysis

Principal components analysis is described in detail in many books on multivariate analysis, for example, Everitt and Dunn (2000) and Krzanowski (1988). In essence, it is a method for finding linear transformations of the original variables that (1) are uncorrelated and (2) account for decreasing proportions of the variation in the original variables. When the first few components account for a suitably large proportion of the variance, they may provide a convenient and parsimonious summary of the data, useful in later analyses or for giving insights into the structure of the data. In particular, for our purposes, they may be used to provide hopefully informative scatterplots of the data.

The results of a principal components analysis of the correlation matrix of the demographic data on states of the United States (after the variables have been log transformed) are shown in Table 7. The first component is essentially a weighted average of the four variables, and the sec-

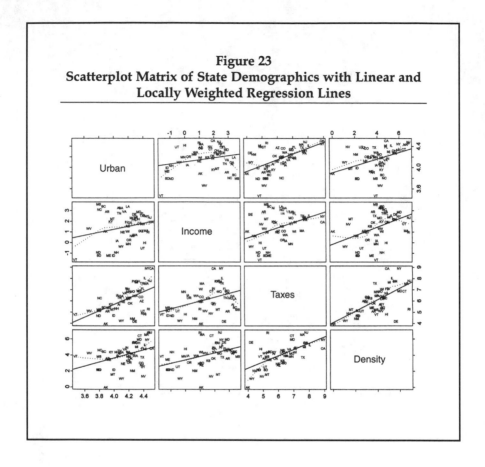

Figure 23
Scatterplot Matrix of State Demographics with Linear and
Locally Weighted Regression Lines

ond is a contrast between the urban and income variables. These two components account for 65% of the variance in the original observations. A plot of the data in the space of these first two components is shown in Figure 25.

Along the first principal components dimension, the states are ordered from those where all four demographic variables are low to those where they are all high. On the second dimension, states at the positive end are those with a high percentage of urban areas and a low percentage of incomes higher than $25,000. At the other end are states where this difference is much less pronounced.

As a slight digression, it is of interest to see how the states are clustered on the basis of their four demographic variable values. Cluster analysis techniques are described in detail by Everitt (1993), but essentially, they are procedures for assessing whether or not there are distinct groups of observations in a set of multivariate data. Application of a *k*-

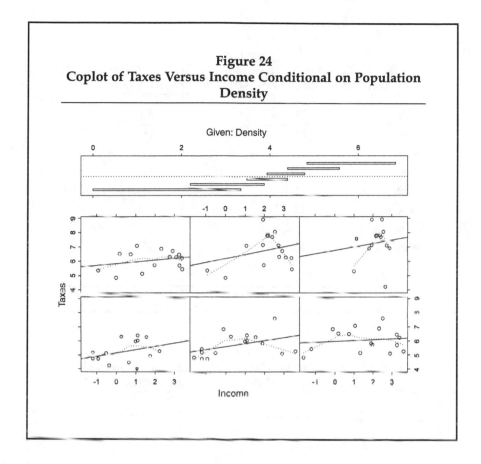

Figure 24
Coplot of Taxes Versus Income Conditional on Population Density

means type algorithm (see Everitt 1993) to minimize the total within-group sum of squares to the log transformed data gives a two-group solution with the means provided in Table 8. In this case, an obvious and highly effective way of displaying the results is by using a map of the United States and labelling states by their cluster number. This is shown in Figure 26.

Multidimensional Scaling

Multidimensional scaling techniques are described in detail by Everitt and Rabe-Hesketh (1997). Such methods are aimed at representing the elements of a *proximity matrix* by a geometrical or spatial model. The proximity matrix may arise directly from experiments in which subjects are asked to assess the similarity of two stimuli or indirectly as a measure of similarity (or dissimilarity) of the two stimuli derived from their raw profile data. The derived geometrical model for the data consists of a set

Table 7
Results of a Principal Components Analysis of Demographic Data on United States After Log Transformation

Variable	PC1	PC2	PC3	PC4
1. Urban	0.466	0.611	0.546	−0.33
2. Income	0.419	−0.770	0.481	0.001
3. Taxes	0.568	0.157	−0.181	0.787
4. Density	0.534	0.001	−0.661	−0.518
Standard Deviation	1.532	0.886	0.732	0.577
Proportion of Variance	0.586	0.196	0.134	0.083
Cumulative Variance	0.586	0.783	0.917	1.000

Figure 25
Plot of Demographic Data in Space of Two Principal Components of the Correlation Matrix

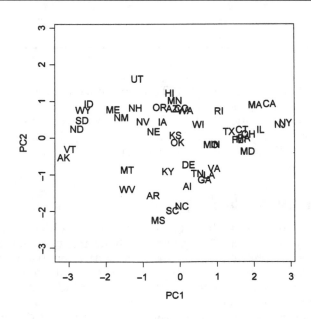

of d-dimensional coordinate values for each stimulus. Both d and the coordinate values need to be determined. In essence, two stimuli that are perceived as highly similar need to be represented in the derived geometrical model by points that are close to each other.

Table 8
Demographic Data Means

| | Means (Log Transformed) | | | |
	Urban	Income	Taxes	Density
Cluster 1:	4.09	0.22	5.40	2.89
Cluster 2:	4.22	2.45	6.73	4.99

Figure 26
States Labelled by Cluster Number

Notes: Numbers provided by a two-cluster solution on the demographic data produced by k-means clustering.

The aim of using multidimensional scaling techniques is primarily to uncover the dimensions on which similarity judgments are being made.

Multidimensional scaling is illustrated in the data shown in Table 9. These data, reported originally by Chakrapani and Ehrenberg (1981), give the percentage of people agreeing with 11 statements about eight brands of cereal. *Classical multidimensional scaling* (see Everitt and Rabe-Hesketh 1997, Chapter 3) applied to the Euclidean distances among cereal brands gives the two-dimensional solution shown in Figure 27.

The first dimension appears to separate the very "traditional" cereals, Weetabix and Cornflakes, from the others. The second dimension ranges from the "fun" cereals, such as Frosties and Sugar Puffs, to those perceived as "good for one's health," such as Special K and All Bran.

Correspondence Analysis

Correspondence analysis is described in detail by Everitt and Dunn (2000). Essentially, this method aims to produce a map of the relationship

Table 9
Attitudes to Brands of Cereal

	1	2	3	4	5	6	7	8	9	10	11
Cornflakes (crfl)	65	64	59	60	40	47	60	27	42	24	17
Weetabix (wtab)	31	40	30	42	50	39	37	38	6	28	12
Rice Krispies (rkrs)	10	32	20	24	17	11	9	9	23	10	57
Shredded Wheat (shrw)	10	23	13	18	31	28	12	26	18	21	5
Sugar Puffs (sgpf)	5	29	15	20	18	6	5	9	13	9	50
Special K (spck)	6	17	7	20	19	15	6	17	8	29	5
Frosties (frst)	6	22	13	19	14	5	5	7	11	9	43
All Bran (albr)	7	11	5	17	19	18	6	17	6	40	0

1: Comes back to

2: Tastes nice

3: Popular with all the family

4: Very easy to digest

5: Nourishing

6: Natural flavour

7: Reasonably priced

8: A lot of food value

9: Stays crispy in milk

10: Helps keep you fit

11: Fun for children to eat

between the categories of two categorical variables linked in the form of a contingency table. Roughly speaking, row categories and column categories that occur close to each other on the derived map indicate cells of the table in which the observed frequency exceeds that expected under independence. When the point representing a row category is distant from that representing a column category, the observed frequency of the corresponding cell is less than that expected under independence.

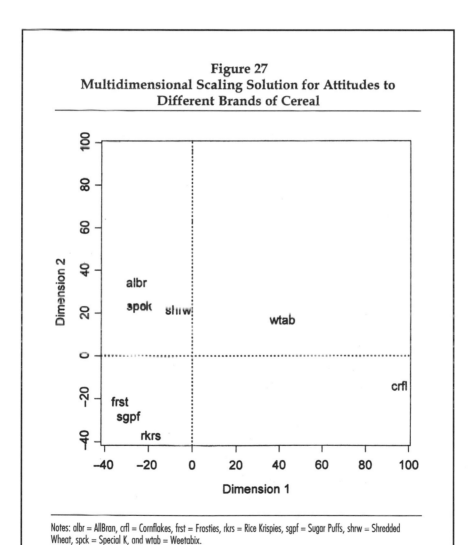

Figure 27
Multidimensional Scaling Solution for Attitudes to Different Brands of Cereal

Notes: albr = AllBran, crfl = Cornflakes, frst = Frosties, rkrs = Rice Krispies, sgpf = Sugar Puffs, shrw = Shredded Wheat, spck = Special K, and wtab = Weetabix.

Table 10
Percentage of Households in Particular Countries that Stock Specific Items of Food

	WG	IT	FR	NS	BM	LG	GB	PL	AA	SD	SW	DK	NY	FD	SP	ID
Ground coffee (GC)	90	82	88	96	94	97	27	72	55	73	97	96	92	98	70	13
Instant coffee (IC)	49	10	42	62	38	61	86	26	31	72	13	17	17	12	40	52
Tea or tea bags (TB)	88	60	96	98	48	86	99	77	61	85	93	92	83	84	40	99
Sugarless sweet (SS)	19	2	4	32	11	28	22	2	15	25	31	35	13	20	—	11
Packaged biscuits (BP)	57	55	76	62	74	79	91	22	29	31	—	66	62	64	62	80
Soup (packages) (SP)	51	41	53	67	37	73	55	34	33	69	43	32	51	27	43	75
Soup (tinned) (ST)	19	3	11	43	25	12	76	1	1	10	43	17	4	10	2	18
Instant potatoes (IP)	21	2	23	7	9	7	17	5	5	17	39	11	17	8	14	2
Frozen fish (FF)	27	4	11	14	13	26	20	20	15	19	54	51	30	18	23	5
Frozen vegetables (VF)	21	2	5	16	12	23	24	3	11	15	45	42	15	12	7	3
Fresh apples (AF)	81	67	87	83	76	94	68	51	42	70	78	72	72	57	77	52
Fresh oranges (OF)	75	71	84	89	76	94	68	51	42	70	78	72	72	57	77	52
Tinned fruit (FT)	44	9	40	61	42	83	89	8	14	46	53	50	34	22	30	46
Jam (shop) (JS)	71	46	45	81	57	20	91	16	41	61	75	64	51	37	38	89
Garlic clove (CG)	22	80	88	15	29	91	11	89	51	64	9	11	11	15	86	5
Butter (BR)	91	66	94	31	84	94	95	65	51	82	68	92	63	96	44	97
Margarine (ME)	85	24	47	97	80	94	94	78	72	48	32	91	94	94	51	25
Olive, corn oil (OO)	74	94	36	13	83	84	57	92	28	61	48	30	28	17	91	31
Yoghurt (YT)	30	5	57	53	20	31	11	6	13	48	2	11	2	—	16	3
Crispbread (CD)	26	18	3	15	5	24	28	9	11	30	93	34	62	64	13	9

Correspondence analysis is illustrated in the data shown in Table 10. These data were collected in a survey of European households and indicate the percentage of all households with various foods in the house at the time of the questionnaire. The two-dimensional correspondence analysis solution for both countries and foods is shown in Figure 28. This "map" clearly indicates the food preferences of different regions of Europe. A plot of the countries only, after rotation, is shown in Figure 29. This mimics quite closely the geographical map of Europe.

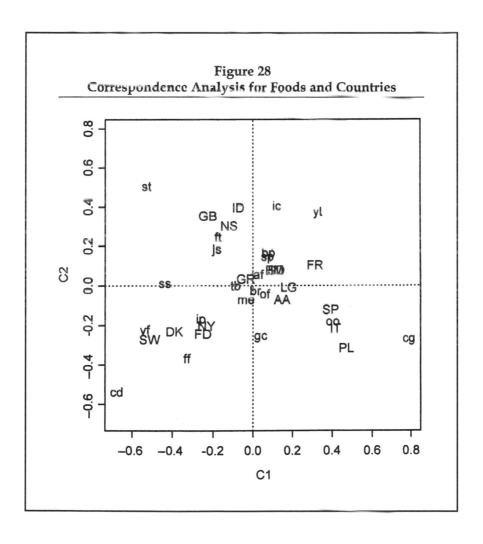

Figure 28
Correspondence Analysis for Foods and Countries

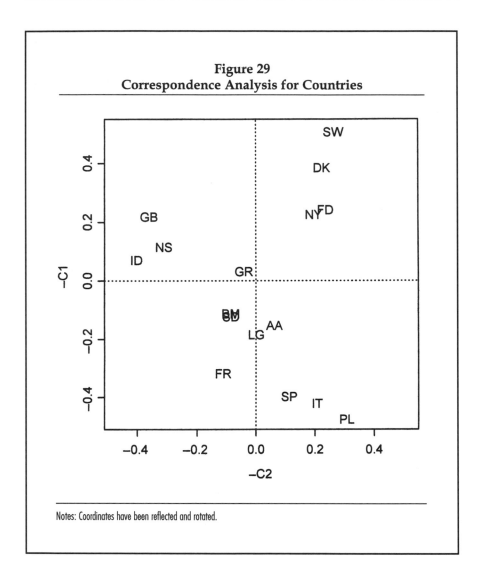

Figure 29
Correspondence Analysis for Countries

Notes: Coordinates have been reflected and rotated.

SUMMARY

According to Wainer (1997, p. 1), "Effectively conveying information in words is a difficult task. When this information is complex, the task often becomes insuperable." The most usual remedy for this problem is to use some form of graphical display instead. In this chapter, a variety of relatively simple but not simplistic graphical procedures have been illustrated. There are, of course, many other possibilities that have not been discussed, including dynamic graphics (Cleveland and McGill 1987). But it is hoped that those methods that have been described will convince readers of the importance of using graphical material in the understanding and presentation of complex data.

BIBLIOGRAPHY

Chakrapani, Chuck and A.S.C. Ehrenberg (1981), "An Alternative to Factor Analysis in Market Research—Part 2: Between Group Analysis," *Professional Marketing Research Society Journal*, 1, 32–38.

Chambers, J.M., W.S. Cleveland, B. Kleiner, and P.A. Tukey (1983), *Graphical Methods for Data Analysis*. Belmont, CA: Wadsworth.

Cleveland, W.S. (1979), "Robust Locally Weighted Regression and Smoothing Scatterplots," *Journal of American Statistical Association*, 74 (3), 829–36.

——— (1993), *Visualizing Data*. Murray Hill, NJ: Hobart Press.

——— (1994), *The Elements of Graphing Data*. Murray Hill, NJ: Hobart Press.

——— and M.E. McGill (1987), *Dynamic Graphs for Statistics*. Belmont, CA: Wadsworth.

Cook, R.D. and S. Weisberg (1994), *An Introduction to Regression Graphics*. New York: John Wiley & Sons.

Everitt, B.S. (1993), *Cluster Analysis*, 3d ed. London: Arnold.

——— and G. Dunn (2000), *Applied Multivariate Data Analysis*, 2d ed. London: Arnold.

——— and S. Rabe-Hesketh (1997), *The Analysis of Proximity Data*. London: Arnold.

Krzanowski, W.J. (1988), *Principles of Multivariate Analysis: A User's Perspective*. Oxford: Oxford Science Publications.

Schmid, C.F. (1954), *Handbook of Graphic Presentation*. New York: Ronald Press.

Tufte, E.R. (1983), *The Visual Display of Quantitative Information*. Cheshire, CT: Graphs Press.

Tukey, J.W. (1977), *Exploratory Data Analysis*. Reading, MA: Addison-Wesley.

Vetter, B.M. (1980), "Working Women Scientists and Engineers," *Science*, 207 (4425), 28–34.

Wainer, H. (1997), *Visual Revelations*. New York: Springer-Verlag.

Wilkinson, L. (1992), "Graphical Displays," *Statistical Methods in Medical Research*, 1, 3–25.

Part IV
Searching for
Structure

I
n searching for the underlying structures, we build marketing models. Models are abstractions of reality. In building models, we smooth out the rough edges, minimize obscurities, and simplify complex phenomena. As a result, models seldom represent reality fully. However, such simplification has some advantages. It makes it easier for us to understand the phenomenon being modeled, even though our understanding may not be complete. As Box once observed, "All models are wrong, but some are useful."[1]

In a sense, in going from data to knowledge, we constantly search for structures. Looking for patterns, applying multivariate techniques to data, developing hypotheses, and deriving lawlike relationships all involve a search for structure. In this part, we apply the term in a narrow sense to cover market mix analysis, market segmentation, and database and data mining techniques.

The first problem tackled in this part of the book is marketing mix analysis, the use of statistical techniques to identify and quantify the impact of key marketing mix elements such as promotion and advertising on sales over time. The tools described by David Gascoigne (Chapter 13) can be applied to a variety of marketing problems: What is the return on investment on my marketing spending? How do I optimize my return on investment? What will happen if I increase the price of my brand? How can I optimize my future marketing activity? Translating a statistical model into something meaningful and actionable to the client is not always an easy task. Gascoigne discusses the considerations and decisions a modeler must make to facilitate this process.

---

[1] See G.E.P. Box, "Mathematical Models for Adaptive Control and Optimization" (1965, *Symp. Series* 4, 61).

The second problem has to do with market segmentation. The market for practically any product is segmented. Segmenting the market is one of the obvious things a marketer can do to understand his or her target market. But segmenting the market raises several issues: Should one use a priori or ad hoc models? How to develop scoring models to exploit past knowledge? How to incorporate the new developments in our segmentation scheme? In Chapter 14, Bill Neal tackles these issues.

The third problem has to do with databases, data mining techniques, and knowledge discovery databases (KDD). The world of marketing research is rapidly changing. Availability of cheap computing power, coupled with the explosive availability of information, has created a need for new ways of analysis. Although the logic of the analyses remains the same, we now need to deal with very large databases. Whereas small sets of data enabled the researcher to test hypotheses, very large databases make new discoveries and hidden relationships possible. In Chapter 15, Peter Peacock provides an excellent introduction to this (relatively) new field and covers database operations, data warehousing and OLAP, data mining, and KDD.

13

Marketing Mix Analysis: A Science ... and an Art

David Gascoigne

What will happen to sales if I increase the price of my brand? What is the impact of a price promotion? What is the Return on Investment (ROI) from my media spending? How can I optimize my future marketing activity? These are some of the most frequently asked questions we at Millward Brown receive from marketing departments in North America and the rest of the world.

Marketing mix analysis is an excellent tool for addressing these issues. The purpose of this chapter is to review some of the practical considerations facing the modeler when conducting marketing mix analysis in a commercial environment. There is a particular emphasis on the pricing and advertising elements.

An introduction to some of the principles of marketing mix analysis is provided, including an overview of the common modeling tools. We then consider the product categories in which the tools may be applied and focus on the recent development of modeling applications for non-packaged goods brands. Detailed pricing and advertising case histories show how conventional methods can be adapted using techniques such as nonlinear regression (NLR), ridge regression, and multistage modeling in order to provide the client with greater insight and actionability.

However, complex modeling formulations can be inappropriate. To illustrate, we show how good data exploratory techniques have been used in an attempt to understand the longer-term contribution of advertising to sales.

A series of case histories is included, so this chapter should be of interest to both the practitioner and the nonpractitioner. Throughout the chapter, there is a common theme. Marketing mix analysis may be difficult, though not necessarily because of the statistics. There are many issues the modeler needs to address, including data availability, clients' objectives, interpretation, and the application of results. Marketing mix analysis is a science—but it is also an art.

PRINCIPLES OF MARKETING MIX ANALYSIS

Marketing mix analysis identifies and quantifies the impact of key marketing mix components on sales, such as price, promotion, distribution, and advertising (Figure 1). These elements are usually considered for both the modeled brand and competitor brands, because competitor activity can also have both positive and negative effects on sales of the modeled brand. Seasonality is inherent in many categories and, though not a marketing factor, should be incorporated where relevant.

Most models developed in a commercial environment are based on multiple linear regression techniques (general linear models), though other tools are available, including NLR, conventional time-series approaches, and neural networks. These alternative approaches may provide a good prediction of sales, but they can be more computationally

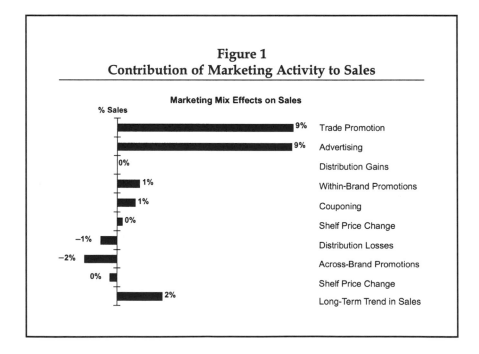

Figure 1
Contribution of Marketing Activity to Sales

Marketing Mix Effects on Sales

% Sales

9%	Trade Promotion
9%	Advertising
0%	Distribution Gains
1%	Within-Brand Promotions
1%	Couponing
0%	Shelf Price Change
−1%	Distribution Losses
−2%	Across-Brand Promotions
0%	Shelf Price Change
2%	Long-Term Trend in Sales

demanding or fail to provide the brand manager with an adequate explanation as to *why* there have been movements in sales.

An example of a model for a retailer shows how accurately we are sometimes able to predict sales (Figure 2). The solid line shows weekly sales, and the dashed line is the model prediction of sales.

The data were modeled at the store level and then aggregated to present the national picture using general linear modeling of the form:

$$y = \beta_0 + \beta_1 x_1 + ... + \beta_p x_p + \varepsilon.$$

In this example, a "good" statistical prediction of sales was obtained by incorporating the following measures:

❑ Regular price and temporary price reduction;

❑ Store inventory, store volume per 1000 households in area, type of store (downtown, mall, etc.), selling square footage;

❑ Magazine, newspaper, radio, outdoor, and television advertising;

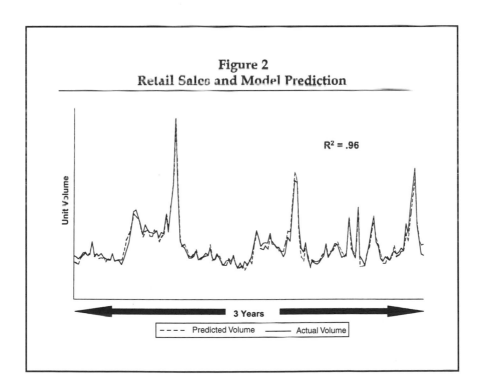

Figure 2
Retail Sales and Model Prediction

$R^2 = .96$

Unit Volume

3 Years

- - - - Predicted Volume ———— Actual Volume

❏ Seasonality;

❏ Underlying trends; and

❏ Promotional/store-type interaction.

The accuracy of the model will usually be influenced by the quality of both the sales data and these explanatory measures. If we do not have the data, we cannot expect good models to be produced.

The model inputs will clearly vary by product category, but we can attempt to incorporate any measure, providing adequate detail and timing of an activity is available.

In this example, we can be reasonably satisfied from the modeling perspective. We have a model that has accuracy and that subsequently satisfied two separate validation processes (in process and hold-out sample). We also tested our data to ensure compliance with important statistical assumptions. Diagnostics include residual analysis, leverage statistics, and influence measures. (Refer to any good statistical textbook for further details.)

So, does this scientific part of the modeling development satisfy our clients' requirements? Not on its own (though good statistical fit and validity are obviously important). We must ensure that the model makes sense.

For example, multicollinearity is caused by having highly correlated measures. This can result in a model having good statistical fit but misleading coefficient weight and signs. As modelers, we would lose all respect from a client if we suggested that an increase in price would result in a sales increase, a reduction in distribution would result in a sales increase, the client's television advertising would have a negative impact on sales, and so on. All these scenarios are statistically possible but do not make intuitive sense (and are more likely to be statistical artifacts).

In the retail example, we could have produced an equally good model fit and short-term projection by using conventional time-series approaches such as Box-Jenkins. Such methods tend to be good forecasting tools but fail to meet the client's objectives, in that they are unable to explain *why* there have been movements in sales.

The summary of marketing mix effects on sales (Figure 1) is inherent in presentations produced by almost every agency that specializes in marketing mix analysis. This provides the client with a useful management summary, though it can be too static and almost too simple in nature for the purpose of future application. We have to make every attempt to explain *why* there have been movements in sales and to estimate the expected impact of future marketing activity and the timing of the activity on sales, as well as how sales can be optimized from future activity given a marketing budget. The client wants to use the model to move his or her business forward. We show how to do this subsequently.

To summarize, we should never lose sight of the client's objectives, and throughout this chapter, an important theme is retained: A successful marketing mix analysis requires not only that the modeler have good statistical practice, but also that the modeler gain a good understanding of the client's issues and apply common sense when building and interpreting the model.

CAN I APPLY MARKETING MIX ANALYSIS TO MY BRAND?

Marketing mix analysis is certainly not new and has been successfully applied across diverse brands for many years. The main prerequisite is to have access to reliable and consistent sales data and marketing inputs over time.

Packaged Goods

Historically, most market mix analysis has been conducted on traditional packaged goods brands. The tool has been publicly presented and had a very high profile for at least 30 years, with every product category modeled at some time, ranging from potato chips and candy to deodorants and haircare products (to name just a few).

Packaged goods clients have the luxury of being able to purchase consistent syndicated sales and causal data from ACNielsen or IRI for their own brand and competitor brands by pack size and variant. These data are typically weekly and available for grocery, drug, and mass merchandise sales channels in the United States (though the sales period can vary by category). Any client purchasing ACNielsen or IRI syndicated sales data can conduct or commission marketing mix analysis projects. Models can also be applied on household panel data (see von Gonten 1998; von Gonten and Donius 1996), though this is less common among practitioners and not covered in this chapter.

Even though product categories are diverse and possess their own unique characteristics and purchase cycles, the consistent delivery and detail of data, the fast moving nature of the product, and the common sensitivity to price and promotion often enable a consistent approach to be adopted.

Nonpackaged Goods

A common myth is that marketing mix analysis can be applied only to packaged goods. This is fortunately nothing more than a myth. In recent years, we have worked with diverse clients ranging from automobiles to pharmaceuticals, financial services to retail, lotteries to alcoholic beverages, telecommunications to mail delivery services, gasoline to milk, and so on.

Many of these projects have features or "quirks" unique to their category that make such projects "nonstandard." However, in most cases, we are able to overcome these difficulties through detailed discussion with the client (and provided adequate data are available).

To illustrate, for a recent telecommunications client providing a monthly subscription service, what sales units should we be modeling? This is not as straightforward as it initially appears. Any of the following sales units could be considered:

❏ New customers,
❏ Repeat customers,
❏ Total new and repeat customers,
❏ The number of telephone calls made, or
❏ The value of the telephone calls.

This becomes more complex when considering the array of tariffs that range from those targeting the "occasional personal user" with low monthly tariff payments but expensive call rates to those aimed at a "heavy business user" with high monthly payments but less expensive call rates.

We recently assessed the ROI of a direct-to-consumer campaign for prescriptions of a drug. We needed to attempt to disentangle the impact of the campaign on the patient from the influence of the campaign on doctors prescribing the drug. There are inevitable time delays caused by potential users of the drug who are influenced by the marketing activity but subsequently need to make an appointment with their doctor before the drug can be purchased. This adds complexity to the problem at hand (though not necessarily to the analysis).

There are additional considerations for nonpackaged goods. First, a category can be heterogeneous and split into several product fields. For example, one of the most diverse categories is financial services. In recent years, we have modeled bank checking and savings accounts, credit cards, automated payment schemes, life assurance, pension schemes, stock exchange investment products, and car and home insurance. We therefore cannot adopt a blanket approach to the modeling of nonpackaged goods at a category level or within a category. The analytical concepts may be similar, but the factors driving each product field clearly differ.

Second, nonpackaged goods clients do not have the luxury of being able to purchase consistent syndicated data for their brand and competitor brands. Their data arrive in many different formats from many different internal and external data sources. In essence, understanding, making sense of, and manipulating these data is the real challenge when modeling for nonpackaged goods clients

Improving Quality of Client Data and the Growth of Modeling in Nonpackaged Goods

Fifteen years ago, a marketing mix analysis on a nonpackaged good brand could have been conducted but with limited benefit and certainly minimal actionability. Sales data would often be monthly or quarterly, and in some cases, only national data rather than market/regional-level data would be available. Such projects would have a relatively simple model formulation and only be able to provide an estimate of the impact of one medium (usually television). This effect would be directional because of the highly aggregated nature of the data.

In recent years, we have seen a sharp increase in the number of marketing mix analysis projects for nonpackaged goods clients. This is in part attributable to the growth of the service sector, new industries, and technological developments. Many clients now have new, innovative, and powerful management information systems that possess detailed sales and inquiry data on *all* customers, both *locally* and *nationally*.

In many cases, we now have access to more powerful sales data than are available from many of our packaged goods clients that buy syndicated data. For example, a U.S. company was recently able to provide telephone inquiries by day, daypart, and time of day. A financial service organization in the United Kingdom was able to provide the date, time of inquiry, whether a subsequent sale was made, and date of subsequent sale where applicable for each customer/potential customer by market and zip code. Advertising spending was also made available by day and daypart. This quality and level of sales data is very powerful.

METHODS

Marketing mix analysis can be a very emotive topic, and there are many schools of thought on the correct methodology, ranging from the statistical purists to those who push the statistical validity to its limits (though sometimes through ignorance) in an attempt to get the answer they want. Fortunately, the latter form the minority, and most practitioners usually balance the desire for sensible results with good statistical practice.

Those of a more academic nature may strive for the most statistically complex solution. Although commendable, this can often be impractical in a commercial environment where tight time constraints are imposed by clients. For example, on a recent project, we attempted to use a structural equation modeling approach. This proved to be very time consuming and then difficult to replicate on products in different markets. Moreover, the results were no more meaningful or insightful than those produced within a shorter time period using a general linear model.

A whole book could be devoted to methodological and data issues surrounding marketing mix analysis approaches. Some argue that store-level data is needed to model packaged goods, others argue that modeling can be conducted at the market level, some argue that there is disaggregation bias at the store level, others argue that there is aggregation bias at the market level, some argue that they have the "best" model because they have the better data, others argue that they have the better model because their model has a more complex formulation or is more flexible ... and so on.

There are clearly no definitive answers to this debate (though those with their own prejudices may not accept this comment). Because the purpose of this chapter is to focus on modeling applications, we do not enter the debate at this stage other than to say that the "best" approach should be governed by the client's objectives and the available data.

Papers discussing methodological issues are referenced for the interested reader. We also make observations on methodology in a subsequent discussion.

PRICE AND PROMOTIONAL ISSUES

Price and promotion invariably have the largest *immediate* effect on sales for packaged goods brands, particularly in the grocery sector. Examples of pricing related promotion include

- ❏ Temporary price reductions ("For this week only, the price is reduced from $1.99 to $1.49"),
- ❏ Extra value ("Get 20% extra for the same price"),
- ❏ Extra packs ("Buy one outer pack containing 12 bars and receive 2 free bars"), and
- ❏ BOGOF ("Buy one get one free").

Promotional incentives can also be provided in the form of free or discounted gifts, instant wins, and so on. Irrespective of the nature of the promotion, its effectiveness will be boosted when supported with a combination of "shelf-talkers" and in-store displays.

There can be a large amount of bias in price and promotion through the aggregation of store-level data to the market/regional level. Some stores promote, whereas others do not, and the promotional effect therefore can be considerably diluted. ACNielsen and IRI specialize in modeling this micro-level trade activity. They have access to detailed store-level data and have developed proprietary models that enable them to model at the store level and report precisely on the impact of such trade promotions. This is done by comparing the impact of sales on stores with and without the different forms of trade activity.

However, this does not imply that other agencies, individuals specializing in commercial modeling, or academics cannot develop meaningful models that provide insight on price and other marketing issues. We therefore focus on how the majority of practitioners can address pricing issues, even though the sales data may only be made available at the market/regional level. We are unable to disentangle the specific impact of all trade promotion, but we can show how the brand reacts to price and pricing-related promotion.

Price Elasticity

Figure 3 shows the power of conducting exploratory analysis before we begin to attempt the modeling process. The solid line is weekly volume share of a leading packaged goods brand in the grocery sector over a three-year period. We refer to this as $Brand_{mod}$. The main competitor for

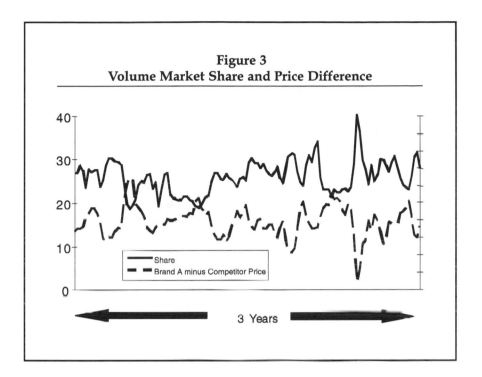

Figure 3
Volume Market Share and Price Difference

this Brand is Brand$_{comp}$. The dashed line is the price of the modeled brand minus the price of the key competitor brand and is simply given by

$$\text{Price Difference} = \text{Brand}_{mod}(\$Sales/Volume\ Sales)$$
$$- \text{Brand}_{comp}(\$Sales/Volume\ Sales).$$

We observe a very strong relationship and almost symmetrical pattern between apparent reductions in price and increase in market share.

Not surprisingly, the inclusion of this price difference term in the model is highly significant. Changes in relative price have a strong influence on sales. For Brand$_{mod}$, we find that a 1% increase in relative price will result in an 0.8% decrease in market share. This is a price elasticity of –0.8.

The elasticity for an additive model can be calculated from the model coefficient, volume, and price:

$$\text{Price Elasticity} = (\text{coefficient for price difference}/$$
$$\text{Brand}_{mod}\text{average volume}) \times (\text{Brand}_{mod}\text{average price}).$$

For a multiplicative model, the input is a price ratio ($Brand_{mod}price/$ $Brand_{comp}price$). The elasticity is obtained directly from the coefficient.

The price elasticity provides an indication of the sensitivity of the brand to changes in price. The elasticity is also useful as a standardized measure, enabling a meaningful comparison of the impact of price changes across all brands, adjusted for the size of the brand (big brands lose more volume in real terms).

In general, the price elasticity implies that if you increase price by 1% and sales volume decreases as a result by this negative percentage, then you would make the same profit as before. Refer to Broadbent (1997) for a more detailed discussion on the concepts of price elasticity.

We typically find that larger, established brands are less sensitive to price changes than smaller or new brands. We also find that price elasticities are not consistent over the different sales channels. For example, a candy product is likely to have greater sensitivity to price in a grocery store, where there is a wide choice of products and a larger amount of promotional activity, than in a convenience store, where the purchase decision is often made more on impulse and products typically demand a higher price.

This leads to a simple consideration that should be applied across all marketing mix analysis projects. We should never assume that the elasticities for promotional spending (or any other marketing mix measures) remain constant over the modeling period. Many agencies specializing in marketing mix analysis present bar charts/pie charts in order to summarize the contribution of the various components of the marketing activity to sales (Figure 1). Although such charts provide a useful overview, they should also specify whether the elasticities have remained constant or changed over time. Failure to do this could lead to misleading conclusions and inappropriate marketing decisions being made.

Figure 4 shows a rolling price elasticity for a packaged goods brand. The average elasticity (the one commonly reported) is –2.7. Focusing on the underlying trend, there has been a slight decrease in the sensitivity of the brand to increases in price. Further investigation showed that this coincided with an increase in both the weight and quality of the television advertising campaigns over the modeling period. This is effectively an indirect long-term impact of advertising on sales of the brand. Price increases are now having a smaller negative impact on sales than they were at the start of the modeling period.

Reporting the average elasticity of –2.7 alone is not incorrect from a statistical viewpoint, but we are failing to provide the brand manager with a true reflection of what is happening to his or her brand due to marketing activity *over time*.

There are also periods of short-term fluctuation. The period around week 95 coincided with a television advertising campaign and strong brand support in-store, though no price promotions. We found that the combined strategy reduced the price sensitivity of the brand for the duration of the campaign.

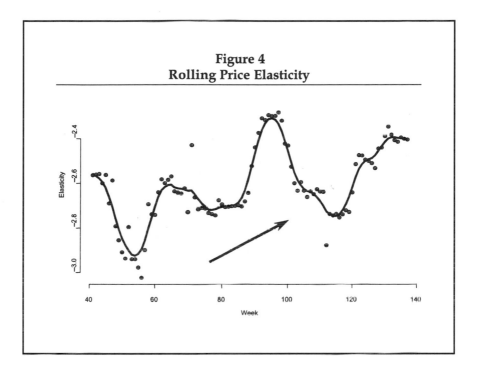

Figure 4
Rolling Price Elasticity

Modeling by Pack Size—Pricing Case History

We now present a detailed case history for a leading brand in the snack category to demonstrate how the concepts on price elasticity can be applied.

Model 1: Total Brand Sales

Total brand sales in the grocery sector were predicted over a three-year period. The primary focus was to understand the contribution of television advertising to sales. A good statistical fit of total brand sales was produced, and we were able to demonstrate that the growth in sales was primarily driven by both excellent television advertising and increased distribution (Figure 5). The average price elasticity for the brand was –2.2.

Model 2: Pack Size Sales

During the next two years, the client obtained improved sales data, and pricing became the primary issue. The key objectives were to determine the combination of pack size promotions that would generate maximum sales for the brand overall and identify the brand's competitor set by pack size.

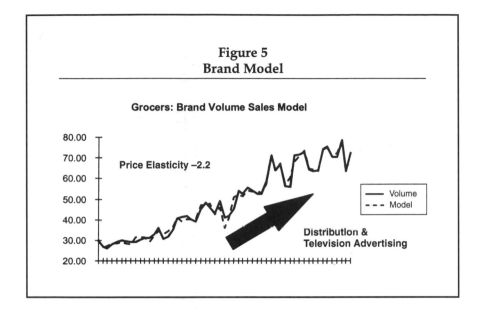

Figure 5
Brand Model

Therefore, three refinements were made to the original modeling approach:

- ❏ Model pack size,
- ❏ Use straight price, and
- ❏ Adopt a multistage modeling approach.

These allow greater insight and actionability for the brand manager by quantifying and explicating the impact of individual elasticities and the extent of cannibalization across pack size. We consider the three model refinements in turn.

Brand Sales Versus Pack Size Sales. Modeling at the total brand level is clearly inappropriate, and we are able to show that this can "hide" potentially key findings (Figure 6). The top chart is total weekly volume sales for the brand – our original unit of measurement. The bottom chart is sales split by the four key pack sizes (small, medium, large, and very large). Points A and B represent two different price promotions.

At point A, the net effect of promoting the small and very large packs results in a positive increase in sales over the promoted period (A*). This is favorable. At point B, the promotion successfully generates sales of the very large pack, but most of these sales appear to be taken from the medium and large packs, and the net effect is minimal (B*). This is unfavorable.

The first refinement was therefore to disaggregate the sales data and model by pack size. This should allow the assessment of pack size inter-

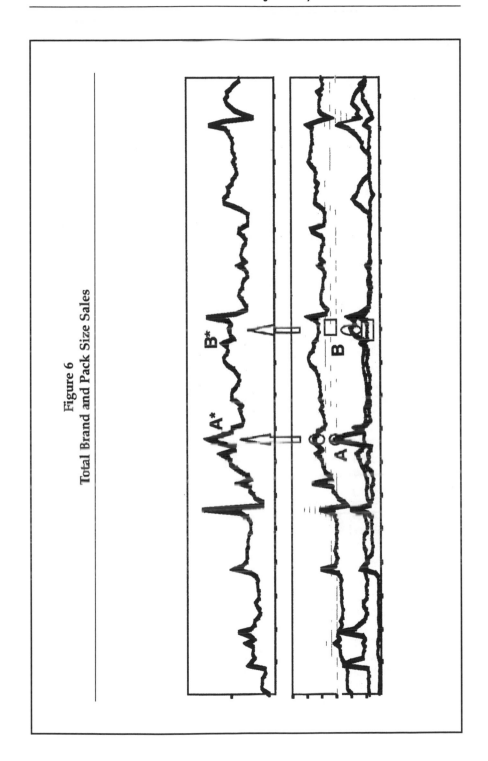

Figure 6
Total Brand and Pack Size Sales

action or cannibalization and indicate where promotions are having the largest impact.

Straight Price. At the same time, we were also considering the merits of using relative price for this new project. Although relative price was adequate for modeling brand sales, this approach does have limitations, particularly as we disaggregate the data. Relative price assumes that a 1% increase in the modeled brand will have the same impact as a 1% decrease in the competitor brand. This tends to work, but conceptually, we would expect a different effect on sales from changing the price of the modeled brand than from changing the price of the competitor brand; the effect is not symmetrical. The second refinement was therefore to use straight price for the client's brand and competitor brands. We should now be able to see the individual contributions of price change.

Competitor Index. We incorporated a straight price term for the modeled brand but were only able to build in the one competitor term. The model worked but was still an unsatisfactory solution for the client who still wanted to know the *competitor set* by pack size and not just the impact of one competitor.

A two-stage modeling approach was therefore adopted. The first phase of the process was to build a model as normal using straight price for the main brand but excluding the competitor prices. The second phase was to model the residuals with only the competitor prices and feed this back into the original model. So, how successful was this approach? Consider the following three observations:

First, a series of pricing terms could now be incorporated across the four models (Table 1). We could also build in a series of other measures (Table 2). Four models were developed explaining between 94% and 96% of variation in sales.

Second, price elasticities are now available for each of the four pack sizes. These are

❏ Small pack, –3.6;
❏ Medium pack, –3.8;
❏ Large pack, –2.8; and
❏ Extra large pack, –2.9.

At this stage, we note that the smaller packs appear to be more price sensitive. This is counterintuitive, as we would expect larger packs to be more price sensitive (most consumers buy in bulk to save money rather than for convenience). We were able to explain this apparent discrepancy. The small and medium packs had been predominantly supported with pricing promotions (temporary price reductions). The larger pack sizes had also been heavily supported with other forms of promotional activity (extra packs for same price). When we combine the price and promotional

Table 1
Model Inputs — Price

Client Brand	Own Label	Other Brands
Small	Small	Brand A Small
Medium	Medium (2 sizes)	Brand A Medium
Large	Large (2 sizes)	Brand B Small
Extra Large	Extra Large (2 sizes)	Brand B Medium
		Brand D Small
		Brand D Medium
		Brand E Large
		Brand F Small
		Brand F Medium
		Brand G Medium

Table 2
Model Inputs — Additional Measures

Promotions	Others
Pack Price Promotion	Theme Advertising
Pack Value Promotion	Promotional Advertising
Extra Pack Promotion	Seasonality
Competitor Promotions	Distribution
	Launch of New Variant

elasticities, the overall elasticities become much stronger for the larger pack sizes.

We also note that price elasticities appear to be considerably greater than those reported two years earlier. Is this evidence to suggest the brand is losing equity and becoming considerably more price sensitive in a relatively short time period? This would have been a disturbing conclusion for the client. Fortunately, this was not the case. The elasticities are no longer comparable because of the change in approach from relative to straight price. The new elasticities are for the individual packs and include the elasticity among brands and within-brand (cannibalization). The original model elasticity was based on competitor brands only. We were able to show that for the new model, the overall elasticity *with other brands* is –2.2, almost identical to what we reported two years earlier using the original formulation.

Third, the multistage modeling approach enabled detailed findings to be identified on the competitor brands and their pack sizes through the development of a competitor index. The competitor index disentangles the contribution of price changes on a set of competitor brands and is obtained from the second phase of the multistage approach.

Figure 7 shows the maximum variation on the sales of the small pack, caused by changes in the six key competitor prices in any one week. For example, changes in price of Competitor Brand A's small size had the largest impact on the sales of the client's small pack brand (up to 90,000 sales units). The next largest variation was due to the client's own medium pack size. This is the cannibalization effect and should be understood and controlled wherever possible. The competitor indices were later validated by other sources of data and research conducted by the client.

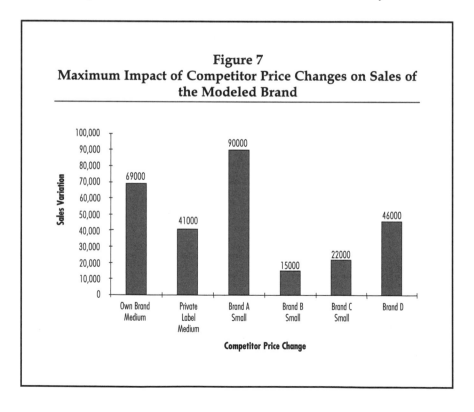

Figure 7
Maximum Impact of Competitor Price Changes on Sales of the Modeled Brand

Spreadsheets can now be provided to help the client generate "what-if" scenarios, understand the implications of changes made to the brand's price, and appreciate the likely impact of competitor price changes. A simple hypothetical example shows the estimated impact on sales of the small pack should five key competitors reduce their price by 5% at the same time (Table 3). This (unlikely) action would result in a volume loss of 3.67%. The models could now be used to deduce the impact of temporary price changes and promotions on individual pack sizes.

If the client reduces the price of the small pack, 97% of the extra sales gained will be taken from competitor branded products of similar pack sizes. This is clearly desirable. The small pack size is not competing with the private label. However, when promoting the medium pack, almost all sales will be generated from those consumers switching from the brand's own small pack (predominantly) and the large pack. The overall sales generated through the medium pack promotion are canceled through the loss in sales of the small and larger packs.

When promoting the large pack, just 15% of sales are taken from competitor brands. The majority of incremental sales are still from existing consumers switching from the medium and extra large packs. In contrast, when the extra large pack is promoted, approximately 55% of sales are taken from competitor brands (mainly private label).

Therefore, if the client wishes to optimize incremental sales for the brand and take sales away from competitor brands, the focus should be on promoting the small packs. If the client wishes to protect the brand market share from the private label, the focus should be on promoting the extra large pack sizes.

Table 3
Price Elasticity Spreadsheet

Price	Before	After	% Change	Volume
Own Brand Medium	1.68	1.68	—	—
Private Label Medium	1.02	0.97	−5	−0.07
Brand A Small	0.90	0.86	−5	−0.18
Brand B Small	0.88	0.84	−5	−0.04
Own Brand Small	1.05	1.05	—	—
Brand C Small	0.99	0.94	−5	−0.07
Brand D	1.41	1.34	−5	−0.04
			Sum Units (100,000's)	−0.40
			Percentage	−3.67

This case history is a good illustration of how the basic concepts can be applied to developed models that meet a client's specific requirements and were certainly actionable. For the practitioner, this analysis shows differences in price elasticities and potential pitfalls when interpreting models. It would have been very easy for a modeler to misinterpret the results of the new pack size elasticities, particularly when making a comparison with previous results. This could have resulted in misguided marketing decisions being made.

TELEVISION ADVERTISING

How Can We Build Television Advertising into a Model?

We begin by considering the common unit of currency for television advertising: a gross rating point (GRP). In its simplest form, 100 GRPs could represent 100% of the target audience having seen the ad once, or 50% having seen it on two occasions, or any other combination. However, straight GRPs rarely produce significant and/or meaningful results. This is because we invariably find that advertising has a carry-over effect beyond the time the advertising has finished. We therefore adopt an approach discussed in detail by Broadbent (1997). The GRPs are converted into advertising stocks, or adstocks, by carrying over a certain proportion of GRPs each week.

Many practitioners have adopted this approach (or slight variations). The following recursive formula can be used on most occasions:

$$\text{Adstock}_n = (\text{Adstock}_{n-1} \times \text{retention factor}) + \text{GRP}_n.$$

An example is provided for a short flight of advertising with a 90% carry-over effect (retention) or, alternatively, a 10% decay (Table 4). We use the adstocks for the purpose of modeling, not the GRPs.

The modeler should determine the appropriate retention level. This is effectively an iterative process and is usually established after generating many models (often hundreds). Where detectable, advertising variations can vary from as little as 50% to as large as 99%.

This certainly has implications for the purpose of media planning. An ad with a 60% retention has a very short carry-over effect. An advertising weight of 100 GRPs in week 1 will have less than half its original effect by the end of the third week. This implies that the campaign only has an impact on sales at the time of the advertising and very shortly afterward. The ad must be constantly on air to retain a sales effect. In contrast, an ad with a 90% retention will still have approximately half its original sales effect by the end of the eighth week and a small sales effect for up to six months. The ad does not need to be constantly on air to maintain a sales effect.

Table 4
Calculating Adstocks with a 90% Retention

Week	GRPs	Carry Over	Adstocks
0	0	0	0
1	100	0	100
2	0	90	90
3	100	81	181
4	0	163	163
5	0	147	147
6	0	132	132

We are sometimes able to detect campaigns with higher levels of retention, which implies sales contributions both in the shorter and longer term. For example, a 98% retention will have half its original impact eight months after the campaign and still have a small sales impact up to two years later.

Various factors can influence the rate of retention, including product category, purchase cycle, promotional/theme-based advertising, and the quality and levels of awareness achieved by the ads.

Short-Term Advertising Contributions

We initially focus on those campaigns with sales contributions over a shorter time period only (those with a 90% retention or lower) and make a brief comparison between the additive and multiplicative formulations.

Additive

We express the advertising contribution in terms of sales generated per GRP. This is easily calculated from the model coefficient, though dependent on the retention factor used in calculating the adstocks. The adstocks form a geometric series given by

$$S_\infty = 1/(1 - \text{retention factor}).$$

The return per GRP is given by

$$\text{Return per GRP} = S_\infty \times \text{modeled adstock}_{coeff}.$$

To illustrate, if we have a 90% retention factor and a model coefficient of 50, the sales return per GRP is 500. However, if we have an 80% retention factor and a model coefficient of 50, the sales return per GRP is 250.

Multiplicative

The advertising impact can be deduced directly from the model coefficients. The results are expressed in terms of a percentage increase in sales given a percentage increase in advertising weight. For example, a 1% increase in advertising weight will generate an additional 0.12% increase in sales.

Both models are useful for the brand manager in assessing the advertising effect, but there can be limitations. The very nature of the additive model can lead to misinterpretation. Suppose we estimate the advertising contribution to be 500 sales per GRP. This implies that we achieve 5000 sales with 10 GRPs, 50,000 sales with 100 GRPs, and so forth. This is unlikely, as the return on sales will be influenced by diminishing returns as the advertising weight increases. This does not invalidate the model; we just need to express caution when interpreting and presenting the results.

The multiplicative model allows for diminishing returns but is conceptually more difficult to interpret. We can convert this percentage contribution back to total sales contribution, but this is less practical. And what do we mean by a 1% increase in advertising? Is this 1% of the total campaign or last week's advertising? This provides little guidance on how future advertising spending should be allocated on a week-by-week basis.

Advertising Response Curves

One approach to improve the actionability of the model is to adapt the additive formulation. Rather than assuming a linear relationship between advertising weight and sales, we use NLR to generate advertising response curves.

Nonlinear regression is certainly more computationally demanding and challenging for the modeler who must address common difficulties, including

❑ *Overparameterised models* where the asymptotic correlation of the parameter estimates show very large positive or negative values for the correlation coefficients.

❑ *Estimating starting values* need to be provided to calibrate the model. Poor starting values can result in a local rather than global solution, nonconvergence, or a physically impossible solution. Many approaches are available to estimate starting values. Perhaps the simplest is to use the results from an initial additive model.

❑ *Computational problems* as we look to produce models that require exponentiation. This may cause an overflow (a number that is too large for the computer to handle) or underflow (a number that is too small for the computer to handle). We therefore may need to transform the appropriate measure(s) to overcome this difficulty.

We can facilitate the modeling process by using a sequential quadratic programming algorithm. This allows the modeler to impose sign constraints for the values of the measures in the model. A good introduction to NLR is provided in the SPSS (1998) *Regression Models Manual*.

Although NLR provides more work for the modeler, when we are able to overcome the difficulties associated with the technique, we generally find that the application improves the overall fit of the model and provides more actionable data and detail for media planning. This is important!

The concave diminishing response curve is often found to define a relationship between sales response and increased advertising weight (Figure 8). This can be given by

$$\text{Sales} = \text{Asymptote} \times (1 - \exp^{[-\text{Gradient} \times \text{Adstock}]}).$$

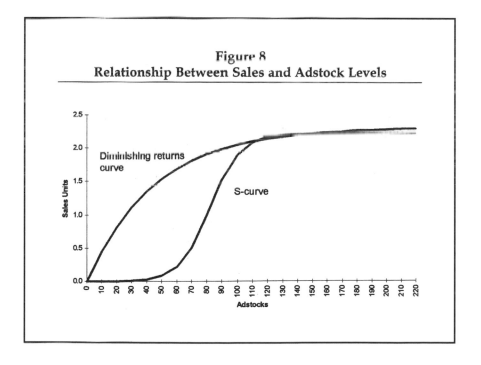

Figure 8
Relationship Between Sales and Adstock Levels

The asymptote is conceptually the maximum number of sales achievable in any one week through television advertising.

We now have an advertising response curve, but how do we use it? The client wanted to optimize sales from the advertising campaign. We were therefore provided with four alternative media plans, each of which had the same total media spending. We ran the plans through spreadsheets that contained the advertising response curve. The shaded areas show the weekly GRPs on the vertical axis (Figure 9). The benchmark is the original plan proposed prior to the modeling work (which also has the same weight).

The first plan is the most *inefficient*. We would expect a 14% reduction in *advertising-related* sales if this flight was executed. There is little to choose between the continuous flighting with lower advertising weights and the drip campaigns (Plans 3 and 4, respectively). Gains of up to 13% of advertising-related sales with the *same media spending* can be expected. This is significant.

There are four observations to be made at this stage. First, other advertising response curves can be considered. For example, many practitioners believe that the S-shaped response curve is more appropriate, though the implications of the two curves differ. To illustrate, for this campaign, we produced two separate models, one with the diminishing

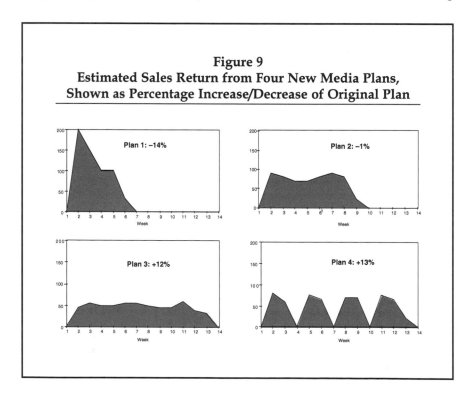

Figure 9
Estimated Sales Return from Four New Media Plans,
Shown as Percentage Increase/Decrease of Original Plan

returns curve and the other with the S-curve (Figure 8). The S-curve only has a small sales effect until a threshold of 60 adstocks is achieved, and then we see a sharp increase in the rate of sales from 60 to 110 adstocks. In contrast, the diminishing returns curve generates a strong sales response with the first 60 adstocks.

Second, we are currently covering the short-term response. There may be merits in exceeding these optimum levels in the longer term that outweigh short-term efficiencies.

Third, we must always remember to assess the media plans in terms of the campaign objectives. For a seasonal, promotional campaign or new product launch, the burst strategy may be the more appropriate.

Fourth, the shape of our advertising response curve and the potential gains from media laydown will largely be influenced by the quality of the ad, or creative. We now consider this particular concept in greater detail.

Television Advertising Campaigns and the Quality of the Creative

The Millward Brown company has been specializing in advertising and communication effectiveness for more than 20 years. We see strong variations in the quality of the creative in terms of persuasion and the ability of the brand to build brand awareness. For example, some advertising is highly persuasive, may coincide with a promotion, or may successfully generate short-term sales but then fail to generate repeat sales or sales in the longer term. Other campaigns may focus on building brand equity and qualities of the brand. They tend to be more successful in generating advertising awareness or recall over a longer time period, which will in turn ultimately have a favorable impact on the underlying level of base sales.

Television advertising should therefore *not* be incorporated as a single measure in the model. Wherever possible, we should attempt to split the advertising into campaigns. The quality of campaigns differ so intuitively that we would expect the corresponding sales response to differ.

The gradient of the advertising response curve is largely influenced and correlated with the efficiency of the ad in generating levels of advertising awareness (Dyson 1998). By advertising awareness, we do not mean awareness of the ad but awareness that the *brand* in question has been advertised on television (or other media) recently.

We investigate awareness in this way because it is vital that the ad gets the brand name across. An ad may communicate certain messages very strongly or be highly motivating, but if these memories of the ad are not remembered in the context of the correct brand, the effect will be greatly reduced.

So, although advertising awareness must never be seen as the only measure by which to evaluate an ad, its importance must not be underestimated because it is fundamental to the success of whatever else the ad is trying to do. The importance of advertising awareness can be seen in the way it relates to sales. Hollis (1994) has shown how the *efficiency* with which an ad generates advertising awareness is directly related to the efficiency with which it generates sales (Figure 10).

The Millward Brown company has been modeling advertising awareness using the current model since 1985 (Brown 1986). The model produces an efficiency statistic called the Awareness Index (AI), which, put simply, measures the rise in advertising awareness per 100 GRPs. Referring to Figure 11, an ad with a higher AI is more likely to hit the maximum weekly sales asymptote quicker than an ad with a low AI (low, straighter response curve). The ad does not need to work as hard to generate the same sales response. We typically find that the greater the AI, the greater is the opportunity to generate more sales with the same media spending but a different media laydown.

Advertising Contributions in the Longer Term

This is the most difficult element of the marketing mix to reliably quantify. We briefly introduce a series of approaches for trying to understand the longer-term contribution.

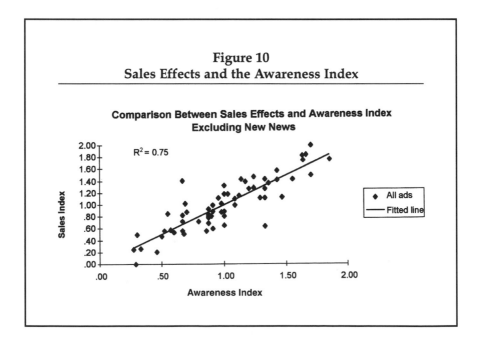

Figure 10
Sales Effects and the Awareness Index

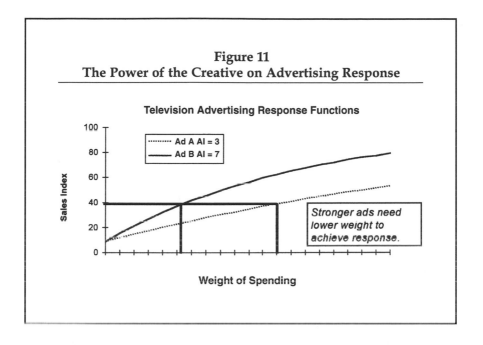

Figure 11
The Power of the Creative on Advertising Response

Television Advertising Response Functions

Regional Variations

"Pictures Paint a Thousand Words". In these days of sophisticated statistical software and complex modeling approaches, the modeler should never forget a key basic principle: Look at your data.

To illustrate, we overlay the volume share of a seasonal packaged goods brand over a three-year period with the television advertising weight (Figure 12). Historically, the brand had generated strong levels of advertising awareness, with the in market AIs being considerably higher than the category norm. During the second year of the modeling period (B), the client decided to switch the television advertising spending to other forms of media, with the exception of just one television region (hence the low advertising weights shown in Figure 12).

We clearly see the gradual decline in the national share of the brand. Following the 18-month advertising hiatus, the brand reverted to national television advertising (C). However, the new creative was weaker and less visible, and the momentum of the decline continued.

A simple comparison of market share was made between the television region retaining support and the rest of the country over the three discrete years (Figure 13). The equity of the brand in the supported region appears to have been maintained during the last two years of the modeling period. Sales were certainly more buoyant than in the rest of the country, whereas traditionally, they had been lower.

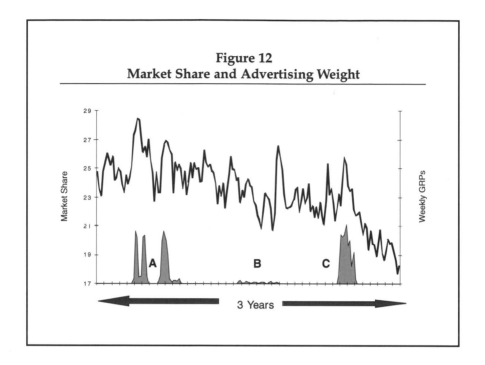

Figure 12
Market Share and Advertising Weight

We therefore have evidence to suggest the difference could be attributable to the long-term impact of cutting the television budget in the rest of the country. This is nothing more than exploratory and is not statistically conclusive. However, it does make intuitive sense because there was no substantial variation in distribution, change in price relative to competitors' during this period, or other changes in the market. Something must have caused the difference. These observations were also supported by the in-market tracking study.

Underlying Trends. Trend variables can be incorporated to detect slow movements in the sales we have been unable to account for within the model. These are often used when the quality of the model inputs are inadequate or the movements are too difficult or slow moving to measure.

The longer-term contribution of advertising is often associated with these trends. Models can be produced at the market or regional level. We can then overlay the gradients of the underlying trend with the weight of television advertising support in those regions.

Accepting that this is a crude approach and again statistically inconclusive, we have seen many cases in which the underlying base level of sales is stronger in the regions retaining a greater television advertising support. (We do need to express caution with the use of trend variables because they can exacerbate difficulties with collinearity.)

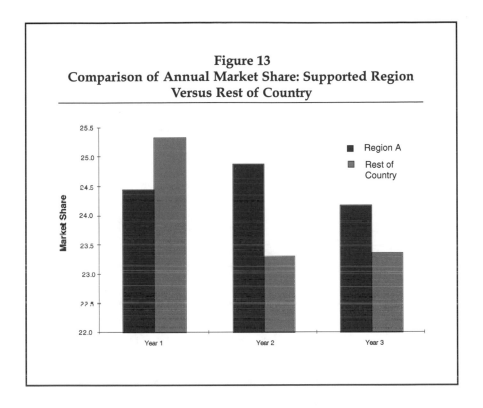

Figure 13
Comparison of Annual Market Share: Supported Region
Versus Rest of Country

Adstocks with High Retention Rates

We attempt to build two components into the model. The first will represent the short-term sales response from television advertising; the second will represent the longer-term contribution. This approach is almost impossible with highly aggregated data because of the collinearity with short- and long-term adstocks, the number of data points we have to work with, and inadequate variation in the model inputs. However, the concepts can be successfully applied if we have detailed regional sales data.

When adopting this approach, a considerable pitfall must be avoided. The long-term advertising component must be calibrated with the carry-over effect from a significant period prior to the start of modeling period. Consider the following hypothetical example: A new brand is launched, and we have 60 GRPs per week for three years. We are to begin modeling at the beginning of year 4, and a support of 60 GRPs per week is retained for the next three years. If we use a long-term retention rate of 99%, the top line represents the true model input starting from just under 5000 adstocks, slowly increasing, and tending toward 6000 adstocks (Figure 14).

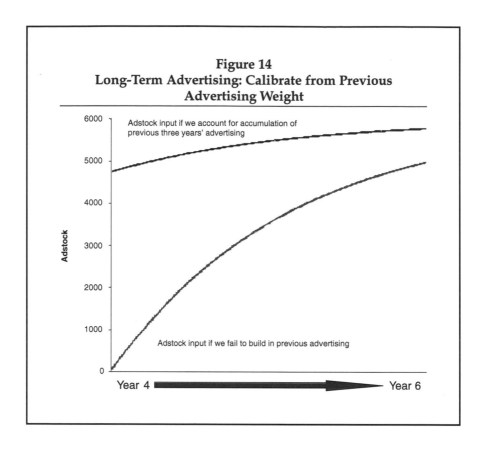

Figure 14
Long-Term Advertising: Calibrate from Previous Advertising Weight

If we do not account for the advertising history, then we could inadvertently build in the lower function to represent the longer-term advertising contribution. This is clearly wrong and is nothing more than a steep trend curve starting from zero and quickly rising to high levels of adstocks. The inclusion of this term could lead to erroneous conclusions and misattribution, particularly if some other activity is happening in the market at the same time (new variant, increase in distribution, and so on).

DISENTANGLING THE IMPACT OF TELEVISION AND PRINT

Collinearity is a common and major problem when conducting marketing mix analysis. Many marketing activities are timed to coincide, and trying to reliably disentangle the true contribution of the different elements of the marketing mix can be a real challenge.

For example, television and print campaigns often occur at the same time, particularly in nonpackaged goods. We usually apply the adstock concept for magazine and newspaper spending but with shorter retention levels because the response to print tends to be more immediate. There are also issues with lagging magazine spending, though this point is beyond the scope of this chapter.

In such cases, conventional general linear modeling methods allow us to quantify the impact of the *advertising campaign* but not necessarily the individual contribution of print and television. The usual methods of least squares can produce estimates that are unstable and have large variances. One possible consequence of this is to have regression coefficients with the wrong sign.

Ridge regression (Hoerl and Kennard 1970) is one tool available to help overcome these difficulties. This is a form of bias estimation that attempts to stabilize the parameter estimates by trading off unbiasedness in estimation for variance reduction. Instead of solving the usual least squares equation

$$b = (X'X)^{-1}X'Y,$$

we solve

$$b(ridge) = (X'X + kI)^{-1}X'Y.$$

The biasing constant k should be small. As k increases, the bias in the parameter estimates increases and variances decrease. The residual sum of squares for the regression also increases with increasing k, so R^2 decreases. A value of k should be selected so that the decrease in variation is greater than the increase in bias (for further detail, see Montgomery and Peck 1982).

A common method for determining the value of k is called the ridge trace, suggested by Hoerl and Kennard (1970). The ridge trace plots the ridge regression coefficient estimates for alternative values of k.

An example from financial services shows the ridge trace for a series of modeled parameters incorporated into a model to predict the sales of a new product. The majority of the modeled parameters quickly stabilize around k = 0.3 (Figure 15).

Focusing on television and press, we observe the change in the sign of the press coefficient (Table 5). The parameter estimates are both highly significant when k = 0.3.

A good macro for running ridge regression is available in SPSS, with a more detailed description of the approach (see the SPSS Advanced Statistics 6.1 Manual, Appendix A). A further example of a ridge regression application is provided in the next section.

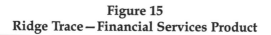

Figure 15
Ridge Trace — Financial Services Product

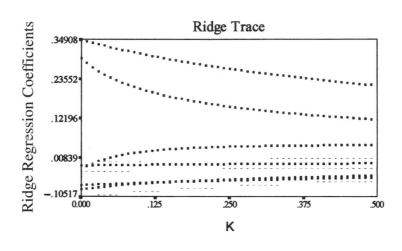

Table 5
Financial Services: Impact of Increasing Biasing Adstock
on Model Estimates for Television and Print

	Coefficients		
K	Television	Press	Adjusted R²
0 (television only)		Excluded from model	
0	0.93*	−2.0*	0.92
0.1	1.54**	0.3	0.91
0.2	0.82	0.9*	0.90
0.3	0.70**	1.1**	0.88
0.4	0.64**	1.3**	0.87
0.5	0.62**	1.4**	0.85

*5% significance level.
**0.1% significance level.

QUANTIFYING MARKETING ROI: A CASE HISTORY

We have discussed several issues, considerations, and concepts the practitioner must consider when conducting a marketing mix analysis. We now share extracts from a detailed case history that has been selected not for its statistical complexity but because it shows how the modeling tools can be adapted to answer one of the most frequently asked questions in marketing: "What is my return on investment?"

In addition, the case history expands on many of the concepts we have introduced in this chapter and shows how the sales effectiveness can be easily underestimated or misinterpreted if we do not consider all aspects of the available data.

Modeling Measures

Although this was our first venture into the modeled product field, the objectives for the client were almost identical to any other nonpackaged goods (and packaged goods client):

❑ The contribution of marketing activity to sales with the particular focus on media spending,
❑ The short- and long-term impact of the marketing activity,
❑ Optimizing media spending, and
❑ What would happen if we stop advertising?

The second part of the modeling period coincides with the client's first significant media campaign for the brand. The initial focus was on new sales, namely, those buying the product or service for the first time.

We were able to build a good model of sales that incorporated the new media campaign (dominated by television and print ads), journal spending to target the business professional, promotional activity, and seasonality. We also attempted to build in Internet activity, which visually correlated with sales. However, the relevant Internet inquiry data were unavailable on a continuous basis, so this measure was excluded from the model.

The sales and model prediction for the last 60 weeks of the modeling period are presented (Figure 16). The sales units have been standardized to hide the identity of the client.

Promotional Activity

Promotional activity (Figure 17) and journal spending have a substantial impact on sales, particularly in the earlier stages of the modeling period. However, the impact does not remain constant over time and is

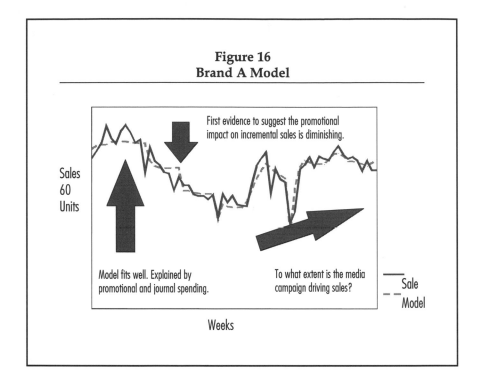

Figure 16
Brand A Model

First evidence to suggest the promotional impact on incremental sales is diminishing.

Sales 60 Units

Model fits well. Explained by promotional and journal spending.

To what extent is the media campaign driving sales?

Sale
Model

Weeks

diminishing toward the end of the modeling period. We also observe that as the weight of promotional spending is reduced, sales quickly fall to a base of approximately 30 sales units. This implies that the promotional activity is successfully generating short-term incremental sales but that the impact quickly diminishes and fails to grow base-level sales. This is a finding we typically observe in modeling both packaged and nonpackaged goods.

The quantifiable ratio of sales return to spending across the whole modeling period is approximately 1:1 (every dollar spent has resulted in a dollar return). However, because the dollar-for-dollar contribution is diminishing over the modeling period, future promotional spending is unlikely to generate profitable incremental sales using the current promotional strategy.

Short-Term Incremental Sales Effects for Television Advertising and Print

We overlay the GRPs with sales of the modeled brand (Figure 18). Eyeballing the data, there appears to be a reasonable association with sales. The first flight generates a sharp incremental lift in sales commonly

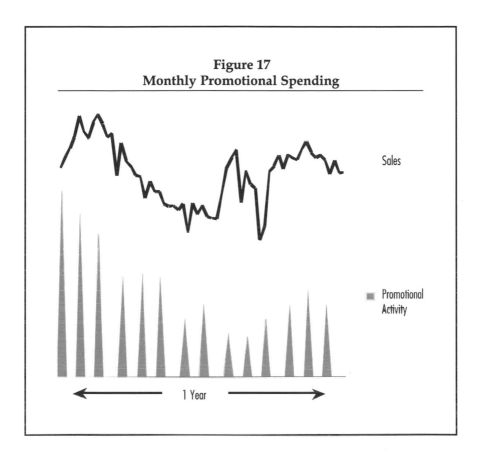

Figure 17
Monthly Promotional Spending

Sales

Promotional
Activity

1 Year

associated with "new news" (Farr 1994), followed by a steadier increase in sales corresponding with subsequent advertising flights.

The impact of television advertising over the modeled period is 123 standardized sales units. Advertising has a carry-over effect beyond the end of the advertising period (see "How Can We Build Television Advertising into a Model?" section). Because there is a reasonable advertising weight at the end of the modeling period, an additional estimate should be made to account for the sales we expect to be generated in subsequent weeks. We were able to use a reliable and validated advertising sales response curve to estimate additional incremental sales of 44 units (making 167 sales units in total).

The additional 44 sales units represent an increase of more than 36% on the advertising contribution initially reported. The level of this return will of course be dependent on many factors, including the quality of the creative (Farr 1994), the rate of decay of the advertising response curve,

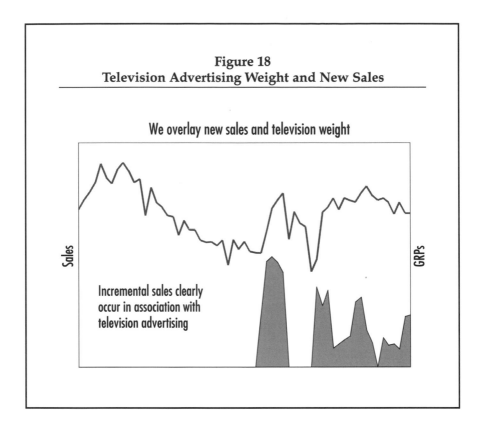

Figure 18
Television Advertising Weight and New Sales

We overlay new sales and television weight

Sales

GRPs

Incremental sales clearly
occur in association with
television advertising

and the weight of advertising in the last few weeks of the modeling period. However, in most cases, this effect will be substantial.

When incremental sales are converted into revenue, these 44 units of potentially unreported sales are worth almost an additional $4 million on the ROI for the advertising campaign.

We now consider the impact of the print campaign that coincided with the second, third, and fourth flights of television advertising. Print is certainly successful in generating short-term incremental sales, and like television, there is a diminishing effect continuing into following weeks. However, this continuing effect is considerably shorter for print spending, which implies that print will generate short-term incremental sales at the time of the print campaign but the impact will become minimal only a few weeks after the campaign.

This has been seen in other marketing mix analysis projects, particularly in the U.K. financial services sector. A strong television advertising campaign may generate and build brand awareness, but the supporting print activity is often the mechanism from which the inquiry or sale will be made. Without the television campaign, the response to print considerably diminishes. To date, we have seen few occasions on which the base level of sales has increased through an unsupported print campaign.

Ridge regression was used to disentangle the effects of television and print. The print campaign on its own generated approximately 43 sales units. This is clearly not as strong as for television, but this is not surprising because the weight of television to print spending is approximately 7:1. However, the ratio of sales is only around 4:1 in favor of television. At first sight, the return for the dollar appears to be greater for print.

On the basis of this evidence, should we switch all future media spending to print? The answer is no. We have not yet completed our ROI calculations, and this decision will become apparent as additional factors are considered. We also observe that we could have completed the modeling at this stage. We had a model that was statistically acceptable, produced an ROI for the media, and concluded that print generated more sales than television dollar for dollar and that the media campaign is unprofitable. This would be wrong yet feasible for those who do not understand the advertising mechanisms and potential paybacks. There are many additional factors we need to consider.

There is a strong synergy with print and television, with the interaction being worth an additional 54 units in short-term incremental sales. This is almost a 26% increase in sales associated with the media campaign. Incremental sales would have been generated with a print campaign only or a television campaign only. However, a complementary print/television effect generates a substantial increase on the ROI and should be considered in all ROI calculations for nonpackaged goods brands. This interaction was worth an additional $4.9 million in revenue for the media campaign

This concept can also be extended to other key components of the marketing mix. For example, many clients place significant dollar spending behind mail drops. Clients typically argue that they know the response rate from the mail drop, but they rarely consider the influence of a television advertising campaign on the mail drop response rate.

Mail drops are irrelevant for the brand in this case history. However, we make brief reference to the field of financial services in the United Kingdom. A bank wanted to encourage current customers of its regular checking account to switch to a new form of bank account that offered additional benefits and services but with a monthly fee. Somewhere in the region of 40% of those switching accounts were directly associated with the response to mail drops. The mail drops coincided with a national television campaign primarily aimed at attracting customers who would be new to the bank. A marketing mix analysis was able to demonstrate a 20% increase in the response rate associated with the television interaction, which would clearly be lost or hidden in the client's internal reporting systems. This figure must be credited to the overall ROI for the advertising campaign and, once again, emphasizes the importance of timing in both the media laydown and additional supporting marketing activity.

Longer-Term Contribution of Media Spending to Sales

We have focused on the short-term incremental sales associated with the media campaign, but is there also a longer-term contribution of advertising to sales? At this stage, we introduce the base that, in the context of nonpackaged goods and in simplistic terms, is a conceptual level of sales expected over a longer time period should you stop all marketing activity. The base comprises components we are typically unable to build into the model and could include measures such as additional promotional activity when data are not readily available, the longer-term impact of PR, and so on (Figure 19).

The base is not static and can be influenced by an increase/decrease in marketing activity, competitor activity, economic measures, and so on. The base is typically the largest component of sales in a marketing mix analysis and represents more than 60% of sales for the brand in this case history. The modeled product is a relatively new brand, and we would expect the contribution of the base to increase further over time (an 80% contribution not being unusual for an established brand). These are effectively "sales in the bag" or "guaranteed weekly sales," and so what happens to the base is important.

Recent developments in the Millward Brown model formulation enable an estimate of the base component directly associated with the

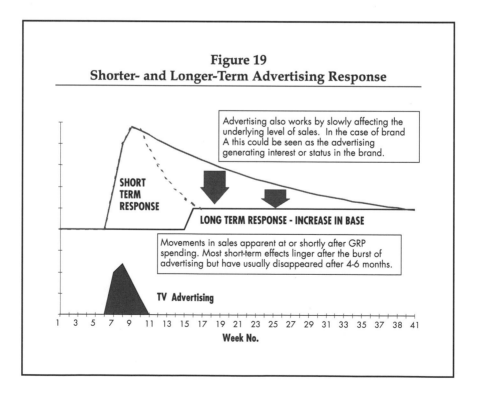

Figure 19
Shorter- and Longer-Term Advertising Response

Advertising also works by slowly affecting the underlying level of sales. In the case of brand A this could be seen as the advertising generating interest or status in the brand.

SHORT TERM RESPONSE

LONG TERM RESPONSE - INCREASE IN BASE

Movements in sales apparent at or shortly after GRP spending. Most short-term effects linger after the burst of advertising but have usually disappeared after 4-6 months.

TV Advertising

1 3 5 7 9 11 13 15 17 19 21 23 25 27 29 31 33 35 37 38 41

Week No.

longer-term impact of television advertising to be calculated. Typically, a minimum of two to three years of sales data is required, and because we only had access to approximately 18 months of sales data, a caveat must be placed on the following estimates. To compensate, we have the full media history for the brand, so, adapting the same modeling concept, we attempted to generate a projected response to estimate the longer-term contribution. This should be reasonably reliable assuming advertising response does not change in subsequent months.

So what is the value? The short-term incremental sales associated with the media campaign are worth 265 sales units. This is approximately the level of sales required to pay back the cost of the media campaign. The projected longer-term contribution attributable to television is an additional 244 units. The overall impact of the television campaign has practically doubled and is worth an additional $21.9 million on the ROI for the television campaign. If we had just considered the short-term effects of advertising, we might have reached the wrong conclusion about the advertising contribution, which could potentially threaten future media campaigns for the brand.

Accepting that this is an estimate at this stage, the findings are supported by other modeling projects conducted by Millward Brown. In some cases, the longer-term effects of advertising can be as much as eight times higher than the short-term effects. Established brands tend to have larger long-term effects, whereas new brands have stronger short-term effects because consumers react to the news value of the launch and may enter the market (Scott and Ward 1997).

Additional Long-Term Contribution to Sales—Repeat Business

The final component of the ROI calculation is to assess the impact on the ROI of the sales generated through repeat business. Unlike conventional modeling of packaged goods brands, repeat sales at the weekly macro-level were provided. The purchase cycle for the modeled brand is monthly.

A very accurate model explaining almost 98% of sales variation (Figure 20) incorporates a term to represent the first repeat purchase (based on new sales four to five weeks prior) and then subsequent four to five week purchases (based on repeat sales).

The calculation of this indirect contribution to sales can be complex. If the advertising is responsible for the initial sale, then all subsequent repeat sales must be included in the ROI. Without the initial sale, there would be no repeat sale.

The short-term incremental sales associated with the media campaign are approximately 265 sales units. The first repeat sale directly associated with the 265 sales units is approximately 21 units. The probability of second, third, and fourth sales (and so on), given someone purchases the product on a second occasion, is high, and an additional 34 units are generated over the duration (and beyond) of the modeling period.

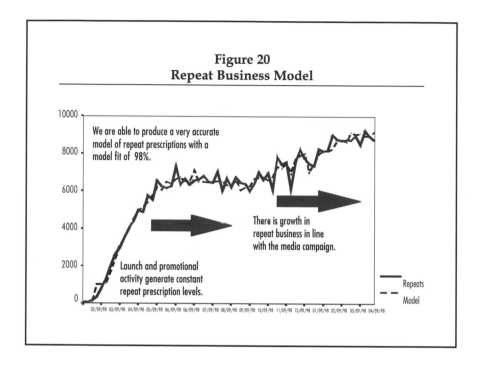

Figure 20
Repeat Business Model

In addition, there are 27 units of repeat business directly associated with the media campaign. These are people who may have become lapsed users, but the strength of the television campaign in enhancing customers' awareness of the product benefits in the context of competitor activity ensured a continued purchase of the product. If we are to use the same rationale, a further 44 sales units could be obtained from future repeat business (though this is more contentious).

The total number of repeat sales associated with the media campaign is therefore a minimum of 82 sales units. This could arguably be 124 sales units or double that if we were to take into account the conventional longer-term contribution of the media spending.

Being in the fortunate position of having access to repeat sales and new sales enables us to calculate the contribution. In essence, this is a second long-term component of television advertising. The repeat purchases may not be directly associated with the brand memorability of the advertising campaign but more with the experiences of the product or service. However, if the initial purchase was attributable to the advertising campaign, then all repeat purchases should be included in the advertising ROI. If we were modeling a packaged goods brand, the majority of the repeat purchases following an initial purchase directly associated with advertising would be lost in the base and difficult to disentangle.

The impact from repeat business is worth a minimum of $7.3 million on the ROI for the modeled brand (this is a conservative estimate).

This mechanism occurs across all product fields and categories. For example, in a recent project in the U.S. automobile market, advertising accounted for approximately 11% of incremental sales. Given information from other sources of research, a purchase or lease of a particular marque or nameplate has a reasonable likelihood of a repeat purchase or lease of the marque within two to four years. Simple probability theory can be applied to determine the expected repeat business associated with the initial incremental sale from the media campaign.

Summarizing the ROI

Many calculations have been included. Table 6 therefore summarizes the ROI for this media campaign. Results presented are factored sales units.

Had we only accounted for the incremental short-term sales effect of print and television, the presented media contribution would have been less than 200 sales units and the campaign would have been unprofitable. This could have had a detrimental effect on future media campaigns for the brand. The additional revenue from the print and television synergy, long-term contribution of television advertising, and repeat business associated with the media campaign are worth an additional $35 million. The campaign is profitable, with the ratio of dollar return to spending being approximately 1.6 to 1, which is considerable given the weight and cost of the media spending.

Table 6
Contribution of the Media Campaign to Sales

Short-Term Incremental Sales:	Sales Units
Television only	167
Print only	43
Television/print interaction	54
Longer-Term Base Sales:	
Television mainly	244
Repeat Sales:	
Campaign	81*
Total	589

*Minimum—more likely to be in the region of 200 units.

Returning to the initial results (see "Short-Term Incremental Sales Effects for Television Advertising and Print" section), the return for dollar spent appeared to be greater for print than television. When adjusting for the additional contributions to the ROI, summarized in Table 1, we find that the sales ratio of television to print is just more than 7 to 1. This is now in line with the respective media spending for the two forms of media. The current strategy appears to work well.

This case history explains in detail the many phases to be considered when identifying the advertising contribution to sales and the extent of the detail we are able to extract from the data. Additional analysis also covered the effect on inquiries, how to optimize the ROI using advertising response curves, and daypart analysis. A full paper was presented and published for the Advertising Research Foundation Week of Workshops in October 1999 (Gascoigne 1999).

OTHER FORMS OF MARKETING ACTIVITY

The main focus of this chapter has been on price and advertising. Many other measures could have been included. To illustrate, we consider *distribution*. A brand with good advertising, competitive price, and a great product is of no benefit if the product is unavailable on the shelf of a grocery store. Many brands may have constant distribution for the duration of the modeling period. There is no variation in the model input, so a distribution term is not required because the contribution will form part of the base sales. If there has been a change in distribution, then this should be incorporated into the model and the subsequent impact on sales should be assessed.

Seasonality is also important because the price, promotional, and advertising elasticities can be affected by the timing of the advertising. There are many approaches for incorporating seasonality, ranging from crude seasonal dummy variables to more sophisticated techniques used in conventional time series (refer to good statistical or econometric textbooks for further detail).

The modeler therefore must use skill and judgment to determine which measures should be incorporated and how they can be incorporated.

SUMMARY AND CONCLUSIONS

Application

Marketing mix analysis can be applied to any brand and in any category providing the client has access to adequate sales and marketing inputs. Many categories have different issues, features, and quirks. Every brand manager believes his or her product category has greater complexity than any other. However, for most projects, the complexity is not in the statistical tools and modeling formulations we employ but in the following:

❑ Application of those tools;

❑ Collation, handling, and manipulation of the client's data, which often arrive from many different sources;

❑ Understanding the client's objectives and issues; and

❑ Correct interpretation and application of the model.

Model Complexity

Most marketing mix analysis is conducted using various forms of general linear modeling. Some modeling formulations can be very simple and applied on highly aggregated data. This is reasonable, providing the modeler understands the limitations and scope of the analysis and conveys this to the client. If more detailed data are available, then more complex formulations can be adopted. However, we should never forget that there can be more error or bias in the sales and model inputs we work with, which can negate the extra efforts involved in producing complex solutions.

Adapting the Conventional Modeling Approach

We considered three examples that showed how the conventional modeling approaches can be adapted to meet clients' specific requirements. First, we applied a multistage modeling approach to produce a competitor index, something that would have been impossible to achieve using multiple regression on the available data. Second, we applied a nonlinear model on a linear model formulation to generate advertising response curves. These can then be used to help optimize sales from future advertising spending by controlling weekly advertising weights to ensure we minimize "wasted" spending (diminishing returns). Third, ridge regression was applied to disentangle the effect of two marketing activities (television and print) occurring at the same time. There is no one standard approach for marketing mix analysis.

Address the Business Issues

The case histories we have used show our approach for addressing the clients' business issues. Other practitioners will have their own approaches. This is fine, providing they always refer back to the objectives and make optimum use of the available data.

For example, a client wants to assess the sales impact of a media campaign. We therefore need to ensure all factors are taken into consideration when assessing the impact of the campaign. We must go beyond reporting the incremental short-term sales during the modeled period. We must try and establish the synergy across the different forms of media and other marketing activity, estimate projected sales expected to occur beyond the modeling period from both the short- and long-term advertising components, and attempt to account for the impact of repeat business. We may not always be able to find the effects with statistical reliability, and in such circumstances, we obviously cannot report such an impact. We may occasionally need to place caveats on the results (as with the ROI case history), but providing the model you are working with is statistically acceptable, this is much better than completely ignoring the contribution (the model can also be further validated at a later stage).

Marketing mix analysis is a science — but it's equally an art.

BIBLIOGRAPHY

Broadbent, Simon (1997), *Accountable Advertising*. Oxfordshire, U.K.: NTC Publications, Ltd.

Brown, G. (1986), "Modeling Advertising Awareness," *The Statistician*, 35 (2), 289–299.

Dyson, P. (1998), "Justifying the Advertising Budget," paper presented at Admap's Monitoring Advertising Performance Conference (January 22).

Farr, A. (1994), "Creating Product Trial," Marketing Week Conference — Understanding How Advertising Works in the FMCG Market Place.

Gascoigne, D.P. (1999), "'Chief Financial Officer — Please Give My Advertising a Chance' — Quantifying and Optimizing My ROI Through Marketing Mix Analysis of Non-Packaged Goods," paper presented at Advertising Research Foundation Workshop — Return on Marketing Investment (October).

Hoerl, A.E. and R.W. Kennard (1970), "Ridge Regression: Applications to Nonorthogonal Problems," *Technometrics*, 12 (February), 69–82.

Hollis, N. (1994), "The Link Between TV Ad Awareness and Sales: New Evidence from Sales Response Modeling," *Journal of the Market Research Society*, 36 (January), 41–55.

Montgomery, D.C. and E.A. Peck (1982), *Introduction to Linear Regression Analysis*. New York: John Wiley & Sons.

Scott, D. and K. Ward (1997), "Measuring the Impact of Marketing Activity on Business Results," paper presented at Advertising Research Foundation Workshop — Return on Marketing Investment (October).

SPSS (1998), *Regression Models Manual, 9.0*. Chicago: SPSS.

von Gonten, M. (1998), "Tracing Advertising Effects: Footprints in the Figures," *Admap*, (October), 43–45.

——— and J. Donius (1996), "Advertising Exposure and Advertising Effects: New Panel-Based Findings," ESOMAR, 205 (November), 147–164.

SUGGESTED READINGS

Advertising Research Foundation (1996), *Marketplace Information for Managing Brands*. New York: Advertising Research Foundation.

Bender, J.D. (1990), "Seasonality in Regression: From the 17th Century Astronomers to the 20th Century Marketing Modellers," The Chicago Marketing Modelers' Group.

Christen, M., S. Gupta, J.C. Porter, R. Staelin, and D.R. Wittink (1997), "Using Market-Level Data to Understand Promotion Effects in a Nonlinear Model," *Journal of Marketing Research*, 34 (August), 322–34.

Gold, L.N. (1992), "Let's Heavy Up in St. Louis and See What Happens," *Journal of Advertising Research*, 32 (6), 31–38.

14
Market Segmentation

William D. Neal

Call it regional marketing, target marketing, micro marketing, niche marketing, one-on-one marketing, or whatever.[1] For most business firms, locating and specifically targeting unique market segments is both a reality and a necessity in today's competitive marketplace. In North America, the assumptions of the mass market no longer hold true for most businesses and product categories. Indeed, in a recent article in *Marketing Management*, marketing guru Fred Webster (1993) questioned whether a sustainable mass market ever existed in North America.

This chapter provides an introduction to the concept of market segmentation, reviews the basic procedures for conducting market segmentation research, provides a view of current practice, and speculates on future developments in the field.

Creative market segmentation strategies often afford the business organization a strategic advantage over its competition. If a firm can address its markets by way of a creative new vision of how that market is structured and operates and can uncover the needs and wants of the segments therein, then it has the opportunity to act on that vision to enhance its own profitability, often at the expense of the competition. It is no secret that foreign firms often enter a domestic market by segmenting the market, uncovering an underserved niche, and then concentrating their marketing and financial resources into that niche. When established, and

---

[1]Much of the material in this chapter is extracted from *A Workshop in Market Segmentation*, written by William D. Neal and copyrighted by SDR, Inc. This same material was the basis for a technical publication by the American Marketing Association on market segmentation written by Steve Struhl, who was then employed by SDR, Inc. See *Market Segmentation: An Introduction and Review* (1992), AMA Marketing Research Techniques Series, Chicago: American Marketing Association.

often dominating in that niche, those market invaders use their dominant position in the niche as a base of operations to expand into and penetrate other segments. One has to only look at what has happened to the North American automobile market over the past 30 years to see evidence of this.

BACKGROUND

Prior to the mid-1950s, product differentiation (that is, the manufacturing of a set of products with varying characteristics or attributes) was considered the accepted method for a producer to address different segments of its market. Marketing research had shown that products in a particular category with different characteristics tend to appeal to different sets of consumers.

An understanding of consumer needs and wants did not drive this process as much as it was driven by what could be manufactured. That is, the process of product differentiation was a function of R&D and plant capabilities. Typically, the R&D folks would tinker around with an existing product and figure out a new variation, and if it could be manufactured, especially at a lower cost, it was. Alternatively, engineers or salespeople would come up with a new idea that they felt would appeal to their customers, then turn it over to R&D to see if it could be made. The resulting product would then be put directly into either the distribution chain or test market to see if it would fly. Obviously, this was an inefficient and costly process.

Product variations produced by this process were sometimes only cosmetic and could border on the ridiculous, such as tail fins on automobiles. Other product variations added true value and could bring a premium price. However, the main point is that, in most cases, these product variations were not in response to quantitative measurement of market demands, but rather were a product of the firm's perceptions of what could or should be done. The process was not marketing-driven.

THE LANDMARK ARTICLE

In July 1956, Wendell R. Smith published an article in the *Journal of Marketing* titled "Product Differentiation and Market Segmentation as Alternative Marketing Strategies." This article is considered the seminal work in defining market segmentation.

In that article, Dr. Smith took the following positions:

- ❏ He rejected classical and neoclassical economic theories of perfect competition and perfect monopoly because of their assumptions of homogeneous supply and demand.
- ❏ He pointed out that the rule in the contemporary marketplace for any product class was heterogeneity on *both* the supply side and the demand side.

❑ Recognizing the realities of a heterogeneous set of demand curves and the usual impossibility of converging those into a single demand curve, manufacturers adopted an alternative policy of product differentiation and market segmentation. Product differentiation accounted for the heterogeneity on the supply side, and market segmentation accounted for the heterogeneity on the demand side.

❑ Dr. Smith then argued that though this strategy appeared to be a single strategy, it was in fact two distinct but closely related strategies, because they call for "differing systems of action at any point in time" and "varying degrees of diversity through time."

❑ He wrote that "While successful product differentiation will result in ... a horizontal share of a broad and generalized market, equally successful application of ... market segmentation tends to produce depth of market position in the segments that are effectively defined and penetrated."

❑ Smith implied that product differentiation strategies should be in response to market segmentation strategies.

❑ He pointed out that there are limits to both market segmentation [if] and product differentiation strategies in the areas of promotional costs and manufacturing costs.

WHAT IS MARKET SEGMENTATION?

In their book *Research for Marketing Decisions*, Paul Green and Donald Tull (1978, p. 540) provide the following, straightforward definition of market segmentation:

> Briefly stated, market segmentation is concerned with individual or inter-group differences in response to market-mix variables. The managerial presumption is that if these response differences exist, can be identified, are reasonably stable over time and [if] the segments can be efficiently reached, the firm may increase its sales and profits beyond those obtained by assuming market homogeneity.

In this definition, Green and Tull make two fundamental points about market segmentation. First, to be true market segments, the people or organizations in each segment must respond differentially to variations in the marketing mix compared with those in other segments. That is, members of each segment will respond differently to variations in product/service attributes, price, promotion/positioning, and/or variations in place/channel. This implies that for any classification scheme to qualify as market segmentation, the segments must exhibit these behavioral response differences.

Second, Green and Tull point out the four basic criteria for segmenting a market:

❑ The segments must *exist* in the environment (and not be a figment of the researcher's imagination),

❑ The segments must be *identifiable* (repeatedly and consistently),

❑ The segments must be reasonably *stable over time*, and

❑ One must be able to *efficiently reach* segments (through specifically targeted distribution and communications initiatives).

In the contemporary marketplace, just about every product and service category can be segmented. The major task is to identify the basis that should be used such that the segments demonstrate significant and differential responses to variations in the marketing mix.

Furthermore, when it is determined that various segments exist and can be identified through marketing research procedures, the question of whether those segments are stable, in terms of time, place, and usage occasion, must be assessed. A market segmentation strategy can be very costly if put in place to address segments that are in significant transition. The necessity for stability is the main reason that market segmentation strategies are most appealing for mature markets and mature product categories. Emerging markets and product categories are often too unstable for an effective market segmentation strategy to be successful.

Then there is the question of reachability. Although the segments may exist and are identifiable and even stable, all of that is useless if those segments cannot be efficiently reached by the distribution and promotion systems available to the firm.

MARKET SEGMENTATION AND STRATEGIC PLANNING

A market segmentation strategy requires a major commitment by the organization. A firm adopts either a mass-market strategy or a market segmentation strategy. There is no in-between. Senior management must be involved, and a strategic decision is required to effectively segment a market. A strategy of market segmentation must permeate the entire organization. The firm's marketing organization must be able to execute alternative marketing strategies and vary pricing, promotion, and/or distribution systems. Also, R&D must be able to execute product variations, and manufacturing must be able to produce those variations. Finance must be able to report costs, profits, and margins by market segment, and marketing research must be able to monitor and measure purchaser response and provide feedback to the organization by market segment.

Usually, market segmentation is a key input to the strategic market planning process. In the May 1980 issue of *Business*, Philip Kotler published a planning model that demonstrated how the strategic planning process and the strategic market planning process interacted. Several years later, I added the strategic research-based protocols that are most often used to support elements of the strategic market planning process. Kotler's model with my additions is shown in Figure 1.

Note that, in this model, market segmentation supports the planning activities of marketing opportunity analysis and target market selection. Typically, the firm will develop market segments for each product category and/or broad geographic market, discern its current and proposed positions within each of those segments, and select its target markets on the basis of the opportunities that exist in each segment. Those opportunities must take into consideration the firm's current perceptual position in each segment and its current capabilities to address the needs of each segment. At that point, initial forecasts of the market demand for each segment will be undertaken. Then, the firm will typically undertake product/service optimization initiatives by fine-tuning its marketing mix to achieve optimal positioning and penetration in each selected target market.

The Research Basics of Market Segmentation

Market segmentation research has evolved rather unevenly since 1960, enjoying various levels of popularity. Likewise, the measures used

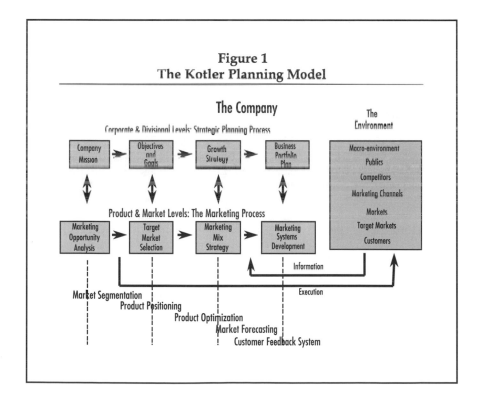

Figure 1
The Kotler Planning Model

as bases for segmentation have varied greatly, moving from demographics to product category attitudes to psychographics, purchase behaviors, usage behaviors, and benefits and then to derived preferences from trade-off exercises. The following section discusses the basics of market segmentation that represent traditional practice in the field.

Methods and Bases for Market Segmentation

When a decision is made to explore a market segmentation policy, two immediate questions must be addressed. First, what *method* is to be used to segment the market, and second, on what *basis* will the market be segmented?

Broadly speaking, there are only two *methods* for segmenting a market: a priori and post hoc methods. However, the *bases* available for segmenting a market are nearly unlimited and can include such things as

- ❏ Product class behaviors,
- ❏ Product class preferences,
- ❏ Product class-related attitudes,
- ❏ Brand selection behavior,
- ❏ Brand-related attitudes,
- ❏ Purchasers' attitudes toward themselves and their environment,
- ❏ Demographics,
- ❏ Geographics, and
- ❏ Socioeconomic status.

A Priori Methods

A priori segmentation is a procedure whereby the organization chooses to break out customer groups by some known and generally accepted classification procedure (i.e., basis) that is assumed to be related to variations in customer purchase or usage of the product category. This grouping may be the result of company tradition, recognized industrial groups, or some other external or internal criteria. Examples of a priori segments include such classification schemes as

- ❏ Standard Industrial Classification (SIC) groups,
- ❏ Geographic regions or sales territories,
- ❏ Basic demographic groups (e.g., sex, age, household composition),
- ❏ Purchase or usage groups (e.g., heavy users, light users, nonusers),
- ❏ VALS (SRI's Values and Life Styles classification system), and
- ❏ PRIZM, or similar geodemographic classification systems.

Again, the basic managerial presumption is that these groups have varying demands in the product or service category and will respond differently to variations in the marketing mix.

As an aside, it has been my experience that a priori market segments that are not based on previous empirical segmentation research are seldom optimal and often quite inefficient from a marketing point of view. Too often, a priori segments are a matter of convenience and/or tradition, not thoughtful or well-executed research.

When Is It Appropriate to Use A Priori Segmentation? Sometimes it is appropriate to use a priori segmentation. Such instances include

1. Previous research, such as a post hoc segmentation baseline study, has already established appropriate market segments. For example, conduct a research study to determine the relative product demand for new product concept X among five customer segments that were established from the firm's original baseline segmentation study.
2. Marketing actions can only be targeted against established or predefined groups. For example, conduct a research study to determine the optimal media buy for brand X print promotion for employed women, 35 to 49 years of age, with household incomes over $40,000. The implication here is that media can only be bought for predefined groups.
3. A presegmentation algorithm or procedure is available and is appropriate for the segmentation under consideration. For example, determine which PRIZM groups would most likely purchase brand X given its price and package size.
4. The objectives of a particular study are to explore or better understand differences between established demographic segments. For example, determine why households with children under 16 years of age consume more processed cheese than do households without children under 16 years of age.
5. When there is no other logical or available basis for post hoc segmentation.

There are several cautions that should be recognized when using a priori criteria for segmenting a market. The following are some major ones:

1. Our society is dynamic! Segmentation studies conducted, or validated, three or four years ago may not be appropriate today. Revalidate segments from baseline studies periodically to check their stability, size, and consistent response to variations in the marketing mix.
2. Do not use a priori segmentation as a substitute for lazy thinking or low research budgets. A missegmented market is often worse for the firm than the mass-market assumption.

3. Segments based on some a priori criteria may be unstable. Consider what has happened to the microcomputer market, and the segments therein, over the past five years.

4. Discernible segments may not exist. For example, regular unleaded gasoline is now a commodity. Segmentation strategies may not be appropriate or worthwhile for this market. Price competition can easily overcome a segmentation strategy when there is little perceived difference between offerings in a product category. That is, the time, effort, and money needed to put a segmentation strategy in place for a perceptually undifferentiated product could be wasted when consumers recognize or perceive that there are no substantial product differences. Competitors can easily defeat the segmentation strategy through price competition.

This last statement has particular importance in the contemporary marketplace. North American producers often will take an undifferentiated product and wrap around a service to add value and differentiate the product from competitors' products. Such a strategy is limited by the perceived value of the service only and not the product. For example, consider two gasoline outlets on opposite corners of a busy intersection, one a full-service center and one a discount convenience outlet. For some gasoline purchaser segments, a minor price differential, say one or two cents per gallon, is sufficient to select the discounter. For other segments, a greater differential is needed to induce them to the discounter. But at some point, there can be a sufficient price differential to induce the majority of the purchaser segments to the discounter. With no differences in product attributes, pricing can often defeat a segmentation strategy, especially if the service wrap-around is marginal in value.

Post Hoc Segmentation Methods and Procedures

Post hoc segmentation is empirically derived, in that it is based on the results of a research study undertaken for the specific purpose of segmenting a market. Segments generated from such a study are formed by aggregating buyers who respond similarly to a set, or sets, of basis questions. These questions may deal with such things as preferences, values, product usage patterns, attitudes toward a product class, attitudes toward brand names, brand-switching behaviors, and so forth. In other words, segments are formed by clustering together respondents on the basis of similarities in their response patterns to various differences in the marketing mix (behavioral-based) or to questions relating to their attitudes toward themselves, their environment, or a product class (attitudinal-based).

The most critical question facing the researcher in conducting a post hoc segmentation study is selecting the basis variables for the segmentation. There is nearly an unlimited set of basis variables that could be chosen. It takes an astute and product-experienced researcher to chose the relevant set. Examples include

❑ Product attribute preferences,

❑ Values,

❑ Product purchase patterns,

❑ Product usage patterns,

❑ Benefits sought,

❑ Brand preferences,

❑ Price sensitivity,

❑ Brand loyalty,

❑ Socioeconomic status,

❑ Deal proneness,

❑ Lifestyles,

❑ Self-image,

❑ Attitudes and opinions toward one's environment,

❑ Dealer loyalty, and

❑ Combinations of these.

The Baseline Segmentation Study. The initial market segmentation research undertaken by an organization to first form its post hoc market segments is usually called a *baseline* segmentation study. The baseline study is often preceded by a considerable amount of research of secondary data sources, a detailed study of previous research in the product category in question, and extensive qualitative research before the quantitative study is designed.

The characteristics of a baseline segmentation study are as follows:

1. The study includes both current and contemplated products.

2. It includes both current and expected purchaser groups.

3. It typically supports strategic planning at the corporate or business unit level and thus requires senior management involvement at the onset.

4. It uses a large sample and a large number of variables to allow for the analysis of alternative bases for segmentation.

5. The selected basis variables are suitable for inclusion in a classification model that will be used in subsequent research to break out the segments discovered in the baseline study.

6. Descriptive media usage variables are usually included in the study to provide major input to the communications and promotional processes.

7. A large amount of time is spent in the data analysis phase of the baseline study to explore alternative segmentation methods and alternative bases.

8. Because of the preceding, baseline segmentation studies tend to be expensive and time-consuming.

A baseline post hoc segmentation study will usually include a large number of nonbasis variables, called *descriptive variables*. These descriptive variables are used to further describe and help delineate the segments that are derived from the basis variables. At a minimum, descriptive variables used in a baseline segmentation study should include extensive demographics and media usage variables.

Writing in the *Journal of Marketing Research*, Yoram Wind (1978) provided this statement about descriptor variables:

> the selection of variables as descriptors of the segments is more complex (than basis variables). This complexity stems from three factors:
>
> 1. The enormous number of possible variables. Most of the variables covered in the consumer behavior literature can and have at some time been considered as segment descriptors.
> 2. The often questionable link between the selected basis for segmentation and the segment descriptors. Segments with varying elasticities to marketing variables may not be identifiable in terms of demographic and other segment descriptors. Conversely, segments defined in terms of demographics and other general customer characteristics tend to be identifiable but may not have varying elasticities to marketing variables. The latter situation restricts management's ability to pursue a segmentation strategy aimed at the given segments (and calls for examination of other possible bases for segmentation). The former situation allows management to follow at least a "self-selection" strategy.
> 3. The question of actionability, which relates to management's ability to use information (on the discriminating descriptors) as inputs to the design of the firm's marketing strategy (e.g., product design, copy execution, media scheduling, distribution coverage).

Algorithms for Post Hoc Segmentation. In general, there are four major classes of traditional algorithms for conducting traditional post hoc segmentation studies. They are

- ❏ Cluster analysis,
- ❏ Correspondence analysis,
- ❏ Search procedures, and
- ❏ Q-type factor analysis.

By a considerable margin, cluster analysis procedures have been the most popular. Correspondence analysis procedures are gaining some popularity in the applied marketing research arena because they can be used with categorical and ordinal measures. Search procedures are also widely used, especially for segmenting large databases. Q-type factor analysis has been mostly discredited and is seldom used (see Stewart 1981).

Cluster analysis is a generic term for a large set of algorithms that are widely available to marketing research professionals. Primarily, the various algorithms cluster together those cases or respondents that respond similarly to a set of basis questions. Clustering algorithms fall into two broad classes: hierarchical and partitioning procedures. In hierarchical procedures, each respondent starts out as an individual cluster, and these clusters are aggregated at each step on the basis of some criterion, such as a minimum or maximum multivariate distance measure. In partitioning procedures, all respondents start off in a single cluster, which is partitioned into successively more groups at each step on the basis of some criterion, such as minimizing the multivariate variance or maximizing the distance between multivariate cluster centroids.

Some clustering algorithms are more appropriate for marketing research than are others. In addition, some clustering programs may provide inconsistent or unstable results. It is extremely important to thoroughly check segments that are generated by clustering procedures. The ways to do this are

1. Use split or holdout samples to verify the results of the initial clustering;
2. Rotate the order of the data, recluster, and determine if the results are nearly identical;
3. Use several different clustering procedures and determine whether the results converge to a single solution; and
4. Use jackknife sample selection procedures to test for convergence of results.

Correspondence analysis (or dual scaling) is a multivariate procedure that develops internal scales of each basis variable. Those scales are then used to cluster respondents on the basis of the similarity of their individual responses to the scales. Its ability to use nominal and ordinal variables as input measures has made this algorithm fairly popular for market segmentation studies.

Search procedures involve the partitioning of a database according to how each of a successive set of variables is correlated to some response variable, such as purchase intent or amount spent in a product category. The most popular of the search procedures are the Automatic Interaction Detector (or AID) and its variation CHIAID (chi-squared–based AID). These techniques typically require very large databases and large amounts of computer processor time.

Because of its tenuous applicability to market segmentation studies, Q-type factor analysis is not addressed.

Some Cautions and Observations Regarding Post Hoc Segmentation.
1. The number and size of segments are not known until after the data analysis phase is completed.
2. The segmentability of the sample (and the population from which it is drawn) is unknown until after the data analysis phase of the study is completed.
3. Segment stability and segment homogeneity are unknown until after the data analysis phase is completed.
4. The size and complexity of subsequent classification models that are generated from a baseline post hoc segmentation study are not predictable and are unknown until the data analysis phase of the study is completed.
5. Spend sufficient time on the front end of the study to obtain management consensus. Design the study carefully. Use previous research, secondary data sources, and qualitative research to target the relevant set of basis variables. Do not rush the data analysis phase of the study under any circumstances.
6. Misspecification of the segmentation model, due to omitted variables or erroneous measurement of those variables, is a distinct possibility and must be addressed by uncovering and delineating sources of error in the study.

Classification or Scoring Models. After a baseline segmentation study is completed, it becomes necessary to report the results of subsequent marketing research studies by market segment. To do this adequately, it is appropriate to develop a set of classification schemes, or scoring models, from the baseline study. If developed correctly, a set of standard questions can be included in every subsequent marketing research study, such that the answers to those questions will enable the researcher to classify respondents into their appropriate market segment with a high degree of accuracy and confidence.

Typically, these classification equations are developed from the basis questions. If the basis measures are "interval" in nature, then an easy way to develop the classification equations is to subject the segment designations (i.e., segment designation as the dependent variable) and basis variables (i.e., the independent variable set) to a standard, stepwise discriminant analysis algorithm and extract the Fisher classification equations that are calculated.[2] A subsample of the original sample should be held out from the discriminant analysis and used to validate the extracted classification equations and estimate the percentage of correct classification.

If the basis variables are "nominal" in nature, then a classification scheme based on a multinomial logit analysis typically works well. The

_____

[2]Fisher classification equations calculate a score for each respondent for each cluster. The higher the score is, the higher the probability that the respondent belongs to the corresponding cluster. The respondent is assigned to that cluster for which he or she has the highest score.

resulting multinomial logit model predicts the probability of segment membership for each case.

In the case in which we are trying to predict segment membership from a larger database, such as a transaction database or customer file, with limited segmentation information, the typical steps are as follows:

1. Merge all of the database elements with the survey data.
2. Crosstab all the database elements against known segment membership from the survey data.
3. Search for significant differences among the database elements using ANOVA or chi-squared statistics, as appropriate.
4. Use variables that show significant differences as the independent set in discriminant analysis, CHAID analysis, and/or logistic/logit regression, as described previously.

This procedure requires a lot of time and patience and may yield only marginal results.

An alternative procedure is to use an artificial neural network (ANN) to develop the scoring model. Recently, the application of ANNs to developing segment scoring models of transaction databases has met with considerable success, mainly because ANNs are not dependent on assumptions regarding data measurement and functional form.

Data Analysis Issues and Some Solutions in Market Segmentation Research

The following represents a list of issues that both management and the research professional must address during the analysis phase of the post hoc market segmentation study.

Factor Scores as Inputs to a Clustering Procedure. In the situation in which the researcher is confronted with a large number of basis variables or there is a high amount of intercorrelation among the basis variables, it is often recommended that a principal components analysis or a factor analysis be executed on the data set. Then, the principal components scores (or factor scores) are used as inputs to a clustering procedure.

Because principal components (and factors) are orthogonal by definition, theoretically this procedure has the effect of reducing the possibility of inadvertently weighting the data by having multiple measures of the same underlying construct, as well as reducing the number of variables necessary to analyze in clustering.

A good rule-of-thumb when inspecting the principal components analysis is as follows: If more than 70% of the total variance is explained by the significant principal components, then one may want to use the principal component scores for each case as the basis variables for clustering. Use extreme caution here! See the following discussion.

If the principal components analysis explains 50 or less of the total variance, it would be more appropriate to use the original or standardized data, possibly throwing out some of the redundant measures prior to clustering.

If the principal components solution explains between 50 and 70%, it is basically a judgment call. Cluster the data both ways and determine which solution makes the most sense.

It has been my experience that clustering on principal component scores will seldom yield the same results as clustering on standardized scores. Indeed, the results may be radically different, even when the principal components represent very high levels of variance in the original data set. See the discussion by Everitt (1993).

Principal component scores are essentially summed correlations. A correlation does not satisfy several of the criteria of a distance measure. The effect of using correlations in a clustering algorithm is to collapse the distance between cases, thus changing the relative locations of those entities in hyperspace.

If the researcher discovers that there is a high amount of intercorrelation in the original data set, as represented by a high level of variance explained in the principal components analysis, then it seems to be a better procedure to select two or three variables that represent each principal component and submit those to clustering in raw form. This procedure has the effect of significantly reducing the number of correlated dimensions in hyperspace (thus reducing overweighing some of the underlying constructs) without radically changing the relative distance between cases.

Outliers. Outliers are isolated cases that are not near any cluster centroid. Outliers distort measures of variance explained, cluster homogeneity measures, and distance measures between centroids. A few outliers can make a "good" clustering solution look like a "bad" one. The key is to identify outliers and throw them out of the analysis.

There are several ways to identify outliers. An easy and simple way is to

> ❑ Pick your "best" cluster solution;
> ❑ Conduct a K-group discriminant analysis in which each cluster is a discriminant group and the basis variables are the independent measures;
> ❑ Rank order cases assigned to each cluster by the "probability of group membership" to that cluster;
> ❑ Throw out cases in the lower 10%, 15%, or 20% of probabilities; and
> ❑ Recluster and retab remaining cases.

It is always a good idea to take the thrown out cases and separately recluster those, just to make sure you have not inadvertently thrown out a meaningful cluster that was hidden in the outliers.

Segmentability

It seldom happens, but sometimes a sample cannot be segmented well. There are two basic reasons this may happen:

1. Important basis variables were not included in the research study, or
2. The market is truly not segmentable, given the bases. That is, response elasticities to marketing mix variables are not significantly different among groups.

In determining whether you have been successful in segmenting a market, four questions should be answered:

1. Did the segmenting algorithm indicate the degree of segmentation, and did this meet expectations in terms of the amount of variance explained compared with the amount of unexplained variance?
2. Does a discriminant analysis between segments (on the basis variables) show significant and sufficient segmentation as measured by both the overall estimated multivariate F (or Wilks' lambda) statistic and the matrix of between-group multivariate F statistics?
3. What are the sources of unexplained variance? Is it based on biased questions, lack of sufficient basis variables, or merely random variation in the sample?
4. Have you really segmented the sample? Does the produced segmentation really make sense? Does it reflect reality?

Although there are rather powerful statistical measures for reviewing the segmentability of the sample, the final determination of whether those segments really exist in the environment is a judgmental one.

What are your options if you get indications of nonsegmentability? You can try a new, reduced, or expanded set of basis variables. You can try a different segmentation procedure or algorithm. Or, you can conclude that the market, as you have measured it, cannot be segmented.

Segment Homogeneity. Questions pertaining to segment homogeneity apply only to the basis variables in post hoc segmentation research. In a priori procedures, the segments are homogeneous by definition. Segment homogeneity is usually measured by calculating the within-segment variance and comparing that variance with the overall variance in the basis variables before the data are clustered.

Segment homogeneity cannot be fully optimized until each respondent in each segment responds identically to the basis questions. Practically speaking, segment homogeneity is seldom optimized because there would be too many segments to deal with effectively. In practice, the maximum number of segments with which the researcher and management can effectively deal usually limits the maximization of intrasegment homogeneity. However, this does not necessarily mean that the researcher should always end up with the maximum number of segments. Some lesser set of segments will, by definition, be less homogeneous, but the increase in intrasegment homogeneity and intersegment variance explained by going to the next higher number of segments may not warrant the additional time and cost necessary to deal with the added segment(s). More important, the managerial and marketing costs of addressing a large number of unique segments may be beyond the resources of the firm.

In any case, given the chosen segmentation procedure, the researcher should establish three criteria dealing with the homogeneity issues during the design of the project. Those criteria are

1. The maximum number of segments that will be considered;
2. The minimum value of the optimization statistic(s) that will be acceptable for intrasegment homogeneity. For example, establish that no cluster will be allowed to have a homogeneity index of greater than 0.8, where the homogeneity index equals the error variance in the cluster divided by the total variance in the data set before clustering; and
3. Segment stability. That is, regardless of the maximum number of segments specified and regardless of the minimum acceptable homogeneity statistic value, if segments do not appear to have stabilized (in a statistical sense), more segments will be explored until stability is acceptable.

By statistical stability (as opposed to market stability, addressed in the next section), we are referring to the amount of respondent cross-over that is taking place at each step of the clustering process. Usually this is a judgment call and is based on whether there are still major new segments being formed at each step of the cluster forming process and whether there are significant improvements to the overall percentage of variance explained with the formation of each new group.

Segment Stability. In market segmentation studies, there are two central issues pertaining to stability:

1. Segment stability over time, and
2. Segment stability over situations or occasions.

The research question is: How likely is it that any person in a segment will remain in that same segment over time and/or over different environmental or market situations? Several factors can have a major effect on segment stability. Among the most obvious are the following:

1. *Changing consumer characteristics.* All consumers go through basic life-cycle changes, even in the short term. Such changes

often are accompanied by changes in product attitudes, usage behaviors, and purchase patterns.

2. *Volatility in the marketplace.* Changes in competitors' activities, plus environmental changes, due to changes in political, legal, cultural, or economic conditions, are likely to disturb the stability of known market segments and increase the likelihood of switching among segments.

3. *The basis of segmentation.* In general, one might hypothesize that the more specific the basis for segmentation (e.g., price sensitivity, brand loyalty), the less stable the segmentation is. Similarly, the more general the basis for segmentation (e.g., benefits sought or needs), the more stable the segmentation is because such basic ideals are typically slow to change. However, the more specific the basis, the more easily one may target marketing solutions to those various segments. Alternatively, the more general the basis, the more difficult it is to target marketing solutions.

The only valid method for testing segment stability is through the use of longitudinal data. Therefore, it is not possible to test for segment stability in a baseline segmentation study. After a baseline study has been conducted, the following steps provide a procedure for checking on segment stability over time:

1. Resurvey a sample from the original baseline population using exactly the same basis questions as were used in the original baseline study;

2. Resegment this new sample using the same algorithm and same procedures as were used in the original baseline study. Produce the same number of segments;

3. Check to make sure that each of the new segments is most closely aligned with its corresponding original segment by inspecting the means (or medians) of each basis variable in both the original and new segments. That is, make sure that cluster 1 in the original study is cluster 1 in the new study;

4. Conduct two-group stepwise discriminant analysis between the original cluster 1 and the new cluster 1, the original cluster 2 and the new cluster 2, and so on, for each set of clusters, using only the basis variables; and

5. If there is a significant difference in any of the discriminant runs (at whatever criteria you choose—90%, 95%, or 99% confidence level), then there most likely has been a significant time or situation shift in the population segments, and a new baseline study may be needed. By closely inspecting the stepwise discriminant printout, you can determine on which variables the shift has occurred. If you are using SPSS or SAS packages and the discriminant programs will not produce the analysis, you may assume that there is no significant difference.

The researcher should conduct such "confirmation" studies on a scheduled basis. The time interval should be based on the purchase cycle or turnover cycle for the particular product category.

Reliability. The true test for segment reliability in these type of studies is to draw two simultaneous and distinct samples from the same population, submit them to the same analytical procedures, and determine if the results are the same, within sampling error. Practically speaking, the researcher involved in segmentation research should collect a sufficiently large sample so that a 20% or 25% holdout sample is available. This holdout sample is then used to test variable distributions, verify the stability of the clustering algorithm, test classification equations, and provide for a quick way to test alternative segmentation bases.

SOME FINAL CONSIDERATIONS REGARDING CONVENTIONAL MARKET SEGMENTATION

Market segmentation studies sometimes fail for various reasons. It has been my experience that most fail for the following reasons:

1. A lack of senior management involvement and recognition that market segmentation is a strategy. A strategy must permeate the firm and the way it deals with the marketplace;
2. A lack of understanding of the concept of market segmentation and its need to identify groups that truly exhibit behavioral response differences to variations in the marketing mix;
3. A presumption that all markets can be segmented on bases that are subject to influence by variations in the marketing mix. There are some that cannot be easily segmented;
4. A researcher too concerned with methods and techniques instead of marketing capabilities and the practicalities of the marketplace;
5. Not tailoring the research parameters to the concept of segmentation; and
6. Selecting the "wrong" set of basis variables.

Some instances in which segmentation research is not useful are

1. The product category is a pure commodity without significant differentiation in product attributes or product/service bundles;
2. The market is so small that marketing to a portion of it is not profitable;
3. A relatively few heavy users make up such a very large portion of the sales volume that they are the only relevant target; and

4. A single brand is the overwhelmingly dominant brand in the market, and therefore, all users are the relevant set.

RECENT ADVANCES IN MARKET SEGMENTATION

Since about 1995, there have been some interesting new developments in market segmentation research. The following sections discuss those recent advancements and include:

❑ Multidimensional segmentation,
❑ Artificial neural networks,
❑ Latent class models,
❑ Fuzzy and overlapping clustering, and
❑ Occasion-based segmentation.

Multidimensional Segmentation[3]

In segmenting markets, most researchers use a single set of basis variables, be they demographics, psychographics, product-category–related attitudes, product-related behaviors, derived importances from conjoint exercises, latent structures, or whatever. However, there is no reason to limit the basis for segmentation to only one type of variable when many criteria actually determine buyers' responses to the selling proposition. These criteria are multidimensional, encompassing attitudes, needs, values, benefits, means, occasions, and prior experiences, depending on the product or service category and the buyer.

A segmentation scheme based on only one set of basis variables may limit the utility of the information to the firm, because its various users have different needs. For example, product development managers may want the market segmented on perceived values and benefits sought; marketing communications managers may want the market segmented into groups of buyers with similar needs, desires, or psychographic profiles; and sales managers may want the market segmented on sales potential or profitability.

How Multidimensional Segmentation Works

A segmentation scheme based on multiple dimensions, using separate segmentation schemes for each one, is often more useful and more flexible for planning marketing strategy and executing marketing tactics. Thus, one may consider different segmentations on a sample of buyers using different bases, say, stated needs, benefits, and amount spent in the category.

---

[3]This discussion was extracted from an article by William Neal (1998).

In the past, such segmentation schemes were deemed too confusing and produced too many segments for marketing managers to address effectively. Yet, in an era of micro-niche marketing and direct marketing tools, many market planners now consider market segmentation schemes that support finer targeting efforts.

Figure 2 shows a three-dimensional segmentation scheme. Here, each segmentation has a different set of basis variables. The X-axis is a needs-benefits segmentation based on derived importances from a conjoint exercise, the Y-axis is a segmentation based on buyers' perceived price range or ability to buy, and the Z-axis is based on clustering the responses to a battery of questions about customer priorities and desires.

Each surveyed customer, now a member of one segment in each of the three segmentation schemes, is assigned to a single cell in the segmentation matrix. Thus, respondents in each cell are similar on all three dimensions and different from respondents in other cells on at least one set of basis variables.

This type of segmentation scheme may have 200 or more cells, so large samples are needed to achieve reliable statistics at the cell level. Even with very large samples, many cells may be sparsely populated; this, however, is acceptable because it indicates that some markets may be too small to be profitable and should be either aggregated with other market segments or dropped from consideration as a specific target.

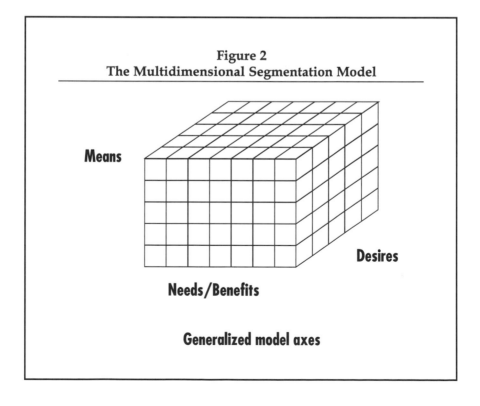

Figure 2
The Multidimensional Segmentation Model

Means

Desires

Needs/Benefits

Generalized model axes

Alone, this segmentation approach provides insight into the marketplace structure. However, each cell of the segmentation scheme, along with means and distributions of all descriptor variables, can be put into a database and manipulated to provide a more dynamic understanding of the market structure and enable the user to reform the cells into new segmentation schemes. With a well-designed segment manager program, the user can aggregate cells into specific market segments on the basis of the varying needs of different internal functional and departmental users while using a common base of homogeneous cells for all of the segmentation schemes in the company. Thus, any specific tactical segmentation scheme can be directly linked to the strategic segments or to any other tactical scheme.

Artificial Neural Networks

Starting in the early 1990s, ANNs have been developed to address a host of analytical problems. Both the appeal and the bane of ANNs are that they do not require any particular underlying model formulation or data structure, as do, say, regression analysis, logit modeling, or factor analysis.

In general, ANNs are given a set of input variables and a set of known outcomes, and the algorithm is asked to find the best relationship between the inputs and the outputs. It does this by initially forming a trial relationship on a subset of the data, called the learning set. The algorithm then backs up through one or more "hidden layers" of input junctures, or neurons, and adjusts the weight of each input to that neuron to maximize its contribution to accurately predicting the outcome. This learning procedure is repeated over and over for each neuron until the process is halted by user specifications or there is 100% accuracy in the prediction of a separate test sample. Results are validated with a third sample, the validation sample.

There are some specialized neural networks that are designed to cluster cases of data. These fall in the class of *unsupervised* neural networks, meaning that the outcomes are not prespecified.

Typically, these algorithms attempt to form clusters on the basis of minimizing variance around a specified set of "seeds" or optimizing a transform function. Currently, one of the best known of these clustering ANNs is the Kohonen Self-Organizing Map. All ANNs of this type require a large number of cases because they need a large learning sample, a large test sample, and a large validation sample.

Results have been mixed — some extremely good, others not so good. The usefulness of the clustering solution seems dependent on the initial selection of seeds or the shape of the transform function. Many alternative runs may be necessary to find an acceptable solution.

Another issue with ANNs is that they can overlearn. That is, the iteration process may optimize the solution for the specific set of data being addressed, but those results cannot be generalized to an additional set of observations. Determining when to stop an ANN from learning is a problem that has not yet been fully solved at the time of this chapter.

Latent Class Models (Mixture Models)

Basically, latent class models (LCMs) allow the user to optimize a function and find clusters of cases based on that function optimization process simultaneously. In general, the model may be applied to almost any dependency model—regression, logit, discriminant, and so forth.

The LCM finds areas in multidimensional space with high densities and estimates a separate set of model parameters for that region. The LCMs (usually) assume densities are either multivariate normal or maximum likelihood.

The basic idea is to determine segments and segment level models simultaneously. For example, using only choice data, determine segment partial probabilities for each parameter in the model, the number of segments, and the size of each. Individuals are assigned to segments on the basis of their posterior probabilities of membership. Software is being rapidly developed to apply LCM to a variety of standard optimization models.

Cohen and Ramaswamy (1998) cite two studies that conclude that latent class conjoint methods are superior to several different segmentation applications to conjoint data in terms of fit, descriptive validity, and predictive validity.

The elegance and appeal of LCM procedures can overshadow a fundamental concern with using this methodology to derive strategic segments. The problem with defining market segments using any of the dependency methods, including LCM and CHAID, is that you are assuming the market is segmented based on optimizing the explained variance in a single dependent variable. This is seldom sufficient for strategic and many tactical market segmentation efforts. However, the methods can be very useful for better understanding market structures.

Fuzzy and Overlapping Clustering

Most clustering algorithms are programmed so that all cases are assigned to one and only one cluster. That is, the algorithms require that the results be mutually exclusive and exhaustive. The basic idea in fuzzy (or overlapping) clustering is to allow a single case to be assigned to more than one cluster. Currently, there is no widely available software to handle this procedure, and there may be little need for it.

There is no reason that cases cannot be duplicated in a data file prior to clustering, such that the case represents two or more sets of measures for each variation of the case.

By way of an example, think about the situation in which you may ask respondents to complete a conjoint trade-off task about their beer selection preferences in different situations, say, at a business social function and at a bar with a group of friends. The conjoint attributes and levels are identical, but respondents' resulting profile preference ratings may be different based on the situation. If you derive importances for each attribute for each of those two occasions for the respondents, you will get two sets of derived importances for each respondent. There is no reason whatsoever that you cannot subject both sets of derived importances for these respondents to a standard clustering routine. The same respondent may then show up in two different clusters, depending on the results from his or her situational preferences. Indeed, this is how most researchers address occasion-based segmentation, as described in the next section.

Most clustering routines assume cases are grouped into hyperspheroids in multidimensional space. Cases are assigned to a cluster on the basis of their multivariate distance from the centroids of the spheroids or their probability of belonging to each spheroid. In the situation in which a particular case is nearly equidistant or has nearly equal probability of belonging to more than one spheroid, the standard clustering program will assign the case to the closest one, even if it takes five decimal points to do it. Many statisticians and research methodologists believe that there should be an alternative for the clustering algorithm to assign the case to each of the clusters.

In theory, that sounds fine. Practice is a different story. The effect of such a procedure would be to increase the variance within each cluster, thus reducing the variance explained by clustering. Cluster homogeneity, discussed previously, would suffer, and the resulting clusters would be much harder to explain because they would be less differentiated. It would seem to be better practice to throw these ambivalent cases out of the analysis using the same procedures for identifying outliers discussed previously.

Throwing out cases that do not fit well is very controversial. However, I believe our objective in market segmentation and the underlying clustering of cases is to identify unique and differentiated markets. Cases that depreciate the differentiation should be held out of the analysis. Thus, I see little need to further develop the concept of fuzzy or overlapping clustering routines.

Occasion-Based Segmentation

A particular challenge in market segmentation analysis is how to address segments when circumstances or occasions drive product preference and selection. For example, it is well known that beer brand preference and brand selection are often driven by the situational circumstances of the purchaser at the time of consumption. Restaurant selection is also well known to be dependent on occasion and circumstance.

Mechanically, occasion-based segmentation is not very difficult. All it takes is a different way of looking at the data input file to standard clustering routines. A case becomes an occasion with individual respondent information appended to each occasion case.

Here is an example. We are measuring the relative influence on brand choice of a set of brands, product attributes, and price variations for carbonated soft drinks for immediate consumption in a variety of store type settings: grocery, convenience, mass merchandise, deli, and drug. Respondents are asked to do a point allocation of importance of each of the attributes, plus price and brand name, on influencing their selection for each store setting that they have experienced in the last ten days. In addition, we ask for demographic and consumption volume profile information to better describe the respondents.

We need to construct the data file as shown here for the first two respondents.

❑ Occasion 1 measures: Respondent 1 profile data;

❑ Occasion 2 measures: Respondent 1 profile data (duplicated);

❑ Occasion 3 measures: Respondent 1 profile data (duplicated);

❑ Occasion 1 measures: Respondent 2 profile data;

❑ Occasion 3 measures: Respondent 2 profile data (duplicated);

❑ Occasion 5 measures: Respondent 2 profile data (duplicated).

Here, each set of point allocation data for each store setting becomes a case. The respondents' profiling data are appended to each set of occasion ratings.

At this point, we have two choices. We could execute a clustering of the point allocation data for each type of shopping trip, thus deriving segments on the basis of the importance drivers for each store type, separately. Alternatively, we could submit all of the point allocation data to a clustering algorithm and find clusters or segments in which the importance drivers are similar within each cluster and different between clusters, regardless of the occasion. The resulting clusters may or may not differentiate between store types. Either way, we have executed an occasion-based segmentation.

SPECULATIONS ON THE FUTURE OF MARKET SEGMENTATION RESEARCH

It seems that the future for market segmentation research is rather rosy from the demand side. Market segmentation has taken on an increasingly important role in business strategy development. Thus, senior management is demanding more segmentation research as a critical input to the strategic planning process.

Our ability to accumulate and manage massive amounts of data on customers and potential customers, aligned with the availability of many more targeted communications capabilities, would seem to ensure that there will be increasing demand for much more and much finer identification of target markets in most product and service categories. The advent and massive use of the Internet only opens up greater possibilities for target marketing.

There are a few downsides. The need for isolating and defining ever smaller target markets will require ever larger research sample sizes and a commensurate increase in the costs of doing excellent market segmentation research. Samples must be pristine and projectable to the larger population from which they were drawn. For a while, this will preclude using the Internet as a respondent recruiting method for segmentation research.

This same demand for finer targeting will force more researchers into the complexities of multidimensional and occasion-based segmentation. These procedures require more time for analysis and reporting, improved methods for delivering and managing results, and the need for leveraging database reporting capabilities.

The ANNs and LCMs will continue to supplant many traditional segmentation algorithms. These require increased methodological and statistical training for their effective use.

The anticipated changes indicate that the implementation of a segmentation strategy will get much more complex for both marketers and researchers.

SUMMARY

Market segmentation is a powerful and well-developed marketing tool. In North America, a strategy of market segmentation is a necessity for most products and services. A properly segmented market can improve marketing, distribution, and manufacturing efficiency and generate additional profits and/or market share.

The basis selected for segmenting a market is key. The creative application of alternative bases for segmentation can often provide a strategic advantage to the innovative firm.

A strategy of market segmentation must be supported at the very top of the organization and must permeate the organization.

Market segmentation research, especially baseline segmentation research, must be carefully planned and executed, using the highest professional research standards. A missegmented market is often worse than making the mass-market assumption.

BIBLIOGRAPHY

Cohen, Steven H. and Venkatram Ramaswamy (1998), "Latent Segmentation Models: New Tools to Assist Researchers in Market Segmentation," *Marketing Research*, 10 (Summer), 15–21.

Everitt, Brian (1993), *Cluster Analysis*, 3d ed. New York: Halsted Press, 26–31.

Green, Paul and Donald Tull (1978), *Research for Marketing Decisions*, 4th ed. Englewood Cliffs, NJ: Prentice Hall, 540.

Kotler, Philip (1980), "Strategic Planning and the Marketing Process," *Business Magazine*, (May-June), 3–4.

Neal, William (1988), "Multidimensional Segmentation," *Canadian Journal of Marketing Research*, 17 (1), 78–81.

Smith, Wendall (1956), "Product Differentiation and Market Segmentation as Alternative Marketing Strategies," *Journal of Marketing*, 20 (July), 3–8.

Stewart, David (1981), "The Application and Misapplication of Factor Analysis in Marketing Research," *Journal of Marketing Research*, 18 (February), 51–62.

Webster, Frederick E., Jr. (1993), "Defining the New Marketing Concept," *Marketing Management*, 2 (October), 22.

Wind, Yoram (1978), "Issues and Advances in Segmentation Research," *Journal of Marketing Research*, 15 (August), 317–37.

15
Database and Data Mining Techniques

Peter Peacock

T his chapter is about databases, data mining, and knowledge discovery in databases (KDD for short) and about what marketing researchers should know of these new developments of the information technology age. We first look at similarities between data mining and traditional marketing research, then we highlight the differences.

What's the Same?

Marketing researchers are working in a rapidly evolving world, a world in which torrents of data are produced by the smallest enterprise, large databases are common, and analytical tools developed by artificial intelligence (AI) researchers are being used alongside or in place of traditional statistical methods. Marketing researchers must become more familiar with these new tools and the database concepts that drive their use. Although terms such as "data mining," "knowledge discovery in data bases," "neural nets," "genetic algorithms," and "decision trees" are new to many marketing researchers, the underlying methodologies to which these terms apply are often recognizable to analytically trained practitioners. In many cases, the underlying methodologies and approaches are no different, in concept at least, than methodologies that marketing researchers have been familiar with and quite comfortable using for many years.

Typically, marketing researchers are applied statisticians who work with relatively small data sets in a deliberate, systematic, and disciplined way. The template-like methodological approach that guides these efforts is well known to almost all marketing researchers (for a good exposition of this methodology, see Hair et al. 1995). As we show subsequently in this chapter, KDD, the analysis hierarchy formulated by AI researchers whose focus is data mining (and which includes data mining as one of its components), corresponds closely to the careful, step-by-step analytical template with which marketing researchers are familiar. Because of this similarity of approaches, adopting data mining and KDD is a natural transition for marketing researchers to make. For many, the transition won't require much more of an effort than learning a new terminology and, of course, becoming familiar with a new tool set (or, as in the cases of SAS and SPSS, learning how to use the new tools that have been recently added to software packages with which marketing researchers are already comfortable).

What's Different?

Major differences between the familiar analysis techniques whose source discipline is classical statistics and the new breed of analytical tools are that the older methods were generally applied to relatively small data sets obtained from samples, and the primary purpose of the research for which the data were collected tended to be the confirmation of existing theories or hypotheses. In contrast, the new tools whose source discipline is AI are often applied to very large data sets; populations, not samples, are the focus of analysis; and the purpose of research is the discovery of interesting relationships rather than the testing of well-constructed hypotheses. Finally, we should emphasize that the data being analyzed with these new tools are *secondary* data, not primary data. For additional thinking on this issue, see Hand (1998, 1999) and Elder and Pregibon (1996), who compare data mining and statistics, point out some of the limitations of popular data mining tools, and call for greater involvement of statisticians in the data mining and KDD fields.

Where Do We Go from Here?

In this chapter, we attempt to introduce some of these new tools and show how they can be employed to solve familiar marketing research problems. However, we start by exploring database concepts with a special emphasis on the relational database model because data mining and KDD apply primarily to data in large databases. Then, in the next section, we introduce the data warehouse and online analytical processing (OLAP), two innovations in information technology that support data mining and knowledge discovery. Next, in the fourth section, we introduce data mining concepts and tools and describe how they can be applied. In the following section, we describe the KDD process. The last section is a summary, and, finally, in the references, we provide traditional reference material and several related Web site addresses.

DATABASE OPERATIONS

As early as the 1960s, increasingly effective approaches to managing large data aggregations on computers were introduced on a regular basis to what is now called the information technology industry. The first such approach was the simple flat file, which, not unlike today's spreadsheet, organized all the data pertaining to a particular process into one file composed of columns and rows. Most marketing researchers are well acquainted with flat files because that is how they usually organize their analysis data sets. Although smaller flat files are conceptually simple and easy to manipulate, large flat files tend to be prone to corruption, wasteful of storage space, and time consuming to traverse.

The second data organization approach is a scheme called ISAM (for Indexed Sequential Access Method).[1] The major advantage of ISAM is that it supports efficient processing of an entire file in one pass or (and in contrast to the flat file case) processing of individual records one at a time. The principal drawbacks to ISAM are the cost and time required to update files, because complex indexing structures must also be updated. These added processing costs are especially burdensome in situations in which frequent updating of large numbers of records is the operational norm.

The next two data organization approaches, unlike the flat file and ISAM structures, are actually database management systems (DBMSs). They are referred to as the *hierarchical* and *network* DBMSs. Both the hierarchical and network DBMSs were designed to support high-volume transaction processing applications and, consequently, possess only limited analytical flexibility. Many companies still use these DBMSs to support customer service systems, airline or hotel reservations systems, or financial applications. These products were not designed to support the multiplicity of views or ad hoc query requirements of decision support systems (DSS) and do not perform well when applied to DSS applications. Both hierarchical and network DBMSs use computer resources efficiently, but they are complex in concept and structure and usable only by highly skilled information technology specialists. Another major drawback of hierarchical and network DBMSs is that their structures are not easily modified when business conditions change.

The Relational Model

The next major innovation was the relational database management system (RDBMS). Commercial RDBMSs have been available for a little more than ten years and are today the most common approach to data

---

[1]This has evolved into VSAM (for Virtual Sequential Access Method), a closely related data organization method.

organization. The basic concept of the relational database (unlike the concepts of earlier database models) is inherently intuitive and easy for the layperson to understand: The well-constructed relational database organizes data into a set of spreadsheet-like *tables* that are *related* to one another by record identifiers called keys and that are arranged such that data redundancy within each table is minimized. A relational structure that minimizes data redundancy within tables is said to be *normalized*. Full normalization is a theoretical objective that is rarely sought in practice because it adversely affects system processing costs. We shall say a little more about normalization and denormalization subsequently.

An Example

As an example of a relational database, consider a system that might be employed for constructing, maintaining, and controlling closed-end questionnaires for a marketing research company that, in keeping with the times, we call "Webstudies Research Inc." Our marketing research firm develops scores of questionnaires annually for marketing research and consumer satisfaction studies conducted in person, by mail, and online. Not surprisingly, many of the questions are common to several questionnaires. Let's also assume that our database is used to store the responses to all of the company's questionnaires.

This simple system has five core tables: (1) a questionnaire table, (2) a question table, (3) an answer table, (4) a questionnaire structure table, and (5) a data table. (We would also expect our questionnaire database to link to several other tables in the company's database—such as a study table, a staff table, and a subject or respondent table, among others—but in the interest of simplicity, these tables are omitted from our example.) A database similar to what we show here could be constructed easily enough with desktop products such as Microsoft Access and with just a bit more effort using "industrial strength" RDBMSs such as Oracle or IBM's DB2.

The five core tables follow. Note that the name of each table as understood by the computer is included in parentheses.

Let's take a closer look at these five tables. The *Questionnaire Table* shown in Table 1 (and labeled "QNAIRE") stores information on the questionnaire *entity* and includes three columns: one for the questionnaire identifier (*insnum*), one for the name of the questionnaire (*questname*), and one for the number of the study to which the questionnaire belongs (*studynum*). Of course, there is nothing sacred about these particular column names; they were assigned as a matter of convenience. In actual practice, we would expect to see additional columns (and this comment applies equally well to the other tables in this example). In Table 1, insnum is the *primary key*; that is, it is the *unique* identifier for the individual rows in the table. Questname, in contrast, is an *attribute* of the questionnaire entity. The third column, studynum, refers or "relates" to another table containing information about the studies and is known as a *foreign key*, which we define to be a column in one table that refers back to the primary key in another table.[2] Note that the studynum key in row 1 refers to study A221, as does the studynum key in row 3. If we were to examine the studies table, however, we would see just one row for study A221.

The *Question Table* ("QSTION") in Table 2 describes the question *entity* and includes every question that Webstudies Research has included in its questionnaires for the past two years. This table is a questionnaire construction resource, and it is added to regularly. Having this table enables the company to use stock questions over and over again and also supports assessment and evaluation of individual questions to determine

---

[2]For every foreign key in one table, there should be a primary key in a second table. This important principle is known as *referential integrity*.

Table 1
Questionnaire Table (QNAIRE)

INSNUM	QUESTNAME	STUDYNUM
I0001	Ajax Foods – Track 0600	A221
I0002	Memphis Conservatory	B506
I0003	Ajax Foods – Product Z	A221

More questionnaire rows

Table 2
Question Table (QSTION)

QUESNUM	QUESTION	DATE	EMPNUM
Q0001	What year were you born?	08/06/98	E253
Q0002	How many people are in your household?	06/22/93	E127
Q0003	How many bedrooms does your home have?	09/10/99	E253
Q0004	Did you buy coffee last week?	08/08/96	E116
Q0005	How many times did you shop online last week?	10/12/98	E127

More question rows

which tend to be valid and reliable and which do not. The primary key for the question table is *quesnum*; the *question* and *date* columns include the actual question text as well as the date when the question was added to our questionnaire construction database. The *empnum* column is a foreign key that maps to a primary key in the employee table and leads us to details about the staff members who have added questions to the question table. Note that there is a *one-to-many* relationship between employees and questions; that is, *one* staff member may add *many* questions to the database.

The *Answer Table* ("ANSWER") in Table 3 represents the answer entity. This table includes all the closed-end answers for the questions in the question table that require precoded response options. Table 3 makes it easy to change the ordering of precoded responses to control for order biases and expand or contract the number of options made available to the respondent. Like the question table, this table is a questionnaire construction resource and is also augmented regularly. The primary key for the answer table is *ansnum*; the *response* column in the answer table includes the precoded response text. Other columns indicate the data *type* associated with the answer (e.g., integer, floating point, character string), the code that indicates the *order* of the response options, the *date* the response options were added to the answer table, and the identifier of the staff member (*empnum*) who added them.

The *Questionnaire Structure Table* ("QSTRUC") in Table 4 supports the construction of online and offline questionnaires by accessing the contents of the three other tables to which it is *joined* or related by a foreign key to a primary key link. Table 4 includes four columns: (1) *insnum*, which links the questionnaire structure table to the questionnaire table; (2) *quesnum*, which links it to the question table; (3) *ordnum*, which governs the order of the questions; and (4) *ansnum*, which links it to the answer table. This table might be constructed using an offline application that permits a staff mem-

Table 3
Answer Table (ANSWER)

ANSNUM	RESPONSE	TYPE	ORDER	DATE	EMPNUM
A0024	Under 19	INT	010	11/17/98	E116
A0025	20 to 29	INT	020	11/17/98	E116
A0026	30 to 39	INT	030	11/17/98	E116
A0027	40 to 49	INT	040	11/17/98	E116

More answer rows

Table 4
Questionnaire Structure Table (QSTRUC)

INSNUM	QUESNUM	ORDNUM	ANSNUM
I0002	Q0001	001	A0024
I0002	Q0001	002	A0025
Additional questions			
I0002	Q0463	084	A0123

Table 5
Data Table (DATA)

SUBNUM	INSNUM	QUESNUM	RESPONSE
S2058	I0002	Q0001	1954
S2058	I0002	Q0002	3
Additional responses			
S2058	I0002	Q0463	125.75

ber to quickly construct a questionnaire using the "objects" from the question and answer tables and then store the completed questionnaire in the questionnaire structure table for online administration or offline output by another application, which might format the questionnaire and send it to a printer.[3] Note that the relationships captured in this table are *many-to-many* relationships. That is, *one* questionnaire may have *many* questions, and *one* question may be incorporated in *many* questionnaires (and similarly in the case of questions and answers).

Finally, the *Data Table* ("DATA") in Table 5 stores the results of the surveys conducted using the questionnaires represented in Table 4. Observe

---

[3]Although we did not show it for this simple example, it is possible to store formatting information in the questionnaire and questionnaire construction tables so that questionnaires can be built online or offline more or less automatically.

that this table identifies the respondent, the questionnaire, and the question number and includes the actual response (or nonresponse) for each combination of respondent, questionnaire, and question. Organizing the data in this fashion makes it easy to compare the response distribution to a particular question for one study with the response distribution for another study (or with the response distribution of *all* other studies). Although the structure of this data table does not look like the data tables to which marketing researchers are accustomed, it is an easy matter to rearrange the data from a table that resembles Table 5 to the flat files that programs such as SPSS, SAS, and S-Plus like to see.

A major advantage of setting up a questionnaire management database like the one in our example is that it can support dynamic Web-based questionnaire construction. By accessing the database, custom "questionnaires" can be developed on the fly in response to the actions of a site visitor from whom one might wish to obtain information.

Benefits of the Relational Model

In addition to its innate intuitiveness, benefits of the relational model include

- ❏ It is much less difficult for the non–technically trained computer user to understand and use an RDBMS than ISAM or the hierarchical or network DBMSs.
- ❏ In contrast to the hierarchical and network DBMSs, it is relatively easy to change a relational DBMS's data structure when the composition of the business or its computer applications changes.
- ❏ An RDBMS enables users to adapt data sets to meet their own requirements rather than the requirements established by the database designers. For example, users can combine different tables in an RDBMS to create *views*[4] of the data that may provide unanticipated insights.
- ❏ Information about the structure of the database (called *metadata*) is maintained in a set of tables, termed the *catalog* or *data dictionary*, that are conceptually identical to all the other tables in a database. This property makes it easy to monitor and understand the structure of any relational database.

Structured Query Language

Developers and users interact with relational databases using Structured Query Language (more commonly known as SQL). Structured

---

[4]A view is a collection of columns pulled from one or more tables. Although a view is only a *virtual* table, it appears to the user to be a separate *physical* table. Views are employed to simplify data visualization and provide security.

Query Language is easier to work with than computer programming languages such as C, Java, and Visual Basic, but working with it can still be a major challenge for the casual user.[5] In many RDBMSs, such as Microsoft Access, graphical query-building tools are available to make the work easier.

The SQL commands can be formulated to create and "drop" (delete) tables, add and drop columns, insert and delete records, and update the cells that represent the intersections of specific columns and rows. It also supports arithmetic calculations such as counts, averages, and totals. By far the most common command type, however, is the SQL select statement used to query a single table or collection of "joined" tables. For example, if we wanted to see all the questions on questionnaire number I0055 that were designed by Jane Smith, whose employee number is 116, we would run the following query:

> SELECT qstion.quesnum, qstion.question, staff.name
>
> FROM qnaire, qstion, staff
>
> WHERE qstion.empnum = staff.empnum
>
> AND qnaire = "I0055"
>
> AND staff.empnum = "E116"

Note that we name the columns we want to see in the first line of the query. Also note that we have "qualified" each column by preceding it with a table name and a dot to remove any ambiguity about the source table for the column. In the next line, we name all the tables from which we plan to draw information. In the third line, we "join" the questionnaire and employee tables on employee number. Finally, the last two lines tell the RDBMS that we only want to consider questionnaire I0055 and questions designed by Jane Smith.

Indexes

One additional concept we should develop here is that of an index. An index on a relational table is a pair of columns maintained in a separate file that permits the table to be accessed in sorted order without needing to actually sort the physical rows of the table itself. For example, say that we wanted to arrange the question table by employee number. One way to do this would be to physically sort the entire table on employee number and save it under another name. For our questionnaire table, such an operation would probably be trivial and shouldn't require much time. For a very large table containing all the data from many question-

---

[5]Indeed, to write the simple query in the following paragraph, a user must know SQL syntax, understand the database structure (i.e., which tables to join), and be familiar with the specifics of each table (e.g., column names, types).

naires administered to many respondents, however, the number of rows to be sorted could easily number in the millions. Performing a physical sort on such a large table could require lots of time and would not be a trivial operation.

In a situation like this, we could index the data table on one or more characteristics, say, questionnaire plus question order number[6] and respondent number (i.e., two criteria). In this case, our index file would have four columns. In the first column are questionnaire number plus question order number; *this column would be in sorted order*. In the second column are the addresses of the physical locations of the records to which the index value points. In the third column are respondent numbers in, say, numerical order (if respondent identifiers were numerical), and in the fourth column is again the address of the actual physical location of the corresponding record. The second and fourth columns would, of course, have different orders.

As we added, deleted, and updated records in our data table, we would make the changes in the physical table, but after each change, the indexes would be updated automatically so that the paths to individual records were always current.

Indexes can increase the speed of locating individual records by orders of magnitude, but they have a downside: As more and more fields are indexed, the update time for a database becomes long, and the indexes consume more and more disk space.

Denormalization

We have used the term *normalize* to refer to the process of placing data related to a process such as questionnaire construction, record keeping, and control in a set of separate, linked tables to minimize redundancy within tables. The relational model ideal referred to previously as the *fully normalized structure* is one in which all of the redundancy is eliminated. Although full normalization is a theoretical ideal that may come close to being realized in RDMSs optimized for managing transactions (e.g., online ordering, inventory processing), it is generally not appropriate for marketing applications, because they usually require many complex queries. The reason the relational structure is denormalized by incorporating redundancy in these situations is that fully normalized structures require many join operations even for simple queries, and these join operations and subsequent accesses to joined tables can impose very large costs in machine time. Stated more simply, fully normalized databases can be very slow databases insofar as query responses are concerned.

---

[6]In this case, we *concatenate* question number and order number by adding their character strings together horizontally.

DATA WAREHOUSING AND OLAP

In this section, we describe data warehouse and OLAP technologies. These closely related technologies are of importance to marketing researchers for several reasons. First, data warehouses and OLAP represent new methods for managing the rising floods of data being produced and stored, and marketing researchers are natural users of these technologies, just as they were natural users of statistical software packages when they first appeared in the 1960s. Second, these technologies signal a not-so-subtle shift in emphasis from primary research to research using secondary data, because data warehouses and OLAP tools lower the cost of performing secondary research relative to the cost of performing primary research. Third, because of these technologies, there is and will continue to be a shift in focus from the planning and front-end quality control typical of the usual primary research project to the back-end cleaning and hygiene so essential to good secondary research. Fourth, marketing researchers need to understand data warehouses and OLAP because they represent the terrain over which researchers will be required to travel to remain competitive with researchers trained in the AI tradition.

The Data Warehouse

Let's begin with a definition:

> The data warehouse is an enterprise-level data repository that draws its contents from critical operational systems such as order entry and billing and selected external data sources. The data warehouse is built according to an enterprise "data model" that must be drawn up ahead of time in an often time- and resource-consuming cross-functional effort. Data warehouses can cost in excess of $10 million to build and take anywhere from one to three years to complete.

When considering data on mainframe computers and other large enterprise servers, most marketers (and perhaps most marketing researchers) probably have a good understanding of what facts have been placed on these machines. They know that most enterprises have transaction processing systems that run on computers and that those systems usually generate large amounts of data on customer purchasing activity. At the same time, however, many marketers often have a naïve view of data *accessibility*. They believe that just because transaction data are collected and written to mass storage devices, they are also forever available, complete, free of error, and readily accessible for analysis.

Until just recently, however, reality bore little resemblance to this imagined situation. In most cases, purchase transaction data were not retained online (if they were retained at all), and they were often incomplete, frequently wrong, and almost completely inaccessible to marketing researchers and analysts who wanted to use them for decision support.

There are many reasons this situation existed. We don't have the space to consider all of them here, but suffice it to say that most data access problems stemmed from the historical facts that transaction processing systems were developed to support the day-to-day operations of the business, that the impact of operational activities on the bottom line is direct whereas the impact of analysis is indirect, and that operational and analytical processing requirements are almost completely at odds. Although this situation meant that analytical requirements were only partially met (when they were met at all), the needs didn't just go away. Indeed, as competitive pressures have increased in recent years, the needs have become ever more salient, especially to marketing managers. Fortunately, plummeting technology costs have provided a solution to the problem: the data warehouse packed with data structured explicitly for decision support.

Figure 1 is a simple schematic showing the essential architecture of the data warehouse. As it illustrates, data from transaction systems are fed into a collection process that performs two broad categories of operations: *data funneling* and *preprocessing*.[7]

Although we describe these operations in greater detail in a subsequent section, because they are included in the KDD process, let's briefly summarize them here. Data funneling includes converting, loading, and then validating data from operational and external systems. The preprocessing operation includes reformatting, standardization, removal of sparse records, and aggregation (for an excellent exposition of the details of these processes, see Kimball 1996).

Data that pass these filtering steps are then stored in the data warehouse, which is usually housed in a separate computer dedicated solely to the warehouse and support of warehouse users. The last element in the diagram is an OLAP server. The OLAP server may be a separate computer whose back end is the warehouse, or it may be a software application that resides on top of the warehouse. Data warehouses tend to be very large—potentially terabytes (trillions of bytes) in size—and house historical data whose purpose is to support intertemporal comparisons. They are updated on a regular schedule using batch processing when regular mainframe transaction processing loads are low; updating may occur daily, weekly, or even monthly in cases in which decision support information changes slowly.

OLAP

As we did previously, let's begin this discussion with a definition:

---

[7]Figure 1 omits an element that represents external sources of data such as IRI, ACNielsen, or Acxiom, but a company's data warehouse could draw from one or more of these external sources.

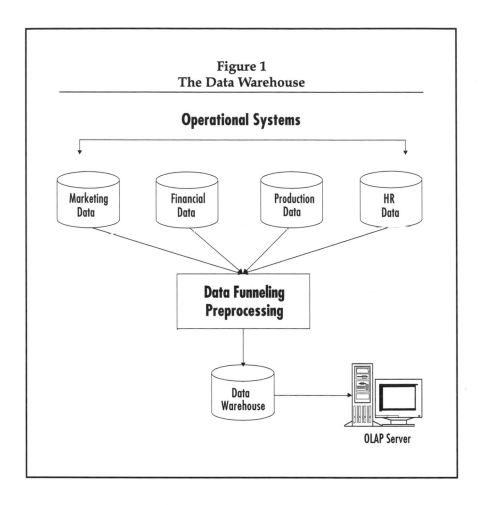

The acronym OLAP refers to a suite of decision support soft-ware tools that resides on top of a database and enables users to manipulate data with great flexibility. Typically, an OLAP tool allows users to select variables from a list, transform them if necessary, "slice and dice" them, and then perform diagnostic operations on them very quickly. If users require more detail about a particular variable, they can usually "drill down" into the data.

In general, the display properties of OLAP systems are configured as cubes in which each axis of the cube represents a different dimension. This arrangement is depicted in Figure 2. This approach is used because three-dimensional data displays can be comprehended quite easily. For example, one dimension might be sales of a company's products, a second dimension might be geographical regions, and a third could be time peri-

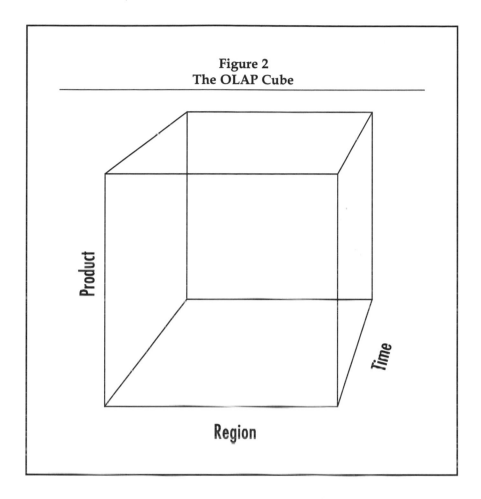

Figure 2
The OLAP Cube

Product

Time

Region

ods. Usually, OLAP systems support more than three dimensions and enable users to easily modify the dimensions displayed.

The easiest way to characterize OLAP systems is to think of them as large-scale exploratory analysis engines. Although some OLAP products incorporate statistical and data mining tools, their primary function is to support very rapid database querying. Almost all OLAP tools support the following capabilities:

❑ Examining data horizontally in rows, often referred to as "slicing;"

❑ Examining data vertically in columns, often referred to as "dicing;"

❑ Aggregating data into totals, averages, and counts, often referred to as "rolling up" data;

❏ Disaggregating data into their component parts so that, for example, dog food brand sales can be broken down by formulation. This capability is often referred to as "drilling down;" and

❏ Applying arithmetic and logical operations to support data transformations and combinations.

DATA MINING

The many articles on data mining that have appeared during the past three to four years in publications that cover a broad range of disciplines reveal some confusion about the meaning of the term "data mining." Data mining is defined by some writers within a quite narrow scope, whereas others define it within a broad scope. Let's try to understand the differences.

Narrow-Scope Data Mining

Narrowly defined, data mining is the *automated discovery* of "interesting," nonobvious patterns hidden in a database that have a high potential for contributing to organizational objectives. As it is used here, the word *interesting* has special meaning for the data mining community; "interesting" patterns are those that are unexpected and that may have an impact on strategy or tactics and ultimately on an organization's performance.

Narrow-scope data mining encompasses computer-based methods that extract patterns or information from data and require only limited human involvement. Most of these methods are of relatively recent origin and have their roots in AI. Examples of machine-learning methods are neural networks, association rules, decision trees, and genetic algorithms.

Note the emphasis here on the process of discovery. Discovery means that we are looking for relationships we did not know about beforehand. The discovery process often involves sifting through massive quantities of data, such as electronic point-of-sale transactions, inventory records, and online customer orders. Although the volumes of data with which marketing decision makers must work are already very large and will become larger still, tools are available to ease the burden. For example, the judicious use of probability sampling, predictive modeling, and machine-learning methods can yield valid results while reducing the data management task significantly.

Broad-Scope Data Mining

In the broad scope,[8] data mining incorporates the following activities:

1. Acquiring data from internal and external sources;

---

[8]Most academic data mining researchers refer to broad-scope data mining as KDD.

2. Translating, cleaning, and formatting the data;

3. Analyzing, validating, and attaching meaning to data (this activity includes the techniques that fall within the span of narrow-scope data mining);

4. Scoring databases;

5. Building and implementing decision support tools and systems to make data mining results available to decision makers and lower-level staff; and

6. Recalibrating models and maintaining delivery systems.

Factors Driving the Data Mining Industry

An often-asked question is, "What is driving the data mining revolution?" We attempt to answer this question in the two subsections that follow.

Despite all the hoopla and media attention received in the past year or two, data mining isn't revolutionary. Its roots reach back to the methodology of John Tukey, a legendary statistician at Princeton and Bell Labs, whose ideas were introduced in the mid-1970s. Tukey (1977) called his methodology "Exploratory Data Analysis," or simply EDA, and EDA continues to be used on a daily basis by researchers and analysts working in a broad range of disciplines. What is different today is that data volumes have gotten so large that analysts are becoming incapable of extracting meaningful information using traditional EDA approaches (which usually required little more in the way of equipment than paper and pencil) or even approaches that incorporate statistical sampling methodologies to reduce the problem of data management. Because data volumes have become so large, data mining professionals are turning increasingly to information technology for support.

The principal differences among EDA of the 1970s, EDA as it continues to be practiced widely today by statisticians and analysts, and narrow-scope data mining are that data mining substitutes machine learning for human learning, *and* data mining is frequently applied to complete data sets (often very large ones) rather than to samples drawn from them.

Several closely related developments have motivated the growth of the data mining industry. We believe grouping them into "supply-side" and "demand-side" factor sets aids in understanding their effects.

Supply-Side Factors

On the supply side are the effects of information technology advances. For example, advances in data storage and data processing technology, such as parallel-processing computers, have led to deep reductions in the cost of collecting and storing the operational data flowing from retail point-of-sale terminals, direct marketing order entry systems, and the interrelated systems of financial services firms.

Another supply-side factor is the declining cost of electronic communication. Not so many years ago, only the analysts working directly with mainframes could gain access to data easily. With today's widespread networks, however, almost anyone with a PC can connect to a corporate network, intranet, extranet, or the Web and work directly with large data files. Also on the supply side is the emergence of new techniques of analysis that have enabled analysts to turn much of the work of discovery over to computers. Examples are neural networks, genetic algorithms (GAs), decision trees, and induction rules. More will be said about these techniques subsequently. To the supply-side factors already mentioned, add the client/server computer architecture revolution and graphical user interfaces. A final supply-side factor is the development of the data warehouse described previously. Lumped together, these technology advances are causing the amount of information in the world to grow exponentially.

Demand-Side Factors

Demand-side factors include the growing need for ever faster analytical results in an increasingly competitive business environment as the relevant market for most industries becomes worldwide in scope, as well as the squashing of the organizational hierarchy. Just a few years ago, marketing managers turned to staff support analysts for the answers they needed. Today, most of the support analysts are gone, and the marketing manager must either become a part-time analyst or sail by dead reckoning. A final demand-side factor is the boomlet in books and articles that focus attention on building and maintaining customer relationships. Perhaps the best known example of this genre is *The One to One Future* by Peppers and Rodgers (1997), but there have been many such publications in recent years.

The Data Miner's Toolkit

A sampling of the literature on data mining indicates that many analytical techniques are classified as data mining tools, but for now at least, agreement on exactly which techniques should and should not be included in the toolset is not widespread. Nonetheless, books and articles in the area indicate that the data miner's toolkit would probably include at least the following six tools or toolsets:

❑ Visualization,
❑ Association rules,
❑ Decision trees,
❑ Case-based reasoning (CBR),
❑ Neural networks, and
❑ Genetic algorithms.

See Berry and Linoff (1997), Dhar and Stein (1996), and Weiss and Indurkhya (1998) for more comprehensive, nontechnical discussions of these data mining methods plus others we have omitted. Goonatilake and Treleaven (1995) present a collection of useful application papers, several of which are somewhat technical.

Of these tools and toolsets, decision trees, association rules, case-based learning tools, neural networks, and GAs are categorized as machine-learning methods. Visualization is more appropriately classified as a *machine-assisted* aid to support human learning. We describe the six categories in the following paragraphs, focusing on how and when they are used.

Visualization

Data visualization is primarily a discovery technique. Visualization is particularly effective for interpreting large amounts of data because it takes advantage of our natural ability to recognize and distinguish between patterns of observable characteristics. Visualization techniques are effective for condensing large amounts of messy data down to a concise, economic, and comprehensible picture. Those used in data mining range from low-level univariate and bivariate analysis tools, such as simple histograms, box plots, scatter diagrams, and link analysis networks, to more advanced tools, such as rotating, multicolored, three-dimensional surface plots that reveal the subtleties in distributions and relationships involving three or more variables.

Association Rules

Association rules are statements about relationships between the attributes of a known group of individuals and one or more aspects of their behavior. These "rules" enable predictions to be made about the behavior of other individuals who are not in the group but who possess the same attributes. Association rules are always stated in dichotomous terms (e.g., make a purchase or not) and usually assign probability-like numbers to actions.

To see how association rules work, consider the following example: Assume we are interested in promoting a ski parka to phone-in customers who have just finished ordering several other items. Promoting the parka to customers who aren't interested will waste the telephone representative's time and may antagonize some callers. Therefore, we want to restrict the offers to just those callers who have a high probability of buying the parka. This is where association rules come in. They use the information in customer purchase histories to formulate probabilistic rules pertaining to subsequent purchases.

Returning to our example, analysis of purchase records with association rule methods may tell us that callers who purchased ski gloves and wool sweaters on one call were far more likely to buy a parka on a subsequent call than, say, callers who ordered chinos, chamois shirts, or dog beds. Therefore, when the association rules are incorporated in our order entry system and the system sees that the customer on the telephone recently ordered ski gloves and a wool sweater, it can trigger the telephone representative to make the offer on a parka. However, if the system finds that the caller bought a chamois shirt and a pair of chinos on the last call, the built-in decision rules incorporate a low probability of a parka order, and the telephone rep is not prompted to make the parka offer.

Decision Trees

Tree-based methods are the most common implementation of what are usually referred to as "induction" techniques, and according to Elder and Pregibon (1996, p. 100), they "dominate work in KDD, machine learning, and expert system communities." These methods construct decision trees from data automatically, yielding a sequence of stepwise rules, such as "If the household has purchased at least twice in the last six months, assign it to this node of the tree." Tree-based methods are good at identifying important variables, nonlinear relationships, and interactions among predictor variables, and they work well when predictors are numerous and many are irrelevant. They also lend themselves well to visualization and, compared with other data mining tools, are relatively easy for users to understand and interpret. Finally, decision tree algorithms are robust to outliers and erroneous data in the predictors or response variable, and they usually run quickly on all but the largest data sets. Leading examples of decision tree algorithms are CHAID, CART, C4.5, and C5.0.

On the negative side, trees use up data rapidly in the training process, so they should not be used with small data sets. They are also highly sensitive to noise in the data, and they tend to overfit data. Therefore, cross-validation of decision tree results is critical.

Case-Based Reasoning

In CBR systems, sets of attributes of new problem "cases" are compared with corresponding attribute sets in a collection of previously encountered cases to find one or more template-like examples that provide generally good outcomes or solutions. Consider the following example of a CBR system that defines the specifications for potential grocery store sites. In this example, specifications might be square footage, number of checkouts, whether the store has a bakery or deli section, and so on. In the application, the essential attributes of a site (e.g., population density, traffic flow, average household income, average age of household heads) might be compared with the rows in a database that contain corresponding attributes for all of the company's existing stores, together with their design specifications and perhaps performance indexes as well.

With the information provided, the CBR system would identify existing locations whose attributes most closely resemble the attributes of the proposed locations and suggest what design specifications they should incorporate. Of course, it would be unusual for all the attributes of any proposed site to duplicate all the attributes of any one or small group of existing sites, and so some modifications of the potential site's design specification would usually be required to accommodate its unique characteristics. In that respect, the most similar case identified by the system is a template; it is a good model, but it is likely to require modification to meet needs that are not inherent in even the most comparable case in the database.

The CBR systems are effective because they convert abstract concepts into real images, forcing users to focus directly on the similarities and differences between different situations in a structured way using the attributes that define the cases. In addition, CBRs are intuitive and easy to understand; they accommodate discontinuous, lumpy relationships between attributes and qualitative data very well, and they are computationally fast. The primary drawback of CBRs is that the solutions included in the case database may not be optimal in any sense because they represent *what has actually been done* in the past, not necessarily *what should have been done* under similar circumstances. Therefore, using them may simply perpetuate suboptimal solutions. Other limitations of CBRs are the time required to establish and maintain the database and the expertise needed to first identify attributes that are related to specific outcomes and then assign weights so that new situations can be matched to the most appropriate outcomes. A final limitation is that CBRs don't work well when there are significant interactions between attributes.

Neural Networks

Neural networks are computer applications that mimic the processes of the human brain that are capable of learning from examples to find patterns in data. There is a multitude of neural network algorithms available for prediction, classification, and clustering, but the algorithm most commonly applied to the prediction problems marketing researchers encounter in practice is the back propagation feedforward procedure (or "backprop model" for short).

Neural nets are good at combining information from many predictors, and they work well when many of the independent variables are correlated and nonlinearities and missing data cause problems for traditional linear models, such as ordinary least squares regression and discriminant analysis. Neural networks have a significant advantage over regression-type models because they detect nonlinear relationships automatically.

A purported advantage of neural networks relative to procedures whose solutions are easier for users to understand (e.g., logistic regression) is the small amount of time required to adjust models to compensate for changes in the relationships they are supposed to capture. In general, rebuilding regression models to accurately represent changes in the relationships they are thought to model is time consuming. As a result, neural networks are considered especially appropriate in dynamic, fast-changing situations when the relationship between behavior (e.g., customer attrition) and a set of predictors is subject to frequent change.

On the negative side, building the *initial* neural network model can be especially time-intensive, because input processing almost always means that raw data must be transformed, and variable screening and selection requires large amounts of analyst time and skill. Also, for the user without a technical background, figuring out how neural networks operate underneath the hood is far from obvious. An even more serious limitation is that, in contrast to regression, neural nets provide little in the way of explanation of the outcomes they produce; they are said to be *opaque*.

Another limitation of neural networks is that they require large training sets, that is, many data points.[9] This requirement is usually not difficult to fulfill in data mining situations, however. Finally, a confusingly large array of neural network procedures exists, so for anyone other than the neural network expert, the multitude of analysis tools available is bewildering.

Genetic Algorithms

Genetic algorithms operate through procedures modeled on the evolutionary biological processes of selection, reproduction, mutation, and survival of the fittest to search for very good solutions to prediction and classification problems. They are used to solve prediction and classification problems or develop sets of decision rules similar to the rules that can be inferred from the output of decision-tree models.

Genetic algorithms are especially effective for solving poorly understood and poorly structured problems, because they attempt to find many solutions simultaneously, whereas a regression model, for example, attempts to find a single best solution. Another strength of GAs is that they can explicitly model any decision criterion in the "fitness function," an objective system used to assess a GA's performance. For example, a GA can explicitly model maximizing the percentage of responses in the top 20% of a direct marketing lift analysis, something logistic regression cannot do. Another benefit of GAs relative to other procedures that can be applied to the same problem (e.g., logistic regression to a prediction problem) is that they may produce novel solutions. For example, they may discover combinations of predictor variables that no one would have expected to be predictive a priori. A final benefit of GAs is that they can be applied fruitfully in cases in which the user doesn't know enough about analytical procedures to select the most appropriate tool for the job. That is, they tend to be forgiving of a user's lack of technical expertise.

---

[9]A regression model is said to be "estimated" by applying a regression procedure to a data set. However, a neural network model is said to be "trained." Conceptually, estimation and training are analogous. Estimation involves reading sample data and then calculating predictor variable weights by using optimization techniques based on calculus. Training involves reading sample data and iteratively adjusting network weights to produce a best prediction. In either case, when weights are determined, new data can be applied to the model to quickly generate predictions.

Although GA software operates very efficiently on relatively small problems with relatively small numbers of variables and can be run effectively on a PC, it tends to operate slowly when large numbers of variables are included. This happens because of the process of evaluation of the fitness function. Therefore, they are not appropriate for automatic searching through very large numbers of candidate variables to find a subset of variables with relatively high predictive power—a task to which decision trees are especially well suited. In addition, the hands-on work associated with constructing GAs is often quite time-consuming, and many runs may be required in the fitting process. Finally, in contrast to regression models for example, GA solutions are difficult to explain. They do not provide interpretive statistical measures that enable the user to understand why the procedure arrived at a particular solution.

THE KNOWLEDGE DISCOVERY PROCESS

To become productively engaged in knowledge discovery activities, marketing researchers should possess a firm grasp of what these activities entail. Figure 3 is a flow chart of the knowledge discovery process. Happily, as we pointed out at the beginning of the chapter, most marketing researchers have been using the "knowledge discovery" approach for years; they have simply not formalized the set of research activities with a catchy name. Although we couch the ensuing discussion of KDD in data mining terms and employ data mining examples, readers will quickly pick up on the similarities between the procedures data miners follow and what they themselves do. See Fayyad, Piatetsky-Shapiro, and Smyth (1996) and Brachman and Anand (1996) for alternative specifications of the KDD process.

The activities represented by the elements in the diagram are described in the following sections. Although Figure 3 omits feedback loops between elements of the diagram, the reader should understand that the KDD process is "iterative" and that there is a substantial flow of information back to prior steps in the process.

Data Funneling

The data funneling element represents the set of procedures that gathers the data together and ensures their suitability for analysis. This is an important step because when data are badly flawed, even the most sophisticated data mining tools perform badly. *Data mining tools assume high data quality levels*; it is not their purpose to identify, correct, or remove data garbage.

Data funneling operations include the identification of internal operational data and external enhancement data appropriate to the data mining objective. They also include moving the internally generated and enhancement data to a central collection point called a "data repository." Finally, they include procedures for evaluating data quality and request-

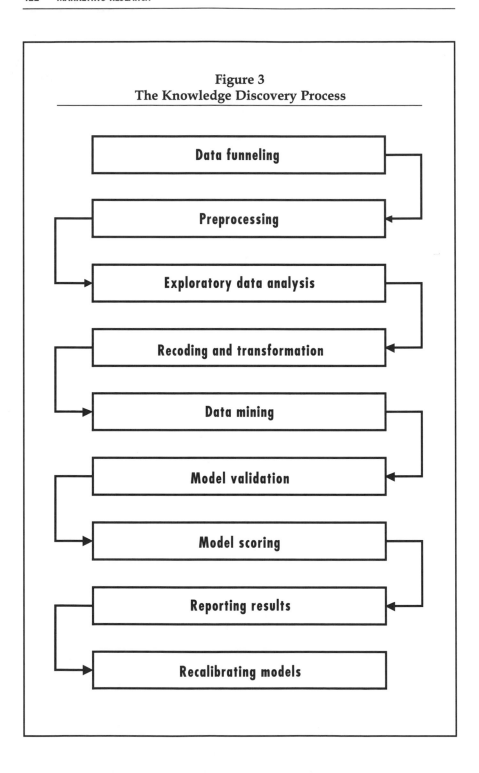

Figure 3
The Knowledge Discovery Process

Data funneling

Preprocessing

Exploratory data analysis

Recoding and transformation

Data mining

Model validation

Model scoring

Reporting results

Recalibrating models

ing that sources retransmit in the event that incoming data do not meet quality standards.

Procedures for assessing data quality include scanning the results by running simple queries, applying basic visualization techniques, and running automatic validation procedures that ensure that incoming data types match expected data types and that individual data items fall within acceptable ranges. Almost all data sets have minor flaws, but it is not the purpose of the screening described here to catch these minor flaws. Rather, its purpose is to identify catastrophic problems, such as data elements that are in the wrong column, numeric elements that have been truncated from seven places to three, or variables that have not been converted from alphabetic representation to numeric. Data funneling also includes selecting the subset of variables to be analyzed from the larger set of all characteristics available in the data repository.

Preprocessing

Data preprocessing includes five operations that ensure that the data mining raw material conforms to input standards:

- ❑ *Reformatting.* Data from different sources are converted to a common format.

- ❑ *Standardization.* It is usually necessary to standardize data attributes, especially text-based attributes, to conform to common external or corporate standard specifications.

- ❑ *Removing sparse records.* When individual records lack data on many important attributes, it makes little sense to retain them in a data mining repository. Thus, specifying criteria for removing sparse records and then physically deleting them from the repository (or making them inaccessible to analysis routines) are important.

- ❑ *Deduplication.* Duplicate instances of the same individual or household resulting from address changes, input keying errors, and fraud are common in databases that are not cleaned regularly. Identifying and removing duplicates is obviously an important preprocessing activity.

- ❑ *Householding.* The natural target unit for many marketing programs is the household rather than the individual. In such cases, individuals must be assigned to households by software that looks for sets of common attributes such as last names, address components, and telephone numbers.

Exploratory Data Analysis

A major purpose of EDA is identifying the anomalies and outliers remaining in a data set after it has passed quality checks and been reformatted and standardized. A second major purpose of EDA is giving the analyst a "sense" or "feel" for the preprocessed data. The analyst looks for largest and smallest values, central tendency (if any), dispersion, the shapes of the distributions of individual variables, and the structure of the relationships among variables. He or she would be on the alert for non-linear relationships and empirical distributions that depart significantly from the classic normal shape. A third major purpose of EDA is the discovery of data patterns and relationships among variables, which suggest hypotheses of cause and effect. Tools that support EDA are query engines such as SQL, descriptive statistics, and visualization techniques.

Recoding and Transformation

In the recoding and transformation phase, some or all preprocessed variables are transformed into new values by, for example, taking their logarithms or square roots or by performing other mathematical operations on their preprocessed values. Preprocessed data may also be recoded into other values using simple decision rules.

Variable transformations are employed to improve the performance of predictive and classification modeling techniques or construct a new predictor or criterion variable whose empirical distribution conforms more closely than the preprocessed variable to an assumed distribution such as the normal. Recoding converts continuous data into a categorical form for use with tools such as neural nets and decision trees, or it converts nominal text label data into numeric values.

Data Mining

This element includes the techniques and algorithms referred to previously as narrow-scope data mining, that is, machine learning from patterns in data performed by the major discovery tools, association rules, decision trees, neural nets, and GAs.

Model Validation

Model validation is another crucial stage in the KDD process because it is the point at which model quality is assessed. Validation is especially critical because a model almost always works better—that is, predicts more accurately—when it is applied to the data set used for estimation or training than when it uses data from an independent sample drawn from the same universe.

A simple approach to model validation is to draw two random samples from the preprocessed data. One sample, usually called the "calibration sample," is used to build the model. The second sample, usually called the "validation" or "holdout" sample, is used to evaluate the model produced using the calibration sample. In general, a well-constructed model produces good results when applied to a validation sample, but some reduction in performance can be expected. It is only when the model performs very poorly—no better than chance, for example—that the analyst must begin the model-building process from scratch.

Model Scoring

In the scoring phase, the validated predictive model or a set of classification rules is applied to the entire database. That is, a model such as $y = b_0 + b_1x_1 + b_2x_2$, developed from a *sample* of the data, is applied to the entire population of records. Scoring is accomplished by substituting corresponding *population* data for the variables (e.g., x_1, x_2, x_3) that were in the sample. The calculated scores, the ys, are placed in a new column in the database.

The predicted values are the *scores*, and the process of applying the equation to the preprocessed variables is called *scoring*. Scoring also refers to the process of coding cluster membership of individual observations when clustering is performed.

Scoring is obviously a crucial step in the KDD process and must be done exactly. Quality assurance is an important four-step supplemental process. First, a set of sample records is selected randomly from the entire database and scored using the newly developed model. Second, these sample records are checked carefully to ensure that the scoring algorithm worked correctly. Third, in a completely separate operation performed under production conditions, the entire database (including the records selected in step 1) is scored with the new model. Fourth, the records matching the sample drawn in step 1 are again pulled from the database and their scores are compared with the scores of the original sample drawn in step 1. The scores of the two samples must match exactly, or the scoring process is defective.

Reporting Results

This stage includes interpreting results and providing support information to decision makers. Decision-support information may be produced in the EDA phase or the discovery phase of data mining, and the results may be in the form of standard paper reports or an electronic document.

Recalibrating the Model

Individual behavior changes, households reconstitute themselves, and the marketing environment of every company evolves, and a model that is best when constructed is unlikely to be best for long. Some models may be productive for two or three years, and others may be useless after only a few months, but all models deteriorate over time. Model recalibration is necessary and should be done regularly and according to a schedule established before the very first model is built. Recalibrating involves rebuilding the model by repeating the model building process with a recently constructed data set. Because business dynamics will cause the data used for recalibration to differ from the data used to build the existing model, the parameters of the recalibrated model will differ from those of the existing model. The recalibrated model may even have a totally different structure—it may include new parameters or its mathematical formulation may differ.

SUMMARY

At the beginning of this chapter, we explained database management systems, the relational model, SQL, and important database concepts. We also described the data warehouse and OLAP systems. Later in the chapter, we defined data mining narrowly and broadly in keeping with existing practice in an emerging industry still groping for its boundaries. We also described the factors driving the data mining revolution and explained why data mining is important to marketing researchers. In addition, we described six of the most commonly used data mining tools, emphasizing how they are used and highlighting their strengths and limitations where appropriate. Finally, the important activities that make up the KDD process were outlined and discussed.

The following reference section was carefully constructed to provide paths to the most important work in the rapidly expanding data mining and KDD fields, while keeping the length of the lists manageable. In addition to individual articles of significance, the suggested readings include several readable and comprehensive overview books on data mining and KDD, several important collections of groundbreaking papers, and two or three well-regarded books focusing on each of the leading data mining methods. Citations are also provided for books on the relational database model and data warehousing. At the end of the reference section, we also provide six Web sites that will lead the patient surfer to every other site connected to data mining and KDD.

BIBLIOGRAPHY

Berry, Michael J.A. and Gordon Linoff (1997), *Data Mining Techniques*. New York: John Wiley & Sons.

Brachman, Ronald J. and Tej Anand (1996), "The Process of Knowledge Discovery in Databases," in *Advances in Knowledge Discovery and Data Mining*, Usama Fayyad et al., eds. Cambridge, MA: AAAI Press/The MIT Press, 37–57.

Dhar, Vasant and Roger Stein (1996), *Seven Methods for Transforming Corporate Data into Business Intelligence*. Upper Saddle River, NJ: Prentice Hall.

Elder, John F. and Daryl Pregibon (1996), "A Statistical Perspective on Knowledge Discovery in Databases" in *Advances in Knowledge Discovery and Data Mining*, Usama Fayyad et al., eds. Cambridge, MA: AAAI Press/The MIT Press, 83–113.

Fayyad, Usama, Gregory Piatetsky-Shapiro, and Padhraic Smyth (1996), "From Data Mining to Knowledge Discovery: An Overview," in *Advances in Knowledge Discovery and Data Mining*, Usama Fayyad et al., eds. Cambridge, MA: AAAI Press/The MIT Press, 1–34.

Goonatilake, Suran and Philip Treleaven (1995), *Intelligent Systems for Finance and Business*. New York: John Wiley & Sons.

Hair, Joseph F. et al. (1995), *Multivariate Data Analysis*, 4th ed. Englewood Cliffs, NJ: Prentice Hall.

Hand, David J. (1998), "Data Mining, Statistics, and More?" *The American Statistician*, 52 (May), 112–18.

———— (1999), "Statistics and Data Mining: Intersecting Disciplines," *SIGKDD Explorations* 1, 1 (June), 16–19.

Kimball, Ralph (1996), *Data Warehouse Toolkit*. New York: John Wiley & Sons.
Peppers, Don and Martha Rogers (1997), *The One to One Future: Building Relationships One Customer at a Time*. New York: Doubleday.
Tukey, John W. (1977), *Exploratory Data Analysis*. Reading, MA: Addison-Wesley.
Weiss, Sholom M. and Nitin Indurkhya (1998), *Predictive Data Mining*. San Mateo, CA: Morgan Kaufmann Publishers.

SUGGESTED READINGS

Agrawal, Rakesh et al. (1996), "Fast Discovery of Association Rules," in *Advances in Knowledge Discovery and Data Mining*, U. Fayyad et al., eds. Cambridge, MA: AAAI Press/The MIT Press, 307–28.
Breiman, Leo et al. (1984), *Classification and Regression Trees*. Belmont, CA: Wadsworth.
Davis, Lawrence (1991), *Handbook of Genetic Algorithms*. New York: Van Nostrand Reinhold.
Fayyad, Usama et al., eds (1996), *Advances in Knowledge Discovery and Data Mining*. Cambridge, MA: AAAI Press/The MIT Press.
Goebel, Michael and Le Gruenwald (1999), "A Survey of Data Mining and Knowledge Discovery Software Tools," *SIGKDD Explorations* 1, 1 (June), 21–33.
Goldberg, David E. (1989), *Genetic Algorithms in Search, Optimization, and Machine Learning*. New York: Addison-Wesley.
Inmon, William (1996), *Building the Data Warehouse*, 2d ed. New York: John Wiley & Sons.
Kolodner, Janet (1993), *Case-Based Reasoning*. San Mateo, CA: Morgan Kaufmann Publishers.
Mitchell, Melanie (1997), *An Introduction to Genetic Algorithms*. Cambridge, MA: The MIT Press.
Piatetsky-Shapiro, Gregory and William Frawley, eds. (1991), *Knowledge Discovery in Databases*. Menlo Park, CA: AAAI Press.
Quinlan, J. Ross (1993), *C4.5: Programs for Machine Learning*. San Mateo, CA: Morgan Kaufmann Publishers.
Teorey, Toby J. (1999), *Database Modeling & Design*, 3d ed. San Francisco: Morgan Kaufmann Publishers.
Thomsen, Erik (1997), *OLAP Solutions: Building Multidimensional Information Systems*. New York: John Wiley & Sons.
Wasserman, Philip D. (1989), *Neural Computing: Theory and Practice*. New York: Van Nostrand Reinhold.
Watson, Ian D. (1997), *Applying Case-Based Reasoning: Techniques for Enterprise Systems*. San Mateo, CA: Morgan Kaufmann Publishers.

SUGGESTED READINGS: DATA MINING LINKS

The following list contains a few links to Web sites that include information about data mining, KDD, and data warehousing. Although many other commercial and noncommercial data mining and KDD Web sites exist, the sites listed should provide paths to all of them. Sites are listed in order of perceived usefulness.

www.kdnuggets.com

www.data-miners.com

www.datamining.org

www.xore.com

home.cnet.com (paste "Data Mining" into the search field)

www.dw-institute.com

Part V
Exploring Extensions

General research techniques can be applied to any functional area. However, each functional area also has its own special problems. For example, international marketing research must take into account cultural differences, pricing research may need to use specialized statistical and econometric models, and measuring equity that is derived from customer relationship may use yet a different set of techniques. Thus, although research techniques are generally common across different functional areas, we also need to add specialized techniques in many cases.

Functional areas in marketing research are endless. To keep the book within a manageable length, I needed to make some compromises. So this section does not cover *all* functional areas. It does not even cover all functional areas that are important. Rather, it covers many of the important functional areas.

Humphrey Taylor (Chapter 16) leads this part with public opinion polls. Should they be banned? What are the issues tackled by opinion polls? What are the methodological issues associated with polls? Can bad polls drive out good?

Roger Wimmer (Chapter 17) addresses issues in advertising research. He provides a critique of current advertising research methods and proposes a three-step research process that includes (1) a comparative rating of an advertisement, (2) the ad's influence in persuading the consumer to buy or rebuy the product/service, and (3) an open-ended description of the advertising message.

Almost all major research houses now have the ability to do international research. Issues in carrying out international marketing research are discussed by Doss Struse (Chapter 18).

An area that has been quietly increasing in importance over the past few decades is the measurement of equity in customer relationships, a topic explored by James Barnes (Chapter 19).

Although in recent years our attention has been increasingly focused on service sectors of the economy, product sectors will always be important. Howard Moskowitz (Chapter 20) reviews different product and package testing techniques.

Pricing is one of the areas of marketing research that makes extensive use of special techniques. David Lyon (Chapter 21) describes several survey-based techniques of marketing research that relate to pricing.

Marketing research is being increasingly used in legal cases, especially in the area of trademark litigation. Ruth Corbin and Neil Vidmar (Chapter 22) survey the role of research in legal disputes.

Each chapter in this part contains many techniques that are specific to the area of inquiry. Taken together, they show the richness of marketing research techniques.

16
Public Opinion Polls

Humphrey Taylor

What Are Opinion Polls?

The words "opinion poll" are used to describe survey research that is intended for publication in the media or for use by politicians, parties, and political candidates. The word "poll" often implies that the research is not conducted as marketing research. To some people, but not the people who conduct them, opinion polls are seen as somehow less serious than "social," "public policy," or marketing research. In reality, opinion polling often requires a degree of accuracy not always required by marketing research.

Whatever else they are, opinion polls are the most visible part of the marketing and survey research industry. When the polls "do well" and accurately predict an election, this is used as evidence that survey research is reliable and can be trusted. When polls do "badly," as they did in the United States in 1948 and in Britain in 1992, and get the election wrong, the survey research industry gets a bad reputation.

Methodologically, therefore, opinion polls are just one application of survey research. However, they measure much more than just opinions. They measure knowledge, behavior ("did you vote?"), future intentions, motivation, salience, preferences, and all the things marketing research surveys measure. It is therefore essential to note that much of what is contained in other chapters of this book is of great relevance to opinion polling. Good survey methodology is just as important to opinion surveys as to all other types of survey research. As with other research, polls can be done well or badly.

This chapter focuses on the use of research to provide results and analysis for publication in the media or for use by political parties and candidates.

THE VALUE OF OPINION POLLS IN A DEMOCRACY

Dictatorships and authoritarian governments usually do not allow the publication of free, independent public opinion surveys. Freely conducted opinion polls often show that governments are unpopular, that the people want change or disagree with some of the policies of their governments, or that, in a free election, governments would lose. Freely conducted preelection and exit polls make it harder for governments to steal elections. Authoritarian and corrupt governments often prevent the publication of poll results that would embarrass them. Even in some democracies, there are recorded examples of governments (including the United States and France) trying to suppress or change the results of polls that they did not like.

The full and free right to conduct opinion surveys and publish the results—regardless of whether these annoy, embarrass, or irritate the political and business establishment—is surely one measure of the freedom of the press and of society generally. That is not to say that all poll results are beneficial to society. Polls provide information, just as economic data or political reporting are information. Polls have shown that the public sometimes supports draconian security measures that many would consider serious violations of important human and civil rights. Polling data, like other information, are value-neutral and can be used to achieve desirable or undesirable objectives.

BANNING THE PUBLICATION OF POLLS

Nevertheless, several countries that consider themselves democracies have banned the publication of election surveys for one, two, or more weeks prior to elections, on the grounds that they have a malign influence on voting behavior. These laws have been triggered by politicians' dislike of (some) poll results and their mistaken belief in bandwagon effects, not by any serious review of the real effects of polls.

The arguments against banning the publication of opinion polls include the following:

❑ Bans violate the freedom of the press (and are therefore unconstitutional in the United States and other countries where press freedom enjoys constitutional or legal protection).

❑ Bans prevent the public from having access to the best (albeit imperfect) information about public opinion without inhibiting the freedom of governments, politicians, and the media to provide dishonest and misleading reports of public opinion.

❑ Much research has failed to demonstrate any persuasive evidence of a bandwagon effect. (However, there is some evidence that polls sometimes have a small effect on turnout; see the section on "The Poll Effect.")

❑ Bans allow political, governmental, and business elite to have access to poll data that the public is legally prevented from reading.

❑ Bans make it much easier for corrupt and dictatorial governments to steal elections and sustain very unpopular policies.

Perhaps the last word on this subject should go to the former British Prime Minister James Callaghan, who wrote that "if people cannot be trusted with opinion polls, they cannot be trusted with the vote" (ESO-MAR 1998, p. 997).

TOPICS FREQUENTLY ADDRESSED IN OPINION SURVEYS

Although opinion polls cover many hundreds of issues, the following is a list of topics frequently addressed by many surveys in many countries:

❑ Politics and public policy
  ❑ Voting intentions;
  ❑ Popularity and performance of government, parties, and political leaders;
  ❑ Importance of different political issues;
  ❑ Government's handling of different issues;
  ❑ Parties' and candidates' abilities to handle different issues;
  ❑ Economic priorities and expectations; and
  ❑ Political crises and scandals.
❑ Specific political issues
  ❑ The economy,
  ❑ Inflation,
  ❑ Unemployment (and job creation),
  ❑ Taxes,
  ❑ Education,
  ❑ Health care,
  ❑ Crime,
  ❑ Environment, and
  ❑ Foreign policy events and issues.
❑ Controversial social issues
  ❑ Death penalty,
  ❑ Abortion,

❑ Euthanasia/doctor-assisted suicide,

❑ Privacy,

❑ Homelessness,

❑ Gay and lesbian rights,

❑ Immigration,

❑ Sports and entertainment,

❑ Popularity (viewing and participation) of different sports, and

❑ Popularity of television/film stars/singers/sports stars and other celebrities.

❑ Societal trends

❑ Confidence in leadership and institutions,

❑ Alienation, and

❑ Prestige/status of different occupations/professions.

❑ Events

❑ Public attitudes and reactions to wars, tragic deaths, and national disasters.

❑ Lifestyles

❑ Leisure activities and hobbies;

❑ Retirement;

❑ Computer use, the World Wide Web, and the Internet;

❑ Smoking;

❑ Exercise;

❑ Nutrition;

❑ Obesity, dieting, and weight control; and

❑ Women and work.

QUOTA SAMPLING VERSUS PROBABILITY SAMPLING

Since the U.S. pollsters debacle of 1948, when the (few) polls that were published indicated a likely Thomas Dewey presidential victory when Harry S Truman actually won, quota sampling has been discredited in the United States. Virtually all public opinion surveys conducted in-person (face-to-face) or by telephone in the United States since then have used some modified version of probability (or random) sampling. Indeed, for U.S. researchers, quota sampling is almost a dirty phrase.

The situation in Europe and in much of the rest of the world has been quite different. The great majority of face-to-face opinion surveys, including election surveys, conducted in France, Germany, Italy, the United Kingdom, and other European countries and in Latin America have used some form of quota sampling, and the interviewers are given considerable latitude to find and select respondents who fit the quota cells (usually based on sex, age, one or two socioeconomic factors, and other variables). Giving the interviewers this freedom to select whom to survey is usually unacceptable in the United States, but the European quota method has worked reasonably well for many years and has been widely accepted, not only by practitioners and their clients, but also by many European academic researchers, something Americans find very puzzling.

The debate about quota versus probability (random) sampling has diminished as telephone surveys have replaced face-to-face surveys for much opinion research. Although many European researchers describe their telephone surveys as quota samples, the interviewers almost always start with a list of telephone numbers selected (however imperfectly) by some more or less random method. The interviewers are no longer as free to pick whom they want to interview.

FACE-TO-FACE AND TELEPHONE SURVEYS: ADVANTAGES AND DISADVANTAGES

In countries with a high telephone penetration—in which well over 90% of all adults live in homes that can be reached by telephone—the advantages of conducting opinion surveys by telephone generally outweigh their disadvantages.

The advantages of telephone surveys over face-to-face surveys generally include (with some national variations)

❏ Lower cost per interview,

❏ Speed (the data can be collected and analyzed faster),

❏ The absence of clustering (there are no benefits to clustering telephone surveys),

❏ The ability to make many callbacks (or recalls) to numbers that do not reply or for which the designated respondent is not available,

❏ The ease of attempting "refusal conversions," and

❏ The relative ease of calling back the same respondent for panel studies.

However, there are many countries where it still is not possible to conduct good telephone surveys. These are countries where:

❏ Telephone penetration is 90% or less (currently only approximately 20 countries have 90% penetration), and

❏ It is necessary to conduct a "secret ballot" because people lie or refuse to reply to the key questions (e.g., voting intention).

It should be noted that in some countries, it is difficult to obtain reliable data on telephone penetration.

A 1996/1997 survey (*Journal of the Market Research Society* 1998) of 83 major survey research firms in 17 countries with high telephone penetration, where most telephone surveys are conducted, found that 45% of these firms believed telephone surveys were more accurate than face-to-face surveys. Only 16% believed face-to-face surveys were more accurate; most of the remainder believed that face-to-face and telephone surveys were equally good.

QUALITATIVE RESEARCH

As with other research applications, opinion research can make good use of qualitative techniques, such as focus groups (discussion groups) and one-to-one in-depth interviews. However, qualitative research does not provide data or percentages and is not a substitute for survey research.

The use of focus groups by private political pollsters working for parties and candidates is widespread. These are often used to test ideas, words, and phrases and to measure reactions to political events and initiatives that politicians might make. Qualitative research is a very valuable tool for improving questionnaire design and developing new hypotheses, but caution should be used in drawing conclusions from qualitative work that has not been confirmed by survey research. Unfortunately, the results of qualitative research are often believed to provide solid evidence of how the general public is thinking or will react, when experience points to the often unrepresentative nature of the small groups of people who agree to participate.

TRACKING SURVEYS

The words "tracking polls" are used to describe frequently repeated surveys that track changes in voting intentions and other key variables. These are often daily tracking surveys, with new data published each day. They were first used in 1970 in Britain but are now widely used in the United States and elsewhere.

Tracking surveys use a variety of different techniques, of which the most frequent are

- ❏ One-day surveys, in which a complete, separate sample is surveyed each day, and
- ❏ Two- or three-day surveys, which may be published separately or as some form of moving average.

There are good reasons for believing that many tracking surveys are less accurate than stand-alone surveys, though there is no inherent reason (except perhaps the cost) they should be. The reasons they are sometimes less accurate include the use of smaller samples and the completion of fieldwork in only one or two days, which tends to produce less effective samples than surveys conducted over three or more days with multiple callbacks.

CRITICAL METHODOLOGICAL ISSUES FOR TELEPHONE SURVEYS OF THE PUBLIC

Opinion surveys, like all surveys, are as good or as bad as the methods used. It should be stressed that though there are clearly many good and bad practices, there are many other methodological issues for which there is no established "best practice." It is noteworthy that the 1996/1997 survey (*Journal of the Market Research Society* 1998) of 83 leading marketing research firms in 17 countries where telephone surveys of the public are widely used, referred to previously, did not find even 2 firms using exactly the same methods. This was true even of 10 leading firms in the United States.

The following is a review of methodological issues that opinion researchers may find useful in improving their methods.

Telephone Penetration

Is the percentage of adults accessible by telephone well over 90%? (If not, there are doubts about the accuracy of telephone surveys.)

Given that those who cannot be reached by telephone are always very different from those who can, what weighting (or other adjustments) should be made to correct the data for nontelephone households?

Random Digit Dialing (RDD)

Although some pollsters have used directories and other lists of publicly available telephone numbers, it is hard to justify not using RDD. There are data showing that people with unlisted numbers are different from people with listed numbers.

Method Used to Select Individual

There are several generally acceptable ways to select the individuals in households called who are to be interviewed.

Some of these methods attempt to give each eligible adult an equal probability of selection. These include a random selection grid (based on some kind of household roster), the next (or most recent) birthday rule, and the use of listed individuals in a few countries where such lists are available.

The other major category of methods attempts to achieve an interview with someone who is at home, while reducing the biases that arise from availability and answering the telephone. These include the so-called youngest male and the rotation youngest methods, which give some degree of preference to younger and/or male adults (who tend to be less available), as well as various forms of quotas to control for demographic variables.

Pure probability methods tend to achieve far too many interviews with older and female adults and require substantial weighting to correct for these biases. Some random selection grids compensate for this problem by intentionally giving younger people and men a higher probability of selection.

Another major problem with pure probability methods is that they achieve interviews in fewer households, and therefore have a lower response rate, than methods that attempt to interview someone who is at home.

The major problem with the nonprobability methods is that they have a strong bias against people who are less often at home and in favor of availability. If availability at home is correlated with any of the key variables being investigated (e.g., use of hotels, airlines, restaurants), it can be a serious source of error. Fortunately, it seems that for many opinion research topics, including voting intentions, there is usually little or no correlation with availability.

Number of Callbacks (Recalls)

Many calls to residential telephone numbers go unanswered. In surveys in which probability methods are used to select the individual, the designated respondent is often not at home. The quality of the sample is therefore critically dependent on the number of times numbers (and/or individuals) are called. However, after several callbacks, such calls tend to produce few new interviews and become expensive. Depending on the importance of the survey and the time available, most polling firms make three or more callbacks on different days (and sometimes at different times).

Major surveys for government agencies and academic research often require many more callbacks, but most published analyses show that these have only a small impact on the final results. The numbers usually do not change significantly because of calls beyond the third or fourth call.

However, a major criticism of surveys conducted over one or two days is that they use few (sometimes no) callbacks and can be seriously biased as a result.

The Use of Demographic Controls (Quotas) During Fieldwork

The 1996/1997 survey already quoted (*Journal of the Market Research Society* 1998) found that virtually all survey firms, including those that describe their methods as "probability sample," use some controls as quotas to reduce biases that would occur otherwise. The most commonly used controls are region, sex (gender), age, and size of place. Some firms also control the sample by occupation, working/not working, education, and (for example, in Canada or Belgium) language.

Refusal Conversion

Refusal rates are a very serious concern and a growing problem in many countries, probably as a direct result of the growth of telemarketing. It is clearly good practice to attempt to convert such refusals. Many firms use supervisors or specially trained interviewers to recall refusals and attempt to convert them so that interviews can be completed.

Weighting

Opinion surveys, like all survey research, produce data with identifiable errors that can, and usually should, be corrected by weighting. These weights may come from census data and/or very high-quality surveys by government agencies or the private sector.

Variables that are widely used to weight opinion surveys include geography (region, big cities, size of place), sex, age, occupation, education, and (in fewer countries) income, race/ethnicity, and working/not working.

Two other types of weight are sometimes used to correct for inevitable design biases; these are number of adults per household (in most surveys in which only one person per household is interviewed, there is a serious bias against people in large households) and (in countries where many homes have two or more telephone lines that can receive incoming calls) the number of telephone lines (numbers) that could be called.

HOW TO JUDGE THE QUALITY OF POLITICAL OPINION SURVEYS CONDUCTED BY TELEPHONE

Telephone surveys are relatively new in many countries. In the United States, almost all public opinion and election polls have been conducted by telephone since 1980. Many of the painful lessons learned in the United States are not being applied in some other countries. Furthermore, in many countries, telephone penetration (i.e., the percentage of people who live in homes where they can be reached by a telephone survey) is lower than it is in the United States, Canada, and several European countries. Adjusting the sample to compensate for people without telephones is a tricky business.

The 1996/1997 survey (*Journal of the Market Research Society* 1998) produced some startling results. One is that no 2 firms among all the 83 leading companies use identical methods. Clearly there is no consensus on best practices. Some of the differences reflect genuine national differences (e.g., different socioeconomic data are more suitable for weighting in some countries than in others). Others seem, to this author at least, to be the result of what looks like gross incompetence—for example, failure to use RDD, to make three or more calls, to include the weekend in the interviewing period, and to weight to adjust for serious biases in all telephone surveys (e.g., number of adults in household, the shortfall in very low-income households). Response rates vary greatly from firm to firm.

Therefore, the following are 11 questions the intelligent poll-watcher should ask. Although there are right and wrong answers to almost all of these questions, genuine and legitimate differences still exist on some of them. However, the polling firms' replies to these questions will tell the questioner a great deal. The good firms will have thought about these questions already and will have sensible answers to them, not only for what they do, but also for why they do it. Some, alas, will probably be addressing them for the first time.

❑ Who paid for the survey (if the payer has a vested interest in the results, look for confirmation from independent polls)?

❑ What list of telephone numbers is used? Does it include all telephone exchanges and numbers currently used, listed and exdirectory (unlisted) numbers?

❑ How is the sample drawn from this list? Does it give all residential numbers an equal probability of selection? Is it limited to numbers in directories, or is RDD used?

❑ How is the individual to be interviewed in the household selected? How is a balance between completing an interview in the household and avoiding a bias because of availability achieved?

❑ How many calls are made to each selected number to try to complete an interview? Are they made over several days at different times?

❑ When is the interviewing done? Does it cover at least three days and include evenings and weekends?

❑ What biases are there in the raw data? Typically, telephone surveys underrepresent poor people, people in large households, and people often away from home.

❑ How are the raw data weighted? Are they weighted by size of household, class or other socioeconomic variables, sex, or age? A key question (where there is much disagreement) is whether to weight by claimed prior voting.

❑ What is the response rate? How many residential numbers (or numbers that may be residential or business) do not reply? How many refusals are there?

❑ How do survey firms compensate for nontelephone households? Do they do more than weight by socioeconomic variables?

And, for preelection surveys:

❑ Do they compensate directly or indirectly for two probable causes of error in the 1992 U.S. presidential election: differential refusal and late swing? If so, how? How do they adjust their final predictions for differential turnout? How do they measure, directly or indirectly, likelihood of voting, and how do they use these data in their final predictions?

INTERNET-BASED POLLS

In 1998, Internet-based surveys were used to attempt to predict the results of 23 U.S. state elections for governor or senator (*Public Perspective* 1999). The predictions made were about as good as the telephone surveys conducted before these elections but not as good as the telephone polls conducted by a major polling firm before recent presidential elections. These are very early days for Internet-based surveys, and it is too soon to know how accurate they may be in a few years as their methods improve.

It is already clear, however, that the words "Internet poll" are being used to describe a wide variety of completely different activities. Many so-called Internet polls make no attempt to develop a representative sample or correct for the many biases in the new data collected online — but some do. Many of these so-called polls are conducted by people or organizations with no experience or expertise in conducting public opinion surveys by telephone, in-person, or any other means — but some are. Most of these so-called polls are conducted by people or organizations that produce no evidence that their results are representative and have no track record of providing reliable survey data — but, here again, there are a few exceptions.

Some critics of Internet-based polling point out that all such surveys must rely on self-selected "volunteer samples" or "convenience samples" and that, because they are not based on probability sampling, they are inherently unreliable. Some proponents of Internet-based polling argue that, over time, we will learn enough about the biases in online data to be able to weight them to correct for the biases that are surely there. Time will tell who is right.

What is clear is that there are huge differences between the better and the worse online "polls" and that these words are often used to describe the replies given by samples that are completely unrepresentative.

SOCIAL DESIRABILITY

A massive source of error in some surveys is the "social desirability bias," in which people claim to do or believe things they do not do or believe. Consciously or unconsciously, some respondents are lying. For example, there is strong evidence that more people than actually do so report that they regularly:

- ❑ Go to church,
- ❑ Clean their teeth,

❏ Have baths or showers,
❏ Wash their hands after using the lavatory/bathroom, and
❏ Are not racist.

In the absence of other data, replies to questions such as these should be treated with considerable skepticism.

In some countries, people have been reluctant to admit to voting for some candidates or parties. Examples include Northern Ireland (where some extreme nationalist and loyalist supporters have apparently lied to pollsters) and several "new democracies" where more people have said they would support government parties than did so. In the United States and Britain, there are examples of people who are apparently unwilling to tell pollsters they would vote against black candidates or for racist ones.

SOME POLLS EXAGGERATE THE NUMBERS OF PEOPLE WITH OPINIONS

Many people ask questions of the public without determining whether people previously had **any** opinion on this topic. This can mislead readers into believing that most people have an opinion when they do not. An easy way to address this problem is to include, as a filter or as an analytical variable, a question asking whether people have "seen, read, or heard" about the topic in question. The large numbers who often do not — who therefore know nothing about issues of burning interest to politicians and the media — often shock and surprise the political elite.

THE "MARGIN OF ERROR" IN POLLS

If ever there was an example of a little knowledge being a dangerous thing, it is the use, by the media, of statements such as "the margin of error for this survey is plus or minus 3%." The truth is that we have no measure of the margin of error; all we have is a theoretical measure of random sampling error if (and only if) we have a pure random sample with 100% response, a perfectly designed questionnaire, no interviewer bias, and completely truthful respondents. We have no way of calculating the probabilities, let alone a maximum possible "margin" of error. Pollsters should tell the media that all surveys, like all censuses, are subject to possible errors that, in the real world, cannot be quantified. The use of the words "margin of error" only misleads people into believing that the survey must be accurate to within the statistical "margin," which of course is not true.

A further problem: Estimates of possible sampling errors assume probability sampling. They should not be applied to quota sampling, Internet-based surveys, or other nonprobability samples. Nor should they be applied to probability samples with substantial nonresponse (which means most of them).

Does that mean that polls have no value? Of course not. The average "error" in all nationwide U.S. polls since 1952 (i.e., the differences between their final estimates of support for major candidates and the actual results) is less than 2% — a pretty good track record. Sometimes the errors have been larger, sometimes they have been smaller. This empirical measure of accuracy, not a measure based on theoretically perfect probability sampling, is much more helpful to readers of the polls.

THREE SOURCES OF ERROR THAT ARE UNIQUELY RELEVANT TO PREELECTION SURVEYS

In addition to the many potential sources of error in all survey research, including all opinion surveys, there are three that are of special relevance to preelection forecasts. These are late swing, differential turnout (or differential abstention), and the poll effect.

Late Swing

Preelection surveys do not actually "forecast." They measure likely voting intentions, and pollsters have generally assumed that these will not change between their final surveys and election day. But there is much evidence that changes in voting intention, including likelihood of voting at all, continue right up to the time that voting is completed.

Fortunately for the pollsters and the research industry, net voting intentions usually do not change much in the last two or three days of most elections; much of the change that does take place is self-canceling, so that the net change is much smaller than the gross change. However, there have been many elections in which parties and candidates appeared to gain or lose ground right up to election day, so that all published polls were out-of-date and reflected voting intentions that subsequently changed.

It is worth noting that this is not a measurement error, but a forecasting error, and polls are judged not on their measurements but on the accuracy of their election forecasts.

There are two main ways to minimize the likelihood of error due to late swing. One is to conduct the final survey as late as possible (but consistent with the even more vital need to obtain a good sample, which normally requires at least three days in the field). The other is to reinterview as many of the people surveyed as possible on the eve of the election day. The results of the last full (i.e., high-quality) survey can then be adjusted by any swings that are detected by the eve-of-poll interviews. (It is important not to use these eve-of-poll interviews by themselves; the sampling biases in such a very fast survey are usually too great.)

Differential Turnout (or Differential Abstention)

It is often said, and it is probably true, that measuring **how** people will vote is much easier than measuring **if** people will vote. Almost all preelection surveys report more people saying they will (or are likely to) vote than actually do so on election day. This may not matter (i.e., it might not affect the accuracy of the final forecast) if the proportion of potential voters for all the candidates or parties who actually vote is the same. But that is often not the case, and pollsters must try to estimate who will and who will not vote. Failure to do this well can make, and often has made, the difference between accurate and inaccurate election forecasts. Indeed, it may well be the single most important source of bad forecasts by otherwise professional and competent researchers.

Several types of questions have been used successfully to help determine the likelihood of potential voters actually voting. These may be used to "screen in" likely votes and "screen out" the rest (i.e., every likely voter has a weight of one, and the rest have a weight of zero). They may also be used to calculate a likelihood of voting (e.g., any number between one and zero), which is then applied to every potential voter. There is no published empirical evidence as to which method consistently works better. Questions that have been used successfully to predict the likelihood of voting include voter registration, prior voting, a likelihood of voting scale, the perceived importance of the election result, and knowledge of where to vote.

The Poll Effect

There is no persuasive evidence that polls create a bandwagon effect or an anti-bandwagon effect, and much evidence that they generally do not.

However, there is some evidence, which is by no means conclusive, that opinion polls published immediately before an election have sometimes had a modest effect on turnout. This effect, if it exists, seems to occur in some elections when the public believes that the leading party or candidate will win with a large majority. And, of course, polls contribute substantially to perceptions of who will win and by how much. The anticipation of a landslide victory seems to depress turnout slightly.

In several elections in several countries, there are survey data that suggest that the winner's majority was slightly reduced because some of the winner's potential voters did not vote because they did not believe their votes were necessary (and, of course, they were right).

This poll effect, if it occurs, is a contributor to the problem of differential turnout; it appears to reduce the turnout of the winner's supporters slightly more than the turnout of the loser's supporters. One reason it has this differential impact is that the winner's supporters tend to believe the polls (that their candidate or party has a big lead), whereas the loser's supporters tend to disbelieve the polls and turn out to vote because they think the race is closer than it is.

POLLING FOR THE MEDIA AND PRIVATE POLITICAL POLLING

Polls done for publication in the media and polls done for politicians differ greatly, even if they use most of the same techniques. Polling for the media is intended to provide "a story" that is newsworthy. Many media commission polls because they make exclusive news and are often reported (so-called secondary reporting) by other media, thereby publicizing the newspaper or television station that commissioned the research.

Responsible pollsters who conduct research for the media are concerned that their work should provide reliable, relevant information. They subscribe to codes of conduct that are designed to encourage the publication of information that adds to public knowledge and does not mislead.

The goals of pollsters who work for politicians, parties, or candidates are very different. They are working to get their clients elected or reelected. Their public utterances and the release of data from their surveys are usually intended to help their clients, not to inform the public. Information released by private pollsters should therefore be treated with great caution by the media. Media reports of private polling should always warn the reader that it may be dangerously misleading if not (as has happened) factually wrong. In 1997, a well-known Republican pollster was censured by AAPOR, the American professional association for survey research, for repeatedly misleading the media and the public about his private poll results in the 1994 election campaign.

PROMOTIONAL (OR CORPORATE LEADERSHIP) SURVEYS: RESEARCH AS A CORPORATE PUBLIC RELATIONS VEHICLE

Public opinion surveys are often commissioned and published by corporations. These surveys are designed to generate widespread media coverage, to provide new information of interest to the sponsoring corporations' customers, to strengthen the sponsors' images, and, in many instances, to provide materials that enhance the sponsors' sales and marketing efforts.

These surveys are often called promotional surveys, but they are quite different from the more obviously self-serving research studies that provide information about consumers who buy, use, or value the companies' products or services. Promotional surveys are not marketing research; they provide their sponsors with little or no marketing information. They provide the public and key audiences of the sponsors with original, interesting, and often useful information.

Marketing researchers are not sure how to describe this use of surveys. It is not marketing research, the purpose of which is to develop and improve competitive marketing strategies. It is not the usual kind of self-serving research that is sometimes published by companies to prove how much people love their products, read their magazines, or support their lobbying positions. And it is not really social or public policy research. The phrase "promotional research" is quite widely used to describe this application of survey research.

Over the years, the use of promotional surveys has grown and developed to the point where it is a recognized arrow in the quiver of many corporate public relations executives and public relations firms in the United States and, to a lesser extent, elsewhere.

The purpose of this research is to increase the visibility and enhance the reputation of corporate sponsors with one or more audiences. Promotional surveys are designed to be published and reported widely, not to inform the sponsoring companies but to interest and attract the audiences they want.

Because these surveys are not marketing research, they are usually paid for out of advertising or public relations budgets. They are an alternative to advertising as a way of reaching key publics with a favorable message about the sponsor.

What benefits do corporate sponsors obtain from these surveys? Promotional surveys are designed to provide them with some or all of the following benefits:

- ❑ Widespread coverage in national, regional, and trade media, including newspapers, magazines, television, and radio. One CEO reported that a single survey costing approximately $150,000 had bought him as much favorable publicity and attention as he would have obtained with $10 million worth of advertising. Surveys commissioned and funded by U.S. companies have been featured many times on such television shows as the *Today Show, Good Morning America,* and evening news programs and in publications such as the *New York Times, The Wall Street Journal, The Washington Post, Time,* and *Newsweek.*

- ❑ The enhancement of the image of the corporation as a responsible leader in its field, providing important and valuable information that is not available from any other source.

- ❑ The strengthening of the image of the corporation as uniquely attentive and responsive to the needs of the public or of their customers. Corporate sponsors can claim that, through such surveys, they are empowering the group surveyed, whether it be the public, small businesses, teachers, or physicians, and making their voices heard to the media and policymakers.

- ❑ The opportunity to make uniquely important speeches and presentations of the survey results to conventions, trade groups, or conferences.

- ❑ The opportunity to place bylined articles in prestigious publications using the survey findings as a platform.

- ❑ As a sales tool that provides their salesforce with a unique door-opener and conversation piece. Insurance companies have given survey reports to risk managers and human resources executives; accounting firms, bankers, and management consultants have used them to get the attention of corporate CEOs; drug companies have sent them to physicians.

❑ The opportunity to present unique information to the White House and federal and state legislators. Special presentations have been arranged to present these surveys to meetings in the White House. Many of these surveys have been used in testimony to congressional committees.

❑ Making top management into celebrities. The CEOs of sponsoring companies have used promotional surveys to greatly increase their visibility and standing with industry groups, government, and the media.

What Promotional Surveys Are Not

It is often necessary to remind corporate sponsors that these surveys are not lobbying surveys designed to prove a point — for example, that the great majority of the public supports the company's position on a piece of proposed legislation. These surveys should not include any questions about the client (e.g., a survey that says that nine out of ten people prefer your product is not what we call a promotional survey). Although the purpose of a promotional or corporate leadership survey is to promote the interests of the sponsor, it should be designed as a "gift to the nation" and not to serve the narrow self-interests of the clients. Obviously, it does serve the sponsor's interest (otherwise why pay for it?). But it does this by making sponsors look like industry leaders, not hucksters.

USING POLLS TO INFLUENCE AND MISLEAD

Many polling firms have been asked by trade associations, companies, special interest groups, and lobbyists to conduct public opinion surveys that are intended for only one purpose: to persuade policymakers and legislators that the voters support their position. Some surveys of this type are honestly conducted and show that the public does support the client's position (or if they do not, they are never published). But some such surveys are carefully designed to produce the results the clients want and, indeed, to mislead.

A skillful researcher can write a questionnaire that, because of the way the questions are asked or their order, can produce results that may mislead unwary legislators into believing public opinion is strongly supportive of a positive when it is not. There are many clients willing to pay for this misleading research. A common abuse is to show the public as having opinions, because respondents answered the question, when they have never heard about or addressed the issue before they were asked about it.

Pollsters need to be on their guard against this abuse of polling and be willing to forgo the easy profits they can earn from it.

REPORTING AND INTERPRETING THE RESULTS: THE ROLE OF THE OPINION RESEARCHER

A debate for which there is no consensus concerns the appropriate role of the opinion pollster. George Gallup used to say that his role was to publish the data—the survey results—and that everybody should be free to interpret them in their own way. Louis Harris was the first of many pollsters who believed that, as experts in public opinion research, they had an obligation to tell the lay reader, including the media and politicians, what the data meant. This school of thought (to which the author subscribes) believes that there are many occasions when the expert, professional researcher is in a much better position to discuss the meaning of the data and interpret the results than someone who is not a professional pollster.

This is an important distinction. Answering the "what if?" and the "so what?" questions and discussing the implications of the results is often much more important than just reporting the results.

Many people who read the polls want to know more than the results; they want to know what the results mean for the future. Politicians want to know how the public will react to events and to steps they may or may not take. This interpretation goes far beyond reporting the data; it is essentially a matter of judgment. The experienced pollster should be better qualified than the layperson to make reliable judgments about his or her survey data.

POLLS ARE OFTEN A MISLEADING GUIDE TO FUTURE PUBLIC OPINION

Politicians who read the polls (and which do not?) to help them decide which policies to support should beware. Although well-conducted polls are the only reliable way to measure current public opinion, they are unreliable predictors of future opinion for two reasons. First, public opinion sometimes changes dramatically; today's polls measure only what people are thinking now. Second, the public itself is not good at predicting how it will react to future or hypothetical events.

This lesson was driven home forcefully by the 1991 Gulf War. The war had four phases: the invasion of Kuwait by Iraq, the U.S. and Allied build-up and economic sanctions, the air war, and finally the ground war.

Seven polling organizations in the United States that conducted surveys just before the air war started all reported that less than 50% (between 44 and 49%) of Americans favored immediate military action, whereas a similar or slightly higher proportion favored allowing more time for sanctions to work. Immediately after the air war began, opinion changed dramatically. The polls reported that between 68 and 84% of the public approved the decision to go to war, whereas those who favored waiting had dropped to between 13 and 26%.

Just before the ground war began, public opinion clearly preferred a continuation of the air war to an invasion. For example, a CBS/*New York Times* poll reported that a massive 79% majority wanted the coalition to "continue with mainly bombing from the air," whereas only 11% favored "beginning the ground war soon" (Taylor 1991). But 11 days later, another CBS/*New York Times* poll reported that a huge 75% majority believed that it was "right to start the ground war" when it was started. Events, not the public's previous expectations, shaped public opinion. In politics, as in much else, nothing succeeds like success or fails like failure.

Long-time students of polls will not find this volatility surprising. A similar pattern of polling data was reported in Britain before, during, and after the Falkland Islands War. Before the first shots were fired, as British forces sailed south, polls showed that most people believed that Prime Minister Margaret Thatcher would not be justified in using force if even very few British lives were lost. In the event, more than 250 were killed, including the sailors who burned to death in the floating inferno of the frigate Sheffield. But, far from flinching, public opinion quickly became overwhelmingly supportive of the military option.

Politicians and their pollsters need to understand that poll data can easily mislead them into making bad decisions, in part because hypothetical questions about how people may react to events in the future are bad predictors of public opinion.

It has been widely reported, and not denied, that early in 1998, when the Monica Lewinsky scandal first broke in the United States, Dick Morris presented President Clinton with a survey that persuaded him that if he admitted to having had an affair with the White House intern, the public would not forgive him. The president decided, apparently with Dick Morris's encouragement, that his best strategy was to deny it, which led indirectly to charges of perjury and obstruction of justice—and his impeachment.

With hindsight, we can see that this was not only unethical, but also terrible political judgment. Dick Morris was quite wrong about public opinion. The public was much more willing to forgive the president for his sex life than for lying to the public under oath. Although most Americans did not want to see him impeached or removed from office, they have not forgiven him for what they believe was perjury and obstruction of justice. His survival depended on having unpopular adversaries who were widely viewed as mean-spirited and "out to get" the president and on the strong economy and low crime rates.

Commercial marketing researchers have known for years not to rely on consumers' own predictions of what they will do or think in the future. In the 1950s, George Katona, at the University of Michigan, demonstrated that many people who say they will buy something will not do so, whereas many others who say they will not buy it will (Taylor 1991). This is equally true when it comes to politics.

CAN BAD POLLS DRIVE OUT GOOD?

To many of the media, a poll is a poll is a poll. "Newsworthiness," not quality or accuracy, determines which polls get reported. The following are some points to watch for:

❏ An unexpected poll finding is more surprising, and hence more "newsworthy," than one that confirms what other polls also report. Bad (i.e., inaccurate) polls are more likely to be surprising and therefore more likely to be reported. Bad polls are cheaper than good polls. A survey of 500 people is less expensive than a survey of 1000. A poll with very few questions is cheaper than one with more questions. High-quality sampling and interviewing cost more than poor-quality, and so on. If the media will report findings regardless of their quality, why spend money on better polls?

❏ One-day "instant" polls are generally much less accurate than polls conducted over three or four days because of all the people they miss. But the media love them because they are the "first with the news" about public reactions to events.

❏ Television call-in polls are not polls. The people who are watching the television shows and choose to telephone in their answers are often very different from the population as a whole.

❏ Poll results are the answers to questions and are therefore critically dependent on the wording and, sometimes, on the order of the questions. Never interpret the results without reading the questions carefully.

❏ Opinion on most issues is more complicated than a yes/no to one or two questions. Polls inevitably simplify and categorize. To really understand public opinion on any issue, from abortion to economic policy, it is necessary to review the answers to a variety of questions addressing the issue in different ways.

❏ A poll is valid only for the population surveyed and for the time of the survey. Surveys of adults, registered voters, or likely voters will all yield different answers.

❏ Qualitative focus groups are not polls. Getting eight to ten people in a room to talk together has many uses, but it does not provide a measure of public opinion as does surveying a representative cross-section of people.

❏ Candidates' polls are often misleading. Polls are leaked not to inform but to influence the media and the public.

❏ Polls do not really predict, they just measure. Good polls report what a representative cross-section of the public (or of likely voters) say when interviewed. The only reason that preelection polls "predict" elections is that most people tell the interviewers how they think they will vote and then actually vote that way. But some people change their minds, and some of those who say they will vote do not. The difference between intentions and behavior, not sampling error, is the main reason good polls sometimes get it wrong.

Does that mean that all polls are worthless? Obviously not. We are better informed with polls than we were without them. But poll readers should recognize that polls differ dramatically in quality and accuracy and that those who pay for and publish polls have differing motives. If nobody cares about the quality of polling, Gresham's law will apply, and cheap and bad polls will drive out good ones.

THE INFLUENCE OF THE POLLS

Historically, many professional pollsters have responded defensively to charges that somehow polls have a negative effect on the democratic process or that they influence elections. Others have argued that polls provide information, which is value-neutral and may, like other information, have positive or negative consequences. In his book *British Public Opinion*, Robert Worcester (1991), of MORI, wrote, "Do polls influence behavior? I believe they do, and I believe this is a good thing."

In the early days of polling, the biggest debate was about a possible bandwagon effect—that voters would rush, lemming-like, to support whichever party or candidate the polls showed to be ahead. Many politicians still seem to fear that this will happen, even though the bandwagon theory is totally discredited. If there was such as effect, polls would systematically underestimate the margin of victory as voters switched their votes to back the leader. If, as others have suggested, there was an anti-bandwagon effect, with voters "voting against the polls," preelection surveys would systematically overestimate the margin of victory as voters switched away from the leaders. Even a cursory review of preelection survey results (not to mention much academic research) is enough to discredit both theories.

However, common sense suggests that opinion polls can, and often do, have the following effects on the political process:

❑ They influence the political agenda. Topics that the polls show the public believes are important get more attention from politicians and the media.

❑ They influence the policies advocated (and sometimes adopted) by governments and politicians.

❑ In the United States and other countries where fund-raising is substantial, they influence the ability of candidates to raise money. People are more reluctant to give money to a candidate with little support in the polls.

❑ They influence the campaign strategies and tactics of parties and politicians who use public and private polls to hone their campaign messages to win votes.

❏ They influence the media reporting of election campaigns. The media often report that the leading candidates are fighting skillful campaigns and that the others are politically incompetent or disorganized.

❏ They become the news, forcing other campaigns' stories and election reporting off the front page.

A review of this list suggests that published polls have much in common with other political reporting and news that can help or harm causes, campaigns, candidates, and governments. Judgments about whether and when this is good or bad are heavily influenced by the political opinions of those making the judgment. Where you stand on the issue often depends on where you sit.

MANIPULATING THE POLLS

In September 1972, a few weeks before the presidential election, pollster Louis Harris received a call from Chuck Colson, a close aide to President Richard Nixon. Colson wanted Harris to know that negotiations between the U.S. government and the North Vietnamese to end the Vietnam war were delicately balanced. If (based on the polls) the Vietnamese believed Democrat George McGovern, a Vietnam "dove," was closing the gap and might defeat Nixon, there would be no peace treaty before the election. If Nixon's big poll lead continued, there was a good chance that there would be a peace treaty and the war would end. Or so he said (Taylor 1998).

In the event, Nixon's big lead was sustained, and he won a landslide victory—and the war continued for two more years. There was no peace treaty. But this was a tough pressure on a pollster.

Compared with some of the things that happen frequently in other countries, however, this was child's play. There are many reports, mostly from the "new democracies," of governments exerting almost irresistible pressures on the media and the pollsters not to publish polls that show they are unpopular. In more than a few countries, most of the media are unwilling to publish such polls, because they believe the government will punish them. In some countries, there are credible reports of pollsters being offered large sums of money by the media and by people close to governments to change their poll results and of not being paid for work done if they would not change them.

Many of the new democracies are not very democratic. Governments are tempted to steal elections, and sometimes do. In Mexico in 1988, early returns showed that the challenger, Cuauhtemoc Cárdenas, was well ahead of the government-supported candidate, Carlos Salinas. Suddenly, the computers tallying the results crashed. When they started working again five hours later, they reported that Salinas had won. Most independent observers believe Cárdenas actually won the most votes.

Stealing elections is not limited to Mexico; governments in many new democracies (like the Democratic party bosses in Chicago and Texas in 1960) have indulged in fraudulent vote counting. It is easier to do this, and get away with it, if the preelection polls and the exit polls point to a government victory. There is strong evidence that in some countries, governments have manipulated both the preelection polls and the exit polls to "predict" the results of elections they then stole.

Far from banning preelection polls, as some countries have done, they should be encouraged in order to provide evidence of election fraud and therefore prevent it. One important measure of democracy is the publication of free, independent polls.

CODES OF CONDUCT FOR OPINION RESEARCH

In many countries, there are codes of conduct for professional membership organizations (e.g., AAPOR, MRS, PMRS) and trade associations (e.g., CASRO, AMSO, CAMRO) that address many issues of importance to the conducting and publishing of surveys. ESOMAR has published *A Guide to Opinion Polls* (ESOMAR/WAPOR 1998) and an International Code of Practice (ICC/ESOMAR 1995) for the publication of public opinion results and guidelines to its interpretation.

In addition, the United States and some other countries have other codes of conduct for firms that publish opinion surveys. These codes usually do not set quality standards; their main function is to list information that must be provided whenever surveys are released. Typically, they require the disclosure of sampling methodology, sample size, fieldwork dates, and questions asked.

Although these codes do not go very far and do not ensure that firms provide all of the information that an informed critic would need to evaluate published surveys, they are very useful and help reduce the likelihood of the public being seriously misled.

BIBLIOGRAPHY
ESOMAR (1998), *Handbook of Market and Opinion Research*. Amsterdam: ESOMAR
ESOMAR/WAPOR (1998), *Guide to Opinion Polls Including the ESOMAR International Code of Practice for the Publication of Public Opinion Results and Guidelines to its Interpretation*. Amsterdam: ESOMAR and WAPOR.
Journal of the Market Research Society (1998), 39 (3).
ICC/ESOMAR (1995), *International Code of Marketing and Social Research Practice and Notes to Its Interpretation*. Amsterdam: ICC and ESOMAR.
Public Perspective (1999), "Heady Days Are Here Again," (June/July), 20.
Taylor, H. (1991), "Polls, Politicians and the Gulf War," *The National Review*, (May 13).
——— (1998), "Pollution," *The National Interest*, (Spring).
Worcester, R. (1991), *British Public Opinion: A Guide to the History and Methodology of Political Opinion Polling*. London: Blackwell.

17
Research in Advertising

Roger Wimmer

Advertising messages are everywhere. There are advertisements on radio, television, billboards, newspapers, magazines, the Internet, matchbook covers, gas pumps, shopping carts, clothing, and on and on. It is probably safe to assume that those who create, sponsor, and use the messages would analyze such a pervasive medium. It is also probably safe to assume that because of the various types of advertising approaches, there are many research methods to analyze the messages. However, before we get to a discussion of the research in advertising, it makes sense to find out what we are planning to investigate. In other words, what is *advertising*?

(Note that because of space limitations, I have assumed that the reader has a basic understanding of qualitative and quantitative research methods and elementary statistics. If a term or concept is used that you do not understand, immediately consult the Internet or the references listed at the end of the chapter for more information. On the Internet, use a search engine such as AltaVista, HotBot, alltheweb.com, or directhit.com. A countless number of sources are available on the Internet for virtually every term or concept discussed in this chapter. In addition, a new search engine called www.ditto.com provides a virtual "look" at statistics and research methodology.)

A COLLECTION OF ADVERTISING DEFINITIONS

A quick search for a definition of *advertising* immediately reveals that the word is not a simple one. It seems as though there are as many definitions of advertising as there are people who work in the industry. And it seems as though there are as many definitions as there are approaches to conduct research on the messages. Just look at some of the variety of definitions available for advertising available from The University of Texas at Austin, Department of Advertising's Web site (www.utexas.edu/coc/adv/research/Topics.html).

There are definitions that equate advertising to sales:

> "The simplest definition of advertising, and one that will probably meet the test of critical examination, is that advertising is selling in print." Daniel Starch, *Principles of Advertising* (1923, Chicago, IL: A.W. Shaw Company, 5).

> "Advertising is selling Twinkies to adults." Donald R. Vance (no source listed).

> "Our job is to sell our clients' merchandise ... not ourselves. Our job is to kill the cleverness that makes us shine instead of the product. Our job is to simplify, to tear away the unrelated, to pluck out the weeds that are smothering the product message." William Bernbach, *Bill Bernbach said...* (1989, New York: DDB Needham Worldwide).

Some definitions of advertising suggest that the method is simplistic:

> "Advertising is what you do when you can't go see somebody. That's all it is." Fairfax Cone (1963), quoted in James B. Simpson, *Contemporary Quotations* (1964, Binghamton, NY: Vail-Ballou Press, 84).

> "Advertising is, actually, a simple phenomenon in terms of economics. It is merely a substitute for a personal sales force—an extension, if you will, of the merchant who cries aloud his wares." Rosser Reeves, *Reality in Advertising* (1986, New York: Alfred A. Knopf, Inc., 145).

> "Advertising is salesmanship mass produced. No one would bother to use advertising if he could talk to all his prospects face-to-face. But he can't." Morris Hite, *Adman: Morris Hite's Methods for Winning the Ad Game* (1988, Dallas, TX: E-Heart Press, 203).

Some definitions claim that advertising is an art, not a science:

> "I warn you against believing that advertising is a science." William Bernbach, *Bill Bernbach said...* (1989, New York: DDB Needham Worldwide).

> "Advertisements may be evaluated scientifically; they cannot be created scientifically." Leo Bogart, quoted in Randall Rothenberg, *Where the Suckers Moon: An Advertising Story* (1994, New York: Alfred A. Knopf, 110).

> "Advertising is fundamentally persuasion and persuasion happens to be not a science, but an art." William Bernbach, quoted in Randall Rothenberg, *Where the Suckers Moon: An Advertising Story* (1994, New York: Alfred A. Knopf, 63).

On the contrary, there are definitions that stress the importance of research in advertising:

> "The most important word in the vocabulary of advertising is TEST. If you pretest your product with consumers, and pretest your advertising, you will do well in the marketplace." David Ogilvy (1963), quoted in Stephen Donadio, *The New York Public Library: Book of Twentieth-Century American Quotations* (1992, New York: Stonesong Press, 70).

> "Advertising people who ignore research are as dangerous as generals who ignore decodes of enemy signals." David Ogilvy, *Ogilvy on Advertising* (1983, New York: Crown Publishers, 158).

Some definitions are somewhat pessimistic:

> "Advertising is legalized lying." H.G. Wells, quoted in Michael Jackman, *Crown's Book of Political Quotations* (1982, New York: Crown Publishing Inc., 2).

Finally, some definitions suggest that advertising is a form of communication:

> "The sole purpose of business is service. The sole purpose of advertising is explaining the service which business renders." Leo Burnett, *100 LEO's* (Chicago, IL: Leo Burnett Company, 30).

This final definition will emerge as significant later in this chapter. Keep it in mind.

This small sample of definitions shows that advertising is defined in a variety of ways, and this suggests that research in advertising should be equally as varied. Let's take a look at some of the current approaches to research in advertising.

APPROACHES IN ADVERTISING RESEARCH

Because there are so many types of advertising, we should expect that there are an equal number of approaches to analyzing advertising. This expectation is verified by a review of any advertising textbook or manual. Let's take a look at some of the methods that are used to conduct research in advertising.

Probably the most prevalent type of advertising research falls under the broad category known as *copy testing*. Although there are many research approaches used in this category of research, the approaches usually focus on such things as layout, design, color, narration (voice-over), music, illustration, size, length, and more. (To get an idea of the range of copy testing or message research, conduct an Internet search for "copy testing.")

As Wimmer and Dominick (2000, p. 347) note,

> Copy testing refers to research that helps develop effective advertisements and then determines which of several advertisements is the most effective. Copy testing takes place at every stage of the advertising process. Before a campaign starts, copy pretesting indicates what to stress and what to avoid. When the content of the ad has been established, tests must be performed to ascertain the most effective way to structure these ideas. For example, in studying the illustration copy of a proposed magazine spread, a researcher might show to two or more groups of subjects an illustration of the product photographed from different angles. The headline might be evaluated by having potential users rate the typefaces used in several versions of the ad. The copy might be tested for readability and recall. In all cases, the aim is to determine whether the variable tested significantly affects the liking or the recall of the ad.

One way to explain the variety of methods used in copy testing research is to consider the dimensions of persuasion discussed by Leckenby and Wedding (1982). The three dimensions, which are appropriate to copy testing research, are the *cognitive dimension* (knowing), the *affective dimension* (feeling), and the *conative dimension* (doing).

Advertising research in the *cognitive dimension* includes research about attention, awareness, exposure, recognition, comprehension, and recall (unaided and aided) of advertising. In other words, what do people (consumers) know about a product, service, concept, or phenomenon after being exposed to advertising messages? Researchers use a variety of methods to collect such information, including focus groups, physiological studies (eye movement, etc.), and consumer panels. In some cases, the research involves a pretest and posttest (measurements are taken before and after exposure to the advertising), whereas other research involves posttest measurements only.

Advertising research in the *affective dimension* typically investigates if (or how) consumers' attitudes toward a particular product or service have changed because of exposure to an advertisement or an advertising campaign. The data are gathered in a variety of ways, including focus groups, telephone studies, central location testing (large groups in an auditorium setting), and a variety of physiological measurements.

The importance of the affective dimension is emphasized by Walker and Dubitsky (1994), who noted that the degree of liking expressed by consumers toward a commercial was significantly related to awareness, recall, and greater persuasive impact. Indeed, several advertising researchers have suggested that liking an ad is one of the most important factors in determining its impact (Wimmer and Dominick 2000, p. 352)

Advertising research in the *conative dimension* deals with actual consumer behavior, particularly buying predisposition (intent to purchase) and actual purchasing behavior. In buying predisposition research, consumers are asked about their probability of purchasing a product or service presented in an advertisement or campaign. In purchasing studies, actual sales are tracked after consumers are exposed to advertising. Sales information is available from private sector research companies such as ACNielsen.

Research in advertising also includes a variety of other approaches including, but not limited to, the following:

❑ *Psychographic* studies to determine the attitudinal and behavioral characteristics of consumers so that advertising can be designed to target these characteristics;

❑ *Market segmentation* studies to find out which types of people like and use which types of products and services. This information, often combined with psychographic data, is also used to create and develop advertising messages;

❑ *Audience size and composition* studies (also known as reach and frequency) to estimate how many consumers were exposed to a message, how many times they were exposed to the messages, and what type of people were exposed to the message(s);

❑ *Market share* studies to investigate a company's share of a product or service before, during, and after an advertising campaign;

❑ *Studies of competitor's advertising* to learn about the products and services competitors are offering and how the competitors communicate this information to their customers; and

❑ *Popularity research* (such as is published in *USA Today*) showing the television commercials consumers say they like the most.

Space limitations do not allow for a complete discussion of the steps involved in all of these advertising research approaches. This information is available from other sources. However, it is important to note that research in advertising must follow the same steps and tenets of scientific research that are used in any other area of research. See Wimmer and Dominick (2000) for additional information about the steps involved in scientific research.

RELIABILITY AND VALIDITY OF ADVERTISING RESEARCH

Anyone who is interested in advertising research probably has two basic questions. First, is advertising research **valid**? That is, do the research studies test what they are *supposed to test*? Second, is advertising research **reliable**? That is, does the research consistently produce similar results? These questions are logical for any type of research and are not limited only to the area of research in advertising. As noted in Wimmer and Dominick (2000, pp. 354–55), to test the assumption that advertising research does, in fact, identify advertising that works well in the marketplace, the Advertising Research Foundation (ARF),

> sponsored a research validity project to determine which copy testing measures were effective (Haley and Baldinger 1991). To begin, ARF selected five pairs of TV commercials. Since one of the ads in each of these pairs had already been shown to produce major sales differences in test markets, ARF researchers used the ads in a field experiment that included many common copy testing measures (for more information, see www.arf.amic.com).

> The experiment revealed a strong correlation between ads that copy tested well and ads that performed well in the marketplace. For example, measuring reaction to commercials on an affective scale (like/dislike) predicted the more effective ad of the pair 87% of the time. Top-of-mind awareness (unaided recall) measures correctly classified the more effective ad 73% of the time. Less effective were measures that asked respondents to recall the main point of the ad.

In addition, as Wimmer and Dominick (2000, pp. 354–55) state,

> The current trend in copy testing is multiple measures of copy research effectiveness. A technique called Advertising Response Modeling (ARM) provides a conceptual model that integrates several measurements to evaluate ad effectiveness (Mehta and Purvis 1997). ARM differentiates between high and low involvement situations and includes measures such as recall, liking, buying interest, and brand rating. The technique highlights that different ads can be successful for a variety of reasons.

The available information about research in advertising verifies that there are many research approaches to seeking a variety of answers. Yet, much of the current advertising research investigates a definition of advertising that may not be correct. However, before we get to that discussion, we need to look at some of the ways advertising research data are collected and analyzed.

DATA COLLECTION METHODS AND STATISTICAL ANALYSIS

Research in advertising uses the same data collection methods and statistical analysis used by all other areas of mass media research. Advertising research uses a variety of qualitative and quantitative research approaches. (Note: The difference between qualitative and quantitative research refers to how the data are collected. In essence, the difference relates to the flexibility of data collection. Qualitative research is flexible and allows researchers to modify immediately the questions respondents are asked, such as in focus groups. Quantitative research uses standardized or static types of measurement instruments in which all respondents are asked the same questions. There is no flexibility in asking unplanned follow-up questions or even questions that were not planned in the research design.)

Some of the types of data collection procedures include, but are not limited to, the following:

❑ Focus groups: Controlled, small group discussions with dozens or hundreds of consumers selected for a specific reason, such as people who purchase a certain type of computer.

❑ Mail surveys: Respondents are sent questionnaires or other product purchasing tracking studies to their home or business.

❑ Telephone surveys: Respondents are called at their home, their work, or other location to gather data.

❑ Online surveys: Perceptions about advertising (print or electronic), evaluations, pretests, and posttests can be conducted using the Internet, where respondents are recruited (or volunteer) to complete a variety of measurement instruments.

❑ Disk-by-mail: Respondents are sent a computer disk to their home or work. The disk contains various measurement instruments, and respondents either send the disk back to the research company or the responses to the instruments are forwarded by the Internet.

❑ CD by mail or purchase: Respondents answer questions contained on a CD they receive from a research company or the company that produces a product or service or on a music CD they purchased from a retail outlet. The completed questionnaire is usually sent back to the research company or manufacturer by the Internet.

❑ In-field surveys or observations: Advertisements, or variations of the same advertisement, are tested on television or cable channels or in different runs of print vehicles to determine if there is a correlation between awareness or sales and the version of the advertisement. In-field studies can also monitor consumer behavior on-site after consumers are exposed to advertising messages.

❑ Shopping center intercepts: Respondents view and respond to advertising messages shown to them by a research company that recruits them in a shopping mall.

❑ Central location testing: Large numbers of respondents, usually 100 or more, are recruited to a setting where they are exposed to various advertising messages at the same time. Pretest and posttest questions are possible, as well as almost any other type of data gathering procedure.

The type of data collection depends on the type of research conducted. If we want consumers to respond to new television commercials, the consumers must view the commercials. This means that a data collection method in which consumers can view the commercials is necessary. However, keep in mind that new technology has expanded the ways in which consumers can view or analyze information (in this case, advertising). For example, prototype television commercials, radio commercials, billboards, or almost any type of advertising can be shown on Internet Web sites or on CDs and DVDs sent to a consumer's home or business.

The types of statistics used to analyze advertising research are also no different than in any other area of mass media research. Limited space in this chapter prohibits a complete discussion of all statistics used in advertising research. Suffice it to say that research in advertising uses all forms of statistics. Research studies may use simple descriptive or summary statistics, such as frequency tables, or measures of central tendency, such as the mean, media, mode, standard deviation, and Z-scores. Other research may use univariate statistics (single dependent measurement), such as the t-test, chi-square, and analysis of variance, or multivariate statistics (multiple dependent measurements), such as factor analysis, cluster analysis, canonical correlation, and discriminant analysis.

Additional information about all of these statistical methods is available from the references listed at the end of this chapter.

A PROBLEM WITH CURRENT DEFINITIONS AND METHODS

The information up to this point is relatively straightforward—an explanation of advertising, types of research used in advertising, and how the data are gathered and analyzed. The problem is that all of the information up to this point is based on antiquated, incorrect, and/or opinion-based definitions of advertising. Most definitions of advertising attribute too much power to the procedure. A more realistic definition of advertising is needed, which means that a more realistic research approach will follow. (Remember the definition of advertising by Leo Burnett, who said that the purpose of advertising is to explain a service that a business renders.)

Leo Burnett hit the nail on the head, and it is time now to conduct research in advertising that addresses what advertising really is, not what it is *thought* to be.

A NEW APPROACH

As mentioned previously, research in advertising covers a wide range of activities, such as copy testing, layout, composition, recall, sales increase/decrease, and more. If we look carefully at all of the types of advertising research, one fundamental concern is always present: Is the advertising effective? This underlying goal seems logical. A lot of time and effort are invested in advertising, and it makes sense to find out if the message or campaign actually "does" anything. Does the advertisement sell anything? Does it increase awareness? Does it increase store traffic? All these questions are valid, but they are missing the point of advertising. They are missing the point of what advertising actually does. This problem must be solved.

Several definitions of advertising were included in the beginning of this chapter, and it is clear from these that there are a variety of definitions available—probably one for every person interested in advertising. However, two frequently used definitions of advertising that I have heard during more than 25 years of experience in mass media research are that advertising is designed to *sell something* or *increase store traffic*. These two reasons are also the major complaints voiced by advertisers when their ads seem to have no effect. I have heard a countless number of advertisers complain that their radio (television, newspaper, magazine) advertising did not work because they did not receive more telephone calls, or their sales did not increase, or the traffic in the store was no greater than before they placed the advertising. "Advertising is a waste of money" is a typical response from these people.

All of these complaints are misdirected; the complaints do not relate to what advertising really is. Sales figures and store traffic are usually the deciding factors in determining if an advertisement or campaign was successful. The "end" is tested but not the "means." That's where things need to change.

The underlying problem with most current advertising research is that there is no universally accepted definition of advertising. Advertisers, creative people, and researchers, among others, attribute too much power to advertising. They falsely attribute powers to advertising that it does not deserve. So what is advertising?

A DIFFERENT APPROACH TO DEFINING ADVERTISING

The sample of advertising definitions included previously in this chapter shows a broad range of perceptions of what advertising is supposed to be and what it is supposed to do. Some definitions say that advertising sells products, others say that advertising replaces a salesperson, and still others say that advertising is an art, not a science. The variety of definitions of advertising is confounding to a researcher. Which definition should be used to analyze advertising? Which definition is correct? Which definition, if investigated, will provide the most useful information to those who create and use advertising? To eliminate this confusion, it is best to search for another definition. We need to look elsewhere.

A good place to start is with an unbiased source, such as *Webster's Dictionary* (Merriam-Webster 1989, p. 59), which defines advertising as

> [T]he action of calling something to the attention of the public, especially by paid announcements.

We can also look at *Webster's* definition (1989, p. 59) of the word *advertise*:

> [T]o make something known to, to make publicly and generally known; to announce publicly especially by a printed notice or a broadcast.

Notice that neither definition mentions sales, increased store traffic, art, science, or research. The definitions do not include cute analogies or metaphors or pessimism. The definitions merely say that advertising is *only communication*. The only thing that advertising does is *communicate a message from one source to another*. If we accept this, we can proceed to how communication (advertising) should be investigated. We first need some discussion about communication.

Again referring to *Webster's Dictionary* (1989, p. 266), communication is defined as

> An act or instance of transmitting; a verbal or written message; a process by which information is exchanged between individuals through a common system of symbols, sings, or behavior.

Do you see the similarity between the definitions for advertising and communication? Do you see that the words "advertising" and "communication" are interchangeable? Both terms are defined in similar ways — advertising and communication are defined as transferring a message from one source to another. In other words,

Advertising = Communication

and

Communication = Advertising.

Accepting this definition of advertising makes the discussion about research in advertising much easier. We now have a goal for any research in advertising: *Analyze communication*. That is, we have a goal to find out if the communication effectively transmits information from one source to another.

Is there a simple way to do this? The answer is "yes." But before we get to the methods of research, we need to take one step backward — a step that will help further define what it is that we are doing when we conduct advertising research.

What we need is more information about the term *communication*. A good place to start is with one of the masters of communication. Let's step back in time to the time of Aristotle, the ancient Greek philosopher. In his book, *The Art of Rhetoric,* Aristotle describes in great detail all of the elements of communication. One of his many conclusions about communication is that communication and persuasion are the same thing. In other words,

$$\text{Communication} = \text{Persuasion}$$
and
$$\text{Persuasion} = \text{Communication.}$$

All communication is persuasion and all persuasion is communication. Taking the information that

$$\text{Communication} = \text{Advertising}$$
and
$$\text{Advertising} = \text{Communication,}$$

we can substitute a few words to produce the following:

$$\text{Advertising} = \text{Persuasion}$$
and
$$\text{Persuasion} = \text{Advertising.}$$

We can even take this relationship one more step. In 1967, Watzlawick, Beavin, and Jackson developed a wonderful argument that *we cannot not communicate.* In other words, everything we do or say communicates a message. The message may be through verbal communication, nonverbal communication, or metacommunication. The bottom line is that no matter what we do, we communicate a message. We always communicate, 100% of the time. There are no exceptions to this rule.

Now, considering the fact that we cannot *not* communicate, let's move one step further and put all of the relationships together:

$$\text{Communication} = \text{Persuasion}$$
and
$$\text{Persuasion} = \text{Communication.}$$

Then,

$$\text{Advertising} = \text{Persuasion/communication}$$
and
$$\text{Persuasion/communication} = \text{Advertising.}$$

Considering that

> We cannot *not* communicate/persuade,

we conclude that

> We cannot *not* advertise

If adverting is only communication/persuasion, how can it be analyzed from any other perspective? How can it be analyzed by investigating increased store traffic or increased sales? Quite simply, it can't. As persuasion, advertising alone does not sell a product. Advertising alone does not increase store traffic. Yet for years, the success of advertising has been measured on the advertisement or the campaign's ability to generate additional sales.

What happens if the advertising communicates to consumers that a manufacture/company has a bad product? What happens if the advertising communicates that the product or service is overpriced? What happens if the advertising communicates that a competitor has a better product? All these things happen. Sales do not increase, and advertising gets the blame. For example, a company can hire an advertising agency to produce print and broadcast advertising that tells consumers that its product is overpriced. In the following weeks, sales for the product do not increase. Where does the blame fall? Not on the company that made the product, but on the advertising. The advertising did not work. The advertising did not "sell" the product. The advertising agency is then blamed for the problem, and the manufacturer might even look for another advertising agency (to then go through the same process all over again). This scenario is repeated thousands and thousands of times every year. Advertising is blamed for the failure of a product or service. The blame rarely, if ever, falls on the company that produced the product or service.[1]

---

[1] The fact that we "cannot *not* communicate" and therefore we "cannot *not* advertise" is something that both individuals and companies often overlook. Let's take a look at a real example based on my own experience. During the past several years, Sears & Roebuck has frequently reported lower-than-anticipated sales figures. A typical press release to stockholders attributes the soft sales to one reason or another (it doesn't matter what the reason is). The bottom line is that fewer customers are shopping at Sears. Why is that? Well, it may be due to competition, or it may be due to the fact that consumers don't like Sears' prices. I'm not sure. The only thing I know is that Sears has forgotten about the fact that they "cannot *not* advertise."

Let me explain. I have been a loyal Sears' shopper for years, the same as my parents. I will admit that my loyalty is to Sears' tools and household appliances, but at least that is something. In the past five visits to Sears to buy tools, I have walked out of the store without making a purchase. I had the product I wanted to buy in

This has been the fundamental problem with most research in advertising: It has focused on investigating things that advertising is not. It's time to change the focus. But to do that, we need to know more about communication/persuasion. (Because these terms are interchangeable, only the word *persuasion* is used in the remainder of this chapter. Please note, however, that whenever the word persuasion is used, the word communication can be substituted.)

How does persuasion work? Since the time of Aristotle, many descriptions of how persuasion works have been presented. In fact, a discussion about the theories of persuasion is contained in almost any book on persuasion or communication. However, the simplest description is probably the *Five Stages of Persuasion*, the five steps that all people pass through in order to make a decision about anything.

---

my hand, but I could not find a salesperson to take my money. What decision did I make? I put the product back on the shelf, walked out of Sears, and went to another store to buy the product. The problem for Sears is that in my past five visits, they advertised (communicated/persuaded) to me that they do not want me to shop in their store. Businesses (and individuals) cannot *not* advertise. From the moment a consumer walks into a store or visits a company Web site or reads a catalog, the store is advertising.

In the case of a retail store, the store advertises a message from the ease of parking, the entrance to the store, the lighting, the product layout, the salespeople, the floor covering, prices, and literally everything else. A store that advertises positive messages through these elements allows a person to move through the Five Stages of Persuasion, and the customer will spend money. If the store advertises negative messages through the elements (such as what Sears does by not having salespeople available), the customer will not spend money. It's that simple.

Sears is a big retail store in the United States (second behind Wal-Mart), so we would think that it would know what to do to correct the situation, and then correct it immediately. That seems logical, but the logic is wrong. Did Sears add more people to help correct the problem of sagging sales? Did it make the buying process easier for customers? The answer to both questions is "no." Instead, Sears changed its advertising campaign. No longer do we hear or see "The softer side of Sears." We now hear and see the new Sears' slogan: "A good life at a great price." As an advertising researcher and customer of Sears, I have to say, "Sorry, the new slogan does not indicate to me that I will be able to buy things when I enter the store." What the slogan says to me is "A good life at a great price for products you can't buy."

The slogan is a plastic bandage for a gaping wound. The slogan says nothing about hiring more salespeople. The slogan says nothing about solving the problem of having to wander around the store trying to find a salesperson. How do I know? I went to Sears just the other day and, you guessed it, put another product back on the shelf and walked across the street to a competitor. It may be that Sears' executives should get out of their offices in Chicago and try to buy something from one of their stores. If they would personally experience the difficulty of buying something in one of their stores, they might make a few changes. And they might decide to change their slogan from "A good life at a great price" to something like "You can now buy things at Sears."

FIVE STAGES OF PERSUASION

The Five Stages of Persuasion are *unawareness, awareness, comprehension, conviction,* and *action.* As mentioned, these stages apply to literally any decision we ever make, from purchases of products and services to decisions about dating, marriage, careers, religion, and everything else. Every human being goes through these stages before making *any* decision. This is a universal behavior. It is another rule without an exception.

The Five Stages of Persuasion is a simple process. A person is first *unaware* of a product, service, or idea, then moves to *awareness* after gathering (being exposed to) some amount of information. The person then passes into the *comprehension* and *conviction* stages after gathering (being exposed to) addition information. The *action* stage is reached when the person buys a product or service, or listens to a radio station, or watches a television program, or believes an idea or philosophy, or takes a specific action.

It's that simple. To persuade anyone to take some kind of action or believe anything, that person must be taken through the five stages. The problem is that the process is not 100% successful.[2] Many people are forever stuck in *unawareness, awareness, comprehension,* or *conviction* and never reach the *action* stage. In addition, some people may reach one stage but then go back to a previous stage. For example, a person may buy something as mundane as Hostess Cupcakes for years, then stop buying for one reason or another. This person, either because of a comment by a friend or relative or because of exposure to an advertisement about Hostess Cupcakes, may say, "I haven't had one of those in years," and then once again enter the action stage by buying Hostess Cupcakes the next trip to the grocery store.

What do we know about the Five Stages of Persuasion? We know that

- ❏ Everyone must pass through the stages for every decision he or she makes;
- ❏ Everyone passes through the stages at a speed unique to him or her. There is no universal timing to the process;
- ❏ Not all people make it to the action stage; and
- ❏ The only way to move people through the Five Stages is through repetition of the message. In most cases, people do not make decisions after only one exposure to a message. The process requires several exposures.

---

[2]Mass communication and the mass media are often said to have a great deal of power over people. One early theory about the power of mass communication was developed during World War II when researchers investigated Adolph Hitler's propaganda. The theory known as the "bullet theory" or "hypodermic-needle theory" suggested that mass communicators need only "shoot" a message at the masses and they would react in universal and predictable ways. However, research in later years did not find evidence for the theory. Additional research found that individual behavior negates the idea that everyone reacts the same way to one specific message or campaign.

There are also several things we don't know about the Five Stages of Persuasion. For example, we don't know

- ❑ How many exposures are required to move a person through each stage;
- ❑ How many people are in each stage of the process at any given time;
- ❑ When people will move from one stage to another;
- ❑ Why people move from one stage to another; or
- ❑ Where people are when they move from one stage to another.

We know that people must pass through the stages to make a decision, but we don't know where, when, how, or why they will pass through the stages. Lucky for us, we do understand that to move people through the stages, we must have repetition of the message. And that's where advertising becomes so important. We repeatedly present advertising messages to consumers because we know they will make a decision only after repeated exposures. In addition, understanding this process changes the way decisions about advertising placement are made. If we don't know where, when, how, or why people get to the action stage, then it makes no sense to schedule or place advertising at a specific time or place. For example, grocery stores have historically included coupons for products in the Wednesday edition of the newspaper. Why is that? Do all people make decisions to buy groceries only on Wednesdays? The answer, of course, is no. But the practice of placing coupons in the Wednesday edition of the paper suggests that the grocery store owner/manager knows when the store's customers make a decision to buy. This is ludicrous.

There is no way to circumvent the Five Stages of Persuasion. There is no company or manufacturer that can slip around the process to sell products or services to consumers. There is no person or group that can slip around the process in an attempt to persuade another person or group to do something or believe in something. There is no parent who can slip around the process to get his or her child to do chores around the house. The process is universal. It is, as mentioned, a rule without exception. Therefore, the Five Stages of Persuasion should be (must be) the basis for all research in advertising. Any other approach is irrelevant to the definition, purpose, and goals of advertising. So how should we conduct research in advertising?

A DIFFERENT APPROACH TO ADVERTISING RESEARCH

The Five Stages of Persuasion model is a simple approach to follow in communication. The Five Stages also relate very nicely with the simple three-step approach for success in any personal or business endeavor. The model for success in business as well as personal life is as follows:

❑ Find out what the people (or person) want(s).
❑ Give it to them (him/her).
❑ Tell them that you gave it to them (him/her).

Think about this three-step approach for a moment, particularly in reference to you. If I find out that you prefer seafood when you go to a restaurant and then decide to take you to a seafood restaurant (a good one), how can I fail? I can't. Or, if you are a student and you find out what your teacher wants you to do to earn an "A," and you provide the teacher with these things, how can you fail? You can't. Finally, consider that a company wants to make a new type of computer. If the company asks people who use computers for suggestions for a new product and then makes the product based on those suggestions, how can the company fail? It can't. (All of these examples assume that the third step of the approach was followed: "Tell them that you gave it to them.")

This three-step process is included here because it also relates to research, in this case, research in advertising. There are two basic approaches we could follow to develop a research methodology for advertising studies. The first is that we could develop what we *think* we need to test or investigate and then administer the measurement instruments to consumers. The second approach is to pay attention to how consumers describe advertising and then develop a research methodology based on what these people say (and do) when *they* discuss and analyze advertising. The second approach is the one I use. For more than 20 years, I have listened to consumers talk about and analyze advertising. These thousands upon thousands of comments have provided the basis for a method to analyze advertising.

It would be gratifying to take personal credit for the discussion of the research methodology about to be presented, but that is not possible. It isn't possible because I didn't develop it. The methodology came from consumers. And in this case, the consumers provided a foundation for a three-step process in analyzing advertising messages. The method is appropriate for any type of print or electronic advertising. You should notice immediately that the consumers helped develop a research methodology based on what advertising really is: *Communication.*

THREE-STEP RESEARCH APPROACH

The three-step research process to analyze the effectiveness of any type of advertising includes the following three steps:

1. An overall rating for the advertisement as compared with all similar advertising,

2. A rating about how successful the advertisement is in encouraging a person to try a product or service for the first time or use the product or service more often, and

3. An open-ended description of the message contained in the advertisement.

After thousands of advertising studies, these three points have emerged as the most successful in determining the success of an advertisement. There is no test of recall, potential for increased sales, or potential for increased store traffic. That is correct. The success of an advertisement is *not* based on a test of recall or a test of increase in sales. *The success of an advertisement is based on its ability to communicate a message successfully and nothing more.*[3]

Considering all of the information up to this point, we now know that the goal of advertising research in any medium should be related to finding out if the advertising communicates the correct message and how well it achieves this task.

Let's look at each of the three steps in advertising research developed by consumers.

Overall Rating

Discussions and debates about learning usually focus on the fact that a person learns things much easier if the new topic or idea relates in some way to something that he or she already understands. Consider, for example, the field of statistics. It is much easier to teach a person how to conduct an analysis of variance if the person already knows how to conduct a t-test. (If you don't know anything about either statistic, conduct a search on the Internet for more information or consult one of the statistics books listed at the end of this chapter.)

Learning something new by associating it with something old is common when discussing advertising with consumers. Consumers almost always compare a new advertisement with something they have already heard, seen, or read. (Consumers also may relate the product or service advertised to something they already know.) When analyzing advertising, consumers may or may not make a product-to-product com-

---

[3]Advertising recall research is a waste of time and money. Generally speaking, recall studies involve showing a person an advertisement and then asking the person to name the product or service or the company that sponsored the ad. Recall is investigated either immediately after exposure to the message or a day or more after the exposure. This research then concludes that an advertisement is successful if it receives high "recall" scores. This makes no sense at all. For example, an advertisement may have high recall scores because it is misleading, false, or irrelevant. Recall of advertising alone means nothing. Recall alone says nothing about the quality of the message. Recall alone says nothing about the advertisement's ability to move people through the Five Stages of Persuasion. The money spent on advertising recall research would be better served if contributed to a favorite charity. It is, again, a complete waste of time.

parison. However, consumers will always compare the advertising they are analyzing with all other advertising in or on that medium. When discussing television commercials, for example, respondents will says things like, "I don't think I will ever buy the product, but the commercial is excellent. It presented the information very clearly, was easy to follow, and was entertaining." Or respondents will say, "I already use that product, but I didn't like the commercial because it went too fast and didn't tell me where I could buy it." In other words, consumers compare advertising in the same way they compare everything else in their lives—with something they already know.

The range of comments consumers have about advertising is almost limitless, but the key is that respondents compare new commercials with old commercials. I have learned over time that consumers have in their minds what constitutes a good advertisement, whether the ad is for dog food, automobiles, or anything else. Because this is true, it makes sense to have consumers rate an advertisement by having them compare it with all other advertisements they have been exposed to—a comparison with an "ideal" commercial. The rating is not across media, but within the same medium. That is, "How do you rate this television commercial against all other television commercials you have seen?" or "How do you rate this newspaper advertisement against all other newspaper advertisements you have ever seen?" This is important, because consumers have difficulty, for example, comparing a television commercial with a magazine advertisement.

The question, "How do you rate this [insert medium] advertisement against all other [insert medium] advertisements you have ever seen [heard]?" is the first question that is asked of consumers when analyzing advertising. The consumers are asked to rate the advertisement as compared with their "ideal" advertisement. Over time, I have learned that a ten-point rating scale is most effective, where "1" means poor, "10" means excellent, and 2 through 9 are in-between.

To summarize, then, assume we are testing a television commercial. The first question asked in an analysis of the commercial is:

> How do you rate this commercial as compared with all television commercials you have ever seen? Please use a scale of 1 to 10, where "1" means poor, "10" means excellent, and 2 through 9 are in-between.

The question can also be posed as

> How do you rate this commercial as compared with all television commercials you have ever seen? Please use a scale of 1 to 10, where the higher the number, the more you liked the commercial.

This rating provides an indication of how attractive the commercial is, how clearly the message is delivered, how easy it is to understand, and how much attention the consumers might pay to it. During the past several years, consumers have shown that an advertisement should have a minimum average score of 7.0 to be considered successful. An advertisement with an average score less than 7.0 does not meet the minimum expectation and will probably not be received well by consumers. Experience in the area has shown that advertisements that achieve average scores of 8.0 or higher are the ads that consumers like to see, hear, and watch over and over. (Recall that people move through the Five Stages of Persuasion because of message repetition.)

Amount of Encouragement

This rating was developed on the basis of consumers saying things like, "The advertisement really convinced me that I need to try the product," and "The advertisement didn't give me any reason to try the product." Listening very closely to consumers' comments highlighted an important point: The consumers were telling the advertisers and advertising community what they want in an advertisement, "explain to me why I need this product or service ... give me some good reasons." (Relate this now to the "Find out what they want and give it to them" step for success.)

Therefore, continuing with the already commonly used ten-point scale, this question asks consumers to rate an advertisement's ability to encourage them to buy or try a new product or service for the first time, buy the product or service again, or buy the product or service more often.

Continuing our hypothetical test of a television commercial, the respondents are then asked:

> How do you rate how *well* this commercial encouraged you to buy the product or service? Please use a scale of 1 to 10, where "1" means it gave you no encouragement at all, "10" means it gave you a lot of encouragement, and 2 through 9 are in-between.

The question can also be asked as

> How do you rate how *well* this commercial encouraged you to buy the product or service? Please use a scale of 1 to 10, where the higher the number, the more encouragement the commercial provided.

This rating provides an indication about the content of the advertisement. It provides an indication of how well the message is delivered, how easy it is to understand, how relevant it is to the person's lifestyle, and how likely the consumer might be to try the product or service for the first time or use the product or service more often.

As before, experience in this area has shown that a successful advertisement must achieve a minimum average score of 7.0 on the ten-point scale. Advertising that does not achieve this minimum will probably not be successful with consumers. However, advertising that achieves average scores of 8.0 or higher will be more successful in moving consumers through the Five Stages of Persuasion more quickly.

The Message

The final step in the three-step advertising research approach is to ask consumers to answer a simple open-ended question about the message the advertisement gave them. Again using the television commercial, the consumers are asked:

> Finally, please explain in your own words what the commercial told you. What did you learn or understand from the commercial?

This question is asked as a "cross-check" for the two ten-point ratings scales. The reason for this is that an advertisement may receive high scores, but the message that is delivered may not be the message intended by the advertiser or those who created the ad. An example should make this clear. Several years ago, I tested a television commercial for a soft rock radio station. The commercial received very high scores: overall 8.4 and encouragement 8.9. The commercial looked very promising, but after reading the open-ended responses by the respondents, it was discovered that almost all the respondents thought the radio station played hard rock music, not soft rock music. In other words, the commercial was *extremely successful in communicating the wrong message*. Needless to say, the commercial was changed to solve this confusion.[4]

After a test is completed, the data summary is quite simple. The average scores are shown along with a summary of the results for the open-ended question. For example, the following summary tables show the results of a test for a radio station's prototype television commercials. The commercials were shown to two focus groups. Group 1 included all men; Group 2 included all women. "Try" is used as a short-form for the "encouragement" rating:

Prototype I	Group 1	Group 2	Average
Rating	7.9	8.6	8.3
Try	8.1	8.3	8.2

Virtually all of the respondents said they like this commercial because it is presented in a very simple way. The commercial is rated highly because it included several examples of the type of music the radio station plays, it showed the station's call letters and frequency throughout the entire commercial, and the infor-

---

[4]This approach to testing advertising messages does not include any specific rating of the creative aspects of the advertisement, though creativity underlies both measurements. An advertisement can be as "new" or "different" as the creators wish to make it. The consumers merely are asked to rate the advertisement on the areas that advertising is supposed to address: How does it relate to other advertising they have already seen? How much encouragement does the advertising provide? What does the advertisement tell you? It is that simple.

mation was presented in an easy-to-understand pace. According to most of the respondents, this commercial is a "home run" for communicating a good message about the radio station.

Prototype II	Group 1	Group 2	Average
Rating	5.2	3.7	4.5
Try	5.6	2.5	4.1

This commercial was not received well by either group. The men criticized the commercial for "going too fast" and "including silly pictures of the DJs." The women did not like the "anti-female" approach of the morning show hosts. Overall, the women agreed that the commercial said, "This radio station is not designed for women, so don't listen." The average scores for Rating and Try indicate that this message will not be successful in communicating a positive message to the radio station's listeners and potential listeners.

As you can see, the data summary for this process is simple. The average scores, along with the comments by the respondents, present an easy way to determine if the advertisement is successful. There is no subjective judgment involved. In addition, because advertising is only communication, the data summary relates only to this area. There is no mention of increasing sales, increasing store traffic, or anything else. It's a pure analysis of communication.

Incidentally, this three-step process of analyzing communications works for all types of advertising including, but not limited to, radio and television, newspapers, magazines, billboards, direct mail, and Internet banner advertising.

THE FUTURE OF ADVERTISING RESEARCH

As mentioned previously in the chapter, both high technology and the Internet have contributed to substantial changes in mass media research. Although still in their infancy, both high technology and the Internet will eventually become commonly accepted methods of research, including research in advertising. Let's look at advertising research in particular.

It is obvious that to test any type of advertising, consumers must be exposed to the messages. For example, we cannot merely ask consumers how they would rate a television commercial or newspaper advertisement without them actually having seen the ad. The consumer obviously must watch, hear, or read the advertisement before he or she can rate and comment on it. Historically, focus groups have been used to test advertising because the methodology allows consumers to hear, see, and read the advertisements. But this procedure can be done with CDs, DVDs, and the Internet. Consumers can be sent a CD or DVD to their home or business and watch the advertisement (print or electronic) on their own equipment. Consumers can also be exposed to advertising through the Internet.

Although there are still questions about control over the testing situation, because we really don't know who is answering the CD, DVD, or Internet questionnaire, the costs of research and the pervasiveness of computers and Internet access will force these methods to be accepted. These high-tech/Internet methodologies save time, money, work, and travel. An example may help support this idea.

In 1999, Wimmer-Hudson Research & Development was contacted by a major music company to investigate how the company could collect opinions from consumers who purchased its products (music CDs) or from radio station program directors who listen to new music and provide comments to the company. Historically, a small response card was included in the CD. Consumers who purchased the CD were asked to complete the small card and mail it back to the music company. In the case of program directors, the music company called these people on the telephone to retrieve their comments about new music releases. Enter the high-technology approach.

Wimmer-Hudson designed a way to include a questionnaire on the music CD. The CD can be played in a normal music system but also works in a computer. Included inside the CD container is a small card that asks consumers to listen to the CD on their normal music system and then take the CD and insert it into their computer. The computer automatically brings up a questionnaire that includes questions about the music selections included on the CD, evaluations of the CD cover, and even a test of introductions for the video planned for one of the songs on the CD. After the consumer answers the questions, he or she is instructed to sign on to the Internet. When on the Internet, the responses to the questionnaire are automatically sent to a secure music company Web site where the executives can view the responses to their new product.

This same procedure can be used to test literally any type of print or electronic advertising.

BIBLIOGRAPHY

Haley, R.I. and A.L. Baldinger (1991), "The ARF Copy Research Validity Project," *Journal of Advertising Research*, 31 (2), 11–32.

Leckenby, J. and N. Wedding (1982), *Advertising Management*. Columbus, OH: Grid Publishing.

Mehta, A. and S.C. Purvis (1997), "Evaluating Advertising Effectiveness Through Advertising Response Modeling," in *Measuring Advertising Effectiveness*, W.D. Wells, ed. Mahwah, NJ: Lawrence Erlbaum Associates, 325–34.

Merriam-Webster (1989), *Webster's Ninth New Collegiate Dictionary*. Springfield, MA: Merriam-Webster.

Walker, D. and T. Dubitsky (1994), "Why Liking Matters," *Journal of Advertising Research*, 34 (3), 9–18.

Watzlawick, P., J.B. Beavin, and D.D. Jackson (1967), *Pragmatics of Human Communication: A Study of Interactional Patterns, Pathologies, and Paradoxes*. New York: Norton.

Wimmer, R.D. and J.R. Dominick (2000), *Mass Media Research: An Introduction*, 6th ed. Belmont, CA: Wadsworth Publishing Company.

SUGGESTED READINGS

Several Web sites are listed here that contain a wealth of information about many of the topics discussed in this chapter. However, keep in mind that Web sites change often, and some of the Web sites listed here may no longer operate.

Advertising publications, references, research, research companies

http://ecommerce.vanderbilt.edu/
http://form.netscape.com/ads/links.html
http://home.inforamp.net/~shirleyu/
http://www.arfsite.org/Webpages/JAR_pages/JAR_primary/jar_issues.htm
http://www.reinartz.com/sci.htm
http://www.zarden.com/marketresearch/services/advres-a.html

Statistics

http://duke.usask.ca/~rbaker/stats.html
http://forum.swarthmore.edu/k12/mathtips/2digit5.html
http://interstat.stat.vt.edu/intersta.htm/
http://members.aol.com/johnp71/javastat.html
http://www.amstat.org/
http://www.cern.ch/Physics/DataAnalysis/BriefBook/
http://www.inria.fr/ariana/demos/MCMCML
http://www.math.washington.edu/~ejpecp/
http://www.math.yorku.ca/SCS/StatResource.html
http://www.maths.uq.edu.au/~gks/webguide/
http://www.maths.uq.oz.au/~pkp/probweb/probweb.html
http://www.stat.ufl.edu/vlib/statistics.html
http://www.statistics.com/
http://www.stats.gla.ac.uk/allstat/
http://www-sci.lib.uci.edu/HSG/Ref.html

Publications

Aronson. B. and R.L. Zeff (1999), *Advertising on the Internet*. New York: John Wiley & Sons.
Babbie, E.R. (1997), *The Practice of Social Research*, 8th ed. Belmont, CA: Wadsworth.
Bissland, J.H. (1990), "Accountability Gap: Evaluation Practices Show Improvement," *Public Relations Review*, 16 (2), 24–34.
Blalock, H.M. (1972), *Social Statistics*. New York: McGraw-Hill.
Block, M.P. and T.S. Brezen (1990), "Using Database Analysis to Segment General Media Audiences," *Journal of Media Planning*, 5 (4), 1–12.
Boyd, H.W., R. Westfall, and S.F. Stasch (1989), *Marketing Research: Text and Cases*, 7th ed. Homewood, IL: Richard D. Irwin.

Broom, G.M., S. Casey, and J. Ritchey (1997), "Toward a Conceptual Theory of Organizational Public Relationships," *Journal of Public Relations Research*, 9 (2), 83–98.

Browne, A. (1997), "Does Your Advertising Work?" *Colorado Business Magazine*, 24 (5), 72–75.

Cohen, J. (1988), *Statistical Power Analysis for the Behavioral Sciences*. New York: Academic Press.

Cook, W.A. and T.F. Dunn (1996), "The Changing Face of Advertising Research in the Information Age," *Journal of Advertising Research*, 36 (1), 55–71.

Davis, J.J. (1996), *Advertising Research: Theory and Practice*. Upper Saddle River, NJ: Prentice Hall.

Fenwick, I. and M.D. Rice (1991), "Reliability of Continuous Measurement Copy Testing Methods," *Journal of Advertising Research*, 31 (1), 23–29.

Fletcher, A. and T. Bowers (1991), *Fundamentals of Advertising Research*, 4th ed. Belmont, CA: Wadsworth.

Fox, S. (1984), *The Mirror Makers: A History of American Advertising and its Creators*. New York: William Morrow and Company, Inc.

Green, H. (1998), "The New Web Ratings Game," *BusinessWeek*, (April 27), 73–78.

Green, P.E., D.S. Tull, and G. Albaum (1988), *Research for Marketing Decisions*. Englewood Cliffs, NJ: Prentice Hall.

Haley, R. (1994), "A Rejoinder to Conclusions from the ARF's Copy Research Validity Project," *Journal of Advertising Research*, 34 (3), 33–34.

Haskins, J. (1976), *An Introduction to Advertising Research*. Knoxville, TN: Communication Research Center.

—— and A. Kendrick (1993), *Successful Advertising Research Methods*. Lincolnwood, IL: NTC Business Books.

Hurlburt, R.T. (1998), *Comprehending Behavioral Statistics*, 2d ed. Pacific Grove, CA: Brooks/Cole.

Jaccard, J. and M.A. Becker (1996), *Statistics for the Behavioral Sciences*, 3d ed. Belmont, CA: Wadsworth.

Jacoby, J. and W.D. Hoyer (1982), "Viewers' Miscomprehension of Televised Communication," *Journal of Marketing*, 46 (4), 12–27.

Kish, L. (1965), *Survey Sampling*. New York: John Wiley & Sons.

Leckenby, J. (1984), "Current Issues in the Measurement of Advertising Effectiveness," paper presented to the International Advertising Association, Tokyo, Japan.

—— and J.T. Plummer (1983), "Advertising Stimulus Measurement and Assessment Research: A Review of Advertising Testing Methods," *Current Issues and Research in Advertising*, 6 (2), 135–65.

Lehmann, E.L. (1991), *Testing Statistical Hypotheses*, 2d ed. Belmont, CA: Wadsworth.

Lloyd, D.W. and K.J. Clancy (1991), "CPMs vs. CPMIs: Implications for Media Planning," *Journal of Advertising Research*, 34 (4), 34–43.

Maleske, R.T. (1994), *Foundations for Gathering and Interpreting Behavioral Data: An Introduction to Statistics*. Pacific Grove, CA: Brooks/Cole.

Mason, R.D., D.A. Lind, and W.G. Marchal (1998), *Statistics: An Introduction*. Belmont, CA: Duxbury.

McQuarrie, E.F. (1996), *The Market Research Toolbox*. Thousand Oaks, CA: Sage Publications.

Moore, D.S. (1998), *Introduction to the Practice of Statistics*. New York: W.H. Freeman.

Nunnally, J.C. and I.H. Bernstein (1994), *Psychometric Theory*, 3d ed. New York: McGraw-Hill.

Percy, L. and J.R. Rossiter (1997), "A Theory-Based Approach to Pretesting Advertising," in *Measuring Advertising Effectiveness*, W.D. Wells, ed. Mahwah, NJ: Lawrence Erlbaum Associates, 267–82.

Raj, D. (1972), *The Design of Sample Surveys*. New York: McGraw-Hill.

Rosenthal, R. and R.L. Rosnow (1969), *Artifact in Behavioral Research*. New York: Academic Press.

Rossi, P. and H. Freeman (1982), *Evaluation: A Systematic Approach*. Beverly Hills, CA: Sage Publications.

Rossiter, J. and G. Eagleson (1994), "Conclusions from the ARF's Copy Research Validity Project," *Journal of Advertising Research*, 34 (3), 19–32.

Ryan, M. and D.C. Martinson (1990), "Social Science Research, Professionalism and PR Practitioners," *Journalism Quarterly*, 67 (2), 377–90.

Schultz, D. and B. Barnes (1994), *Strategic Advertising Campaigns*. Lincolnwood, IL: NTC Business Books.

Skinner, B.F. (1953), *Science and Human Behavior*. New York: Macmillan.

Toothaker, L.E. (1996), *Introductory Statistics for the Behavioral Sciences*, 2d ed. Pacific Grove, CA: Brooks/Cole.

Tukey, J.W. (1986), *The Collected Works of John W. Tukey*. Belmont, CA: Wadsworth and Brooks/Cole.

Williams, F. (1992), *Reasoning with Statistics*, 2d ed. New York: Holt, Rinehart & Winston.

18
International Research

Doss Struse

T he state of international marketing research is simply a reflection of the information needs of modern corporations. Whatever the causes, there is no question that business has been rising on a tide of globalization. With this has come the ancillary globalization of key business functions such as finance, planning, purchasing, manufacturing, R&D, and, perhaps most of all, marketing. In support of global marketing, the marketing services industries are becoming dominated by large international firms that can provide support around the globe. Of marketing services firms, advertising agencies are the most evolved toward a global model, with marketing research, graphic design, and PR firms rapidly consolidating into global networks in the 1990s.

The largest international marketing research firms have now become the largest firms in most major countries. ACNielsen, IMS, VNU, Taylor Nelson Sofres Interscarch (TNSI), NFO, Gartner Group, Research International, Aegis, IPSOS, UIG, Millward-Brown, and others are large both because they operate in many countries and because they have become the leaders in most of those countries. One major beneficial effects of the rise of these large international firms has been the development of a more sophisticated infrastructure for conducting marketing research in virtually all countries around the world. A second, related benefit has been the leveling of differences in marketing research capabilities and competencies among countries.

The focus of this discussion is on survey, sales tracking, and media research — that is, on research that is focused on collecting and analyzing information from customers and consumers — rather than on secondary research based on government economic or social statistics.

A LOOK BACK

To best appreciate the current state of international research, it is well to reflect back on what it was like just a single career lifetime ago, circa 1969.

A Client-Oriented Perspective

The emphasis of international businesses was to establish operations in countries and then grow this "local" business. The challenge was first market entry, then expansion from this beachhead, and only later optimization of the business. The management model used was a typical multilocal model with headquarters serving as the planning and coordinating arm. Headquarters might be deeply involved in market entry but would shift to a coordinating role after a market was opened. The role played by marketing research supported this model. Not uncommonly, headquarters might do research to identify which of the company's products might be most easily adapted to a local market and might undertake the first adaptations of the selected products. However, as the company was established in a country, the market research would shift to the local company. Given the limited role for international research per se, the range and complexity of international research was fairly circumscribed. It would not be unfair to characterize this as consisting mostly of studies such as

- ❑ Habits and practices,
- ❑ Target market definition,
- ❑ Concept appeal,
- ❑ Product performance and fulfillment, and
- ❑ Introductory advertising.

Although clients might conduct a study in multiple markets to assist in prioritizing markets for order of entry, the emphasis was on understanding consumers' response within a given market. There might have been some comparison of results at a macro level across markets, but the emphasis was on analysis and interpretation within market.

Market researchers of this period did not have the benefit of fax machines, e-mail networks, the Internet, low-cost jet services to any point on the globe, overnight express delivery services, the spread of English as the lingua franca, personal computers, cell phones, a highly evolved research company infrastructure, or another 30 years of accumulated experience in international business.

Researchers of the time had the encumbrance of wildly varying socioeconomic infrastructures among countries, widely varying laws and regulations affecting commerce and research, widely varied cultures, and a smaller pool of people with experience in multiple cultures and languages. Anyone working in the field at that time had at least one, and probably many more, horror story of how the products to be tested were barred from entry to the test country by health inspectors or customs officials, how the completed questionnaires were held in customs for three weeks before being released for shipment to the supplier's data processing center, how the translation of the test concept or product name meant something horrible in the local language, how the critical survey questions were mistranslated into nonsense in half the countries, or how the instructions for using the test product didn't take into account local conditions.

Doing international research was a slow, time-consuming process fraught with the opportunity for things to go wildly amiss because of misunderstandings and lack of sensitivity to local cultural and political factors. Given the time and professional labor required and the risk of mishaps, it isn't surprising that international research was a small segment of the total marketing research industry. Nor is it surprising that companies localized their research activity to a great extent after they were established in a country.

A Research Company–Oriented Perspective

Given the behavior of clients, research suppliers would have seen less demand for international research than for "local" research services. In many cases, the international research associated with a client's preparation for entering into a country would dry up when the client had entered the market and be supplanted by a local demand for services. Not surprising is the limited investment that research firms made in building up explicitly international capabilities. Companies interested in expansion were most likely to invest in building their home market business or expanding as client companies did by opening or acquiring operations in other countries to serve the local demand in that country.

The widely varying levels of economic development, social infrastructure, and government policy toward international business across countries discouraged research companies from building elaborate infrastructures of their own to support international research.

International research was labor intensive, slow, dependent on local knowledge, and risky because so many things could go wrong. Also, the demand for international research was less steady than that for "local" research. Just as clients of this time have their horror stories of projects gone awry, suppliers have even more, because they are more intimately involved in the logistics of working across borders and cultures.

This confluence of factors channeled the research companies interested in international expansion into a multilocal model parallel to that used by their clients. Perhaps a good example of this multilocal research model would be the ACNielsen Company. Nielsen had moved early to expand internationally, establishing operations as local companies throughout Europe, South America, and Austral-Asia. Nielsen's expansion served the needs of consumer goods companies operating as multilocals. The Nielsen companies operated to a common set of operational standards but operated independently. Nielsen had very little capability to integrate information across countries to provide regional or "world-wide" summaries for clients until the 1980s or later. This was not due to any inherent limitation in the information it was producing for clients but to the absence of sufficient infrastructure. ACNielsen is not alone in this regard but is simply a visible prototype for most of the industry.

A counterexample to this multilocal model (and harbinger of later developments) is IMS. Although one might argue that IMS was founded later than Nielsen, the real driving force for IMS to provide international and global information products was the industry it served. The pharmaceutical industry has adopted and operated on a global model, especially in R&D, far earlier than other industries. This is driven by disease, and therefore the consumer needs, being primarily a human condition rather a social or cultural condition. The ability to pay may be largely a social phenomenon, but the needs for ethical drugs are more universal. Although IMS operates on as wide a scale as Nielsen, it has provided global products and services in addition to local products from its inception.

The Special Challenges of International Research

International research and especially multicountry studies have several special challenges beyond the complicated logistics of a large project in various locations. Researchers responsible for multicountry work must be prepared to deal with problems in

- ❑ Sampling,
- ❑ Culture,
- ❑ Language,
- ❑ Literacy and education,
- ❑ Attitudes toward research,
- ❑ Regulation, and
- ❑ Context.

Depending on the specific countries included in a multicountry survey, one may have either readily available, high-quality sampling frames in the form of computerized databases or an absence of any adequate sampling frame, which forces a geographic approach or building one's own sampling frame. Usually the availability of adequate lists or databases is correlated with the degree of economic development. Some countries experiencing rapid economic development will offer a special challenge of good sampling frames for the core urban centers but poor capabilities for the areas surrounding the core of the city and for secondary cities or the hinterland.

Culture has various effects that are intertwined with, but independent of, language. These may be as obvious as the prohibition of certain foods or beverages or as subtle as downplaying negative opinions.

Language receives significant attention from researchers because it is so central and has such direct impact on the research process and content. Although access to major European languages has not been a significant barrier, the ready access to the less commonly used languages and dialects can be. If nothing else, the process of translation and verification of translations has historically been time consuming. Language has another effect on the management of research projects. Unless one has coders fluent in each language, it is necessary to do coding locally. One impact is that researchers may shy away from using unstructured or open-ended questions in multicountry studies because of the complexities of coding in multiple languages and the costs of doing so. There has been a move also to do data entry locally for the same reasons.

An effect sometimes overlooked by researchers from highly developed cultures is that of literacy and educational levels. Some of the seemingly straightforward questions used extensively in marketing research involve highly sophisticated concepts and ways of thinking about objects. People with less exposure to education and less experience in reading may interpret the task posed by research in a totally different way. The notion of numerically scaling one's feeling about a brand is a relatively modern concept. The average person in nineteenth-century America might not have had any idea of how to respond to such a line of questioning.

Not unrelated to the level of social development and education are attitudes toward doing research itself. Whereas in western, developed societies, research has been accepted as legitimate and providing some overall economic benefit, this may not be the case in all societies or all segments of society. A suspicious consumer or a consumer who does not see the potential benefits of research is less than an ideal subject. This is especially tricky, in that when information has been recorded on a survey form or captured in a data file, it tends to be seen as real. The limitations of respondents may be lost unless they provide nonsensical or inconsistent answers.

In some areas, governments have regulations that directly or indirectly affect how one can do research or the content of research. In some cases, this is as broad as prohibiting making comparative tests of competitors' products or commercials. Or, it may be that interviewers must be licensed and register with the local police station before doing any interviewing in an area.

Although there is a movement of cultures toward "one world," there are still differences in what is available to consumers from place to place. Imagine doing a "market basket" study in which one is trying to compare local prices paid for a market basket of equivalent, commonly purchased goods. You will have trouble including, say, a McDonald's hamburger in your portfolio of products if you are working in a country where beef is not an accepted food.

Unfortunately, there is no formula or cookbook solution to all of the problems that may arise.

Regional Variations

This scenario did vary by region. Those U.S. corporations with a huge home market had less reason to turn to international expansion as early as did European companies. Europe and European companies had a long tradition of international trade, as well as extensive experience over centuries of social and economic interaction across cultural and political borders. European companies with relatively small home markets and relatively modest distances between countries turned quickly to international expansion, though there was relatively little emphasis initially to develop even Pan-European brands, let alone world brands.

This international experience soon led European-based companies to expand beyond Western Europe into the Middle East, Africa, and Asia. The multilocal model was again the basis for managing these far-flung organizations. As this expansion unfolded, marketing research companies were founded locally or expanded on a multilocal model to serve the country-by-country needs of clients.

Other regions generally did not have the industrial base or level of development for their indigenous corporations to expand through entry into Europe or the United States. Consequently, the research industry generally developed as a local business, with new entries by European, or occasionally U.S., research companies.

Japan was to prove an exception as it brought a different managerial and production model to certain industries. Japan centralized product development and manufacturing in Japan, where it could benefit from economies of scale and the "experience curve effect." Japan initially built what was an export business, only establishing local operations under pressure or much later when the advantage of scale or experience was no longer a significant competitive advantage.

Because Japan initially targeted developed economies — such as the United States, Canada, and later Europe — with sophisticated, value-added products, it was able to purchase marketing and marketing research services in these markets fairly easily, because these countries were the ones with the most highly evolved marketing and research infrastructures.

Given this context, it is not surprising that the epicenter of the international research industry was Europe rather than the United States or another region.

Seeds of Change

Several factors have been at work to fundamentally change the world and the world of business. Political stability and relative peace has enabled the continued lowering of barriers to free trade and the free movement of capital. The continued vitality of capitalism has reduced disparities in the standard of living between regions as the quest for profit has pushed manufacturing to lower cost regions. Continued deregulation of industry has enabled the spread of competition, which lowers prices and increases choice for buyers. The net is a continued expansion of the world economy, greatly expanded interaction among countries, and a rising tide of prosperity.

As the competitive, capitalistic business model has spread and as deregulation has continued, economies of scale have become more valuable than ever. Advantage of scale has been accentuated by the rise of "monoculturism," that is, the convergence of interests, aspirations, and preferences among people of similar socioeconomic status regardless of their cultural or ethnic origins. At the same time, corporations have recognized the value of brands and the accelerating expense of establishing new brands in a highly competitive, global marketplace. Economies of scale have moved to marketing and advertising in the 1990s.

Whereas a previous generation of business managers operated from core technologies and products adapted to local conditions and marketed locally, the business managers of the 1990s operate from the basis of core brands under central direction and global or regional production supported by local sales and distribution.

A LOOK AT INTERNATIONAL RESEARCH TODAY

Marketing research practice and the marketing research industry have evolved in response to the changes taking place in the world economy and as expressed in client needs.

In contrast to 30 years ago, international marketing research has become a large business in its own right. Of the $12 to $14 billion spent for marketing research annually, international research accounts for more than 25%, according to data compiled by *Advertising Age* (1999a, b), Honomichl (1999), and ESOMAR (1998). The remainder of the bulk of the spending is done by clients that are principally global in scope, though the specific projects commissioned may be "local." The top 25 marketing research companies account for more than 50% of the total industry. Among these companies, nearly half their revenues are derived from outside their home countries.

This growth in the market has been driven by clients' needs to establish, build, and maintain brands that transcend the boundaries of countries. Clients need a much wider range of research today than 30 years ago, in addition to needing to study multiple countries and segments simultaneously.

The growth of global research organizations has followed a parallel path with the evolution of global ad agencies and communication companies and has been intertwined with their evolution. This close connection has perhaps slowed the evolution of the research companies at times. Robert Maxwell moved aggressively in the 1980s to build an information empire as well as a mass communications empire. Maxwell acquired AGB/NFO/SRG, forming the most extensive global research network of the time. However, the aftermath of the collapse of Maxwell's companies was to splinter this network.

The various pieces have reformed in other combinations to be important components of three different companies today—Nielsen, NFO, and TNSI.

WPP moved early to build an international research network, acquiring Research International, Millward-Brown, and BMRB. However, the financial difficulties faced by WPP in the early 1990s limited the expansion of these businesses for several years other than through alliances and licensing deals. Although both companies have grown strongly in recent years, there is no telling what they might have been like if not constrained by WPP's problems at that time.

Key Enablers of Change

It is difficult to overestimate the effects of fax machines, e-mail networks, the Internet, video conferencing, low-cost jet transportation, express delivery services, English becoming the language of business, personal computers, and cell phones on the practice of international research. These have immeasurably made communication immediate, extensive, continuous, and personal. In addition to directly accelerating the planning and coordination of research, they have also directly accelerated implementation. Questionnaires can be sent around the world in minutes. Just consider the savings in the time required for translating a questionnaire into various languages and then having "back translations" done to check the adequacy of the original translation. Or, consider how much time can be saved in briefing local field agencies by using video conferencing or even by flying the field supervisors to a common briefing location. Or, consider how much time is saved by entering data locally through PCs and electronically transmitting the data file to the coordinating center rather than physically shipping paper questionnaires, which might be held in customs, mislaid in transit, or even lost.

Professional societies and education have also proved to be important enablers, though their effects may be less obviously visible than the impacts of technology. However, the steady spread of professional associations and standard-setting groups from country to country has helped build both the industry infrastructure and the pool of trained professionals. There can be no question that without the indigenous professional societies, the growth of the market research industry would have been slowed.

International research is still slower than domestic work. However, this difference is not due to slow communications but rather to differing levels of data collection capacity across countries. That is, the difference in speed is more a function of scheduling and capacity rather than communications, whereas in the "old days," the delays were more often than not due to slow communications.

A Client-Oriented Perspective

In contrast to the past when clients were focused on relatively straightforward issues of which products to use to enter countries, clients today are dealing with how to most efficiently market brands across as many countries as possible. That is, marketers are wrestling with how to evolve brand identities and brand equities across multiple countries and cultures and how to optimize their marketing investments across as many countries as possible. With this has come a shift in the analytic and interpretative focus of research. The emphasis has become to understand the similarities and differences among countries or market segments. In addition to classic, basic research designs, clients are now expecting to be able to execute more sophisticated types of studies in the areas of benefit segmentation, occasion and need-based segmentation, brand positioning, brand equity, return on advertising, customer relationship management, and so on across any number of countries and geographic areas as necessary. In most cases, the unit of analysis is not the country but a type of consumer or customer. Countries may vary in the mix of various segments but are not regarded as having materially different segments of any relevance.

Implementing international research, even highly complex studies, has become significantly easier, less labor intensive, and faster in the past 30 years. Also, international research has become much less risky; although misunderstandings are still possible, these are much less common due to modern communications, the evolution of the research industry, and the development of a modern infrastructure for marketing research.

It would be fair to state that though the degree of complexity and sophistication of "domestic" and "international" research designs was quite far apart 30 years ago, there are few, if any, systematic differences today. To illustrate, it is common to have clients commissioning studies such as

- ❏ A latent-class segmentation study of the personal computer market across 30 countries;
- ❏ A discrete choice study to estimate demand for new financial services products across 40 countries;
- ❏ A tracking study of customer satisfaction in a business-to-business market across 25 countries;
- ❏ A tracking study of consumer response to advertising in more than 100 countries;
- ❏ A study to track brand equity in more than 30 countries for an IT (information technology) product; and
- ❏ Studies to track brand equity, consumer satisfaction, and price elasticity in more than 100 countries for a consumer product sold through company retail outlets.

International still takes more time than domestic research. It takes more management time. And, it costs substantially more than domestic research, though it is not clear if this is due to the nature of the work or to the way most of the large international research firms are managed.

Beyond the ability of international marketing research firms to fulfill clients' needs for sophisticated multicountry research, the entire marketing research industry has become more capable. Through the example set by the leading multinational clients, many "local" research agencies have been exposed to the most sophisticated research designs. Through these multinational companies' local operations, local research companies have been exposed to the sophisticated research practices. The result is that research firms in virtually any part of the world can now design, implement, and analyze a range of fairly sophisticated work. This has been accelerated by the widespread availability of powerful PCs and statistical software packages. The net is that the difference in expertise and sophistication between the most developed and least developed countries has diminished, if not disappeared.

This improvement in the availability of competent marketing research firms is producing some redefinition in the role of the international research firm. Clients have discovered that it is now easier and less risky than ever before to organize their own "virtual" international network of research agencies and manage projects directly. The principal benefit is lower costs at the expense of more managerial time. In some cases, this is resulting in pressure on international firms to reexamine their practices in coordinating international research projects to lower costs without lowering profits.

Although research companies have responded to the need for sophisticated, comparable research across many countries, there are several factors that still make life difficult for clients and suppliers. Despite a rising tide of prosperity and the emergence of a monoculturalism, the social infrastructure of countries still varies widely. The impact is that though the same classes of research can be conducted virtually everywhere, the specific method for collecting data will vary locally. For example, the virtually universal penetration, acceptance, and usage of home telephones in the United States has led to roughly 50% of consumer research in the United States being carried out by telephone. However, in Europe, despite similar levels of prosperity, only one-third as much research is done by telephone, and it is even less in South America and Asia. Consequently, to reach the same sector of the population in a variety of countries, it may be necessary to use the telephone in some countries and personal interviewing in others. Similarly, in the United States, the concept of the "mail panel" is well established, with at least three vendors maintaining standing panels in excess of 250,000 households each. Until recently, this capability had not been widely available outside the United States.

There are other factors that mandate a degree of specialization in international research by both suppliers and clients, including some vexing technical issues yet to be fully resolved.

A Research Company-Oriented Perspective

Marketing researchers had a foreshadowing of the changes that would affect the research industry in observing the changes reshaping the advertising agencies during the 1980s and continuing through the 1990s.

Ad agencies were the first of the marketing services to feel the need of clients developing and maintaining global brands. The initial attempt to create broad international presence by affiliations with local agencies in various countries was insufficient. The next wave was based on acquisitions, mergers, and expansions to create an integrated global presence.

Just as clients discovered that economies of scale operated more strongly than ever in today's economic environment, ad agencies too discovered this, which set off a rapid consolidation in this industry. Saatchi & Saatchi was perhaps the prototypical ad agency that seized on this trend of consolidation to propel itself to the first rank for a period. However, Interpublic, Omnicom, True North, WPP, and others quickly followed suit, accelerating the consolidation underway.

Clients' emerging need for building and maintaining global brands soon manifested itself in demand for more multicountry research, more sophisticated research, and more sophisticated analysis. The research industry had to move from providing what was, in effect, basic one-country-at-a-time market research to complex multicountry studies with analysis that differentiated local phenomena from "global" phenomena.

The marketing research companies' initial response was like that of the ad agencies: They built their reach through loose affiliations with indigenous local research companies. It was not uncommon even a few years ago for a visitor to the leading local research company in Thailand to see a wall of company logos from all of the Western research companies with which it was affiliated. The inherent lack of control and consistency in these loose affiliations led the larger research firms to invest in acquiring local partners or starting their own indigenous operations. Beginning in the late 1980s and continuing through the present, large global research networks comparable to the ad agency networks were being built, principally through acquisitions and mergers. Although integrating newly acquired businesses is anything but easy, the large international firms have been able to bring common standards into their operations, common training and education for their staffs, and common communications and logistics systems. The emergence of these more tightly integrated networks is a major factor in the continuing progress by the industry in seamlessly implementing more and more complex international research.

Regional Differences

Because the effort to build global brands originated with clients' headquarters, the effect on the industry was quite different by region. The major corporations driving globalization were typically headquartered in a few countries—the United States, the United Kingdom, Germany, Japan, Benelux, France, and Italy. Not surprisingly, the research companies building the most extensive global capabilities have been originated in these countries. The exception is Japan. Firms in the United States, with the exception of ACNielsen, were relatively late to take advantage of the trend toward globalization. This was probably a legacy of the United

States' historic tendency to isolationism and of the United Kingdom's historic tendency toward international trade. With U.S. research companies in the past not having extensive experience internationally and with relatively easy access to U.K. research companies offering both this experience and the convenience of working in English, many U.S. corporate clients chose to work with U.K. research agencies rather than their normal U.S. suppliers. This is one of the factors that makes London disproportionately important in the research industry. It is arguably the "capital" for international research.

With modern communications, English becoming the language of business, and the growth of the large international research networks, it is increasingly common to find clients based in one country dealing directly with a supplier team based in another country. In general, these arrangements work well for research design and analysis; however, conflicts often arise over the management of project logistics. Or, more accurately, conflicts arise over the management of communications of project logistics. American clients are oriented to being very involved in the day-to-day management of projects and are likely to make "on the fly" modifications to the study during the first few days of implementation. This is not the practice in much of Europe or the rest of the world. This is related partly to differences in data collection modes and partly to professional practice. Whereas a U.S. computer-assisted telephone interview (CATI) center may provide real-time updates on project progress, this is not common elsewhere. Weekly updates might be more common, especially because the interviewing mode might be face-to-face rather than telephone. This can be an area of considerable stress and frustration on both sides unless expectations are explicitly managed from the outset.

A VIEW OF LEADING PRACTICES

Major international research companies have invested significantly in communications networks to tie together their operations around the globe. Although only a few years ago this might have included only telephone and fax systems in every office, today every office has a company e-mail system and Internet access. The most sophisticated companies have established wide area networks to enable working groups that cut across physical boundaries. These advanced communication systems further enable the deployment of common standards, methods, and training. All these lead to greater consistency, predictability, and timeliness.

The premier companies are building integrated knowledge bases to capture their research expertise, client knowledge, local business and cultural knowledge, and so forth in order to extend this knowledge to any professional in the company. These systems also make it possible to centrally manage and distribute knowledge and experience across the entire company. Straightforward examples are a central registry of all projects, a master database of incidence levels across countries, and a master database of interviewing costs, which could be accessed from any office.

Although advanced communications systems speed the flow of information regarding the planning and implementation of research projects, a few companies are moving to reengineer and automate the entire project management process rather than continue to rely on manual scheduling and control methods. One area on which leading international research companies are focusing involves using technology to accelerate the development of questionnaires, the preparation of accurate CATI or CAPI (computer-assisted personal interview) scripts if computer-assisted interviewing is called for, the translation of questionnaires, and the set-up of the basic tabulation or analysis of the data collected. Considerable progress has been made in developing libraries of commonly used survey questions along with the correct associated translation into the most common languages. These libraries, coupled with software for visually building questionnaires with "drag and drop" tools and with software that generates CATI/CAPI scripts automatically from questionnaires, offer significant reductions in the time and labor required to prepare and field international research projects.

These same companies are also in the forefront of extending the reach of technology right to the respondent, investing heavily in CATI and CAPI systems for more automatic interaction with respondents. Most recently, companies have begun exploring the Internet as the next generation of automated exchanges with respondents.

Greatly increased communications have enabled a change in organization within research companies. In the past, it was common to either have duplicated expertise in several countries or centralize important types of expertise in the "home" country. Now it is possible to have a distributed base of expertise with the location driven by where the expertise is most easily obtained. Increasingly, the leading companies have multiple competency centers. For example, it is not uncommon for expertise in IT research to be centered in the United States, expertise in alcoholic beverages to be in London, and expertise for luxury goods to reside in Paris.

The aspiration of the leading firms is to provide seamless service globally, regionally, and locally to clients from any location. There is no question that the leaders have made significant progress toward this goal.

Considerations in Doing an International Project

As noted previously, there is no universally applicable cookbook method for managing international research. There are many special factors that still must be taken into account today, despite all of the tremendous progress in building a more uniform research infrastructure.

There are, however, five "rules" that anyone undertaking multicountry research should follow:

1. *Get someone who knows more than you do.* Although working through one of the larger, global research companies will appear to cost more, these companies provide a coordination

and quality control service that is worthwhile in its own right. These companies also provide the experience and knowledge needed to ensure a successful project.

2. *Focus on what you are trying to accomplish rather than how you would do it.* In short, let the experts you hire advise you on how to accomplish the objective. To do this, you must be blindingly clear about what your objectives and goals are and stay a step removed from the implementation details.

3. *Set expectations explicitly for the end users, the researchers, and yourself.* International projects cannot be run as they would be in your home country. For example, it may simply be impossible to guarantee daily project updates, even though these are common in the United States. Similarly, research vendors will have different views on how they interact with their clients and who holds the responsibility for certain actions. These expectations by all parties need to be made explicit, and appropriate compromises must be struck.

4. *Be realistic.* It should go without saying than one must deal with reality rather than simply one's wishes. There are some things you can change but others that are beyond any client's ability to influence. It is critical to make this distinction as early as possible.

5. *Don't waste people's time.* A common "sin" is to request cost quotes from 30 countries for ten different variations of study parameters. If every client does this, every research company will need to have a dedicated staff of people doing nothing but cost variations. ESOMAR (1999) publishes surveys of costs by country for a variety of types of research, and these data provide a useful basic benchmark to gauge the prices quoted by suppliers and initiate the discussion of how to achieve a fair value for both client and supplier.

THE NEXT ADVANCES

Transnational Research and Transnational Research Companies

As marketers evolve toward global branding and global marketing and as the world edges toward monoculturalism, countries become less important as an organizing or operating basis than specific consumer or customer segments. The challenge for research companies is to move their operations from a largely multilocal basis to a transnational basis.

The steps toward distributed competency centers are consistent with moving to a transnational model. Universally accessible knowledge systems are consistent with the transnational model. However, it will be necessary to move data collection and the management of data collection from being multilocal to transnational.

Some tentative steps have been taken by leading companies in setting up CATI centers that operate regionally. Several firms have the capability to do telephone interviewing throughout Europe from the United Kingdom or Belgium with native language speakers covering all of the European languages. These centers are also capable of conducting interviews in the United States and Canada. At least one U.S. research company has the capability of conducting international telephone research into most European, Latin American, and Austral-Asian countries. In Austral-Asia, several centers are offering regionwide telephone interviewing.

Codification of Knowledge

Marketing researchers have developed an extensive battery of experience carrying out international research in the past 30 years, and especially the past 10 years. However, much of the useful, practical lore is resident in specific experts with research suppliers or clients rather than formally codified. The knowledge management systems being developed by research companies and other professional service companies will accelerate translating this lore into knowledge available to a broader range of professionals. The benefits ultimately will be more appropriate research designs, more consistent quality, faster project implementation, less rework and waste, and more actionable results.

Overcoming Cultural and Methodological Biases

There are several sources of bias stemming from cultural and methodological factors common in international research. The research industry will need to address and resolve these if international research is to continue to grow in value:

❑ Currently, any extensive multicountry study involves multiple modes of interviewing. What has not been fully addressed are the biases affected due to the mode of the interview. That is, there are indications that CAPI interviews will yield different answers to certain types of questions relative to paper-and-pencil face-to-face interviews or telephone interviews.

❑ Different cultures appear to have differing tendencies in how rating scales are used. Although adjustment methods have been proposed, these are cumbersome to apply in practice across the extensive batteries of scales used in most segmentation or brand equity research. Although normalization of responses within culture and within respondent eliminates some types of bias, it also eliminates any information regarding the absolute level of response and preserves only relative levels.

❑ The availability of accurate and complete sampling frames varies immensely across countries, which makes it problematic to easily implement equivalent sampling plans in all areas.

❏ The willingness of the population to cooperate in surveys is quite different across countries and is rapidly changing, especially in countries with the largest research industries.

The Internet

The degree of change implied by these steps to transnational data collection will accelerate as the Internet becomes a significant vehicle for collecting information from consumers. Although the Internet would require respondents to have a local Internet service provider, the research capability could be managed from a single site, given access to a variety of language skills.

The impact of the Internet, though still some ways off in large parts of the world, on the marketing research practice will be vastly more profound than any other technology of the past 50 years. The Internet will enable marketing researchers to engage and interact with consumers and customers as "stakeholders" rather than as "subjects" in an investigation. Bringing a richly interactive and adaptive information-sharing experience into the home or the workplace will offer new possibilities for deeper understanding and insight into the relations between consumers and the products and services they confront. In many cases, marketing research learning will become embedded in the very nature of the exchanges between customers and marketers rather than standing apart as a separate stream of activities.

Beyond additional learning, Internet research may bring unprecedented speed, enabling researchers to deliver answers in real time rather than in weeks or months.

And perhaps most exciting, the Internet-enabled methods may provide the key to address marketing accountability; that is, what return do the investments made in marketing programs produce over time? This is the "Holy Grail" that marketers and researchers have sought but have never quite been able to grasp.

Virtual Reality

The rapid development of visualization and graphic processing power will bring true virtual reality to the PC of the near future. Virtual reality will enable consumers to experience new products and services before these exist, experience new advertising and communications stimuli before companies commit millions to their production and distribution, and interact with researchers and marketers in new ways. In many cases, consumers' behavior in the virtual reality presented them will be the critical observations rather than their verbal responses to a battery of questions.

Integration of Attitudinal and Behavioral Information

The technologies underlying e-commerce, the Internet, and virtual reality will contribute to a better fusion of attitudinal and behavioral data.

With an ability to interact with the same consumers over time will come a greatly enhanced ability to develop knowledge of changes in their attitudes and behaviors. This will be a first step to building the connections between these.

AN OUTLOOK ON THE INDUSTRY

International marketing research will continue to grow in importance given the course set by the large, global companies dominating the world's economies. The continued leverage afforded by economies of scale in global branding and marketing ensures the continued growth and maturation of international research as a professional discipline and an industry segment. As the capital intensity of this segment increases, the consolidation of the industry underway will further intensify.

BIBLIOGRAPHY

Advertising Age (1999), "Research Business Report," (May 24), [available at www.adage.com].
—— (1999), "International Research," (May 19), [available at www.adage.com].
ESOMAR (1998), *Annual Study on the Market Research Industry.* Amsterdam: ESOMAR.
—— (1999), *1998 Press Study.* Amsterdam: ESOMAR.
Honomichl, J. (1999), "Honomichl Global 50," *Marketing News,* (August 16), H1–H23 [available at www.ama.org/pubs/mn].

SUGGESTED READINGS

Advertising Research Foundation (1996), "Global Research: The Critical Component for International Success," 2nd Annual Global Research Workshop, New York.
Agres, Stuart J. and Tony M. Dubitsky (1996), "Changing Needs for Brands," *Journal of Advertising Research,* 36 (1), 21–31.
Barnard, Philip (1999), "The Expanding Universe of Marketing Research," presented to the British Marketing Research Association Conference.
Bartlett, C.A. and S. Ghoshal (1989), *Managing Brands Across Border: The Transnational Solution.* London, Random House
——and —— (1995), *Transnational Management: Text, Cases, and Readings in Cross-Border Management.* Burr Ridge, IL: Richard D. Irwin.
Bartram, Peter (1990), "The Challenge for Research Internationally in the Decade of the 1990s," *Journal of Advertising Research,* 30 (6), RC3–RC6.
Buzzell, Robert D., John A. Quelch, and Christopher Bartlett (1995), *Global Marketing Management: Cases and Readings.* Reading, MA: Addison-Wesley.
Drucker, P. H. (1993), *Post-Capitalist Society.* New York: Harper Business.
Fujitake, Kikuharu (1990), "The Transition and Future of Marketing Research," *Journal of Advertising Research,* 30 (2), 58–67.
Funakawa, Atsushi (1997), *Transcultural Management: A New Approach for Global Organizations.* London: Jossey-Bass.
Hickson, David J. and Derek Pugh (1996), *Management Worldwide: The Impact of Societal Culture on Organizations Around the Globe.* London: Penguin.

Huysman, B. (1998), "Telephone Research in Asia—The Wave of the Future?" *Quirk's Marketing Research Review,* (November), 32–36 [available at www.quirks.com].

Kotabe, Masaaki and Kristiaan Helsen (1997), *Global Marketing Management.* New York: John Wiley & Sons.

Leavitt, T. (1983), "The Globalization of Markets," *Harvard Business Review,* 61 (May/June).

Lunn, S. (1999), "Coordinating Multi-Country Research," presentation at the Marketing Research Association Conference.

Marquardt, Michael J. (1998), *The Global Advantage: How World Class Organizations Improve Performance Through Globalization.* Houston, TX: Gulf.

McDonald, C. and P. Vangelder, eds. (1998), *ESOMAR Handbook of Market and Opinion Research,* 4th ed. Amsterdam: ESOMAR

Mirza, Hafiz, ed. (1999), *Global Competitive Strategies in the New World Economy: Multilateralism, Regionalization and the Transnational Firm.* Northampton, MA: Edward Elgar.

Mueller, Barbara (1995), *International Advertising: Communicating Across Cultures.* Belmont, CA: Wadsworth.

Ohmae, K. (1995), *The End of the Nation State, the Rise of Regional Economies.* New York: The Free Press.

Quelch, John A. and Christopher A. Bartlett, eds. (1998), *Global Marketing Management,* 4th ed. Reading, MA: Longman.

Redwood, J. (1993), *The Global Marketplace: Capitalism and Its Future.* London: Harper Collins.

Yip, George S. (1992), *Globalizing Strategy.* Englewood Cliffs, NJ: Prentice Hall.

19
Measuring the Equity in Customer Relationships

James G. Barnes

I n this chapter, we discuss the need to measure how well a firm or organization is doing in the creation and management of customer relationships. The implication of this is that a company cannot begin to improve on the relationships it has with customers until it knows the current health of those relationships—where they are strong and where they are weak, which customers have the strongest relationships and where relationships are at risk, which aspects of the relationships should be shored up, and what the customer finds appealing or unappealing.

SHAREHOLDER VALUE

In recent years, considerable attention has been turned in corporate circles to the creation of *shareholder value*. This focus results from the realization that one of the most important (if not the most important) responsibilities of management is the enhancement on behalf of shareholders of their investment in the company. Although there is certainly good reason to advocate that the interests of other stakeholders—among them employees, customers, and communities—should also be protected, the current focus of most large, publicly traded companies is on the creation of shareholder value. But there is no generally accepted definition of what shareholder value involves. How, exactly, does management go about the creation of shareholder value?

Historically and today in many companies, shareholder value is equated with current stock price. Management is perceived to be advancing the interests of shareholders if the stock price moves upward each quarter. Corporate performance and the compensation of CEOs are closely tied to such short-term financial measures as return on capital invested, earnings per share, and operating income.

There is growing disillusionment in some quarters with the nature of such corporate performance measures and with the focus on historic, short-term, internal financial measures to guide investors and assess shareholder value creation. Some authors such as Henry Mintzberg (1999) and Peter Drucker (Andrews 1999) are openly critical of corporations that tie CEO compensation to short-term movements in the stock price and to corporate performance measures that are entirely financial and historic, arguing that the achievement of such objectives may not really add value for the shareholder.

There has been a recent movement toward a reliance on additional measures of corporate performance and, by extension, of shareholder value. This development has sparked a burgeoning movement within and outside the accounting profession that is focused on the development of other measures of corporate performance and on the acceptance in the accounting and investment communities of the legitimacy of nonfinancial, intangible measures as a basis for evaluating performance.

Historically, businesses have measured the things that have been easy to measure or whose performance is automatically captured, because they had to *for accounting purposes*. Companies measure sales because they need to issue invoices to customers and because they have to pay the tax department. They measure productivity per employee because it represents a basis for compensation and because increased productivity is a good thing. They measure things that are easily measured and that are quantifiable in easily accepted units: dollars, minutes and seconds, number of defects, number of complaints, and so on.

A focus on a "balanced scorecard" has emerged in the 1990s as stock exchanges, regulatory bodies, professional accounting organizations, some companies themselves, and various critics have come to the realization that historic, financial measures are an inadequate reflection of the actual performance of the corporation or of its ability to create *future* shareholder value for those investors whose time horizon extends beyond the next quarter.

Attention has turned at the most senior levels of management to the measurement and reporting of more intangible measures of corporate performance, things that are not reported in dollars or minutes and that have typically not been measured in most organizations. Some of these include customer satisfaction and retention, customer turnover, customer service standards, employee turnover, employee training, new product development, innovation, partnerships, and strategic alliances (Brancato 1997). The movement toward the establishment of new corporate performance measures is entirely consistent with a management emphasis on customer retention and relationships, which makes it all the more important that companies begin to measure these key corporate assets.

Short-term value creation is focused on managing the stock price so that sales and profit targets are met. Because stock price is so volatile, linked as it often is to the quarterly reporting of earnings, management is encouraged to drive revenues through promotions that may, in fact, have the effect of diminishing long-term customer loyalty and to cut costs, often by reducing staff and thereby impairing customer service. The effect, in the short run, is to achieve profitability and financial targets. But this is not the achievement of shareholder value, except possibly for those shareholders who wish to cash out on the back of an inflated stock price.

Real shareholder value is created by guaranteeing the long-term viability and growth of the company. Shareholder value creation is, therefore, intimately tied to customer loyalty, for it is this loyalty that will deliver the stream of earnings needed to drive sales growth. Customers deliver revenue, and they do so in perpetuity as long as they are satisfied. Long-term customer satisfaction drives customer relationships. Indeed, genuine customer relationships will never develop unless the customer is continually satisfied with the company and the way in which he or she is treated.

The links, then, are obvious. Management must pay attention to the creation of value for customers, which drives customer satisfaction, which leads to the creation of customer relationships, which leads to the retention of customers and to their long-term patronage, which contributes to shareholder value.

UNDERSTANDING CUSTOMER VALUE

It is important that marketing practitioners and others within the firm understand the connection between the various components of the chain that links customer value creation to shareholder value. Simply put, marketing is all about *creating value* for customers. Many companies today profess to be dedicated to value creation or adding value for their customers. The sad fact is, however, that few really understand their customers well enough to know exactly how they should go about creating or adding value in ways that customers will recognize and appreciate. Many firms fall into the trap of attempting to create value for customers, using as a definition management's own view of what the customer values. The result, while costing the company money to implement and deliver, leaves the customer cold because it simply does not represent a valued addition to the offer or, as it has come to be called in many firms, the *value proposition*.

This calls out for research directed at understanding value, as defined by the customer. Customers see value in many places and in many forms. It is not simply value for money. Value can be created and added for customers through many different actions and activities of the company. Value creation does not require product modification or price discounting. In fact, in many cases, lower prices are counterproductive to creating a value proposition that customers will really appreciate. It makes a great deal more sense for companies to focus on creating value for customers through improved service delivery, increasing contributions to the community in which the customer lives, and making it easier for the customer to deal with them. Value relates to how the customer is served, how he or she is treated and made to feel.

Value can be added by making improvements in a company's service delivery processes and systems. Again, research is generally useful to determine where service quality meets customer expectations and where it is deficient. It is necessary to measure service quality at a series of different levels and not to focus only on the technical delivery of service. Although time and space do not permit a review of the details of service quality measurement, suffice it to say that the customer defines service as more than the functional provision of the product or service. It is important to examine the nature of the core service, the systems and processes that the firm has in place to support service delivery, the accuracy and timeliness of service delivery, and the interaction among the customer, the firm, and its employees and systems.

The value that is created for the customer by the firm contributes to the customer's level of satisfaction with the company, how it conducts its business, and what it has to offer. Again, there is more to customer satisfaction than meets the eye. Many firms take the pulse of customer satisfaction from time to time but measure the concept far too simplistically. We need to ask, satisfaction with what? It is, for example, entirely possible that customers may be quite satisfied with a company's core products or services, and even with support services such as delivery and billing, but may be so dissatisfied with the manner in which they are treated by staff that they will refuse to deal with the company ever again. Satisfaction is a function of the customer's interaction with the company on a number of different levels. All of these must be taken into account if we are to have an accurate picture of satisfaction levels and the factors that contribute to them.

Customer relationships are the result of long periods of customer satisfaction. If a customer is not satisfied with his or her dealings with a company, it is highly unlikely (barring unusual circumstances) that a close, positive, genuine relationship will develop. It takes a certain time for awareness to develop into familiarity and familiarity into a special relationship. Satisfaction is one of the conditions necessary for a genuine relationship to emerge. Companies need to know how far along they are in creating relationships with their customers. They need to know where relationships are strong and where they are at risk. They need to know the health of their customer relationships as compared with those of their competitors.

Long-standing customer relationships represent a company's most valuable assets. These are assets that will pay dividends well into the future. By knowing how much equity really resides in its customer relationships, a company can have a very good understanding of how these relationships will pay returns to shareholders in the future through their contribution to a stream of revenue on which the company can rely.

The measurement of concepts such as service quality, customer satisfaction, and customer relationship equity must be tied directly to strategy. Many companies have established a corporate strategy of "relationship marketing," the premise being that they will achieve success through the creation and enhancement of customer relationships. We set aside for the moment the question of whether or not many firms really understand the nature of customer relationships and what it takes to establish and sustain them. If a company subscribes to such a strategy, it is imperative that its success in delivering on such a strategy be measured.

But this creates another problem, namely, that of deciding how to measure performance against such an intangible objective. How do we know when a genuine relationship is in place? How do we know when it has been improved or when it is in danger of deteriorating? The very idea of measuring something as intangible as a relationship will immediately create skepticism in the minds of many managers. And yet, much progress has been made in recent years in gaining acceptance that other intangible indicators of performance can and should be measured. More and more firms are measuring customer satisfaction and service quality. The measurement of customer relationships is but a small step farther along the path.

THE NATURE OF RELATIONSHIPS

Customer relationships, as with all human relationships, are formed over time. They have both behavioural and psychological or attitudinal components or indicators. Both are usually present to indicate that a relationship exists. The emotive or attitudinal component is in fact the more important of the two. It is possible, as is evidenced in certain industries in which the repurchase cycle is very long, for a strong emotive bond to exist between a company and its customers even in the absence of *buying* behaviour. It is, of course, possible that other forms of positive behaviour may be taking place even though buying is not. For example, although a family may not buy more than one home from a real estate agent, that does not prevent them from recommending that agent to friends who are in the market for a new home. Thus, it is important for marketing executives to be aware of both the behavioural and the emotive sides of the relationship they have with customers. They must have information not only on the observable, customer contact forms of behaviour, but also (and more important) on the state of the emotive connection with customers and insights into their nonobservable behaviour toward the firm and its brands.

What is it about relationships that cause some to express confusion or blanch at the thought that they can be measured, let alone managed? To quote Brian Quinn (1992, p. 242), "A phenomenon to be understood or managed must first be delineated and measured." Many organizations that purport to be practising "relationship marketing" do not understand the essence of a relationship, particularly as the customer is likely to define it. To delineate a relationship is to deconstruct it into its characteristics and essential components. A relationship is, above all, an emotional concept. It is impossible to conceive of a genuine relationship that is not characterized by emotions. If the interaction between a company and the customer is not characterized by certain emotions, then no relationship exists. The customer's response is "this is not a relationship; I rarely think of them; I never hear from them; they don't seem to care about me." Genuine relationships with businesses *do* exist, and they are, in this context as in all aspects of our lives, characterized by emotional bonds such as trust, affinity, commitment, empathy, caring, and two-way communications.

The Relationship Continuum

I often ask students and seminar participants why a relationship is like beauty. In some groups, a more cynical member will respond "because it is skin-deep." In some cases, that may unfortunately be true, but the answer that I am looking for is that it exists in the eye of the beholder. In other words, no relationship exists unless the customer says it does. Also, as with other related and similar concepts, relationships may be seen to exist on a continuum. Some relationships are perceived to be (and may be rated by the customer to be) stronger than others, closer, longer-lasting, more likely to endure, and so on.

There is no denying that relationships are personal, emotional, and ephemeral constructs. In short, they are difficult to define and difficult to describe. But the individual *knows* when he or she is in one. For example, when participants in a focus group are asked to describe their relationship with their electricity supplier, a quizzical look is likely to appear on their faces, and one participant may well say something like "that's not a relationship; I never hear from them" or "I don't have any dealings with them; to me they are just a bill!"

Therefore, a *relationship* is in the same league as quality, service, value, and other marketing-related concepts that exist largely in the eye of the consumer. These concepts also share the characteristics of complex attitudinal concepts that have their origins in psychology and that are measured on a regular basis by clinical psychologists so that they can assess the nature of attitudes toward certain objects, concepts, ideas, and behaviours.

In many ways, the concept of a "relationship" can be approached in the same way that social psychologists approach "attitudes." They can be deconstructed into components or dimensions.

Spurious Relationships

There are, of course, other forms of relationships that companies have with their customers. These are fleeting contacts that do not warrant the label "relationship" and include the meal at the roadside restaurant or in an airport cafeteria while on a business trip or vacation. The likelihood of ongoing contact or of a genuine relationship developing is remote. Recently, many companies have established frequent-buyer programs or clubs to encourage repeat buying—the behavioural side of a relationship. These marketing tools generally fall into a category that might be labeled "spurious" or "artificial" relationships. They are predicated on an incentive to encourage customers to come back again and again, with the promise of a reward for their "loyalty." What distinguishes such a program from a genuine relationship is the possible absence of an emotional connection with the company. This is not to say that such an emotional connection cannot coexist with a frequency marketing or club-card program—it is not at all unlikely, in fact, that membership in such a program may evolve into a genuine relationship—but rather that such a program is not synonymous with and does not naturally lead to the establishment of a genuine customer relationship.

The establishment of airline frequent-flyer programs and other such "loyalty" programs are designed to produce a behavioural result, namely, repeat buying and the related effect, increased "share of wallet." In that sense, they are no more than a modern-day, database-driven equivalent of the trading stamp programs that reached their peak of popularity in the 1950s. It is, in fact, quite interesting to now witness the relaunch of S&H "Green Stamps" in a electronic version to compete against the established frequency marketing programs such as air miles. But such programs must be seen for what they are, namely, incentives to increased repeat buying, not evidence of genuine customer relationships.

Customer Relationships as Assets

Customer relationships have generally been considered by progressive managers in most companies as assets that need to be managed strategically. Bill Birchard (1999, p. 318), writing recently in *Fast Company*, observed that "In the new economy, the most valuable assets have gone from solid to soft, from tangible to intangible. Instead of plant and equipment, companies today compete on ideas and relationships." Betsey Nelson, FCO of Macromedia Inc., a Web software company, calculates value on the basis of how close her company can get to its customers. She observes, "We're looking at the value over time of a relationship.... One thing that we know is that it's extremely valuable to us to own that customer relationship" (Birchard 1999, p. 318).

Nelson goes on to observe that her interest is in the "core drivers of value." This may (or must) be examined at least at two levels. Nelson's focus is on the creation of value for shareholders, and in that context, she is interested in what drives long-term customer value. But an incredibly important precursor to shareholder value is the creation of value for customers. Indeed, if a company is not successful in creating value for its customers, it can forget about achieving customer satisfaction or the long-term customer value that leads to a relationship and eventually to shareholder value.

Customer relationships may be viewed as long-term customer commitment or loyalty, which results from the fact that customers are satisfied not only by the company's products and services, but also by how they are treated by the company and its employees and by how they are made to feel as a result of their contact and association with the company. Thus, relationships result from successively satisfying customers. Brian Quinn (1992, p. 247) quotes the CEO of *Reader's Digest* as saying, "Our relationship with the reader is the key to the success of this entire company." Jacques Nasser, President and CEO of the Ford Motor Company, speaking of the automotive business, recently observed that "This industry is being transformed from a nuts and bolts industry into a consumer one, and from a transaction industry into a relationship business" (Burt 1999, p. 24). Mercedes-Benz's advertising in North America at the end of the twentieth century is focused on the relationship between the customer and the Mercedes-Benz dealer and brand.

Yet few companies measure the health of that relationship. Few companies know the cost of losing a customer or the payback to be gained through the cultivation of long-term solid customer relationships.

Driving Customer Satisfaction

To understand how relationships are formed, we need an insight into the factors that contribute to customer satisfaction. In my opinion, many companies demonstrate a very narrow view of these factors, assuming that if they get the core product right and deliver it quickly and conveniently, the customer will be satisfied. My research over the past 30 years has convinced me that the drivers of customer satisfaction are much more complex than that. It is, for example, quite possible that a company can get its product right (in fact, may have absolutely the best product or service in the market), deliver it conveniently and quickly, and still not satisfy the customer, who may be turned off by the interpersonal contact that he or she has with the employees of the company. We need to appreciate that customer satisfaction is driven not only by functional aspects of product and customer service, but also by softer, much more "fuzzy" components that relate to how the customer is treated and made to feel.

Essentially, as many authors have recognized in recent years, customer satisfaction is all about value creation. We must therefore ask ourselves how we are creating value for the customer.

Brand Relationships

The importance of relationships with customers is limited not only to those situations in which customers come into contact with a company and its employees. In fact, one of the most interesting and relevant applications of relationship thinking lies in the area of branding. Customers establish relationships with brands, just as they do with companies and other organizations. As consumers, we certainly develop brand loyalties, which are predicated on much more than repeat buying. There emerges over time an emotional attachment to a brand. Well-established names such as Kraft, Kellogg's, Volvo, Michelin, and Tide are examples of brands that have succeeded in creating such an emotional tie. Such brands add *meaning* to the lives of those who buy and use them. They become an important part of the lives of those consumers. By extension, consumers develop emotionally charged relationships with sports teams and rock bands. The unswerving loyalty of fans in the province of Quebec to the Montreal Canadiens is evidence of such a relationship, as is the extraordinary international popularity of European football clubs such as Juventus and Manchester United. These too are brands. As such, it is not sufficient for marketing executives to examine in their research such concepts as brand characteristics and brand personality; they must have insight into brand relationships as well.

WHY MEASUREMENT IS IMPORTANT

We have discussed four concepts that are integral to a complete understanding of the concept of customer relationships: value, satisfaction, relationships, and payback. The latter focuses on the creation of shareholder value. It is important for management to understand from the customer's perspective how well the company is performing in each of these areas. There is therefore a need to measure them all on an ongoing basis. Simply put, if we do not measure such things, it is impossible to know how well we are doing in creating value for our customers or maintaining positive customer relationships.

Many managers probably believe measurement of such intangible concepts as customer value and relationships is impossible; it isn't! In fact, measurement is essential for feedback. If management does not measure such integral strategic elements, then it is impossible to know what underlies customer relationships, how well the company is doing at creating those relationships, and how the company is benefiting from them. Only by measuring the health of the customer relationship can management understand how it can be strengthened.

I have always been intrigued by discussions I have had over the years with senior managers of some large firms about their understanding of how to best manage customer relationships. In too many cases, the response is that this is done by capturing sales data at the checkout or analyzing the sales volume of individual customers. In some cases, these managers infer that customers who purchase more products and services must have a stronger relationship with the company. Why would they continue to purchase items if they did not have a relationship with the company? This is reminiscent of a view that many bankers hold (or maybe used to hold) that if a customer has four or more products with the bank, then he or she has a relationship. This is, of course, entirely a behavioural definition of a relationship. It ignores the essential attitudinal and emotional sides.

In cases such as these, the idea of measuring relationships may be accepted. The problem is that managers with this behavioural view do not understand that they are measuring the wrong things and obviously do not have a fundamental understanding of the nature of a true relationship, one that is built on emotions. Measuring customer relationships is different from measuring customer satisfaction or service quality, both of which many companies do, and some do well. But measuring customer satisfaction and service quality is not enough. Measuring satisfaction without measuring the factors that contribute to satisfaction produces a global number — "we're at 8.2, on average, on a ten-point scale" — but tells management little about what contributes to that score or what it can do to get the number up to 8.5 within six months.

Measuring service quality is a move in the right direction, in that it allows a company to delve a little deeper into what contributes to satisfaction. Companies that do it well examine service quality along a series of service dimensions, looking at functional service delivery, timeliness, accuracy of fulfillment, responsiveness, and increasingly the interaction between the customer and employees: How friendly are they? How knowledgeable, understanding, polite?

But measuring satisfaction and service quality, though it provides management with valuable information on how the company is performing in creating satisfied, loyal, and committed customers, will give management only some of the information it needs to create genuine long-term customer relationships. This is because, just as many factors other than service contribute to satisfaction, it takes more than excellent service delivery to create a relationship. The essential question that must be asked is: How good are we at creating value for our customers? This presumes that value may be created in many different ways and that excellent service provision is but one of those.

We have all heard the old cliché that "you can't manage what you can't measure." Indeed, this is aptly applicable to the assessment of customer relationships. The key is to understand not that measurement is important but to understand exactly what needs to be measured.

CREATING LONG-TERM CUSTOMER VALUE

Most companies cannot even begin to calculate the value of customer relationships or the cost of losing a customer. Although a large percentage of companies will acknowledge the importance of customer relationships and their contribution to the creation of shareholder value, most have no idea what that contribution is or could be. It is critical that the importance of relationship building be demonstrated in measurable terms if management is to be persuaded of the payback to be realized from an investment in customer relationship building. A number of authors have recently begun to argue for the treatment of customer relationships as an investment (Gummesson 1999) and for a clear demonstration of the link between relationship marketing and shareholder value (Gordon 1998).

The building of customer relationships makes considerable sense only if one agrees with the impact on the creation of long-term customer value. Shareholder value in the future is dependent in large part on the loyal customers the company can rely on to deliver the stream of earnings referred to previously. What then contributes to long-term customer value? It is more than the total amount that the customer can be expected to spend with the company over his or her purchasing lifetime. In fact, that is quite a narrow view of customer value. It is, however, an important component.

A customer who is truly loyal contributes *directly* to the stream of earnings flowing to the company in two ways. The first is through retention. If the customer is retained as a customer for many years, then the company or brand gains the benefits from that prolonged patronage. This is the essence of the argument for creating customer loyalty. In its simplest manifestation, if we assume a typical automobile buyer buys an average of ten cars over a lifetime and spends an average of $25,000 each time, then his or her lifetime value may be $250,000. Research clearly demonstrates that a stronger, closer customer relationship very definitely leads to a greater likelihood of customer retention — that the customer will be more loyal and will remain a customer much longer (Barnes 1997a).

Long-term customer value is, therefore, much more than the simple forward projection of current spending levels. Ideally, we would like to be able to calculate the long-term profitability of a customer, but few firms capture the costs associated with serving a customer and fewer still are able to associate specific costs with specific customers. In the absence of cost information, it makes sense to focus on the potential value of the customer in terms of the revenue that he or she can generate directly or influence.

The second component of a customer's *direct* long-term value relates to the concept of *share of spend*. Not only will the customer who feels a certain closeness and a relationship to the company and the brand remain a customer, but he or she will give that company a greater share of total business in the category as well. This is the so-called share of wallet phenomenon. The research results presented subsequently in this chapter also clearly demonstrate that bank customers, for example, will give their financial institutions a greater share of their total business if a strong relationship is in place. Thus, not only will the customer stay longer, but he or she will spend more, thereby adding to long-term value.

There are other, even more difficult-to-measure aspects of why a long-term loyal customer is more valuable. These relate to the fact that they are likely to be prepared to pay higher prices once they get to know the company and its employees and are almost certainly less likely to quibble over price. They are easier to please and take far less time to court and woo. They are also much more likely to be receptive to new products and services that are introduced by the company.

The financial, more direct aspects of long-term customer value can, in fact, be measured objectively using internal customer data. An examination of the customer records of many organizations will likely reveal that those customers who have been "on the books" for a long time are less likely to spread their business around and more likely to buy higher-priced products and services and give the company a bigger share of their total spending in the category. They come back to do business again and again and require little marketing effort or expense. They are obviously the company's most valuable assets.

What is less obvious is the value of the loyal customer that is more difficult to observe and measure but may in fact be a greater contributor to long-term customer value. This refers to the related concepts of word-of-mouth and sphere of influence. Customers who have a solid, mutually beneficial relationship with a company, where they are treated well and made to feel important and valued, will delight in telling their friends. They become advocates for the company and bring in untold volumes of business, simply by telling friends, family, and associates.

Simon Cooper, former CEO of Delta Hotels, would motivate his employees to provide exceptional service to their guests by telling them that every business guest at a Delta Hotel has a potential lifetime value of $300,000. Even the most roadweary business traveler would take many years to rack up this volume of business in room charges alone. But, if one factors in the possibility that the customer concerned may influence the travel policy for his or her company or is on the national executive board of a professional organization that must decide where to hold its annual convention, then it is easy to see how one guest may have the potential to influence much more than $300,000 in total future sales. This illustrates the dual concepts of referral business and sphere of influence. Yet few companies make any attempt to measure the extent to which their customers are prepared to engage in such referral behaviour.

Respondents' future intentions are related to the relationship he or she has with the organization. Two primary aspects of future intentions are the likelihood of the organization being the main supplier of products or services in the future and the likelihood of recommending the organization to friends and family. These measures should be included in survey instruments to provide insights into future spending patterns and behavioural intentions.

Calculating the long-term value of a customer is not an easy prospect for most organizations. For some it is virtually impossible. The reason for this is that the vast majority of organizations have no way of measuring the costs of serving a customer or of capturing the direct costs involved in that service. This represents a barrier if we are interested in calculating the profitability of each customer. But many companies do not even have the ability to collect sales data, so they do not even know what volume of revenue is being brought in by each customer, let alone the profitability of that business. This is especially difficult in retail environments in which the customer is anonymous. Such a problem has prompted many retail organizations to establish frequent-buyer clubs so that most of the members' purchasing can be "observed" by virtue of the fact that the club card is used to record purchases. This is not the most accurate means of assessing the value of a customer, but it represents a step in the right direction. There are clearly deficiencies in the information collected, just as there are in such database approaches to estimating customer value.

For example, companies that rely on automatic data capture usually have no way of knowing what *share* of a customer's business they are enjoying. A bank, watching the customer's account balances and investments grow, may be deluding itself into thinking that it has a growing percentage of the customer's business, or even all of it, or even that it has a relationship with that customer. Not knowing all the details of the customer's life, the bank may be enjoying only a declining portion of the customer's rapidly expanding portfolio and of his or her family's business as the customer systematically places his or her financial business with other institutions.

MEASURING CUSTOMER RELATIONSHIPS

My understanding of customer relationships has come, in part, from many years of analyzing and interpreting data collected from hundreds of focus groups and customer surveys. Largely through the comments made by consumers, I came to the realization not only that consumers indeed develop close, enduring relationships with certain companies and brands, but also that much of what business managers and authors consider relationships to be are not, or at least not in the minds of consumers. I also developed an interest in understanding more about customer relationships in the early 1990s as the concept of "relationship marketing" began to emerge in the mainstream of marketing thought. Much of what was written in the early years of relationship marketing was, however, focused on three definitions or interpretations of customer relationships. The first of these related to frequent-buyer or similar "club" programs, the second to a database approach to interacting with customers, and the third to the creation of some form of contractual arrangement to lock in customers.

My view was then and is now that such interpretations of customer relationships are far too narrow and that these are, in fact, not genuine relationships at all but rather approaches to marketing that may well stimulate repeat buying behaviour but fall short in terms of creating an emotion-based, genuine customer relationship. My response was to attempt to understand more about what constituted a genuine relationship, as defined by the customer. Because a relationship is essentially a psychological concept, I delved into the very rich literature in social psychology dealing with interpersonal relationships (Sheaves and Barnes 1996). This literature revealed a vast resource of information on and insights into what constitutes a genuine relationship in any context. I have been applying the principles ever since.

One of the most obvious conclusions to be drawn from social psychology is that a relationship is a multidimensional construct and that, if it is to be measured, it must be approached as a series of relevant dimensions. It is necessary to deconstruct a consumer's relationship with a company or a brand into a series of dimensions that would include trust, reliability, responsiveness, communications, respect, affection, understanding, and other characteristics that are associated with any kind of relationship. To measure customer relationships, we must approach the task through the measurement of the dimensions of a relationship.

Typically, the approach I use to measure customer relationships relies on a series of Likert-scaled agree–disagree statements that are generated from focus groups or depth interviews or that are constructed through reference to batteries of psychological scales used to measure various psychological constructs such as trust or mutuality of interest. Examples of such agree–disagree statements are presented in Table 1.

Three other aspects of customer relationships have proven integral not only to the understanding of genuine relationships, but also to the measurement of the health of those relationships. Those are relationship closeness, its emotional tone, and its strength.

Closeness is a concept that appears to underlie many aspects of relationships. Social psychologists have developed approaches to the measurement of closeness in interpersonal relationships that are appropriately applied to the measurement of customer relationships. Thus, any approach to assessing the health of a customer relationship should incorporate a measure of the closeness of the relationship (Barnes 1997a). A

Table 1
Examples of Agree–Disagree Statements to Measure Relationship Dimensions

- "I get the feeling that _____ really cares about me."
- "_____ really understands my needs."
- "I am treated with respect by _____."
- "I often feel intimidated when dealing with _____."
- "I feel my business is safe with _____."
- "I deal with _____ because I want to, not because I have to."
- "Moving my business to another bank is just not worth the effort."
- "I can count on _____ to be there when I need them."
- "I never seem to be able to contact _____."
- "I feel comfortable dealing with _____."
- "_____ is an important part of the community where I live."
- "Dealing with _____ is like dealing with friends."
- "I really wouldn't deal with _____ if I didn't have to."
- "The employees at _____ really know their business."
- "_____ is a company that understands people like me."

measure of the customer's satisfaction with the relationship is also appropriate, in keeping with the argument that these two constructs are interrelated, in that it is not possible for customers to be satisfied with a relationship without feeling that the relationship is particularly close.

Acknowledging that a relationship cannot be thought to exist without emotional content, it is appropriate also to focus on the emotional tone of the relationship to assess its closeness and, therefore, its likelihood of lasting. An *emotional tone* index may be developed, which consists of various positive and negative emotions or feelings and involves respondents indicating the extent to which they experience each in their dealing with a particular company or brand (Barnes 1997b).

It is also important to consider the relative *strength* or *depth* of a customer relationship. Several approaches may be employed to identify that aspect of a relationship that implies the likelihood of its continuing. A measure of relationship strength might also incorporate the depth of customers' interactions with the company in question by including a measure of the share of their category business that they give to the company and addressing the extent to which they feel strongly about the relationship by examining whether they feel that they will still be dealing with the company in the future and whether they would recommend the company to others. These three variables then represent indicators of the strength of the relationship that a customer has with a company or brand.

I have found that measurement is not only possible but also can be instrumental in identifying areas in which the relationship is weak. The key to achieving this is to understand what should be measured: the dimensions of the relationship. This includes traditional relationship dimensions such as trust and commitment, as well as others such as affiliation, affection, empathy, reciprocity, understanding, respect, communication, and vulnerability.

THE PAYBACK FROM SOLID CUSTOMER RELATIONSHIPS

For management to be convinced of the value of investing in the creation and maintenance of customer relationships, it must see that a payback will be realized from such an investment. It must be clear that launching a relationship management program that will move a customer along a relationship equity scale from a score of, say, 76 to a score of 85 will produce a certain payback for the company. There will be an investment required on the part of a company that strategically manages its customer relationships. That investment will come in the form of human resources, communications, and service improvement programs that are designed to create value for the customer, which leads to greater satisfaction and greater likelihood of customer retention through relationship creation.

The payback from strong, close relationships comes from several sources. These are principally but not exclusively (1) the increased likelihood that the customer will continue to be a customer, (2) the length of time the customer is likely to remain a customer, (3) the greater percentage of his or her business that the customer will give the firm, and (4) the greater likelihood that the customer will recommend the company to friends and family members.

We can clearly demonstrate that stronger relationships, as reflected in greater closeness, higher positive emotional tone, and a higher overall score on the relationship equity index, will produce higher payback on each of these output or payback measures. It is the extent of this payback that is often surprising to clients.

For example, the data in Table 2, taken from telecommunications, financial services, and retail grocery businesses, demonstrate that by creating closer customer relationships a company can achieve demonstrable payback in many forms. Clearly, those customers who consider their relationships with their telecommunications service provider, bank, or supermarket to be very close are significantly more likely to be satisfied in their dealings with those companies — the first step in the creation of long-term relationships. The closer relationships are also much stronger, which indicates that they are much more likely to last.

Those customers who feel closest to the service providers in each of these industries are also significantly more likely to give that company more of their business. Those who feel less close are more likely to spread their business around. For example, in the banking business, those customers who feel very close to their main financial services provider give that company 94.3% of their banking business, whereas those who feel less close give their main bank only 88.4% of their business.

It is in the areas of customer retention and referrals that the numbers become even more dramatic. Those customers who feel closest to their service providers in these industries are significantly more likely to indicate that they are very likely to still be a customer two years from now. Only 64.0% of bank customers who do not feel particularly close are confident that they will still be a customer in two years, as compared with 94.3% of those who feel very close to their bank. Similarly, 83.6% of those who feel very close say that they are very likely to recommend their bank to friends and family members. The corresponding percentage of those who do not feel particularly close is 36.0%, a number that should make bankers everywhere sit up and pay attention because it represents the future of the customer franchise.

By considering measures such as these, it is possible for management to calculate the payback to be realized by increasing the closeness in customer relationships. Similar analyses may be performed by examining the emotional content of the relationship or by focusing on an aggregate score for relationship equity. Armed with such input data as average weekly or annual spending and by making reasonable assumptions relating to length of time as a customer and the number of others influenced through referral business, it is possible to attribute a certain value to existing cus-

Table 2
Exploring the Impact of Customer Closeness©

Customers from three industries (telecommunications, banking, and retail grocery) were asked to indicate how close they felt toward their main service provider in each industry. The respondents were then divided into three groups on the basis of their present level of closeness with their main telecommunications company, bank, or grocery retailer. The groups were as follows:

Group #	Description Telecom	Banking	Grocery	
Group #1	"Less than close" (Rated their closeness as 1 to 5)	54.5%	32.7%	38.9%
Group #2	"Fairly close" (Rated their closeness as 6 or 7)	23.8%	27.1%	25.3%
Group #3:	"Very close" (Rated their closeness as 8 to 10)	21.7%	40.2%	35.8%

Very significant differences were found in each industry across the three closeness groups on all of the critical relationship and loyalty variables. Note that for the telecommunications industry, share of business is the percentage of customers who also buy their long-distance telephone service from their local telephone service provider.

	Telecom	Banking	Grocery
Relationship Satisfaction**			
Group #1	7.2	6.7	7.0
Group #2	7.9	8.3	7.9
Group #3	9.1	9.1	9.1
Relationship Strength**			
Group #1	8.8	7.9	7.9
Group #2	9.1	9.0	8.7
Group #3	9.5	9.4	9.0
Share of Business*			
Group #1	83.9%	88.4%	76.6%
Group #2	92.4%	92.1%	79.3%
Group #3	92.9%	94.3%	82.6%

Table 2
Continued

	Telecom	Banking	Grocery
Very Likely to be with Main Telecom/Bank/Grocery Store Two Years from Now**			
Group #1	80.3%	64.0%	63.0%
Group #2	85.5%	83.2%	74.4%
Group #3	84.0%	94.3%	84.3%
Very Likely to Recommend Main Telecom/Bank/Grocery Store to Others**			
Group #1	57.5%	36.0%	48.3%
Group #2	58.6%	71.7%	63.3%
Group #3	86.3%	83.6%	77.9%

*Significant differences exist at level .05.
**Significant differences exist at level .001.

tomer business and the stream of that business and referral business well into the future. Thus, it *is* possible to calculate the value of a long-term customer relationship and determine the loss to a business when a customer leaves to go elsewhere.

TRACKING RELATIONSHIP EQUITY

Measuring the strength of customer relationships at a single point in time is not sufficient. An initial study benchmarks the starting point of the measurement exercise and will identify where the relationship is strongest, where it is weakest, and the customer segments that are most receptive to strengthening the relationship. The results will also point to areas in which something has to be done to strengthen the relationship. Strategies then need to be developed and implemented. These typically come in the form of the development and implementation of communications programs, improved systems and processes, and forward-thinking human resources policies.

This is not the end of the measurement exercise but rather the beginning. It is imperative that the measurement be repeated, perhaps quarterly or semiannually, to identify where weaknesses have been improved or, ideally, overcome. The benchmarking also enables management to understand how the company compares with companies in other industries and competitors.

The utopia in managing customer relationships is reached when customers become a company's personal spokespersons. This can only occur when they have had such resoundingly positive experiences that they *want others* to have the same experiences.

Measurement programs such as the one proposed here are able to identify the expected payback to be received from the implementation of a customer relationship management strategy. Payback can be quantified in terms of improvements in customer satisfaction and strengthened customer relationships. The payback can be observed in the form of greater share of customer spending, increased loyalty and retention, and increased propensity to recommend the company to others.

STRATEGIC IMPLICATIONS

Introducing a program to measure the health of customer relationships on a regular basis will provide very valuable information to guide management in the implementation and management of a customer relationship program. In the first place, a measurement program such as the one described in this chapter will identify the overall health of the customer relationship and enable the company to track that critical measure over time to determine whether the relationship management program is successful in creating stronger, closer relationships with customers.

In the second place, the program will allow management to deconstruct the relationship into its component dimensions to determine where the relationship is strong and where it is weak. The examination of the relationship in terms of its various dimensions is also useful in determining which dimensions contribute most to the overall health of the relationship and customer satisfaction.

Typically, analysis of the data collected will reveal the overall position of the company on its "relationship equity index," which is composed of the various dimensions of the relationship. It will also reveal which of the dimensions of the relationship are most important in predicting and explaining the overall relationship index score. This then allows management to focus efforts on those dimensions of the relationship that are most important to the target customer group and examine the company's relative performance on each of the dimensions.

It is not uncommon to find that a company is performing well on several dimensions of the relationship and less well on others. If the dimensional analysis reveals, for example, that the company is not performing well on dimensions such as responsiveness and communications, this should send management in search of solutions that will bolster performance on those dimensions of the customer relationship.

Analysis of the information obtained from a customer relationship measurement program will also allow management to determine how well the company is performing in building solid relationships with certain segments of customers. It is common, for example, to find that certain customer groups have stronger, closer relationships than others. This points out to management where relationships are weakest and where they are in danger of disintegrating. It will reveal those segments of customers that are most likely to be "defectors" or "switchers" and those where the relationship is superficial or artificial. By focusing on those relationships that are most vulnerable, management can put in place programs to repair those relationships, assuming that appropriate long-term customer value can be generated by doing so.

Further analysis of relationship measurement data will reveal those segments of customers that have certain kinds of relationships with the company. It will be revealed, for example, that some customers may be quite satisfied with their dealings with the company, even though their relationship may not be particularly close. Often, in addition to asking customers to indicate how close their relationships is with a company, we ask them how close they would like their relationship to be. In general, we find that approximately 30% to 40% of respondents will indicate that their relationship is just about right in terms of closeness; in other words, their current closeness and desired closeness are the same. Usually, 50% to 60% or more will indicate that they would want their relationship with the company to be closer, thus providing management with clear direction that it should get closer to its customers.

What is most interesting is that we consistently find approximately 10% of respondents who indicate that they would want their relationships to be *less close* than they are at present. These results are reminiscent of a participant in a focus group that I was moderating many years ago who told the group that he had an "ideal" relationship with his bank, one that was, for him, totally satisfying. When asked to describe that relationship, he replied, "It's simple; I don't call them and they don't call me." Clearly, customers who desire a more distant relationship need to be managed in a different way than those who want to be contacted on a regular basis.

By examining the state or health of customer relationships by customer segment, a company will be in a position to examine what actually constitutes value from the perspective of the members of each segment. The value to be derived from strengthening or making the relationship closer with particular segments will direct management toward the most profitable solution. For example, analysis of the results of a customer relationship measurement program may reveal that relationships with certain high-yield customers are less strong than they should be. By examining the details of that relationship and developing appropriate strategies to shore up the relationship on those dimensions on which it is weakest, management can direct resources toward programs that will produce the greatest payback.

The approach to measuring the equity of customer relationships that has been described in this chapter has applications in several related areas. Although we have tended to describe the approach using large-scale service providers such as banks and supermarkets as examples, the same principles apply when brand relationships are being examined. The principles of relationship building are the same, whether we are talking about relations with retailers and other service providers or with national and international brands such as Nike, Michelin, or President's Choice. Similarly, the same approach can be used with other stakeholders of interest to management. Many companies are today directing attention to the relationships that they have with employees, shareholders, suppliers, donors, and other important groups. The principles inherent in our customer relationship measurement program are equally applicable in those and other contexts.

One application that is just now attracting the attention of managers relates to the management of customer relationships using technology and particularly over the Internet. As more and more companies develop a Web presence and direct their attention to dealing with customers and others over the Internet, they are becoming increasingly concerned with what this technology-based interaction does to customer relationships. Banks, for example, should be particularly interested in knowing whether their customer relationships are strengthened or weakened when customers move from a branch and ABM-based approach to banking to one that involves banking on the Internet. Are large catalogue retailers such as Lands' End and J. Crew successful in establishing and maintaining relationships over the Internet?

DIRECTION FOR MANAGEMENT

The approach to the measurement of customer relationships that has been described in this chapter is one that provides management with a clear direction for action to be taken to improve the state of customer relationships. It is a strategic approach, one that is focused on an understanding of the higher-order needs of customers and on the creation of satisfying, meaningful relationships with them as a means to ensuring long-term corporate success. The results of this research are actionable because they produce for management a clear picture of the details of the relationship that the company has with its important segments of customers. Thus, different strategies can be developed for the management and cultivation of relationships with each segment.

Results are actionable also in that the relationship is broken down into its constituent parts and examined in terms of its emotional content. It is therefore possible to report to management that customers in critical segment "A" are less trusting of the company, do not feel that the company is responsive enough, and say they rarely hear from the company. Results such as these have clear implications for management, not only in terms of how the company conducts its marketing programs — *the implications may be less significant for marketing than for other departments of the company* — but particularly in areas such as employee training and staffing levels, customer contact strategy, marketing communications, service delivery systems, customer service levels, and even sponsorships and community relations.

This approach to the quantification of customer relationships allows management to tie together such critically important concepts as customer value creation, customer satisfaction, relationships, and shareholder value. It allows for the quantification of these complex concepts and brings them to an actionable level. It also permits the calculation of the payback to be obtained from an investment in the enhancement of customer relationships, thereby establishing a direct link with shareholder value creation. Such knowledge within a company certainly provides that firm with a strategic competitive advantage.

BIBLIOGRAPHY

Andrews, Fred (1999), "Drucker Disdains Corporate Myopia," *The Globe and Mail*, (November 18), B19.

Barnes, James G. (1997a), "Exploring the Importance of Closeness in Customer Relationships," presented at the Relationship Marketing Conference of the American Marketing Association, *New and Evolving Paradigms: The Emerging Future of Marketing*, Dublin, Ireland (June 12-15).

———— (1997b), "Closeness, Strength and Satisfaction: Examining the Nature of Relationships Between Providers of Financial Services and their Retail Customers," *Psychology and Marketing*, 14 (December), 765–90.

Birchard, Bill (1999), "Intangible Assets + Hard Numbers = Soft Finance," *Fast Company*, (October), 316–36.

Brancato, Carolyn Kay (1997), *Institutional Investors and Corporate Governance*. Chicago: Richard D. Irwin.

Burt, Tim (1999), "Ford Chief Takes a New Direction," *Financial Times*, (November 15), 24.

Gordon, Ian H. (1998), *Relationship Marketing*. Toronto, ON: John Wiley & Sons Canada Limited.

Gummesson, Evert (1999), *Total Relationship Marketing*. Oxford: Butterworth-Heinemann.

Mintzberg, Henry (1999), "How Fat Cats Can Slim Down," *Financial Times*, (October 29), 13.

Quinn, James Brian (1992), *Intelligent Enterprise*. New York: The Free Press.

Sheaves, Daphne and James G. Barnes (1996), "The Fundamentals of Relationships," in *Advances in Services Marketing and Management*, Vol. 5, Teresa A. Swartz, David E. Bowen, and Stephen W. Brown, eds. Greenwich, CT: JAI Press, 215–46.

20
Product and Package Testing

Howard Moskowitz[1]

PART 1: PRODUCT TESTING OVERVIEW

Objectives of Product Testing

I n the world of market research, product testing occupies a venerable place. Manufacturers need to know how their products perform. In the main, product testing methods have been developed and advanced, as well as used, by researchers involved in fast moving consumer goods (e.g., beverages, shaving creams). The objectives of the research have varied from measuring basic acceptance (is the product good or bad, accept versus reject), to providing consumer feedback for ongoing formulation, to assessing concept–product fit, and even to estimating market share or expected volume. The many uses of product testing mean that there is no one discipline or set of knowledge that encompasses the world of evaluation that we call "product testing." The stage at which the test is commissioned, the knowledge base of the researcher doing the test, and the use of the data all dictate different types of tests.

The Different "Players" in the Product Testing World

Market researchers are only one group of professionals involved in the evaluation of products. When looking at the professionals involved and the technical literature cited, the reader might come across disciplines

---

[1]The author acknowledges the assistance of Margaret Mirabile in the preparation of this article for publication.

as different as product developers, sensory analysis (R&D–oriented), quality control (production-oriented), consultants to management (process-oriented, for the development process), market researchers, advertising agencies, statisticians, and many more. For health and beauty aid products, one might also cross knives with perfumers. In durables, one might also meet up with engineers (Gacula 1993; Meilgaard, Civille, and Carr 1987; Moskowitz 1983, 1984, 1985, 1994; Stone and Sidel 1985). Each of the players in the product-testing world tests for a specific reason. As we will see, the different players in turn bring to bear their predilections and biases about what data should be, what respondents should do, and even language.

What Type of Data Does the Researcher Present— The Difference Between Early-Stage Guidance and Late-Stage Confirmation

Most researchers in the market research industry are familiar with late-stage product testing. In late-stage testing, most of the developmental work has finished. The R&D department has probably finished creating its prototypes, tested these among consumers (more about that later), and arrived at one or two potentially acceptable prototypes. Criteria for selecting these prototypes for a confirmatory test may include success in earlier stage testing. The products may be promising because they are not distinguishable from the current gold standard (e.g., in the case of cost reduction, in which the goal is to maintain product quality with cheaper ingredients) or because they fit a marketing-driven concept.

Late-stage product testing usually does not call for action, beyond a pass/fail (though a fail may call for additional work). Rather, the late-stage product test provides the necessary information to confirm that R&D has developed an appropriate product. In common parlance, late-stage (confirmatory) product testing acts as a "disaster check" (though it is unclear how a potentially disastrous product, with low acceptance, could have even reached this stage of testing).

In contrast to late-stage confirmatory tests are early-stage development studies. Variously called "research guidance tests," "R&D hall tests," and the like, these early-stage tests serve the purpose of guiding R&D. Typically, these tests are commissioned to screen winning products from among a wide variety of contenders (for future work), identify the characteristics of a product that drive acceptance (for brand learning), segment consumers on the basis of sensory preference (for targeted development/marketing), and so forth. Early-stage tests may be run by R&D but often are run by market researchers as well. Early-stage tests encompass a far wider range of questions and applications than do late-stage confirmatory tests. Typically, these early-stage tests provide a plethora of information that could not otherwise be obtained.

Types of Problems to Be Answered

The key to correct (or better, "appropriate") product tests is to identify a problem and then match the right test method to the problem. As simple as this seems, this dogma is violated as often as it is fulfilled. For example, it is not unusual for researchers to use paired comparisons tests (head-to-head preference tests) to guide product developers, even though the data do not really help the developers who receive the report. Nor is it particularly unusual for researchers to rely on in-house expert panels who select products on the basis of "liking" or "preference" or to go forward with these products for further development—despite the fact that the in-house expert panelists are not the relevant consumers of the product and their preferences may be irrelevant to the population at large.

Product testing can address many different types of problems, depending on the agenda and needs of researchers. Many of those who commission product tests simply want some type of single number such as significance (is my product better than a competitor's?) or scoreboard rating (how high do I score?). Others using product testing want to learn about the product (e.g., what drives liking, are there segments in the population that have different preferences, along what particular attributes is the product strong or weak?). Typically, these different questions come from different audiences that commission the research.

PART 2: PRODUCT TESTING SPECIFICS

Affective Tests—How Much Do I Like this Product?

Traditionally, most product tests have been commissioned to answer questions about liking. These tests may comprise paired comparisons (in which one product is paired against a standard, such as the market leader). In other cases, the researcher will use a scale of liking (e.g., the nine-point hedonic scale, varying from dislike extremely to like extremely; Peryam and Pilgrim 1957). Still other researchers use appropriateness as a measure of acceptance, rather than degree of liking (Schutz 1989). Paired comparisons are often used when the marketing objective is to beat or at least equal a specific product. (Marketers think in terms of performance in comparison with a competitor or with a gold standard.) Scales of liking are used when the researcher wants to determine the degree of acceptance or even whether the product is liked at all (viz., classification). Table 1 presents various scales for liking that have been used by researchers (Meiselman 1978).

Liking can be further refined in these tests by having the respondent assess the different components of the product as they appear to the senses (e.g., like appearance, fragrance/aroma, taste/flavor, texture/feel). Quite often, these attribute liking ratings correlate highly with overall liking, which suggests that respondents may have a hard time differentiat-

Table 1
Verbal Descriptors for Hedonic Scales

Scale Points	Descriptors
2	Dislike, unfamiliar
3	Acceptable, dislike (not tried)
3	Like a lot, dislike, do not know
3	Well liked, indifferent, disliked (seldom if ever used)
5	Like very, like moderately, neutral, dislike moderately, dislike very
5	Very good, good, moderate, tolerate, dislike (never tried)
5	Very good, good, moderate, dislike, tolerate
9	Like extremely, like very much, like moderately, like slightly, neither like nor dislike, dislike slightly, dislike moderately, dislike very much, dislike extremely
9	FACT Scale (Schutz 1964): Eat every opportunity, eat very often, frequently eat, eat now and then, eat if available, don't like—eat on occasion, hardly ever eat, eat if no other choice, eat if forced

ing overall liking from attribute liking. (Respondents do differentiate the different senses, however, in terms of scaling amount of an attribute, rather than liking of an attribute, as we will see.)

It is worth noting that quite often researchers use these affective tests along with action standards. An action standard dictates that the product will move forward in the development or marketing process (i.e., to further development or even to market introduction) if the product meets specific objectives (i.e., achieves a certain minimum acceptance level).

Paired Preference Tests

In consumer research, the role of the paired preference test appears to be sacrosanct, whether deserved or not. Paired preference simply means putting one product up against another and instructing the respondent to indicate which one he or she prefers. The preference measure does not show how much one product is liked (or how much more one product is liked versus another). Rather, the paired preference test is simply a head-to-head match, with "winner take all" (on at least a person-by-person basis). The results of paired preference tests are reported in percentages, rather than in degree of liking (as would be reported in a scaling exercise).

Paired preferences tests can extend to other attributes, because the researcher can also ask the respondent to indicate which product has more of a specific characteristic. The characteristic need not even be a sensory one (such as depth of color, thickness, graininess of texture). Rather, the characteristic could even be an image (e.g., one product is "more masculine").

Paired preference tests, popular as they are, provide relatively little information. The conventional (yet unproven) wisdom is that consumers make choices by implicitly comparing products with one another. Thus, the typical paired test pits a new product against either the gold standard that it is to replace or the market leader (and only the market leader) against which it is thought to compete.

The positives of paired preference testing are the simplicity of the test in the field execution and the ease of understanding (viz., a paired comparison result). The negatives are that the demand for head-to-head comparison may focus attention onto small, irrelevant differences that exist (especially when the respondent is searching for a hook on which to hang the comparison) and that the data cannot be used for much beyond the comparison results. Paired comparison data are not particularly useful for product development because they give no real guidance.

It is worthwhile digressing for a moment here to understand a little of the intellectual history of paired testing, because of the widespread use of the methods and its limitations (which do not appear to affect the use or misuse of the procedure). Paired testing got its start more than a century ago. The German psychologist, physiologist, and philosopher Gustav Theodor Fechner (Boring 1929) was interested in the measurement of sensory perception. However, according to Fechner, the human being is not able to act as a simple measuring instrument in the way that we understand these instruments to operate. (Today's researchers, especially those in experimental psychology and psychophysics, would vehemently disagree with Fechner, but keep in mind that we're dealing with the start of subjective measurement, not with its well-developed world today.) According to Fechner, one way to measure sensory perception was to ask people to discriminate between samples. From their behavior, Fechner was able to determine the magnitude of difference needed between two samples to generate a difference. The psychometrician L.L. Thurstone (1927) carried this analysis one step further by developing paired comparison methods, in which respondents judged which sample was stronger, heavier, liked more, and so forth. From the paired comparison data (the ancestor of our paired preference tests), Thurstone developed a subjective scale of magnitude. Thurstone's scaling methods were soon adopted by researchers to erect scales of sensory magnitude and liking, from which developed the long-standing acceptance of paired methods in applied product testing. Thurstone, publishing in the academic literature, was thus able to influence subsequent generations of applied market researchers, many of whom do not know the intellectual origins of this test.

Sensory Questions—How Much of a Characteristic Does My Product Possess?

Respondents can act as judges of the amount of a characteristic. Sometimes these characteristics or attributes can be quite simple, such as the sweetness of a beverage. Other times the attribute may be more complex, such as the "tomato flavor," which calls into play a host of sensory attributes. Still other times the attribute may be simple but require explanation (e.g., the ginger burn of a ginger candy).

There is an ongoing debate in the scientific literature (especially for fragrance, but also for food) about the degree to which a respondent can validly rate sensory characteristics. On one side of this dispute are those who believe that the only attribute that a consumer can validly evaluate is liking. These researchers believe that it is improper to have consumers rate sensory attributes. On the other side of the dispute are those (including this author) who believe that a well-instructed respondent can validly rate sensory attributes, and indeed, such a respondent (not an expert, mind you) can switch focus from liking to sensory to sensory directional (see the next section) for many attributes.

The dispute is simple enough to solve through experimentation. In cases in which experts and consumers rate the same products, it has been shown that their ratings correlate with each other (Moskowitz 1995) and with known physical variations of the product (Moskowitz and Krieger 1998). The scientific literature suggests that consumers can validly rate sensory attributes and that their attribute ratings line up with known physical changes in the stimulus. Literally thousands of scientific articles in all manner of disciplines related to sensory perception suggest that the unpracticed respondent can assign numbers whose magnitude matches the physical magnitude of the stimulus (see Stevens 1975). One could ask for no clearer validation of a respondent's abilities.

Sensory Directionals or "Just Right" Information— What To Do

Quite often in developmental research, a key question is, "What's wrong with this product (if anything), and what does the consumer think we should do to correct this problem?" When a respondent is asked to evaluate problems, the typical question is known as a sensory directional. The question may be phrased somewhat as follows: "Please describe this product: 1 = far too dry ... 5 = perfect on dryness/wetness ... 9 = far too wet." Note that the respondent is assumed to know both the "ideal" level of dryness/wetness and the degree to which the product deviates from that ideal.

Respondents often find this type of question fun to answer, because the question allows them to become experts by telling R&D product developers what to do. Sensory directionals are surprisingly on target for visual attributes (viz., the respondent knows the optimal or ideal level of darkness or stripes), usually on target for texture, but sometimes on target and other times off target for taste/flavor. The directions are generally off target for certain types of emotion-laden attributes such as "real chocolate flavor," perhaps because these attributes are hedonic attributes (liking) disguised as sensory attributes. No chocolate ever has enough "real chocolate flavor." Even if the developer were to use a lot of chocolate flavoring, the product would still taste too bitter.

Typically, product developers use rules of thumb by which they translate these just right scales to direction. Thus, when a respondent says that a beverage lacks "real fruit flavor," the product developer knows that often the respondent means that the product is not sweet enough — or, that changing the amount of sugar will change the fruit flavor.

Where Do Sensory and Other Product Test Attributes Come From?

Because much of product testing involves finding a way to have consumers communicate with product developers, it is important that the questionnaire cover the key sensory attributes of the product. A glance at different questionnaires will reveal a remarkable range of attributes, from the very general (overall appearance, aroma, taste, flavor, texture) to the very specific (e.g., amount of pepper flavor, even amount of black pepper flavor). Some questionnaires are filled with specifics; other questionnaires appear to be probing the surface, without much depth in the quality of information being generated. Table 2 shows an example of an attribute list for beer (Clapperton, Dagliesh, and Meilgaard 1975).

The novice researcher asked to create a product questionnaire often feels at a loss. In general, there is no fixed list of attributes. In many corporations, there may be a so-called laundry list of attributes that has been used over the years by various researchers involved in the product category. All too often the laundry list is a legacy list, comprising so many attributes as to be daunting and formidable. Yet, many practitioners in product testing are loathe to dispense with any attributes lest these attributes somehow be discovered "critical" to decision making.

Besides legacy lists, or laundry lists, many practitioners use focus groups to elicit consumer-relevant attributes. The focus groups are set up with consumers who first discuss and then sample the product, all the while rating attributes relevant to the product. For many products that are used at home (e.g., laundry, personal care, food prepared at the stove), the respondents may be given products ahead of the focus group, asked to use the products, and then asked to discuss the attributes in the group session. The number of attributes emerging from this exercise can be enormous, requiring, at the end of the exercise, the researcher to pare down this large number to a workable few that can be used in the questionnaire.

In addition to legacy lists and focus groups, in recent years there have sprung up other, more general lists of attributes. These lists, appear-

Table 2
A Comprehensive Attribute List for the Sensory
Characteristics of Beer

	First-Tier Term	Second-Tier Term
1	Spicy	
2	Alcoholic	Warming, vinous
3	Solvent-like	Plastic-like, Can liner, Acetone
4	Estery	Isoamyl acetate, Ethyl hexanoate, Ethyl acetate
5	Fruity	Citrus, apple, banana, black currant, melon, pear, raspberry, strawberry
6	Floral	Phenylethanol, geraniol, perfumy, vanilla
7	Acetaldehyde	
8	Nutty	Walnut, coconut, beany, almond
9	Resinous	Woody
10	Hoppy	
11	Grassy	
12	Straw-like	
13	Grainy	Corn grits, mealy
14	Malty	
15	Worty	
16	Caramel	Primings, syrupy, molasses
17	Burnt	Licorice, bread crust, roast barley, smoky
18	Medicinal	Carbolic, chlorophenol, iodoform, tarry, Bakelite
19	Diacetyl	Buttery
20	Fatty acid	Soapy/fatty, caprylic, cheesy, isovaleric, butyric
21	Oily	Vegetable oil, mineral oil
22	Rancid	Rancid oil
23	Fishy	Amine, shellfish
24	Sulfitic	
25	Sulfidic	H_2S, mercaptan, garlic, lightstruck, autolyzed, burnt rubber
26	Cooked vegetable	Parsnip/celery, dimethyl sulfide, cooked cabbage, cooked sweet corn, tomato ketchup, cooked onion
27	Yeasty	Meaty

	First-Tier Term	Second-Tier Term
	Table 2	
	Continued	
28	Ribest	Black currant leaves, catty
29	Papery	
30	Leathery	
31	Moldy	Earthy, musty
32	Sweet	Honey, jammy, oversweet
33	Salty	
34	Acidic	Acetic, sour
35	Bitter	
36	Metallic	
37	Astringent	
38	Powdery	
39	Carbonation	Flat, gassy
40	Body	Watery, characterless, satiating

ing in a variety of publications (e.g., Civille and Lyon 1995), provide a start for the researcher. Unfortunately, many of these attribute lists cover such a wide range of characteristics that only a few attributes are relevant. The researcher, confronted with the task, then simply uses judgment, typically extracting one or two promising attributes from the list, going back to the legacy lists, and perhaps running a focus group. In the end, however, the list chosen is a personal one, dictated by the specific product, the experience and insight of the researcher, and the momentary needs for information.

Scales—What's the Right Metric to Measure Subjective Responses?

Over the years, researchers have fought with one another, often passionately, about the appropriate scales to use. We saw that there are a variety of scales to measure liking. We are talking here of a more profound difference in scaling—the nature of the scale and the allowable transformations. The standard nine-point hedonic scale (Peryam and Pilgrim 1957) is an example of a category scale. Category scales are assumed to be interval scales; the differences between adjacent category points is assumed to be equal up and down the scale. However, there is no fixed zero point. Interval scales (like Fahrenheit or centigrade) allow the researcher to do many statistical analyses, such as calculate the mean and the standard deviation, perform T-tests and regression, and so on. The interval scale has no fixed zero, however, so that one cannot calculate ratios of scale values. On a nine-point scale of liking, we cannot say that the liking of 8 is twice as much liking as that of 4. Other scales, such as ratio scales (with a fixed zero) do allow the researcher to make these ratio claims. Weaker scales, such as ordinal scales (viz., "rank order these products in degree of liking"), just show an order of merit. One cannot even talk about the differences being equal between ranks 1 and 2 versus ranks 2 and 3.

In the end, most researchers end up with the scale that they find easiest to use. The category scale is by far the most widely used because it is simple and can be anchored at both ends. (Sometimes the researcher anchors every point in the scale as well.) Many academic researchers use ratio scales to study the magnitude of perception, and from time to time, ratio scales have been used in the commercial realm of product testing. Many researchers in business use rank order or ordinal scaling. They need to be careful not to interpret differences in ranks as reflecting the magnitude of differences in subjective magnitude.

Product-to-Concept Fit

Beyond simply measuring acceptance or sensory attributes, researchers want to discover whether a product and a concept fit together. The concept sets the expectations for the product. When a consumer buys a product, there are often some expectations about the appearance, the taste, and the texture of the product, along with nonsensory expectations (e.g., aspirational expectations such as sophistication). Products can be tested within the framework set up by these expectations in the concept–product test.

The actual test execution is quite simple. In one variation, the respondent reads the concepts; an opportunity to form expectations is given. The respondent then evaluates one or several products. For each product, the respondent rates the degree to which the product delivers what the concept promises. The scale is also simple—the product delivers too little, just right, or too much of what the concept promises. The scale sounds easy enough to use, and in actuality, it is easy (at least respondents say that they have no problems).

One of the key issues that keeps emerging in the evaluation of concept–product fit is whether respondents really have an idea of what a product should taste like, smell like, or perform like. If the concept promises a specific flavor (e.g., an Italian flavor) or a specific performance (e.g., 366 MHz processor in a computer), respondents can easily ascertain whether the product lives up to the concept. For many aspirational concepts, however, such as those developed for perfumes, it is difficult, if not impossible, to truly show that a product and concept agree with each other. The respondent may try to articulate the reasons for the concept–product fit, but the reasons will be different for each person.

Base Size—How Many Respondents Are Enough?

The issue of base size continues to appear in product testing, perhaps because base size more than any other factor influences the cost of a project. The greater the number of respondents in a study (viz., the larger the base size), the more comfortable the researcher should feel about the results — presuming, of course, that the respondents participating are the correct respondents. This has led to recommendations or at least rules of thumb dictating 100 or more respondents for conventional product tests but far more (e.g., 300 or more) for claims substantiation tests (Smithies and Buchanan 1990).

Base size issues are not as simple as they might appear. The statistician would aver that the reason for the large base size is that it reduces the uncertainty of the mean. The standard error of the mean, a measure of the expected variation of the mean were the study to be repeated, drops down with the square root of the number of respondents. That is, one feels more comfortable about obtaining the same mean the next time if one uses a large enough base size in the first place. Matters can get out of hand, of course, if this requirement for uncertainty reduction in itself demands a base size so large that the test is unaffordable. (Many novice researchers, in fact, become so fearful about the uncertainty that they refuse to do studies unless there is an enormous base size, preferring to do qualitative research instead.)

Another way to look at base size is to consider the stability of the mean rating with an increasing number of respondents. The first rating is, of course, the most influential rating in determining the average, for it is the only data point. Each additional rating affects the average less and less (viz., by $1/n$, where n = number of ratings). It has been shown that the mean stabilizes at about 50 ratings, whether the attribute deals with liking or sensory judgments, and that this number appears to hold even when the data comprise ratings from a homogeneous population of individuals with the same preference pattern (Moskowitz 1997). Therefore, it appears that the researcher will not be in particular danger if the base size exceeds 50. A base size of 100 might be better (or at least appear so psychologically), but the mean will not change much from 50 ratings to 100 ratings, assuming the sampling rules are maintained for choosing the respondents.

How Many Products Can a Respondent Validly Taste or Smell?

A recurring bone of contention in product tests is the number of samples that a respondent can evaluate without becoming fatigued. Some of the conventional (but not necessarily correct) "wisdom" avers that the typical respondent can evaluate only two or three samples before fatigue sets in. Scientific research in the senses of taste and smell (where fatigue is most likely to occur) suggest that the human senses are far more robust, that we can evaluate many more samples than is commonly thought, and that perhaps the reason for fatigue is boredom with the task rather than some sensory loss. If in fact the consumer respondent knows that the task will last an hour and has prepared for that eventuality, then no fatigue sets in, as long as the respondent is motivated and the samples are spaced out with enough time to rinse the mouth (see Table 3).

Perhaps some of the concern of fatigue can be traced to what is observed to occur in a corporate environment, when team members in product work (marketers, R&D, sensory analysts) meet to evaluate many samples and decide on the next steps. The tasting and evaluation is so haphazard that after a few samples most participants remark that they cannot remember the first sample they tasted. Despite R&D's best attempts to present the samples in a coherent order, the team members end up tasting the samples rapidly, trying to keep all the information in their head. They would be better off simply rating each sampling and then tallying the results at the end of the tasting.

What Is the Best Venue in Which to Test Products?

Product evaluation can range from the simple testing of one or two snack chips to the complex preparation and evaluation of many frozen entrees. Traditionally, market researchers have been used to fairly simple types of tests, in which the preparation and the respondent task is correspondingly simple (e.g., "Which of these two carbonated beverages do you prefer;" "Rate each carbonated beverage on these ten attributes").

Product tests are done in three different types of venues. The simplest product tests are done at home. The respondent takes home one (or more) products, uses the products, evaluates the products on attributes, and records the ratings. The interviewer may call the respondent on the telephone and record the ratings, or the respondent may return with the completed ratings (and either be finished with the study or receive a new set of products to evaluate), mail in the ratings, or even punch in the ratings on the Internet.

Sometimes the researcher wants to have more control over the samples. Control is necessary when the samples must be tested absolutely "blind" (viz., no hint as to brand, which is hard to do at home, unless the product is repackaged) or when the samples must be tested under tight control or prepared appropriately. The interview can be set up as a mall intercept or as a hall/prerecruit test. In a mall intercept, the interviewer sets up a test station somewhere in the mall (e.g., at a store front, in an office right off the mall, even at an electronic kiosk). The respondent is intercepted by an interviewer and invited to participate for a short interview, lasting 5 to 30 minutes, and then the study begins. Quite often respondents refuse to participate. This is called a "refusal," and the refusal rates are increasing as shoppers become tired of the interruption. Nonetheless, the mall intercept method is frequently used.

Table 3
Maximum Number of Products that Should Be Tested
(Max) and Minimum Waiting Time Between Samples in
Minutes (Wait)

Product	Max	Wait	Comments
Carbonated soft drink (regular)	15	7	Little adaptation or residual exists
Pickles	14	10	Garlic and pepper aftertaste build up
Juice	12	10	Watch out for sugar overload
Yogurt	12	10	
Coffee	12	10	
Bread	12	4	
Cheese	10	15	Fatty residue on tongue
Carbonated soft drink (diet)	10	10	Aftertaste can linger
French fries	10	10	Fatty residue on tongue
Cereal (cold)	10	10	
Milk-based beverage	10	10	
Soup	10	10	Can become filling
Sausages	8	15	Fat leads to satiety
Hamburgers	8	15	Amount ingested must be watched
Candy—chocolate	8	15	
Croissants	8	10	Fat leads to satiety
Salsa	8	10	Longer waits necessary for hot salsas
Cereal (hot)	8	10	Amount ingested must be watched
Ice cream	8	10	Fat leads to satiety
Mousse	6	15	Combination of fat + sugar yields satiation
Lasagna	6	10	Amount ingested must be watched

Notes: Prerecruit, four-hour, central location test.

For more elaborate tests, the researcher may hire a hall or a test facility and pay the respondent to participate for an extended period. In this extended test, the respondent provides a great deal of information. Of course, the respondent may be well paid to participate, but the quality of the data and the need to test several samples with the same respondent more than compensates for the extra cost. Table 4 compares home use and central location tests.

Choreographing a Product Test

During the past 25 years, market researchers specifically, along with sensory analysts, have begun to test many different products in a single evaluation session. Rather than limiting the test to a few products (e.g., three or four at most), the researchers have recognized the value of obtaining data on a large set of products, with each respondent evaluating many products. These product tests, done in a prerecruit central location or at home, obtain data from a single individual on far more products than traditionally has been the case. With such extensive data, however, the researcher has been afforded the opportunity to do far more complex analyses than were ever considered possible.

Sometimes the number of products may be as high as 10 to 15. (Despite what purists say, it is fairly straightforward to evaluate this many products. One need only ensure adequate motivation and time between samples.) A typical example of choreographed evaluation appears in Table 5. The approach is set up so that the respondent is prerecruited and paid to participate (increasing or at least maintaining motivation). The session may last several hours, which enables the evaluations to proceed at a leisurely pace. Most important, the choreographed test session is set up to acquire data from respondents in an optimal fashion. One can almost envision the evaluation session to be a "factory," with most of the time being spent acquiring the data. Very little of the interview time is

Table 4
Central Location Versus Home Use Tests: Advantages Versus Disadvantages

Aspect	Central Location	Home Use Test
Control over ingestion and evaluation	High	Low
Test site versus typical consumption	Unnatural	Natural
Amount of product to be evaluated	Limited	Unlimited
Number of different products tested	Many	Few
Measure satiation and wearout	No	Yes
Mix many concepts and many products	Yes, easy	No, hard
Number of panelists/products for stability	20–50	50–100

spent briefing the respondent, making the respondent feel comfortable, delivering the product, or then finishing a session. These activities in a short intercept evaluation may take up 5 to 10 minutes in a 20-minute interview, or 25% to 50% of the time. In contrast, in a 120- to 240-minute interview, these 5 to 10 minutes are negligible.

Table 5
Choreography of an Extended Product Evaluation Session

Step	Activity	Rationale
1	Study is designed to test multiple products within an extended one- or two-day session.	Maximizes amount of data and motivation of respondent.
2	Respondents are recruited to participate for an extended session.	Must be telephone recruited. Typically not a problem if the study is run on the evening or on a weekend.
3	Respondent shows up, and the chief interviewer orients the respondent as to the purpose of the study.	Usually 25 people show up for the test. The orientation is important because it secures cooperation.
4	Interviewer guides respondent through first product.	This is slow, because the interview guides the group through all the attributes. Respondents are unsure at the start, but have no problem going through the evaluation with an interviewer guiding the group. The products are randomized across respondents.
5	Respondent completes first product, waits for second product. Where appropriate, an interviewer checks the data.	Neither the interviewer nor the respondent knows the "correct ratings," but this checking maintains interest and motivation.
6	Respondent waits a specified time and proceeds with second product.	Waiting, order of products is strictly controlled.
7	Respondent finishes the evaluations, proceeds to an extensive classification.	Data provide information on respondent attitudes, geodemographics, purchase patterns, etc.
8	Respondent is paid and dismissed.	Respondent maintains ongoing motivation and interest throughout the entire evaluation.

PART 3: ANALYSES OF PRODUCT TEST DATA

Basic Data: Product × Attribute Profiles

In the past three decades, researchers have begun to recognize that there is much to be learned by obtaining profiles of multiple products on multiple attributes. These profiles, or report cards, are analyzed in a variety of ways. Fundamentally, they require the respondent to rate each product on different characteristics, with all of the products rated on the same characteristics. The scales are similar. These report cards, or matrices, enable the researcher to glance quickly through the data set to determine the scores of a particular product on different attributes or, more important, the scores of many products on the same attribute. The ability to compare many products on a scorecard basis creates a deeper understanding of the product category and is far easier to comprehend than a series of paired comparisons among all of the products. Respondents may rate the product on sensory, liking, or image attributes or even their fit to different concepts. Table 6 shows an example of such data.

Drivers of Liking and the Inverted U-Shaped Rule for Products

At a higher level of analysis, these matrices enable the researcher to understand what characteristics drive acceptance (or drive other attributes). In days gone by, the researcher might simply correlate all of the attributes with overall liking to determine which particular attribute drives liking. The correlation statistic, assuming as it did a linear relation between two variables, often failed to show the importance of sensory attributes as drivers of liking. Rather, attributes such as good quality and good taste correlated with overall liking. This is somewhat of a tautology. One approach to understand drivers of liking plots overall liking on the ordinate and attribute liking on the abscissa. The equation that describes this relation is: Overall Liking = A + B (Attribute Liking). The slope, B, indicates the relative importance of the attribute. High values of slope B mean that the attribute is important; *unit increases in the liking of the attribute correspond to high increases in overall liking.* Conversely, low values of slope B mean that the attribute is unimportant (Moskowitz and Krieger 1995)

More recently, it has been the fashion to plot overall liking versus sensory attributes and fit a curve to the data, as shown in Figure 1 (Moskowitz 1981). The curve, a quadratic function, shows that liking first increases with sensory attribute level, then peaks, and then drops down. The specific form of this inverted U-shaped curve will depend on the specific product being tested, the sensory range achieved, and the preferences of the respondents. Sometimes the curve will be flat, showing that

Table 6
Example of Product × Attribute Profile

Product	A	B	C
Appearance			
Like appearance	61	54	59
Brown	57	43	62
Flecks	59	30	73
Tomato pieces/amount	22	42	64
Tomato pieces/size	18	35	40
Vegetable pieces/size	11	15	38
Aroma/Flavor			
Like aroma			
Aroma	45	44	57
Like flavor	61	57	18
Flavor strength	61	57	76
Tomato flavor	55	59	49
Meat flavor	13	25	56
Mushroom flavor	16	24	36
Onion flavor	25	20	36
Green pepper flavor	11	9	30
Vegetable flavor	18	18	36
Herb flavor	52	36	70
Black pepper flavor	19	14	36
Garlic flavor	30	20	34
Cheese flavor	11	32	5
Salt taste	25	24	23
Sweet taste	37	28	19
Aftertaste	48	44	70
Sour taste	26	36	54
Oily flavor	26	23	24
Texture/Mouthfeel			
Like texture	58	63	60
Crisp vegetable texture	35	34	40
Oily mouthfeel	29	24	25
Thickness	53	41	47

Notes: All scales are rated 0 to 100. For sensory scales, 0 = none at all and 100 = extreme. For liking scales, 0 = hate and 100 = love.

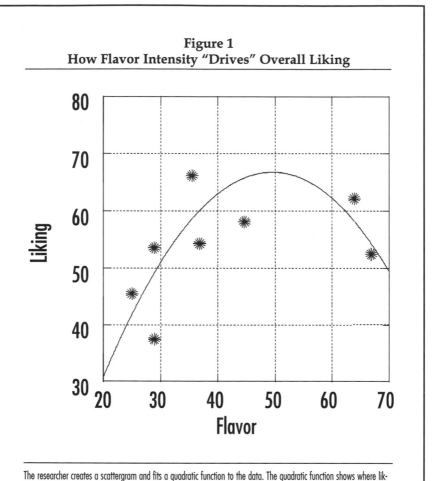

Figure 1
How Flavor Intensity "Drives" Overall Liking

The researcher creates a scattergram and fits a quadratic function to the data. The quadratic function shows where liking tends to peak and reveals the degree to which liking covaries with a single sensory attribute.

though respondents differentiate the product on a sensory attribute, the sensory differences do not drive liking (at least on a univariate basis). Sometimes the curve will show an inverted U-shaped curve; other times the curve will increase and perhaps flatten out slightly as if it were reaching an asymptote. In other situations, the curve will show a downward sloping relation, which suggests that, as the sensory attribute increases, liking actually decreases. There is usually quite a pronounced relation between flavor/aroma sensory levels and liking but less of a relation between texture or appearance and liking. We know from basic research (perception and liking of flavor) that the chemical senses (taste, smell) provoke more hedonic reactions (like versus dislike) than do the visual, auditory, and tactile senses. Thus, for consumer goods (whether food or health and beauty aids), we should not be surprised to see these strong sensory-liking curves for the flavor attributes but not for many of the appearance or texture attributes.

Sensory Preference Segmentation

Marketers are the first to recognize that consumers differ from one another. It should come as no surprise that product test results are often reported by total panel and by key subgroups. Traditionally, these key subgroups comprise individuals falling into different geodemographic classifications or into different brand usage patterns (e.g., users of brand X versus brand Y, heavy versus light users of Brand Z, users versus nonusers). Some of these segmentations also may be based on responses to a battery of questions, which divide people into groups on the basis of preset classifications (Mitchell 1983). For the most part, these segmentations, whether by brand, by geodemographics, or by other, overarching psychological schemata, do not show particularly striking differences in the consumer responses to products. That is, in a product test, these different subgroups of individuals appear to show quite similar reactions to the products themselves.

Psychologists interested in the basic science of perception have introduced newer concepts of segmentation. The fundamental idea behind sensory-based segmentation begins with the previously suggested relation: As a sensory attribute increases, liking first increases, peaks (at some optimal sensory level), and then drops down with further increases in sensory attribute (Moskowitz, Jacobs, and Lazar 1985). It is important to keep in mind that the segmentation is based on the sensory level at which a person's liking rating peaks, not on the magnitude of liking. (A short digression is appropriate here. Segmentation based on the pattern of liking ratings, rather than relations between liking and sensory attributes, could introduce artifacts. Respondents showing similar sensory–liking patterns may fall into different segments if one respondent assigns high numbers to products and the other respondent assigns low numbers to the same products.) When applied to product test results (more than six products must be evaluated by each respondent), this segmentation, based on the sensory–liking patterns, reveals that there are often two, three, or more groups in the population with distinct sensory preference patterns. That is, each segment shows a different sensory level at which liking peaks. There may be individuals who like strong-flavored products, individuals who like weak-flavored and lighter-colored products, and so on. (See Figure 2, which shows data for coffee.)

Sensory preference segments transcend geodemographics, brand usage, and values. Consumers in different segments may use the same brand, have the same values, and so forth. This organizing principle for

Figure 2

Sensory Segmentation: Results from a Five-Country Study of Coffee

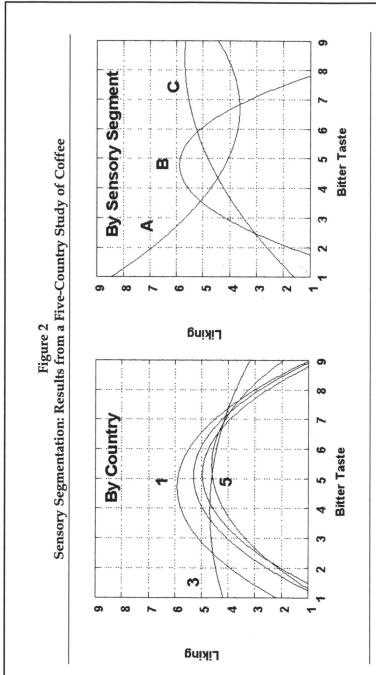

The left panel shows how overall liking for respondents from each of five countries (1–5) is driven by perceived bitterness. The right panel shows the same liking–bitterness relation, this time using data from sensory segments obtained from the five countries. Note that each segment is represented in each country, albeit in different proportions.

product development, emerging from product test results (and from basic psychophysics), is forming the foundation of new approaches for consumer research and applied product development.

Product Mapping and Creating a Product Model from the Map

At an even higher level of analysis, the matrix of product × attribute rating is used to map products into a geometrical space (see Figure 3). The geometrical space may comprise one, two, three, or many more dimensions (though it is difficult to visualize a space of more than three dimensions). Product mapping is done typically with disconnected products, usually those current in the product category, but occasionally with prototypes (so-called category appraisal, aptly named because the approach considers the full range of products currently in a category without regard to the connectedness of their underlying formulation; Munoz, Chambers, and Hummer 1996).

The locations of the product in the map are usually based on the sensory properties of the products, and products located close together are sensorially similar to each other. Brand managers and product developers

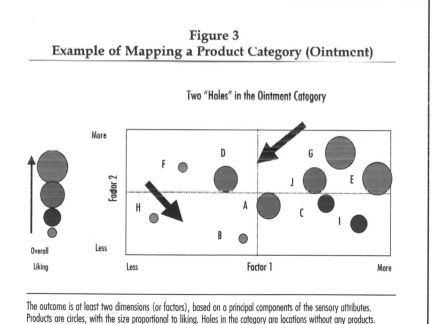

Figure 3
Example of Mapping a Product Category (Ointment)

Two "Holes" in the Ointment Category

The outcome is at least two dimensions (or factors), based on a principal components of the sensory attributes. Products are circles, with the size proportional to liking. Holes in the category are locations without any products.

use these brand maps as heuristics to understand how the consumer perceives the products as a set of interchangeable (or noninterchangeable)
items.

When the coordinates of the brand map are factor scores (from factor
analysis), the map serves double duty. First, the map locates the products
in a space as the heuristic to visualize. Second, the coordinates of the map
(viz., the dimensions) act as independent variables in a regression model.
(The map coordinates, being factor scores, are parsimonious and statistically independent so that no violence is done to the data.) As a consequence, the researcher builds a set of equations (one per attribute, such as
liking, image rating, sensory rating), and the independent variables are
the factor scores. (The models are not just linear equations, but also quadratic equations.) At the end of the day, the researcher is able to identify a
location in the map and estimate the full sensory profile and liking rating
corresponding to the location in the map. This type of analysis can only
occur if the researcher tests multiple products (at least six, but preferably
ten or more). Such an approach using mapping and modeling (with factor scores as independent variables and all rating attributes as dependent
variables) typically would occur early in the research process, when the
objective is to understand the categories, discover drivers of liking, and
then identify unfilled holes in the product category.

Product Optimization

Originally, optimization was done using the relation between liking
and sensory attributes (Schutz 1983). This is called R–R or
response–response analysis, because the optimization model uses relations between two dependent or response variables (viz., liking is a rated
attribute, as are sensory attributes). More recently, however, attention has
focused on the variables under the developer's control (rather than on the
sensory–liking relation). This is called S–R or stimulus–response analysis,
because the optimization model uses the relation between variables under
the developer's control and consumer-rated attributes.

Several decades ago, statisticians developed systematic arrays of variables with the property that the variables were independent of one another.
These are called experimental designs (Box, Hunter, and Hunter 1978;
Khuri and Cornell 1987; Plackett and Burman 1946). Product developers
use these designs to create arrays of products that comprise known variations (e.g., in ingredients or process conditions). By varying the independent variables (viz., features under the developer's control) and obtaining
reactions (e.g., consumer liking, cost of goods, yield, sensory attributes,
even image attributes), the developer can link the variables under direct
operational control to what the consumer responds. Furthermore, these
experimental designs lend themselves to statistical modeling by regression.
It is a short step from the experimental design + consumer reaction to modeling, and another short step from modeling (or equation building) to optimizing (viz., identifying the combination of the variables under design that

produces the highest liking, or the highest liking constrained to a given cost). Table 7 shows two experimental designs—one a screening design (allowing the researcher to investigate many different variables, each at two levels), and the other a more complex experimental design (called a Box Behnken design). The Box Behnken, or response surface, design enables the researcher to create a quadratic model that relates formulation to liking, cost, and other attributes and to optimize liking or any other variable, subject to explicit constraints (viz., the formulation must stay within the range tested) and implicit constraints (viz., one or more attributes of the product, such as a sensory attribute or even cost of goods, must remain within specified constraints). Table 8 shows results for the optimization of a commercial pizza that varied on six formula variables.

Table 7
Example of Two Experimental Design Systems Commonly Used in Product Development

Prod	A	B	C	D	E	F	G	H	I	J	K	Prod	A	B	C
1	1	1	0	1	1	1	0	0	0	1	0	1	3	3	3
2	1	0	1	1	1	0	0	0	1	0	1	2	3	3	1
3	0	1	1	1	0	0	0	1	0	1	1	3	3	1	3
4	1	1	1	0	0	0	1	0	1	1	0	4	3	1	1
5	1	1	0	0	0	1	0	1	1	0	1	5	1	3	3
6	1	0	0	0	1	0	1	1	0	1	1	6	1	3	1
7	0	0	0	1	0	1	1	0	1	1	1	7	1	1	3
8	0	0	1	0	1	1	0	1	1	1	0	8	1	1	1
9	0	1	0	1	1	0	1	1	1	0	0	9	3	2	2
10	1	0	1	1	0	1	1	1	0	0	0	10	1	2	2
11	0	1	1	0	1	1	1	0	0	0	1	11	2	3	2
12	0	0	0	0	0	0	0	0	0	0	0	12	2	1	2
												13	2	2	3
												14	2	2	1
												15	2	2	2

Notes: The left system (11 variables, A–K, 12 runs) is a Plackett-Burman screening design. The design is used to identify key drivers of a response. Each variable (A–K) appears at two options (1 = new, high, on; 0 = old, low, off, respectively). The right system (3 variables, A–C, 15 runs) is a central composite design. It is used to identify optimal levels of a process or an ingredient.

Table 8
Example of an Optimization Run (for Pizza)

Optimize	Total	Total	Total	Total
Constraint # 1	None	Cost < 200	Cost < 150	Cost < 175
Constraint # 2	None	None	None	Cheese Flavor > 63
Ingredient				
Pepperoni	1.25	1.31	1.02	1.07
Mushroom	0.30	0.29	0.27	0.18
Sausage	2.00	1.78	1.20	0.99
Beef	2.00	0.00	0.00	0.00
Cheese A	2.56	2.21	2.22	2.59
Cheese B	3.00	2.42	1.67	3.00
Ratings				
Cost	286	199	150	174
Liking: Total	76	72	69	71
Beef: Amount	65	11	9	5
Cheese: Amount	76	73	68	77
Cheese: Flavor	61	62	58	63
Crust: Amount	63	69	69	67
Crust: Bready	54	58	58	57
Crust: Hardness	45	45	45	46
Mushroom: Amount	21	20	20	14

Notes: Six ingredient were varied systematically according to a central composite design. The results led to a product model, interrelating formulations (under the developer's control), and ratings (acquired by the researcher). Data from optimization studies let the researcher quickly identify the most promising formulations.

Consumer research has taken 25 years to recognize the value of experimental design and product optimization. The product development process used to be far more circuitous and tortuous, with the developer creating a prototype, the researcher testing it and providing feedback (e.g., directional ratings, liking ratings, sensory ratings), and then everyone returning to the drawing boards to give it one more try. With experimental design, the developer creates a set of products, and then the researcher evaluates these products, creates a design, and either identifies the optimum product (meeting consumer needs) or shows that the optimum lies further out. The process repeats, but usually the procedure generates an optimum fairly quickly (viz., in one or two iterations).

Product optimization is run occasionally by market researchers and occasionally by product developers using small-scale R&D efforts (called research guidance panels). Optimization procedures, long in coming to consumer research, provide one of the most promising technologies for improving the usefulness of product tests, because the data generate a database both for future use and for immediate, concrete action to solve the current problem in an actionable fashion.

Emerging Product Test Methods—Observation

Up to now, we have dealt exclusively with paper-and-pencil (or computer-based) questionnaires. Recently, the ethnographic approach to product testing has begun to gain favor, especially in R&D facilities of larger companies. Ethnography studies behavior in the normal environment. Similarly, ethnographic product testing studies how respondents use specific products. Right now, the goal of ethnographic product research is to identify the ways that products are used in order to improve them or to come up with new ideas. Ethnographic research is not typically (but is sometimes) used to evaluate different products. We can trace ethnographic research back to a combination of two sciences: anthropology (which examines the behavior of people in their environment) and human factors (a branch of psychology that examines the behavioral interaction of a person and a machine or a person and a stimulus). Ethnographic research is only in its infancy for product evaluation, but it is a trend that bears watching.

Emerging Product Test Methods—Satiety Evaluation

Home use evaluation is supposed to capture the "real" nuances of product use. One area of evaluation that is coming into play, especially for fast moving consumer goods of different sensory characteristics, is known as "satiety evaluation." The goal here is to identify the factors that make consumers stop consuming a product. We know that people stop eating foods when they are satiated. We know that there is variety seeking among consumers (van Trijp 1995), so that eventually consumers habituate, or get bored with, the same soap fragrance or the same cereal and buy another fragrance, another cereal, or the same product but in a different flavor. Consumer researchers are now turning their attention to identifying the factors underlying this boredom, defined as either short-term satiation (just can't eat or drink any more) or long-term habituation (just got tired of the taste and wanted to try something new). Like ethnographic methods, satiety and boredom aspects of product testing are just in their infancy. The jury is out as to what will be found, but these new methods are part of the evolving growth of product research.

The Estimation of Volumetrics

Many marketers use concept–product tests to estimate the amount of a product that they will sell. Through years of experience, researchers have developed databases and then models that show the relation among concept scores (before product usage), product scores (during usage), and estimated volume. These approaches, expanded by ACNielsen Bases® (1999), use models that interrelate many of the marketing variables. Concept scores and product scores are only two of the variables. Other factors considered are awareness (or some surrogate of advertising) and distribution.

The most widely used volumetric modeling is Bases® II (ACNielsen Bases 1999). This system assesses the appeal and market potential for products on the basis of the reaction of consumers to the concept (simulating the marketplace reality of advertising first), followed by reaction to the product (again simulating marketplace reality). Bases® II estimates Year 1 sales volume after launch, as well as volume for Years 2 and 3. In contrast to the methods described previously, the market potential analysis calls into play many factors, not just the product itself.

These market models differ from the developmental models previously discussed because the market models come into play at the end of the development process. There is no search for patterns because these studies concentrate on one product, one concept, and the response from many individuals. Quite often, however, the widespread popularity of these test market simulators has led to their use as "de facto" concept–product tests. Unlike conventional concept–product tests that look only at the fit of the product and concept, volumetric testing incorporates many more aspects of the marketing mix.

PART 4: PACKAGE DESIGN RESEARCH

A Short Overview

Package research is often the neglected child in consumer testing of price, positioning, product, and package. Until recently, little attention had been given to the product package. Companies might launch new products and involve their in-house package design professionals as well as outside design houses. However, much of the research done was either qualitative (focus groups) or none at all. Part of this lack of research stems from the perception that the package is not particularly important — it is just a vehicle in which to enclose the product (especially in fast moving consumer goods). Part of the lack of research can be traced to the design houses, which perceive their work as artistic and incapable of judgments. (No design house wants consumers to design the package for it.) As a consequence, there is a paucity of research literature on package design, though there are scattered articles here and there and many well-respected companies specializing in package research. (We can compare this dearth of literature with the extremely high volume of literature on advertising testing, perhaps because many more dollars are spent on advertising, so it is immediately more important to be "right.")

Today, however, with increased competition in many categories, the package is assuming renewed importance, and researchers are rising to the occasion. Manufacturers are sponsoring short in-house courses on the importance of package design. Package design firms, once the bastion of the artist, are welcoming quantitative research. (It should be acknowledged that these design firms always welcomed qualitative research, because that research, like qualitative in advertising, probed and revealed aspects of the package that were important for the designer.) Package design firms are also adopting a more holistic approach to the design process. According to researchers at Cheskin (1999), a brand identity and design firm, commenting on the design of a beer package, "Beyond helping you manage clients, research can actually help you create better design — not by dictating color and form, but by informing your intuition.... When your job is to make a product sell itself at the point of sale, how do you know that your design will deliver the goods?... What does the package say about the beer inside?... How should your client position the product?... If you just look at the packages, what would you say about the beer?"

What Should Package Testing Provide?

Package testing serves several purposes, the most important of which is to confirm or disconfirm the objectives of the package designer. Typically, package designers create packages (either graphics or structures) with some objective in mind, such as reinforcing the brand, communicating new benefits, or enhancing the chances that the product will be selected. In all of these objectives, package testing must provide some idea as to whether or not the new package is successful. A modicum of sensitivity to the creative process is also in order, because package testing often reflects on the creative abilities of the designer, who is both an artist and a business-responsive individual.

Focus Groups

For many years, the conventional package evaluation consisted of focus groups. Focus groups, properly conducted, can be very valuable in the creative process, especially in the up-front developmental stage. The focus group is private, does not come out with hard and fast results, and can cover a great deal of territory in a warm, informal manner. In a package design focus group, the respondent can verbalize reactions to package features, identify key features that elicit interest, and talk about the coherence between the package itself and the brand. A sensitive package designer gets a great deal out of focus groups because the designer can see and hear how the consumer reacts to the packages. By presenting different possible packages, the designer can see which "work" and which do not. Focus groups provide the designer with a great deal of feedback, generally in a nonthreatening, nonjudgmental manner (viz., not judged by another professional, though consumers could reject the package). It should come as no wonder that this type of qualitative research has been welcomed by designers, because in essence, it reflects how they would intuitively go about obtaining feedback about their creations.

Focus groups can, however, backfire in several ways. First, they can be misused. In a focus group, people say many different things, and the listener can select specific phrases to suit his or her own purpose and agenda. Second, and even more important, respondents often like to "play designer." Respondents like to tell designers what to do, even if the designers aren't really interested in following the sage advice (Glass 1999). Consequently, there may develop an antagonism between the client/respondent (with the client wanting to follow the respondent's suggestions) and the designer (who has a basic artistic and business idea in mind and simply wants feedback).

Profiling Packages

At the simplest level, the researcher can determine whether the package is acceptable to the consumer or fits the brand. This type of testing typically involves attitudinal measures. The researcher shows the package to the respondent and obtains a profile of ratings, similar to the way that the researcher obtains product ratings. The key differences are that the researcher may obtain profiles of the expectation of the product (based on the package), as well as ratings of the package itself. The attributes can vary substantially from one product category to another. Some of the ratings may deal with interest in the package (or in the product, based on exposure to the package). Other ratings may deal with one's expectation of the product based on the package. If the respondent actually uses the product in the package, the researcher can obtain ratings of person–package interaction (including ease of carrying or gripping the product, ease of opening, ease of removing the product, and ease of storing the package). This type of information is extremely valuable to the package designer, who wants to find out whether or not the package is on target.

Typically, the designer receives only the simplest of "briefs" or project descriptions, such as the requirement that the package be upscale, that it live up to the brand, and that it communicate an effective or good-tasting product. The data from the evaluative package tests provide the diagnostics to demonstrate whether the package as designed actually lives up to the requirements set by the client's package design group.

Behavioral Measures—T-Scope and Speed of Recognition

At a more behavioral level, the package testing may involve behavioral measures. One behavioral measure is the ability to identify whether a package is actually on the shelf during a very short exposure time. The rationale behind this type of testing (called T-Scope or tachistoscope testing) is that the typical shopper spends relatively little time inspecting a store shelf. Therefore, for a package to make its impact, it is important that the package "jump off" the shelf (visually). It is assumed by the researcher that those packages that are perceived in the short interval permitted by the T-Scope have shelf presence. In some demonstrations, Elliot Young (1999) has demonstrated that in these T-Scope tasks the speed at which the stimulus information is available is often so low that the respondent must use color and design cues, rather than brand names. Well-known brands with distinctive package features (e.g., Tide® brand detergent, with its concentric halos) are rapidly recognized, even if the brand name is incorrect. If the research interest focuses on the recognizability of the single package, then one can present single packages and determine the fastest shutter speed (viz., the least time needed) for the package to be correctly identified. If the research interest focuses on the "findability" of the package on the shelf, then the researcher can place the test package at different locations on the shelf and then parametrically assess the contribution of package design and location on the shelf as joint contributors to findability.

Eye Tracking and the Features of a Package

Eye tracking is another method for testing the shelf. The typical shelf is an extremely complex array of package designs over which the consumer's eye wanders. The objective of package designers is to guide the consumer to the package. This action then constitutes the first step in selecting the product. Eye tracking allows the researcher to identify the pattern that the eye follows. Is the eye drawn to the client's particular package? Does the eye wander away from the package (thus diminishing the chances that the customer will select the product)? Young (1999) has also demonstrated the use of eye tracking technology, based on military research developments in the 1970s. The eye tracking technology traces the location of the line of sight. It shows how the consumer, when presented with either a shelf set or a single package, explores the stimulus, then it tracks how the eye wanders and records what the eye sees. When done for a single stimulus (e.g., an over-the-counter medicine), the eye tracking technology can show if, when, and for how long key messages are looked at (but not whether these are good or not). When done for the entire shelf, the eye tracking technology can identify whether the package is even looked at and for how long. On the basis of these analyses, Young and his associates have amassed a variety of generalizations about where on the shelf the package should be, how many facings the package should have, and so on.

Optimizing Package Design—Can Art and Science Mix?

One of the most intriguing developments is the advance of conjoint measurement (systematic stimulus variation) into package design. Conjoint measurement comprises the experimental variation of components in a concept in order to understand the underlying dynamics of how the components perform. The respondent evaluates full combinations of these components (e.g., benefits, prices), and from the ratings, researchers estimate the partworth contribution of each component. The same research paradigm (viz., systematic variation of components) has begun to enter package research, but this time the components are features of the package (e.g., different names, colors, graphics), and the concepts are full packages comprising these systematically varied features. From the responses of consumers to test packages (e.g., created on the computer screen), the researcher and package designer quickly discover

Figure 4
Components of Package Design Research

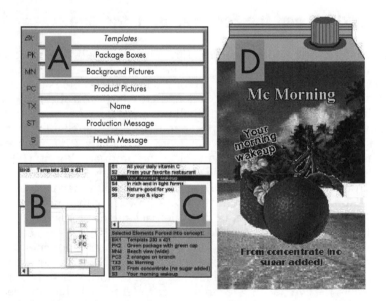

Notes: A = categories or sets of features; B = specific template used to embed graphic features; C = features in specific designed package; D = juice package corresponding to the specific set of designed features.

what every design feature contributes to consumer interest, communication, and such.

Some of the power of the conjoint approach applied to graphics design can be seen by inspecting Figure 4 (showing the template, components, one finished package, and a table of utilities). The conjoint system enables the designer to rapidly understand the effectiveness of each concept element and then create new and better combinations by incorporating high performing graphic elements and discarding poor performing elements. Of course, attention must always be paid to the artistic coherence of the design. Unlike concept testing using conjoint measurement, however, there is far less in the literature (and in actual practice) using systematically varied package features. The best explanation for this is that package design is still an artistic endeavor, resisting research on the one hand and yet welcoming research insights on the other.

Package Design—An Overview

In contrast to product (and concept) development, package research development is still in its infancy. For the most part, researchers are only beginning to recognize the importance of the "package" as a key factor. Up to now, it was the artistic aspects of package design, along with the role of the package as a secondary factor, that hindered the full flowering of package research. That unhappy situation is beginning to remedy itself as the competitive environment forces recognition of package research as a key new source of information, useful to maintain or to achieve competitive advantage in the marketplace.

BIBLIOGRAPHY

ACNielsen Bases (1999), sales brochure (available at www.Bases.com).

Boring, E.G. (1929), "Sensation and Perception," in *The History of Experimental Psychology*. New York: Appleton Century Crofts.

Box, G.E.P., J. Hunter, and S. Hunter (1978), *Statistics for Experimenters*. New York: John Wiley & Sons.

Cheskin, Inc. (1999), "Five Bottles of Beer," *Critique: The Magazine of Design Graphic Thinking*, (Spring), 89–95.

Civille, G. and B.G. Lyon, eds. (1995), *FlavLex, Version 1.15*. West Conshohocken, PA: Softex, American Society for Testing and Materials.

Clapperton, J., C.E. Dagliesh, and M.C. Meilgaard (1975), "Progress Towards an International System of Beer Flavor Terminology," *Master Brewers Association of America Technical Journal*, 12, 273–80.

Gacula, M.C., Jr. (1993), *Design and Analysis of Sensory Optimization*. Trumbull, CT: Food and Nutrition Press.

Glass, Alan (1999), personal communication.

Khuri, A.J. and J.A. Cornell (1987), *Response Surfaces*. New York: Marcel Dekker Inc.

Meilgaard, M., G.V. Civille, and B.T. Carr (1987), *Sensory Evaluation Techniques*. Boca Raton, FL: CRC Press.

Meiselman, H.L. (1978), "Scales for Measuring Food Preference," in *Encyclopedia of Food Science*, M.S. Petersen and A.H. Johnson, eds. Westport. CT: AVI, 675–78.

Mitchell, A. (1983), *The Nine American Lifestyles*. New York: MacMillan.

Moskowitz, H.R. (1981), "Relative Importance of Perceptual Factors to Consumer Acceptance: Linear Versus Quadratic Analysis," *Journal of Food Science*, 46, 244–48.

———— (1983), *Product Testing and Sensory Evaluation of Food: Marketing and R&D Approaches*. Westport, CT: Food and Nutrition Press.

———— (1984), *Cosmetic Product Testing: A Modern Psychophysical Approach*. New York: Marcel Dekker Inc.

———— (1985), *New Directions in Product Testing and Sensory Analysis of Food*. Westport, CT: Food and Nutrition Press.

———— (1994), *Food Concepts and Products: Just In Time Development*. Trumbull, CT: Food and Nutrition Press.

———— (1995), "Experts Versus Consumers," *Journal of Sensory Studies*, 11 (1), 19–35.

———— (1997), "Base Size in Product Testing: A Psychophysical Viewpoint and Analysis," *Food Overall Quality and Preference*, 8, 247–56.

————, B.E. Jacobs, and N. Lazar (1985), "Product Response Segmentation and the Analysis of Individual Differences in Liking," *Journal of Food Quality*, 8, 168–91.

———— and B. Krieger (1995), "The Contribution of Sensory Liking to Overall Liking: An Analysis of Six Food Categories," *Food Quality and Preference*, 6 (2), 83–91.

———— and ———— (1998), "International Product Optimization: A Case History," *Food Quality and Preference*, 9 (6), 443–54.

Munoz, A.M., E. Chambers IV, and S. Hummer (1996), "A Multifaceted Category Research Study: How to Understand a Product Category and Its Consumer Responses," *Journal of Sensory Studies*, 11 (4), 261–94.

Plackett, R.L. and J.D. Burman (1946), "The Design of Optimum Multifactorial Experiments," *Biometrika*, 33, 305–25

Peryam, D.R. and F.J. Pilgrim (1957), "Hedonic Scale Method of Measuring Food Preferences," *Food Technology*, 11, 9–14.

Schutz, H.G. (1964), "A Food Action Rating Scale for Measuring Food Acceptance," *Journal of Food Science*, 30, 202–13.

———— (1983), "Multiple Regression Approach to Optimization," *Food Technology*, 37, 47–62.

———— (1989), "Beyond Preference: Appropriateness as a Measure of Contextual Acceptance of Food," in *Food Acceptance*, D.M.H. Thomson, ed. London: Elsevier, 115–34.

Smithies, R.A. and B.S. Buchanan (1990), *Substantiating a Taste Claim*, Transcript Proceedings, NAD Workshop. New York: Council of Better Business Bureaus, Advertising Research Foundation.

Stevens, S.S. (1975), *Psychophysics: An Introduction to its Perceptual, Neural and Social Prospects*. New York: John Wiley & Sons.

Stone, H. and J.L.H. Sidel (1985), *Sensory Evaluation Practices*. New York: John Wiley & Sons.

Thurstone, L.L. (1927), "A Law of Comparative Judgment," *Psychological Review*, 34, 273–86.

van Trijp, J.C.M., (1995), "Variety-Seeking in Product Choice Behavior—Theory with Applications," in *The Food Domain*, Vol. 1. Wageningen, The Netherlands: Wageningen University.

Young, E. (1999), personal communication.

21
Pricing Research

David W. Lyon

INTRODUCTION AND CONTEXT

Pricing is both one of the most common research topics and one of the most difficult tasks to perform well. Many of the issues involved are quite fundamental and easily understood, and most are not unique to pricing research, only exacerbated relative to other research topics. But in practice, these fundamental issues are frequently ignored, even in the context of methodologies founded on otherwise sophisticated statistical and psychological theories. These contrasts of popularity versus difficulty and elementary issues versus sophisticated models make the commercial practice of pricing research at the turn of the millennium a fascinating microcosm of many of the successes and embarrassments of marketing research as a whole.

The simple term "pricing research" can, of course, cover a broad range of objectives, topics, and approaches. In this chapter, we focus on how to relate potential demand for a product or service to its price using primary, or survey-based, marketing research. To place our focus in a broader context, let us briefly mention a few important kinds of pricing research that we will *not* explore in detail.

By focusing mostly on the price–demand relationship, we exclude a host of affective questions about pricing. What price, or pricing structure, will buyers perceive as "fair"? What pricing is consistent with the other positioning elements of a product? How do consumers assimilate information about a product and its competitors to form price expectations? What price will trigger unwanted regulation or bad publicity? How will competitors, as opposed to buyers, react to our product's pricing? What is the optimum role of price-based promotions or "deals" in the marketing mix compared with advertising? How will pricing affect the rate of diffusion (or "uptake curve") of a new product? All these questions are reasonable to ask, and all are "pricing research." Each leads to very different and intriguing considerations, theories, and research approaches. But each is also much less commonly addressed in commercial practice and beyond our scope here.

We do not consider secondary pricing research, which typically involves analysis of past pricing history and the concomitant demand changes. Neither do we explore pricing research based on comparisons of test markets in which prices differ. Each of these approaches has serious limitations. Historical analysis fails if there is little past price variation, if all competitors' prices tend to move together, or if recent market shifts have changed the market relationships. Thus, it is typically of little or no help in pricing new products, especially if they are significant innovations. Test markets are critically dependent on successful "matching" of the markets at each price level and subject to competitive disruptions. They are often used for new product pricing in consumer packaged goods, but they too are unsuitable for new products of the sort that cannot easily be manufactured and delivered in test quantities before a full-scale launch decision is made.

The drawbacks of historical analysis and test markets just cited are often pointed out by survey research practitioners, but the other side of the coin often goes unmentioned. Both these techniques offer something that the techniques we focus on cannot: They are based on real buyers' real behavior in the real world. In contrast, survey-based pricing research generally assumes not only that respondents can accurately determine how they would behave in a hypothetical future situation, but also that they will truthfully report that determination to us.

This assumption is so fundamental to so much survey-based marketing research that it often goes unrecognized and unexamined. This was made memorably clear to me when I watched an audience of economists react with mystification and confusion to the first few minutes of a talk on stated preference discrete choice modeling. Their problem became clear when one suddenly understood what was being said and exclaimed, "You mean you *ask* people what they're going to do? And then you *believe* them?"

The members of the audience did not simply disagree with the idea that respondents can and will predict their future behavior. They found it so astonishing that they initially failed to even comprehend what the idea was. This reaction to something taken so much for granted in marketing research practice should fuel continuing concerns about, and attention to, what questions we ask and how we ask them. A recurring theme will emerge as we discuss pricing research approaches: They succeed or fail largely because of the answers they demand of respondents. The details are sometimes obvious and sometimes not, but in case after case, the statistical and mathematical properties pale in importance relative to the effects of how respondents react to questions.

DIRECT QUESTIONING

Willingness to Pay

Perhaps the simplest approach to primary pricing research is to demonstrate or describe a product or service and then baldly ask, "What would you be willing to pay for this?" When marketers unfamiliar with research want to measure "willingness to pay," this is often exactly the question they intend to ask.

The most obvious problem with this is its invitation to respondents to "lowball" the answer. It is impossible to hide the focus on price and virtually impossible to hide in which product's price we are interested. On hearing such a question, many respondents immediately shift into their "used car lot" mode and produce "opening offers" that are not remotely accurate.

The one significant advantage of this question is its completely open-ended nature. If we genuinely have no idea what price might be appropriate, we are not forced to select a handful of price points to study (as is required by many other approaches). Despite this, the question is sometimes asked with a presupplied list of multiple-choice answers. Not only does that negate the one advantage, but it also motivates respondents to avoid being seen as a miser or spendthrift by not giving the lowest or highest answers suggested.

That this question is not at all uncommon in practice, despite its obvious problems, is an unfortunate testament to how frequently the peculiarities of pricing research are ignored. Note that it is an analog of a type of question that is quite reasonable in other contexts. "What color would you like your next car to be?" should produce perfectly reasonable answers. "How fast should it accelerate from 0 to 60?" may invite some exaggeration of the real need, but probably not much. But "How much would you be willing to pay?" invites huge problems.

The Buy Response Question

An equally simple and far more reliable direct question is simply "Would you buy this product?" This again would be asked after an initial demonstration and/or description of the product. The question is pricing-related if the explanation happens to mention the price of the item or if the example happens to carry a price tag. From the researcher's point of view, we are asking, "Would you buy it for $x?" but it is critically important that the respondent's attention not be called to the price by actually using such phrasing. The price should be presented unobtrusively and matter-of-factly, so that it is just one feature of the product among many others.

In its simplest form, this is known as a "buy response" question—the response is either "buy" or "no buy." If carefully executed, it engenders essentially no price-related bias. It can also avoid any tendency to overstate willingness to buy the product being researched if it is placed in the context of a full set of competitors and their prices and phrased as "Which, if any, would you buy?" Of course, for new products that require presenting specific advance information, the ability to conceal which product is of interest will be lost.

The obvious problem with a single buy response (or purchase likelihood) question is that it does not inform us about price per se. It is nothing more than a simple concept test on the overall product as priced, with no information as to whether some other price would be better. We need to ask the question at two or more price points to learn something about price effects.

Monadic Tests

Monadic tests split the overall survey sample into several separate cells and ask a single buy response question with a different price in each cell. Well-executed monadic tests are clearly the least biased, most defensible way we now have to measure price sensitivity in a survey context. This is because no respondent ever knows what other prices are being tested. Indeed, no respondent knows that *any* other prices are being tested or even that price is the object of the research. With a monadic test, we can be certain that the differences we see from one price point to the next are not due to bias in the responses. If carefully presented in a full competitive context, we can also feel confident in the absolute share levels we estimate (for an excellent description of painstaking execution of monadic tests for both pricing and other purposes, see Marder 1997).

Monadic tests are very simple, very defensible, and very widely used. But they also suffer from a major problem that impels many to use other approaches. That problem is the sampling variance that arises from having independent samples for each price point. With 100 respondents in each sample cell, the 95% confidence interval for the percentage buying in a cell can be as much as plus or minus 10 percentage points. The confidence interval around the difference of two such results can be plus or minus up to 14 percentage points. So, if we see that 43% of 100 respondents will buy at $7, but 56% of 100 others buy at $5, then we can be 95% confident that the true difference is somewhere between 1% fewer buying at $5 and 27% more buying at $5. Such wide degrees of uncertainty can make the results virtually useless for managerial action.

Surprisingly, many monadic tests are executed and used with little or no consideration of their levels of sampling errors. Cell sizes of 100, or even less, are not uncommon, and cell sizes of 500 or more are rare. This means that sampling errors are relatively large, and paradoxical reversals of the expected price–demand relationship are relatively routine.

Variance Reduction in Monadic Tests

How can the sampling error and its impact be reduced while maintaining the basic framework and virtues of monadic tests? There are several options sometimes available. First, we can increase the sample cell sizes. This may provide a strong budgetary incentive to use mail (or, increasingly often, the Web) as the data collection medium. Marder (1997) describes many such mail studies in the context of very carefully controlled monadic experiments.

Second, we can try to control variance by careful matching of the sample cells. Quota controls, and sometimes dynamic cell assignment schemes, can be used to get the same mix in each sample cell on potentially purchase-related variables such as the age, gender, income, and education of consumers or the size, industry, and growth rate of business concerns. Less desirably but more easily, we can also match the cells post hoc using weighting, including multivariate "raking" schemes.

Third, we can minimize the number of separate cells tested and space their prices widely. If two cells see very different prices, a straight line price curve drawn between their two results will be much more stable relative to the sampling variance than one between two very close prices. And, using only two cells, say, instead of three or more means that each cell can be larger for the same budget. However, we are then forced to rely on assumptions of linear price effects between the points we measure. If we suspect that there are distinct threshold prices in the market, this is unacceptable. Indeed, although the basic advice to use few, widely spaced cells is very valid and practical, we can easily take it to the extreme of studying prices far removed from those we care about, thereby losing all face validity.

Fourth, we can try to minimize the variance in the respondent-level data. One frequent way to do this is to replace the buy response question with a purchase likelihood question, "How likely would you be to buy this item? Will you definitely buy it, probably buy it, might or might not buy it, probably not buy it, or definitely not buy it?" Variations abound, of course, in the number and labeling of the scale points.

From a scaling standpoint, a buy response question has only two scale points, and we are always at one extreme or the other. By providing intermediate scale points, the purchase likelihood question can reduce variance at the source and improve the stability of our likelihood versus price curves. But this is true only if we can somehow translate the purchase likelihood scale into actual purchase probabilities or some other unit we are willing to treat as interval-level data. This is often not possible and always entails some degree of uncertainty. Surprisingly often, purchase likelihood questions are asked but then analyzed using the "top box" or "top two box" percentages. This not only converts the results back to two-point scales with all the variance of buy response, thus negating the advantage of the original question, but also requires an arbitrary decision as to how many of the top scale points will count as purchase surrogates.

Another option for reducing the scale variance is to ask for some form of purchase allocation rather than a simple buy/no-buy question. When the product of interest is being tested in the context of a full set of competitors, we can ask respondents to allocate points, chips, or stickers among the options in proportion to their relative purchase interest. If 10 points are allocated, we effectively have an 11-point scale. Although it seems natural to treat this as an interval scale, the key question now becomes whether the allocations are in fact proportionate to true purchase probabilities and/or market shares.

Marder (1997) has used such allocation approaches frequently and reports favorable external validation results for them. One intriguing finding he reports is that sticker tests perform better than verbal point allocations or chip tests, illustrating in a surprising context that simple respondent psychology drives what works. Putting all the points or chips in one place saves the respondent effort, whereas placing ten stickers requires essentially the same amount of work whether they all go in one place or are spread around. Thus, stickers are spread around more than are chips or points, reduce variance more, and are more reflective of the true distribution of purchases and/or probabilities.

The allocation approach is difficult or impossible to use unless competitive offerings are included in the respondent stimulus. Correspondingly, using purchase likelihood questions makes it difficult or impossible to disguise which product is of interest, and that lessens the value of providing the competitive context. These considerations often drive the choice between allocation and likelihood scales.

Series of Price Questions

An entirely different way to address the variance problems of monadic designs is to directly attack the root of the problem by abandoning the monadic framework altogether. We can simply ask each respondent a series of buy response (or purchase likelihood) questions, each about the same product but at different prices.

This approach is also widely used with varying details. Some practitioners always ask about the prices in increasing sequence, some in decreasing sequence, and some in randomized or rotated orders or with other ways of balancing one or more orders across the sample. When a buy response is the basic question, some ask about an intermediate price point first and then search up for the no-buy point or down for the buy point, as the initial response dictates.

Terminology also varies. The term "sequential monadic" borders on the oxymoronic, but it is often used, based on the idea of doing a sequenced series of "monadic" tests. The Gabor-Granger technique, more commonly used in Europe than in North America, is essentially the use of purchase likelihood questions in a randomized price order.

The overwhelming problem with all these variants is the response bias based on price. The first question in the sequence can be asked in unbiased fashion. But there is no way to ask the second or subsequent questions without making it obvious that nothing has changed but the price of one product. To illustrate the problem, consider Figure 1, which shows data on videodisk player rentals, adapted from Brennan (1995). Brennan uses an 11-point Juster scale, translated to mean purchase probabilities, but the same pattern is routinely seen with simple buy response questions as well.

When prices were asked about in low to high order, a huge number of respondents balked at the first price increase they were asked about and even more at the second. Figure 1 shows such a steep decline in the price–demand curve that we would strongly recommend a low price (sub-

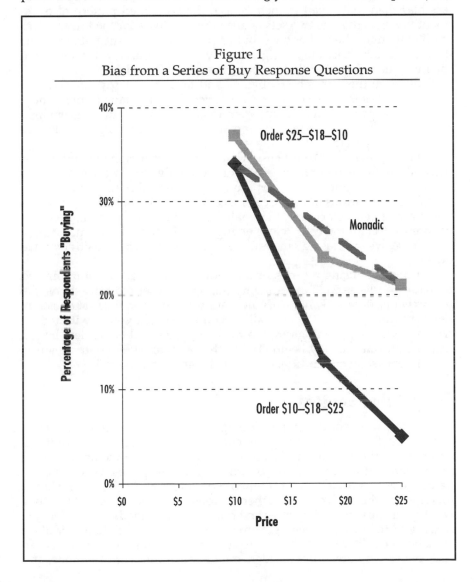

Figure 1
Bias from a Series of Buy Response Questions

ject to cost and profit considerations, of course). When asked about in declining order, however, we find a 21%, not a 5%, probability of buying at the highest price. The price–demand curve is now shallow enough that the highest price is clearly the one that will maximize revenue and profits.

This huge discrepancy in results must be due to bias induced by the series of price questions. As we would expect, a monadic analysis using just the first questions answered (shown by the dashed line in Figure 1) shows less price sensitivity than either series alone. In this case and in many others, the series of questions asked in declining order shows much less bias than that asked in increasing order. A related pattern also frequently seen is that the two sets of answers are closer for the lower prices studied than for the higher ones. In this particular case, the data from the declining order series are not significantly or substantively different from the monadic results, but that is not a generalizable finding.

Although the bias is both obvious and fairly well known, a series of price questions is quite common in practice. The dramatic improvement in sampling errors it offers is apparent in any study. But the bias entailed is only visible if two or more different orders of questions actually are used and compared.

One popular practice is to use what amounts to a monadic design but then ask about the other price points subsequently simply because "it's so quick and easy" and "can't hurt anything." The thinking is that, if the data from the various monadic cells seem close enough, they can be combined across cells. Of course, the smaller our samples are, the more likely we are to declare the cells "close enough" and proceed. But in virtually every case, we are biasing our results toward excess price sensitivity if we do so.

In practice, using a series of questions often leads to compromised monadic results as well. In setting up the first of a series of questions, the researcher is far less likely to disguise interest in price in the first question. Even the first question then literally becomes "Would you buy it for $x?" which alerts the respondent to the focus on price and engenders biased responses from the very beginning. In the Brennan (1995) data, this was in fact done, so even the "monadic" results are not unbiased.

Competitive Contexts

In most forms of direct questioning, there is much to be gained from conducting the questioning in the context of a full set of assumptions specified by the researcher. This context should usually include showing the respondent the competitive offerings and their prices. When respondents are not reminded about competitive options and prices or are left to imagine for themselves what other options they should entertain, they will typically overstate buy rates and purchase likelihoods and understate sensitivity to price differences. Sometimes it is not feasible to specify a realistic competitive context (perhaps the market is highly fragmented, so each buyer is aware of or considers only a small number of options, and we do not want to create artificial awareness of all the options and prices). In those cases, it is often possible and usually desirable to use background questions about current ownership, brand awareness, last price paid, price awareness, and so forth, to at least call any information each respondent already has to the forefront of his or her mind.

In some markets, one must include other details about the purchase occasion as well. In what, if any, type of store should the respondents imagine themselves shopping? How urgently is the product needed and for what purpose? Many businesses buy similar products for a variety of different internal uses. The specific use the respondent is thinking of will often dictate both price sensitivity and willingness to buy at all.

These considerations of context may strike the reader, as they do me, as obvious to the point of banality, yet many pricing tests are routinely conducted with no reference to the decision environment at all.

The van Westendorp Price Sensitivity Meter

The van Westendorp "Price Sensitivity Meter," or PSM, was first proposed in 1976 (van Westendorp 1976). It is a form of direct questioning whose use in commercial practice appears to have increased in the past five years or so. As is discussed subsequently, its popularity owes more to its simplicity, ease of implementation, and intuitive appeal than to any theoretical foundation for its analysis.

Questions and Underlying Rationales

The PSM technique first exposes respondents to a product description or sample (in practice, usually a new product). After initial familiarization with the product, four questions are asked, along the lines of the following:

- ❏ At what price would you consider this item to represent a good value? (the "inexpensive" question);
- ❏ At what price would you say this item is getting expensive, but you would still consider it? (the ""expensive" question);
- ❏ At what price would you say this item is so expensive that you would no longer consider it? (the "too expensive" question); and
- ❏ At what price would you say this item is so inexpensive that you would begin to question its quality? (the "too inexpensive" question).

The questions can be adapted to apply to an entire product category, and sometimes are. The last question, in particular, may be rephrased to apply to the category if the original product example is concrete enough to unequivocally establish its quality independently of price. Practitioners who advocate using the PSM technique are sometimes passionate, but, amusingly, not unanimous, about the correct order in which to ask the questions. The order here is that given in van Westendorp's (1976) original paper.

In formulating these questions, van Westendorp was guided by two psychological principles. The "theory of reasonable prices" holds that prospective buyers can examine an item and formulate a rough notion of what they would expect the item to cost or at least the range into which they would expect it to fall. Furthermore, it says that if an item is priced within a buyer's "reasonable range," then price will not be a factor in the final decision. In other words, an unreasonable price disqualifies the item from consideration, whereas a reasonable one results in the final decision being made on other grounds. The first two questions establish a respondent's "normal range" of prices for the item, and the last two establish his or her "acceptable range." The normal and acceptable ranges are two different ways to operationalize the "reasonable range" idea.

The second principle is simply the idea of price signaling quality, which leads to the idea that some price is too low. In some markets, this seems untenable, so practitioners occasionally ask only the first two questions and conduct an abbreviated analysis.

Analysis

The analysis proposed by van Westendorp (1976) involves plotting the empirical cumulative distribution functions for the four questions and then interpreting various points at which those distribution curves cross, as is illustrated in Figure 2. On the basis of his experience with a small number of studies, he supplies interpretations for each point. For example, at the price he defines as the "indifference price point," the number of respondents finding that price below their normal range is equal to the number for whom it is above their normal range. Van Westendorp claims that this price maximizes the percentage of respondents for whom the price is in the normal range and that it typically represents the price of the market leader and/or the price at which most transactions occur in the market.

This analytic approach is not the only one possible but is still widely used despite some major problems. Mathematically, there is no guarantee that some of the pairs of distribution curves will ever cross. In practice, the curves for the last two questions, which intersect to give the "optimum price point," often fail to intersect and their analysis then devolves into using the most extreme answers to each question to set an "optimal range." Van Westendorp's (1976) claims that certain points maximize the percentage of respondents for whom a price is normal or acceptable are simply wrong (except under very strong assumptions as to the smoothness and symmetry of the distribution curves). From a validation standpoint, I am unaware of any published validation in the 24 years since van Westendorp's original paper. Indeed, there have been exceptionally few publications addressing this method at all.

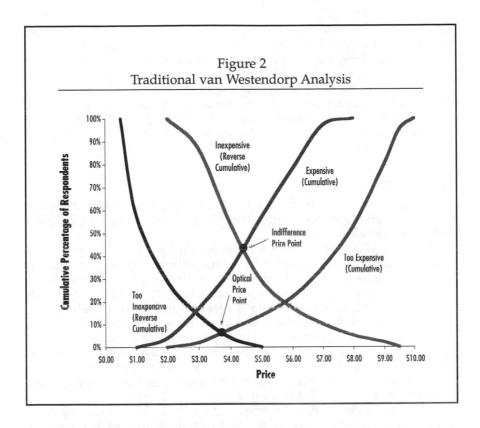

Figure 2
Traditional van Westendorp Analysis

Further underscoring the lack of theory behind the analysis, it is not uncommon to see practitioners define two of the points based on a different pair of curve crossings than did van Westendorp. This seems to be due to an error introduced as the technique was passed from researcher to researcher without reference to the original paper.

Two other major problem areas should be mentioned. The first is the very practical problem that remarkably many respondents give four answers that do not show the expected relationships (e.g., their "too inexpensive" price is higher than their "inexpensive" price). Van Westendorp (1976) refers to a few percent having this problem and to automatically cleaning the data (in an unspecified way). I have seen 20% or more of respondents with inconsistent data. This discrepancy probably results from the common practice today of asking the questions over the telephone, as opposed to van Westendorp's original in-person administration. Both respondents and interviewers find it harder to track answers and check consistency on the telephone, and because of household or workplace distractions while on the telephone, some respondents give less attention to the exact wording of the questions than they would in person. The lack of any published specifics on how to correct these problems means that each practitioner must invent his or her own method.

The second problem is much more fundamental. Each of the four questions is a close relative of the basic "How much would you pay for this?" question. As such, each is an open invitation to responses biased low. That bias may be somewhat ameliorated because the questions actually ask about price expectations rather than outright willingness to pay. But asking about expectations also means that we cannot directly relate market shares to price.

Discussion

Despite these major issues, the PSM technique is popular and appears even to be gaining in popularity. Why? There seem to be both practical and more theoretical reasons.

From a practical standpoint, it requires only four quick and easy questions and can be administered in any data collection mode (if we ignore the data inconsistency issue). Another important practical consideration is that the results virtually always have face validity. Respondents simply do not look at $2.00 packaged goods items and pronounce them a good value at 10¢ or say that a $30 coffee maker is not getting expensive until $300. Virtually all responses are in ranges considered reasonable by marketers, and the ultimate results are little influenced by those that are not. Thus, the results are never embarrassing or inexplicable. By the same token, however, we should wonder how much real knowledge is being added when we never find real surprises.

The more theoretical and rational reason for PSM's popularity is the intuitive appeal to marketers of the four questions. Indirectly, the appeal of the questions testifies to our willingness to accept the theories of reasonable prices and psychological pricing from which van Westendorp (1976) started.

Newton, Miller, and Smith's Modification of PSM

The appeal of the questions has not just led to their popularity; it has also motivated attempts to find a more rational way to analyze them. In particular, Newton, Miller, and Smith (NMS; 1993) proposed adding two additional questions and using a completely different analytic approach. One appeal of their method is that it actually produces a price–demand curve as its output rather than a set of price points not explicitly linked to shares.

The two new questions NMS propose to ask after the first four are "At (*the price just named as [inexpensive or expensive]*), how likely would you be to actually buy the item?" Just before asking these two new questions would be an ideal time to explicitly remind respondents of competitive alternatives and prices, and possibly their own level of need for any such product, to avoid gross demand overestimation.

The NMS (1993) analysis converts the purchase likelihood scale to numeric purchase probabilities using knowledge obtained from previous validation studies on the category or related ones (for many consumer packaged goods and some other categories, such data are available from several firms specializing in "simulated test markets"). When no such knowledge exists, their method cannot be used, but as we demonstrate subsequently, their basic analytic idea can still be distilled into a very simple and useful analysis.

For each respondent, a purchase probability curve as a function of price is produced using those two data points plus assumptions of zero purchase probability at and above the too expensive price point and at and below the too inexpensive price points. The probability curve is assumed to be piecewise linear between those points. For an example, see Figure 3. Those curves are then averaged over respondents to produce an overall market share curve as a function of price. The assumption of zero purchase at the too inexpensive price means that the share curve is not uniformly downward sloping; it tends to peak in the general area in which many respondents find the price within their normal range. If that assumption of psychological pricing in a category seems unnatural, then different assumptions about purchase probabilities at prices less than the inexpensive price can be easily incorporated.

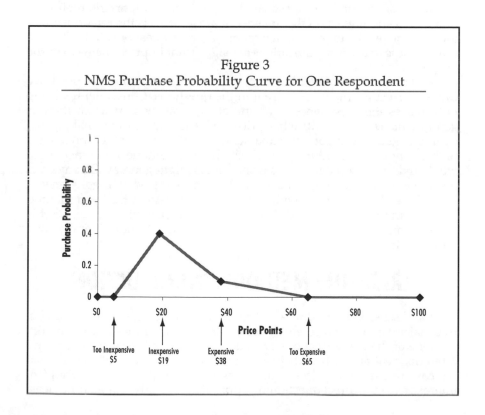

Figure 3
NMS Purchase Probability Curve for One Respondent

Another Analytic Approach

If no calibration data are available, we can discard the extra questions NMS (1993) propose but retain a very simplistic version of their analysis. Consider a "curve" for each respondent that is one at and between the inexpensive and expensive price points and zero everywhere else. This simple "normal range" indicator curve is a very simpleminded analog to NMS's purchase probability curve. If we average these curves over all respondents, we have a plot of the percentage of respondents for whom each price is in the normal range. Inspection of this curve will indicate what price is in the normal range for the maximum possible proportion of respondents. According to the original theory of reasonable prices, this is a natural price to seek; it is the price that the most people would regard as normal or reasonable. Indeed, it is the price incorrectly claimed to be represented by the indifference price point in the original analysis. A parallel analysis using the acceptable range can also be conducted, which leads to an improved analog of the optimum price point.

Both the NMS (1993) analysis and the simplification just described require us to accept some assumptions that are clearly too simplistic. But those assumptions are not unnatural and not out of character with the simplicity of the theory of reasonable prices. Just as important, their relationship to and impact on the final result are clear, as is the relationship of the analytic results to the original theory and the questions. In both these senses, these analytic modifications are significant improvements over the original approach.

Even when the full NMS (1993) approach is available and used, we cannot correct for the bias inherent in the questions. Consequently, using PSM makes the most sense as an initial exploratory step when there is genuine uncertainty as to what price range is appropriate, making the open-ended question format valuable. Use of PSM is most reasonable for highly innovative products for which there is genuine ignorance as to what kinds of reasonable ranges respondents might generate. In any case, the range of prices suggested by PSM—and somewhat higher ones—should then be further studied with monadic tests or a trade-off method before being finally accepted. Unfortunately, in current practice, PSM is used far more widely and its results are taken much more literally than they should be.

TRADE-OFF METHODS: INTRODUCTION

We discuss several "trade-off" methods, including conjoint analysis, two major variants of discrete choice modeling, and brand–price trade-off.

One of the key attractions of trade-off methods is that they can, and often do, treat all the brands in a market symmetrically. This means that we can measure the price–demand response not just for one brand of interest, as in the direct questioning approaches, but also for all (or at least several) of the brands in the market. Thus, they let us compare our product's price sensitivity with that of other brands in the market.

Furthermore, trade-off models offer the ability to measure and/or simulate cross-elasticities. Knowing which products' demands will be most affected by our price indicates from whom we might expect a competitive response. It also lets us evaluate whether lower prices are only cannibalizing our own other brands rather than drawing net share from the competitive entries. How our price affects another product's demand can also be measured with direct questioning *if* we are able to provide a full competitive context and obtain buy responses, allocations, or purchase likelihoods for the competitors as well as for our own brand. Direct questioning approaches cannot, however, measure how other products' price changes affect our brand's demand because they do not vary the other products' prices. Cross-elasticities in that direction tell us which competitors' prices we should monitor most carefully and react to most strongly.

Having self-elasticities for all brands in the market and a full set of cross-elasticities means that we can model market shares for all products under a variety of different pricing scenarios. With trade-off methods that address more than just pricing, we can determine how pricing trades off against other product attributes and simulate overall product performance as a function of both design details and pricing. These modeling capabilities are often a major motivation for choosing trade-off methods.

On the surface, trade-off methods would seem to share common response bias issues as well. When the respondent task treats all brands symmetrically, it is no longer apparent which brand we are focusing on, so one important source of bias should be reduced or eliminated. However, all trade-off methods involve asking multiple related questions of a single respondent, which makes them subject to at least some bias. As with a series of direct questions, there is a gain in statistical (i.e., sampling) precision when we do not have to deal with independent samples answering different questions. The issue is whether the bias is large enough to overwhelm the variance reduction we gain, as it usually is in the case of a series of direct questions.

The bias inherent in trade-off methods is one major argument against using them (others include their cost, complexity, and time requirements). As we show, however, both the severity of the bias and the direction in which it operates depend critically on the details of the respondent task and, thus, vary from one trade-off method to the next. Rather than simply making a blanket condemnation of trade-off methods because of bias or a blanket decision to accept the bias because of their modeling capabilities, it is important to understand and consider the differences in their bias sources and actual performance.

Conjoint Analysis

Conjoint analysis gained considerable popularity starting in the 1970s and came into widespread use in the 1980s. In the new millennium, however, its use has probably peaked and is declining, particularly for pricing purposes, in favor of discrete choice analysis. Despite that decline, it remains a very widely used technique.

Textbooks typically describe conjoint analysis as a product design method. In practice, however, it is very often used as a pricing method. The large majority of commercial conjoint studies at least include price as one variable; I believe that half or more are actually motivated primarily by an interest in pricing.

At this point, a note on terminology is in order. What we call here "conjoint analysis" or simply "conjoint" is also known as "full-profile, ratings-based conjoint." What we call "discrete choice" analysis or modeling is sometimes known as "choice-based conjoint." With our choice of terminology, comments about "conjoint" are emphatically *not* to be taken as applying to discrete choice. We will also not specifically address "adaptive conjoint analysis," a term usually taken to refer to a highly popular, partial-profile, ratings-based version of conjoint implemented in a software product, ACA, from Sawtooth Software. However, many of our comments about the use and performance of conjoint analysis would also apply, at least in general terms, to the use of ACA for pricing research.

Review of Conjoint Mechanics

A full introduction to conjoint analysis is far beyond our scope here, but a thumbnail sketch of the basics, particularly of the variant we wish to focus on here, may be useful.

Conjoint analysis, as we have defined it, studies a small number (often in the range of 5 to 15) of "attributes" of products or services in a category. For each attribute, some small number (usually only 2 to 4) of distinct "levels" are studied. When price is studied, it is one attribute and the particular price points to be studied are its levels. Other attributes might include almost any other aspect of products or services, such as the size, color, performance, reliability, or warranty of products or the speed and hours of provision of services, among many others. An experimental design is used to generate some number (usually 8 to 32, often 16 or 18) of "profiles" of possible products or services on the basis of the attributes and levels. Each profile lists one level on each of the attributes being studied (hence "full-profile") and is intended to represent a hypothetical version of the product or service. The respondent task is to rate or rank these profiles in terms of relative preference. Often, the profiles are typed on separate cards, which respondents are then instructed to sort into order or place in piles according to their relative appeal.

The analysis recovers a "utility" for each level of each attribute. Differences between the utilities of two levels of an attribute are comparably scaled to similar differences for every other attribute. This means we can examine issues like whether a given product change, such as increasing its size, will add enough utility to offset the utility lost by another change, such as a price increase. In fact, the utility value of each possible product improvement can be reexpressed as the amount of the price change required to produce an equal but opposite utility change. This sort of analysis is one of the major results examined when conjoint is used for pricing purposes. In most cases, utilities are produced separately for each respondent. This means we can easily segment respondents according to their price sensitivity and profile the other characteristics (including the other utilities) of those who are most or least price sensitive.

If the attributes and levels have been chosen suitably, we can use the utilities to perform simulations. This involves describing two or more competitors in terms of the attributes and levels studied, computing the total utility for each of the resulting profiles, and then allocating a share among alternatives on the basis of those utilities. Most simply and most often, this is done for each respondent, and the entire share represented by that respondent is allocated to the single competitive profile that has the highest total utility (the "first-choice model"). By varying the price assumptions and repeating the simulation, we can generate price–demand curves for any product and also observe the effects its price changes have on the other products in the simulation. In saying this, we implicitly assume that the simulation outcomes represent "demand" or "market share." Most practitioners are rightly careful to label these outcomes "share of preference" and avoid claims that they measure actual demand or share. Many marketers ignore those cautions and use the simulation results as if they represent real shares anyway.

Usefulness for Pricing Research

We have already said that conjoint has been and is widely used for pricing research. This is so despite some fundamental mechanical limitations imposed by the design and analysis framework. For example, experimental designs for conjoint usually produce profiles that include every possible combination of levels between any two attributes, with only limited exceptions. Thus, if brand and price are both attributes, we typically generate at least one profile for each possible combination of brand and price point. In markets in which different brands or different types of products are actually at very different price points, this may be undesirable and produce profiles that make no sense to respondents.

Even when we are content to use the same price levels for each brand, we may be unwilling to accept having identical price utilities for each. Conjoint analysis produces only one set of price utilities that applies to all brands or types of products. In real markets, of course, we often find that the market leader shows less price sensitivity than do less powerful competitors.

In cases in which we can live with these limitations (and there are certainly many such cases), how well would we expect conjoint analysis to work for pricing applications? From the standpoint of pricing-engendered response bias, we might suppose that conjoint would perform quite well. After all, conjoint studies are not obviously about price. They are about several, or even many, attributes of a product, one of which just happens to be price. In most cases, price is an important and natural feature of a product, and its inclusion in the task does not call excessive or undue attention to it.

Surprisingly, we find in practice a consistent pattern of sizable bias in the pricing results. Conjoint tends always to show low price sensitivity! In study after study, price is sufficiently unimportant that the ideal product appears to be one with every possible feature added, with price correspondingly increased to levels far beyond anything seen in the real market. One of my earliest conjoint studies had me telling the managers of a major hotel chain that they could raise room rates $15 to $25 per night if they would provide free parking with each room. Management pointed out that parking at the time only cost $6 to $8 per night in the first place and, even more damningly, that only 20% of its clientele even brought cars to the hotel. Similarly, in a study of the market for move-up homes for working professional couples, Batsell and Elmer (1990) found that price utilities barely varied at all across a range of $95,000 to $125,000. If the utility of other attributes were converted to price equivalents, their data would imply that an extra bedroom or study would be worth hundreds of thousands of dollars. Put another way, the data imply that if every other attribute studied was at its maximum possible level, one could add millions of dollars to the price of a house without affecting its overall utility. Similar anecdotes are abundant among frequent users of conjoint.

Why Does Conjoint Underestimate Price Effects?

Why does this happen? There does not appear to be broad consensus on just *why* this occurs, though there is widespread recognition that it is a problem. My belief as to the reason is consistent with that of Tull and Hawkins (1990, p. 368):

> [P]rice is often used as an indicator of quality, particularly for image items and items for which it is difficult to determine quality. If the quality of such a product is explicitly stated in the research design and price is also included, the importance of price can be understated compared to actuality.

In the sense in which Tull and Hawkins (1990) use "quality," one could construe almost *any* other attribute to describe the quality of a product. In other words, no matter what the profile says about the other attributes, no matter what instructions might have been given about assuming "all else is equal," some respondents treat price as reflecting quality and sort or rate the profiles accordingly.

When we examine individual respondent-level utilities, it is not uncommon to find 20% or more of respondents having higher utilities for high prices than for low ones. These are not just cases in which two adjacent price points have a utility reversal, but ones in which the overall pattern is backward. This implies that, all else being equal, these respondents prefer higher prices. Now, there may well be respondents who really do prefer higher prices. But if they prefer them because they imply higher quality, then they most assuredly do *not* prefer higher prices *all else being equal*. In a conjoint context, a reversed price curve tells us to simply raise our price and our utility, preference, and share will go up too. Such results are simply illogical in conjoint; rather than being informative, they simply indicate respondents who ignored the instructions and would not "play the conjoint game."

We might consider finding such respondents and eliminating them from our analysis. Unfortunately, even so drastic a measure (entailing much bias potential in itself) would not solve the problem. Along with those whose price utilities are actually reversed are others for whom price as a proxy for quality operates to only *some* degree. The effect in their case is not so extreme to reverse the price utility curve but only to flatten it somewhat. Thus, we have some unknown, but often large, number of respondents for whom price effects were attenuated, though not actually reversed, due to the use of price as a proxy for quality. In any aggregate summary, be it average utilities or simulated preference shares, the result is that the effect of price is understated.

If we accept for the moment that respondents' use of price as a proxy for quality is what causes the problem, then what causes them to do that? I believe the answer lies in the relatively hypothetical nature of many conjoint tasks. The more hypothetical a product profile, the harder it is to read, comprehend, and take at face value and the more a respondent will seek other cues as to how to react to it. The more specific and realistic a profile, the easier it is to react naturally without needing other cues. Many conjoint designs produce profiles that seem very hypothetical, in part because some attributes, often brand, must be omitted to avoid conflicts with others.

Brand is often omitted from conjoint designs because the "every possible combination" feature of the experimental designs creates problems when brand is included. As an example, imagine a hotel conjoint in which Hyatt Regency and Holiday Inn Express are two levels of the brand attribute, and a lobby attribute has the levels "small, functional lobby" and "large, visually spectacular lobby." Can we imagine each of those brands with each of those lobby types? Realistically, we cannot. One attribute or the other needs to go. Such problems could arise between any two attributes, but it is not hard to see that brand attributes are very often involved in such conflicts. In countless markets, brands have such strong identities that, once buyers know the brand, they assume or expect specific levels on many of the other attributes. Consequently, brand is often excluded from conjoint designs. Some practitioners actually go so far as to make a blanket recommendation that brand should not be used in a conjoint study.

The great value of including brand is from a response psychology standpoint: It provides a powerful and concrete link to specific real products with which the respondent is familiar. In a sense, it provides a "hook" on which to hang the profile description or a framework around which to drape it. But that is also exactly the reason for excluding brand—the hook or framework is often too rigid to allow the variations from current reality expressed by the other attributes. In any event, the frequent exclusion of brand would be expected to aggravate any tendency to use price as a proxy for overall quality.

Another View of the Price Understatement Problem

Fiedler (1988) also finds understatement of price effects in conjoint but characterizes the problem somewhat differently. He reports on results from two conjoint studies of pricing of condominiums in two high-rise towers in New Jersey, directly across the Hudson from Manhattan. Each of the two conjoint studies could be validated externally. The first study's results were compared with the actual initial sales patterns of the condominiums (i.e., which floor plans, view sides, and floors sold out most rapidly), and a later study's results were compared with the prices commanded by each unit when later resold. Although neither study used the particular form of conjoint analysis we have focused on (his early study used nonmetric factor analysis, the later one used ACA), in each case he found that price had more effect in the real world than was indicated by the conjoint:

> The conjoint model overestimates the effects of those attributes which may be more emotionally laden, such as the benefits of a glorious view or the consequences of living on the lowest tier of floors. Correspondingly, the model underpredicts the more concrete attributes such as price and floor plan.

> These methodological findings suggest that in the design of conjoint measurement research, there is great risk in attempting to measure across attributes, some of which are concrete descriptors and others of which are more benefit oriented. (Fiedler 1988, pp. 34–35)

In Fiedler's (1988) view, the problem is not a *price* problem per se but a problem of mixing what we might term "hard" and "soft" attributes (in fact, his discussion focuses more on overstatement of view utilities than understatement of price effects, but they are two sides of the same coin). It may be worth noting, however, that price is, in many respects, the epitome of a "hard" attribute. From that point of view, Fiedler's formulation of the problem would still lead us to expect *some* degree of price understatement, even if all the other attributes are relatively "concrete" and not "emotionally laden."

Fiedler's (1988) results provide no support whatsoever for our previous argument that lack of specificity, or excessively hypothetical profiles, is the underlying cause of the problem. In his later study, the respondents were current owner/residents of the condominiums in question, to whom the topic and all the attributes would have been exceptionally specific and familiar.

Discrete Choice Modeling

Discrete choice modeling (DCM), or discrete choice analysis, originated in econometrics in a form now known as "revealed preference" discrete choice. In the 1980s, a series of articles by Louviere and his associates (see Louviere and Woodworth [1983] for a general theoretical treatment, or Louviere [1986] and Louviere and Hensher [1983] for specific applications with a pricing component) showed how to combine the underlying theory with attribute and level experimental designs like those used in conjoint analysis, which leads to "stated preference" discrete choice.

The names of the two branches of discrete choice reflect an issue raised in this chapter's introduction. To wit, "revealed preference" investigates past real-world decisions (which "revealed" the underlying preference), whereas "stated preference" relies on what respondents "state" their preferences would be. Revealed preference models, then, are one way of studying historical data, using individual-level history rather than just aggregate market shares. Although they may be assisted by surveys to collect the demographics or consideration sets of the buyers, the fundamental strengths and weaknesses of revealed preference models derive from their foundation on real decisions and are those of other historical analysis approaches, not of survey-based approaches. Stated preference discrete choice is more firmly rooted in surveys, and we focus on it here.

Stated preference discrete choice, hereafter simply "discrete choice" or "DCM," came into commercial use in the 1980s but has gained widespread acceptance and popularity only in the past decade. Today, it is probably more popular than conjoint analysis and has certainly led to a decline in the use of conjoint. As that statement suggests, it serves many of the same purposes as conjoint. Its relative popularity can be attributed to several factors. Theoretical considerations include an explicit underlying error theory, a clear link between the data collected and the final simulation models, and the idea that the response task it requires is more natural to respondents, thus yielding more valid responses and often being easier or faster as well. Practical issues include much greater flexibility in how attributes and levels relate to each other and, especially, to brands and in the structure and size of the respondent task.

The flexibility in how respondent tasks are designed and structured means that different DCM tasks are not as obviously related to one another as different conjoint designs typically are. It also means that, to understand how well DCM performs for pricing purposes, we need to consider several general styles of DCM design.

Conjoint-Like Discrete Choice

In the DCM designs that most closely resemble conjoint analysis, we define attributes and levels and create profiles from them, much as we would in conjoint analysis. We then group the profiles into several "choice sets," each containing at least two, and often up to six or eight or so, profiles. This is done according to some type of design strategy, sometimes as simple as randomly assigning profiles to choice sets. Fixed choices other than the profiles (such as "none of these") may be added to each choice set as well. Respondents are asked to examine all the profiles in a single choice set, interpret them as the competitive choices available in the marketplace, and indicate which of the profiled products they would choose to buy, if those were the available choices. Having done so, they are then presented with a second choice set and asked what they would do in that new market situation. This process is repeated several times. There is no need for a respondent to answer every choice set in the design, and indeed, some randomizing design approaches present entirely different choice sets to each respondent.

How many choice sets a single respondent can or should see is a subject of considerable debate and controversy based on differing views and experiences as to respondent fatigue and bias issues, but a range of 6 to 20 choice sets per respondent would undoubtedly include most studies. Choice sets are typically printed on separate sheets of paper (or displayed on a computer screen) and often described to respondents as "shopping situations" or "scenarios." In addition to "scenario," "task" is sometimes used to mean a single choice set or the paper stimulus representing the choice set. However, we use "task" here to mean the entire set of choice sets to which a respondent is exposed. (Thus, we would say, "The task included twelve choice sets, or twelve scenarios," not "Each respondent completed twelve tasks.")

If brand is included in this type of design, it is treated like any other attribute, as it would be in conjoint. The issues around whether to include brand are much the same as in conjoint analysis, except that DCM designs often (not always) grant much more (but not unlimited) flexibility in eliminating undesirable combinations of attributes. Drawing on the hotel example used for conjoint, we might be able to "prohibit" the combination of Hyatt Regency and a small, functional lobby from ever appearing.

As in conjoint analysis, discrete choice analysis recovers a "utility" for each level of each attribute. Utilities can be analyzed much as they are in conjoint analysis. A major difference is that, as DCM is most often practiced today, the utilities are at the aggregate level, not the individual respondent level (but as is discussed subsequently, this is rapidly changing). With some design approaches, particularly random ones that generate different profiles and choice sets for each respondent, another major difference is that interactions in utilities may be estimated. From a marketing perspective, this means we can find different price utilities for each brand, for example, thereby overcoming one major limitation of conjoint for pricing work. The utilities are usually derived from a multinomial logit (MNL) model or some variant of one. These details are not discussed here, but some of their important implications are explored subsequently.

As with conjoint analysis, we can use the utilities to simulate. Using the underlying MNL model, it is a straightforward prediction exercise to simulate results for any hypothetical choice set that could have been generated under our design approach. With suitable strong assumptions, we can simulate for very different choice sets as well. For example, we could use only two profiles in each choice set but simulate a market with 20 competitors or the reverse.

This type of DCM design is widely used, both for pricing and other purposes. One could point to several general advantages it offers over conjoint analysis not particularly related to pricing research. A key issue, however, is whether it shares the same bias issues as standard conjoint does. I have only limited personal experience with this type of design and am also unaware of any convincing assessments of its performance for pricing. However, there would appear to be little to shield it from the same underestimation of price effects found in standard conjoint, for the same reasons. The profile generation process is still essentially that of standard conjoint, with the profiles no less hypothetical than in conjoint. If our hypothesis as to why conjoint understates price effects is correct, it must apply equally here.

Price-Only Discrete Choice

An important version of DCM for pricing work is a price-only discrete choice design. In it, the same basic set of brands appears in each choice set. The only differences among choice sets are the prices of the brands. This is sometimes viewed as using brand and price as the only two attributes. It is more illuminating, however, to use a different paradigm and say that brand is not simply an attribute, it is what defines the basic alternatives or choices that populate each choice set. Neither is there "a price attribute." Instead, we have a separate price attribute for each brand. Viewed this way, it becomes immediately apparent that each brand can be tested at a set of price levels appropriate to it, possibly completely different from the prices of other competitors. This removes another of the obvious mechanical limitations of conjoint analysis. In addition, we can use a different number of levels of price for each brand, perhaps to better reflect our substantive interests or to simply optimize some aspect of the experimental design or task size.

In addition to studying different levels of each product's price, we are able to compute utilities separately for each product's price. When this is possible in a conjoint-like DCM, it would typically be described as computing brand–price interactions. Here, however, the separate price effects are all main effects in both the experimental design and the analysis — each comes from a different attribute.

As mentioned previously, brand is no longer an attribute but an identifier of the alternatives in a set. In many markets, brand alone is inadequate for this purpose, and the real need is to unequivocally identify the exact product in the choice set. Although it might be reasonable in standard conjoint to generate a dishwasher profile that says "Maytag, five cleaning cycles, low energy consumption, two-year warranty, $500," we would not be content in a price-only DCM to describe a choice as simply "Maytag, $500." Instead, we would need to specify something conceptually equivalent to "Maytag model KPX273-4, $500." Ideally, we would let respondents examine the particular Maytag model we have in mind before beginning the DCM task and could effectively refer to "the Maytag you just saw" or "Dishwasher A, the Maytag one." If restricted to written descriptions, we might simply give a detailed description, in some ways not unlike a conjoint analysis profile. That description might be repeated without variation on each scenario but would more often be presented once in advance (as a real dishwasher would be when possible) and then kept available for reference.

In terms of potential biases, there is an obvious objection to price-only DCM. Because prices are the only differences among scenarios, it is obvious that the exercise is about pricing. Logically, this must result in over-sensitivity to price in the results and might even trigger conscious efforts to bias the results in favor of lower prices.

Surprisingly, that bias is not large enough to be obvious in practice. In actual practice, this technique finds some markets to be very price sensitive and others not to be. If the bias were severe, we would expect to find case after case of very price-sensitive markets. But in practice, we do not, and the face validity of price-only DCM results is generally excellent. The apparent bias is much smaller than that experienced with conjoint analysis (and presumably with conjoint-like approaches to DCM), as well as being in the opposite direction.

Why is this obvious potential for bias not significantly realized? I believe that the answer lies in the same issues of realism and specificity that explain the tendency to use price as a proxy for quality in conjoint analysis. Here, we are dealing with specific products, right down to exact models and, when possible, concrete examples or demonstrators of them. Even in cases in which the model descriptions are written and complex, they do not vary from one scenario to the next, so they need only be read and "decoded" once, unlike the situation in conjoint analysis. The strong connection to reality and the absence of a need to read and interpret a constantly changing parade of profiles make it easier for respondents to focus on how they would really behave.

In addition, respondents usually will not know which product is the topic of the research because all or most of the prices vary. And because they vary according to an experimental design and the scenario order is randomized, patterns in the price variations are eliminated.

In summary, the use of real, specific products removes any need to use artificial simplifications to either understand or answer the task. At the same time, the seemingly random price variations obscure the product of focus and make it less obvious how to deliberately influence the results, so respondents find it simplest to just answer honestly, at least to the best of their conscious ability.

Although the term "price-only discrete choice" is highly descriptive, neither it nor any other single term is widely accepted as a standard name. It has also been called "the pricing conjoint" and "price elasticity choice modeling" and is marketed commercially under a variety of proprietary trademark names. The approach itself, however, is very widely used.

Our discussion of the technique as a form of discrete choice modeling tends to imply the use of MNL as the underlying analytic model, and the earliest published description (Mahajan, Green, and Goldberg 1982) indeed used a logit model. A more accessible and influential early article (Wyner, Benedetti, and Trapp 1984) described the use of separate linear probability models (LPMs) on each product (i.e., simple regressions of share on prices) rather than MNL. It was in this simpler form that the approach first achieved commercial popularity, and the LPM approach is often still used today. A practical problem is that a LPM will sometimes forecast a share below zero, particularly if prices are varied over a very wide range or the product studied is very price sensitive. Using an MNL model avoids this, as well as offering theoretical advantages.

Disguised Price-Only Discrete Choice

If price-only discrete choice makes it obvious that price is the topic, an obvious improvement is to vary other attributes as well simply to disguise our interest in price. Johnson and Olberts (1991) outline one version of this idea in which the attributes describing the purchase occasion or context were varied; more often, one varies a few other attributes of the products themselves.

There are some obvious costs involved in doing this. In some cases, it may be difficult to find other attributes that can be varied plausibly without detracting from the realism and specificity that typify the approach and help it work well. Varying other attributes will usually necessitate a larger experimental design, which leads to more scenarios per respondent and possibly more respondents being needed. When we can fit additional attributes into a design of the same size that would have been used for prices only, the cost of estimating more effects (i.e., the additional ones for the disguising variables) is that we degrade the statistical precision of the price effects about which we actually care.

Because price-only DCM does not show obvious systematic biases in the first place, it is far from clear that these costs of adding other attributes are justified by the benefits of disguising our interest in price. However, when the other attributes are of direct research interest themselves, this is a very reasonable and often used approach with the same generally successful performance that price-only DCM enjoys.

Cross-Effects in DCM Models

The analysis of discrete choice data is most often based on MNL models. The MNL model has a well-known property called "independence of irrelevant alternatives," or IIA, which is problematic in many marketing applications and especially so for pricing research.

Rather than showing an algebraic derivation or discussing how the name IIA arises, we illustrate the importance and nature of the IIA property and problem with a simple example. Suppose that we have a discrete choice model using MNL for four products. Further suppose that for some set of prices (and some set of levels on any nonprice attributes) that we call "the base case," the modeled shares are as shown in the first line of Table 1. Now suppose we cut the price of product A relative to the base case, leaving all the other attribute and level assumptions of the base case unchanged. Suppose that our model now forecasts a share of 50% for product A, an increase of ten percentage points from the prior product A share of 40%. The issue that concerns us is whence the 10% share gained by product A comes. Which products lose how much share to allow that gain for product A?

In a simple MNL model, there is only one possible answer: Each other product contributes share in proportion to the share it had originally. In our example, the 10% gain for product A represents a one-sixth aggregate share loss for the other three products, so each contributes one-sixth of the share it had in the base case. In marketing terms, this is often called the "fair share draw" property, in that the new share product A draws is drawn from the others "in fair share" to what they have.

The problem here is not that the IIA answer is unreasonable; one could argue strongly that if one answer must be assumed, then that given by IIA is the most reasonable one to choose. The problem is that any answer is assumed in the first place. The question of which products gain or lose share when one changes its price is usually a key part of what we need to measure and model. It is reflective of the structure of a market and, in real markets, usually does not follow the IIA or "fair share draw" rule. We cannot simply assume the answer; we must let the data dictate it.

This is accomplished in the MNL context by adding "cross-effect" terms to the model, which creates a generalization of the MNL known as a "mother logit" model. The basic idea behind cross-effects is that a given product's utility is no longer solely a function of its own price and other attributes, as in MNL, but is also a function of some or all of the other products' prices and other attributes. In any given model, many cross-effects are possible. In our example with four products, each could have a cross-effect arising from each of the three others, for a total of 12 possible

Table 1
Illustration of the IIA Property or Assumption

	Product A	Product B	Product C	Product D
Initial ("base case") shares	40.0%	30.0%	20.0%	10.0%
Price of A is cut	50.0%	?	?	?
The IIA Answer	50.0%	25.0%	16.7%	8.3%

cross-effects. The usual practice is to test each for statistical significance and include only the significant ones in the final model. This effectively says that we will accept IIA except when the data argue strongly (i.e., significantly) against it.

Unfortunately, much of the software used for DCM modeling makes the use of cross-effect terms in models cumbersome or even impossible. It is partly for this reason that the LPM approach to price-only discrete choice (Wyner, Benedetti, and Trapp 1984) remains somewhat popular. The LPMs are implemented with ordinary regression, making it easy to add cross-effects. An LPM with cross-effects amounts to nothing more than a regression of one product's share on all products' prices. The coefficient for its own price is an "own effect," whereas the other coefficients, for the other products' prices, are cross-effects.

Experimental designs must support cross-effects terms before they can be added to models. In general, this requires that a single design control all attributes simultaneously, making them all approximately orthogonal to one another. A design approach sometimes known as "split plot" makes use of separate, approximately orthogonal designs for different products or different subsets of attributes, which are then randomly joined to obtain the overall design. This type of design does not support cross-effects in the analysis and has become much less popular in the last few years as the importance of cross-effects has become more widely understood. The designs used in practice for conjoint-like variants of discrete choice are often, but not necessarily, ones that will *not* support cross-effects in the modeling, whereas designs used for price-only DCM almost always support cross-effects.

Other Issues in Discrete Choice

A recent and rapidly developing trend in DCM is the use of hierarchical Bayes (HB) models to develop individual respondent-level parameter estimates for the discrete choice model (Allenby 1999). Such models are complex and computationally demanding; their details are beyond our scope here. The key issue relative to pricing research is the idea that HB models obviate the need for cross-effects in the model. With individual-level models, IIA operates for each individual but not in the aggregate model formed by totaling results from the individual models. Because of this, some practitioners believe the IIA problem is no longer an issue in HB discrete choice models (see, e.g., Orme 1999). Others are more skeptical, arguing that the continued existence of IIA at the individual level remains problematic. Ultimately, the resolution of this debate should be empirical. Some data have already been presented showing that HB models without cross-effects predict about as well in the aggregate as a traditional aggregate model with cross-effects, depending on the number of scenarios each respondent answers (Renken and Sigler 1998). To my knowledge, no one has yet investigated how much, if at all, an HB model with cross-effects improves on either an HB model without cross-effects or an aggregate model with them. In the next few years, these issues will likely be settled, and the need for cross-effects in pricing models may be either eliminated in an HB context or further confirmed as necessary even there.

In conjoint analysis, it has been shown that the size of the effects found for an attribute is increased when the attribute is measured at more levels, even when the range of levels studied is held constant (Wittink, Krishnamurthi, and Reibstein 1989). This is also true after correcting for some computational artifacts that partially cause the problem (for those corrections, see Karson and Mullet 1989). The reason for this is not completely clear, but one plausible explanation is that respondents subconsciously realize that attributes with more levels matter more to the researcher and accordingly react to them more. Although I am unaware of specific studies of the problem in a discrete choice context, the explanation just proposed would appear to hold equally well in DCM. If so, the common practice of studying different numbers of price levels for each brand (often more for the client brand than for any other) is a mistake.

In some markets, respondents' real-world decisions are not pure choices. For example, in business-to-business marketing, buyers spread their purchases among alternatives for a variety of reasons. In these cases, it is common commercial research practice to ask respondents to allocate their purchases by percentage, or "times out of the next ten" or the like, instead of simply choosing one option. This can be viewed as invalidating the underlying error theory and derivation of the MNL, and it further complicates already messy issues of variance estimation. From a purely heuristic point of view, however, practitioners find it trivial to adapt the point estimates of utilities to work from allocation data rather than true choice data. From a marketing point of view, allowing respondents to allocate rather than choose makes the task much more realistic and useful, so allocation tasks are often used and sometimes cited as another advantage of DCM methods over conjoint analysis.

Although the details are beyond the scope of this chapter, DCM approaches to pricing research are also popular because of the flexibility they offer in modeling complex marketing situations. It is comparatively straightforward to reparameterize the price attributes to enforce required premium or discount relationships between related products (e.g., the deluxe model always costs more than the regular model). It is also easy to build models in which several prices or price components directly affect each product. This capability can be used to study products that have separate prices for purchase and service, or list price versus discount situations, or different underlying price contributions for each level of nonprice attributes (as in bundling situations) (Lyon 1998; Lyon and Luery 1996). Models with multiple price components can also sometimes be implemented using conjoint analysis but are often more straightforward when discrete choice is used.

Brand–Price Trade-Off

Brand–price trade-off, or BPTO, is a technique that is not particularly widespread in current North American practice, but we discuss it briefly here for two reasons. First, it remains fairly popular in Europe, which leads to frequent brief reappearances here. Second, it provides another excellent illustration of how response psychology determines success in pricing research. The BPTO respondent task appears superficially to be very similar to price-only discrete choice analysis. But the differences are enough to bring into play a very different set of respondent psychology issues and doom the usefulness of the technique.

Review of BPTO Mechanics

Initially, BPTO was described in a working paper by Johnson (1972) and a more accessible article by Jones (1975). As in a price-only discrete choice design, one selects a set of prices to be studied for each of several brands. Each brand can have different price levels and a different number of price levels, as desired. Some current practitioners are comfortable with up to 15 brands having up to ten price levels each.

Respondents are presented with the set of brands, with each initially shown at the *lowest* of its price levels, and asked which they would choose under that pricing scenario. Up to this point, from a respondent's point of view, the task is indistinguishable from a price-only DCM task. In actual practice, BPTO users tend to do an excellent job of specifying and exemplifying the exact products being studied, as was recommended previously for pricing applications of DCM.

After a respondent makes the initial choice, the price of the brand chosen is increased to the next level under study. No other prices change, and the respondent is again asked what he or she would choose under the slightly revised pricing scenario. Again, the price of whichever brand is chosen is raised one level. To facilitate this process, the prices for each brand are often bound together with rings and sometimes positioned below the product examples on a shelf to facilitate "flipping up" a single price level at a time. The process continues until some product has been chosen at the highest price level under study. At that point, the task may either end altogether or continue with that product being no longer available. In some versions, a "none of them" option is also offered, and the task ends after it is chosen.

Discussion

Just as in price-only DCM, this respondent task involves making choices in a series of different pricing scenarios, each of which involves the identical products with only price varying. But in a price-only discrete choice, an experimental design dictates which price combinations are tested, and the order of combinations is randomized across respondents.

The result is that the respondent sees no consistent pattern in the series of questions. In a BPTO task, the pattern is very simple and clear. After a few scenarios, the respondent can very nearly predict what the next scenario will be even before giving his or her answer to the current one. Even in the article that originally popularized the technique, Jones (1975, p. 77) recognized that "the repetitiveness of the task poses some problems since a 'game playing' situation may develop."

The method's inventor put the problem more pointedly in a later paper (Johnson and Olberts 1991, p. 4):

> [R]espondents soon became self-conscious. Some, apparently regarding it as an intelligence test, meticulously chose the lowest price each time. Others, apparently regarding it as a challenge to their brand loyalty, remained faithful to their preferred brand, even as its price increased to unreasonable levels.

Of course, both those behaviors are perfectly acceptable *if* they accurately reflect real-world behavior, so we cannot simply reject respondents with those behavior patterns. We can, however, reject the face validity of a method that produces those patterns as frequently as BPTO usually does. In that paper, Johnson and Olberts (1991) go on to recommend using what is essentially price-only DCM but with some situational or contextual variation added to create greater realism in the task.

The analytic details of BPTO are intriguing and include some distinct strengths as compared with discrete choice. But, as in so many other aspects of pricing research, basic issues of how respondents react to and answer questions trump all other considerations. Consequently, BPTO is a very poor approach to pricing research.

SUMMARY

We have reviewed many pricing research techniques in widespread use today and have seen that which ones work well and which do not is often a question of basic response psychology and how our questions bias the answers we get. By far the safest and most defensible research approach is the venerable monadic test, simply because it is least subject to bias arising from what we ask respondents to do. Other forms of direct questioning, such as willingness to pay and a series of buy response questions, generally invite very strong biases toward excess price sensitivity. The van Westendorp (1976) technique, though useful in very early explorations of price for innovative products, is also subject to high response biases and often analyzed with a dubious approach.

Trade-off methods all accept some degree of bias as a result of asking multiple related questions. Their payoff is a reduction in sampling variance and, most seductively, the power to model and simulate results under a variety of pricing scenarios and for more than just one brand. Experience with trade-off methods shows that their bias is sometimes in nonintuitive directions and to surprisingly great or small degrees. Discrete choice methods designed around specific real products seem to perform best, and DCM continues to be an extremely active area of methodological research, particularly with the advent of hierarchical Bayes methods. Even a well-designed discrete choice model, however, should only be used when the marketing problem clearly dictates that a monadic design will not answer the objectives and with a full recognition of the potential biases.

Acknowledgments

Much of the material presented here originated in American Marketing Association tutorials I originally codeveloped with Mike Zicha. David Luery and I have also shared many materials and copresented on pricing research and related topics. I thank both for the discussions, assistance, and occasional prodding, without which this chapter would never have been possible. Of course, the responsibility for errors and controversial opinions is entirely mine.

BIBLIOGRAPHY

Allenby, Greg M. (1999), "Hierarchical Bayes Modeling: Applications in Discrete Choice Analysis," tutorial presented at American Marketing Association's Advanced Research Techniques Forum, Santa Fe, NM (June).

Batsell, Richard R. and John B. Elmer (1990), "How To Use Market-Based Pricing to Forecast Consumer Purchase Decisions," *Journal of Pricing Management*, 1 (Spring), 5–15.

Brennan, Mike (1995), "Constructing Demand Curves from Purchase Probability Data: An Application of the Juster Scale," *Marketing Bulletin*, 6, 51–58.

Fiedler, John A. (1988), "Conjoint Predictions: 15 Years Later," in *Proceedings of the Sawtooth Software Conference on Perceptual Mapping, Conjoint Analysis, and Computer Interviewing*. Sun Valley, ID: Sawtooth Software, 25–35.

Johnson, Richard M. (1972), *A New Procedure for Studying Price-Demand Relationships*. Chicago: Market Facts, Inc

—— and Kathleen Olberts (1991), "Using Conjoint Analysis in Pricing Studies: Is One Price Variable Enough?" presented at American Marketing Association's Advanced Research Techniques Forum, Beaver Creek, CO (June).

Jones, D. Frank (1975), "A Survey Technique to Measure Demand Under Various Pricing Strategies," *Journal of Marketing*, 39 (July), 75–77.

Karson, Marvin J. and Gary M. Mullet (1989), "Conjoint Utility Limits as Affected by Conjoint Design and Estimating Program," *Marketing Research*, 1 (December), 27–32.

Louviere, Jordan J. (1986), "A Conjoint Model for Analyzing New Product Positions in a Differentiated Market with Price Competition," in *Advances in Consumer Research*, Vol. 13, Richard J. Lutz, ed. Provo, UT: Association for Consumer Research, 375–80.

—— and David A. Hensher (1983), "Using Discrete Choice Models with Experimental Design Data to Forecast Consumer Demand for a Unique Cultural Event," *Journal of Consumer Research*, 10 (December), 348–61.

————— and George Woodworth (1983), "Design and Analysis of Simulated Consumer Choice or Allocation Experiments: An Approach Based on Aggregate Data," *Journal of Marketing Research,* 20 (November), 350–67.

Lyon, David W. (1998), "Using Trade-Off Methods for Pricing Research," tutorial presented at Institute for International Research's Conjoint & Choice Based Modeling Essentials: A Tools & Techniques Forum, Chicago, IL.

————— and David A. Luery (1996), "Survey-Based Approaches to Pricing Research: Session 2: Advanced," tutorial presented at American Marketing Association's Advanced Research Techniques Forum, Beaver Creek, CO (June).

Mahajan, Vijay, Paul E. Green, and Stephen M. Goldberg (1982), "A Conjoint Model for Measuring Self- and Cross-Price Demand Relationships," *Journal of Marketing Research,* 19 (August), 334–42.

Marder, Eric (1997), *The Laws of Choice: Predicting Customer Behavior.* New York: The Free Press.

Orme, Bryan K. (1999), "Predicting Actual Sales with CBC: How Capturing Heterogeneity Improves Results," presented at American Marketing Association's Advanced Research Techniques Forum, Santa Fe, NM (June).

Newton, Dennis, Jeff Miller, and Paul Smith (1993), "A Market Acceptance Extension to Traditional Price Sensitivity Measurement," presented at American Marketing Association's Advanced Research Techniques Forum, Monterey, CA (June).

Renken, Tim and Patty Sigler (1998), "Disaggregate Discrete Choice Analysis: Because Not All Consumers Are the Same," tutorial presented at Institute for International Research's Conjoint & Choice Based Modeling Essentials: A Tools & Techniques Forum, Chicago, IL.

Tull, Donald S. and Del I. Hawkins (1990), *Marketing Research: Measurement & Method.* New York: Macmillan Publishing Company.

van Westendorp, Peter H. (1976), "NSS – Price Sensitivity Meter (PSM) – A New Approach to Study Consumer Perception of Prices," in *Venice Congress Main Sessions.* Amsterdam: European Marketing Research Society (ESOMAR), 140–66.

Wittink, Dick R., Lakshman Krishnamurthi, and David J. Reibstein (1989), "The Effect of Differences in the Number of Attribute Levels on Conjoint Results," *Marketing Letters,* 1 (2), 113–23.

Wyner, Gordon A., Lois H. Benedetti, and Bart M. Trapp (1984), "Measuring the Quantity and Mix of Product Demand," *Journal of Marketing,* 48 (Winter), 101–109.

22
Survey Research Goes to Court

Ruth M. Corbin and Neil Vidmar

SURVEY RESEARCH AS EXPERT EVIDENCE: A FAST-GROWING FIELD

O ne of the most exciting developments in survey research during the past 30 years has been its appearance in the courtroom as expert evidence, shoulder to shoulder with other sources of finely honed expertise. These past thirty years have seen survey research evolve from a "wannabe science," greeted at best skeptically by lawyers and judges, to a powerful evidentiary tool considered de rigcur in many legal applications. What took survey research so long to attain that respected standing? What are its most significant applications? And where is it headed in the future? These are the questions tackled in this chapter.

The trend toward increased reliance on surveys as expert evidence is consistent in many countries. Although the nuances of the laws are different in each country (see Coleman and Mackay 1995; Gatowski et al. 1996), this chapter focuses on those principles of law for which survey evidence is applicable across international borders. Examples from actual cases will necessarily arise from individual jurisdictions, but the lessons for survey research are universal.

Put most simply, survey research has an opportunity to come into play in any legal disputes in which it is important to know what certain groups of the public experience or believe. Along with a growing appreciation of the value provided by surveys, courts are discovering another undeniable truth: There is no such thing as a perfect survey. Despite advancements in its usefulness, survey research remains an inexact science, with competing views about methodologies and standards. "Each year courtrooms are littered with the smoldering wreckage of consumer surveys that appeared rigorous and valid when launched, but were shot down at trial," writes Keller (1992, p. 403) in a journal of the American Bar Association. That having been noted, far too many surveys are discarded for major flaws that could have been readily avoided. The frequency of such disasters can undoubtedly be reduced through persistent documentation of experience and learning in this growing field.

The bulk of applications of survey evidence has occurred in the context of intellectual property disputes, particularly with respect to protecting trademarks and shutting down misleading advertising. Applications are also reasonably developed in criminal law with respect to potential jury bias. The adaptation of survey evidence to other fields continues to emerge and holds much untapped potential. Although judges are reluctant to permit their decision-making authority to be usurped by an expert,[1] properly prepared survey evidence can be a compelling source of influence and sometimes a determinative one (e.g., *Big Sisters Association of Ontario v. Big Brothers of Canada* 1996).

A review of published cases leads us to observe at least five well-developed application areas of survey research to courtroom issues:

❑ Protecting trademarks through establishing confusion in trademark infringement and passing-off proceedings; establishing reputation, distinctiveness, or secondary meaning in trademarks; or supporting trademark oppositions on the grounds that a mark is or has become "generic" in the public perception;

❑ Detecting deceptive advertising and isolating the sources within any given advertisement;

❑ Providing estimates of damages in civil law suits;

❑ Measuring potential jury bias in criminal proceedings by supporting requests for change of venue, challenge for cause, or trial by judge alone or assessing the likely impact of defense arguments on juries (sometimes referred to as "marketing a verdict"); and

❑ Establishing community standards wherever application of a statute accommodates existing standards and mores.

The following section gives examples from each of these applications to illustrate the theoretical issues that have arisen in each context. The

---

[1]For example, Rouleau made the following observation in *Choice Hotels International Inc. v. Hotels Confortel Inc.* (1996; 67 C.P.R. [3d] 340 at 348–49): "In this case, the survey ... by Ms. Ruth M. Corbin obviously is not binding on this court, which yields to no one in its assessment of the facts. However, this survey is a tool that we cannot dismiss, since it provides additional evidence that there is a reasonable risk of confusion between the appellant's COMFORT INN trade-mark and the respondent's CONFORTEL trade-mark evidence that the respondent was unable to contradict or even challenge" (see Coleman and McKay 1995, note 2; Freckelton 1997; Gatowski et al. 1996, note 2).

examples also demonstrate the nature of questions and tests used by survey researchers to give everyday meaning to legal terminology.

AREAS OF APPLICATION

Trademark Proceedings and Passing-Off Actions

Tests of Confusion

Trademark disputes frequently involve allegations that one company is infringing on another's trademark by causing confusion. Confusion is a term of art in the legal profession. In layperson's terms, the use of a trademark causes confusion with another trademark if people would be likely to infer that the products or services associated with those trademarks originate from or are licensed by the same source (Lipton 1987; McCarthy 1996; *Seagram and Sons Ltd. v. Seagram Real Estate Ltd.* 1990; Simonson 1994). A related area for establishing confusion is passing-off actions. Passing off is a common-law cause of action that entails a misrepresentation to consumers, which injures the goodwill of another company's product or service in a material way.

Confusion may be observed in actual decisions or behaviour of misled consumers. Behavioural evidence of *actual* confusion is difficult for lawyers to locate. Survey evidence designed to show that confusion is *likely* to happen can be the next best thing. One of the principal tests of confusion involves direct questioning of consumers about their belief about the company that manufactures or sells a given product. We refer to this as the "named-source test." Illustration of the effectiveness of the named-source design is readily apparent from the decision in *McDonald's Corp. v. Peter MacGregor Ltd.* (1987). In 1979, Peter MacGregor Limited filed an application to register the trademark "MacSteak" based on proposed use in Canada in association with a meat product. McDonald's opposed the application on the grounds that the mark was confusing with several of its registered trademarks, including Big Mac, MacSundae, and McDonald's. A survey was conducted in Toronto with the pivotal question: "If you were to see or hear of a product called MacSteak, who do you think would make or market this product?" Of 200 completed interviews, 63% of the respondents replied "McDonald's," a nine times greater percentage than the next most common response. Backed by this evidence, McDonald's was successful in opposing the registration of MacSteak on the grounds of likelihood of confusion.[2]

Another example is contained in *Cartier Inc. v. Cartier Optical Ltd.* (1988), in which the plaintiff was the well-known jewellery company. The

---

[2]McDonald's was similarly successful in the earlier decision of *McDonald's Corp. v. Silverwood Industries Ltd.* (1984; 4 C.P.R. [3d] 68 [T.M.O.B.]) in opposing registration of the mark "MacFreeze" for soft ice cream. The MacSteak survey was virtually identical to the survey used to successfully oppose MacFreeze.

defendant had begun to operate and advertise using "Lunettes Cartier" and similar variations in association with eyeglasses. The plaintiff tendered a survey in which respondents were shown actual advertisements of the defendant displaying the impugned mark. Respondents were asked to offer their opinion as to the name of the company that manufactured the products shown in the advertisement. Of the respondents who had an opinion as to the company, 62% named "Cartier" and less than 2% named "Lunettes Cartier." Combined with other conclusions that could reasonably be drawn from the survey evidence, the Court enjoined the defendant.

Surveys of the design offered in *Cartier Inc. v. Cartier Optical Ltd.* (1988) are generally vulnerable to criticism unless a true cause-and-effect inference can be drawn. For example, in the case of the Cartier advertisement, an expert must be able to rule out the possibility that, when people are asked the name of the manufacturing company, they are not simply repeating the name on the advertisement, which happens to be the same name as the plaintiff's company. In other words, the survey must be designed so that it can be unambiguously concluded that respondents answering "Cartier" meant "Cartier" the plaintiff company. Two techniques would assist in this regard: a further "probe" question to confirm what respondents meant and a scientific control condition to confirm the inference of cause and effect (Diamond 1997).

A likelihood of confusion survey that is based on the named-source test is clearly only effective if the manufacturing/owner source is a recognized name. The named-source design would not be effective in a situation in which the consumer is still likely to be confused as to source, but the name of the source is unknown, which is an accepted proposition in trademark law. For example, Thermasilk Shampoo may be a well-known brand in Canada but not necessarily associated with its manufacturer, Lever Ponds. In that case, the standard named-source test would not be effective in attempting to illustrate the confusion induced by another company's brand. Similar design problems arise when the mark at issue, say, the product's brand name, is also the name of the trademark owner.

Survey experts have devised clever designs to capture the likelihood of confusion when the trademark owner is the single, unknown source. Consider, for example, the U.S. case of *Squirtco v. Seven-Up Co.* (1980), in which Squirtco, producers of a grapefruit-flavoured soft drink named "Squirt," charged the Seven-Up Company with trademark infringement in naming its lemonade-flavoured soft drink "Quirst." Three surveys were introduced into evidence by Squirtco as evidence of confusion, one of which was particularly interesting in design. Respondents in three stores in Phoenix, Ariz., were intercepted and given a coupon worth 50¢ off the regular price of one six-pack of 12-ounce cans of any nonalcoholic beverage except colas. The main purpose of the 50¢ coupon was to increase the efficiency of the survey by stimulating the purchase of non-cola soft drinks. After the customers had completed their shopping and were preparing to leave the store, they were intercepted by an interviewer and questioned as to the product they had bought. Seventy people claimed to have bought the soft drink Squirt, but three of them had in fact purchased Quirst.[3] The judge found this 4.3% level of error to be sufficient for confusion. On appeal, the finding of a likelihood of confusion was upheld. However, the Court of Appeal commented that a 25% level of error was sufficient to support an inference of a likelihood of confusion, implicitly suggesting that 4.3% should not be considered the norm.[4]

The concept of confusion extends to confusion about sponsorship or affiliation. Such confusion is recognized as actionable and can be regarded as indirect or secondary source confusion. An example is provided in *National Football League Properties, Inc. v. Wichita Falls Sportswear, Inc.* (1982). The method used in that case has come to be known as the "NFL Test" and has been accepted in at least three U.S. courts (Amend and Johnson 1992). The respondent is shown the defendant's product and asked whether he or she believes that the company that made the product had "to get authorization or sponsorship, that is, permission, to make it?" If the respondent answers affirmatively, then he or she is asked from whom such permission must be obtained.

Finally, confusion extends to trade dress. Laws about trade dress constitute a category of trademark law in which a nonfunctional but distinctive aspect of a business may indicate that a product or service comes from a specific source without its necessarily having acquired secondary meaning (Davis 1996; Handler and McCarthy 1996). The leading U.S. case in this area is *Two Pesos v. Taco Cabana* (1991, 1992; see also *Fuddruckers Inc. v. Doc's B.R. Others Inc.* 1987). The U.S. Supreme Court held that a trade dress that is inherently distinctive is protectable under the Lanham Trademark Act without a demonstration that it has acquired secondary meaning. The trade dress must be nonfunctional for the operation of the business and involve total image and overall appearance (i.e., not individual elements but rather "the whole collection of elements taken together").

Taco Cabana and its affiliate Ta Casita operated a chain of fast food Mexican restaurants. The restaurant described its trade dress as a festive atmosphere that involved the dress of waitstaff; particular types of artifacts, colors, and murals; a floor plan; an outside patio that was capable of being sealed off from the inside patio by garage doors; and distinctive colors, designs, and awnings on the exterior of the building. Two Pesos opened a restaurant that was generally similar in motif to Taco Cabana

---

[3]Serious questions can be raised as to whether the court was justified in relying on these data because the small numbers of confused customers may have been a chance occurrence.

[4]Certainly of assistance to the Court in the *Squirtco* case were the two other surveys, both designed and executed in a more traditional manner. These two surveys essentially asked the question, "Do you think Squirt and Quirst are put out by the same company or by different companies?" Twenty-three percent of the respondents in the first survey thought it was the same company, whereas 34% of those in the second survey thought so.

restaurants. In an ensuing lawsuit against Two Pesos, Taco Cabana introduced a survey intended to show that customers were likely to associate or confuse a Taco Cabana restaurant with a Two Pesos restaurant.

Customers in Taco Cabana restaurants were asked if they had previously eaten at a Ta Casita or Taco Cabana or Two Pesos Restaurant. If the answer was yes, the respondents were asked which ones. Then they were asked, "Do you think that any of these stores are owned or operated by the same company?" and if so, "Why do you think that?" Sixty-five percent of Taco Cabana customers had been to a Two Pesos restaurant. Sixty-one percent of respondents indicated that they believed Two Pesos and Taco Cabana restaurants were affiliated or owned by the same company. The open-ended questions asking respondents to explain why produced the following: same food, similarity of buildings, same style operation, menu similarity, and same decoration and color.

Two Pesos also introduced a survey of its customers. Half were asked, "Have you ever gone to another restaurant by mistake when you intended to go to a Two Pesos restaurant?" and the other half were asked, "Have you ever gone to a Two Pesos restaurant by mistake when you intended to go to another restaurant?" On appeal, the Fifth Circuit decision gave little credence to the Two Pesos study, not only because a small number of respondents confessed to a "rather silly mistake," but also because, in the Court's words, "[t]he issue is not whether consumers can read signs and menus that identify different restaurants, but whether consumers assume some affiliation between Taco Cabana and Two Pesos." The Court considered the Taco Cabana survey probative of the legal issues in dispute.

The Taco Cabana survey had some weaknesses with regard to its sample of respondents but was perceived as clearly superior to the Two Pesos survey. The open-ended responses were especially helpful because they provided the court with direct information about why the respondents might have been confused.

Tests of Reputation, Distinctiveness, and Secondary Meaning

Reputation, distinctiveness, and secondary meaning are related terms in trademark law. Each refers to the perception of a particular mark, symbol, or logo that permits it to act as a trademark, that is, to communicate to the consumer a single business origin. Establishment of reputation, distinctiveness, or secondary meaning in a name or mark determines the owner's latitude in protecting it and is typically required to support a passing-off action.

Reputation includes the extent to which a trademark has become known. It is often measured through standard survey tests of awareness.

Proof of distinctiveness of a name, or even a nickname, would arise from evidence that consumers associate the name in question with a single, particular source.

Secondary meaning is said to be present when terms or symbols with general and ordinary meanings become distinctive through use and association with a particular product, service, or business. Secondary meaning allows certain ordinary words or symbols to adopt legal force as trademarks. The issue to be addressed in gathering evidence for secondary meaning is whether the consumer believes, in a given context, that the mark denotes a single source for the product. The onus is to demonstrate clearly that a descriptive term has become so distinctive to the wares in question that the acquired secondary meaning will not normally be confused with the primary meaning of the word.

Survey formats have evolved to measure the presence of reputation, distinctiveness, or secondary meaning in trademarks and trade names. For example, affidavits were filed in *Sunkist Growers Inc. v. Sunkist Fruit Market Toronto Limited* (1995; unreported), in which each side argued the extent of its established reputation in consumer markets. Reputation was operationalized in a survey instrument for Sunkist Growers as the association of the word "Sunkist" with products of Sunkist Growers Inc. and the strength of awareness of Sunkist oranges. Individual questions included the following: "When you hear the word Sunkist, what one thing first comes to mind? What else, if anything, do you think of when you hear the word Sunkist? For about how many years have you connected the word Sunkist with [oranges or fruit market, depending on answers to the previous questions]? Have you ever seen or heard of Sunkist oranges? Are you aware of any store in the province of Ontario named Sunkist Food Markets?" Survey evidence established a remarkably high awareness of Sunkist oranges and geographically limited, relatively small awareness of Sunkist Food Markets.

Reputation and distinctiveness may also accrue to a design element. One of the earliest known templates for measuring reputation and distinctiveness in a design appeared in *Oneida v. National Silver* (1940). Oneida had produced silver-plated silverware in a popular design called "Coronation." National Silver produced a copied pattern that it called "Princess Royal." Oneida's survey consisted of showing housewives a picture of a piece of cutlery bearing the Princess Royal pattern (with the name hidden from view) and asking the following two questions (among others): "Who do you think puts out this silverware?" and "If you wanted to buy a set of this silverware, how would you ask for it?" A sizable percentage of the 1000 respondents identified the piece as Oneida's. Only one person named Princess Royal. The evidence was accepted by the judge, in conjunction with viva voce evidence of an additional 24 women who claimed to have been personally confused.

Surveys in disputes regarding secondary meaning of a word or term must test whether the relevant population associates the term with a particular source. The word "Canadian" provides a good example. In 1982, Molson sought to register "Canadian" as a trademark for use in association with beer (*Molson v. Carling Breweries* 1984). Molson had been using Canadian in association with beer products since 1959. Carling Breweries opposed the registration on the ground that the word "Canadian" is a word in common use by manufacturers of beers, serves to distinguish the place of origin of the product, and is not distinctive of wares of any particular entity.

In response to Carling's opposition to its proposed registration of Canadian, Molson filed survey evidence seeking to establish that it had indeed become distinctive of its beer product by reason of its extensive use and advertising. The survey evidence entailed having interviewers pose as restaurant and bar customers who asked servers for "a Canadian." In the majority of cases, they were served a Molson beer of that brand. The opposition was initially decided in Molson's favour, and the application to register Canadian as a trademark in association with beer was allowed.

On appeal to the Federal Court, however, Carling was successful in overturning the Canadian Trademark Opposition Board's decision. On appeal, the Court raised doubts about the value of the survey research and put more stock in criticisms of the research raised by the opponent's expert. One of the more important criticisms was that restaurant servers are accustomed to deciphering limited cues about what people want when they order and therefore are an inappropriate population for assessing distinctiveness. Another criticism was that the request for a Canadian was made in the context of requests by other people at the table for other brands of beer. This context of ordering by brand was thought to give too significant a clue to the servers about the nature of the product being ordered. What Molson should have done, suggested the Court, was survey the actual consumers who used the product to determine whether Canadian had become distinctive of Molson:

> In my view, the only evidence which can be given much weight is that which relates to perceptions of the mark in or about 1971. The principal evidence relevant for this purpose was the material filed with the application consisting of an affidavit of Mr. Thomas King of International Surveys Limited as to a survey conducted by his company in 1971 and 1972 of a sample of beer-vendors, together with some 59 affidavits from those in the beer retail business such as bar managers, waiters, waitresses, etc. The survey was conducted predominantly in a few urban locations and the majority were places where beer is consumed on the premises as compared to those engaged in sale of beer for off-premises consumption. The survey indicated that in the majority of such situations when the surveyors asked for a "Canadian" they were served a Molson's beer of that brand. Similarly, the affidavits were predominantly from those engaged in on-premises sales and they were to the general effect that when customers asked such persons engaged in the retail beer trade for a "Canadian" they served their customers a Molson's beer of that brand. They also indicated that a high percentage of consumers of this brand asked for it by the name "Canadian," or sometimes "Molson's Canadian." While this evidence is not without value I do not find it convincing. The appellant/opponent in the proceedings before the Registrar

filed the affidavit of Charles S. Mayer, a professor of marketing at York University and an expert on market surveys. In his affidavit he analyzed a similar survey done on behalf of the applicant/respondent in 1977 ... and he strongly criticized the methodology employed in that survey which, it appears, was deliberately done on essentially the same basis as the one conducted in 1971-1972. Among the weaknesses he pointed out was the fact that the sampling was unrepresentative, and that those surveyed were "professionals who are used to responding to incomplete cues and thus, are representative of the wrong population." In effect, he was saying that to ascertain whether a descriptive word has really become distinctive of a particular product it is necessary to survey the people who use the product, and this was not done. I find that to be a telling criticism of both surveys; even if I should be wrong in finding that the relevant date for establishing distinctiveness was December 10, 1971, instead of February 13, 1975, the date of the filing of the opposition, I think the result would be the same. The principal evidence of distinctiveness in 1975 would probably be the survey conducted in 1977 but this is flawed in the same way as is the earlier survey. (*Molson v. Carling* 1984, §197–98)

In other words, Molson failed to design and execute a survey that tested the perception of the relevant population for the product and mark at issue.[5] As illustrated here and subsequently elaborated, the selection of the relevant population is frequently critical in influencing the weight that a survey will be given. At times, the relevant universe will comprise two or more discrete groups, and it might be desirable to design separate surveys for each group.

When Trademarks Become Generic

Legislation and common law deny exclusive trademark rights to words that are or become the name of a product, product category, or service. These are sometimes referred to as "generic" terms. Valid trademarks may have their registration cancelled if they become generic. Generic terms cannot generally be exclusively appropriated. Examples of terms that have been held to be generic include aspirin (in the United States and Britain), brassiere, cellophane, cola, escalator, kleenex, lanolin, linoleum, shredded wheat, thermos, trampoline, and yo-yo. Examples of terms that have been challenged as generic but have been held by courts to be valid trademarks are Coke, Levi's, Polaroid, and Teflon.

---

[5]In addition to those who purchase and consume beer as consumers, surely those who purchase and serve beer as owners and employees of bars, restaurants, and the like would also form part of the relevant population on the facts of this case. Nevertheless, the survey design itself was fundamentally flawed in this instance and was correctly given little or no weight.

The 1936 U.S. case involving "cellophane" appears to be the first serious attempt to introduce surveys to determine whether a trademark had become generic (*DuPont Cellophane Co. v. Waxed Products Co.* 1934).[6] Retail dealers were interviewed in one of the surveys. Results showed that 88% of the dealers knew no name other than "cellophane" to order that type of product. In a second survey, 17,000 subscribers of popular magazines — including *Good Housekeeping, The Saturday Evening Post, Delineator,* and *Ladies Home Journal* — were polled and asked whether they believed "cellophane" to be a trademark. Among respondents, 72% indicated that it was. As it turned out, neither survey played a significant role in the decision. The Court nevertheless found fault with the survey of magazine subscribers because it was accompanied by flattering correspondence and offers of prizes that "might well have stimulated a search for a registered trademark that theretofore had been unknown.... Such proofs have no great weight" (*DuPont v. Waxed Products* 1934, §337).

The first Canadian case to introduce survey evidence on the issue of genericism was *Aluminium Goods Ltd. v. Registrar of Trade Marks* (1954). Aluminium Goods sought to register "Wear-Ever" as a trademark used in association with cooking utensils. A survey was conducted to ascertain consumer and dealer knowledge of the word "Wear-Ever":

> [The survey house] conducted the survey throughout Canada by its own employees who, in personal interviews, submitted a series of non-leading questions to 3007 housewives and 505 dealers in cooking utensils in 64 cities, towns and rural communities. The question submitted to housewives differed somewhat from those submitted to dealers, but in each case I am satisfied that no objection could be taken to the form of the questions or to the manner in which the survey was conducted. I am satisfied that the report indicates a fair sampling of both consumer and dealer knowledge throughout Canada.
>
> I do not propose to state in detail the contents of the report and the accompanying documents. It is sufficient to state that as a result of the questioning, 91% of 3007 housewives and 96.5% of 505 dealers identified "Wear-Ever" as a brand. It is a significant fact that while 44% of the dealers questioned did not deal in "Wear-Ever" utensils, 96.5% of all identified "Wear-Ever" as a brand, thus indicating the widespread knowledge among deal-

---

[6]In this case, DuPont Cellophane, owner of the registered mark "Cellophane," sued Waxed Products, a wholesaler and converter of transparent cellulose sheets. Waxed Products purchased its transparent wrapping from a competitor of DuPont. DuPont alleged that when Waxed Products received orders for "cellophane," it delivered the competitor's product. The Second Circuit found "that 'cellophane' [was] used to designate the cellulose product we are concerned with, far more commonly than any other term, and is certainly the descriptive word in general use."

ers of the manner in which the word was used. (*Aluminium Goods v. Registrar of Trade Marks* 1954, §97)

Two basic survey design approaches have been used to assess genericism versus distinctiveness. They have come to be referred to in the literature as the "thermos test" and the "Teflon test" (Leiser and Schwartz 1983). Both tests appear to be based on the assumption that consumers will use a name either as a generic term or a trademark. The objective of the surveys is to estimate the percentage size of each group.

The thermos test relies on "product category" questions that focus on what words consumers use to describe or ask for a certain type of product. It first arose in the U.S. case of *American Thermos Products Co. v. Aladdin Industries, Inc.* (1962). Questions asked of the 3300 interviewees included the following:

1. Are you familiar with the type of container that is used to keep liquids such as soup, coffee, tea, and lemonade hot or cold for a period of time?

2. Have you yourself ever used (or filled) such a container — that is, the type to keep liquids cold or hot?

3. What was the occasion for using such a container?

4. If you were going to buy one of these containers tomorrow — that is, the type that keeps food and beverages hot or cold — what type of store would you select to make your purchase?

5. What would you ask for — that is, what would you tell the clerk you wanted?

6. Can you think of any other words that you would use to ask for a container that keeps liquids hot or cold?

7. If you were going to describe one of these containers to a friend of yours, what words would come to your mind first to describe a container that keeps liquids hot or cold?

8. Do you or does anyone else within your household own a container such as we have been talking about?

9. How many are owned by all members of your household?

10. What do you call this (these) container(s)?

11. Do you know the name of any manufacturers that make these containers that keep liquids hot or cold? Can you name any trademarks or brand names that are used on these containers?

Seventy-five percent of those familiar with these types of containers called them a "thermos," 11% called them "vacuum bottles," and 12% named "Thermos" as a trademark for these containers. In *American Thermos* (1972), this survey was actually offered by the defendant rather than the trademark holder. The trademark holder's survey asked respondents to name trademarks or brand names used for vacuum bottles, insulated bottles, or other containers that kept the contents hot or cold.

The approach taken by the Teflon test to assess genericism versus distinctiveness is a series of brand awareness questions that require consumers to classify various words (including the disputed mark) as brand or common names. It originated with a dispute over the name Teflon in *E.I. duPont de Nemours & Co. v. Yoshida International Inc.* (1975). In a Teflon test, survey respondents are told that there are two ways to name products: the common name, which refers to all products of a given class, and the brand name, which refers to a specific product within that class. The respondents are then given a list of terms, including the term in question, and asked whether each term on the list is a common or a brand name. The original Teflon test in *E. I. duPont* (1975) proceeded as follows:

> I'd like to read eight names to you and get you to tell me whether you think it is a brand name or a common name; by brand name, I mean a word like Chevrolet which is made by one company; by common name, I mean automobile which is made by a number of different companies. So if I were to ask you, "Is Chevrolet a brand name or a common name?" what would you say?
>
> Now, if I were to ask you, "Is washing machine a brand name or a common name?" what would you say?

If the respondent indicated understanding the distinction, the survey would continue. If the respondent did not understand, the explanation would be given again. If the respondent still did not understand the distinction, the interview would be concluded.

Thereafter, the eight names were administered in the context of the question: "Now, would you say _____ is a brand name or a common name?" The eight words used in the original Teflon survey were STP, thermos, margarine, Teflon, Jell-O, refrigerator, aspirin, and Coke. The results of the Teflon survey appear in Table 1.

The Teflon Survey produced results for thermos that were markedly different from the results for thermos obtained in the Thermos case. There are several possible explanations for this, including the amount of time between the two surveys, but it also suggests the possibility that the distinct survey formats may have influenced the results.

A further approach to surveying the issue of genericism can be found in *Institut National Des Appellations D'Origine Des Vins et Eaux-de-Vie v. Andres Wines Ltd.* (1987). The issue was the meaning the Canadian public attributed to the term "champagne." A telephone survey conducted by the plaintiff posed the following questions to interviewees who were all at least 19 years of age:

1. What, if anything, does the word Champagne mean to you?
2. When you think of Champagne do you think of any particular country or countries or not?
3. What country or countries do you think of?

Table 1
Results of Teflon Test

Name	Percentage Answering Brand	Percentage Answering Common	Percentage Answering Don't Know
STP	90	5	5
Thermos	51	46	3
Margarine	9	91	1
Teflon	91	31	2
Jell-O	75	25	1
Refrigerator	6	94	0
Aspirin	13	86	0
Coke	76	24	0

Interestingly, the Court found the survey of little assistance for the purpose for which the plaintiff had introduced it, namely, what people associate with the term "champagne" and whether, in the their minds, it is connected to any particular country. Instead, the Court found the survey to be of assistance for the defendant's allegation that "champagne" was generic:

> Indirectly, the plaintiffs' survey sheds light on the defendants' allegation that the term has become generic because of its use in describing high quality commercial products or simply sparkling wines from anywhere in the world.

> All the evidence in this regard has been compelling and the court has no difficulty in finding that the word "champagne" has acquired generic attributes. (*Institut National v. Andres Wines* 1987, p. 432)

Deceptive Advertising

Survey evidence in misleading advertising cases has been less routine and more controversial than the more established applications in trademark disputes. There are few templates or standard models on which to rely. Most surveys used in misleading advertising disputes have required a highly customized approach. Misleading advertising studies are also typically more costly to carry out than other types of studies because of the necessity to show the advertisements in question to interviewees in person. For these reasons, research in the misleading advertising area is a less developed field than in other types of litigation support (see Craswell 1997; Diamond 1989; Preston 1989).

Two specific principles of misleading advertising claims have established the opportunity and direction for survey research support. The first is that the determination of whether an ad is misleading is to be made not from the perspective of an expert analyst but from the perspective of the "average person." The second is that the test of whether an ad is misleading is not to be based on its literal meaning but on its general impression. As the court stated in *American Brands* (1976), "a statement acknowledged to be literally true and grammatically correct [may] nevertheless [have] a tendency to mislead, confuse or deceive.... The question in such cases is — what does the person to whom the message is addressed find to be the message?"

The principles of average person and first impression were the bases of evidence in *Beatrice Foods Inc. v. Ault Foods Limited* (1995). In that case, Beatrice attempted to restrain Ault Foods from launching an advertising campaign for its new Purfilter milk. Beatrice alleged that Ault's emphasis on the removal of miniscule levels of bacteria from milk would unjustifiably taint public perception of the safety of ordinary pasteurized milk.

In support of its application, Beatrice submitted survey evidence. It incorporated an experimental design, whereby one group was shown the Purfiltre milk ad and another was not and both groups were asked to rate the milk they currently drink at home. The misleading advertising analysis was addressed by statistically comparing the average ratings between the control and test groups on 11 image questions pertaining to the milk that respondents drank at home.

Although the research contained sound experimental design, it was criticized severely by the opposition and the Court on four grounds:

❑ The research had failed to test the exact version of the offending advertisement;

❑ The researchers had extrapolated too loosely from the results, attributing unsubstantiated generalizations to the population;

❑ The open-ended (qualitative) data had been ignored in interpreting the results; and

❑ The research test had not directly addressed the relevant sections of the Competition Act; for example, it failed to demonstrate that buying decisions would be affected.

In addition to illustrating the tests of the average person and general impression, the decision also sets standards for validity criteria that researchers will be expected to address in misleading advertising cases in the future.

In *Maple Leaf Foods v. Robin Hood Multifoods Inc.* (1994), the defendant argued that the information in its ads was factually accurate, in that Maple Leaf's frozen pie crusts were limited to bottom crusts that would need to be reshaped if required to serve as top crusts. The plaintiff took issue with the *implication* in the defendant's ads that consumers could not achieve an acceptable-looking top pie crust by following instructions written on the package. The evidence established that they could. Justice Jarvis held that the overall impression of the advertisement conveyed false and misleading representations. Survey evidence had not been tendered but could have been by either party on the matter of the overall impression gained by a representative group of pie crust consumers.

Determining Damages

Survey research also has been used to determine damages. In *Harold's Department Stores Inc. v. Dillard Department Stores* (1996), a jury found Dillard liable for a copyright infringement of fabric designs on 37,000 dresses that were sold for less than Harold's price. Harold's clientele was mostly college students. A marketing professor surveyed a sample of 1231 college-age women who had visited a Harold's store or seen a Harold's catalog and visited a Dillard store during the time that Dillard had the dresses for sale. The respondents were asked (1) if they had seen any print skirts at Dillard that they thought of as unique to Harold's and (2) how likely they were to purchase clothes from Harold's during the next year. The survey found that, in contrast to women who had visited both stores but did not see the skirts at Dillard, approximately 33% of women who saw the skirts at Dillard indicated that they would be less likely to buy clothes from Harold's during the next year. Projecting from the survey to nationwide sales, the expert estimated that Harold's suffered damages to goodwill, reputation, and sales to future and prospective customers at between $226,367 and $517,809. Following testimony on these findings by the expert, the jury awarded Harold's $312,000.[7]

Canadian applications of survey research to calculation of damages in Canada are less well developed than in the United States, at least with respect to reported cases. Corbin and McIntyre (1995) brought attention to the potential of survey research in this regard.

---

[7]In several other cases, courts themselves have fashioned surveys to assess damages in complex cases involving hundreds or thousands of claimants. See *Cimino v. Raymark Industries, Inc.* (1990), 751 F. Supp.649; *In re Estate of Ferdinand E. Marcos Human Rights Litigation* (1997), 910 F. Supp. 1460 (1995); and *In Re Chevron U.S.A.* (1997), 109 F.3d. 1016. The importance of these cases for this chapter is the recognition by courts of the utility of survey methodology in determining damages.

Potential Jury Bias

Survey research finds important applications in criminal law, particularly in trials involving juries. Canadian law, for example, recognizes that jury members must be unbiased, "indifferent between the Queen and the accused" (Canadian Criminal Code, §567[1][6]). But bias may creep into their judgments in the form of a predisposition to believe that the defendant is more likely guilty than innocent. The most common situation that is thought to lead to bias is that pretrial publicity may have set community sentiments against the accused or put inadmissible evidence in the minds of potential jurors. Two of the remedies for such situations are change of venue (Canadian Criminal Code, §527[1])[8] and challenges for cause (Canadian Criminal Code, §567[1]).

Change of Venue

Change of venue entails seeking a jurisdiction where a body of unbiased jurors is more likely to be found. Survey evidence can be tendered to help with decisions on whether pretrial publicity has hurt the chances for assembling a fair jury or whether other sources of community sentiment would induce social pressure among jurors to decide one way rather than another (for a discussion of research on pretrial prejudice in the United States, see Kramer, Kerr, and Carroll 1990; Mehrkens et al. 1999; though England and Australia have been wary of admitting survey evidence regarding pretrial publicity, see Chesterman 1999; Lloyd-Bostock and Thomas 1999).

The first successful use of survey evidence for change of venue applications in Canada occurred in *R. v. Brunner* (Vidmar and Judson 1981). In July 1977, Brunner was arrested in Middlesex County, Ontario, and charged with fraud contrary to section 338(1) of the Criminal Code. He was alleged to have misrepresented his business ties with a building products company and sold overpriced materials and services by fraudulent means. Because the question of pretrial publicity is germane to this story, it is important to point out that Brunner had previously entered a guilty plea in a related fraud trial known through newspaper accounts as the "Bevlen Conspiracy." That so-called conspiracy was the subject of a highly publicized, sensational trial with fully 600 citizens called as potential jurors, testimony by elderly men and women describing how they were cheated of their life savings, wiretap evidence of conversations between Bevlen salesmen and their victims, and aspects of the case being debated in the Ontario legislature. The trial set records for the longest criminal trial and longest jury deliberations in Middlesex County, and

---

[8]The Canadian Criminal Code, §527(1), allows that "a court ... or a judge ... may at any time before or after an indictment is found ... order the trial to be held in a territorial division in the same province other than that in which the offense would otherwise be tried if ... it appears expedient to the ends of justice."

eight of the defendants were found guilty. More than 100 separate newspaper stories, accompanied by major headlines and dramatic reporting of testimony, had been published in the county's leading newspaper.

Brunner was coming to trial on subsequent charges several months after the Bevlen case ended. Defense counsel applied for a change of venue, asserting that the Bevlen case would cause continuing prejudice in the community. The Crown contested the application.

The defense submitted two surveys bearing on the claim that Brunner could not receive a fair trial in Middlesex County. The first survey sampled the population with approximately the same procedures that would be used to select a jury. (This and other attempts to simulate the "real-life" aspects of the survey were later used to explain its success.) A 19-item questionnaire was designed. The following were the important questions: "Does the Bevlen conspiracy trial mean anything to you?" If the answer was yes, respondents were asked to tell the interviewer about it as a check on accuracy of recall. If the answer was no or recall was inaccurate, the interviewer provided the following prompting statement and question: "The Bevlen trial involved salesmen for the Bevlen Building Products Company who were accused of fraudulent practices in selling people siding and other home improvements; does this information make the Bevlen trial familiar to you?"

Thereafter, four questions assessed presumptions of guilt toward an accused involved in Bevlen who was subsequently charged with additional fraudulent practices; the questionnaire moved from general attitudes to more specific beliefs about how the respondent would behave in a courtroom. A follow-up experiment was designed to interpret the source of the biases discovered in the first survey.[9] Overall, the two market tests indicated that approximately three and one-half months after the end of the main publicity and headlines following the Bevlen conspiracy, it remained a well-known, notorious event in Middlesex County. The presiding judge ordered the trial to be moved to another venue.

Another example is found in *R. v. Theberge* (Case Law Order No 005/121/050), in which James Theberge of Timmins, Ontario, was accused of murdering 17-year-old Susan Hall. Evidence showed that Timmins's newspaper, *The Daily Press*, published 15 stories about the murder. Justice Robert Boissonneault found the articles to be objective and nonprejudicial to the accused. However, the victim's father was a local doctor who saw more than 400 patients per month. He was also on retainer for the town's largest corporate employer. Expectations of potential community bias were confirmed in a survey of 250 people, in which 33% admitted to a biased predisposition and 18% claimed to have an open mind when other of their responses indicated they did not. The importance of these data was heightened because the trial occurred more than three years after the killing, yet evidence of prejudice persisted.

---

[9]It is useful to note that it was designed as a controlled experiment rather than as a representative survey.

An expert witness called by the Crown testified that the poll was not valid because of certain debatable technical flaws. The judge, however, rejected the prosecution's witness because of his lack of experience in jury selection and allowed a change of venue, writing, "I conclude it is improbable a fair and impartial jury can be chosen."

Challenge for Cause

Courts may turn down requests for change of venue but still consider the survey evidence used in the request to have weight in the proceedings. In such cases, the court may be amenable to a request for challenge for cause. Challenge for cause entails questioning potential jurors as to their prejudices and requesting their exclusion on those grounds. Such challenges have been common in many U.S. jurisdictions, and U.S. lawyers are sometimes permitted to take a great deal of license in the nature of their questioning of potential jurors.

Such challenges were rare in Canada until recently. Their more frequent use has been spurred by a growing body of case law recognizing that parts of Canadian society are marked by racism and other prejudices that might jeopardize the right of an accused to a fair trial (Vidmar 1999a). There has also been a growing awareness of the power of the mass media to create a climate of prejudice against an accused.

A case in point is *R. v. Iutzi* (Vidmar and Melnitzer 1984). In May 1978, a 14-month-old boy was found dead of head injuries in Thamesford, Ontario. Both parents were charged with second-degree murder; each denied having committed the killing. An image of vagrant irresponsibility surrounded them; for example, neither had a stable job history, they were frequently seen hitchhiking, and they had become subjects of community gossip. Before the trial, they reported threats against themselves, and law students working for defense counsel were also threatened by people in the street.

Suspecting community prejudice through word-of-mouth rumour, defense counsel commissioned a telephone survey to assess the degree of community prejudice. On the basis of the findings, the defense counsel was granted the right to challenge for cause. This involved putting up to 12 questions to each potential juror and having two peers assess whether the juror could be expected to judge the case in an unbiased manner. The challenge for cause process then became the final basis for selecting jurors, though that process itself is thought to be imperfect (Vidmar and Melnitzer 1984).

Another high-profile case occurred with *R. v. Paul Bernardo* (1994). Bernardo was accused of the first-degree murder of two teenage girls. Survey evidence established that many members of the public had a predisposition to believing that Bernardo had killed the girls, that they would not be able to keep an open mind as a juror, and that they doubted that his wife could have been directly involved in the murders. This evidence of bias in the public was part of the basis for both the defense and

Crown obtaining a wider latitude in questioning potential jurors than might otherwise have been permitted.

Decisions of Trial by Judge Alone

Another solution to the problem of not being able to find an impartial jury is to have a trial by judge alone. The Canadian Charter of Rights (§ 7, 11[d]) gives accused persons the right to a trial by an independent and impartial tribunal. But what if an impartial jury is unlikely to be found? The Criminal Code provides a solution by stating that all murder trials must be heard by a judge and jury *unless* the provincial attorney general waives that provision. And even the Crown's refusal to waive has been overruled in at least one case in which the judge decided the accused could not get an impartial jury trial.

That case was as follows: In November 1991, Colin McGregor was accused of killing his estranged wife with a crossbow in broad daylight on an Ottawa street (*R. v. McGregor* 1992). The killing sparked an avalanche of publicity, exacerbated by the broader public sentiment regarding female victims of male violence. McGregor's lawyer used survey evidence to successfully argue for a trial by judge alone. The survey revealed high awareness of the murder, high concern about crime and violence against women, and a preexisting bias against McGregor's intended defense of insanity.

Contempt of Court

In England, Australia, and New Zealand, newspapers or other mass media are sometimes charged with contempt of court for publishing material that is considered to potentially jeopardize an accused person's right to a fair and impartial trial (see Chesterman 1997; McGrath 1988). Survey methodology was introduced in a recent case in Australia, *Attorney General for NSW v. John Fairfax Publications* (1999), in which the *Sydney Morning Herald* newspaper was charged with contempt of court. A lead headline and stories accompanied by large, color photographs describing the accused, a Vietnamese immigrant, as a drug boss were published five months before the accused was scheduled for trial on drug charges. Although such contempt of court citations are ordinarily issued immediately after publication of the alleged prejudicial publicity, in this case, the charges were brought *after* the accused was brought to trial and the charges dismissed on a technicality. The *Herald* was placed in the difficult position of proving that the article on the drug boss would have had no long-lasting effects on public opinion. Had the contempt charges been made before the trial, a public opinion survey could have assessed the longer-term effects of the publicity. But how could it offer evidence after the fact? There is a body of research indicating that public memory for news articles is brief, but it cannot speak directly to the specific facts alleged in the charges against the *Herald*. The *Herald* decided to argue in court that it was put in a situation that required it to produce "next-best " evidence because it was not possible to produce the most direct evidence.

The *Herald* commissioned a survey that attempted to assess the effects of the article through a simulation experiment (Vidmar 1999b). Readers of the *Herald* were recruited by a marketing firm for a study of newspaper readership behaviour. Some of the respondents were randomly selected to be provided with copies of the complete edition of the *Herald* that contained the article in dispute, and some were provided with that edition plus two additional editions that had follow-up stories involving the drug trade. The remainder of respondents served in control conditions and read either one or three editions of the *Herald* that were of a later date and contained no mention of drug bosses. All respondents were instructed to read the newspapers in the way that they would ordinarily read their newspaper. At the end of the session, all respondents filled out a questionnaire about which ads they had found most interesting, which articles they had read, and other questions intended to disguise the true purpose of the experiment.

In the second part of the experiment, the respondents were called two weeks later and asked a series of open- and closed-ended questions about the news stories they had read. The respondents were quizzed regarding whether they could recall the names of persons associated with the drug trade, specific names of persons identified as "drug bosses," and recognition of the actual name of the person who had been identified as a drug boss that had led to the charges against the *Herald*. After a period of only two weeks, only one of the respondents was able to identify the person who had been named as a drug boss. There were additional findings, but the main finding was that the results were consistent with other literature and indicated that memory decay following exposure to news stories that are one-time events is very rapid. Given that there were almost no effects of the article after two weeks, the likelihood of effects after five months would be even less likely.

The experiment is open to the criticism that the simulation may have not captured all of the conditions existing at the time of the story. However, an alternative argument is that if the articles had had an effect at the time, rereading the articles in the experiment should have triggered recall of the original information. There was no evidence of recall in either the experimental or control conditions. In short, the research provided next-best evidence for a defendant placed in a difficult situation. Eventually, the judge decided for the defendant on other grounds and gave little weight to the survey and other social science testimony in his written judgment. However, the research demonstrates how experimental approaches can provide novel evidence in legal settings.

Jury Selection Criteria and "Marketing" a Verdict

A related area of survey development is research that tests various arguments on mock juries to find out what is likely to "win" in the courtroom. The field is reasonably well developed in the United States and received wide publicity in the preparation of the O.J. Simpson trial. In one of the widely read commentaries on the Simpson case (Bugliosi 1997, pp. 116–17), the failure of the prosecution was blamed in part on its not taking into account the impressions of simulated jurists and not properly exploiting jury selection surveys:

> Once [the case was transferred downtown], there is evidence that the prosecution only made a bad situation much worse .... A national authority in the field of litigation support ... offered his firm's services free to Garcetti, and Garcetti accepted.... In the ... important area of assisting in jury selection, he says that although Garcetti was amenable, Marcia Clark was not.... Clark looked askance, as so many trial lawyers still do, at the emerging field of jury consultants. After the second day of jury selection, she told him she didn't feel there was any need for his services.

Apparently, the expert's early research on jury selection showed that black women were more vociferously in support, or forgiving, of O.J. Simpson than black men. Black women also viewed Marcia Clark "extremely negatively, actually calling her names like 'bitch'. They saw her as a pushy, aggressive white woman who was trying to bring down and emasculate a prominent black man" (Bugliosi 1997, pp. 116–17). Clark nevertheless settled for a jury with six black women and two black men — by the end of the trial, the jury had changed composition to reflect an even higher proportion of black women. The prosecution team had also minimized the expert's role in the challenge for cause questionnaire submitted to potential jurors, though the defense's expert in jury selection played an instrumental role. Bugliosi cites this mismanagement of jury selection experts as one illustration of the "incredible incompetence of the prosecution."

Many claims made by jury consultants are exaggerated (Hans and Vidmar 1986). Commentators on jury experts have drawn a strong distinction between courtroom selection of jurors and the use of jury simulations and focus groups undertaken in advance of trial. There is evidence that surveys of the community may be able to assess some gross attitudinal characteristics of individual jurors that may predict their likely tilt toward one side or another at trial (see Goodman, Loftus, and Greene 1990; Penrod 1990. For a general review of survey and other evidence bearing on attitudes of jurors toward corporate defendants, see Hans 1998. For questions bearing on juror attitudes toward issues in criminal and civil cases, see Ginger 1984; Krauss and Bonora 1983). For example, research has uncovered that some jurors hold strong anti-plaintiff biases in personal injury lawsuits, which have developed out of perceptions that greedy plaintiffs and their lawyers are trying to get compensation they do not deserve. In other civil cases, some jurors may hold strong attitudes against a defendant. In criminal cases, some prospective jurors may hold anti-defendant or anti-prosecution attitudes. The distribution and degree of these attitudes may vary in the community or differ between communities and are relevant to varying degrees from case to case. Survey research and focus groups may provide the kind of information that can assist lawyers in devising questions and identifying persons with strong attitudinal biases.

Nevertheless, despite the claims of some jury experts, no credible scientific evidence has been produced that shows that experts can select individual jurors with a precise degree of accuracy (Diamond 1990; Saks 1976). There are several reasons to expect that experts cannot accurately predict the proclivities of individual jurors. Neither demographic characteristics nor courtroom observations of behaviour are capable of revealing the rich histories and experiences of jurors that may lead them to lean one way or another. Jurors often do not reveal their true views during voir dire questioning. The process of jury selection is misleading; it is actually a process of "deselecting," that is, rejecting jurors who are randomly called to the jury box through challenges for cause or peremptory challenges. Even when a juror appears likely to be favourable to one side, lawyers for the other side are likely to reject the juror. Even more important, evidence matters! Jurors pay attention to the judge's instructions to decide the case on the evidence. They do not rely exclusively on their own prejudices or the lawyers' opening and closing statements (Vidmar 1999a, c).

However, pretrial simulations or focus groups can assist the legal team in discovering weaknesses in their case and encourage them to seek additional evidence (Boyll and Parshall 1998). In addition, this type of research also allows the lawyer to devise trial strategies and improve ways of communicating with the jury. Pretrial jury research in civil cases may also assist a lawyer in deciding whether to pursue a case to trial or attempt to settle it through negotiation. In addition, pretrial research of this type may assist a lawyer in forming questions in the taking of depositions.

Pretrial research on juries has come to play a role in many major civil and criminal trials in the United States. It has been used less often in Canada because of a lack of a tradition of jury experts, potential disapproval of Canadian judges if they learned of the activity, and the costs of such exercises. Nevertheless, the second author of this chapter has conducted pretrial research for several important Canadian criminal cases, as well as cases in the United States, and it is possible that this type of research has occurred, without public reporting, in other Canadian cases.

Evidence of Community Standards

Survey research has been used to argue community standards, particularly in obscenity cases. One of the legal tests for obscenity involves determining whether the material in question violates community standards of decency and whether any public that may be served by the material is outweighed by social harm. Community standards clearly depend on judgments and perceptions of citizens of the community, which may vary over time and between communities. Survey evidence is a natural measurement tool for community perceptions.

Some early Canadian cases on obscenity rejected survey evidence on methodological and policy grounds (Lamont 1972-73). However, such evidence gradually gained consideration. The leading case in Canada is *R. v. Prairie Schooner News Ltd.* (1970), which dealt with the possession of obscene matter for the purpose of distribution. In that case, an opinion poll was submitted by the defense to establish the relevant community standard regarding obscenity. The survey was eventually rejected for poor sampling quality, among other things, but it did give the Court the opportunity to confirm that survey evidence on public views of obscenity would be considered relevant and acceptable under appropriate sampling standards. *Towne Cinema Theatres Ltd. v. The Queen* (1985) is another of the foundation cases in which experts incorporated survey evidence in testimony about the effects of pornography.[10]

Similar use of survey evidence bearing on obscenity occurs in U.S. cases. Although the law does not require the prosecution to produce evidence that the material in question is obscene (*Paris Adult Theatre I v. Slayton* 1973), defendants generally have the right to introduce survey data as evidence bearing on contemporary community standards (*Smith v. California* 1959). In *People v. Nelson* (1980), an Illinois appeals court ordered a new trial for a convicted defendant because the trial judge did not allow a survey and thereby denied the defendant "the right to introduce the best evidence he can gather on the issue."

Similar to Canadian standards, the admissibility and weight to be given to the research depends on the appropriateness of the sample as defined by the prevailing obscenity statute, the nature of the questions, and other matters similar to those that arise in other legal contexts. In *People v. Nelson* (1980), the appeals court approved of a series of questions that asked respondents whether in their opinion it was currently all right in Illinois for adults to purchase magazines that depict nudity and actual or pretended sexual activities, for movie theatres to show films that depict nudity and actual or pretended sexual activities, and so forth. However, other courts have raised the issue of whether such general questions are sufficiently probative when the legal issue involves a particular magazine (*Carlock v. Texas* 1980). Linz and colleagues (1991) describe an experimental study involving a sample of adults, obtained by random digit dialing, that was exposed to the actual sexually explicit films that were the subject of the obscenity charges. A control sample of respondents viewed nonexplicit films. Following the viewing, respondents were asked questions about community tolerance and their own personal tolerance of the materials. This study came about as close as practically possible to assessing

---

[10]A similar outcome occurred in *R. v. Times Square Cinema* (1971; 4 C.C.C. [2d] 229) — a rejection of survey evidence due to poor sampling but an endorsement of the value of survey evidence (if properly collected) in deciding community standards of tolerance.

informed opinion about community attitudes on obscene materials. Yet it is open to the criticism that there was a selection bias, because the respondents were volunteers and constituted approximately 21% of persons contacted and only 45% of the 284 respondents who agreed to participate after learning about the general nature of the study. The lesson is that research on obscenity faces considerable methodological obstacles.

Public opinion polls have also played a role in litigation involving the issue of whether capital punishment is inconsistent with "evolving community standards" and, therefore, contrary to the U.S. Constitution's Eighth Amendment's proscription of cruel and unusual punishments (Vidmar and Ellsworth 1974). In *Gregg v. Georgia* (1976), for example, Justice Marshall's dissenting opinion considered findings from a survey (Sarat and Vidmar 1976) involving experimental conditions that shed light on his hypothesis that a public informed about the actual facts involved in the administration of the death penalty would be opposed to capital punishment.

HOW SURVEY RESEARCH MADE IT THIS FAR

Survey research is now at a stage of development that most social scientists will acknowledge that, if done properly, it lives up to all the process standards that proper scientific methods demand. Historically, however, courts were slow to accept this type of data as evidence; evidentiary rules against hearsay and restrictions on the use of the opinion evidence rule presented obstacles to the acceptance of survey research as evidence.

The Hearsay Rule

Hearsay is an out-of-court statement that is presented in court to prove the truth of a matter. Rules of evidence provide that this type of statement is inadmissible because the statement is not made under oath, and the party making the statement is not available for cross-examination.

Surveys are, by definition, reports of what other people say. For this reason, survey evidence was initially treated as a violation of the hearsay rule. The historical rejection of surveys on the basis of hearsay is well illustrated in the decision of the Exchequer Court of Canada in *Building Products Ltd. v. B.P. Canada Ltd.* (1961), a trademark infringement action. At trial, both the plaintiff and the defendant offered into evidence surveys designed and conducted by "experts." The Court held that all such surveys were inadmissible on the basis that they were hearsay. The Court went to great lengths to explain why the surveys were hearsay and, as a result, inadmissible. The judgment is illustrative of the historical difficulties in tendering survey evidence:

In general, the survey is a public opinion and matters of this sort consist of a number of questions put by interviewers to a selected number of members of the public, either at large, in specified areas, or to a number of persons in the trade. The questions are prepared by the organization conducting the survey, after consultation with the client - employer. They are then distributed to a number of survey supervisors throughout the chosen area who are given instructions as to the manner of conducting the survey. The supervisor in turn instructs the required number of interviews as to the method of approach to be adopted and supplies questionnaires to be submitted to those interviewed. The answers to the questions submitted are supposed to be taken down verbatim by the interviewer and are then forwarded to the office of the survey company where they are checked and the answers tabulated according to the responses received. Finally, a written report is prepared — such as those I have mentioned — and an official of the survey company presents the report as evidence and comments on its contents, including his opinion as to what the report may indicate.

This type of evidence is no doubt useful and may be admissible in certain enquiries and before certain administrative tribunals not bound by the laws of evidence. In my view, however, it is purely hearsay evidence and not within any of the exceptions to the rules excluding such evidence. No matter what attempts may be made to ensure that the survey is conducted in an impartial and objective fashion, the fact remains that the witness who tenders the report (or even brings in the questionnaires as did Mr. Haynes) has no personal knowledge as to the manner in which the questions were submitted or that the recorded answers are those actually made by those interviewed. But the main objection to such evidence is that the witness is endeavouring to state certain conclusions based on opinions said to have been expressed by individuals who are not before the Court and whose opinions consequently are not expressed under the sanction of an oath or subject to the test of cross-examination. In my opinion, the interviewer who asked the questions would not be allowed to say, "Mr. Jones told me that." How, then, can an official of a survey company who has not participated in the questioning, but who bases his opinion on tabulations made by others of reports of supervisors who have collected written statements by interviewers of what others said, be allowed to express an opinion as to what "bp" means to others, or whether its use by several companies would or not cause confusion? Such an opinion or report would be utterly valueless and in my view inadmissible. Another very serious objection with the receipt of such evidence is the fact that the interviewers, in going from door-to-door to submit their questions, can not possibly create in the minds of those interviewed marketing conditions similar to those encountered by persons actually going to purchase the various wares in questions, even if they are showing samples of the marks.... For

608   MARKETING RESEARCH

these reasons, I must reject the evidence. (*Building Products v. B.P. Canada* 1961, 128–130)[11]

There is an important nuance regarding the use of hearsay statements that eventually convinced judges to allow surveys into evidence in both the United States and Canada. A statement such as "A told me that she had seen B steal the money" would be inadmissible hearsay if the intent was to rely on A's statement as proof that B had stolen the money. But it would not be hearsay when used as evidence that A had in fact made the statement. The difference is that the witness has direct knowledge that A made the statement.

Provided that survey evidence is offered merely to show that certain statements were made by the interviewees and not to prove the truth of the statements themselves, such evidence does not offend the rule against hearsay. As such, it is argued that the hearsay rule is not violated by survey research, because the evidence that is tendered is that the statements made by interviewees were made in response to certain questions without attempting to assess whether these statements were true (see Potvin and Leclerc 1992; Stitt and Huq 1988).[12]

The foundation for the acceptance of the view that the hearsay rule is not violated by the nature of survey evidence is set out in *Subramaniam v. Public Prosecutor* (1956, p. 970):

> Evidence of a statement made to a witness by a person who is not himself called as a witness may or may not be hearsay. It is hearsay and inadmissible when the object of the evidence is to establish the truth of what is contained in the statement. It is not hearsay and is admissible when it is proposed to establish by the evidence, not the truth of the statement, but the fact that it was made.

Judicial acknowledgment that survey evidence does not offend the hearsay rule was first noted in Canada in the case of *Canadian Schenley Distilleries Ltd. v. Canada's Manitoba Distiller Ltd.* (1975):

> There will be no objection to evidence being admissible when the poll is put forward not to prove the truth of the statements it contains, but merely to show the basis of an expert's opinion ... or an assessment of the results of the survey.

---

[11]See also, for example, *Imperial Oil Ltd. v. Superamerica Stations* (1965; 47 C.P.R. 57 [Ex. Ct.]) and *Paulin Chambers Co. Ltd. v. Rowntree Co. Ltd.* (1966; 51 C.P.R. 153 [Ex. Ct.], av'd [1968] S.C.R. 134).

[12]There may be a tenuous distinction being made here that is open to challenge: Are the respondents' statements accurate reflections of their views? In other words, do they say what they really think? This is an issue of survey validity that we discuss subsequently.

The rule expressed in *Canadian Schenley* (1975) has been consistently followed in Canada, though with continuing refinement, and is now considered one of the leading cases on the matter of admissibility of survey evidence in Canada (Potvin and Leclerc 1992).

At approximately the same time the decision in *Canadian Schenley* (1975) was released, the first edition of Sopinka and Lederman's (1994, p. 321–22) treatise on *The Law of Evidence in Civil Cases* was beginning to draw attention away from the hearsay nature of the evidence and toward the quality of the evidence:

> [C]ourts ... have indicated a willingness to accept expert evidence of surveys ... as long as it can be demonstrated that approved statistical methods and social science research techniques have been employed. With respect to this kind of evidence, the courts have been more concerned about the procedures and techniques utilized by the experts than they have been about the hearsay aspect of such evidence.

Jurisprudence in the United States followed a similar course, though on an earlier time frame. Views were clearly set against survey evidence in the early part of the twentieth century. In the case of *Elgin National Watch Co. v. Elgin Clock Co.* (1928), Elgin National Watch submitted survey evidence of an expert witness that purported to show that the word "Elgin," used in connection with time pieces, signified to retail jewellers the products of the plaintiff. In rejecting the evidence, District Judge Morris wrote (*Elgin National Watch v. Elgin Clock* 1928):

> While recognizing the practical difficulties [of calling in a large group of witnesses] ... I am not convinced to make the innovation [of allowing the substitution of a survey] suggested by the plaintiff.... [T]he affidavit submitted for filing is one based, not upon personal knowledge of the affiant nor upon facts admitted in evidence, but, on the contrary, is predicated solely upon the unverified statements or opinions of persons not called as witnesses.

In *Oneida v. National Silver* (1940), the judge expressed reluctance to allow the survey in as evidence and was more confident in relying on the supporting evidence of 24 viva voce witnesses. "Such evidence has greater weight," he wrote, "than that obtained in the survey" (*Oneida v. National Silver* 1940).

By 1948, the U.S. judicial system was warming up to surveys, as evidenced when Circuit Judge Frank introduced one he had conducted himself! In *Triangle Publications v. Rohrlich* (1948), the publisher of *Seventeen* magazine (Triangle) brought an action against manufacturers of Miss Seventeen Girdles (Rohrlich) based on an assertion of the likelihood of confusion between these names:

> As neither the trial judge nor any member of this court is (or resembles) a teen-age girl or the mother or sister of such a girl,

> our judicial notice apparatus will not work well unless we feed
> it with information directly obtained from 'teen-agers' or from
> their female relatives accustomed to shop for them. As we have
> no staff [of suitable investigators] I have questioned some ado-
> lescent girls and their mothers and sisters, persons I have cho-
> sen at random. I have been told uniformly by my questionees
> that no one could reasonably believe that any relation existed
> between plaintiff's magazine and defendant's girdles.

Judge Frank's opinion was the dissenting one, and there was indeed
a finding of infringement against Rohrlich based on likelihood of confusion. Several years later, the United States introduced a Federal Rule of
Evidence (201), which barred independent judicial investigations of the
type conducted by Judge Frank on the grounds that the degree of consumer confusion between two products is not "capable of accurate and
ready determination by resort to sources whose accuracy cannot reasonably be questioned." This Rule of Evidence served to emphasize the need
to have evidence whose accuracy could be questioned in Court.

By the time of *Zippo Manufacturing Co. v. Rogers Imports, Inc.* (1963),
the admissibility of survey evidence had become clear:

> The weight of case authority, the consensus of legal writers, and
> reasoned policy considerations all indicate that the hearsay rule
> should not bar the admission of properly conducted public sur-
> veys. Although courts were at first reluctant to accept survey
> evidence or to give it weight, the more recent trend is clearly
> contrary.

In the United States, surveys overcame the hearsay objection on two
technically distinct bases. The first was that mentioned previously, which
held that surveys are not offered to prove the truth of what the respondents have said but rather simply to prove that they have said it. The second basis on which survey research has overcome the hearsay rule, as
confirmed in *Zippo* (1963), is that statements of beliefs, attitudes, or states
of mind at a specific point in time are recognized exceptions to the
hearsay rule (Federal Rule of Evidence 803[1]). The *Zippo* case is generally
considered to have marked the end of the hearsay objection to survey
evidence in trademark cases in the United States and the beginning of the
routine use of that type of research and expert evidence in providing consumer confusion.

Expert Witness Exceptions to the Opinion Evidence Rule

A related obstacle to the acceptance of survey research as evidence in
judicial proceedings has been the opinion evidence rule. The opinion evidence rule is often said to limit witnesses to testifying only as to their personal knowledge and not as to inferences or conclusions they may draw
from their perceptions. However, a major exception to the opinion evi-

dence rule is recognized in the case of expert witnesses, whose opinions or inferences arise from special skills that less-experienced people are unlikely to have.

Experts have also been given latitude in interpreting the hearsay rule beyond the limits described previously. In particular, they have been permitted to substantiate their own opinions about the conclusions to be drawn from research data based on what respondents have said in surveys. In *The City of Saint John v. Irving Oil Co. Ltd.* (1966), an expert witness conducted a survey regarding the value of a certain parcel of land and then used the results to draw conclusions of his own regarding the true land value.

Despite the latitude given to experts in interpreting survey evidence, there may still be some expectation that they assure themselves first-hand of the integrity and credibility of the survey process. In explaining the little weight to be accorded the survey evidence in *Molson Breweries, a Partnership v. John Labatt Limited et al.* (1988), the Court noted:

> The Pye affidavit was sworn by the designer of the survey, who hired another company to actually conduct it. The affiant was not present while the surveys were conducted, was not involved in the survey's completion, and can provide no direct evidence of the manner in which questionnaires were completed.

Is Survey Evidence Now de Rigeuer?

Many trademark lawyers today recommend the use of survey evidence in establishing an assertion of trademark reputation or confusion. Not only do these proponents value having survey evidence available to prove their case, but they are also concerned about the adverse inference that might be drawn by not offering such evidence in appropriate circumstances. For example, one Canadian trademark practitioner has written that "the use of research in trade-mark litigation has become so prevalent ... that a judge might be suspicious of any litigant who did not offer a survey to prove likelihood of confusion or the converse" (Borookin 1988, p. 49).

Some judges appear to agree. Justice MacFarland stated in *Sun Life Assurance Co. v. Sunlife Juice Ltd.* (1998):

> Without such evidence, how am I to otherwise determine whether there is likely to be confusion ... what I think personally is immaterial.

Judges in the United States have been more explicit in making adverse inferences when survey evidence has not been tendered in appropriate circumstances, taking the position that failure by a plaintiff to undertake a survey suggests that a properly done survey would have been adverse to the plaintiff's position (Diamond 1977). Specific examples in the U.S. judiciary include the following:

❏ In *Mushroom Makers, Inc. v. R.G. Barry Corp.* (1979), in which the defendant did not introduce any survey evidence: "This omission is underscored given the fact that the defendant is a substantial corporation with the means to have undertaken either a survey or an investigation to establish instances of actual consumer confusion."

❏ In *Information Clearing House, Inc. v. Find Magazine* (1980): "It is also significant that plaintiff, though possessed of the financial means, did not undertake a survey of public consumer reaction to the products under actual market conditions."

❏ In *Bonny Prods. v. Robinson Knife Mfg. Co.* (1989): "There is no evidence in this case that would support a finding that the public identifies the oblong shaped white colored handle with a slit found on Bonny's kitchen tools with either Bonny or any single source. Plaintiff failed to offer any consumer surveys to demonstrate such an association, which is the most persuasive and desirable evidence of secondary meaning."

❏ In *Brunswick Corp. v. Spinit Reel Co.* (1987): "In a case such as this in which confusion as to product source is a material issue, a survey may be the only available method of showing the public state of mind."

❏ In *Processed Plastic Co. v. Warner Bros., Inc.* (1982): "If plaintiff truly believed that the survey was inaccurate or unreliable, it could have taken one itself and let the results be compared."

❏ In *Warren Corp. v. Goldwert Textile Sales, Inc.* (1984), the court denied the plaintiff's request for a preliminary injunction to disallow an allegedly deceptive label on a competitor's fabric. "There was, it should be noted, ample time in which plaintiff might have conducted some research, if only to document an informal survey, among purchasers of its camel's hair fabric."

Weight

The admissibility of surveys as expert evidence is now soundly established, at least in the intellectual property field and most notably in the trademark area. However, courts are also aware of the imperfections of such evidence. As aptly observed by McCarthy (1984, p. 779), "it is notoriously easy for one survey expert to appear to tear apart the methodology of a survey taken by another." Judge Anderson in the United States made a similar observation in the famous thermos case (*King-Seeley Thermos Co. v. Aladdin Industries* 1962), with a view to accommodating the inherent weaknesses of survey evidence: "Any conclusion in this area cannot be reduced to a figure of unimpeachable accuracy but must, at best, be an approximation." The proper approach is to view survey evidence with some appreciation of the many sources of variability in conducting a survey. Technical defects, assuming they are not fatal to the credibility of the survey as a whole (e.g., *Irwin Toy Ltd. v. Marie-Anne Novelties Inc.* 1986), may be used to diminish the overall weight to be given as evidence rather than to reject the results out-of-hand. Justice McKeown (1997, p. 4) of the Federal Court of Canada commented that "the weight given to survey evidence is ultimately in the judge's discretion. [It is incumbent on counsel and expert to] persuade the court that the risks, bias or inaccuracies were minimized."

This is not to say that a survey with technical defects should always be tendered in evidence. If not carried out using acceptable scientific standards, a survey may fail to meet the minimum criteria for admissibility. This was the case in *Labatt Brewing Company v. Molson Breweries* (1996), in which, citing the ambiguity of questions used in the survey, the problematic data analysis, and the absence of a scientific control condition, the Court found the plaintiff's survey evidence to be inadmissible. "If I am wrong in that conclusion," wrote Justice Vickers, "I would have given little weight to the evidence."

Similarly, if the expert does not disclose sampling methods and assurances that the survey was conducted in conformity with statistical principles, the expert evidence will generally be inadmissible or given no weight, as follows:

> Because Mr. de Vries has not qualified himself as an expert with respect to statistical sampling methods, and because I am unable to conclude that his survey was designed or conducted in conformity with statistical principles, I regard Mr. de Vries' and Mr. Butcher's evidence as having no probative value. (*Bio Generation Laboratories v. Parton I Corp.* 1991, p. 550)

In conclusion, survey evidence, in principle, has passed the threshold of legal tests relating to admissibility. It may still be impeachable on the grounds of technical integrity. The United States has had the longest history of testing the many dimensions of survey validity.

WHAT CONSTITUTES "GOOD" SURVEY EVIDENCE IN THE VIEW OF THE COURTS

To be accorded its full potential weight, a survey must be properly designed and conducted. Opponents are justifiably avid in their efforts to draw the court's attention to any shortcomings of a survey. Details in design, methodology, and implementation are mercilessly probed. For this reason, the importance of quality controls and attention to detail cannot be overemphasized. The research must stand up to the closest scrutiny.

As in other areas of the common law, there has gradually developed a body of jurisprudence with respect to surveys, their admissibility, and the weight to be accorded to them in specific circumstances. Although appropriate parameters for a survey are, to a certain extent, factually and legally dependent, there are several universal standards against which admissibility and weight have been judged. They include the following:

❑ The survey sample should be representative of the relevant universe or, as it is sometimes known, the pertinent population. This criterion has proven to be critical to the weight, or even admissibility, accorded to hundreds of surveys examined in the course of our review;

❑ Survey objectives should specifically address the relevant issues in dispute; a survey designed previously for other purposes runs the risk of having irrelevant questions, an inappropriate sample, and measures that are not quite on the mark of the evidentiary requirements of a particular litigation;

❑ The time period for the survey should not be biased by seasonality or changing markets;

❑ Although the real-life context of the consumer's experience need not be reproduced exactly, elements of that context critical to the legal analysis should not be omitted;

❑ The survey sample should be sufficiently large to draw reasonable conclusions;

❑ Questions should be free from bias;

❑ Responses should allow interviewees freedom of expression, not unduly restrict their answers;

❑ Coding of open-ended questions should be thorough and not overly restrictive;

❑ Interviewer instructions and all respondents' answers must be disclosed;

❑ Interviewers should be well-trained but should have no knowledge of the litigation or purpose of the survey;

❑ The data should be analyzed in accordance with accepted statistical principles and accurately reported; and

❑ The objectivity of the entire process should be assured.

It is difficult to say which criteria are most important and which are least important. The absence of any of them raises concerns for the trier of fact in assigning weight. If the time and means are not available to have each of these requirements addressed, it would be preferable to have no survey evidence at all. A "quick and dirty" survey that cuts corners is likely to be a waste of time, effort, and money.

Detailed discussion of these requirements is set out in Corbin, Gill, and Jolliffe (2000).

Distinguishing Validity from Reliability

The research terms "reliability" and "validity" have sometimes been used interchangeably by the courts, as they might be in dictionaries. However, the words reliability and validity have technical definitions in the history of social science. It has proved useful to apply these definitions to expert survey evidence for two reasons. First, it is desirable to have a common denominator of language between the court and its appointed experts. Second, the distinction in definition has helped categorize criteria for evaluation and weight.

Reliability refers to the likelihood of getting the same results if one were to repeat the measurements on another sample on another day, using the same instrument and methodology. Therefore, if the questionnaire is tested on a sample of people that is distinctly unrepresentative of the population, its reliability should be called into question. If there is lack of consistency in interviewer style or inconsistent interviewer training, then reliability is also threatened. If coding is not done with strict rules or there is any lack of objectivity in the survey process, reliability is not assured. However, if such conditions are reasonably well controlled, then the reliability of the survey sample is adequately described by the margin of error.

Reliability standards are almost always under the control of the survey researcher, insofar as he or she makes design decisions and oversees the quality controls of the interviewing process. In reviewing survey evidence submitted in litigation, it is straightforward to evaluate adherence to reliability standards. In most cases, it should be possible to attach quantitative estimates (e.g., margin of error) to reliability. Although there can never be 100% reliability, the standard of 90% to 99% is usually considered adequate to give confidence to the results. Counsel may freely delegate responsibility for adherence to reliability standards to the hired expert, assuming that person is well versed in quality control requirements and is prepared to attend to fine detail.

Validity of a survey refers to the extent to which a test or questionnaire meets its intended purpose. Is the concept that requires measurement being accurately captured by the test questions? If not, what *is* being measured? And is it an acceptable surrogate for the necessary evidence?

The issue of validity bears on whether the right questions have been asked in the right way in the right circumstances, all in order to provide the measurements essential to the inquiry. For example, in *Kraft Jacobs Suchard (Schweiz) AG v. Hagemeyer Canada* (1998), both parties brought summary judgment motions with respect to trademark infringement and passing off involving the Toblerone chocolate bar. Survey evidence was tendered by each of the parties on the issue of likelihood of confusion. The defendant's survey evidence was rejected outright because it measured so-called product confusion, not source confusion. That is, it measured whether consumers thought that the Hagemeyer bar, called Alpenhorn, was actually a Toblerone bar. The Court reviewed the law applicable to infringement and passing off actions and found that confusion as to the manufacturing source was the real issue ("Do consumers believe that the bars originate from the same source?"), not whether people mistook one product for the other. The plaintiff's survey measured source confusion and was accepted. From the decision:

> The Corbin survey measured the likelihood of confusion as to the source of the Alpenhorn chocolate bar. It is significant to note that people were asked the following question after they were shown the Alpenhorn product.

Q: Which company do you believe puts out the brand of chocolate product you just saw?

Inappropriately the Liefeld study measured what I will call product confusion. The first question put to the public was as follows
and the question had some built-in direction for the question.

Q: Looking at these (point to Alpenhorn display) do you think
the Alpenhorn bar is an actual Toblerone bar, or do you have
no opinion?

For reasons I shall set out in my analysis, I find that the proper
test was conducted by the Corbin study and accept those results
over the Liefeld study. I find that a significant percentage of the
public believes the source of the Alpenhorn bar to be the manufacturer of Toblerone, that is to say that the two products were
made by the same company. I also find that a statistically significant portion of the confusion was attributable to a combination of three distinguishing indicia: the shape of the box, the let-
tering font and the picture of the sectioned chocolate on the
outside of the Alpenhorn package.

...Whether it be a claim for trade-mark infringement or passing
off, the proper legal test for confusion is what I will describe as
source confusion, that is to say Section 6 of the Act sub-section
(2) provides that the use of a trade-mark causes confusion with
another trade-mark if the use of both trade-marks in the same
area would be likely to lead to the inference that the wares or
services associated with those trade-marks are manufactured,
sold, leased, hired or performed by the same person whether or
not the wares or services are the same general class....

[With reference to Section 7 of the Act, in respect of passing off,
as well as to previous relevant decisions] I, therefore, find that
pursuant to the Act and the common law, the legal test for
infringement of trade-mark and passing off is the same with
respect to confusion and that is "source confusion" as set out in
the Corbin study and not "product confusion" as set out in the
Liefeld study. (*Kraft Jacobs Suchard v. Hagemeyer* 1998)

This case is a clear and simple example of the importance of counsel
and survey expert discussing the legal issues involved in the action.
Otherwise, there is a risk that the survey expert will produce reliable evidence that is potentially invalid in terms of measuring the real facts at issue.

There is good reason for separating reliability and validity criteria in
assessing whether survey research meets acceptable standards. It is well
established on most questions of reliability what the "right" answer is.
Therefore, judges may wish to apply a high standard to expert survey evidence in this regard; reliability standards are sufficiently well taught and
known that survey researchers should not be submitting evidence that
does not thoroughly address issues of reliability. Validity issues, in contrast, entail more ambiguity and creative challenge and are more open to
debate. Counsel must be integrally involved in ensuring the validity of

the survey instrument. Counsel is in the best position—or should be—to know the legal issues that are to be put to rigorous test through the survey design.

Assurance of validity in surveys is at the heart of circumventing the hearsay rule, which traditionally was the basis for excluding survey evidence. Recall from our previous discussion that survey evidence became a recognized exception to the hearsay rule because survey experts report only on what people say, not whether their statements are true. Yet, for survey evidence to play a role in deciding legal matters, survey experts are often obliged to assume that people's statements regarding their impressions and purchase intentions *are* true. Thus, unless survey questions are "valid" and accurately measure the concept at issue in the case, the results should be discounted. In short, survey experts must design questions that encourage people to say what they mean.

There is recent evidence that courts are concerning themselves more with the validity of tests brought to bear on litigation, though they do not explicitly allude to the validity criterion.

The case of *New Balance Athletic Shoes, Inc. v. Matthews* (1992) is a case in point. Although it appears not to have created excitement for precedents for legal issues, it seems to be an important case for precedents for validity of survey research.

In that case, Matthews filed to register the mark Balance & Design based on proposed use for men's clothing. New Balance Athletic Shoes opposed the application because it had registered a similar name, namely, New Balance, for certain categories of clothing and luggage.

Matthews relied on a consumer survey conducted in the Vancouver area. Interviewers presented individuals with two cards, each card with six different trademarks. One of the six marks on one card was the applicant's mark, Balance & Design, and one of the six marks on the other card was the mark New Balance. Respondents were asked the name of the company that they associated with each mark. They were then asked what products they associated with each mark. The researcher presenting the results argued that the 11% confusion result was insufficient to warrant rejection of Matthews's application.

In rejecting the survey evidence, D.J. Martin of the Trade Marks Opposition Board listed several problems. Some were standard issues of reliability, such as

❑ The survey was restricted to the Vancouver area, despite the reach of the application being all of Canada;

❑ The bias of the sample toward women, despite the application being for men's clothing; and

❑ The insufficient interviewer instructions.

However, more important are his decisive comments on various issues pertaining to validity. First (p. 141), he suggests that words taken out of context limit the validity of the test:

The applicant's mark was presented to consumers as it appears in use but the opponent's mark was presented as two words "new balance" when the evidence reveals that its mark usually appears in a different format.

Second (pp. 145–46), he identifies questions as "leading" if they put the respondent in a frame of mind in which they might otherwise not be:

The initial question asked in the survey was leading. That question was: "What is the name of the company you associate with that trade mark?" Where a trade mark includes or comprises ordinary words, it seems likely that a number of people would respond to that question by assuming that the name of the associated company incorporates the words of the trade mark whether or not they have any knowledge of the actual company that is associated with the mark. In other words, if consumers were shown a card with the trade mark RHINOCEROS on it and were asked the survey question, a certain number would answer "Rhinoceros" even though they had no knowledge of any specific associated company.

Psychologists would probably phrase the same argument as a "context effect" or taking cues from the environment to make judgments. It is how the human brain works in everyday circumstances and will continue to work when put in the artificial circumstances of an experimental test.

Third, Martin's comments also suggest a disapproval of word-association quizzes. Fourth (p. 141), he sets guidelines for implementing a test for confusion:

The test is whether or not a consumer familiar with one trade mark and the associated goods is likely to infer that the goods associated with a second trade mark come from the same source, whether or not that source is known.

And later (p. 148),

[I]t is a matter of first impression and imperfect recollection.

He also gives rather more explicit direction to the survey profession for implementation of these tests than we have seen before (p. 147):

It is preferable to design a survey that elicits a consumer's first impression by the use of open-ended questions such as "What do you think of when you see (or hear) this mark?" or "What word comes to mind when you see this mark?" This allows a respondent to reply in any number of ways. He might state that the mark reminds him of another mark, that it reminds him of a particular company, that he associates it with particular wares or services, that he associates it with a particular emotion or feeling, etc. Such a question should be followed up by one or

more prompts in which the respondent is asked if there is anything else he thinks of when he sees the mark. This allows for a
more complete assessment of the respondent's first impression,
which is the essence of the test for confusion.

The *New Balance* case is noteworthy because of the lengths to which
the presiding officer went in commenting on how to validly measure the
disputed issues in the litigation. The case makes important progress in
bringing validity issues to the attention of the legal profession, at least in
the sector of intellectual property.

FUTURE TRIALS

Survey research has had to battle four levels of assessment by the
legal profession to be given its full due in the courtroom:

❏ Scientific legitimacy,
❏ Admissibility as to rules of evidence,
❏ Admissibility as to quality control, and
❏ Weight.

The field has reached a level of professionalism at which there is now
no excuse for unsound research to be filed that would not pass at least the
first three tests. The fourth test, weight, will continue to pose a challenge
as survey researchers struggle with the creative demands of designing
valid operational measures of legal concepts.

A major opportunity for surveys to next conquer in legal applications
is the prediction of future impacts of certain corporate actions. For example, when there is a breach of contract in distribution agreements between
a corporation and its distributor, a distributor may seek damages for
future lost sales. How much could it have sold of the company's goods if
the contract had not been breached? This very typical type of dispute is
usually analyzed by expert accountants using theoretical forecasting
models. Market input, through surveys, would certainly be an enhancement. In our experience, the use of such surveys is just now seeing the
kind of growth that trademark surveys saw 20 years ago. Yet to be
evolved are the precedents and standards developed for other types of
surveys. Surveys about future buying entail a thorny issue not present in
standard surveys—consumers themselves are often uncertain of their
own future behaviour, so how could they report it to others? The state of
what is known on this issue and recommendations for questionnaire
design are contained in a review article by Corbin and McIntyre (1997).

Further potential exists for this type of survey in interlocutory injunctions. Interlocutory injunctions are an extraordinary form of relief in
which a party seeks a court order for another party to stop temporarily an
offending action—such as misleading advertising or selling a product

bearing an allegedly infringing trademark — until a future scheduled trial. Interlocutory injunctions require three standards to be met: proof that a serious issue exists, demonstration that the balance of convenience (or inconvenience) in corporate impact favours the plaintiff, and evidence that irreparable harm would accrue to the plaintiff during the period awaiting trial. The irreparable harm criterion is the most important factor in the granting of an interlocutory injunction and, typically, the hardest to prove. Social science evidence could be exploited far more than it has to date in assisting parties to an interlocutory injunction with this most important criterion. Such evidence could be directed toward showing that business *will* be lost and, once lost, will be impossible to retrieve or fully compensate. Alternatively, evidence could be produced by the defendant demonstrating that damages could readily be measured through survey research.

The final, qualitative challenge we raise is that of making the courts comfortable with the imperfections of surveys. We all know there is no such thing as a perfect survey, nor is there perfection in any other form of scientific research. Seeking to discredit a survey, opposing counsel will sometimes pounce on the smallest detail to plant seeds of doubt in the court's mind. The challenge to survey researchers is, perhaps, to explain the inevitable imperfections and avoid all others. Surveys appear to remain the best measurement instrument currently available to the courts in drawing conclusions about broad populations.

Acknowledgment

This article has benefited from the input of Kelly Gill, law partner with Gowling Strathy and Henderson. Some excerpts appear, without further acknowledgment, from a book he coauthored with Dr. Corbin (*Trial by Survey*), currently in press by Carswell Publishers.

BIBLIOGRAPHY

Aluminium Goods Ltd. v. Registrar of Trade Marks (1954), 19 C.P.R. 93 (Ex.Ct.).

Amend, J.M. and P. Johnson (1992), "Types of Surveys in Trademark and Trade Dress Litigation," address to the American Bar Association — Section of Patent, Trademark and Copyright Law's Annual Spring Education Program.

American Brands, Inc. v. R. J. Reynolds Co. (1976), 413 F. Supp. 1352 (S.D.N.Y.).

American Thermos Products v. Aladdin Industries Inc. (1962), 134 U.S.P.Q. 98 (D.Conn.).

Attorney General for the State of NSW v. John Fairfax Pty. Limited (1999), NSWSC 318.

Beatrice Foods Inc. v. Ault Foods Ltd. (1995), 59 C.P.R. (3d).

Bereskin, D. (1988), "The Use of Surveys in Legal Trade-Mark Litigation," *Canadian Journal of Marketing Research*, 7, 49–58.

Big Sisters Association of Ontario v. Big Brothers of Canada (1996), 77 C.P.R. (3d) 177 (F.C.T.D.).

Bio Generation Laboratories Inc. v. Partron I, Corp. (1991), 37 C.P.R. (3d) 546 at 550 (T.M.O.B.).

Bonny Prods. v. Robinson Knife Mfg. Co. (1989), 14 U.S.P.Q. 2d 1666, 1667 (S.D.N.Y.).
Boyll, Jeffrey and Donald Parshall (1998), "Using Early Jury Focus Research," *For the Defense*, (July), 25–28.
Brunswick Corp. v. Spinit Reel Co. (1987), 832 F. 2d. 513, 4 U.S.P.Q. 2d 1497 (10th Cir.).
Bugliosi, V. (1997), *Outrage: The Five Reasons Why O.J. Simpson Got Away with Murder.* New York: Dell.
Building Products v. B.P. Canada (1961), 36 C.P.R. 121 at 128–130 (Ex. Ct.).
Canadian Schenley Distilleries Ltd. V. Canada's Manitoba Distiller Ltd. (1975), 25 C.P.R. (2d) 1 (F.C.T.D.).
Carlock v. State (Texas) (1980), 609S.W. 2d 787.
Cartier Inc. v. Cartier Optical Ltd. (1988), 20 C.P.R. (3d) 68 at 77-8 (F.C.T.D.).
Chesterman, Michael (1997), "OJ and the Dingo: How Media Publicity Relating to Criminal Cases Tried by Jury Is Dealt with in Australia and America," *American Journal of Comparative Law*, 45, 109–47.
——— (1999), "Criminal Trial Juries in Australia: From Penal Colonies to a Federal Democracy," *Law and Contemporary Problems*, 62, 69–102.
The City of Saint John v. Irving Oil Co. Ltd. (1966), S.C.R. 581.
Coleman, A.M. and R.D. Mackay (1995), "Psychological Evidence in Court: Legal Developments in England and the United States," *Psychology, Crime and Law*, 1, 261–68.
Corbin, R., K. Gill, and S. Jolliffe (2000), *Trial by Survey.* Toronto: Carswell.
——— and D. McIntyre (1995), "Evidence of Irreparable Harm in Interlocutory Injunction Applications," 74 C.P.R. (3d), 289–305.
——— and ——— (1997), "Evidence of Irreparable Harm in Interlocutory Injunction Applications," *Canadian Patent Reporter*, 74, 289–306.
Craswell, Richard (1997), "Compared to What? The Use of Control Ads in Deceptive Advertising Litigation," *Antitrust Law Journal*, 65, 793–812.
Davis, Theodore (1996), "Copying in the Shadow of the Constitution: The Rational Limits of Trade Dress Protection," *Minnesota Law Review*, 80, 595.
Diamond, Shari Seidman (1977), "Legal Applications of Survey Research," in *Modern Scientific Evidence: The Law and Science of Expert Testimony*, D.L. Faigman, David H. Kaye, Michael J. Saks, and Joseph Sanders, eds. St. Paul, MN: West Publishing Co., 185–219.
——— (1989), "Using Psychology to Control Law: From Deceptive Advertising to Criminal Sentencing," *Law and Human Behavior*, 13, 239–54.
——— (1990), "Scientific Jury Selection: What Social Scientists Know and Do not Know," *Judicature*, 73, 178–83.
——— (1997), "Legal Applications of Survey Research: Applications of Survey Research," in *Modern Scientific Evidence: The Law and Science of Expert Testimony*, David L. Faigman, David H. Kaye, Michael J. Saks, and Joseph Sanders, eds. St. Paul, MN: West Publishing, Chapter 5.
DuPont Cellophane Co. v. Waxed Products Co. (1936), 30 U.S.P.Q. 332 (2nd Cir. C.A.), modifying 22 U.S.P.Q. 167 (E.D.N.Y. 1934), cert denied 299 U.S. 601.
E.I. duPont de Nemours & Co. v. Yoshida International Inc. (1975), 185 U.S.P.Q. 597 (E.D.N.Y.).
Elgin National Watch Co. v. Elgin Clock Co. (1928), 26 F. 2d 376 (District Ct., District of Del.).
Freckelton, Ian (1997), "Child Sex Abuse Accommodation Evidence; The Travails of Counterintuitive Evidence in Australia and New Zealand," *Behavioral Sciences and Law*, 15, 247–83.
Fuddruckers Inc v. Doc's B.R. Others, Inc. (1987), 826 F.2d. 837 (9th Cir.).

Gatowski, Sophia et al. (1996), "The Diffusion of Scientific Evidence: A Comparative Analysis of Admissibility Standards in Australia, Canada, England and the United States, and Their Impact on Social and Behavioral Sciences," *Expert Evidence*, 4, 86–92.

Ginger, Ann Fagan (1984), *Jury Selection in Civil and Criminal Trials*. Tiburn, CA: Law Press Corp.

Goodman, Jane, Elizabeth Loftus, and Edith Greene (1990), "Matters of Money: Voir Dire in Civil Cases," *Forensic Reports*, 3, 303–29.

Gregg v. Georgia (1976), 428 U.S. 153.

Handler, Arthur and Eileen McCarthy (1996), "Conopco—Consumer Confusion Remains the Touchstone of Trade Dress Infringement," *Trade Mark Reporter*, 86, 595–610.

Hans, Valerie (1998), "The Illusions and Realities of Jurors' Treatment of Corporate Defendants," *DePaul Law Review*, 48, 327–53.

——— and Neil Vidmar (1986), *Judging the Jury*. New York: Plenum.

Harolds Department Stores, Inc. v. Dillard Department Stores (1996), U.S. Ct Appeals, Tenth Cir., 83 F.3d 1533.

Information Clearing House Inc. v. Find Magazine (1980), 492 F. Supp. 147, 161, 209 U.S.P.Q. 936, 947 (S.D.N.Y.).

Institut National des Appellationd d'Origine des Vins et Eaux-de-Vie v. Andres Wines Ltd. (1987), 16 C.P.R. (3d) 385 (Ont.H.C.), aff'd 30 C.P.R. (3d) 279.

Irwin Toy Ltd. v. Marie-Anne Novelties Inc. (1986), 12 C.P.R. (3d) 145 (Ont. H.C.J.).

Joseph E. Seagram & Sons Ltd. v. Seagram Real Estate Ltd. (1990), 33 C.P.R. (3d) 454, 38 F.T.R. 96, 23 A.C.W.S. (3d) 486 (F.C.T.D.).

Keller, B.P. (1992), "A Survey of Survey Evidence," *Journal of the Section of Litigation of the American Bar Association*, 19 (1), 403.

King-Seeley Thermos Co. v. Aladdin Industries, Inc. (1963), 321 F. 2d 577, 579, 138 U.S.P.Q. 349, 351 (C.A. 2nd Cir.), aff'g sub nom *American Thermos Products Co. v. Aladdin Industries, Inc.*, 207 F. Supp. 9, 134 U.S.P.Q. 98 (D. Conn., 1962).

Kraft Jacobs Suchard (Schweiz) AG v. Hagemeyer Canada (1998), 78 C.P.R. (3d) 464 (Ont.Ct.Gen.Div.).

Kramer, Geoffrey, Norbert Kerr, and John Carroll (1990), "Pretrial Publicity, Judicial Remedies and Jury Bias," *Law and Human Behavior*, 14, 409–38.

Krauss, Elissa and Beth Bonora (1983), *Jurywork: Systematic Technics*. New York: Boardman.

Labatt Brewing Company v. Molson Breweries, A Partnership dba Carling O'Keefe Breweries (1996), 73 C.P.R. (3d) 544.

Lamont, H. (1972–73), "Public Opinion Polls and Survey Evidence in Obscenity Cases," 15 C.L.Q. 135.

Leiser, A. and C. Schwartz (1983), "Techniques for Ascertaining Whether a Term Is Generic," *Trademark Reporter*, 73 (July/August), 376–90.

Linz, Daniel et al. (1991), "Estimating Community Standards: The Use of Social Science Evidence in an Obscenity Prosecution," *Public Opinion Quarterly*, 55, 80.

Lipton, Jack (1987), "Trademark Litigation: A New Look at the Use of Social Science Evidence," *Arizona Law Review*, 29, 639–65.

Lloyd-Bostock, Sally and Cheryl Thomas (1999), "Decline of the Little Parliament: Juries and Jury Reform in England and Wales," *Law and Contemporary Problems*, 62, 7–40.

Maple Leaf Foods v. Robin Hood Multifoods Inc. (1994), 58 C.P.R. (3d), 54 (Ont. Ct. Gen. Div.), leave to appeal refused (1994), 58 C.P.R. (3d) 54.

McCarthy, J.T. (1984), *Trademarks and Unfair Competition*, 2d ed. Rochester, NY: Lawyers Publishing Cooperative, 779.

———— (1996), *McCarthy on Trademarks and Unfair Competition*, 4th ed. Deerfield, IL: Clark Boardman Callaghan.

McDonald's Corp. v. Peter MacGregor Ltd. (1987), 15 C.P.R. (3d) 433 (T.M.O.B.).

McGrath, John (1988), "Contempt and the Media: Constitutional Safeguard or State Censorship?" *New Zealand Law Review*, 371–88.

McKeown, William J. (1997), "Expert and Survey Evidence in Patent and Trade-Mark Cases: Proposed Federal Court Case Management Procedures," 14 C.I.P.R. 1 at 4, presented in an address to the Third Annual continuing Education Symposium on Intellectual Property Law of the Patent and Trademark Institute of Canada (March 15).

Mehrkens, Nancy et al. (1999), "The Effects of Pretrial Publicity on Juror Verdicts: A Meta-Analytic Review," *Law and Human Behavior*, 23, 219–36.

Molson v. Carling Breweries (1984), 1 C.P.R. (3d) 191 at 197-98 (F.C.T.D.).

Molson Breweries, a Partnership v. Johnn Labatt Ltd. et al. (1998), Court File No. T-162-96, Unique No. 98204055 (F.C.T.D.).

Mushroom Makes Inc. v. R.G. Barry Corp. (1979), 441 F. Supp. 1220, 196 U.S.P.Q. 471 (S.D.N.Y., 1977) aff'd 580 F. 2d 44, 199 U.S.P.Q. 65 (C.A. 2nd Cir., 1978), cert. denied 200 U.S.P.Q. 832 (1979).

New Balance Athletic Shoes, Inc. v. Matthews (1992), 45 C.P.R. (3d) 140 (T.M.O.B. Canada).

Oneida v. National Silver (1940), Supreme Court of New York, Madison County, 25 N.Y.S.2d 271.

Paris Adult Theatre I v. Slayton (1973), 93 S.Ct. 2628.

Penrod, Steven (1999), "Predictors of Jury Decision Making in Criminal and Civil Cases: A Field Experiment," *Forensic Reports*, 3, 261–77.

People v. Nelson (1980), 410N.E 2d.476.

Potvin, J. Guy and Alain M. Leclerc (1992), "Survey Evidence—A Tool of Persuasion," *Canadian Intellectual Property Review*, 9, 158–71.

Preston, Ivan (1989), "False or Deceptive Under the Lanham Act: Analysis of Factual Findings and Types of Evidence," *Trademark Reporter*, 79, 508–53.

Processed Plastic Co. v. Warner Bros. Inc. (1982), 218 U.S.P.Q. 86, 89 (N.D. Ill.).

R. v. Bernardo (1994), Ont. Ct. J. (Gen. Div.) 214/94; 95 C.C.C. (3d) 437.

R. v. McGregor (1992), Ontario Court of Justice (General Division), unreported.

R. v. Prarie Schooner News Ltd. (1970), 1 C.C.C. (2d) 251 (Man. C.A.).

Saks, Michael (1976), "The Limits of Scientific Jury Selection," *Jurimetrics Journal*, 17, 3–19.

Sarat, Austin and Neil Vidmar (1976), "Public Opinion, the Death Penalty and the Eighth Amendment," *Wisconsin Law Review*, 171–206.

Simonson, I. (1994), "Trademark Infringement from the Buyer Perspective: Conceptual Analysis and Measurement Implications," *Journal of Public Policy & Marketing*, 13 (2), 181–199.

Smith v. California (1959), 80 S.Ct. 215.

Sopinka, John and Sidney N. Lederman (1974), *The Law of Evidence in Civil Cases*. Toronto: Butterworths.

Squirtco v. Seven-Up Co. (1980), 207 U.S.P.Q. 897 (8th Cir.).

Stitt, M.J. and N. Huq (1988), "The Legal Status of Survey Research," *Canadian Journal of Marketing Research*, 7, 42–48.

Subramaniam v. Public Prosecutor (1956), 1 W.L.R. 965 (P.C.), at p. 970.

Sun Life Assurance Co. v. Sunlife Juice Ltd. (1998), 22 C.P.R. (3d) 244 (Ont. H.C.J.).

Taco Cabana Int'l. Inc. v. Two Pesos Inc. (1991), 932 F.2d 1113, 1122, 19 U.S.P.Q. 2d 1253 (5th Cir.).

Towne Cinema Theatres Ltd. v. The Queen (1985), 18 C.C.C. (3d) 193, 18 D.L.R. (4th) 1 (S.C.C.).

Triangle Publications v. Rohrlich (1948), 167 F.2d 969 (2nd Cir. C.A.).

Two Pesos v. Taco Cabana (1992), 112 S.Ct. 2753.

Vidmar, Neil (1999a), "The Canadian Criminal Jury: Searching for a Middle Ground," *Law and Contemporary Problems*, 62, 141–72.

———— (1999b), "An Analysis of the Potential Effects of Pretrial Publicity Regarding *Regina v. Van Ia Duong*," report submitted in evidence in *Attorney General for the State of NSW v. John Fairfax Pty. Limited* (1999), NSWSC 318.

———— (1999c), "The Performance and Functioning of Juries in Medical Malpractice Cases," ALI-ABA Course: Litigating Medical Malpractice Claims, San Francisco, CA (November 11–13).

———— et al. (1999), "Amicus Brief Filed in *Kumho Tire Company, Ltd. v. Carmichael*," 119 S.Ct. 1176.

———— and Phoebe Ellsworth (1974), "Public Opinion and the Death Penalty," *Stanford Law Review*, 26, 1245–70.

———— and John W.T. Judson (1981), "The Use of Social Science Data in a Change of Venue Application: A Case Study," *Canadian Bar Review*, 59, 76–102.

———— and Julius Melnitzer (1984), "Juror Prejudice: An Empirical Study of a Challenge for Cause," *Osgoode Hall Law Journal*, 22 (3), 487–511.

Warren Corp. v. Goldwert Textile Sales Inc. (1984), 581 F Supp 897, 902, 222 USPQ 816 (SDNY), at 902 fn 5, 222 USPQ at 820.

Zippo Manufacturing Co. v. Rogers Imports Inc. (1963), 216 F. Supp. 670 (D.Ct., S.D.N.Y.).

Part VI
Envisioning the Future

Uncommonly brilliant minds have warned us about the difficulty of predicting the future. From Niels Bohr to John Kenneth Galbraith, we have been repeatedly told that predictions are fraught with many pitfalls. The future tends to be unpredictable, and we know that what we predict today may never come to pass. So why bother?

The main advantage of forecasting is that it creates a comfort level and provides us with a basis for planning. As we move into the future, we revise our forecasts, and as a result, our plans may change. We all know and accept this. It is somewhat like a firm forecasting its sales for the next five years, *every year*. No firm with a five-year forecast waits for another five years to work on its next forecast. The fact that the forecasts may change every year does not diminish the usefulness of the forecasting procedure itself. Sometimes, of course, we attempt to predict just for the fun of it.

Jack Honomichl examines the entrenched trends that are now strong and, at least on current evidence, moving inexorably into the future. Such trends include

- ❑ More exacting and continuous measurement of human behavior enabled by recent and continuing technological innovations;
- ❑ Concentration of power, with approximately 25 research companies controlling two-thirds of all research around the world;
- ❑ Broadening the scope of research, with an emphasis on information that includes MIS/IT, CSM, custom research, business intelligence, and syndicated data services;
- ❑ Change in leadership, with the prime movers of the industry being technocrats and professional managers rather than researchers themselves; and
- ❑ Less public cooperation.

The forces that give rise to these trends (such as technology and internationalization) already have been set in motion and will propel the industry along a fairly predictable path. All we need is a keen industry analyst who can identify, clarify, and integrate these trends and project them into the future. As a keen, long-time observer of marketing research industry trends, Jack Honomichl is in a unique position to identify and isolate such trends.

23
Looking to the Future

Jack Honomichl

Large, round-numbered anniversaries serve a useful purpose. They can justify an especially lavish commemorative conference; they can spawn a book that otherwise would never have been written; and they can prompt some to reflect on where our industry has been and, extrapolating from that, where it is going—always keeping in mind the admonition of the late Niels Bohr, world-renowned physicist/philosopher: "Prediction is extremely difficult. Especially about the future."

Those readers on the "sunny side" of 60 years of age probably don't know this, but 40 years ago survey research practitioners paid homage to sampling—probability sampling to be exact. Not surprisingly, most practitioners in those days had, or pretended to have, one foot in academia and the other in crass commerce. They wanted to project an image of an academic bringing scientific discipline to business's investigation of the commonweal. They wanted the best of both worlds, the trappings of academia and the better pay of commerce.

Also in those long-ago days, many survey practitioners had academic training in the social sciences, such as psychology, cultural anthropology, sociology, and so forth. MBAs were yet to be born. Can you imagine a world without MBAs? That's how primitive things were 40 years ago.

Interviewing was door-to-door or on street corners. Trained interviewers held clipboards and talked directly, eyeball to eyeball, with respondents. The elite, the gold standard of the day, was the field force built by Paul Smelser, founder of the market research department at Procter & Gamble (P&G). Smelser, who came with a Ph.D. in economics from John Hopkins University, believed in professionalism, and he practically invented the concept of field interviewing. The program he put together at P&G called for recruiting bright young women right out of college, training them seriously, and then sending them into the field in crews with strict supervision. They were supposed to dress formally, as if on the way to an office.

So as not to intimidate respondents, interviewers (P&G called them "investigators") were trained to memorize questions and the answers and return to their cars before filling out the questionnaires. Teams of such well-groomed, disciplined, and professional young women toured the United States doing surveys and product placement tests and checking retail stores for evidence of new products coming from competitors. Eventually, more than 3000 such investigators passed through P&G's system before the company switched over to telephone interviewing in the mid-1960s.

A colorful insight into door-to-door data collection came from the famous author Margaret Atwood at PMRS's (Professional Marketing Research Society's) 25th anniversary conference in 1985. Atwood, the featured speaker, regaled the audience with snippets about her early days when employed as a field interviewer by Canadian Facts. One story related to a door-to-door taste test in which the product, a fruit drink, was prepoured in little paper cups on a tray, which then was presented to respondents at their doorways. The problem was, it was winter and the test product froze. Field organizations wised up in later years and moved inside big malls, where working conditions were far better.

"High-tech" at that time started—and stopped—at IBM card sorters, and employees who could wire those monsters were prized indeed. Who then could have imagined the awesome computer power available today, when processing time is measured in nanoseconds?

Almost all market research firms in the 1950s were privately held, and they considered their financials—revenues and profits—highly confidential. Many firms were founded and led by flamboyant, high-profile researchers such as Alfred Politz, who came to the United States from Germany with a Ph.D. in physics in 1937 and asked himself this question: "What do I do? Which profession makes the most money with the least intelligence? The answer was advertising, but my English was not good enough for this field." Just six years later, he founded his own research firm after being fired by Compton Advertising, where he had been research director. Politz, like many early research industry leaders, strove to deal directly with the CEOs of client companies. He wanted immediate application of his survey "findings," and research departments hated that. The important thing is that Politz trained hundreds of fledgling survey research practitioners, and his firm came to be known as "Politz University." Almost all of them went on either to start their own research firms or to corporate United States and Canada as directors of research departments.

In addition, research methodology sparks came from Politz's public debate with his arch rival for fame, Ernest Dichter, the Vienna-born champion of motivational research, which Politz tended to ridicule. Accounts of these debates made their way into daily newspapers.

Today, large research firms tend to be led by people with a financial background or an MBA, and methodological niceties are relegated to underlings.

If anything typified the survey research industry in those early days, it was this joke that made the rounds time and again:

Why is a survey like a baby elephant?

Well, for one, it is conceived at a high level amidst much commotion and trumpeting in a cloud of dust. Then there is a 22-month gestation period. And then, when this ugly thing is born, covered by the blood of corporate politics, everyone stands around and says, "Whose idea was this?"

Now, fast forward to November 1999. NFO Worldwide, one of the world's largest research conglomerates, announced a new affiliated company, InsightExpress. The avowed purpose of InsightExpress is to provide "automated" or, if you will, "professional do-it-yourself" surveys on the Internet, untouched by human hands and paid for in advance by company credit cards. NFO has raised $25 million in venture capital, not to develop this service, but to promote it through advertising and publicity. The average project they envision will cost approximately $1,000, and the turnaround time would be between 12 and 72 hours.

All of this is to be accomplished through a joint venture NFO has with Engage Technologies, which is a public start-up controlled by CMGI, an investor in controlled Web sites (e.g., Flycast, Alta Vista, AdForce, AdKnowledge, and AdSmart). CMGI has been a darling of Wall Street.

Engage Technologies has a database of 35+ million Internet users (based on CMGI Web sites) that has been built using "cookies" on users' browsers, plus user-volunteered information and anonymous user profiles. There are 800 such databases, for example, people who somehow have expressed an interest in skiing, taking a cruise, or biking. These are continuously updated, and the depth of interest can be quantified. In turn, NFO has developed more than 80 "templates" that include, for example, lifestyle questions or demo batteries.

Clients, as individuals, can come to the InsightExpress facility online and pick an interest group, the questions, and the number of respondents needed. The rest is automated, and tabulated results will be shipped online over the Internet as soon as the quota is reached. Any brand manager who wants something quick to plug into a presentation or marketing plan can bypass his or her company's research department and order direct, with a quick turnaround. It could be as easy as calling in an order to Lands' End or Club Med.

This is not to say that NFO's InsightExpress is the wave of the future or that, if it is a financial success, competitors will spread rapidly. But it could be a harbinger, given the almost fanatic interest these days in anything Internet, coupled with the desire for instant gratification.

So, these are bookends of PMRS's lifespan. At one end are quasi-academic, cumbersome, face-to-face inquiries; at the other are automated, faceless, prepackaged gropes for information that has some fleeting utility. I am reluctant to use the word "revolution," but evolution at an ever-increasing pace is appropriate. And that makes predictions of what is coming in the future dicey at best.

But, putting Bohr's admonition aside, I'll make a stab at it. There are now some well-defined trends driving the marketing/advertising/public opinion research industry, and most can be documented. Since these trends are so strong, it is safe to say that they will prevail into the foreseeable future. Let's look at them and at least get a glimmer of what is down the road.

IMPACT OF TECHNOLOGY

Innovations like NFO's InsightExpress are made possible by access to the Internet by the general population. To future adults now stewing in grade and high school, access to the Internet will be commonplace and taken for granted. Put another way, InsightExpress may be running a bit ahead of the wave, but in a few short years, it will be riding a crest. You could liken it to the advent of the telephone, rare at first but then omnipresent. That opened the door to interviewing by telephone, and research purists at the time howled, especially about the bastardization of sampling purity. But all those field interviewers, like Margaret Atwood, could come in out of the cold. Then came WATS line capability, which helped the cost problem, and one could consider nationwide surveys by telephone. And then came other technological innovations, such as random and autodialing, and so on. Telephone interviewing became automated, and thanks to computers, complex questioning could be managed by CATI programs. The rest is history.

But there was still a problem. The telephone did not permit exposing respondents to visual stimuli. But that can be bypassed by communicating to the respondent through his or her PC wired to the Internet and, maybe down the road, through picture phones. It should be noted that, at least in the United States, it is now common to conduct television copy testing by telephone. Homes with VCRs are recruited, and a videotape of the test copy is mailed to the respondent's home. After self-exposure at the respondent's leisure, a telephone interview is conducted to obtain the usual measures of copy impact. The tape destroys itself as it runs so that respondents cannot run it twice and there is less chance that the proposed copy falls into competitors' hands.

In a similar development, a dynamic pioneer named Arthur C. Nielsen Sr. built his worldwide empire (still the largest market research organization in the world, with revenues of more than $1.4 billion) by drawing a sample of retail food outlets, such as supermarkets, and having a nationwide field staff (young men recruited just out of college, like the young women recruited by Smelser at P&G) visit the chosen stores periodically to "audit" movement. From that came extrapolations of market size and share of market. Nielsen had turned packaged goods marketing into a horse race, and only he had the score card.

And then came the UPC, the Universal Product Code, that little zebra strip made mandatory by supermarket chains for purposes of inventory control and automatic reordering of low stocks. Product movement data could now be captured at checkout, in toto, every hour of the day. And market tracking firms such as ACNielsen could buy these data from grocery chains in finite detail at the individual store level, amalgamate them, and continuously produce a virtual Niagara Falls of data. Software was developed to harness these data and sift out information, much as generators create power along St. Lawrence spillways.

What made all this possible? Computers and ever-improving scanning equipment deployed at checkout counters in almost every store today did.

Before you make the mistake of pooh-poohing NFO's InsightExpress, reflect on what the telephone did to face-to-face interviewing and what the UPC code and computer did to Mr. Nielsen's box counters.

Several research firms in the United States are now gearing up to offer online interviewing over the Internet. One such firm is Harris Black International, a well-established survey firm based in Rochester, N.Y. It has changed its name to HarrisInteractive, and the corporate focus now is on being a field/tab house for research firms that want to conduct traditional surveys online. To facilitate this, Harris joined with Excite@Home to recruit a panel of 4.2 million online panelists who have agreed to participate in surveys, and Harris claims it can field surveys from both large, representative samples of the overall population and targeted subsets (a lot of weighting there).

As for technology, Harris touts a high-speed customized e-mail system that makes possible rapid formatting, targeting, and delivery of more than 290,000 e-mails per hour to invite panelists to cooperate with a specific project. Then there is a "sophisticated" survey engine that can be programmed to conduct up to 144,000 interactive, five-minute surveys an hour in any language supported by Microsoft Word. There's more, but you get the idea.

HarrisInteractive went public in late 1999 to raise $75.4 million to develop this facility and expand into countries outside the United States. It is not alone. There are other research firms in the United States doing basically the same thing, and they too are looking to public offerings for financial energy.

Radio stations have long lamented the holes in radio audience measurement services. The Arbitron Company has a monopoly in the United States on local market measurement of audience size and station (program) popularity via self-administered diaries in which respondents log for a week. The big hole is out-of-home listening, which can be as large, maybe larger, especially during commuter driving hours.

Relief may be on the way from computer miniaturization. I might add that much of the technological progress in this area is rooted in research conducted for the military, the fruits of which are now spilling over into the public sector. This relief, now in test in Canada and the United Kingdom and operating for real in Switzerland, consists of a small (approximately four ounces), portable "receiver," which a respondent can wear on person. It continuously picks up the radio signals to which the respondent is exposed, including those away from home in an auto, at work, or at a beauty parlor or barber shop. At night, this receiver slips into a fixture attached to a telephone through which the data are "emptied" into a central computer over the telephone line, and the battery is recharged.

The idea is to go into an explicit market, recruit, say, 1000 people, and have them carry this receiver around for a week. The technology has been around for a long time; the problem was to get the receiver small enough that respondents would not consider it cumbersome. Apparently, that time has come, and if Arbitron's technology proves to be the best, it could help solidify its monopoly position on radio audience ratings in the United States. And, if this gadget works for radio, can television be far behind?

I could go on, but these few examples illustrate how technology — computer, UPC scanner, Internet — has already made possible more exciting and continuous measurement of human behavior, all at a much faster rate and usually at a much lower cost than ever before. And that opens up a world of analytical possibilities that have not existed before.

As for the impact on analytical power, imagine doing a factor analysis with 40 attributes without a powerful computer and software at hand.

So, the technology trend is well established and powerful, and it is destined to be so into the future, à la the illustration of radio (and perhaps television) audience measurement. But it is difficult to say just when or how. Who could have imagined a service like NFO's InsightExpress just two years ago? Surely more such innovation is coming, rapidly and dramatically, and more common practices in the market research industry will be clobbered into obsolescence.

Some will make the case that the awesome impact of technology has dehumanized the research process and, if anything, that understanding of consumers and what makes them tick is further away. I could write another chapter for this book in defense of that thesis, but let it rest for now. Deal with the harsh reality of technology.

CONCENTRATION OF POWER

By my reckoning, the world's largest 25 marketing/advertising/public opinion research conglomerates control approximately 65% to 67% of the world spending for research services. The balance is divided up among an army — more than 400 — of other research firms of any consequence around the world. For the record, of 1998's top 25 firms, 15 call the United States home, 3 each are based in the United Kingdom and Japan, 2 are based in Germany, and France and Brazil are home to 2 others.

Much of this concentration is due to mergers and acquisitions. Specifically, if you look at just the world's 25 largest marketing research conglomerates as of 1998, in the three-year period 1997, 1998, and 1999, they acquired 77 research firms that had, in toto, revenues of $1.483 billion at time of acquisition. If I had gone back five years, this acquisition mass would be even more staggering. But the most current three years make the point. The trend is concentration of power in the hands of just a handful of multinational conglomerates, and their acquisitions span Greece, Korea, South Africa, Israel, Bulgaria, Norway, Denmark, India, Switzerland, and Canada, as well as the usual suspects: the United States, United Kingdom, France, Germany, and the Netherlands.

These statistics do not reflect numerous other top 25 firms' moves toward an international presence through joint ventures, the opening of branch offices outside their home country, or the many cases in which one of the top 25 acquired less than a controlling interest in a market research firm in another country.

Canada is a good case in point. One by one, major Canadian market research firms (e.g., Canadian Facts, Market Facts of Canada, Goldfarb Consultants, ISL, Canada Market Research, Thompson Lightstone, and Elliott Research) have been acquired by large conglomerates based in the United Kingdom, France, or the United States. Add in the biggest players of all—ACNielsen, Nielsen Media Research, and IMS Health, all U.S. companies—and it seems that only one Canadian research organization of note, namely BBM, is still Canadian-owned. BBM, being a trade association of sorts, can't be sold, I assume, but it does have a joint venture with a British firm, Taylor Nelson Sofres Intersearch.

This is not to single out Canada, though; much the same could be said for Spain, Greece, Norway, Australia, and other major nations around the world.

So what is driving all this acquisition activity? There are two causes. One is that many of the multinational marketers are hastening to expand their global reach. Just look at the annual reports of such giants as Coca-Cola, Gillette, and IBM. For many, from 50% to 70% of their profits come from operations outside their home country.

If a U.S. research firm depends heavily on, say, P&G and P&G's main interests are outside the United States, that research firm wants to be able to say, "We can serve your research needs outside the United States just as we do in the United States." And of course, the British research conglomerates want to say the same to British multinationals, and the German research firms want to say the same to German multinationals, and so on. Just follow the money.

The other driving force is public ownership. Today, there are 13 marketing research conglomerates that are publicly listed on the New York Stock Exchange, the London Stock Exchange, NASDAQ, the Amsterdam exchange in the Netherlands, or Germany's Frankfort Exchange. Others are subsidiaries of larger, nonresearch conglomerates (e.g., WPP Group), but their revenues and profits are put into the public domain.

For these big companies, hyping the stock is the name of the game. But if annual revenues are, say, $100 million or more, natural growth, even though commendable, is not necessarily exciting to institutional investors. To get exciting, double-digit growth, these public companies turn to growth through acquisition, and because they have common stock, that often can be used to pay for acquisitions. Need more, just issue more.

This is an oversimplification, but the basic truth is that much of the acquisition frenzy in the research industry in recent years has been driven in large part by the desire to groom a stock and make it more exciting.

Of course, some of the acquisitions have been made to round out geographic coverage—for example, buying a research firm network in the Pacific Rim to cater to clients' interest in expansion there. Also, strategically, foreign research companies wanted to establish a foothold in the U.S. market, and U.S. firms wanted to establish a foothold in the European community (EC) market. Acquisition was the easiest and fastest way to accomplish that.

Whatever the motivation, though, the end result is the same: Many of the world's largest research conglomerates have scooped up desirable research firms around the world.

Will this trend continue? Yes, but with a twist. So far, this activity has been characterized by top 25 firms buying smaller firms for some strategic reason. But now, most of the really desirable midsized firms have been acquired (or that option rejected), and the top 25 are starting to acquire one another. There have been three such instances in recent years. We should expect more of this, and the end result in a few years could be that as few as ten worldwide marketing/advertising/public opinion research conglomerates will control, say, two-thirds of the world's spending for research services.

It is also important to recognize that the rank-and-file of people working in the research industry do not realize how far this concentration of power has gone or the names of those firms most apt to make it into the elite ten. Unfortunate, but true.

There is another deviation in this acquisition trend: that is, "outsiders"—large corporations with no previous involvement in the research industry—buying large research firms. They don't see "research" firms; instead, these outsiders see themselves as buying into the "information" industry or firms that are basically "database" creators. The main concept is that, unlike custom ad hoc survey firms, where key employees can split off and take their clients' business with them, the database firms and their revenue flow are relatively stable and much less vulnerable to the whims of individuals.

Does this concentration trend mean that the smaller research firms will be wiped out? Not at all. There will always be room for the small, specialized boutiques that perform valuable research that the conglomerates ignore or that do it much better and earn the label "expert." That, coupled with highly personalized service and thoughtful analysis, will keep these relatively small firms alive and profitable. But those firms that do not provide services that are unique or especially valuable, well....

INTELLIGENCE

Another trend I think worthy of note is the fading relevance of the word "research" as an industry describer. As I have noted up front, the word "research" fell into place back in the early days when market research practitioners had one foot in academia and desired the intellectual cachet associated with it, including the Ph.D. title if they had one to flaunt.

But, it seems to me the word "research" has always been a misnomer and a drag. Reflect for a minute. What people in our industry do is measure things that someone out there is willing to pay to have measured. Want to know how many households bought ice cream last month or how many put ice cream on a piece of cake, or how many people are apt to vote in the next election and how they are predisposed to vote, or how well the main selling point in a television commercial sticks in people's minds after exposure, or how many people consider themselves religious or actually attend church regularly, or how many people think intrusive telephone calls from pollsters as they sit down to eat should be banned? Well, we know how to measure all those things, for a price.

Some things are much easier to measure than others, and in the end, all such measures are really estimates, not precise measures in the ruler sense of the word. Still, they have utility to clients, and that makes a business.

Today the key buzzword (and concept) is "information," and how that information is developed (the process) is really a secondary consideration for those who pay the piper. The business press is awash with news about the "information" industry, which seems to be a nondescript catchall for all kinds of knowledge, no matter the source. Corporate leaders seem to be subscribing to British statesman Benjamin Disraeli's belief, "As a rule, he who has the most information will have the greatest success in life."

Quick to spot a trend, many major market research firms in the United States have dropped "research" and adopted instead—in news releases, annual reports, and sales literature—the term "information" or "marketing information" to describe their corporate mission. Information, goes the perception, leads to smart, and smart leads to "intelligence," and that is the trend I see brushing "research" aside.

Some background: There has come to be the concept of a corporate intelligence officer, a top executive in the corporate hierarchy, and it follows that the market research function logically fits into the CIO's organization. To put that into perspective, look up the word "intelligence" in the dictionary. It appears as an aggressive, action-oriented word with these key connotations:

❑ Ability to learn, acquire knowledge;
❑ Ability to respond quickly;
❑ Using reason to solve problems; and
❑ Secret information, à la military applications.

We all use the word "intelligence" in a personal context as it relates to individual traits. Now apply the concept of intelligence to a top-level corporate function.

This concept is catching on fast. In 1986, there was founded in the United States a new trade association, the Society of Competitive Intelligence Professionals (SKIP). There are now more than 6700 individual members of SKIP, and it seems that approximately 25% of them are directors of market research at major multinational corporations, and approximately 25% work in companies outside the United States. Some are retired executives from U.S. intelligence agencies, and you'll find such at companies like Intel, Kellogg, 3M, and IBM. One of the leading proponents of SKIP in Europe reportedly is the director of marketing research at Nestlé in Switzerland.

There are SKIP chapters in the United States, Belgium, Switzerland, Germany, South Africa, Mexico, the Netherlands, Italy, the United Kingdom, and Canada. More than 1800 executives paid to attend the annual conferences of SKIP, which are held in major cities around the world (Chicago, Berlin, and Montreal in 1999).

SKIP defines its mission as identifying information sources, data gathering, and information analysis—but applying cutting-edge tools and techniques that range from "war game" strategy exercises to "data mining" corporate operational files and "technology scouting" the areas in which competitors are likely to make a breakthrough.

So, what functions would report to the CIO? I suggest the following logically would, and this is much the way it would work in large multi-nationals in time:

- ❏ *Management Information Systems*: A database focused on the most important asset a business has, its consumer franchise, without which naught.

- ❏ *Customer Satisfaction Measurement (CSM)*: CSM measures are too important to be left to operations management, and CSM results should be known to a firm's CEO on a continuous, summary basis and prepared and analyzed by a third party, namely, the corporate CIO. This is closely linked to the most important corporate asset, its consumer franchise.

- ❏ *Custom Market Research*: Custom, proprietary surveys, or studies if you will, are the ultimate in commercial espionage. Ad hoc surveys can be used not only to study potential markets and the most effective way to exploit them, but also to study the weakness of competitive brands/services and how best to exploit them. Equally important, generally speaking, the market research department in many corporations is a support function of marketing management. In all too many cases, that makes the research practitioner a toady to some brand manager's tactical decisions. By making the marketing research function part of the CIO's organization, it might well be used more to address high-level corporate strategy decisions—a big step up in prestige.

- ❏ *Business Intelligence*: To continuously monitor anything a competitor does, including personnel changes, new production construction, financials, acquisitions, and so on. Most of the input comes from public domain sources.

❑ *Syndicated Data Services*: There are different data availabilities industry by industry, but in high-volume packaged goods, for example, there are many well-established market tracking services syndicated to anyone who will pay the price. The CIO's operation would view input from such services not only to study his or her employer's own brands, but also to continuously study the strengths and weaknesses of competitive brands.

The CIO's job would be to coordinate the work of these five functions and front the corporate intelligence input into total corporate planning and marketing strategy, including the recommendation of defensive moves to competitor actions.

In different corporations, the name may be something other than "intelligence" and the CIO's exact span of responsibilities might be a bit different from the ideal structure I just described, but I do believe that there is an inexorable march toward the concept of "intelligence." Market research will become just an arrow in the CIO's quiver; in a roundabout way, that will inject a new vitality into the research process. If you doubt, recall SKIP.

LEADERSHIP

As noted previously, most of the founders of market research firms in the industry's early days were themselves prominent researchers; they were practitioners who became entrepreneurs. Some grew into competent businessmen or women, but most did not. (One exceptional case was Arthur C. Nielsen Sr., who founded Nielsen Marketing Research, by far the largest research organization in the world. He was also the first to take a marketing research firm — or any service firm, for that matter — public: NASDAQ in 1956. He was, by any measure, the most outstanding, professional manager this industry has ever seen.)

As the pioneers died off, retired, or sold out and the research business became more complex, there came a new breed of top executive, and he or she usually came equipped with an MBA. Then, as research firms started to become much larger and subsidiaries of public firms, many of the largest found themselves headed by a person with a financial background. The end result is that, today, few of the larger multinational research firms are headed by CEOs who would claim to be "researchers."

Thanks in part to the explosion of research interest in the Internet for data collection, there is a new breed. This phenomenon was explained in a recent interview given by Tod Johnson, CEO of the NPD Group, the tenth largest U.S. marketing research conglomerate. It is very active in survey interviewing over the Internet, and its subsidiary, Media Metrix, is the leading firm in the measurement of Internet audience size and behavior.

Referring to the young executives driving the Internet part of NPD's business base, Johnson said,

> I don't think they feel as much a part of the marketing informa-
> tion industry; they're part of a real technology-driven sphere
> Internet industry, and their skills are very different. They under-
> stand the new technologies and the Internet environment, and
> they take computers and what they can do as second nature.
> They're very, very experimental and try different things.... Work,
> exciting work, is what motivates such people. I don't think the
> historical management skills are going to be what's needed to
> drive this [market research] industry in the next 10 or 20 years.

As of the end of 1999, young, tech-driven people in conventional
industries (including market research) are being recruited by start-ups in
the Internet world, especially those with an information mission. The lure
is stock options and the feeling of being in on what is a fast-growth industry geared to the future.

In addition, one of the biggest problems of traditional market
research is a shortage of skilled employees. Granted that today there are
several university programs that offer an MBA in marketing research, or
some such, but the number of students they spill out each year is small
and quickly absorbed by the companies that support those programs.
And, as it pertains to top management, it is difficult to recruit good people because most of those who have desirable credentials are already
locked in by an equity position, or some equivalent, with the company
that is employing them.

Given all this, I suggest that the existing shortage of key employee
skills, which has existed for the past eight years or so, will continue into
the future and, in some way, crimp the industry's growth. The market
research industry is a "people business," and it takes bright, well-
educated people to drive its growth. Some large, sophisticated research
firms recruit out of university and then train to solve this problem, but
most firms have neither the resources nor the time to take this course.

A byproduct of all this is that extremely desirable people will be in
short supply, which runs up salaries and, probably, as Mr. Johnson
pointed out, the need for employers to provide an "exciting, forward-
looking" work atmosphere.

PUBLIC COOPERATION: A WITHERING RESOURCE

In the early days, it was almost a given that the general population's
willingness to cooperate with surveys and other data collection techniques (e.g., panels) was, for all practical purposes, boundless. It was perceived to be an unlimited resource, something that could be exploited at
will.

Well, those days are gone. Respondents' cooperation turned out to be
a withering resource, one that could cripple the marketing/advertis-
ing/public opinion research industry. It has been eroding for a long
period of time, and there have been many contributing factors, including

❑ Abuse by those who turned loose ill-trained, ill-mannered interviewers on an unsuspecting public, often armed with long, laborious questionnaires, all too many of which were designed for ease of data processing rather than involvement with the respondent;

❑ Dramatic increases in the amount of interviewing, which increased the prospects of individual homes being questioned more often. This is especially true of relatively high-income households simply because the higher the disposable income, the greater the commercial interest is;

❑ An avalanche of telemarketing, some of which is disguised as a survey of public opinion but is in fact a screening device to sort out prime prospects for some service or product. This greatly increased the times an average household might be contact with what is perceived to be an invasive telephone call; again, this activity focuses more on the wealthy in society;

❑ Public distaste with some survey subjects, an example being political polling during election waves; and

❑ Clients who knew, sparingly, of the ever-decreasing completion rates but really did not want to be bothered with the details, even as many truly conscientious researchers wanted to face up to the problem and suggest remedies, albeit ones that would add to the cost of doing good work. What once were referred to as "samples" were reduced to "quotas."

On top of this there came to be a technological barrier: the telephone answering machine. Data show that penetration is relatively low among older people and those living in rural areas. But among well-educated, urban residents, the penetration is sky-high (75% in the United States), and to most newly emerging adults, telephone answering machines are nearly as commonplace as telephones. Many use them to screen all calls.

Also, there came to be a breed of politicians who saw gold in "them there invasion-of-privacy hills." This has led and will lead to legislation at both the state and national level to somehow limit the invasiveness of telemarketing, and survey research is often lumped into that category. This has led to an ever-increasing, ever more expensive effort by research trade organizations to hire lobbyists who try to teach technocrats in government the difference between telemarketing and legitimate data collection for surveys. This effort is going on in major counties all around the world.

Moreover, in most modern countries, politicians have found it rewarding to take a strong stand against "invasion of privacy." In the EC, for example, it has been decreed that individuals (read: respondents) cannot be asked about "sensitive" areas without their written permission. Areas considered sensitive include religion, political affiliation, health matters, and, I think, involvement with unions. Taken literally, such stipulations mean that you could not do a telephone survey regarding a health matter, such as asking people what medicines they take to treat a cold, without prior written consent. The degree to which these strictures are enforced country by country, I don't know, but the intention — Big Brother protecting the little people from exploitation by crass commerce — is all too real.

Take these trends, add a dash of public skepticism from those who resent being interrupted at dinner time by a stranger who wants to know into what income bracket they fall, shake well, and you have the environment in which the present-day researcher must operate. No wonder completion rates are abysmal.

These are the major forces I see driving the research industry in the next era: the ever-increasing impact of technology, an ever-increasing concentration of ownership (power), a shift from "research" to "intelligence," a dramatic change in leadership requirements, and the withering resource of respondent cooperation. We will be impacted by all of them for years to come.

Is this bad? There will always be those who are spooked by change and those who welcome change for the opportunities it offers those smart enough to take advantage and solve problems. The research industry was populated from the start by individuals of imagination, tenacity, and vision, such as Arthur C. Nielsen Sr., an outstanding example. Those pioneers faced many problems that far exceed those facing would-be researchers today, and they prevailed (and got rich). So will the most able of us today.

About the Contributors

James G. Barnes

Jim Barnes is Professor of Marketing at Memorial University of Newfoundland, Canada. He served as Dean of the Faculty of Business Administration from 1978 to 1988. He holds undergraduate degrees in Commerce and Economics from Memorial University, an MBA from the Harvard Business School, and a doctorate from University of Toronto. Barnes is a widely published author, having written six books, including *Fundamentals of Marketing*, the best-selling textbook in Canada, which is soon to be published in its ninth edition. He is regarded as a leading authority on marketing research, services marketing, and customer relationships. For his contribution to management education in Canada, Barnes received the inaugural national Leaders in Management Education award from *The Financial Post* in 1997. In 1999, he was elected a Fellow of the PMRS of Canada. Barnes is also Chairman of the Bristol Group, a full-service marketing consultancy with three offices in Canada.

John Bound

John Bound is Visiting Research Associate, South Bank University. He received his education at University of Southampton (B.Sc. in Economics, 1947) and Institute of Statisticians. He has previously worked for University of Southampton, the U.K. government, Quaker Oats Company, University of Strathclyde, and London Business School. Bound has published various books, including *Coastwise Shipping and the Small Ports*, with P. Ford, and *The Marketing Research Process*, with M. Crimp. He has been published in *Journal of the Royal Statistical Society Series A*, along with various conference papers and book reviews. He has served as council member of the Royal Statistical Society, council member of the Market Research Society (UK), and book review editor of *Journal of the Market Research Society*.

Chuck Chakrapani

Chuck Chakrapani is president of Standard Research Systems, adjunct professor at the DeGroote School of Business at McMaster University, chairman of the Investors Association of Canada, Fellow of the Royal Statistical Society, and the former executive director and past president of the PMRS. Chakrapani has held academic appointments at the London Business School and University of Liverpool. He is the editor-in-chief of *Canadian Journal of Marketing Research*, editor of *Money Digest*, and the author of more than ten books and 500 articles on marketing research and investing. His books include *How to Measure Service Quality and Customer Satisfaction*, *Marketing Research: Methods and Canadian Practice* (with Ken Deal), and *Statistics for Market Research* (to be published in 2001). Chakrapani has conducted workshops and seminars in England, the United States, Australia, Canada, Asia, and the Middle East. He was elected Fellow of the PMRS for his "outstanding contributions to marketing research in Canada." He works internationally, and his clients include several multinational companies, marketing boards, and government bodies.

Peter Chan

Peter Chan is vice-president, Statistical Services and Information Technology, with Canadian Facts (CF) Group Inc. He holds an MSc degree in Statistics and Applied Mathematics, Concordia University, and a BSc degree from McGill University. With more than 20 years of hands-on experience in a variety of quantitative methods, Chan provides CF Group Inc. with expertise in multivariate analysis techniques, sampling theory, and a broad range of statistical applications. Since joining CF, Chan has been responsible for the development and enhancement of statistical and micro computing services throughout the company. He is also experienced in applying many recent statistical techniques developed by academic and research institutions, such as Bell Laboratory of AT&T. Prior to joining CF in 1981, Chan was responsible for a variety of statistical functions in the design and analysis of consumer and marketing research for Bell Canada. Chan is a member of the PMRS, the AMA, and the American Statistical Association.

Ruth M. Corbin

Ruth M. Corbin is president and chief executive officer of Decision Resources Inc., a marketing sciences company specializing in research and business analysis, as well as research support for litigation and regulatory matters. She is also an adjunct professor in the Faculties of Management and Medicine, University of Toronto. She holds a bachelor's degree in Applied Mathematics and Psychology, University of Toronto, and MSc and doctoral degrees from McGill. Corbin has held several appointments, including the Boards of Directors for MDS Inc., Trimark Financial Corporation, Unihost Corporation, Alphanet Telecommunications Inc., and the Royal Conservatory of Music. She is a member of the Dean's Advisory Council, University of Toronto Faculty of Management, an editor of the *Journal of Forecasting*, and serves as a member of the editorial board of the *Canadian Journal of Marketing Research*. Author of several articles and chapters and a book on social science evidence in litigation, Corbin is a frequent speaker to audiences on marketing strategy, consumer trends, and business forecasting.

Ken Deal

Ken Deal is Chairman of Marketing, McMaster University, and president of Marketing Decision Research, Inc. He has served as vice president and president of PMRS. With a doctoral degree in marketing and management science, he has been a professor of marketing at McMaster University since 1973. Deal's expertise is in providing sophisticated marketing research insights that help organizations build and enhance marketing strategies. Deal has experience in the energy sector, aviation industry, financial and government services, pharmaceutical research, clinical trials of medical devices, and environmental issues. He has provided expert testimony to the Supreme Court of Ontario and the Federal Court of Canada. He also has presented executive seminars in strategic marketing for private, public, and nonprofit sectors in marketing research, pricing, and other topics. He is an active teacher, researcher, and practitioner in marketing research, modeling, and management. The second edition of his book, *Marketing Research: Methods and Canadian Practice*, is now in progress.

Ian Dey

Ian Dey (MA, Social Administration, PhD) is a senior lecturer in Social Policy, University of Edinburgh. His current interests lie in the field of family policy, though he has also undertaken research on changing work patterns and employment programs. Dey became interested in computer-based methods of qualitative data analysis in the late 1980s and developed an application (Hypersoft) to support his research projects. He has participated in international conferences on computer-based analysis and has consulted on qualitative projects. As well as presenting and publishing papers on using computers to assist qualitative analysis, Dey is author of *Qualitative Data Analysis: A User Friendly Guide*, a book on the practical issues raised by the use of software for qualitative analysis. His latest book, *Grounding Grounded Theory: Guidelines for Qualitative Inquiry*, is a critical review of grounded theory and is widely cited as an analytic framework by software developers and qualitative researchers who use compter-assisted methods of analysis.

A.S.C. Ehrenberg

A.S.C. Ehrenberg has been Professor of Marketing at South Bank University since 1993. He previously spent 23 years at the London Business School and worked in industry for 15 years. He has also held academic appointments at Cambridge, Columbia, Durham, London, NYU, Pittsburgh, and Warwick. Ehrenberg is former chairman of the Market Research Society and a gold medallist in 1969 and 1996. With his colleagues, he has published some ten books and more than 300 articles in various journals, including *Nature, Journal of the Market Research Society, Admap, Journal of the Royal Statistical Society, Journal of Advertising Research, Journal of Marketing Research*, and *Journal of Marketing*. A frequent speaker and active consultant on both sides of the Atlantic, Ehrenberg now leads a small research team for the SBU's "R&D Initiative." Its agenda includes branding, advertising, promotions, distribution, pricing, media, modeling, and information management.

Brian Everitt

Brian Everitt is Professor of Behavioural Statistics and Head of the Biostatistics and Computing Department at the Institute of Psychiatry, King's College, London. After obtaining a degree in statistics at

University College, London, he worked briefly for the civil service before undertaking an academic career, first at Queen Mary College, London, and then at the Institute of Psychiatry, a postgraduate school of the University of London. He is the author of more than 30 books on statistics, including *Cluster Analysis, A Handbook of Statistical Analyses using SPLUS, The Cambridge Dictionary of Statistics*, and *Statistical Aspects of the Design and Analysis of Clinical Trials*. His most recent book is an attempt at a more popular text on probability and risk, entitled *Chance Rules*. His hobbies include running, cooking, playing the guitar (badly), and coping with his seven-year-old daughter and two young grandchildren.

Brian Fine

Brian Fine is executive chairman of AMR Interactive. Prior to the formation of AMR in 1991, Fine was managing director of Australia Market Research, which he established in 1984. Fine holds a bachelor's degree in Psychology and an HNC in Business Studies. He has experience on both the supplier and user sides of the business, including time spent at Market Research Africa, research and planning director at J Walter Thompson in Canada, vice president with Attitude and Behaviour Measurement in Canada, and general manager of Audience Studies in Australia. He specializes in strategic and advertising research and brand equity, customer satisfaction, and loyalty measurement. More recently, his focus has been on the challenges and opportunities of Internet research. Fine was national chairman of the Market Research Society of Australia from 1993 to 1996 and past president of the Council of the Marketing Services Association. He is also executive chairman of Media Metrix Australia.

David Gascoigne

David Gascoigne is vice president, Millward Brown (US). He heads the Advanced Analytical Group in North America, providing client servicing and technical support for Salesdynamics. Before that, Gascoigne was head of the Statistics Group, Millward Brown (UK). He has managed almost 50 projects in financial services, telecommunications, pharmaceuticals, the music industry, and automobiles. In 1988, Gascoigne graduated with an honors degree in Applied Statistics, Sheffield and Hallamshire University. He has 12 years' experience as a statistician, obtaining early experience in the steel industry (statistical quality control), finance sector (actuarial), and health sector (epidemiology) before becoming the principal in information management and statistics for a water utility in the United Kingdom. He has served on the committee of the West Midlands group of the Royal Statistical Society and on the steering committee for Matching Education, Assessment and Employment Needs in Statistics, a two-year funded project based at the Center for Statistical Education, University of Nottingham, England.

Naomi R. Henderson

Naomi Henderson is chief executive officer, RIVA Market Research Inc., Bethesda, Md. Henderson has talked to more than 25,000 respondents in the 35-year span of her research service career that started with door-to-door interviews in the 1960s. She has held positions as a senior analyst at Resource Management Corporation (Washington, DC) and Opinion Research Corporation (Princeton, NJ). She holds degrees in education and psychology (BA 1964, MEd 1968) from American University and has completed course work at George Washington University in group dynamics. She founded RIVA Training Institute, a division of RIVA, Inc. that trains researchers in the art and science of effective qualitative techniques. She is a member of the Qualitative Research Consultants Association, the Marketing Research Association, the AMA, the National Association of Female Executives, and the International Women's Writers Guild, on whose advisory board she serves. Since 1987, she has been listed in the annual directory of *Who's Who in American Women*.

Jack J. Honomichl

Jack Honomichl is president of Marketing Aid Center, Inc., a firm he founded in 1978. He has held executive positions with Marketing Information Center, a research subsidiary of Dun & Bradstreet; Audits & Surveys; MRCA Information Services; and *The Chicago Tribune*. Honomichl has been a featured speaker at the national conventions of almost every research industry trade association in North American and Europe. He also has been a guest lecturer at several U.S. universities on the subject of information assimilation in the decision-making process. He founded *Inside Research*, a newsletter addressed to top management in the worldwide marketing, advertising, and public opinion research industry and is a columnist for *Marketing News* and *Advertising Age*. He has published more than 400 articles, as well as the textbook *Honomichl on Marketing Research*. Honomichl received his bachelor's degree from the Kellogg School of Management, Northwestern University, and his AM degree from the University of Chicago.

Vinay Kanetkar

Vinay Kanetkar is an associate professor, Department of Consumer Studies, University of Guelph. He received his doctorate from the Faculty of Commerce, University of British Columbia. His doctoral research, which focused on determining the impact of television advertising on consumer price sensitivity using scanner panel data, was published in *Marketing Science Journal*. Kanetkar has also published in *Journal of Marketing Research, Journal of Public Policy & Marketing*, and many other academic journals. He is particularly interested in various forms of price leaders in the marketplace and the extent to which such strategic pricing orientation results in organizational objectives. Kanetkar enjoys teaching research methods, management of product development, and statistical applications to marketing decision making. Before joining Guelph, he taught at the Faculty of Management, University of Toronto, where he implemented results on the use of electronic data collection for decision-making purposes. In addition, he serves as a consultant to several market research companies.

David W. Lyon

Dave Lyon is principal of Aurora Market Modeling, which he founded in 1996 as a vehicle for consulting on multivariate research design, implementation, and interpretation for both research companies and direct end users of research. Previously, Lyon served for more than six years each at Total Research Corporation and Opinion Research Corporation. At those firms, he consulted with clients on applications of multivariate techniques, the main focus of his marketing research experience. Trade-off techniques, including discrete choice modeling, conjoint analysis, and their variants, are of particular interest to him. Lyon has worked with clients in a wide variety of industries, particularly pharmaceuticals but also telecommunications, packaged goods, small appliances, financial services, and information services. Lyon is a member of the AMA, the American Statistical Association, the Association for Computing Machinery, and the Institute for Operations Research and Management Sciences. He is a 1971 honors graduate of Princeton University, where he majored in statistics.

Naresh K. Malhotra

Naresh K. Malhotra is Regents' Professor, which is the highest academic rank in the university system of Georgia, DuPree College of Management, Georgia Institute of Technology. He has been listed in *Who's Who in America* since 1997 and *Who's Who in the World* as of 2000. Malhotra was ranked first in the country on the basis of articles published in *Journal of Marketing Research* between 1980 and 1985. He holds the record for the maximum number of publications in the *Journal of Health Care Marketing* and *Journal of the Academy of Marketing Science* from its inception through 1995. He has published a book entitled *Marketing Research: An Applied Orientation*, now in its third edition, which has been made into international, European, and Australian editions, as well as translated into Spanish. The book's wide adoption at both the graduate and undergraduate levels has led to its use in more than 100 universities in the United States.

Eric Marder

Eric Marder is chairman of Eric Marder Associates, Inc., the company he founded in 1960. He pioneered the use of controlled experiments in surveys, developed various research techniques, including STEP, VEST, SUMM, and Ad-Weight, and applied these techniques to solving practical business problems for *Fortune* 500 companies. In the course of his work, Marder earned intensely loyal support from his clients, and though his work has not been publicaly available until the publication of his book *The Laws of Choice: Predicting Customer Behavior*, he has influenced thinking in the field for many years. Marder's background cuts across the physical and social sciences. He has a bachelor's degree in electrical engineering and a master's in sociology. Before starting his firm, he was vice-president of marketing research at Kenyon & Eckhardt, then a major advertising agency. He also spent several years as an instructor of physics at the University of Rhode Island and at Rutgers University.

Howard R. Moskowitz

Howard Moskowitz is president and chief executive officer of Moskowitz Jacobs Inc. Moskowitz is an experimental psychologist in the field of psychophysics (the study of perception and its relation to physical stimuli). In 1975, he introduced psychophysical scaling and product optimization for consumer product development. In the 1980s, his contributions in sensory analysis were extended to health and beauty aids. His research and technology developments have led to concept and package optimization (IdeaMap®), integrated and accelerated development (DesignLab®), and the globalization and democratization of concept development (IdeaMap® Wizard). Moskowitz has a doctoral degree in experimental psychology, Harvard University. He has written/edited 11 books, published more than 180 articles, has lectured in the United States and abroad, serves on the editorial board of major journals, and has won many awards. In 1992, Moskowitz founded a $2,000 prize for young scientists working in the psychophysics of taste and smell, administered through the Association of Chemoreception Scientists.

William D. Neal

William D. Neal is Founder and Senior Executive Officer of SDR, Inc., a professional services and consulting firm specializing in advanced marketing research methods, procedures, and technologies. Neal has personally authored more than 40 articles, tutorials, and seminars on marketing research methods and procedures. He is considered a national expert in the fields of applied market segmentation, product positioning, product optimization, brand value, brand equity, and advanced research methods. He is on the editorial review boards of *Marketing Management* and *Marketing Research* magazines and is an ad hoc reviewer for several other marketing management and marketing research publications. Neal has been very active in the AMA since 1978, serving as President of the Atlanta Chapter and Regional Vice President and Vice President of the Marketing Research Division. From 1991 to 1995, he served on the Association's Executive Committee, and from 1991 to 1993 as the Association's Chairman-Elect and Chairman of the Board of Directors.

Peter Peacock

Peter Peacock is Associate Professor of Marketing and Information Systems at the Babcock Graduate School of Management, Wake Forest University. Peacock teaches graduate courses in marketing research, database marketing, and information systems. His current research is in the area of data mining with special emphasis on response modeling and prospect profiling. He is also conducting research on the linkage between large firm business strategies and the scope and complexity of the relational data structures employed to implement those strategies. His varied research interests have resulted in articles published in the *Journal of*

Business, Journal of Consumer Research, Journal of Marketing Research, Journal of Office Systems Research, Business Horizons, and *Marketing Management.* He has been a consultant in data mining, database marketing, marketing research, and information technology to Bridgetree, Inc., R. J. Reynolds Tobacco Company, Novartis, and Sara Lee. He received his doctoral degree in business from the University of Chicago.

Doss Struse

Doss Struse is senior vice president of InterSurvey, an Internet-based research firm. Previously, he was chairman and CEO of Research International, USA. He ran RIUSA from 1996 to 1999, making it the second-biggest unit within the world's foremost custom research company. Prior to that, he was Senior Vice President of Marketing for Nielsen, working in both the U.S. division and at its international headquarters in Brussels. Struse spent the first part of his career in client companies, principally in the food industry. He was Director of Marketing Research for General Mills, Carnation/Nestlé, and Oscar Mayer & Company. He started his career with Foote, Cone & Belding Advertising. In addition to his positions, Mr. Struse has been active in the AMA, Advertising Research Foundation, Marketing Science Institute, and other professional groups. Struse holds a master's in sociology from the University of Michigan and a bachelor of arts from Princeton University.

Humphrey Taylor

Humphrey Taylor is chairman of Harris Poll, a service of Harris Interactive. Taylor began working in survey research in Britain in 1963. In 1966, he found Opinion Research Centre. Taylor conducted all of the private political polling for the Conservative Party and was an advisor to Prime Minister Edward Heath in the 1970 campaign and subsequently to Margaret Thatcher. In 1970, his firm was acquired by Louis Harris and Associates. Taylor was appointed president of Harris in 1981, chief executive officer in 1992, and chairman in 1994. He is chairman of the National Council on Public Polls and a trustee of the Roper Center, Royal Society of Medicine Foundation, and American Academy of Ophthalmology. In addition to writing many articles, Taylor has written editorials for the *New York Times, The Wall Street Journal,* and the *Times* (London). He has been a guest lecturer at Harvard, Oxford, New York University, and University of California, San Francisco.

Neil Vidmar

Neil Vidmar is Professor of Law at Duke Law School and holds a secondary appointment in the Psychology Department at Duke. He received his doctorate in social psychology from University of Illinois in 1967 and subsequently joined the University of Western Ontario. Vidmar serves as a faculty member for judicial education courses in Canada and the United States. He is coauthor of *Judging the Jury* and author of *Medical Malpractice and the American Jury* and *World Jury Systems*. He has written approximately 90 articles on such topics as the jury system, exemplary damages, privacy, reliability of eyewitnesses, attitudes toward the death penalty, and battered women and rape trauma syndromes. His current research projects include an investigation of expert evidence in the litigation process, a project on *pro se* claimants in the Dalkon Shield Trust resolution process, and a study on the dynamics of retribution. He has consulted about trial prejudice issues in the United States and abroad.

Roger D. Wimmer

Roger D. Wimmer is president, CEO, and cofounder of Wimmer-Hudson Research & Development, Denver, Colo., a full-service research company that specializes in audience and programming research for the mass media as well as Internet-related research. Prior to this company, Wimmer was president, CEO, and cofounder of The Eagle Group Inc.; president, general partner, and cofounder of Paragon Research; president of Surrey Research; and Manager of Research for Cox Broadcasting in Atlanta, Ga. Before entering private sector research, Wimmer was an associate professor at University of Georgia and assistant professor at University of Mississippi. He holds a doctorate in mass media research from Bowling Green State University (Ohio). He has published many articles and chapters in books and is the senior editor of *Mass Media Research: An Introduction*, currently in its sixth edition. In his spare time, Wimmer is an avid Harley-Davidson rider, woodworker, painter, Adjunct Professor of Journalism at University of Colorado-Boulder, and father.

Index

653

ABOUT THE AMERICAN MARKETING ASSOCIATION

The AMA is the world's largest and most comprehensive professional association of marketers. With more than 45,000 members, the AMA has more than 500 professional and collegiate chapters throughout North America. The AMA sponsors 25 major conferences per year and publishes eight marketing publications that serve the academic, research, and marketing management areas. AMA can be reached at www.ama.org.

ABOUT THE PROFESSIONAL MARKETING RESEARCH SOCIETY

The PMRS is a nonprofit organization for marketing research professionals engaged in marketing, advertising, social, and political research. The PMRS was founded in 1960 and now serves more than 1500 members across Canada, with local chapters in British Columbia, Manitoba, Ottawa, Quebec, Toronto, and the Atlantic. PMRS can be reached at www.pmrs-aprm.com.